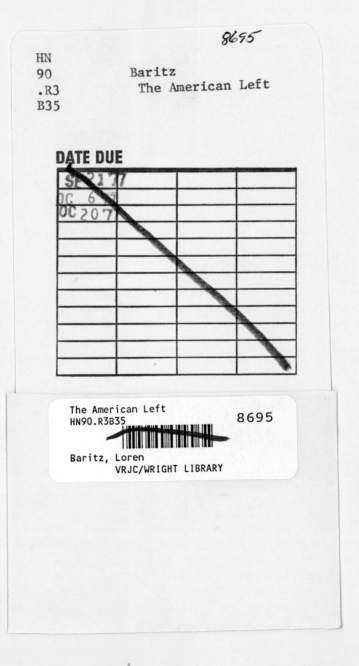

The American Left

THE AMERICAN LEFT / Radical Political Thought in the Twentieth Century

EDITED BY Loren Baritz

BASIC BOOKS, INC., PUBLISHERS

New York / London

To Bill Gum,

without eulogy as it

would be premature.

PREFACE

L ET it be acknowledged immediately that radicalism has failed in twentieth-century America. It has produced neither socialism nor revolution, nor the immediate likelihood of either. It has not succeeded in transferring power from those who have it to those who do not. Other, easier, criteria for judging success run a very high risk of sentimentality, wish-fulfillment, and can be used only with the possibility of damaging the mind. I mean to be saying that the test of radicalism's success is the existence of the social order that radicalism demands. Modern American radicalism may point to a partly courageous and partly insane record, to partial victories and short-run achievements, but on the grounds set out here it cannot avoid the charge of failure. What follows, then, are the most important statements which have punctuated this history of failure.

This apparently hard-headed approach to American radicalism is partly impertinent, for radicalism must fail, must always fail, so long as society encourages or allows injustice. This side of utopia, radicals must always be pushing their rock up the hill, and the distance of the summit or the weight of the rock is an absolute but not a conclusive criterion. For radicalism's only fatal failure will be to let loose of the rock, to quit. Despite political intimidation and harassment of the most intense kind, despite apathy and hostility, despite internal confusion and autocannibalism, despite stupid external direction and stupid internal obeisance, despite all this and even more, American radicals have not quit and show no signs of doing so. In the light of this, the absolute failure to reconstruct American society can, without sentimentality, be fitted into its proper context. But here it is not how the game is played that matters. Winning is what matters. The redistribution of power is what matters.

A better understanding and even appreciation of the work that radicals have done in the recent past may add a little strength to the present struggle. The record assembled here, after all, is filled with dumb ideas as well as good ones, with stupendous mistakes that ought not to be duplicated for the sheer exhilaration of failing stupendously, and with wisdom and political tact that are instructive. There is too much work to be done to waste effort on reinventing ideas already worked out by others. My best hope is that this collection will teach somebody something that he needs to know, something that he will not therefore have to think through from scratch alone; this could permit an escape from the sort of barbarism that believes that it is freshly come on a virgin world never before imagined or analyzed. Others have pushed on our rock; let us learn at least where they found it impossible to go, and why this was so.

It has been said that America has no radical tradition. This collection should prove that such a conclusion is silly. It is also said that America has not had something called an "indigenous" radical tradition, one that sprang from, and related to, the concrete details of American life. This collection should throw light on this assumption, and will, I believe, show that at times, especially during the period of Soviet ideological and cultural hegemony, this assertion is reasonably accurate. But it is a mistake to confuse the American radical tradition with the worst and most mechanical excesses of the 1930's. The plea for less fake scientism in social theory, for a more creative response to this particular place, has been almost constant in the history of radicalism. Although such efforts under the slogan of "American exceptionalism" were once condemned as heresy by the Comintern, this is precisely the area where American radicals have done their best work. Before the Russian Revolution, before the enormous prestige of the Soviet Union as the only revolutionary state and the greatest exemplar of applied socialism, and after this prestige was weakened by the rise of China, the political liberation movements in the Third World, and the Soviet Union's own international excesses, American radicals were freer to think about the United States in more sensitive, more intelligent and successful ways. Perhaps this explains the great excitement and movement in American radicalism before World War I and the Russian Revolution, and again in the period beginning roughly with the decade of the 1960's. Whatever the explanation of these two moments of greatest activity, there is ample evidence to refute the charge that this nation has not produced a native radicalism. I suppose that it is not necessary to argue that a reliance on Marx does not prove that a political system or vision is by definition alien. I also suppose that a mechanical and inappropriate application of Marxism to the facts of American life does not prove that the fault belongs to Marx.

Too much of our political information comes from inside, from the defenders, so of course it is suspect. To ignore radicalism is to be passive under capitalism's party line, to offer one's nose for leading. Under this circumstance it would be astonishing and even disappointing if the powerful self-servers did not serve themselves as powerfully as possible by manipulating the society's perception and consciousness. This manipulation takes as many forms as the changing circumstances require and as the ingenuity of the defenders allows. We can be distracted by Theodore Roosevelt's fake fight about good and bad trusts, by false dreams of two chickens in every garage, by illusory fears and phantoms whether in the guise of Franklin Roosevelt or Khrushchev, and by the truly beautiful packaging of "the following commercial message which makes this program possible."

The very mythology of American patriotism and nationalism demands that we not think too critically about our corporate and technocentric political economy. For if we do, something will have to change. Thus every well-developed skill available to corporate America will necessarily be used to prevent, discredit, or digest criticism. This means that the individual citizen must learn to withstand the vast, powerful, attractive, and ubiquitous communication furies that corporate capitalism directs. *Time* magazine, for instance, concludes a review of an anthology of new Left thought this way (never mind that its opinion is wrong, as will be shown by many of the selections representing the new Left in the following pages): "But New Leftese mostly favors ideas that can be daubed on a placard. American radicalism is in danger of making itself voluble without making itself articulate." [1] Daubed?

This sort of direct attack, however supercilious in *Time's* attitudinizing manner, is unusual. The corporate communications industry has apparently concluded that radical criticism is best ignored or coopted, that the advertising industry's smooth assurance that personal deficiencies—dullness, drabness, stinks of various kinds, etc.—can be repaired with the stuff it sells is the best answer to radical America. From its point of view it *is* the best answer and, in that all-American phrase, it seems to work. Radicalism has to fight the entire organization of advertising, public relations, all the media, all organized and sponsored communication, not in order to win the day, whatever that now means, but in order merely to be heard and to survive.

Publishing, as this book may show, is the only significant exception to all this. But then one must hurry to ask about the significance, in a large social sense, of books in a television age. Well, through books radicals can read each other, and the liberal intelligentsia can exercise itself. In a kind

[1] *Time,* 5 January 1970, p. 58.

of sad, little popular song, Peggy Lee sings "is that all there is?" Yeah, that's all, kid, so let's dance and booze and write a book (two-thirds of this statement is probably sensible).

The book business and scholarship have their own problems with radical criticism in America. There are instances of publishers rejecting a manuscript because it is too radical, but these books have been, and can be, published somewhere and somehow, even if the biggest, most commercial, and most prestigious firms will not do so, and they usually will. The problem here is with the authors, not with something called the capitalistic, profit-mad, fascist-pig publishers. A publisher may be all these things, of course, but whatever the person is he would be hard-pressed to locate substantial radical criticism or a responsible treatment of radicalism in any academic discipline. This is the fault of scholarship, not the publishing industry. The problem is scholarly self-censorship, not heavy-handed thought-control imposed by external force. Whether this relative freedom from imposed political orthodoxy would survive the death of self-censorship is clearly something else.

The history of American radicals and of radicalism in America has not yet been written. There are some excellent biographies of individual radicals, as well as several valuable analyses of discreet moments or developments in the history of radicalism, but these do not yet add up to a view of radicalism as an integrated aspect of American political and cultural life. Because our knowledge of radicalism is as yet so fragmentary, it follows, if one assumes as I do that radicalism is an indispensable dimension of the shifting realities of America, that our view even of dominant or established power is therefore also fragmentary. For all the overemphasis on politics and economics in American historical scholarship, the radical prosecuting attorney has been run out, or laughed out of court. Without the radical critique we can never get the story straight. Whenever scholarship proceeds from the assumptions of the *New York Times,* and then leads to its conclusions, it must be that scholarship fails to do its essential job of innovation, challenging received social wisdom, and finding new abrasive truth.

The story of radicalism remains obscure not because it has been repressed, not because historians and others have deliberately stuffed what they know down a memory hole, but because of the general American assumption that the doings and undoings of radicals do not matter. It is often assumed that a detailed understanding of radicalism is a sort of scholarly subspecialty that will not really contribute to an understanding of social change in twentieth-century America. There is no doubt that American radicalism has not been able to play the numbers game with success. It has never successfully achieved the mass base of popular support necessary for certain kinds of political success.

In quantitative electoral terms, 1912 was the peak of success, at least for the Socialist Party. In this year there were about 150,000 members of the party, Eugene Debs polled close to 900,000 votes (6 percent of the total) for the presidency, and there were hundreds of Socialists in office, mostly in municipal government (56 mayors, over 300 aldermen), and one congressman in the U.S. House of Representatives. The states giving the Socialists the most votes in 1912 were California (79,000), Illinois (81,000), New York (63,000), Ohio (90,000), Oklahoma (42,000), Pennsylvania (84,000), Washington (40,000), and Wisconsin (33,000). This year was the quantitative peak, with paid membership in the Socialist Party thereafter beginning to skid.

From 1900 through World War II the tougher Socialist Labor Party never won more than 50,000 votes in a national election (and it got less than 13,000 votes in 1936, in the middle of the Depression). In its first national campaign the Communist Party got 33,000 votes in 1924, running with, and against, La Follette's third-party effort that the Socialists and the American Federation of Labor and others supported to the tune of almost 5 million votes. Thereafter the Communists collected 49,000 votes in 1928, 103,000 in 1932, 80,000 in 1936, and 49,000 in 1940. After the war, Henry Wallace's Progressive Party got just over 1 million votes in 1948, while Norman Thomas got about 90 percent less on the Socialist Party ticket.

After this the story remains essentially unchanged. With the exception of the Progressives who got 140,000 votes in 1952, none of the left splinter parties were to assemble more than 55,000 votes in any national election. The Socialists reached a catastrophic low of 2,126 votes in Eisenhower's year of 1956. This is a perfectly clear tale of the utter failure of the American Left to succeed within the established electoral system. And with the increasing importance of the expensive media, especially TV, this will not soon, if ever, change. American radicals have had no sustaining success in American politics, as politics has been defined by tradition, law, and political money.

There are other definitions of success, however, having to do with sheer staying power, or the quality of thought, or, most important, the kind of political and cultural struggle that lays the groundwork for future action. Because it is now clear that action directed toward electoral victory will fail, the question has been, and will be, asked about what other action is meaningful to the Left. Building a base, always building, running for office in order to win minds not votes, especially if winning means the sort of sellout, dilution, and distraction that it has usually meant. Sometimes the Left knows these things, and sometimes not. In fact they are not always true. Right now black radicals, for some good reasons, are less wary of electoral politics than the white Left. In any case, no intellectual fetish will free anybody, and the Left will always have to be rethinking the possibilities and risks of electoral effort.

Another almost standard explanation of why Americans know so little about American radicalism is the maddening bickering, jealousies, and schisms of American radicals. It is enough to concede partial validity to this charge. But such validity neither explains nor justifies ignorance. If neuroses, silliness, or rigidity of the subject justified ignorance, none of us would know anything about social and political life. There is then no way to explain this sniffish attitude toward the radical past and present on any other than political grounds. This of course is a very serious charge, the accuracy of which can be tested by assessing the treatment of radicalism in any standard history of twentieth-century America, in any journalistic attempt to supply "background," in the mindless insistence of sociologists to view radicalism as "deviance" (on a statistical "norm" whose applicability to a dangerous world merely shows that middle-aged complacency is now a scholarly "norm" in a "deviant" world), in the failure of political scientists to think about the normative dimension of what they do and what they fail to do, and in the almost obsessive concentration of economists on the nuts and bolts of the given, that is, the provided, that is, corporate capitalism (again, an international perspective will show how self-satisfied national parochialism may distort scholarship just as it does diplomacy).

The struggle to make black people visible in our history is the same sort of struggle that must occur if radicalism is ever to surface. The claim here is that radicalism must be brought to full historical consciousness partly for the sake of the accuracy of the record, and also that we may all better understand the meaning of experience in this time and place. And that we may then act on what we newly understand. The view from the left is not merely interesting. It is a vital vantage point that alone permits a fully critical analysis of the political economy to be made. Political and scholarly debate in the absence of the prosecutor has not, and cannot, rise above whatever assumptions are current or chic at any moment. There is then no impulse or mechanism for change except the sharpening techniques and demands of already established power. The technique of social change that established power almost always employs may be perceived in its now fashionable desperation to find ways to clean up the environment by exhortation, public relations, and other toothless expressions of deep concern.

There is an apparent contradiction between saying that the ignorance about radicalism is not the result of repression and that this ignorance is a consequence of American political orthodoxy. It is not that radicalism has been swept under the rug because of political fear of its power. Rather, the perceptual mode induced by standard American politics operates as blinders. Cutting off peripheral vision, the American center literally does not see leftward except when it is scared out of its wits. The "majoritarianism" of the American center necessarily celebrates itself by celebrating numbers, so that any minority will therefore have to struggle for mere visibility. Self-induced sensory numbness rather than political viciousness explains much, but not all, of the politics of center scholarship in America.

The radical papers assembled here must contribute to a better appreciation of the very high level of some radical thought, and of the devotion of some to a more humane social order. The criteria for selecting the papers were reasonably clear. Radicalism itself was defined as a commitment to, and advocacy of, transferring cultural, political, and economic power to the mass of powerless people; although Marxism is a usual commitment of the American left, this was not made into a mechanical requirement for admission into this book.

Among the vast number of radical papers available, those were selected for inclusion which most usefully or cogently diagnosed America's political economy. There is thus no intention in this collection to illustrate the history of radicalism as such, but rather to allow the radical perception of the unfolding American reality to emerge. There is also no desire to illustrate the organizational and internal difficulties of American radicalism, although some critical moments in the history of radicalism cannot otherwise be understood, and so these are included and explained.

Despite the length of this anthology, there are many people and much intelligent comment that have been omitted. I have tried to avoid things already very familiar or easily accessible. Some may object to the exclusion of the original *Masses,* but I suggest that the talented circle around this journal has already received too much attention for a balanced assessment of radicalism. Because our radical past was more than a literary affair, I have tried to underplay it. Stressing literary radicalism also may be a way to domesticate radicalism, and although this collection is not blind to the literary left, it does not follow along every possible, or perhaps even desirable, literary path. More serious is the omission of the more purely academic radicals. This means the absence, among others, of Thorstein Veblen, C. Wright Mills, William A. Williams, and Herbert Marcuse. In a real sense, these men are indispensable to understanding the radical past. But I want to give the people involved in political work and action this platform, not, in this case, to correct a distortion, but because of the importance of what they also had to say. All the work of these central radical academics is easily available, as most of the work reprinted here is not.

And finally I have decided to focus this collection on political radicalism, thereby slighting the cultural radicalism that has become increasingly important. I say that cultural insurgency is as, or more, important than the more strictly political variety, but this is another, more subtle and complex, story. So the Yippies are absent, along with mini-skirts, Chaplin, relevant aspects of film and radio, something of the flapper, the politics of booze and sex and crime and sport and etc. This is all too bad because of its importance and its fun, but the politicos, with their sometimes decayed humor, their occasional grimness and ploddingness, have, and will, carry the greatest weight in any fight for redistributing power. And so this collection is what it is for open, if not for generally accepted, reasons. For those of you who still insist on a different assortment, all I can say is: Go make your own.

I hope that these voices of the left will help to teach us to look at America with greater courage, with less self-serving squinting and winking, and with results that will encourage people who believe in humane change to keep at it.

John Kaufmann and Stuart Ewen provided materials of the most recent radical past that otherwise would have been inaccessible to me. Mr. Barry Nadler did much of the library work.

LOREN BARITZ

April 1971

CONTENTS

PART V

Debs   83

PART VI

The War to Make the World Safe
for Capitalism   107

PART VII

PART VIII

PART IX

PART X

Depression   233

PART XI

The Black Beginning   271

PART XII

PART XIII

PART XIV

PART XV

PART XVI

PART XVII

The American Left

PART I
The Class Struggle

DANIEL DE LEON (1852–1914) was the leading intelligence behind revolutionary socialism in the 1890's. An effective public speaker, a passionate and occasionally venomous editorialist, he was also the most lucid theoretical Marxist in America. He was born in Curaçao, educated at the University of Leyden and at the Columbia Law School from which he graduated with honors when he was twenty-six years old. After an improbable stint as a practicing lawyer in Texas, he returned to teach Latin American foreign policy and international law at Columbia. He was not promoted after the customary six-year trial period, probably because of his growing involvement with radical labor causes. His leftward movement is illustrated by a Cooper Union speech he gave in defense of the men condemned to death in the Haymarket Affair trial; he put his career on the line when he said that the nation's record would "be blood-stained by a judicial crime as the one contemplated in Chicago."

He fleshed out his already good education by seriously reading Marx in the late eighties and nineties, when he also joined the Socialist Labor Party. This organization had been formed in 1877, and under De Leon's leadership, especially his editorship of *People,* the official English-language weekly, the SLP became, for about a decade, the home of revolutionary socialism in the United States.

De Leon's diagnosis of America's political economy was the source of his strengths and his weaknesses. He believed that labor needed both political and economic weapons in order to destroy capitalism. The lure or hope of cooperation, peaceful coexistence, between labor and capital was a smokescreen thrown up by capitalists and their perhaps unwitting agents in labor to hide the necessity of struggle between irreconcilable interests. So he viewed the American Federation of Labor's voluntary refusal to become political as a kind of self-castration that would inevitably convert the

3

AFL into an agent of capitalism. The Socialist Labor Party, as he understood it, was the appropriate *political* arm of revolutionary socialism, and the need to create an economic or industrial arm occupied much of his attention for most of the rest of his life.

Because the SLP viewed the AFL as hopelessly corrupt, De Leon abandoned the idea of "boring from within," a favorite trade union slogan of the time. At least the old but moribund Knights of Labor were still committed to industrial, not craft, unionism, and the SLP tried to take it over. But De Leon failed with the Knights, and this led to the decision to create a new and independent industrial union. At Cooper Union, on Friday, 13 December 1895, in front of a defiant red banner, De Leon won the overwhelming approval of an overflow crowd for the creation and support of the Socialist Trade and Labor Alliance. This was supposed to be the industrial army of the Socialist Labor Party's political revolution.

The creation of the STLA led to dual unionism, to the charge that De Leon was dividing and thus weakening labor's actual and potential power. Samuel Gompers, the president of the AFL, described the STLA as being "conceived in iniquity and brutal concubinage with labor's double enemy, greed and ignorance, fashioned into an embryonic phthisical dwarf, born in corruption and filth."

After its initial impressive growth, the STLA declined, eventually merging with the Industrial Workers of the World at the founding convention in 1905. De Leon's ideological clarity, his refusal to cooperate with muddled bleeding-hearts, "labor fakirs," well-meaning liberals who sought ways to avoid violence at a time when he thought that the class struggle must become increasingly intense, led him to try to rid his party of compromise and vacillation. His fixity finally led to a rebellion of the rightwing—the reformers and the progressives—of the SLP which formed the Socialist Party in 1901. Thereafter the SLP became increasingly pure and increasingly isolated, while the more moderate Socialists supported existing unions, even the AFL, criticized dual unionism, built a heterogeneous base, committed itself to short-range victory within established political channels, and shaped itself to be reformist, evolutionary, and democratic.

De Leon's most revealing and typical speech was given during the textile workers' strike at New Bedford, Massachusetts, 11 February 1898. In *What Means This Strike?* he explained the labor theory of value in language that anyone could understand, and defended dual unionism because, as he said, labor conflict without socialism must fail. The speech was to be reprinted dozens of times, and it has become a little classic of socialist theory in ordinary language. Gompers also went before the New Bedford strikers to call for unity within the AFL, and although De Leon's appeal won converts to the STLA, his revolutionary group could not take over New Bedford.

De Leon has had the reputation of an aloof, scholarly, crabbed, dried-out, inflexible tyrant more devoted to the purity of abstractions than to winning a better life for American workers. Although there is something in such a characterization, it is partly unfair. Because he was a revolutionary without a revolution, he can sound doctrinaire. Lenin's [1] appreciation of De Leon's work may hint at their similarities, at least in approach. De Leon's unfortunate reputation, during his life and since, is a consequence of his unbending belief that revolution was necessary. He is condemned for not being what on principle and ideology he refused to be. Perhaps the reforming mentality must condemn the revolutionaries simply to even the score. This internal struggle on the left may finally be seen to be not internal at all, but a necessary battle between natural enemies.

De Leon's New Bedford speech shows him at his best, and his more moderate opponents on the left must even now find a way to deal with it. His final reputation will depend on the outcome of his long-range predictions as well as on his intellectual acuity, and that is probably the way he would have wanted it.

---

[1]

WHAT MEANS THIS STRIKE?

DANIEL DE LEON

WORKING men and working women of New Bedford; ye striking textile workers; and all of you others, who, though not now on strike, have been on strike before this, and will be on strike some other time————:

It has been the habit in this country and in England that, when a strike

[1] In an interview printed in the *New York World,* 4 February 1919, p. 2, Lenin said: "The American Daniel De Leon first formulated the idea of a Soviet government, which grew up in Russia on his idea. Future society will be organized along Soviet lines. There will be Soviet rather than geographical boundaries for nations. Industrial unionism is the basic thing."

SOURCE: Daniel De Leon, *Speeches and Editorials* (New York: New York Labor News Co., n.d.), vol. 1.

is on, "stars" in the Labor Movement are invited to appear on the scene, and entertain the strikers; entertain them and keep them in good spirits with rosy promises and prophesies, funny anecdotes, bombastic recitations in prose and poetry; stuff them full of rhetoric and wind—very much in the style that some generals do, who, by means of bad whiskey, seek to keep up the courage of the soldiers whom they are otherwise unable to beguile. Such has been the habit in the past; to a great extent it continues to be the habit in the present; it was so during the late miners' strike; it has been so to some extent here in New Bedford; and it is so everywhere, to the extent that ignorance of the Social Question predominates. To the extent, however, that Socialism gets a footing among the working class such false and puerile tactics are thrown aside. . . . Our organization sends us out to teach the workers, to enlighten them on the great issue before them, and the great historic drama in which most of them are still unconscious actors. Some of you, accustomed to a different diet, may find my speech dry; if there be any such here, let him leave; he has not yet graduated from that primary school reared by experience in which the question of wages is forced upon the workers as a serious question, and they are taught that it demands serious thought to grapple with, and solve it. If, however, you have graduated from that primary department, and have come here with the requisite earnestness, then you will not leave this hall without having, so to speak, caught firm hold of the cable of the Labor Movement; then the last strike of this sort has been seen in New Bedford; then, the strikes that may follow will be as different from this as vigorous manhood is from toddling infancy; then you will have entered upon that safe and sure path along which, not, as heretofore, eternal disaster will mark your tracks, but New Bedford, Massachusetts, and the nation herself will successively fall into your hands, with freedom as the crowning fruit of your efforts. (Applause.)

Three years ago I was in your midst during another strike. The superficial observer who looks back to your attitude during that strike, who looks back to your attitude during the strikes that preceded that one, who now turns his eyes to your attitude in the present strike, and who discovers substantially no difference between your attitude now and then might say, "Why, it is a waste of time to speak to such men; they learn nothing from experience; they will eternally fight the same hopeless battle; the battle to establish 'safe relations' with the capitalist class, with the same hopeless weapon: the 'pure and simple' organization of labor!" But the Socialist does not take that view. There is one thing about your conduct that enlists for and entitles you to the warm sympathy of the Socialist, and that is that, despite your persistent errors in fundamental principles, in aims and methods, despite the illusions that you are chasing after, despite the increasing poverty and cumulating failures that press upon you, despite all that you preserve manhood enough not to submit to oppression, but rise in the rebellion that is implied in a strike. The attitude of workingmen engaged in a bona fide strike is an inspiring one. It is an earnest that slavery will not prevail. The slave alone who will not rise against his master, who will meekly bend his back to the lash and turn his cheek to him who plucks his beard—that slave alone is hopeless. But the slave, who, as you of New Bedford, persists, despite failures and poverty, in rebelling, there is always hope for. This is the reason I have considered it worth my while to leave my home and interrupt my work in New York, and come here, and spend a few days with you. I bank my hopes wholly and build entirely upon this sentiment of rebellion within you.

Whence Do Wages Come and Whence Profits?

What you now stand in need of, aye, more than of bread, is the knowledge of a few elemental principles of political economy and of sociology. Be not frightened at the words. It is only the capitalist professors who try to make them so difficult of understanding that the very mentioning of them is expected to throw the workingman into a palpitation of the heart. The subjects are easy of understanding.

The first point that a workingman should be clear upon is this: What is the source of the wages he receives; what is the source of the profits his employer lives on? The following dialogue is not uncommon:

Workingman—"Do I understand you rightly, that you Socialists want to abolish the capitalist class?"

Socialist—"That is what we are after."

Workingman—"You are! Then I don't want any of you. Why, even now my wages are small; even now I can barely get along. If you abolish the capitalist I'll have nothing; there will be nobody to support me."

Who knows how many workingmen in this hall are typified by the workingman in this dialogue!

When on payday you reach out your horny, "unwashed" hand it is empty. When you take it back again, your wages are on it. Hence the belief that the capitalist is the source of your living, that he is your bread-giver, your supporter. Now that is an error, an optic illusion. . . .

The fact is just the reverse of the appearance: that, not the capitalist, but the workingman, is the source of the worker's living; that it is not the capitalist who supports the workingman, but the workingman who supports the capitalist (Loud applause); that it is not the capitalist who gives bread to the workingman, but the workingman who gives himself a dry crust, and sumptuously stocks the table of the capitalist (Long and loud applause). This is a cardinal point in political economy; and this is the point I wish first of all to establish in your minds. Now, to the proof.

Say that I own $100,000. Don't ask me where I got it. If you do, I would have to answer you in the language of all capitalists that "such a question is un-American." You must not look into the source of this my "original accumulation": it is un-American to pry into such secrets. (Laughter.) Presently I shall take you into my confidence. For the present I shall draw down the blinds, and keep out your un-American curiosity. I have $100,000, and am a capitalist. Now, I may not know much; no capitalist does; but I know a few things, and among them is a little plain arithmetic. I take a pencil and put down on a sheet of paper "$100,000." Having determined that I shall need at least $5,000 a year to live with comfort, I divide the $100,000 by $5,000; the quotient is 20. My hair then begins to stand on end. The 20 tells me that, if I pull $5,000 annually out of $100,000, these are exhausted during that term. At the beginning of the 21st year I shall have nothing left. "Heaven and earth, I would then have to go to work if I wanted to live!" No capitalist relishes that thought. He will tell you, and pay his politicians, professors and political parsons to tell you, that "labor is honorable." He is perfectly willing to let you have that undivided honor, and will do all he can that you may not be deprived of any part of it; but, as to himself, he has for work a constitutional aversion; the capitalist runs away from work like the man bitten by a mad dog runs away from water. I want to live without work on my $100,000 and yet keep my capital untouched. If you ask any farmer, he will tell you that if he invests in a Durham cow she will yield him a supply of 16 quarts a day, but, after some years, the supply goes down; she will run dry; and then a new cow must be got. But I, the capitalist, aim at making my capital a sort of $100,000 cow, which I shall annually be able to milk $5,000 out of, without her ever running dry. I want, in short, to perform the proverbially impossible feat of eating my cake, and yet having it. The capitalist system performs that feat for me. How?

I go to a broker. I say, Mr. Broker, I have $100,000; I want you to invest that for me. I don't tell him that I have a special liking for New Bedford mills' stock; I don't tell him I have a special fancy for railroad stock; I leave the choosing with him. The only direction I give him is to get the stock in such a corporation as will pay the highest dividend. Mr. Broker has a list of all of these corporations, your New Bedford corporations among them, to the extent that they may be listed; he makes the choice, say of one of your mills right here in this town. I hire a vault in a safe deposit company and I put my stock into it. I lock it up, put the key in my pocket, and I go and have a good time. If it is too cold in the north I go down to Florida; if it is too hot there I go to the Adirondack Mountains; occasionally I take a spin across the Atlantic and run the gauntlet of all the gambling dens in Europe; I spend my time with fast horses and faster women; I never put my foot inside the factory that I hold stock of; I don't even come to the town in which it is located, and yet, lo and behold, a miracle takes place! . . .

I can lie flat on my back all day and all night; and every three months my manna comes down to me in the shape of dividends. Where does it come from? What does the dividend represent?

In the factory of which my broker bought stock, workmen, thousands of them, were at work; they have woven cloth that has been put upon the market to the value of $7,000; out of the $7,000 that the cloth is worth my wage workers receive $2,000 in wages, and I receive the $5,000 as profits or dividends. Did I, who never put my foot inside of the mill; did I, who never put my foot inside of New Bedford; did I, who don't know how a loom looks; did I, who contributed nothing whatever toward the weaving of that cloth; did I do any work whatever toward producing those $5,000 that came to me? No man, with brains in his head instead of sawdust, can deny that those $7,000 are exclusively the product of the wage workers in that mill. That out of the wealth thus produced by them alone, they get $2,000 in wages, and I, who did nothing at all, I get the $5,000. The wages these workers receive represent wealth that they have themselves produced; the profits that the capitalist pockets represent wealth that the wage workers produced, and that the capitalist, does what?—let us call things by their names—that the capitalist steals from them.

The Stock Corporation

You may ask, But is that the rule, is not that illustration an exception?— Yes, it is the rule; the exception is the other thing. The leading industries of the United States are today stock concerns, and thither will all others worth mentioning move. An increasing volume of capital in money is held in stocks and shares. The individual capitalist holds stock in a score of

9

concerns in different trades, located in different towns, too many and too varied for him even to attempt to run. By virtue of his stock, he draws his income from them; which is the same as saying that he lives on what the workingmen produce but are robbed of. Nor is the case at all essentially different with the concerns that have not yet developed into stock corporations.

"Directors"

Again, you may ask, The conclusion that what such stockholders live on is stolen wealth because they evidently perform no manner of work is irrefutable, but are all stockholders equally idle and superfluous; are there not some who do perform some work; are there not "Directors"?—There are "Directors," but these gentlemen bear a title much like those "Generals" and "Majors" and "Colonels" who now go about, and whose generalship, majorship and colonelship consisted in securing substitutes during the war. (Applause.) These "Directors" are simply the largest stockholders, which is the same as to say that they are the largest sponges; their directorship consists only in directing conspiracies against rival "Directors," in bribing Legislatures, Executives and Judiciaries, in picking out and hiring men out of your midst to serve as bell-wethers that will lead you like cattle to the capitalist shambles, and tickle you into contentment and hopefulness while you are being fleeced. The court decisions removing responsibility from the "Directors" are numerous and increasing; each such decision establishes, from the capitalist Government's own mouth, the idleness and superfluousness of the capitalist class. These "Directors," and the capitalist class in general, may perform some "work," they do perform some "work," but that "work" is not of a sort that directly or indirectly aids production;—no more than the intense mental strain and activity of the "work" done by the pickpocket is directly or indirectly productive. (Applause.)

"Original Accumulation"

Finally, you may ask, No doubt the stockholder does no work, and hence lives on the wealth we produce; no doubt these "Directors" have a title that only emphasizes their idleness by a swindle, and, consequently, neither they are other than sponges on the working class; but did not your own illustration start with the supposition that the capitalist in question had $100,000, is not his original capital entitled to some returns?—This question opens an important one; and now I shall, as I promised you, take you into my confidence; I shall raise the curtain which I pulled down before the question, Where did I get it? I shall now let you pry into my secret.

Whence does this original capital, or "original accumulation," come? Does it grow on the capitalist like hair on his face, or nails on his fingers and toes? Does he secrete it as he secretes sweat from his body? . . . Read the biographies of any of our founders of capitalist concerns by the torch-light of . . . his biography, and you will find them all to be essentially the same, or suggestively silent upon the doings of our man during the period that he gathers his "original accumulation." You will find that "original capital" to be the child of fraudulent failures and fires, of high-handed crime of some sort or other, or of the sneaking crime of appropriating trust funds, etc. With such "original capital,"—gotten by dint of such "cleverness," "push," and "industry,"—as a weapon, the "original" capitalist proceeds to fleece the working class that has been less "industrious," "pushing" and "clever" than he. If he consumes all his fleecings, his capital remains of its original size in his hands, unless some other gentleman of the road, gifted with greater "industry," "push" and "cleverness" than he, comes around and relieves him of it; if he consumes not the whole of his fleecings, his capital moves upward, million-ward.

The case is proved: Labor alone produces all wealth. Wages are that part of Labor's own product that the workingman is allowed to keep; profits are the present and running stealings perpetrated by the capitalist upon the workingman from day to day, from week to week, from month to month, from year to year; capital is the accumulated past stealings of the capitalist—corner-stoned upon his "original accumulation." (Long applause.)

Who of you before me fails now to understand, or would still deny that, not the capitalist supports the workingman, but the workingman supports the capitalist; or still holds that the workingman could not exist without the capitalist? If any there be, let him raise his hand and speak up now.

None? Then I may consider this point settled; and shall move on.

The pregnant point that underlies these pregnant facts is that, between the Working Class and the Capitalist Class, there is an irrepressible conflict, a class struggle for life. No glib-tongued politician can vault over it, no capitalist professor or official statistician can argue it away; no capitalist parson can veil it; no labor fakir can straddle it; no "reform" architect can bridge it over. It crops up in all manner of ways, like in this strike, in ways that disconcert all the plans and all the schemes of those who would deny or ignore it. It is a struggle that will not down, and must be ended only by either the total subjugation of the Working Class, or the abolition of the Capitalist Class. (Loud applause.)

Thus you perceive that the theory on which your "pure and simple" trade organizations are grounded, and on which you went into this strike, is false. There being no "common interests," but only HOSTILE INTERESTS, between the Capitalist Class and the Working Class, the battle you are waging to establish "safe relations" between the two is a hopeless one.

Put to the touchstone of these undeniable principles the theory upon which your "pure and simple" trade organizations are built, and you will find it to be false; examined by the light of these undeniable principles the road that your false theory makes you travel and the failures that have marked your career must strike you as its inevitable result. How are we to organize and proceed? you may ask. Before answering the question, let me take up another branch of the subject. . . .

Development of Capitalist Society

Let us take a condensed page of the country's history. For the sake of plainness, and forced to it by the exigency of condensation, I shall assume small figures. Place yourselves back a sufficient number of years with but ten competing weaving concerns in the community. How the individual ten owners came by the "original accumulations" that enabled them to start as capitalists you now know. (Laughter.) Say that each of the ten capitalists employs ten men; that each man receives $2 a day, and that the product of each of the ten sets of men in each of the ten establishments is worth $40 a day. You know now also that it is out of these $40 worth of wealth, produced by the men, that each of the ten competing capitalists takes the $20 that he pays the ten men in wages, and that out of that same $40 worth of wealth he takes the $20 that he pockets as profits. Each of these ten capitalists makes, accordingly, $120 a week.

This amount of profits, one should think, should satisfy our ten capitalists. It is a goodly sum to pocket without work. Indeed, it may satisfy some, say most of them. But if for any of many reasons it does not satisfy any one of them, the whole string of them is set in commotion. "Individuality" is a deity at whose shrine the capitalist worships, or affects to worship. In point of fact, capitalism robs of individuality, not only the working class, but capitalists themselves. The action of any one of the lot compels action by all; like a row of bricks, the dropping of one makes all the others drop successively. Let us take No. 1. He is not satisfied with $120 a week. . . . As all the wealth produced in his shop is $40 a day, he knows that, if he increases his share of $20 to $30, there will be only $10 left for wages. He tries this. He announces a wage reduction of 50 percent. His men spontaneously draw themselves together and refuse to work; they go on strike. What is the situation?

In those days it needed skill, acquired by long training, to do the work; there may have been corner-loafers out of work, but not weavers; possibly at some great distance there may have been weavers actually obtainable, but in those days there was neither telegraph nor railroad to communicate with them; finally, the nine competitors of No. 1, having no strike on hand, continued to produce, and thus threatened to crowd No. 1 out of the market. Thus circumstanced, No. 1 caves in. He withdraws his order of wage reduction. "Come in," he says to his striking workmen, "let's make up; Labor and Capital are brothers; the most loving of brothers sometimes fall out; we have had such a falling out; it was a slip; you have organized yourselves in a union with a $2 a day wage scale; I shall never fight the union; I love it, come back to work." And the men did.

Thus ended the first strike. The victory won by the men made many of them feel bold. At their first next meeting they argued: "The employer wanted to reduce our wages and got left; why may not we take the hint and reduce his profits by demanding higher wages; we licked him in his attempt to lower our wages, why should we not lick him in an attempt to resist our demand for more pay?" But the labor movement is democratic. No one man can run things. At that union meeting the motion to demand higher pay is made by one member, another must second it; amendments and amendments to the amendments are put with the requisite seconders; debate follows; points of order are raised, ruled on, appealed from and settled;—in the meantime it grows late, the men must be at work early the next morning, the hour to adjourn arrives, and the whole matter is left pending. Thus much for the men.

Now for the employer. He locks himself up in his closet. With clenched fists and scowl on brow, he gnashes his teeth at the victory of his "brother" Labor, its union and its union regulations. And he ponders. More money he must have and is determined to have. This resolution is arrived at with the swiftness and directness which capitalists are able to. Differently from his men, he is not many, but one. He makes the motion, seconds it himself, puts it, and carries it unanimously. More profits he SHALL HAVE. But how? Aid comes to him through the mail. The letter-carrier brings him a circular from a machine shop. Such circulars are frequent even to-day. It reads like this: "Mr. No. 1, you are employing 10 men; I have in my machine shop a beautiful machine with which you can produce, with 5 men, twice as much as now with 10; this machine does not chew tobacco; it does not smoke (some of these circulars are cruel and add: this machine has no wife who gets sick and keeps it home to attend to her: it has no children who die, and whom to bury it must stay away from work); it never goes on strike, it works and grumbles not; come and see it."

Invention

Right here let me lock a switch at which not a few people are apt to switch off and be banked. Some may think: "Well, at least that machine capitalist is entitled to his profits; he surely is an inventor." A grave error. Look into the history of our inventors, and you will see that those who really profited by their genius are so few that you can count them on the fingers of your hands, and have fingers to spare. The capitalists either take advantage of the inventor's stress and buy his invention for a song; the inventor believes he can make his haul with his next invention; but before that is perfected, he is as poor as before, and the same advantage is again taken of him; until finally the brown of his brains being exhausted, he sinks into a pauper's grave, leaving the fruit of his genius for private capitalists to grow rich on; or the capitalist simply steals the invention and gets his courts to decide against the inventor. From Eli Whitney down, that is the treatment the inventor, as a rule, receives from the capitalist class.

Such a case, illustrative of the whole situation, happened recently. The Bonsack Machine Co. discovered that its employees made numerous inventions, and it decided to appropriate them wholesale. To this end, it locked out its men, and demanded of all applicants for work that they sign a contract whereby, in "consideration of employment," they assign to the company all their rights in whatever invention they may make during the term of their employment. One of these employees, who had signed such a contract, informed the company one day that he thought he could invent a machine by which cigarettes could be held closed by crimping at the ends, instead of pasting. This was a valuable idea; and he was told to go ahead. For six months he worked at this invention and perfected it; and, having during all that time, received not a cent in wages or otherwise from the company, he patented his invention himself. The company immediately brought suit against him in the Federal Courts, claiming that the invention was its property; and—THE FEDERAL COURT DECIDED IN FAVOR OF THE COMPANY, THUS ROBBING THE INVENTOR OF HIS TIME, HIS MONEY, OF THE FRUIT OF HIS GENIUS, AND OF HIS UNQUESTIONABLE RIGHTS!! (Cries of "Shame" in the hall.) "Shame"? Say not "Shame"! He who himself applies the torch to his own house has no cause to cry "Shame!" when the flames consume it. Say rather "Natural!" and smiting your own breasts say "Ours the fault!" Having elected into power the Democratic, Republican, Free Trade, Protection, Silver or Gold platforms of the capitalist class, the working class has none but itself to blame, if the official lackeys of that class turn against the working class the public powers put into their hands. (Loud applause.)—The capitalist owner of the machine shop that sends the circular did not make the invention.

The Screws Begin to Turn

To return to No. 1. He goes and sees the machine; finds it to be as represented; buys it; puts it up in his shop; picks out of his 10 men the 5 least active in the late strike; sets them to work at $2 a day as before; and full of bows and smirks, addresses the other 5 thus: "I am sorry I have no places for you; I believe in union principles and am paying the union scale to the 5 men I need; I don't need you now; good-bye. I hope I'll see you again." And he means this last as you will presently perceive.

What is the situation now? No. 1 pays, as before, $2 a day, but to only 5 men; these, with the aid of the machine, now produce twice as much as the 10 did before; their product is now $80 worth of wealth; as only $10 of this goes in wages, the capitalist has a profit of $70 a day, or 250 per-cent more. . . .

Now watch the men whom his machine displaced; their career throws quite some light on the whole question. Are they not "American citizens"? Is not this a "Republic with a Constitution"? Is anything else wanted to get a living? Watch them! They go to No. 2 for a job; before they quite reach the place, the doors open and 5 of that concern are likewise thrown out upon the street.—What happened there? The "individuality" of No. 2 yielded to the pressure of capitalist development. The purchase of the machine by No. 1 enabled him to produce so much more plentifully and cheaply; if No. 2 did not do likewise, he would be crowded out of the market by No. 1; No. 2, accordingly, also invested in a machine, with the result that 5 of his men are also thrown out.

These 10 unemployed proceed to No. 3, hoping for better luck there.

But what sight is that that meets their astonished eyes? Not 5 men, as walked out of Nos. 1 and 2, but all No. 3's 10 have landed on the street; and, what is more surprising yet to them, No. 3 himself is on the street, now reduced to the condition of a workingman along with his former employees.—What is it that happened there? In this instance the "individuality" of No. 3 was crushed by capitalist development. The same reason that drove No. 2 to procure the machine, rendered the machine indispensable to No. 3. But having, differently from his competitors Nos. 1 and 2, spent all his stealings from the workingmen instead of saving up some, he is now unable to make the purchase; is, consequently, unable to produce as cheaply as they; is, consequently, driven into bankruptcy, and lands in the class of the proletariat, whose ranks are thus increased.

The now 21 unemployed proceed in their hunt for work, and make the round of the other mills. The previous experiences are repeated. Not only are there no jobs to be had; but everywhere workers are thrown out, if the employer got the machine; and if he did not, workers with their former employers, now ruined, join the army of the unemployed.

What happened in that industry happened in all others. Thus the ranks of the capitalist class are thinned out, and the class is made more powerful, while the ranks of the working class are swelled, and the class is made weaker. This is the process that explains how, on the one hand, your New Bedford mills become the property of ever fewer men; how, according to the census, their aggregate capital runs up to over $14,000,000; how, despite "bad times," their profits run up to upwards of $1,300,000; how, on the other hand, your position becomes steadily more precarious.

No. 1's men return to where they started from. Scabbing they will not. Uninformed upon the mechanism of capitalism, they know not what struck them; and they expect "better times,"—just as so many equally uninformed workingmen are expecting today; in the meantime, thinking thereby to hasten the advent of the good times, No. 1's men turn out the Republican party and turn in the Democratic, turn out the Democratic and turn in the Republican,—just as our misled workingmen are now doing (Applause), not understanding that, whether they put in or out Republicans, Democrats, Protectionists or Free Traders, Goldbugs or Silverbugs, they are every time putting in the capitalist platform, upholding the social principle that throws them out of work or reduces their wages. (Long applause.)

But endurance has its limits. The Superintendent of the Pennsylvania Railroad for the Indiana Division, speaking, of course, from the capitalist standpoint, recently said: "Many solutions are being offered for the labor question; but there is just one and no more. It is this: Lay a silver dollar on the shelf, and at the end of a year you have a silver dollar left; lay a workingman on the shelf, and at the end of a month you have a skeleton left. (Loud applause.) "This," said he, "is the solution of the labor problem." In short, starve out the workers. No. 1's men finally reach that point. Finally that happens that few if any can resist. A man may stand starvation and resist the sight of starving wife and children; but if he has not wherewith to buy medicine to save the life of a sick wife or child, all control is lost over him. On the heels of starvation, sickness follows, and No. 1's men throw to the wind all union principles; they are now ready to do anything to save their dear ones. Cap in hand, they appear before No. 1, the starch taken clean out of them during the period they "lay on the shelf." They ask for work; they themselves offer to work for $1 a day. And No. 1, the brother of labor, who but recently expressed devotion to the union, what of him? His eyes sparkle at "seeing again" the men he had thrown out; at their offer to work for less than the men now employed, his chest expands, and, grabbing them by the hand in a delirium of patriotic ecstasy, he says: "Welcome, my noble American citizens. (Applause.) I am proud to see you ready to work and earn an honest penny for your dear wives and darling children (Applause); I am delighted to notice that you are not, like so many others, too lazy to work (Applause); let the American eagle screech in honor of your emancipation from the slavery of a rascally union (Long applause); let the American eagle wag his tail an extra wag in honor of your freedom from a dictatorial walking delegate (Long applause); you are my long-lost brothers (Laughter and long applause); go in my $1-a-day brothers!" and he throws his former $2-a-day brothers heels over head upon the sidewalk. (Long and prolonged applause.)

When the late $2-a-day men have recovered from their surprise, they determine on war. But what sort of war? Watch them closely, and you may detect many a feature of your own in that mirror. "Have we not struck," argue they, "and beaten this employer once before? If we strike again, we shall again beat him." But the conditions have wholly changed.

In the first place, there were no unemployed skilled workers during that first strike; now there are; plenty of them, dumped upon the country, not out of the steerage of vessels from Europe, but by the native-born machine.

In the second place, that very machine has to such an extent eliminated skill that, while formerly only the unemployed in a certain trade could endanger the jobs of those at work in that trade, now the unemployed of all trades (virtually the whole army of the unemployed) bear down upon the employed in each; we know of quondam shoemakers taking the jobs of hatters; quondam hatters taking the jobs of weavers; quondam weavers taking the jobs of cigarmakers; quondam cigarmakers taking the jobs of "machinists"; quondam farm hands taking the jobs of factory hands, etc., etc., so easy has it become to learn what is now needed to be known of a trade.

In the third place, telegraph and railroads have made all of the unemployed easily accessible to the employer.

Finally, different from former days, the competitors have to a great extent consolidated; here in New Bedford, for instance, the false appearance of competition between the mill owners is punctured by the fact that to a great extent seemingly "independent" mills are owned by one family. . . .

Not, as at the first strike, with their flanks protected, but now wholly exposed through the existence of a vast army of hungry unemployed; not, as before, facing a divided enemy, but now faced by a consolidated mass of capitalist concerns; how different is now the situation of the strikers! The changed conditions brought about changed results; instead of VICTORY, there was DEFEAT (Applause); and we have had a long series of them. Either hunger drove the men back to work; or the unemployed took their places; or, if the capitalist was in a hurry, he fetched in the help of the strong arm of the government, now HIS GOVERNMENT.

Principles of Sound Organization

We now have a sufficient survey of the field to enable us to answer the question, How shall we organize so as not to fight the same old hopeless battle?

Proceeding from the knowledge that labor alone produces all wealth; that less and less of this wealth comes to the working class, and more and more of it is plundered by the idle class or capitalist; that this is the result of the working class being stripped of the tool (machine), without which it cannot earn a living; and, finally, that the machine or tool has reached such a state of development that it can no longer be operated by the individual but needs the collective effort of many;—proceeding from this knowledge, it is clear that the aim of all intelligent class-conscious workingmen must be the overthrow of the system of private ownership in the tools of production because that system keeps them in wage slavery.

Proceeding from the further knowledge of the use made of the Government by the capitalist class, and of the necessity that class is under to own the Government, so as to enable it to uphold and prop up the capitalist system;—proceeding from that knowledge, it is clear that the aim of all intelligent, class-conscious workingmen must be to bring the Government under the control of their own class by joining and electing the American wing of the International Socialist party—the Socialist Labor party of America, and thus establishing the Socialist Co-operative Republic. (Applause.)

But in the meantime, while moving toward that ideal, though necessary, goal, what to do? The thing cannot be accomplished in a day, nor does election come around every twenty-four hours. Is there nothing that we can do for ourselves between election and election?

Yes; plenty.

When crowded, in argument, to the wall by us New Trade Unionists, by us of the Socialist Trade and Labor Alliance, your present, or old and "pure and simple" organizations yield the point of ultimate aims; they grant the ultimate necessity of establishing Socialism; but they claim "the times are not yet ripe" for that; and, not yet being ripe, they lay emphasis upon the claim that the "pure and simple" union does the workers some good NOW by getting something NOW from the employers and from the capitalist parties. We are not "practical" they tell us; they are. Let us test this theory on the spot. Here in New Bedford there is not yet a single New Trade Unionist organization in existence. The "pure and simple" trade union has had the field all to itself. All of you, whose wages are NOW higher than they were five years ago, kindly raise a hand. (No hand is raised.) All of you whose wages are now lower than five years ago, please raise a hand. (The hands of the large audience go up.) The proof of the pudding lies in the eating. Not only does "pure and simpledom" shut off your hope of emancipation by affecting to think such a state of things is unreachable now, but in the meantime and RIGHT NOW, the "good" it does to you, the "something" it secures for you "from the employers and from the politicians" is lower wages. (Prolonged applause.) . . .

The New Trade Unionist knows that no one or two, or even half a dozen elections will place in the hands of the working class the Government of the land; and New Trades Unionism not only wishes to do something now for the workers, but it knows that the thing can be done, and how to do it.

"Pure and Simple" or British trade unionism has done a double mischief to the workers: besides leaving them in their present pitiable plight, it has caused many to fly off the handle and lose all trust in the power of trade organization. The best of these, those who have not become pessimistic and have not been wholly demoralized, see nothing to be done but voting right on election day—casting their vote straight for the S. L. P.

This is a serious error. By thus giving over all participation in the industrial movement, they wholly disconnect themselves from the class struggle that is going on every day; and by putting off their whole activity to a single day in the year—election day, they become floaters in the air. I know several such. Without exception they are dreamy and flighty and unbalanced in their methods.

The utter impotence of "pure and simple" unionism today is born of causes that may be divided under two main heads.

One is the contempt in which the capitalist and ruling class holds the working people. In 1886, when instinct was, unconsciously to myself, leading me to look into the social problem, when as yet it was to me a confused and blurred interrogation mark, I associated wholly with capitalists. Expressions of contempt for the workers were common. One day I asked a set of them why they treated their men so hard, and had so poor an opinion of them. "They are ignorant, stupid and corrupt," was the answer, almost in chorus.

"What makes you think so?" I asked. "Have you met them all?"

"No," was the reply, "we have not met them all individually, but we have had to deal with their leaders, and they are ignorant, stupid and corrupt. Surely these leaders must be the best among them, or they would not choose them." . . .

In Washington there is a son of a certain labor leader with a Government job. He is truly "non-partisan." Democrats may go and Republicans may come, Republicans may go and Democrats may come, but he goeth not; the Democratic and the Republican capitalists may fight like cats and dogs, but on one thing they fraternize like cooing doves, to wit, to keep that son of a labor leader in office. Who is the father of that son?—Mr. Samuel Gompers, "President of the A. F. of L." . . .

The ignorance, stupidity and corruption of the "pure and simple" labor leaders are such that the capitalist class despises you. The first prerequisite for success in a struggle is the respect of the enemy. (Applause.)

The other main cause of the present impotence of "pure and simple" unionism is that, through its ignoring the existing class distinctions, and its ignoring the close connection there is between wages and politics, it splits up at the ballot box among the parties of capital, and thus unites in upholding the system of capitalist exploitation. Look at the recent miners' strike; the men were shot down and the strike was lost; this happened in the very midst of a political campaign; and these miners, who could at any election capture the Government, or at least, by polling a big vote against capitalism announce their advance towards freedom, are seen to turn right around and vote back into power the very class that had just trampled upon them. What prospect is there in sight of such conduct, of the capitalists becoming gentler? Or of the union gaining for the men anything NOW except more wage reductions, enforced by bullets? None! The prospect of the miners and other workers doing the same thing over again, a prospect that is made all the surer if they allow themselves to be further led by the labor fakirs whom the capitalists keep in pay, renders sure that capitalist outrages will be repeated and further capitalist encroachments will follow. Otherwise were it if the union, identifying politics and wages, voted against capitalism; if it struck at the ballot box against the wage system with the same solidarity that it demands for the strike in the shop. Protected once a year by the guns of an increasing class-conscious party of labor, the union could be a valuable fortification behind which to conduct the daily class struggle in the shops. The increasing Socialist Labor Party vote alone would not quite give that temporary protection in the shop that such an increasing vote would afford if in the shop also the workers were intelligently organized, and honestly, because intelligently, led. Without organization in the shop, the capitalist could outrage at least individuals. Shop organization alone, unbacked by that political force that threatens the capitalist class with extinction, the working class being the overwhelming majority, leaves the workers wholly unprotected. But the shop organization that combines in its warfare the annually recurring class-conscious ballot, can stem capitalist encroachment from day to day. The trade organization IS impotent if built and conducted upon the impotent lines of ignorance and corruption. The trade organization IS NOT impotent if built and conducted upon the lines of knowledge and honesty; if it understands the issue and steps into the arena fully equipped, not with the shield of the trade union only, but also with the sword of the Socialist ballot.

The essential principles of sound organization are, accordingly, these:

1st—A trade organization must be clear upon the fact that, not until it has overthrown the capitalist system of private ownership in the machinery of production, and made this the joint property of the people, thereby compelling every one to work if he wants to live, is it at all possible for the workers to be safe. (Applause.)

2nd—A labor organization must be perfectly clear upon the fact that it cannot reach safety until it has wrenched the Government from the clutches of the capitalist class; and that it cannot do that unless it votes, not for MEN but for PRINCIPLES, unless it votes into power its own class platform and programme: THE ABOLITION OF THE WAGES SYSTEM OF SLAVERY.

3rd—A labor organization must be perfectly clear upon the fact that politics are not, like religion, a private concern, any more than the wages and the hours of a workingman are his private concern. For the same reason that his wages and hours are the concern of his class, so is his politics. (Applause.) Politics is not separable from wages. For the same reason that the organization of labor dictates wages, hours, etc., in the interest of the working class, for that same reason must it dictate politics also; and for the same reason that it execrates the scab in the shop, it must execrate the scab at the hustings. (Applause.)

The Work of the Socialist Trade and Labor Alliance

Long did the Socialist Labor Party and New Trade Unionists seek to deliver this important message to the broad masses of the American proletariat, the rank and file of our working class. But we could not reach, we could not get at them. Between us and them there stood a solid wall of ignorant, stupid, and corrupt labor fakirs. Like men groping in a dark room for an exit, we moved along the wall, bumping our heads, feeling ever onwards for a door; we made the circuit and no passage was found. The wall was solid. This discovery once made, there was no way other than to batter a breach through that wall. With the battering ram of the Socialist Trade & Labor Alliance we effected a passage; the wall now crumbles; at last we stand face to face with the rank and file of the American proletariat (Long and continued applause); and we ARE DELIVERING OUR MESSAGE (Renewed applause)—as you may judge from the howl that goes up from that fakirs' wall that we have broken through.

I shall not consider my time well spent with you if I see no fruit of my labors; if I leave not behind me in New Bedford Local Alliances of your trades organized in the Socialist Trade & Labor Alliance. That will be my best contribution toward your strike, as they will serve as centers of enlightenment to strengthen you in your conflict, to the extent that it may now be possible.

In conclusion, my best advice to you for immediate action is to step out boldly upon the streets, as soon as you can; organize a monster parade of the strikers and of all the other working people in the town; and let the parade be headed by a banner bearing the announcement to your employers:

We will fight you in this strike to the bitter end; your money bag may beat us now; but whether it does or not, that is not the end, it is only the beginning of the song; in November we will meet again at Philippi, and the strike shall not end until, with the falchion of the Socialist Labor Party ballot, we shall have laid you low for all time! (Loud applause.)

This is the message that it has been my agreeable privilege to deliver to you in the name of the Socialist Labor Party and of the New Trade Unionists or Alliance men of the land. (Prolonged applause.)

PART II
Revolutionary
Unionism

A s a result of the Western Federation of Miners' demand for a more universal and militant labor organization, a secret meeting of radical labor people was held in Chicago early in 1905. As the chairman of this group, Big Bill Haywood (1869–1928) opened the meeting by banging a piece of wood on the table and by asserting that the new organization's purpose was to transfer ownership of the means of production from capitalists to workers. Among the thirty-two people present (said to represent about 100,000 workers) were Eugene Debs, Daniel De Leon, A. M. Simons, and Mother Jones. The manifesto (the beginning of Document 2) sent out by this group condemned all earlier labor organizing as limited and fragmentary, as any craft structure like the AFL had to be. One universal, tough union was wanted. The solution had to match the problem, so labor unity and aggressiveness had to be stronger than that of capitalism.

The response to the manifesto was a convention (extracts of the proceedings are in Document 2) in Brand's Hall in Chicago of over 200 delegates who represented, in varying estimates, from 60,000 to 300,000 workers. The twelve labor organizations that finally joined the new union actually represented 49,010 workers, of whom 27,000 were members of the Western Federation of Miners. Two hundred thousand copies of the manifesto were distributed on 27 June 1905, the first day of the founding convention of the Industrial Workers of the World, the "Wobblies." The convention lasted for about two weeks, and the basic ideological and tactical conflict on the left was perfectly reflected in its proceedings. Was the road to socialism direct economic action or political organization? Or some combination of both?

Haywood, the convention's chairman, tried to ease the conflict by saying that political organization would inevitably flow from economic power. T. J. Hagerty, a defrocked Catholic priest, read the divisive preamble to the delegates. This document flatly asserted that labor should not affiliate politically with any present party or group, but that labor would take political power after it had taken economic power. De Leon, as could be expected from the guiding spirit of the Socialist Labor Party and representative of the Socialist Trade and Labor Alliance, and as a more thorough-going Marxist, insisted on political organization while he pointed out that established politics were so corrupt that labor would have to go its own political way. (Each of these documents and reactions is reprinted in the following extracts from the IWW convention.)

Even though the preamble passed the convention with no substantial amendment, the inability to satisfactorily resolve this conflict eventually led to Debs's withdrawal from the IWW, to a purge of De Leon, and to the victory of Hagerty, Vincent St. John, and Haywood (who was, however, not quite so single-minded in his commitment to violence and industrial sabotage). Now the IWW demanded that labor seize industry rather than merely strike against it, a prelude of the sitdown strikes of the 1930's as well as of the civil rights and campus seizures of the 1960's.

The problem of direct action versus political action was resolved for the Wobblies in 1908 in a new preamble which stated that the world's workers must organize as a class, "take possession of the earth and the machinery of production, and abolish the wage system." Political radicalism was driven from the IWW.

Congress authorized the creation of an Industrial Relations Commission in 1912 to investigate recent industrial conflict, especially the Lawrence strike. Woodrow Wilson appointed the commission members with Frank P. Walsh, a midwestern lawyer, as chairman.

The following testimony (Document 3) of "The Saint," Vincent St. John (1873–1929), is a clear and detailed description of how the Wobblies perceived their own tactics and strategy. With Bill Haywood, St. John had been a member of the Western Federation of Miners and a founder of the IWW. He was instrumental in the expulsion of De Leon, and was the General Secretary of the Wobblies from 1908 until he quit in 1914 (to be succeeded by Haywood). St. John was among the Wobbly leaders arrested for suspected sabotage or espionage during the war.

In his testimony before this Senate commission, St. John defended the Wobblies' condemnation of other labor organizations, his willingness to destroy the property of capitalists, and his belief in violence against persons in self-defense. Whether the members of the commission could make anything of St. John's description of government as a committee empowered to serve the capitalists, or of his prediction that government would "die of dry-rot" after the working class took control of industry, is doubtful. St. John apparently did not think it was necessary to hide his position from this creature of the U.S. Senate, and his testimony revealed the inner workings of the Wobblies.

The Wobblies, alone among the organized American left, had style and local color. The "hallelujah I'm a bum" mentality was both joyous and prideful, and the sometimes wild exuberance of Wobbly actions contributed to both their failures and successes. They could go further and faster than their organization could sustain, but their courageous and intelligent leadership of the Lawrence strike of 1912 resulted in an important victory for the textile workers and an important defeat for the state-municipal-police establishment. Their free speech struggles in the West (an anticipation of the Free Speech Movement crisis at Berkeley in the mid-sixties) led to arrests, violence, defeats, and success, and through it all the Wobbly tough-as-hell, no-pie-in-the-sky camaraderie was maintained. The image of this most uniquely American splinter of the Left remained that of the brothers swapping tales of struggle around a western camp fire.

The IWW opposition to World War I led to their disintegration. Haywood and a hundred others were arrested, and convicted of, espionage in a mass Chicago trial, and the leadership was broken. Haywood finally fled to the Soviet Union, where he died; his ashes still rest in an honored place in the Kremlin wall. With him a significant chapter of the Left *seemed* to close, but some of the young radicals of the 1960's were walking his path, whether they knew about him or not. It must be that the same impulses drove them both, the same despair about political organization, the same cultural defiance and toughness, the commitment to direct action as the necessary tactic on the way to socialism. But the strongest link is style, a belief in the community of brothers and sisters, and a positive celebration of living and fighting outside of—underneath—the American mainstream.

PROCEEDINGS OF THE FIRST CONVENTION OF THE INDUSTRIAL WORKERS OF THE WORLD

MR. [William D.] Haywood: The reading of the Manifesto will take place at this time.

Mr. A. M. Simons, of Chicago, then read the Manifesto calling for the convention, as follows:

Manifesto

Social relations and groupings only reflect mechanical and industrial conditions. The *great facts* of present industry are the displacement of human skill by machines and the increase of capitalist power through concentration in the possession of the tools with which wealth is produced and distributed.

Because of these facts trade divisions among laborers and competition among capitalists are alike disappearing. Class divisions grow ever more fixed and class antagonisms more sharp. Trade lines have been swallowed up in a common servitude of all workers to the machines which they tend. New machines, ever replacing less productive ones, wipe out whole trades and plunge new bodies of workers into the ever-growing army of tradeless, hopeless unemployed. As human beings and human skill are displaced by mechanical progress, the capitalists need use the workers only during that brief period when muscles and nerves respond most intensely. The moment the laborer no longer yields the maximum of profits, he is thrown upon the scrap pile, to starve alongside the discarded machine. A *dead line* has been drawn, and an age-limit established, to cross which, in this world of monopolized opportunities, means condemnation to industrial death.

The worker, wholly separated from the land and the tools, with his skill

SOURCE: *Proceedings of the First Convention of the Industrial Workers of the World, Founded at Chicago, June 27–July 8, 1905* (New York: New York Labor News Co., 1905), pp. 3–7, 153–157, 220–221, 223–228.

of craftsmanship rendered useless, is sunk in the uniform mass of wage slaves. He sees his power of resistance broken by craft divisions, perpetuated from out-grown industrial stages. His wages constantly grow less as his hours grow longer and monopolized prices grow higher. Shifted hither and thither by the demands of the profit-takers, the laborer's home no longer exists. In this helpless condition he is forced to accept whatever humiliating conditions his master may impose. He is submitted to a physical and intellectual examination more searching than was the chattel slave when sold from the auction block. Laborers are no longer classified by differences in trade skill, but the employer assigns them according to the machines to which they are attached. These divisions, far from representing differences in skill or interests among the laborers, are imposed by the employers that workers may be pitted against one another and spurred to greater exertion in the shop, and that all resistance to capitalist tyranny may be weakened by artificial distinctions.

While encouraging these outgrown divisions among the workers the capitalists carefully adjust themselves to the new conditions. They wipe out all differences among themselves and present a united front in their war upon labor. Through employers' associations, they seek to crush, with brutal force, by the injunctions of the judiciary, and the use of military power, all efforts at resistance. Or when the other policy seems more profitable, they conceal their daggers beneath the Civic Federation and hoodwink and betray those whom they would rule and exploit. Both methods depend for success upon the blindness and internal dissensions of the working class. The employers' line of battle and methods of warfare correspond to the solidarity of the mechanical and industrial concentration, while laborers still form their fighting organizations on lines of long-gone trade divisions. The battles of the past emphasize this lesson. The *textile* workers of Lowell, Philadelphia and Fall River; the *butchers* of Chicago, weakened by the disintegrating effects of trade divisions; the *machinists* on the Santa Fe, unsupported by their fellow-workers subject to the same masters; the long-struggling *miners* of Colorado, hampered by lack of unity and solidarity upon the industrial battle-field, all bear witness to the helplessness and impotency of labor as at present organized.

This worn-out and corrupt system offers no promise of improvement and adaptation. There is no silver lining to the clouds of darkness and despair settling down upon the world of labor.

This system offers only a perpetual struggle for slight relief within wage slavery. It is blind to the possibility of establishing an industrial democracy, wherein there shall be no wage slavery, but where the workers will own the tools which they operate, and the product of which they alone will enjoy.

It shatters the ranks of the workers into fragments, rendering them helpless and impotent on the industrial battle-field.

Separation of craft from craft renders industrial and financial solidarity impossible.

Union men scab upon union men; hatred of worker for worker is engendered, and the workers are delivered helpless and disintegrated into the hands of the capitalists.

Craft jealousy leads to the attempt to create trade monopolies. Prohibitive initiation fees are established that force men to become scabs against their will. Men whom manliness or circumstances have driven from one trade are thereby fined when they seek to transfer membership to the union of a new craft.

Craft divisions foster political ignorance among the workers, thus dividing their class at the ballot box, as well as in the shop, mine and factory.

Craft unions may be and have been used to assist employers in the establishment of monopolies and the raising of prices. One set of workers are thus used to make harder the conditions of life of another body of laborers.

Craft divisions hinder the growth of class consciousness of the workers, foster the idea of harmony of interests between employing exploiter and employed slave. They permit the association of the misleaders of the workers with the capitalists in the Civic Federations, where plans are made for the perpetuation of capitalism, and the permanent enslavement of the workers through the wage system.

Previous efforts for the betterment of the working class have proven abortive because limited in scope and disconnected in action.

Universal economic evils afflicting the working class can be eradicated only by a universal working class movement. Such a movement of the working class is impossible while separate craft and wage agreements are made favoring the employer against other crafts in the same industry, and while energies are wasted in fruitless jurisdiction struggles which serve only to further the personal aggrandizement of union officials.

A movement to fulfill these conditions must consist of one great industrial union embracing all industries,—providing for craft autonomy locally, industrial autonomy internationally, and working class unity generally.

It must be founded on the class struggle, and its general administration must be conducted in harmony with the recognition of the irrepressible conflict between the capitalist class and the working class.

It should be established as the economic organization of the working class, without affiliation with any political party.

All power should rest in a collective membership.

Local, national and general administration, including union labels, buttons, badges, transfer cards, initiation fees, and per capita tax should be uniform throughout.

All members must hold membership in the local, national or international union covering the industry in which they are employed, but transfers of membership between unions, local, national or international, should be universal.

Workingmen bringing union cards from industrial unions in foreign countries should be freely admitted into the organization.

The general administration should issue a publication representing the entire union and its principles which should reach all members in every industry at regular intervals.

A *central defense fund,* to which all members contribute equally, should be established and maintained.

All workers, therefore, who agree with the principles herein set forth, will meet in convention at Chicago the 27th day of June, 1905, for the purpose of forming an economic organization of the working class along the lines marked out in this Manifesto.

Representation in the convention shall be based upon the number of workers whom the delegate represents. No delegate, however, shall be given representation in the convention on the numerical basis of an organization unless he has credentials—bearing the seal of his union, local, national or international, and the signatures of the officers thereof— authorizing him to install his union as a working part of the proposed economic organization in the industrial department in which it logically belongs in the general plan of organization. Lacking this authority, the delegate shall represent himself as an individual.

Adopted at Chicago, January 2, 3 and 4, 1905.

A. G. SWING	W. L. HALL	THOS. J. HAGERTY
A. M. SIMONS	CHAS. H. MOYER	FRED D. HENION
W. SHURTLEFF	CLARENCE SMITH	W. J. BRADLEY
FRANK M. MCCABE	WILLIAM ERNEST TRAUTMANN	CHAS. O. SHERMAN
JOHN M. O'NEIL	JOS. SCHMIDT	M. E. WHITE
GEO. ESTES	JOHN GUILD	WM. J. PINKERTON
WM. D. HAYWOOD	DANIEL MCDONALD	FRANK KRAFFS
MOTHER JONES	EUGENE V. DEBS	J. E. FITZGERALD
ERNEST UNTERMANN	THOS. J. DE YOUNG	FRANK BOHN . . .

Speech of William D. Haywood

William D. Haywood being called by the convention said:

It has been said that this convention was to form an organization rival to the American Federation of Labor. That is a mistake. We are here for the purpose of organizing a LABOR ORGANIZATION (laughter and applause); an organization broad enough to take in all of the working class. (Applause.) The American Federation of Labor is not that kind of an organization, inasmuch as there is a number of the international bodies affiliated with it that absolutely refuse to take in any more men. When this organization is properly launched there will be a place for every man that has been refused. They may place us on record as being dual, but remember that the United Workers of the Industrial Union will recognize those men as union men. There will be a label adopted by this convention, and it will be the duty of every member of this organization to patronize that label in preference to any other label. (Applause.)

We recognize that this is a revolutionary movement, and that the capitalists are not the only foes that you are to fight, but the most ardent enemy will be the pure and simple trades unionist. But there is only a few of him. He is not very well organized. You have got a tremendous field to work in. There are at least twenty million unorganized wage workers in the United States of America to say nothing of Canada. This industrial union movement is broad enough to take in all of them, and we are here for the purpose of launching that union that will open wide its doors to the working class. I care not for the skilled mechanic, particularly the pure and simple trades unionist who enforces an apprenticeship for the benefit of the man that will close down the factory or the mine at a moment's notice and throw out the men who have devoted their time to become skilled for his especial benefit. What I want to see come from this organization is an uplifting of the fellow that is down in the gutter. (Applause.) And there must be arrangements made for others than wage earners. Now, don't misunderstand me. I mean, for the unemployed, the man that would like to be a wage earner (applause), and the purpose of this organization will be to reduce hours sufficiently to give that fellow an opportunity to work. (Applause.) There will be no maximum scale of wages, I take it, established by this organization. There will be no agreement that will tie you up over night. (Applause.) I voice these sentiments because I am imbued with them, being a member of the Western Federation of Miners, a revolutionary industrial labor organization. We have not got an agreement existing with any mine manager, superintendent or operator at the present time. We have got a minimum scale of wages. The Western Federation of Miners has established in nearly all the cities throughout the West and the entire Province of British Columbia the eight-hour day, and we did not have a legislative lobby to accomplish it. (Laughter and applause.)

Now, I would suggest this conundrum: If the American Federation of Labor spends $5,000 a year maintaining a legislative lobby and gets through absolutely none of the measures that they advocate, how long will it take the American Federation of Labor to bring the working class to the full product of their toil? (Laughter.) Now, it is not the purpose of the American Federation of Labor to bring about such a condition. As Mr. Gompers has said on a number of occasions, "We want a little more, until we get what belongs to us." But he has never gone on record as saying what belongs to the working class. (Applause.) He should know—he is a Republican—that one of the greatest Republicans in this country said that inasmuch as labor produces nearly all of the good things of life, the duty of the government and its greatest aim should be to see that the producers of that wealth or of those things shall enjoy the full product of their labor. That was Abraham Lincoln; not quite correctly quoted, but nearly so. (Applause.) Gompers does not seem to recognize that labor produces all wealth, and it has always been somewhat of a marvel to me that they should be continually chasing after the Western Federation of Miners to reaffiliate with them, because inscribed on the charter of the Western Federation of Miners is the motto, "Labor produces all wealth; wealth belongs to the producer thereof." (Applause.) And we are striving to carry that motto into its fulfillment. That is the reason that we have come out of the West and come to Chicago to meet in convention with our brothers and sisters, realizing that we must all be uplifted at the same time (applause), that society can be no better than its most miserable. If you will assist us in establishing a plane of living for the working class whereby every man and woman will enjoy a decent livelihood, we will at least have the satisfaction of knowing that our children will never get below that condition. It is worth making an effort for, delegates, and I believe that your most earnest consideration will be directed toward that end; and if it is so directed you will have the earnest and hearty support of the Western Federation of Miners. (Applause.)

As the delegates that have previously spoken remarked, strength does not always come from numbers. The American Federation of Labor is two millions strong.

A Delegate: No! no! !

Del. Haywood: Nearly so.

The Delegate: Six hundred thousand.

Del. Haywood: Well, two million may be too many for any one to grasp the meaning of. It may be only one million. Say it is one million. The Western Federation of Miners comes in here with twenty-seven thousand. The capitalist class of this country fear the Western Federation of Miners more than they do all the rest of the labor organizations in this country. (Applause.) And we have given them a better run for their money (applause), and every time that it becomes necessary for us to make a stand against that class they begin to clean out their cannons and burnish up their bayonets. There has not been a strike in the mines by the Western Federation of Miners but what we have been confronted with the militia, the judiciary, the county and the state and municipal officers. In 1892 in the Coeur d'Alene, they had out the entire militia of the State. In 1894 in the Cripple Creek district, they had out the entire militia, but for once in the history of the labor movement it was on the workingman's side. (Applause.) In 1896, in Leadville, as Delegate O'Neil will bear me out, the members of that organization had to live on bacon and beans or beans straight for a number of days. In 1899, again, in the Coeur d'Alene, they had out the militia. And you know something about the recent strike in Colorado. So that the history of the Western Federation of Miners has been a militant one. We are known as a progressive and an aggressive organization, sufficiently aggressive to keep the other fellows busy all the time. (Applause.) And during the brief period of our existence we have improved the conditions of our membership. We have lessened their hours to a greater extent than any other labor organization, and during the last two years, although it was the set purpose and intention of the capitalist class of the entire West —they were all in hearty accord—to defeat and annihilate the Western Federation of Miners, we went into our last convention three thousand stronger than we were at the previous convention. (Applause.) And we are continuing to grow. We want you to join hands with us, to stand shoulder to shoulder with us and see if we will not be able to infuse in the working class of this country the same militant spirit with which the Western Federation of Miners is imbued. (Applause.) I want to say that if that is accomplished, not only Gompers but the capitalists will begin to tremble. Mr. Gompers, in a recent editorial of the American Federationist, referred to this, the then coming convention, as the coming "gabfest." There has been some talking done here in this convention, but there has not been a delegate that took the floor but said something, and that something meant something; it meant something for the working class, and it meant the doom and the burial of such fakirs as Samuel Gompers. (Applause.) . . .

I do not desire to take up the time of the convention. I just want to reiterate that in coming here we come in good faith. We are prepared to install the Western Federation of Miners in this new industrial movement. I am delighted to see the extreme political forces joining hands on this economic middle-ground. This is what I regard as the basis of all political parties, a solid foundation from whence an organization can be built where the workers can come into a solid and grand formation, and just as surely as the sun rises, when you get the working class organized economically it will find its proper reflection at the polls. Let this movement be not for political purposes, but bear this well in mind that it is for the purpose of supervising; that it is for the purpose of saying to the operators of Illinois that "you cannot close down the mines, for the work that we do in these coal mines means bread and butter to our wives and our families, and when you take away from us the means of life you are murdering us, and we are not going to tolerate it any longer." (Applause.) You have seen stalwart men right here in the city of Chicago, and you will find many of them, with their emaciated wives and their babies dying on dried-up breasts, and these men haven't got nerve enough to go out and steal. (Applause.) The purpose of this organization is to give every man an opportunity to work. That is not asking very much, just the opportunity to work. The other fellow don't want to work. We want to work, and we want to make it impossible for the operators to close down a coal mine when that mine is ready for operation, and we want it to be operated for the benefit of the people. We want to make it impossible for them to close down the factories when there are people needing clothes. We want to insist that production shall be carried on for the benefit of all of the people all of the time, and to give all of the people work whenever they want it and need it. (Applause.) . . .

The Chairman: Reports of standing committees. The Committee on Constitution.

Del. T. J. Hagerty [of the Industrial Workers club, Chicago] secretary of the Committee on Constitution: The Committee on Constitution has the following Preamble to report. . . .

(Reading Preamble): "The working class and the employing class have nothing in common. There can be no peace so long as hunger and want are found among millions of working people, and the few who make up the employing class have all the good things of life. Between these two classes a struggle must go on until all the toilers come together on the political as well as on the industrial field, and take and hold that which they produce by their labor, through an economic organization of the working class without affiliation with any political party. (Applause.) The rapid gathering of wealth and the centralization of the management of industry into fewer and fewer hands make the trades unions of to-day unable to cope with the ever-growing power of the employing class, because the trades unions foster a state of things which allows one set of workers to be pitted against another set of workers in the same industry, thereby helping to defeat one another in wage wars. The trades unions aid the employing class to mislead the workers into the belief that the working class have interests in common with their employers. These sad conditions can be changed and the interests of the working class upheld only by an organization formed in such a way that its members in any one industry or in all industries, if necessary, shall cease work whenever a strike or lockout is on in any department thereof, thus making an injury to one the concern of all. Therefore, we the workers unite under the following constitution." (Applause.)

The Chairman: You have heard the reading of the Preamble offered by your Committee on Constitution. What is the pleasure of the convention? . . .

Del. [Joseph] Gilbert: I would like to say, Mr. Chairman and Fellow Delegates, that it is quite impossible for us to split hairs and to analyze with fine accuracy the scientific interpretation of this or any other document. But one of the things that pleased me particularly about that Preamble was this, that while possibly it was not stated in absolutely scientific terms, it seems to me it was stated in the terse, ordinary language of the plain people, and that is what we want. We do not want to put out from this convention an academic statement. We want simply to put out a statement that will carry conviction to the mind of the humble toiler, and when you talk about there being nothing in common between them the average common horse sense knows that. Therefore I would move you the adoption of that first clause, without wasting the time of the convention. (Seconded.)

The Chairman: The motion is out of order.

Del. [M. E.] White [of the United Brotherhood of Railway Employees]: I have heard a good many Preambles read, and this is the first time I have seen a Preamble that has not got the ear marks of too many professors.

The language sounds good to me. I believe we can go before the working class of this country with it and that they can understand the report without having to get dictionaries and find out what is meant. What we want is to go before the common people with a Preamble so plain that every honest Tom, Dick, and Harry, including ourselves, can understand it. I am in favor of the entire Preamble as reported by the Committee. . . .

Del. [A. M.] Simons: It seems to me we are trying to adopt something that is almost ridiculous in statement. If you will analyze that as it stands, it says that we are in favor of political action without any political party. I am absolutely in favor of no endorsement whatever of any political party. At the same time the wording of that is contradictory and confusing, and there ought to be something done to straighten that out. It either ought to be split into two sentences, or else it ought to state more clearly what it does mean. As it stands now it practically says no political action, without a political party. I object to that. I have not a copy here, and so cannot make an intelligent amendment.

A delegate moved as an amendment that the word "political" be stricken out.

Del. [Lincoln] Wright: I want to say that that paragraph does not contradict itself, in my opinion. I will point out the reason. The first part of the paragraph merely places it upon the plane of the existing civilization, the existing conditions under which we live in the United States; that is, wherever it is possible to get at the mass of working people and present a program of the international revolutionary proletariat by methods which give us that chance. Furthermore, it says, "without affiliation with any political party," which is correct. We can pursue the method of appearing before the working class with this program without affiliation, and I believe that the sentence or paragraph stands upon its feet, not that it comes out clear, but enough to enable you to study it out, and I think that any person who will follow that closely will see exactly the status of it.

Del. [H. M.] Richter: The paragraph reads, "between these two classes a struggle must go on." Why must it go on?

Del. [J. S.] Schatske: Until it is finished.

Del. Richter: "Until the toilers come together on the political as well as economic field and take and hold what they produce." It says that the moment you bring the workers together on the political and economic field the struggle ceases. As a matter of fact, it just starts then. "That which they produce," why should they take it? Doesn't it belong to them? If I have something I don't need to take it. To take it implies that I take it from something outside of me, but not from myself. This says, "what they produce by their labor, through an economic organization of the working class without affiliation with any political party." Why should that statement be in the Preamble "without affiliation with any political party"? The form of the organization will give expression thereto. Although this phrase was in the Manifesto calling this convention, I do not see any need to have it in the Preamble. Mr. Chairman, I move that this paragraph be stricken out and the following substituted: "There can be no peace as long as an increase of wages of the whole working class means a corresponding decrease of profit to the capitalist class, and vice versa. From these conditions a struggle arises which will not cease until the worker is lifted out of his present merchandise or wage slavery position through the collective ownership of the tools of production and distribution. Until such a change is possible the wage workers must unite and organize as a class on the industrial as well as political field, having for their aim an effort to realize their class interests and to support and protect them in their struggle for existence."

Del. [W. Roscoe] Parkes: I second the motion to adopt the substitute, to get it before the house.

The Chairman: It has been regularly moved and seconded that paragraph two be stricken out and the substitute offered by Delegate Richter be adopted instead. Are you ready for the question?

Del. [Daniel] De Leon [of the Socialist Trade and Labor Alliance]: The paragraph, if you will let me read it over again, says: "Between these two classes a struggle must go on until all the toilers come together on the political as well as the industrial field and take and hold that which they produce by their labor, through an economic organization of the working class without affiliation with any political party." This is the language as offered. I wish to speak for the clause as a member of that committee, and against the proposed substitute. The argument has been made by Delegate Simons that that is contradictory; that this clause proposes political action without a political party. Now, let me invite your attention to the Manifesto, to the promise and invitation under which this convention is gathered, and under the terms of which it is convened. You will find on page four of this issue of this form of the Manifesto (holding up a copy), this passage: "Craft divisions foster political ignorance among the workers, thus DIVIDING THAT CLASS AT THE BALLOT BOX as well as in shop, mine, and factory"; and on the next page of the Manifesto you find this clause: "It (this organization) should be established as the economic organization of the working class WITH-OUT AFFILIATION WITH ANY POLITICAL PARTY." If to recognize the necessity of uniting the working people on the political field, and in the same breath to say that the taking and the holding of the things that the people produce can be done without affiliation with any political party—if that is a contradiction; if it can be said that these two clauses in this proposed paragraph are contradictory, then the contradiction was advocated by Delegate Simons himself, who was one of the signers of this Manifesto. (Applause.) Here you have his signature (holding up the page of the Manifesto with Simons' signature). But, delegates, there is no contradiction, none whatever; and I consider that these two passages in the Manifesto, if any one thing was to be picked out more prominent than any other, are indeed significant of the stage of development, genuine capitalistic development in America. This Manifesto enumerates a series of evils that result from the present craft division:—it shatters the ranks of the workers and renders industrial and financial solidarity impossible; union men scab it upon one another; jealousy is created, and prohibitive initiation fees are adopted; "craft divisions foster political ignorance among the working class, thus dividing them at the ballot box." If this, the division of the working class on the political field, is an evil, then it follows that unity of the working people on the political field is a thing to be desired. And so it is; and this clause in the Preamble correctly so states it. That being so, does this other sentence sound contradictory, the sentence that provides that the new organization shall be without affiliation with any political party? The situation in America, as presented by the thousand-and-one causes that go to create present conditions, removes the seeming contradiction. That situation establishes the fact that the "taking and the holding" of the things that labor needs to be free can never depend upon a political party. (Applause.) If anything is clear in the American situation it is this: That if any individual is elected to office upon a revolutionary ballot, that individual is a suspicious character. (Applause.) Whoever is returned elected to office on a program of labor emancipation; whoever is allowed to be filtered through by the political election inspectors of the capitalistic class;—that man is a carefully selected tool, a traitor of the working people, selected by the capitalist class. (Applause.)

It is out of the question that here in America—I am speaking of America and not Europe—that here in America a political party can accomplish that which this clause demands, the "taking and the holding." I know not a single exception of any party candidate, ever elected upon a political platform of the emancipation of the working class, who did not sell them out as fast as elected. (Applause.) Now, it may be asked, "that being so, why not abolish altogether the political movement? Why, at all, unite the workers on the political field?" The aspiration to unite the workers upon the political field is an aspiration in line and in step with civilization. Civilized man, when he argues with an adversary, does not start with clenching his fist and telling him, "smell this bunch of bones." He does not start by telling him, "feel my biceps." He begins with arguing; physical force by arms is the last resort. That is the method of the civilized man, and the method of civilized man is the method of civilized organization. The barbarian begins with physical force; the civilized man ends with that, when physical force is necessary. (Applause.) Civilized man will always here in America give a chance to peace; he will, accordingly, proceed along the lines that make peace possible. But civilized man, unless he is a visionary, will know that unless there is Might behind your Right, your Right is something to laugh at. And the thing to do consequently is to gather behind that ballot, behind that united political movement, the Might which is alone able, when necessary, to "take and hold." Without the working people are united on the political field; without the delusion has been removed from their minds that any of the issues of the capitalist class can do for them anything permanently, or even temporarily; without the working people have been removed altogether from the mental thraldom of the capitalist class, from its insidious influence, there is no possibility of your having those conditions under which they can really organize themselves economically in such a way as to "take and hold." And after those mental conditions are generally established, there needs something more than the statement to "take and hold"; something more than a political declaration, something more than the permission of the capitalist political inspectors to allow this or that candidate to filter through. You then need the industrial organization of the working class, so that, if the capitalist should be foolish enough in America to defeat, to thwart the will of the workers expressed by the ballot—I do not say "the will of the workers, as returned by the capitalist election inspectors," but the will of the people as expressed at the ballot box—then there will be a condition of things by which the working class can absolutely cease production, and thereby starve out the capitalist class, and render their present economic means and all their preparations for war absolutely useless. (Applause.) Then, the clause "between these two classes a struggle must go on until all the toilers come together on the political as well as industrial field, and TAKE AND HOLD that which they produce by their labor"—through what?—THROUGH AN ECONOMIC OR-GANIZATION OF THE WORKING CLASS, "without affiliation with any political party," stands out in all the clearness of its solid foundation and challenging soundness. That clause is a condensation, I should say, of hundreds of volumes now in the libraries of the country, and of many more volumes that have not yet been written, but the facts upon which they are based are coming forward. One of the facts, a fact of great importance, is that curious apparition—the visionary politician, the man who imagines that by going to the ballot box, and taking a piece of paper, and looking about to see if anybody is watching, and throwing it in and then rubbing his hands and jollying himself with the expectation that through that process, through some mystic alchemy, the ballot will terminate capitalism, and the Socialist Commonwealth will arise like a fairy out of the ballot box. That is not only visionary; it is the product of that cowardice which we find very generally in the politics of some men who claim to represent the working class (applause), on account of which we find that such politics in nine cases out of ten degenerate into what is called "possibilism." It brings about a repetition of the methods of the Christian church, which raises a fine, magnificent ideal in the remote future, to be arrived at some time, sooner or later —rather later than sooner—eventually if not later—and in the meantime practices all "possible," "practical" wrong. (Applause.) I maintain that this clause, consequently, is not contradictory, but states the four-squared fact. (Applause.)

The Chairman: Your time is up.

Del. De Leon: I am done.

[3]

TESTIMONY OF VINCENT ST. JOHN

Mr. [O. W.] Thompson: For the purpose of the record, will you kindly give us your name and address?

Mr. St. John: Vincent St. John, Chicago, Ill.

Mr. Thompson: What is your official position?

Mr. St. John: General secretary and treasurer of the Industrial Workers of the World.

Mr. Thompson: How long have you occupied that position?

Mr. St. John: Since January 1909.

Mr. Thompson: How long have the Industrial Workers of the World been in existence as a definite organization, if you know?

Mr. St. John: Since July 27, 1905. . . .

Mr. Thompson: What are the purposes, general scope, and plan of the Industrial Workers of the World? Take your time and make your statement in regard to that.

Mr. St. John: The primary purpose is the organization—to organize the working class on a class basis. That is, to organize and educate the workers with the understanding that the workers of this and every other country constitute a distinct and separate economic class in society, with interests that are distinct and separate from the employing class, as such, in society. That is, the organization divides society to-day into two broad classifications—the employing class on the one hand and the wageworking class on the other. The purpose of the organization is to organize and educate the wageworking class into a knowledge of economic position for the purpose of gaining requisite power in order to advance their interests, defend their interests, and advance them wherever possible, with the ultimate object of placing the control and operation of industries in which workers work into the hands and under the jurisdiction of the organized wageworkers of the country, so that the result of their efforts, the wealth produced by them and by their collective efforts, will accrue to those who are responsible for its creation without having to pay tribute to any employing class over any other parasitical

SOURCE: U.S. Congress, Senate, *Industrial Relations: Final Report and Testimony Submitted to the Congress by the Commission on Industrial Relations . . .* , 64th Cong., 1st Sess., 1916, pp. 1445–1455.

class whatever. It is proposed to accomplish that by organizing the workers in such a manner that it will be possible for them, through their organization, to control their labor power, their brain and muscular energy that is used from day to day and year to year in the operation of industries, which to-day is a commodity sold on the labor market under the same rules, governed by the same conditions, that any other commodity is sold; and the Industrial Workers of the World propose that the wageworkers organize in such a manner that they will control a sufficient amount of this commodity required to operate the industries so that they will be able to dictate the terms upon which it is used.

I think, for a general statement, that covers the matter, so far as I can go.

Mr. Thompson: Is there anything in respect to the plan of your organization, its form, that you have not stated in your answer to the previous question?

Mr. St. John: Nothing that I can recollect. It is simply a general statement. It might not be clear to the commission or to yourself, but the only way I see to make it clearer is simply by a line of questions.

Mr. Thompson: What is the present membership of the Industrial Workers of the World?

Chairman Walsh: Might I interpolate a question there to see if I cannot open it up?

How would you apply what you have said in your general statement, if you had the power to do so at once, to the transportation industry; that is, the general transportation industry of the country?

Mr. St. John: How would we apply it?

Chairman Walsh: Yes, sir.

Mr. St. John: Well, the transportation industry is subdivided into four component parts, under the scheme of organization, our plan of organization. Marine, steam railroads————

Chairman Walsh: Well, just take steam railroad.

Mr. St. John: Well, the steam railroad?

Chairman Walsh: Yes.

Mr. St. John: They would be organized at different points into local unions: that is, division points of the railroad, local unions, or industrial unions of railway employees would be instituted or organized. These local unions would embrace all employees of the railroads entering that particular point in that local union. It would not make any difference what their occupation happened to be, from the section man to the engineer, and men and women engaged as clerks in the office, telegraphers, station

43

agents; it would include every wageworker on the systems of the railroads working out of that point. They would be members of that particular industrial organization; and they would be branched inside of that local industrial union as their experience and their particular requirements of the industry might dictate.

Chairman Walsh: Who would determine that?

Mr. St. John: They would determine that themselves, the membership.

Chairman Walsh: Individually?

Mr. St. John: What?

Chairman Walsh: Individually?

Mr. St. John: No, sir; the local union.

Chairman Walsh: The local union would determine which were the best fitted?

Mr. St. John: They would determine the branch formation of the local union. They would determine whether it was necessary to have a branch consisting of engineers and firemen or whether one branch would be sufficient to get the required administrative functions by taking in the entire train crew in a branch. That would be determined by the experience of the members of the branch who were actually employed in the industry.

Chairman Walsh: What else have you to say in this game of transportation industry?

Mr. St. John: The different industrial unions would be brought together, forming a national industrial union of the transportation industry. That would comprise all of the employees of all of the railroad systems in the United States in the National Industrial Union.

Chairman Walsh: Would it include the president?

Mr. St. John: How?

Chairman Walsh: Would it include the president, superintendents, etc.?

Mr. St. John: It would include only what is recognized as the wage-working element of the railroad.

Chairman Walsh: It would not include the administrative part?

Mr. St. John: It would not include those that were looked upon as the officials of the system at all.

Chairman Walsh: Now, after that union was formed the local unions were formed, and you had this national union, what means would you propose to see that those men get the profit of their own labor? What means would you adopt to see that these men so formed into a union would receive what I believe you said was the product of their toil and not divide it with anyone else?

Mr. St. John: That would be impossible, so far as the railroad workers themselves were concerned. They could not accomplish that individually; that is, it would be impossible for the employees of the different railroad systems to arrange matters to that extent simply as the employees of the railway system, of the railway industry. The ultimate object of the organization would have to stand until such time as the organization in all of the industries reached the point that gave them the required power to attain that object.

Chairman Walsh: Will you please pick out some industry, for instance, now? We are going to try to put this into operation. Will you pick out some industry that you might indicate to the commission that would be the first one that you would start on, considering the fact that you have made a study of the subject?

Mr. St. John: I am trying to state that, as far as the organization is concerned, we would not try to put any such plan into operation for a particular industry. The achievement of that ultimate object of the organization will depend upon the existence of an organization in all industries and about the same power.

Chairman Walsh: That would not fit them unless there was an entirely changed industrial system?

Mr. St. John: Well, that is the purpose of the organization. It is to change the industrial system.

Chairman Walsh: Are you attempting to organize in specific industries? You are, aren't you?

Mr. St. John: Yes, sir.

Chairman Walsh: Organize the workers?

Mr. St. John: Yes, sir.

Chairman Walsh: Assume that you completed a perfect organization in the meat-provision industry, which employs, as I understand, a large number of what might be common or unskilled laborers.

Mr. St. John: Yes, sir.

Chairman Walsh: Suppose, now, you effect a complete organization in the packing industry. What means would you take, if you can give it briefly and generally, the means you would adopt to put into form the general objects of your organization as you have stated them in the record here?

Mr. St. John: All that we could hope to accomplish with an organization of that kind, if it was confined to one industry alone, would simply be to extend the control of the workers as so organized, so that they would be able to dictate better conditions for themselves, better returns for their labor; and the revenues of an organization so formed would be used in extending the organization to other industries to bring them up to the same standard. So there would be a requisite amount of control exercised not only in one industry alone but in all the industries sufficient to be able to dictate the terms under which those industries would operate; that is, we would have, through the organization, control of a sufficient amount of labor power to prevent the operation of the industries by withdrawing it or to allow it to operate on terms satisfactory to the membership of the organization.

Chairman Walsh: Assuming, Mr. St. John, that you succeed in perfecting such an organization in the leading industries of the Nation, the large employers of labor, what steps would you then take to bring about the conditions that you mentioned in the statement of your general object, to wit, that the workers should have the product of their own labor and not give any proportion or divide it with the parasitical class or with the class of nonworkers?

Mr. St. John: Well, when that stage arrives the organization will have gradually increased its control over the industries.

Chairman Walsh: How is that?

Mr. St. John: I say when that stage arrives the organization will have gradually increased its control and domination over industry to such an extent that they will be able to operate the industry and exchange the products through the medium of our own organization.

Chairman Walsh: At what point would you take in what you call the officials or the administratives?

Mr. St. John: Whenever we were strong enough to dominate them and know that they would work for our interest.

Chairman Walsh: Would your plan require a political action?

Mr. St. John: I don't know what you mean by political action.

Chairman Walsh: That is, would it require control of the legislative body of the Nation?

Mr. St. John: No, sir.

Chairman Walsh: Or of the various States, or a change in the organic law of the Nation, or constitutions of the various States?

Mr. St. John: None, whatever.

Chairman Walsh: That is all.

Mr. Thompson: I understand, Mr. St. John, from your answers to the chairman's questions, that what you stated in reference to the program of your organization in regard to the production and distribution of wealth is a future program. That at present you are concerned with the organization of the workers to better their hours and their working condition and to increase their wages.

Mr. St. John: The organization, in order to represent the interests of the working class, must necessarily have a twofold function. It has to be able to handle the everyday problem of the workers, which is one of shorter hours, better wages, and improved shop conditions, and ultimately the education of the workers, so that they can assume control of industry. The fundamental purpose of the organization is to drill, have the workers drilled, and to educate themselves so that they can control industry; and as a training school or preparation for that task, the everyday struggle of the workers is the first struggle in front of the organization.

Mr. Thompson: Mr. St. John, what is the method of organization you pursue in any given industry, if you have such?

Mr. St. John: The method of organization?

Mr. Thompson: Yes, sir.

Mr. St. John: You mean by that how we build up an organization—start it?

Mr. Thompson: Yes. Do you have any organized? Do you have any distinct plans, different from those of other labor organizations that are commonly understood and known?

Mr. St. John: Well, I think that is the general proposition. All organization work is pretty much the same. The plan the I. W. W. follows is by organizers. For a local union in a given locality it carries on the organization work, through its members, through its membership, educational work, the distribution of leaflets, circulation of the papers of the organization, holding of public meetings in halls and on the streets, in front of factory gates, in fact any method by which the attention of the workers employed can be attracted; either carrying on agitation inside or outside of the factories.

Mr. Thompson: When as a result of such methods as you may use for basing an organization in a given city or factory, how do you present or make your demands to such factory, in reference to any subject which you take up? Do you have a shop organization?

Mr. St. John: We have a shop organization. If the local, if the industry in question has several different establishments in the same locality, the workers in the shops have meetings of their own wherein they take up the questions that they are interested in, with a view to the particular shop that they are working, and their demands or ideas are formulated into demands, and these different shops, branches, elect delegates who receive the report from the meetings of the shop branches; that is, the demands formulated for the different shops, and harmonize the whole. That is, they compile from the different demands a general set of demands, embracing whatever particular demands may apply to each shop or each establishment, either combined into a set of demands covering the entire district or the jurisdiction of that industry, or that industrial charter, or whatever it may be; and they are presented to whoever has the authority to receive them on the part of the employers.

Mr. Thompson: Who in the cases you have mentioned would present such demand on your organization?

Mr. St. John: The committee elected by the different branches of the workers involved.

Mr. Thompson: What, if any, arrangement does your organization countenance with the different factories that you may have an organization in?

Mr. St. John: What arrangement do we countenance?

Mr. Thompson: Yes. Do you carry out systems of collective bargaining?

Mr. St. John: We do not make any agreements for any stated length of time; but, as an example, if there was a—if the effort to gain better conditions resulted in a strike and this strike resulted in a victory for the workers involved, work would be resumed simply upon the representatives of the employer, the qualified representatives of the employer, saying that they agreed to the terms for which the workers were fighting, and a notice posted in the mill to that effect. That is the extent of the effect of any agreement we enter into. . . .

Mr. Thompson: That is to say that the fundamental policy of your organization is this: That they do not countenance any time agreements, and that the making of a time agreement automatically severs the organization making it from your parent body?

Mr. St. John: That has been the policy in the past; yes, sir.

Mr. Thompson: And consequently and naturally you would not encourage the carrying out of such an agreement? That goes without saying.

Mr. St. John: Certainly not.

Chairman Walsh: Mr. Thompson, inasmuch as the time is drawing to a close, could we shorten it by having him explain the difference in the operations of his organization and that of the American Federation of Labor, for instance?

Mr. Thompson: We can take it up that way, Mr. Chairman, but that was not the plan that I had outlined.

Chairman Walsh: I will not call your attention, then, when the 40 minutes are up.

Mr. Thompson: When demands are made by your organization on the factory or firm, and they are not acceded to, what are the general plans of your organization for enforcing such plans, if you have any?

Mr. St. John: Well, we have no general plan, because the circumstances surrounding each particular case is what determines the plan of operation. The general plan might be stated as the withdrawing of the labor power from the establishment in question, or from the industry in question, in that locality, and if necessary from the industry in question throughout the country, in an effort to stop production in that manner. That is generally known as a strike. If circumstances were such as to prevent, such as to indicate that a strike would probably not give the results, would be inopportune, the conditions in the industry were not favorable, why, different methods would be resorted to; we would try to slow up the production in the factory; turn out poor work; in fact, interfere with the process of production so as to destroy the possible chance for revenue or profit accruing to the owners from that particular industry or mill.

Mr. Thompson: Is that what you call sabotage?

Mr. St. John: That is what it is generally known as; yes, sir.

Mr. Thompson: How else do you carry that principle out? Say, when you are out on a strike and not in the mill, how would you carry that same principle out?

Mr. St. John: If we were out on strike?

Mr. Thompson: Yes.

Mr. St. John: We couldn't very well carry that principle out if we were out on a strike, excepting it would be to interfere with the products turned out in that particular mill, in transportation, or interfere with the raw material going into the mill. We would make an effort, if the organization was in shape, to control an influence sufficient with the isolated plant in question, so that no raw material or anything they use in the manufacture got very far.

Mr. Thompson: If, in carrying it out, it is necessary to destroy property, would your organization countenance that?

Mr. St. John: If the destruction of property would gain the point for the workers involved, that is the only consideration we would give to it. The fact that property was destroyed would not have anything to do with determining whether we adopted the plan or not.

Mr. Thompson: Then, the criterion of your action on a strike is whether or not the proposed action will gain the point of the strike?

Mr. St. John: That is the only one.

Mr. Thompson: Would that same reasoning apply to questions of violence against persons?

Mr. St. John: Certainly.

Chairman Walsh: Please turn this way, Mr. St. John, and speak a little louder; this is a difficult place to hear.

Mr. Thompson: I understood he said yes.

Mr. St. John: I said certainly.

Mr. Thompson: I wish you would explain the reasons why your organization would not make a time agreement, and why you countenance the destruction of property or the injury of persons in order to carry out any desired point as workmen?

Mr. St. John: Well, in the matter of the time agreements, the entering into time agreements is of no value to the working class. It is of no value to that particular part of the working class who are directly involved in the agreement. It is, as a rule, a distinct—it places them at a disadvantage for the future period. In the first place, it is simply saying to the employer that on a certain date, after the lapse of a certain number of months, we are going to make a demand on you for increased wages or change in the working conditions. That is what it means to them. The consequence is that if he has any semblance of intelligence at all he prepares for it, and he has got a year's time to get ready for it. He makes up his stock ahead—his warehouse is piled with stock where he is dealing in goods that he can handle that way; and when the time comes and you make your demands, he has made arrangements so that he is able to get along without you. He places you at a disadvantage.

Another thing, it prevents the workers from taking advantage of any favorable opportunity that might arise during the term of this agreement, by which they could get better conditions. For instance, the market or demand for the commodities that were being produced might become lively, and the plant become rushed with orders, why, from that circumstance the workers . . . [have] an advantage in making terms and demands. There is an added demand for the commodity they are selling —their labor power; and there is that added demand there, and they are in a more favorable position to force recognition for their claims and gain what they are after.

In addition to that, it destroys the active spirit in an organization to work under a contract period. The membership, as a rule, working under a time contract, as soon as the contract is signed and they are back to work, they lose everything except a mere passing interest in their organization; and they think things are settled for the time being, and they do not need to bother . . . [until] their contract is about to expire. Those are a few of the reasons; and as far as the destruction of property is concerned, the property is not ours. We haven't any interest at all in it; it is used simply—it is used to make the lot of the workers, as a class, harder; and the only property that we have, experience in the past has shown that the employers, as a class, are not at all particular whether they injure our property or not. They take us into the mills before we are able—before we have even the semblance of an education, and they grind up our vitality, brain and muscular energy into profits, and whenever we cannot keep pace with the machine speeded to its highest notch, they turn us out onto the road to eke out an existence as best we can, or wind up on the poor farm or in the potter's field. And we think what is good for the working class—rather, what is good for the employing class is certainly good for us. And he has not shown any respect at all for our property, that it is not incumbent upon us to show any respect for his property; and we do not propose to do it; and we do not propose to make any bones about having that attitude clearly understood; that we are getting somewhat intelligent, and at least beginning to notice things. And the same holds true with regard to life and violence. Not that the Industrial Workers of the World are advocating the destruction of life to gain any particular point or the use of violence; because the destruction of life is not going to gain any point, and if life happens to be lost in strikes that we are implicated in, the blame generally, and has been up to date, on the other side. But we are not going to tell our membership to allow themselves to be shot down and beat up like cattle. Regardless of the fact that they are members of the working class, they still have a duty that they owe to themselves and their class of defending themselves whenever they are attacked and their life is threatened. Violence is not always the choosing of the working class; as a general rule, it is forced on them as a simple act of self-defense. They have to strike back when they are struck at, and that is the spirit and that is the idea the organization is trying to educate the workers into.

We do not—we do not want to be understood as saying that we expect to achieve our aims through violence and through the destruction of human life, because, in my judgment, that is impossible. The achievement of success—the success of this organization—the realization of what it is striving for—depends on one thing only, and that is gaining the control of a sufficient amount of the labor power that is necessary in the operation of industry. Now, when we have that control, then through organization the necessity for violence will be reduced; in fact, it will almost disappear. It will disappear. The necessity for using any tactics that will lead to violence will disappear, and the protection and the safeguarding of human life will increase just in proportion as we have that control. And we will not only be able to take care of ourselves, and therefore it will become unnecessary for us to injure anybody else so far as life is concerned.

Mr. Thompson: In getting your control of an industry, Mr. St. John, do you—and in your advocacy of the method of gaining that control, do you tell your membership only to use force in case it is necessary for self-defense?

Mr. St. John: We don't tell them anything of the kind. They are supposed to have sense enough to know that. If they did not have sense enough to know when to take care of themselves, no amount of telling on our part would do them any good.

Mr. Thompson: In other words, your general policy is that whatever violence is necessary to carry the point, and if violence will carry the point, they must use it to gain the point?

Mr. St. John: Most assuredly; yes.

Mr. Thompson: Yes.

Chairman Walsh: What is the answer?

Mr. St. John: Most assuredly; yes.

Mr. Thompson: That is to say, if violence will bring the point that the workers want, then it is countenanced?

Mr. St. John: Well, violence is not going to bring the point that the workers want except in rare instances.

Mr. Thompson: Take the case of workers filling the place of strikers, for instance. If your people believe that by committing acts of violence against the people who take the places, they would cause a determination of the struggle in favor of the strikers, then you would countenance such violence?

Mr. St. John: Certainly.

Commissioner Harriman: I would like to ask you, Mr. St. John, what was the underlying cause for the creation of your organization?

Mr. St. John: Well, the organization came into existence mainly because of the lack of unity on the part of labor as it was and is organized to-day.

Commissioner Lennon: I wish the witness would face that way [indicating audience], and we could hear just as well.

Mr. St. John: Strikes in different sections of the country were fought out and lost by the workers, not because they did not put up a good fight themselves, those that were directly involved—not because of the fact that the employers were in an advantageous position, but simply because that, in addition to fighting the employers who were solid as a unit on the proposition, they also had to contend against the assistance rendered to the employers by workers in the same industry or in other industries. The only show for the winning of a strike is stopping the production of the commodity that is being manufactured by the workers that are on strike, curtailing the profits of the corporation or the individual who has title to that establishment; and as long as he can transfer his work to other workers or operate his factories with scab labor and the product turned out by scab labor are distributed around the country by union men with union cards in their pockets, and the raw materials are furnished to the scab labor in this particular factory and pass through the hands of men with union cards in their pockets, the chances of any body of workers winning a strike in any important industry are reduced to a minimum, to say the least. And it was to overcome that state of affairs that the union has come into existence.

Commissioner Harriman: Do you think that cooperation between employers and the wage-earning class is possible or impossible—peaceful cooperation?

Mr. St. John: It is not possible except by a loss to the wage earners. It might be brought about, but the only ones that would gain by it would be the employers. The wage earners would be the ones to suffer.

Commissioner Harriman: I would like to ask you what is the attitude of your organization toward the Government?

Mr. St. John: Toward the Government?

Commissioner Harriman: Yes.

Mr. St. John: Well, they simply look on the Government as a committee employed to look after the interests of the employers. That is all the Government means to it. It is simply a committee employed to police the interests of the employing class.

Commissioner Lennon: Mr. St. John, I understood you to answer Mr. Harriman that the reasons for starting the I. W. W. were, your view as to the inefficiency—because of your ideas of lack of cooperation in the existing organizations. Is that true?

Mr. St. John: Yes.

Commissioner Lennon: Where have you found in your observations that the unions that you are criticizing have been less successful than the I. W. W. in strikes and lockouts and contests of that character?

Mr. St. John: What do you want, definite examples?

Commissioner Lennon: Yes.

Mr. St. John: Well, the industrial history of the country is full of them for the last 15 years.

Commissioner Lennon: Well, I know something of that history myself.

Mr. St. John: The strike of the subway and elevated railroad men in the city of New York in 1905 is one instance.

Commissioner Lennon: Yes.

Mr. St. John: The strike of the miners in Leadville, Colo., in 1896 is another instance. The loss of the A. I. U. strike in 1894 is another instance, and the garment workers' strike in Chicago in 1908, I think that was another instance. The loss of the————

Commissioner Lennon: While those strikes were, in the main, lost, but not entirely—that is another phase of the matter. Are you not aware of the fact that hundreds and even thousands of strikes were gained in the meantime?

Mr. St. John: Well, that might hold true, but the strikes that were gained were possibly of less economic importance or involved fewer people than those that were lost. As a matter of fact, in the past 15 or 20 years in this country organizational workers have practically been wiped out in every basic industry—been wiped out after struggles, after fights, after strikes, and they have been wiped out, and there is no gainsaying the fact that today, in basic industries in this country, they have no efficient organization.

Commissioner Lennon: Have the Industrial Workers an efficient organization in those industries?

Mr. St. John: No, sir; we haven't, and more is the pity.

Commissioner Lennon (inaudible): Are you in the same position now in regard to strikes as the old organization has long been?

Mr. St. John: Yes; some of them.

Commissioner Lennon: In other words, you are in the same position as the other unions, although not quite so successful?

Mr. St. John: We are in the same condition of the other unions for this simple reason: We not only have to fight the employers, but have to fight all other unions besides. For some reason or other, all unions think it is a badge of honor to scab on the I. W. W. They are encouraged in that viewpoint by all parties and by every agency of the country and that is an added handicap, but it is no criterion—it is no criterion of whether the methods of the I. W. W. are correct or not. . . .

Commissioner Lennon: Do you maintain that the idea of collective bargaining or agreements should not be recognized? You said that in industry you don't believe in collective agreements.

Mr. St. John: I don't believe in collective agreements, so far as the wage-workers are concerned; no.

Commissioner Lennon: Well, then, as between men. Do you believe that men ought to agree with each other?

Mr. St. John: I am not interested in that. That is not a part of the labor question.

Commissioner Lennon: It is not a part of the labor question?

Mr. St. John: No.

Commissioner Lennon: The labor question covers all questions.

Mr. St. John: What is that?

Commissioner Lennon: I have no right to argue with you; I don't want to argue with you. That is all right. What are you striving for? What is the ideal that you are working for?

Mr. St. John: Working-class control of industry.

Commissioner Lennon: Is that collective ownership?

Mr. St. John: We don't care anything about ownership; all we want is control of it.

Commissioner Lennon: What are you going to do with it? What will you do with it?

Mr. St. John: When we control it, we will control the products produced by it, and we will distribute them to those whose efforts are responsible for producing them.

Commissioner Lennon: For the benefit of those that are organized, or for the benefit of all?

Mr. St. John: For the benefit of those actively contributing in the effort necessary to produce. Whenever the working class has control of industry, they will all be organized. There will be no question about organized and nonorganized at that time.

Commissioner Lennon: All right.

Commissioner Ballard: You spoke a minute ago of expelling from your organization. What would constitute such offense as to merit the expulsion from the I. W. W.?

Mr. St. John: Violation of the principle of the organization—that is, the fundamental principle of the organization. The signing of a contract with employers by local unions, the repudiation of the principle of the organization with regard to the employing class, and the wage-working class having no interests in common. That is, for instance, if any local of the organization were to take the stand that the employers and workers had a mutual interest and that they should meet and try to arrive at some mutually satisfactory understanding, why, that would automatically expel them from the organization.

Commissioner Ballard: Have any of your men been expelled for any of those causes?

Mr. St. John: One local union was expelled for entering into an agreement with the employers in Great Falls, Mont.

Commissioner Ballard: You spoke of not believing in organized government. If, for instance, the I. W. W. could eventually control the working class, would there any longer be any need for a Government as we have it now?

Mr. St. John: I did not say anything about not believing in organized government. Somebody asked me what we thought of the political government of today, and I said that we recognized it as a committee of the employing class. So far as organized government is concerned, whenever the workers are organized in the industry, whenever they have a sufficient organization in the industry, they will have all the government they need right there.

Commissioner Ballard: What would become of our present United States Government?

Mr. St. John: It would die of dry-rot.

PART III
Sexual Oppression

It is one of the critical instincts of the Left to search out the institutional and systemic causes of oppression and repression. Political liberals will often blame individuals for social dislocations, as conservatives will usually accuse human nature. In politics as in medicine different diagnoses led to different prescriptions. So conservatives will try to prevent change for which they believe people to be incapable, liberals will want to change the leaders, and radicals must demand a structural reorganization of society's basic institutions.

In the following selection, Emma Goldman (1869–1940), an anarchist devoted to a social vision of free association and voluntary communism, attacked the institution of marriage as a microcosm of capitalism. Absolutely incompatible with love, she argued that marriage was a system for exploiting women; it incapacitated them for independence, produced ignorance, poverty, and dependence, and led to a profound alienation that must eventually explode. Although more and more women were working, American society, along with every other culture built on private property, socialized women in the direction of expecting marriage rather than work. This sexual pacification program absolutely deformed the girls' self-perception by inculcating the myth of masculine supremacy and feminine passivity.

Emma Goldman understood that the freedom of women depended on revolution. Her politics were thus necessarily more inclusive than "the woman question," as it once was quaintly put. She arrived in the United States in 1886, and after seven years was jailed for inciting to riot at a rally for Eugene Debs. When McKinley was assassinated by a mad anarchist who really believed in the propaganda of the deed, she was arrested again but released for lack of evidence of her alleged complicity. Because of her opposition to World War I and the draft, she was sentenced to two years in jail. Finally, in 1919, she and Alexander Berkman, with whom she had worked for a long time, were deported to Russia. Disillusioned with the Soviet experiment, she split openly with Lenin and Trotsky and fled in 1921. After taking an active part in the Spanish Civil War, she died of a stroke in Toronto.

Her lyrical and passionate plea for women's liberation in the name of voluntary love (then and since misunderstood as "free love") echoed through the generations, until the young women of the late sixties took up the cause. Although they probably do not know of Goldman's earlier struggle, the causes remain almost constant for her rebellion and theirs. In both cases the issue of women's liberation has been correctly perceived as the single most explosive demand of the Left, the one whose acceptance would most thoroughly change society's way of muddling through.

---

[4]

MARRIAGE AND LOVE

EMMA GOLDMAN

THE popular notion about marriage and love is that they are synonymous, that they spring from the same motives, and cover the same human needs. Like most popular notions this also rests not on actual facts, but on superstition.

Marriage and love have nothing in common; they are as far apart as the poles; are, in fact, antagonistic to each other. No doubt some marriages have been the result of love. Not, however, because love could assert itself only in marriage; much rather is it because few people can completely outgrow a convention. There are today large numbers of men and women to whom marriage is naught but a farce, but who submit to it for the sake of public opinion. At any rate, while it is true that some marriages are based on love, and while it is equally true that in some cases love continues in married life, I maintain that it does so regardless of marriage, and not because of it.

On the other hand, it is utterly false that love results from marriage. On

SOURCE: Emma Goldman, *Anarchism and Other Essays* (New York: Mother Earth Publishing Co., 1910), pp. 233–245.

rare occasions one does hear of a miraculous case of a married couple falling in love after marriage, but on close examination it will be found that it is a mere adjustment to the inevitable. Certainly the growing-used to each other is far away from the spontaneity, the intensity, and beauty of love, without which the intimacy of marriage must prove degrading to both the woman and the man.

Marriage is primarily an economic arrangement, an insurance pact. It differs from the ordinary life-insurance agreement only in that it is more binding, more exacting. Its returns are insignificantly small compared with the investments. In taking out an insurance policy one pays for it in dollars and cents, always at liberty to discontinue payments. If, however, woman's premium is a husband, she pays for it with her name, her privacy, her self-respect, her very life, "until death doth part." Moreover, the marriage insurance condemns her to life-long dependency, to parasitism, to complete uselessness, individual as well as social. Man, too, pays his toll, but as his sphere is wider, marriage does not limit him as much as woman. He feels his chains more in an economic sense.

Thus Dante's motto over Inferno applies with equal force to marriage. "Ye who enter here leave all hope behind."

That marriage is a failure none but the very stupid will deny. One has but to glance over the statistics of divorce to realize how bitter a failure marriage really is. Nor will the stereotyped Philistine argument that the laxity of divorce laws and the growing looseness of woman account for the fact that: first, every twelfth marriage ends in divorce; second, that since 1870 divorces have increased from 28 to 73 for every hundred thousand population; third, that adultery, since 1867, as ground for divorce, has increased 270.8 per cent; fourth, that desertion increased 369.8 per cent.

Added to these startling figures is a vast amount of material, dramatic and literary, further elucidating this subject. Robert Herrick, in *Together;* Pinero, in *Mid-Channel;* Eugene Walter, in *Paid in Full,* and scores of other writers are discussing the barrenness, the monotony, the sordidness, the inadequacy of marriage as a factor for harmony and understanding.

The thoughtful social student will not content himself with the popular superficial excuse for this phenomenon. He will have to dig down deeper into the very life of the sexes to know why marriage proves so disastrous.

Edward Carpenter says that behind every marriage stands the life-long environment of the two sexes; an environment so different from each other that man and woman must remain strangers. Separated by an insurmountable wall of superstition, custom, and habit, marriage has not the potentiality of developing knowledge of, and respect for, each other, without which every union is doomed to failure.

Henrik Ibsen, the hater of all social shams, was probably the first to realize this great truth. Nora leaves her husband, not—as the stupid critic would have it—because she is tired of her responsibilities or feels the need of woman's rights, but because she has come to know that for eight years she had lived with a stranger and borne him children. Can there be anything more humiliating, more degrading than a life-long proximity between two strangers? No need for the woman to know anything of the man, save his income. As to the knowledge of the woman—what is there to know except that she has a pleasing appearance? We have not yet outgrown the theologic myth that woman has no soul, that she is a mere appendix to man, made out of his rib just for the convenience of the gentleman who was so strong that he was afraid of his own shadow.

Perchance the poor quality of the material whence woman comes is responsible for her inferiority. At any rate, woman has no soul—what is there to know about her? Besides, the less soul a woman has the greater her asset as a wife, the more readily will she absorb herself in her husband. It is this slavish acquiescence to man's superiority that has kept the marriage institution seemingly intact for so long a period. Now that woman is coming into her own, now that she is actually growing aware of herself as a being outside of the master's grace, the sacred institution of marriage is gradually being undermined, and no amount of sentimental lamentation can stay it.

From infancy, almost, the average girl is told that marriage is her ultimate goal; therefore her training and education must be directed toward that end. Like the mute beast fattened for slaughter, she is prepared for that. Yet, strange to say, she is allowed to know much less about her function as wife and mother than the ordinary artisan of his trade. It is indecent and filthy for a respectable girl to know anything of the marital relation. Oh, for the inconsistency of respectability, that needs the marriage vow to turn something which is filthy into the purest and most sacred arrangement that none dare question or criticize. Yet that is exactly the attitude of the average upholder of marriage. The prospective wife and mother is kept in complete ignorance of her only asset in the competitive field—sex. Thus she enters into life-long relations with a man only to find herself shocked, repelled, outraged beyond measure by the most natural and healthy instinct, sex. It is safe to say that a large percentage of the unhappiness, misery, distress, and physical suffering of matrimony is due to the criminal ignorance in sex matters that is being extolled as a great virtue. Nor is it at all an exaggeration when I say that more than one home has been broken up because of this deplorable fact.

If, however, woman is free and big enough to learn the mystery of sex without the sanction of State or Church, she will stand condemned as utterly unfit to become the wife of a "good" man, his goodness consisting of an empty brain and plenty of money. Can there be anything more outrageous than the idea that a healthy, grown woman, full of life and passion, must deny nature's demand, must subdue her most intense craving, undermine her health and break her spirit, must stunt her vision, abstain from the depth and glory of sex experience until a "good" man comes along to take her unto himself as a wife? That is precisely what marriage means. How can such an arrangement end except in failure? This is one, though not the least important, factor of marriage, which differentiates it from love.

Ours is a practical age. The time when Romeo and Juliet risked the wrath of their fathers for love, when Gretchen exposed herself to the gossip of her neighbors for love, is no more. If, on rare occasions, young people allow themselves the luxury of romance, they are taken in care by the elders, drilled and pounded until they become "sensible."

The moral lesson instilled in the girl is not whether the man has aroused her love, but rather is it, "How much?" The important and only God of practical American life: Can the man make a living? Can he support a wife? That is the only thing that justifies marriage. Gradually this saturates every thought of the girl; her dreams are not of moonlight and kisses, of laughter and tears; she dreams of shopping tours and bargain counters. This soul poverty and sordidness are the elements inherent in the marriage institution. The State and the Church approve of no other ideal, simply because it is the one that necessitates the State and Church control of men and women.

Doubtless there are people who continue to consider love above dollars and cents. Particularly is this true of that class whom economic necessity has forced to become self-supporting. The tremendous change in woman's position, wrought by that mighty factor, is indeed phenomenal when we reflect that it is but a short time since she has entered the industrial arena. Six million women wage workers; six million women who have the equal right with men to be exploited, to be robbed, to go on strike; aye, to starve even. Anything more, my lord? Yes, six million wage workers in every walk of life, from the highest brain work to the mines and railroad tracks; yes, even detectives and policemen. Surely the emancipation is complete.

Yet with all that, but a very small number of the vast army of women wage workers look upon work as a permanent issue, in the same light as does man. No matter how decrepit the latter, he has been taught to be independent, self-supporting. Oh, I know that no one is really independent in our economic treadmill; still, the poorest specimen of a man hates to be a parasite; to be known as such, at any rate.

The woman considers her position as worker transitory, to be thrown aside for the first bidder. That is why it is infinitely harder to organize women than men. "Why should I join a union? I am going to get married, to have a home." Has she not been taught from infancy to look upon that as her ultimate calling? She learns soon enough that the home, though not so large a prison as the factory, has more solid doors and bars. It has a keeper so faithful that naught can escape him. The most tragic part, however, is that the home no longer frees her from wage slavery; it only increases her task.

According to the latest statistics submitted before a committee "on labor and wages, and congestion of population," 10 per cent of the wage workers in New York City alone are married, yet they must continue to work at the most poorly paid labor in the world. Add to this horrible aspect the drudgery of housework, and what remains of the protection and glory of the home? As a matter of fact, even the middle-class girl in marriage cannot speak of her home, since it is the man who creates her sphere. It is not important whether the husband is a brute or a darling. What I wish to prove is that marriage guarantees woman a home only by the grace of her husband. There she moves about in *his* home, year after year, until her aspect of life and human affairs becomes as flat, narrow, and drab as her surroundings. Small wonder if she becomes a nag, petty, quarrelsome, gossipy, unbearable, thus driving the man from the house. She could not go, if she wanted to; there is no place to go. Besides, a short period of married life, of complete surrender of all faculties, absolutely incapacitates the average woman for the outside world. She becomes reckless in appearance, clumsy in her movements, dependent in her decisions, cowardly in her judgment, a weight and a bore, which most men grow to hate and despise. Wonderfully inspiring atmosphere for the bearing of life, is it not?

But the child, how is it to be protected, if not for marriage? After all, is not that the most important consideration? The sham, the hypocrisy of it! Marriage protecting the child, yet thousands of children destitute and homeless. Marriage protecting the child, yet orphan asylums and reformatories overcrowded, the Society for the Prevention of Cruelty to Children keeping busy in rescuing the little victims from "loving" parents, to place them under more loving care, the Gerry Society. Oh, the mockery of it!

Marriage may have the power to bring the horse to water, but has it ever made him drink? The law will place the father under arrest, and put him in convict's clothes; but has that ever stilled the hunger of the child? If the parent has no work, or if he hides his identity, what does marriage do then? It invokes the law to bring the man to "justice," to put him safely behind closed doors; his labor, however, goes not to the child, but to the State. The child receives but a blighted memory of its father's stripes.

As to the protection of the woman,—therein lies the curse of marriage. Not that it really protects her, but the very idea is so revolting, such an outrage and insult on life, so degrading to human dignity, as to forever condemn this parasitic institution.

It is like that other paternal arrangement—capitalism. It robs man of his birthright, stunts his growth, poisons his body, keeps him in ignorance, in poverty, and dependence, and then institutes charities that thrive on the last vestige of man's self-respect.

The institution of marriage makes a parasite of woman, an absolute dependent. It incapacitates her for life's struggle, annihilates her social consciousness, paralyzes her imagination, and then imposes its gracious protection, which is in reality a snare, a travesty on human character.

If motherhood is the highest fulfillment of woman's nature, what other protection does it need, save love and freedom? Marriage but defiles, outrages, and corrupts her fulfillment. Does it not say to woman, Only when you follow me shall you bring forth life? Does it not condemn her to the block, does it not degrade and shame her if she refuses to buy her right to motherhood by selling herself? Does not marriage only sanction motherhood, even though conceived in hatred, in compulsion? Yet, if motherhood be of free choice, of love, of ecstasy, of defiant passion, does it not place a crown of thorns upon an innocent head and carve in letters of blood the hideous epithet, Bastard? Were marriage to contain all the virtues claimed for it, its crimes against motherhood would exclude it forever from the realm of love.

Love, the strongest and deepest element in all life, the harbinger of hope, of joy, of ecstasy; love, the defier of all laws, of all conventions; love, the freest, the most powerful moulder of human destiny; how can such an all-compelling force be synonymous with that poor little State and Church-begotten weed, marriage?

Free love? As if love is anything but free! Man has bought brains, but all the millions in the world have failed to buy love. Man has subdued bodies, but all the power on earth has been unable to subdue love. Man has conquered whole nations, but all his armies could not conquer love. Man has chained and fettered the spirit, but he has been utterly helpless before love. High on a throne, with all the splendor and pomp his gold can command, man is yet poor and desolate, if love passes him by. And if it stays, the poorest hovel is radiant with warmth, with life and color. Thus love has the magic power to make of a beggar a king. Yes, love is free; it can dwell in no other atmosphere. In freedom it gives itself unreservedly, abundantly, completely. All the laws on the statutes, all the courts in the universe, cannot tear it from the soil, once love has taken root. If, however, the soil is sterile, how can marriage make it bear fruit? It is like the last desperate struggle of fleeting life against death.

Love needs no protection; it is its own protection. So long as love begets life no child is deserted, or hungry, or famished for the want of affection. I know this to be true. I know women who became mothers in freedom by the men they loved. Few children in wedlock enjoy the care, the protection, the devotion free motherhood is capable of bestowing.

The defenders of authority dread the advent of a free motherhood, lest it will rob them of their prey. Who would fight wars? Who would create wealth? Who would make the policeman, the jailer, if woman were to refuse the indiscriminate breeding of children? The race, the race! shouts the king, the president, the capitalist, the priest. The race must be preserved, though woman be degraded to a mere machine,—and the marriage institution is our only safety valve against the pernicious sex awakening of woman. But in vain these frantic efforts to maintain a state of bondage. In vain, too, the edicts of the Church, the mad attacks of rulers, in vain even the arm of the law. Woman no longer wants to be a party to the production of a race of sickly, feeble, decrepit, wretched human beings, who have neither the strength nor moral courage to throw off the yoke of poverty and slavery. Instead she desires fewer and better children, begotten and reared in love, and through free choice; not by compulsion, as marriage imposes. Our pseudo-moralists have yet to learn the deep sense of responsibility toward the child, that love in freedom has awakened in the breast of woman. Rather would she forego forever the glory of motherhood than bring forth life in an atmosphere that breathes only destruction and death. And if she does become a mother, it is to give to the child the deepest and best her being can yield. To grow with the child is her motto; she knows that in that manner alone can she help build true manhood and womanhood.

Ibsen must have had a vision of a free mother, when, with a master stroke, he portrayed Mrs. Alving. She was the ideal mother because she had outgrown marriage and all its horrors, because she had broken her chains, and set her spirit free to soar until it returned a personality, regenerated and strong. Alas, it was too late to rescue her life's joy, her Oswald; but not too late to realize that love in freedom is the only condition of a beautiful life. Those who, like Mrs. Alving, have paid with blood and tears for their spiritual awakening, repudiate marriage as an imposition, a shallow, empty mockery. They know, whether love last but one brief span of time or for eternity, it is the only creative, inspiring, elevating basis for a new race, a new world.

In our present pygmy state love is indeed a stranger to most people. Misunderstood and shunned, it rarely takes root; or if it does, it soon withers and dies. Its delicate fiber cannot endure the stress and strain of the daily grind. Its soul is too complex to adjust itself to the slimy woof of our social fabric. It weeps and moans and suffers with those who have need of it, yet lack the capacity to rise to love's summit.

Some day, some day men and women will rise, they will reach the mountain peak, they will meet big and strong and free, ready to receive, to partake, and to bask in the golden rays of love. What fancy, what imagination, what poetic genius can foresee even approximately the potentialities of such a force in the life of men and women. If the world is ever to give birth to true companionship and oneness, not marriage, but love will be the parent.

PART IV
The Emerging Soviets

T HE following brief selections show a part of the American Left's perception of the swirl of events during the Russian Revolution. In the first article (Document 5), the author obviously has his fingers crossed, and he uses the occasion to take a crack at the more central socialists in America who were still wedded to the idea that significant change could come about through strictly political activity. In the second statement (Document 6), the National Secretary of the Socialist Labor Party joins what was to become a favorite indoor sport of the American Left: arguing about which local splinter group more nearly resembled the ideas of the instantly mythological heroes of the Russian Revolution.

The third selection (Document 7) is the opening chapter of *Ten Days That Shook the World* (1919) by John Reed (1887–1920). Reed was an effective reporter, a dedicated radical, and an incorrigible romantic. Although he voted for Wilson in 1916, and only joined the Socialist Party in the summer of 1917, he moved quickly and stylishly leftward. His reportage of the Mexican Revolution and of World War I both resulted in books, but it was his excited, detailed, and sometimes lyrical report of the Russian Revolution in *Ten Days That Shook the World* that made his reputation. After he returned to the United States following the October Revolution, he was arrested several times for alleged sedition; he went back to Russia, now as the international delegate of the brand-new Communist Labor Party, and he was not given permission to return home again. Viewed by Lenin as a colleague in the revolution, Reed was honored and celebrated in Moscow, where he died of typhus a few days before his thirty-third birthday. His grave is now alongside of the Kremlin wall.

5

THOUGHTS ABOUT RUSSIA

PHILLIPS RUSSELL

THE most fascinating thing in the world just now in Russia. One day the news from there is glorious. The next day it is depressing. The third day it is doubtful. No first-born of anxious parents was ever watched so eagerly as is this infant nation by a distracted world. What is Russia going to do? How will she emerge from her present struggles? What system will her social and economic life be governed by when finally she is free from her old trappings? These are the unspoken questions in the heart of every rebel the world over.

Tho it is risky to attempt comment on the movements of any people 5,000 miles away, it appears that Russia is the battleground in a struggle for mastery between the bourgeoisie and the proletariat, between the employer and the workingman, between the forces that want a republic controlled by businessmen and those that demand an industrial democracy.

The autocracy does not figure any more. The reason the Russian autocracy vanished so suddenly was because it never existed in fact. It was simply a mental concept. It had no power other than that bestowed upon it by the imagination of the Russian people. When the masses no longer conceded any power to it, it had none. It simply dissolved like the chimera it was.

There is a lesson for us all here. The kind of a revolution we need first is a revolution in the minds of men and women. Economic development always makes physical conditions ripe for a change long before the brains of human beings catch up with the process. For aught we know, we could sweep away capitalism tomorrow if the working people were *mentally* prepared to do it.

We all hope for the best from Russia, but we must make up our minds not to expect too much from her. Because the Russian workers have won political liberty, it does not follow that they have achieved industrial freedom.

SOURCE: Phillips Russell, "Thoughts about Russia," *International Socialist Review,* 18, no. 1 (July 7, 1917): 21.

The news from Petrograd on the day this was written was to the effect that in a municipal election [take note] the Socialists were victorious. Of course, we cannot altogether trust the dispatches from Petrograd, since most of the foreign correspondents there are probably ignorant of social movements. But if this news is accurate, it is not very comforting. It indicates that the Russian comrades, in constructing a new regime, are making use of the old-fashioned, futile political machinery which is in bad enough odor even in political democracies like the United States, England, and France.

Let us pause here a moment and think over these fundamentals:

It is not the business of revolutionists to elect governors or mayors or sheriffs or pound-keepers to fill the seats left open in the machinery of a republican form of government, which, as experience shows, is abundantly suited to capitalism, but to organize a new world.

In erecting the framework of this new society, we must organize from the bottom upward.

The unit of that new society will be not the municipal council, not the political cabinet, not even the Socialist party branch, but the *labor union*.

We no longer need a government of persons, but an administration of things.

Modern nations no longer have their bases in political subdivisions, but in industrial organizations.

The congress, the parliament, the council of the future must be composed not of representatives from states or provinces or districts or counties, but of representatives from industries.

It is the business of the producers and distributors of the modern world to maintain not a political but an *industrial* democracy.

Russia may be merely experimenting till she finds herself. She may show us some things yet. But let us hope, for the sake of Russia's working men and women, that they won't wake up to find that they have destroyed a brutal autocracy and replaced it with a greedy capitalism.

6

SOCIALIST LABOR PARTY, 1917–1919

ARNOLD PETERSON

THE theories of the Socialist Labor Party have received a startling, and in a certain sense, unexpected vindication in Russia. To be sure, Russia economically was not so situated as to present a most favorable soil for the application of the Socialist Labor Party's principles. But so far advanced, generally, is capitalism now, that Russia, under the leadership of Lenin, soon found it necessary to proceed along the lines laid down by the Socialist Labor Party, namely, to discard the political state machinery and to organize the workers and peasants along occupational lines. This process of organization, and the result—the Soviets, corresponds to the industrial union program long ago formulated by the Socialist Labor Party, with such differences, of course, as naturally result from the differences between the two countries (Russia and the United States of America). Furthermore, the soundness of the principles of the Socialist Labor Party has been recognized by no less an authority than Lenin himself, who, it is said, has been much impressed with Daniel De Leon's writings, which it is further reported, are being translated into the Russian language.

Thus, while the party as such has not increased much in membership and votes, it can, nevertheless, look back with satisfaction upon the harvest so far reaped, and look forward with confidence to the harvest yet to be reaped, and, if all signs do not fail, a harvest to be reaped in a not too distant future.

SOURCE: Arnold Peterson, "Socialist Labor Party, 1917–1919," *American Labor Year Book, 1919–1920* (New York, 1920), pp. 420–421.

[7]

TEN DAYS THAT SHOOK
THE WORLD

JOHN REED

Background

Towards the end of September 1917, an alien Professor of Sociology visiting Russia came to see me in Petrograd. He had been informed by businessmen and intellectuals that the Revolution was slowing down. The Professor wrote an article about it and then travelled around the country, visiting factory towns and peasant communities—where, to his astonishment, the Revolution seemed to be speeding up. Among the wage-earners and the land-working people it was common to hear talk of "all land to the peasants, all factories to the workers." If the Professor had visited the front, he would have heard the whole Army talking Peace. . . .

The Professor was puzzled, but he need not have been; both observations were correct. The property-owning classes were becoming more conservative, the masses of the people more radical.

There was a feeling among businessmen and the *intelligentsia* generally that the Revolution had gone quite far enough, and lasted too long; that things should settle down. This sentiment was shared by the dominant "moderate" Socialist groups, the *oborontsi* Mensheviki and Socialist Revolutionaries, who supported the Provisional Government of Kerensky.

On October 14th the official organ of the "moderate" Socialists said:

The drama of Revolution has two acts; the destruction of the old regime and the creation of the new one. The first act has lasted long enough. Now it is time to go on to the second, and to play it as rapidly as possible. As a great revolutionist put it, "Let us hasten, friends, to terminate the Revolution. He who makes it last too long will not gather the fruits. . . ."

Among the worker, soldier and peasant masses, however, there was a stubborn feeling that the "first act" was not yet played out. On the front

SOURCE: John Reed, *Ten Days That Shook the World* (New York: International Publishers, 1967), pp. 1–13. Reprinted by permission of International Publishers Co., Inc.

the Army Committees were always running foul of officers who could not get used to treating their men like human beings; in the rear the Land Committees elected by the peasants were being jailed for trying to carry out Government regulations concerning the land; and the workmen in the factories were fighting black-lists and lock-outs. Nay, furthermore, returning political exiles were being excluded from the country as "undesirable" citizens; and in some cases men who returned from abroad to their villages were prosecuted and imprisoned for revolutionary acts committed in 1905.

To the multiform discontent of the people the "moderate" Socialists had one answer: Wait for the Constituent Assembly, which is to meet in December. But the masses were not satisfied with that. The Constituent Assembly was all well and good; but there were certain definite things for which the Russian Revolution had been made and for which the revolutionary martyrs rotted in their stark Brotherhood Grave on Mars Field, that must be achieved, Constituent Assembly or no Constituent Assembly: Peace, Land and Workers' Control of Industry. The Constituent Assembly had been postponed and postponed—would probably be postponed again, until the people were calm enough—perhaps to modify their demands! At any rate here were eight months of the Revolution gone, and little enough to show for it. . . .

Meanwhile the soldiers began to solve the peace question by simply deserting, the peasants burned manor-houses and took over the great estates, the workers sabotaged and struck. . . . Of course, as was natural, the manufacturers, land-owners and army officers exerted all their influence against any democratic compromise. . . .

The policy of the Provisional Government alternated between ineffective reforms and stern repressive measures. An edict from the Socialist Minister of Labour ordered all the Workers' Committees henceforth to meet only after working-hours. Among the troops at the front, "agitators" of opposition political parties were arrested, radical newspapers closed down, and capital punishment applied—to revolutionary propagandists. Attempts were made to disarm the Red Guard. Cossacks were sent to keep order in the provinces. . . .

These measures were supported by the "moderate" Socialists and their leaders in the Ministry, who considered it necessary to co-operate with the propertied classes. The people rapidly deserted them, and went over to the Bolsheviki, who stood for Peace, Land, and Workers' Control of Industry, and a Government of the working-class. In September, 1917, matters reached a crisis. Against the overwhelming sentiment of the country, Kerensky and the "moderate" Socialists succeeded in establishing a Government of Coalition with the propertied classes; and as a result, the Mensheviki and Socialist Revolutionaries lost the confidence of the people forever.

An article in *Rabotchi Put* (Workers' Way) about the middle of October, entitled "The Socialist Ministers," expressed the feeling of the masses of the people against the "moderate" Socialists. . . .

A Congress of delegates of the Baltic Fleet, at Helsingfors, passed a resolution which began as follows:

We demand the immediate removal from the ranks of the Provisional Government of the "Socialist," the political adventurer—Kerensky, as one who is scandalising and ruining the great Revolution, and with it the revolutionary masses, by his shameless political blackmail on behalf of the bourgeoisie. . . .

The direct result of all this was the rise of the Bolsheviki. . . .

Since March, 1917, when the roaring torrents of workmen and soldiers beating upon the Tauride Palace compelled the reluctant Imperial Duma to assume the supreme power in Russia, it was the masses of the people, workers, soldiers and peasants, which forced every change in the course of the Revolution. They hurled the Miliukov Ministry down; it was their Soviet which proclaimed to the world the Russian peace terms—"No annexations, no indemnities, and the right of self-determination of peoples"; and again, in July, it was the spontaneous rising of the unorganised proletariat which once more stormed the Tauride Palace, to demand that the Soviets take over the Government of Russia.

The Bolsheviki, then a small political sect, put themselves at the head of the movement. As a result of the disastrous failure of the rising, public opinion turned against them, and their leaderless hordes slunk back into the Viborg Quarter, which is Petrograd's *St. Antoine.* Then followed a savage hunt of the Bolsheviki; hundreds were imprisoned, among them Trotzky, Madame Kollontai and Kamenev; Lenin and Zinoviev went into hiding, fugitives from justice; the Bolshevik papers were suppressed. Provocators and reactionaries raised the cry that the Bolsheviki were German agents, until people all over the world believed it.

But the Provisional Government found itself unable to substantiate its accusations; the documents proving pro-German conspiracy were discovered to be forgeries; and one by one the Bolsheviki were released from prison without trial, on nominal or no bail—until only six remained. The impotence and indecision of the ever-changing Provisional Government was an argument nobody could refute. The Bolsheviki raised again the slogan so dear to the masses, "All Power to the Soviets!"—and they were not merely self-seeking, for at that time the majority of the Soviets was "moderate" Socialist, their bitter enemy.

But more potent still, they took the crude, simple desires of the workers, soldiers and peasants, and from them built their immediate programme. And so, while the *oborontsi* Mensheviki and Socialist Revolutionaries involved themselves in compromise with the bourgeoisie, the Bolsheviki rapidly captured the Russian masses. In July they were hunted and despised; by September the metropolitan workmen, the sailors of the Baltic Fleet, and the soldiers, had been won almost entirely to their cause. The September municipal elections in the large cities were significant; only 18 per cent of the returns were Menshevik and Socialist Revolutionary, against more than 70 per cent in June. . . .

There remains a phenomenon which puzzled foreign observers; the fact that the Central Executive Committees of the Soviets, the Central Army and Fleet Committees, and the Central Committees of some of the Unions —notably, the Post and Telegraph Workers and the Railway Workers— opposed the Bolsheviki with the utmost violence. These Central Committees had all been elected in the middle of the summer, or even before, when the Mensheviki and Socialist Revolutionaries had an enormous following; and they delayed or prevented any new elections. Thus, according to the constitution of the Soviets of Workers' and Soldiers' Deputies, the All-Russian Congress *should have been called in September;* but the *Tsay-ee-kah* would not call the meeting, on the ground that the Constituent Assembly was only two months away, at which time, they hinted, the Soviets would abdicate. Meanwhile, one by one, the Bolsheviki were winning in the local Soviets all over the country, in the Union branches and the ranks of the soldiers and sailors. The Peasants' Soviets remained still conservative, because in the sluggish rural districts political consciousness developed slowly, and the Socialist Revolutionary party had been for a generation the party which had agitated among the peasants. . . . But even among the peasants a revolutionary wing was forming. It showed itself clearly in October, when the left wing of the Socialist Revolutionaries split off, and formed a new political faction, the Left Socialist Revolutionaries.

At the same time there were signs everywhere that the forces of reaction were gaining confidence. At the Troitsky Farce Theatre in Petrograd, for example, a burlesque called *Sins of the Tsar* was interrupted by a group of monarchists, who threatened to lynch the actors for "insulting the Emperor." Certain newspapers began to sigh for a "Russian Napoleon." It was the usual thing among bourgeois *intelligentsia* to refer to the Soviets of Workers' Deputies (Rabotchikh Deputatov) as *Sabatchikh* Deputatove —Dogs' Deputies.

On October 15th, I had a conversation with a great Russian Capitalist, Stepan Georgevitch Lianozov, known as the "Russian Rockefeller"—a Cadet by political faith.

"Revolution," he said, "is a sickness. Sooner or later the foreign powers must intervene here—as one would intervene to cure a sick child, and teach it how to walk. Of course, it would be more or less improper, but the nations must realise the danger of Bolshevism in their own countries —such contagious ideas as 'proletarian dictatorship,' and 'world social revolution.' . . . There is a chance that this intervention may not be necessary. Transportation is demoralised, the factories are closing down, and the Germans are advancing. Starvation and defeat may bring the Russian people to their senses."

Mr. Lianozov was emphatic in his opinion that whatever happened, it would be impossible for merchants and manufacturers to permit the existence of the workers' Shop Committees, or to allow the workers any share in the management of industry.

"As for the Bolsheviki, they will be done away with by one of two methods. The Government can evacuate Petrograd, then a state of siege declared, and the military commander of the district can deal with these gentlemen without legal formalities. . . . *Or if, for example, the Constituent Assembly manifests any Utopian tendencies, it can be dispersed by force of arms. . . .*"

Winter was coming on—the terrible Russian winter. I heard business men speak of it so: "Winter was always Russia's best friend. Perhaps now it will rid us of Revolution." On the freezing front miserable armies continued to starve and die without enthusiasm. The railways were breaking down, food lessening, factories closing. The desperate masses cried out that the bourgeoisie was sabotaging the life of the people, causing defeat on the Front. Riga had been surrendered just after General Kornilov said publicly, "Must we pay with Riga the price of bringing the country to a sense of its duty?"

To Americans it is incredible that the class war should develop to such a pitch. But I have personally met officers on the Northern Front who frankly preferred military disaster to co-operation with the Soldiers' Committees. The secretary of the Petrograd branch of the Cadet party told me that the break-down of the country's economic life was part of a campaign to discredit the Revolution. An Allied diplomat, whose name I promised not to mention, confirmed this from his own knowledge. I know of certain coal mines near Kharkov which were fired and flooded by their owners, of textile factories at Moscow whose engineers put the machinery out of order when they left, of railroad officials caught by the workers in the act of crippling locomotives. . . .

A large section of the propertied classes preferred the Germans to the Revolution—even to the Provisional Government—and didn't hesitate to say so. In the Russian household where I lived, the subject of conversation at the dinner table was almost invariably the coming of the Germans, bringing "law and order." . . . One evening I spent at the house of a Moscow merchant; during tea we asked the eleven people at the table whether they preferred "Wilhelm or the Bolsheviki." The vote was ten to one for Wilhelm. . . .

The speculators took advantage of the universal disorganisation to pile up fortunes, and to spend them in fantastic revelry or the corruption of Government officials. Foodstuffs and fuel were hoarded, or secretly sent out of the country to Sweden. In the first four months of the Revolution, for example, the reserve food supplies were almost openly looted from the great Municipal warehouses of Petrograd, until the two years' provision of grain had fallen to less than enough to feed the city for one month. . . . According to the official report of the last Minister of Supplies in the Provisional Government, coffee was bought wholesale in Vladivostok for two roubles a pound, and the consumer in Petrograd paid thirteen. In all the stores of the large cities were tons of food and clothing; but only the rich could buy them.

In a provincial town I knew a merchant family turned speculator— *maradior* (bandit, ghoul) the Russians call it. The three sons had bribed their way out of military service. One gambled in foodstuffs. Another sold illegal gold from the Lena mines to mysterious parties in Finland. The third owned a controlling interest in a chocolate factory, which supplied the local Co-operative societies—on condition that the Co-operatives furnished him everything he needed. And so, while the masses of the people got a quarter pound of black bread on their bread cards, he had an abundance of white bread, sugar, tea, candy, cake, and butter. . . . Yet when the soldiers at the Front could no longer fight from cold, hunger and exhaustion, how indignantly did this family scream "Cowards!"—how "ashamed" they were "to be Russians." . . . When finally the Bolsheviki found and requisitioned vast hoarded stores of provisions, what "Robbers" they were.

Beneath all this external rottenness moved the old-time Dark Forces, unchanged since the fall of Nicholas the Second, secret still and very active. The agents of the notorious *Okhrana* still functioned, for and against the Tsar, for and against Kerensky—whoever would pay. . . . In the darkness, underground organisations of all sorts, such as the Black Hundreds, were busy attempting to restore reaction in some form or other.

In this atmosphere of corruption, of monstrous half-truths, one clear note sounded day after day, the deepening chorus of the Bolsheviki, "All Power to the Soviets! All Power to the direct representatives of millions on millions of common workers, soldiers, peasants. Land, bread, an end to the senseless war, an end to secret diplomacy, speculation, treachery. . . . The Revolution is in danger and with it the cause of the people all over the world!"

The struggle between the proletariat and the middle class, between the Soviets and the Government, which had begun in the first March days, was about to culminate. Having at one bound leaped from the Middle Ages into the twentieth century Russia showed the startled world two systems of Revolution—the political and the social—in mortal combat.

What a revelation of the vitality of the Russian Revolution, after all these months of starvation and disillusionent! The bourgeoisie should have better known its Russia. Not for a long time in Russia will the "sickness" of Revolution have run its course. . . .

Looking back, Russia before the November insurrection seems of another age, almost incredibly conservative. So quickly did we adapt ourselves to the newer, swifter life; just as Russian politics swung bodily to the Left—until the Cadets were outlawed as "enemies of the people," Kerensky became a "counter-revolutionist," the "middle" Socialist leaders, Tseretelli, Dan, Lieber, Gotz and Avksentiev, were too reactionary for their following, and men like Victor Tchernov, and even Maxim Gorky, belonged to the Right Wing. . . .

About the middle of December, 1917, a group of Socialist Revolutionary leaders paid a private visit to Sir George Buchanan, the British Ambassador, and implored him not to mention the fact that they had been there because they were "considered too far Right."

"And to think," said Sir George, "one year ago my Government instructed me not to receive Miliukov, because he was so dangerously Left!"

September and October are the worst months of the Russian year—especially the Petrograd year. Under dull grey skies, in the shortening days, the rain fell drenching, incessant. The mud underfoot was deep, slippery and clinging, tracked everywhere by heavy boots, and worse than usual because of the complete break-down of the Municipal administration. Bitter damp winds rushed in from the Gulf of Finland, and the chill fog rolled through the streets. At night, for motives of economy as well as fear of Zeppelins, the street-lights were few and far between; in private dwellings and apartment houses the electricity was turned on from six o'clock until midnight, with candles forty cents apiece and little kerosene to be had. It was dark from three in the afternoon to ten in the morning. Robberies and house-breaking increased. In apartment houses the men took turns at all-night guard duty, armed with loaded rifles. This was under the Provisional Government.

Week by week food became scarcer. The daily allowance of bread fell from a pound and a half to a pound, then three-quarters, half, and a quarter-pound. Towards the end there was a week without any bread at all. Sugar, one was entitled to at the rate of two pounds a month—if one could get it at all, which was seldom. A bar of chocolate or a pound of tasteless candy cost anywhere from seven to ten roubles—at least a dollar. There was milk for about half the babies in the city; most hotels and private houses never saw it for months. In the fruit season apples and pears sold for a little less than a rouble apiece on the street corner. . . .

For milk and bread and sugar and tobacco one had to stand in *queue* long hours in the chill rain. Coming home from an all-night meeting I have seen the *kvost* (tail) beginning to form before dawn, mostly women, some with babies in their arms. . . . Carlyle, in his *French Revolution,* has described the French people as distinguished above all others by their faculty of standing in *queue.* Russia had accustomed herself to the practice, begun in the reign of Nicholas the Blessed as long ago as 1915, and from then continued intermittently until the summer of 1917, when it settled down as the regular order of things. Think of the poorly-clad people standing on the iron-white streets of Petrograd whole days in the Russian winter! I have listened in the bread-lines, hearing the bitter, acrid note of discontent which from time to time burst up through the miraculous good nature of the Russian crowd. . . .

Of course all the theatres were going every night, including Sundays. Karsavina appeared in a new Ballet at the Marinsky, all dance-loving Russia coming to see her. Shaliapin was singing. At the Alexandrinsky they were reviving Meyerhold's production of Tolstoy's "Death of Ivan the Terrible"; and at that performance I remember noticing a student of the Imperial School of Pages, in his dress uniform, who stood up correctly between the acts and faced the empty Imperial box, with its eagles all erased. . . . The *Krivoye Zerkalo* staged a sumptuous version of Schnitzler's "Reigen."

Although the Hermitage and other picture galleries had been evacuated to Moscow, there were weekly exhibitions of paintings. Hordes of the female *intelligentsia* went to hear lectures on Art, Literature and the Easy Philosophies. It was a particularly active season for Theosophists. And the Salvation Army, admitted to Russia for the first time in history, plastered the walls with announcements of gospel meetings, which amused and astounded Russian audiences. . . .

As in all such times, the petty conventional life of the city went on, ignoring the Revolution as much as possible. The poets made verses—but not about the Revolution. The realistic painters painted scenes from mediaeval Russian history—anything but the Revolution. Young ladies from the provinces came up to the capital to learn French and cultivate their voices, and the gay young beautiful officers wore their gold-trimmed crimson *bashliki* and their elaborate Caucasian swords around the hotel lobbies. The ladies of the minor bureaucratic set took tea with each other in the afternoon, carrying each her little gold or silver or jewelled sugar-box, and half a loaf of bread in her muff, and wished that the Tsar were back, or that the Germans would come, or anything that would solve the servant problem. . . . The daughter of a friend of mine came home one afternoon in hysterics because the woman street-car conductor had called her "Comrade!"

All around them great Russia was in travail, bearing a new world. The servants one used to treat like animals and pay next to nothing were getting independent. A pair of shoes cost more than a hundred roubles, and as wages averaged about thirty-five roubles a month the servants refused to stand in *queue* and wear out their shoes. But more than that. In the new Russia every man and woman could vote; there were working-class newspapers, saying new and startling things; there were the Soviets; and there were the Unions. The *izvoshtchiki* (cab-drivers) had a Union; they were also represented in the Petrograd Soviet. The waiters and hotel servants were organised, and refused tips. On the walls of restaurants they put up signs which read, "No tips taken here—" or, "Just because a man has to make his living waiting on table is no reason to insult him by offering him a tip!"

At the Front the soldiers fought their fight with the officers, and learned self-government through their committees. In the factories those unique Russian organisations, the Factory-Shop Committees, gained experience and strength and a realisation of their historical mission by combat with the old order. All Russia was learning to read, and *reading*—politics, economics, history—because the people wanted to *know*. . . . In every city, in most towns, along the Front, each political faction had its newspaper—

sometimes several. Hundreds of thousands of pamphlets were distributed by thousands of organisations, and poured into the armies, the villages, the factories, the streets. The thirst for education, so long thwarted, burst with the Revolution into a frenzy of expression. From Smolny Institute alone, the first six months, went out every day tons, car-loads, train-loads of literature, saturating the land. Russia absorbed reading matter like hot sand drinks water, insatiable. And it was not fables, falsified history, diluted religion, and the cheap fiction that corrupts—but social and economic theories, philosophy, the works of Tolstoy, Gogol, and Gorky. . . .

Then the talk, beside which Carlyle's "flood of French speech" was a mere trickle. Lectures, debates, speeches—in theatres, circuses, schoolhouses, clubs, Soviet meeting-rooms, Union headquarters, barracks. . . . Meetings in the trenches at the Front, in village squares, factories. . . . What a marvellous sight to see Putilovsky Zavod (the Putilov factory) pour out its forty thousand to listen to Social Democrats, Socialist Revolutionaries, Anarchists, anybody, whatever they had to say, as long as they would talk! For months in Petrograd, and all over Russia, every street-corner was a public tribune. In railway trains, street-cars, always the spurting up of impromptu debate, everywhere. . . .

And the All-Russian Conferences and Congresses, drawing together the men of two continents—conventions of Soviets, of Co-operatives, Zemstvos, nationalities, priests, peasants, political parties; the Democratic Conference, the Moscow Conference, the Council of the Russian Republic. There were always three or four conventions going on in Petrograd. At every meeting, attempts to limit the time of speakers voted down, and every man free to express the thought that was in him. . . .

We came down to the Front of the Twelfth Army, back of Riga, where gaunt and bootless men sickened in the mud of desperate trenches; and when they saw us they started up, with their pinched faces and the flesh showing blue through their torn clothing, demanding eagerly, "Did you bring anything to *read?*"

What though the outward and visible signs of change were many, what though the statue of Catherine the Great before the Alexandrinsky Theatre bore a little red flag in its hand, and others—somewhat faded—floated from all public buildings; and the Imperial monograms and eagles were either torn down or covered up; and in place of the fierce *gorodovoye* (city police) a mild-mannered and unarmed citizen militia patrolled the streets —still, there were many quaint anachronisms.

For example, Peter the Great's *Tabel o Rangov*—Table of Ranks— which he riveted upon Russia with an iron hand, still held sway. Almost everybody from the schoolboy up wore his prescribed uniform, with the insignia of the Emperor on button and shoulder-strap. Along about five o'clock in the afternoon the streets were full of subdued old gentlemen in uniform, with portfolios, going home from work in the huge, barrack-like Ministries or Government institutions, calculating perhaps how great a mortality among their superiors would advance them to the coveted *tchin* (rank) of Collegiate Assessor, or Privy Councillor, with the prospect of retirement on a comfortable pension, and possibly the Cross of St. Anne. . . .

There is the story of Senator Sokolov, who in full tide of Revolution came to a meeting of the Senate one day in civilian clothes, and was not admitted because he did not wear the prescribed livery of the Tsar's service!

It was against this background of a whole nation in ferment and disintegration that the pageant of the Rising of the Russian Masses unrolled. . . .

PART V
Debs

In all the confusion and ugly in-fighting on the early Left, Eugene V. Debs (1855–1926) usually stayed clean, stayed away from the worst slug-fests, and so stayed a little aloof. Because of his unwillingness to battle in the mud of factional ambition and political mindlessness, he was for decades the most unifying personal force on the left. But his frequent absences from the worst battles were better for him personally than for the Left, for he could have been more of a force for internal sanity. It is true, however, that his unique position would have been compromised had he been more clearly identified with one or another faction. But, again, would the factions have been quite as hostile if he had fought harder for unity? He did, however, speak for the Left to America with a more domestic accent and with more success than anyone else.

Coming out of the organized labor movement of railroad workers, Debs threw himself into the Pullman strike of 1894, for which he was thrown into jail for six months. He converted to socialism while in the Woodstock jail, and he later formed a socialist political party which joined with the bolting rightwing of the Socialist Labor Party to form the Socialist Party in 1901. He was the Socialists' presidential candidate five times, the last, when he received about 900,000 votes, while serving time in the Atlanta penitentiary.

Debs's genius for unity must not obscure his passion, his willingness and ability to whip himself and his audiences into a flaming revolutionary anger. For instance, when Bill Haywood, Charles Moyer, and George Petti-bone, officers of the Western Federation of Miners, were arrested in Denver in 1906 on a trumped-up murder charge and sent to prison in Idaho without extradition proceedings, Debs published "Arouse, Ye Slaves!" (Document 8). He published this in March 1906 in the *Appeal to Reason,* a social-ist newspaper that then had a circulation of about half a million, cost 25 cents a year, and was an authentic voice of midwestern American socialism. Debs obviously wrote this piece with clenched fists and in white heat; so Theodore Roosevelt sent a copy to his Attorney General with a note: "This is an infamous article. Is it possible to proceed against Debs and the proprietor of this paper criminally?" [1] TR failed to ban the *Appeal* or to get Debs, but in a few years Wilson succeeded with both.

Typical of his political acuity and dedication to socialism, Debs began to worry about the electoral successes of the Socialist party. In 1911 he said that there was "Danger Ahead" (Document 9) if Socialists compromised revolutionary principle to win votes. The almost standard politician's response of "you can't achieve anything unless you're elected first" is definitively answered here by Debs. He feared cooptation, obviously, but he was also concerned about the effect on Socialists of yielding when the goal for which they compromised could not be reached through compromise.

The IWW's leadership of the Lawrence strike precipitated a debate over tactics on the left. Debs was moved to explain his own view of the relationship of tactics to principles, and of violence to success, in an article called "Sound Socialist Tactics" (Document 10) which originally appeared in the *International Socialist Review* in February 1912. The Left's agony over tactics was a battle for life and death, as Debs saw it, so he could say that between tactics and strategy, the revolution would ultimately depend more on the tactics. He came down squarely for working-class solidarity in opposition to capitalist property values and laws, but he could not abide individual criminal violence, including industrial sabotage so important to the Wobblies. That his view prevailed within the Socialist Party is recorded in the fact that it repudiated direct action and sabotage at its 1912 convention. In fact, after the relatively satisfactory outcome of Debs' campaign in the same year, the conservative wing of the party, controlled by Morris Hillquit and Victor Berger, wanted to purge the party of Haywood as a symbol of IWW direct actionism. A referendum was held early in 1913 which removed (24,000 to 11,000) Haywood from the SP National Executive Committee on the grounds that he advocated violence; he and other syndicalists quit the party, and the gradualists tightened their control.

One of the most important speeches Debs ever made was delivered to a state convention of the SP in a park at Canton, Ohio, 16 June 1918 (Document 11). For giving this speech Debs was convicted of violating the Es-

[1] Quoted in David Shannon, *The Socialist Party of America* (New York, 1955), p. 30.

pionage Act and was sentenced to ten years in jail. During his trial, he refused to allow anyone to testify in his defense, and his conviction was ultimately upheld by a unanimous Supreme Court. Before he was sentenced he told the court that "while there is a lower class I am in it; while there is a criminal element, I am of it; while there is a soul in prison, I am not free." On advice from his Attorney General, A. Mitchell Palmer, Woodrow Wilson refused to intervene, and Debs remained in Atlanta for thirty-two months until Harding finally had him released late in 1921. It is clear that Debs was imprisoned months after the armistice for delivering a speech that, even according to the Justice Department, was not illegal.

The Canton speech is memorable because its rhetorical heat burned and can still be felt, rather than because of its content. It was an inspirational call to socialism, a hand of solidarity extended to the persecuted Wobblies, to the Bolsheviks, and to oppressed people of the world. Debs could fire an audience as could no other radical of these early decades, and his crime, as the legal criminality of wartime hysteria defined it, should have been extraordinary human decency, not sedition.

---

[8]

AROUSE, YE SLAVES!

EUGENE V. DEBS

THE latest and boldest stroke of the plutocracy, but for the blindness of the people, would have startled the nation.

Murder has been plotted and is about to be executed in the name and under the forms of law.

Men who will not yield to corruption and browbeating must be ambushed, spirited away and murdered.

That is the edict of the Mine Owners' Association of the western states and their Standard Oil backers and pals in Wall Street, New York.

These gory-beaked vultures are to pluck out the heart of resistance to their tyranny and robbery, that labor may be left stark naked at their mercy.

SOURCE: Eugene V. Debs, *Writings and Speeches* (New York: Hermitage Press, Inc., 1948), pp. 256–258.

Charles Moyer and William D. Haywood, of the Western Federation of Miners, and their official colleagues—men, all of them, and every inch of them—are charged with the assassination of ex-Governor Frank Steunenberg, of Idaho, who simply reaped what he had sown, as a mere subterfuge to pounce upon them in secret, rush them out of the state by special train, under heavy guard, clap them into the penitentiary, convict them upon the purchased perjured testimony of villains, and strangle them to death with the hangman's noose.

It is a foul plot; a damnable conspiracy; a hellish outrage.

The governors of Idaho and Colorado say they have the proof to convict. They are brazen falsifiers and venal villains, the miserable tools of the mine owners who, themselves, if anybody, deserve the gibbet.

Moyer, Haywood and their comrades had no more to do with the assassination of Steunenberg than I had; the charge is a ghastly lie, a criminal calumny, and is only an excuse to murder men who are too rigidly honest to betray their trust and too courageous to succumb to threat and intimidation.

Labor leaders that cringe before the plutocracy and do its bidding are apotheosized; those that refuse must be foully murdered.

Personally and intimately do I know Moyer, Haywood, Pettibone, St. John and their official co-workers, and I will stake my life on their honor and integrity; and that is precisely the crime for which, according to the words of the slimy "sleuth" who "worked up the case" against them, "they shall never leave Idaho alive."

Well, by the gods, if they don't, the governors of Idaho and Colorado and their masters from Wall Street, New York, to the Rocky Mountains had better prepare to follow them.

Nearly twenty years ago the capitalist tyrants put some innocent men to death for standing up for labor.

They are now going to try it again. Let them dare!

There have been twenty years of revolutionary education, agitation and organization since the Haymarket tragedy, and if an attempt is made to reapeat it, there will be a revolution and I will do all in my power to precipitate it.

The crisis has come and we have got to meet it. Upon the issue involved the whole body of organized labor can unite and every enemy of plutocracy will join us. From the farms, the factories and stores will pour the workers to meet the red-handed destroyers of freedom, the murderers of innocent men and the arch-enemies of the people.

Moyer and Haywood are our comrades, staunch and true, and if we do not stand by them to the shedding of the last drop of blood in our veins, we are disgraced forever and deserve the fate of cringing cowards.

We are not responsible for the issue. It is not of our seeking. It has been forced upon us; and for the very reason that we deprecate violence and abhor bloodshed we cannot desert our comrades and allow them to be put to death. If they can be murdered without cause so can we, and so will we be dealt with at the pleasure of these tyrants.

They have driven us to the wall and now let us rally our forces and face them and fight.

If they attempt to murder Moyer, Haywood and their brothers, a million revolutionists, at least, will meet them with guns.

They have done their best and their worst to crush and enslave us. Their politicians have betrayed us, their courts have thrown us into jail without trial and their soldiers have shot our comrades dead in their tracks.

The worm turns at last, and so does the worker.

Let them dare to execute their devilish plot and every state in this Union will resound with the tramp of revolution.

Get ready, comrades, for action! No other course is left to the working class. Their courts are closed to us except to pronounce our doom. To enter their courts is simply to be mulcted of our meagre means and bound hand and foot; to have our eyes plucked out by the vultures that fatten upon our misery.

Capitalist courts never have done, and never will do, anything for the working class.

Whatever is done we must do ourselves, and if we stand up like men from the Atlantic to the Pacific and from Canada to the Gulf, we will strike terror to their cowardly hearts and they will be but too eager to relax their grip upon our throats and beat a swift retreat.

We will watch every move they make and in the meantime prepare for action.

A special revolutionary convention of the proletariat at Chicago, or some other central point, would be in order, and, if extreme measures are required, a general strike could be ordered and industry paralyzed as a preliminary to a general uprising.

If the plutocrats begin the program, we will end it.

DANGER AHEAD

EUGENE V. DEBS

THE large increase in the socialist vote in the late national and state elections is quite naturally hailed with elation and rejoicing by party members, but I feel prompted to remark, in the light of some personal observations during the campaign, that it is not entirely a matter for jubilation. I am not given to pessimism, or captious criticism, and yet I cannot but feel that some of the votes placed to our credit this year were obtained by methods not consistent with the principles of a revolutionary party, and in the long run will do more harm than good.

I yield to no one in my desire to see the party grow and the vote increase, but in my zeal I do not lose sight of the fact that healthy growth and a substantial vote depend upon efficient organization, the self-education and self-discipline of the membership, and that where these are lacking, an inflated vote secured by compromising methods, can only be hurtful to the movement.

The danger I see ahead is that the Socialist party at this stage, and under existing conditions, is apt to attract elements which it cannot assimilate, and that it may be either weighted down, or torn asunder with internal strife, or that it may become permeated and corrupted with the spirit of bourgeois reform to an extent that will practically destroy its virility and efficiency as a revolutionary organization.

To my mind the working class character and the revolutionary integrity of the Socialist party are of first importance. All the votes of the people would do us no good if our party ceased to be a revolutionary party, or only incidentally so, while yielding more and more to the pressure to modify the principles and program of the party for the sake of swelling the vote and hastening the day of its expected triumph.

It is precisely this policy and the alluring promise it holds out to new members with more zeal than knowledge of working class economics that constitute the danger we should guard against in preparing for the next campaign. The truth is that we have not a few members who regard vote-

SOURCE: Eugene V. Debs, "Danger Ahead," *International Socialist Review* (January 1911), pp. 413–414.

getting as of supreme importance, no matter by what method the votes may be secured, and this leads them to hold out inducements and make representations which are not at all compatible with the stern and uncompromising principles of a revolutionary party. They seek to make the socialist propaganda so attractive—eliminating whatever may give offense to bourgeois sensibilities—that it serves as a bait for votes rather than as a means of education, and votes thus secured do not properly belong to us and do injustice to our party as well as to those who cast them.

These votes do not express socialism and in the next ensuing election are quite as apt to be turned against us, and it is better that they be not cast for the Socialist party, registering a degree of progress the party is not entitled to and indicating a political position the party is unable to sustain.

Socialism is a matter of growth, of evolution, which can be advanced by wise methods, but never by obtaining for it a fictitious vote. We should seek only to register the actual vote of socialism, no more and no less. In our propaganda we should state our principles clearly, speak the truth fearlessly, seeking neither to flatter nor to offend, but only to convince those who should be with us and win them to our cause through an intelligent understanding of its mission.

There is also a disposition on the part of some to join hands with reactionary trade-unionists in local emergencies and in certain temporary situations to effect some specific purpose, which may or may not be in harmony with our revolutionary program. No possible good can come from any kind of a political alliance, express or implied, with trade-unions or the leaders of trade-unions who are opposed to socialism and only turn to it for use in some extremity, the fruit of their own reactionary policy.

Of course we want the support of trade-unionists, but only of those who believe in socialism and are ready to vote and work with us for the overthrow of capitalism.

The American Federation of Labor, as an organization, with its Civic Federation to determine its attitude and control its course, is deadly hostile to the Socialist party and to any and every revolutionary movement of the working class. To kow-tow to this organization and to join hands with its leaders to secure political favors can only result in compromising our principles and bringing disaster to the party.

Not for all the vote of the American Federation of Labor and its labor-dividing and corruption-breeding craft-unions should we compromise one jot of our revolutionary principles; and if we do we shall be visited with the contempt we deserve by all real socialists, who will scorn to remain in a party professing to disreputable methods of ward-heeling be a revolutionary party of the working class while employing the crooked and politicians to attain their ends.

Of far greater importance than increasing the vote of the Socialist party is the economic organization of the working class. To the extent, and only to the extent, that the workers are organized and disciplined in their respective industries can the socialist movement advance and the Socialist party hold what is registered by the ballot. The election of legislative and administrative officers, here and there, where the party is still in a crude state and the members economically unprepared and politically unfit to assume the responsibilities thrust upon them as the result of popular discontent, will inevitably bring trouble and set the party back, instead of advancing it, and while this is to be expected and is to an extent unavoidable, we should court no more of that kind of experience than is necessary to avoid a repetition of it. The Socialist party has already achieved some victories of this kind which proved to be defeats, crushing and humiliating, and from which the party has not even now, after many years, entirely recovered.

We have just so much socialism that is stable and dependable, because securely grounded in economics, in discipline, and all else that expresses class-conscious solidarity, and this must be augmented steadily through economic and political organization, but no amount of mere votes can accomplish this in even the slightest degree.

Voting for socialism is not socialism any more than a menu is a meal. . . .

---

[10]

SOUND SOCIALIST TACTICS

EUGENE V. DEBS

SOCIALISTS are practically all agreed as to the fundamental principles of their movement. But as to tactics there is wide variance among them. The matter of sound tactics, equally with the matter of sound principles, is of supreme importance. The disagreements and dissensions among Socialists

SOURCE: Eugene V. Debs, *Writings and Speeches* (New York: Hermitage Press, 1948), pp. 350–353.

relate almost wholly to tactics. The party splits which have occurred in the past have been due to the same cause, and if the party should ever divide again, which it is to be hoped it will not, it will be on the rock of tactics.

Revolutionary tactics must harmonize with revolutionary principles. We could better hope to succeed with reactionary principles and revolutionary tactics than with revolutionary principles and reactionary tactics.

The matter of tactical differences should be approached with an open mind and in the spirit of tolerance. The freest discussion should be allowed. We have every element in every shade of capitalist society in our party, and we are in for a lively time at the very best before we work out these differences and settle down to a policy of united and constructive work for socialism instead of spending so much time and energy lampooning one another.

In the matter of tactics we cannot be guided by the precedents of other countries. We have to develop our own and they must be adapted to the American people and to American conditions. I am not sure that I have the right idea about tactics; I am sure only that I appreciate their importance, that I am open to correction, and that I am ready to change whenever I find myself wrong.

It seems to me there is too much rancor and too little toleration among us in the discussion of our differences. Too often the spirit of criticism is acrid and hypercritical. Personal animosities are engendered, but opinions remain unchanged. Let us waste as little as possible of our militant spirit upon one another. We shall need it all for our capitalist friends.

There has recently been some rather spirited discussion about a paragraph which appears in the pamphlet on "Industrial Socialism," by William D. Haywood and Frank Bohn. The paragraph follows:

When the worker, either through experience or study of Socialism, comes to know this truth, he acts accordingly. *He retains absolutely no respect for the property "rights" of the profit-takers. He will use any weapon which will win his fight.* He knows that the present laws of property are made by and for the capitalists. *Therefore he does not hesitate to break them.*

The sentences which I have italicized provoked the controversy.

We have here a matter of tactics upon which a number of comrades of ability and prominence have sharply disagreed. For my own part I believe the paragraph to be entirely sound.

Certainly all Socialists, knowing how and to what end capitalist property "rights" are established, must hold such "rights" in contempt. In the *Manifesto* Marx says: "The Communist (Socialist) revolution is the most radical rupture with traditional property relations; no wonder that its development involves the most radical rupture with traditional ideas."

As a revolutionist I can have no respect for capitalist property laws, nor the least scruple about violating them. I hold all such laws to have been enacted through chicanery, fraud and corruption, with the sole end in view of dispossessing, robbing and enslaving the working class. But this does not imply that I propose making an individual law-breaker of myself and butting my head against the stone wall of existing property laws. That might be called force, but it would not be that. It would be mere weakness and folly.

If I had the force to overthrow these despotic laws I would use it without an instant's hesitation or delay, but I haven't got it, and so I am law-abiding under protest—not from scruple—and bide my time.

Here let me say that for the same reason I am opposed to sabotage and to "direct action." I have not a bit of use for the "propaganda of the deed." These are the tactics of anarchist individualists and not of Socialist collectivists. They were developed by and belong exclusively to our anarchist friends and accord perfectly with their philosophy. These and similar measures are reactionary, not revolutionary, and they invariably have a demoralizing effect upon the following of those who practice them. If I believed in the doctrine of violence and destruction as party policy; if I regarded the class struggle as guerrilla warfare, I would join the anarchists and practice as well as preach such tactics.

It is not because these tactics involve the use of force that I am opposed to them, but because they do not. The physical forcist is the victim of his own boomerang. The blow he strikes reacts upon himself and his followers. The force that implies power is utterly lacking, and it can never be developed by such tactics.

The foolish and misguided, zealots and fanatics, are quick to applaud and eager to employ such tactics, and the result is usually hurtful to themselves and to the cause they seek to advance.

There have been times in the past, and there are countries today where the frenzied deed of a glorious fanatic like old John Brown seems to have been inspired by Jehovah himself, but I am now dealing with the twentieth century and with the United States.

There may be, too, acute situations arising and grave emergencies occurring, with perhaps life at stake, when recourse to violence might be justified, but a great body of organized workers, such as the Socialist movement, cannot predicate its tactical procedure upon such exceptional instances.

But my chief objection to all these measures is that they do violence to the class psychology of the workers and cannot be successfully inculcated as mass doctrine. The very nature of these tactics adapts them to guerrilla warfare, to the bomb planter, the midnight assassin; and such warfare, in this country, at least, plays directly into the hands of the enemy.

Such tactics appeal to stealth and suspicion, and cannot make for solidarity. The very teaching of sneaking and surreptitious practices has a demoralizing effect and a tendency to place those who engage in them in the category of "Black Hand" agents, dynamiters, safe-blowers, hold-up men, burglars, thieves and pickpockets.

If sabotage and direct action, as I interpret them, were incorporated in the tactics of the Socialist Party, it would at once be the signal for all the *agents provocateurs* and police spies in the country to join the party and get busy. Every solitary one of them would be a rabid "direct actionist," and every one would safely make his "get-away" and secure his reward . . . when anything was "pulled off" by their dupes, leaving them with their necks in the nooses.

With the sanctioning of sabotage and similar practices the Socialist Party would stand responsible for the deed of every spy or madman, the seeds of strife would be subtly sown in the ranks, mutual suspicion would be aroused, and the party would soon be torn into warring factions to the despair of the betrayed workers and the delight of their triumphant masters.

If sabotage or any other artifice of direct action could be successfully employed, it would be wholly unnecessary, as better results could be accomplished without it. To the extent that the working class has power based upon class-consciousness, force is unnecessary; to the extent that power is lacking, force can only result in harm.

I am opposed to any tactics which involve stealth, secrecy, intrigue, and necessitate acts of individual violence for their execution.

The work of the Socialist movement must all be done out in the broad open light of day. Nothing can be done by stealth that can be of any advantage to it in this country.

The workers can be emancipated only by their own collective will, the power inherent in themselves as a class, and this collective will and conquering power can only be the result of education, enlightenment and self-imposed discipline.

Sound tactics are constructive, not destructive. The collective reason of the workers repels the idea of individual violence where they are free to assert themselves by lawful and peaceable means.

The American workers are law-abiding and no amount of sneering or derision will alter that fact. Direct action will never appeal to any considerable number of them while they have the ballot and the right of industrial and political organization.

Its tactics alone have prevented the growth of the Industrial Workers of the World. Its principles of industrial unionism are sound, but its tactics are not. Sabotage repels the American worker. He is ready for the industrial union, but he is opposed to the "propaganda of the deed," and as long as the I. W. W. adheres to its present tactics and ignores political action, or treats it with contempt by advising the workers to "strike at the ballot box with an ax," they will regard it as an anarchist organization, and it will never be more than a small fraction of the labor movement.

The sound education of the workers and their thorough organization, both economic and political, on the basis of the class struggle, must precede their emancipation. Without such education and organization they can make no substantial progress, and they will be robbed of the fruits of any temporary victory they may achieve, as they have been through all the centuries of the past.

For one, I hope to see the Socialist Party place itself squarely on record . . . against sabotage and every other form of violence and destructiveness suggested by what is known as "direct action."

It occurs to me that the Socialist Party ought to have a standing committee on tactics. The art or science of proletarian party tactics might well enlist the serious consideration of our clearest thinkers and most practical propagandists. . . .

---

[11]

THE CANTON, OHIO SPEECH

EUGENE V. DEBS

COMRADES, friends and fellow-workers, for this very cordial greeting, this very hearty reception, I thank you all with the fullest appreciation of your interest in and your devotion to the cause for which I am to speak to you this afternoon. (Applause.)

SOURCE: Eugene V. Debs, *Writings and Speeches* (New York: Hermitage Press, 1948), pp. 417–433.

To speak for labor; to plead the cause of the men and women and children who toil; to serve the working class, has always been to me a high privilege; (Applause) a duty of love.

I have just returned from a visit over yonder (pointing to the workhouse), where three of our most loyal comrades [who were imprisoned for opposing the war] are paying the penalty for their devotion to the cause of the working class. (Applause.) They have come to realize, as many of us have, that it is extremely dangerous to exercise the constitutional right of free speech in a country fighting to make democracy safe in the world. (Applause.)

I realize that, in speaking to you this afternoon, there are certain limitations placed upon the right of free speech. I must be exceedingly careful, prudent, as to what I say, and even more careful and prudent as to how I say it. (Laughter.) I may not be able to say all I think; (Laughter and applause) but I am not going to say anything that I do not think. (Applause.) I would rather a thousand times be a free soul in jail than to be a sycophant and coward in the streets. (Applause and shouts.) They may put those boys in jail—and some of the rest of us in jail—but they can not put the Socialist movement in jail. (Applause and shouts.) Those prison bars separate their bodies from ours, but their souls are here this afternoon. (Applause and cheers.) They are simply paying the penalty, that all men have paid in all the ages of history, for standing erect, and for seeking to pave the way to better conditions for mankind. (Applause.)

If it had not been for the men and women, who, in the past, have had the moral courage to go to jail, we would still be in the jungles. (Applause.) . . .

There is but one thing you have to be concerned about, and that is that you keep four-square with the principles of the international Socialist movement. (Applause.) It is only when you begin to compromise that trouble begins. (Applause.) So far as I am concerned, it does not matter what others may say, or think, or do, as long as I am sure that I am right with myself and the cause. (Applause.) There are so many who seek refuge in the popular side of a great question. As a Socialist, I have long since learned how to stand alone. (Applause.) . . .

I never had much faith in leaders. (Laughter.) I am willing to be charged with almost anything, rather than to be charged with being a leader. I am suspicious of leaders, and especially of the intellectual variety. (Applause.) Give me the rank and file every day in the week. If you go to the city of Washington, and you examine the pages of the Congressional Directory, you will find that almost all of those corporation lawyers and cowardly politicians, members of Congress, and misrepresentatives of the masses—you will find that almost all of them claim, in glowing terms, that they have risen from the ranks to places of eminence and distinction. I am very glad I can not make that claim for myself. (Laughter.) I would be ashamed to admit that I had risen from the ranks. When I rise it will be with the ranks, and not from the ranks. (Applause.) . . .

They who have been reading the capitalist newspapers realize what a capacity they have for lying. We have been reading them lately. They know all about the Socialist party . . . except what is true. (Laughter.) . . .

Why should a Socialist be discouraged on the eve of the greatest triumph in all the history of the Socialist movement? (Applause.) It is true that these are anxious, trying days for us all—testing days for the women and men who are upholding the banner of labor in the struggle of the working class of all the world against the exploiters of all the world; (Applause) a time in which the weak and cowardly will falter and fail and desert. They lack the fibre to endure the revolutionary test; they fall away; they disappear as if they had never been. On the other hand, they who are animated by the unconquerable spirit of the social revolution; they who have the moral courage to stand erect and assert their convictions; stand by them; fight for them; go to jail or to hell for them, if need be— (Applause and shouts) they are writing their names, in this crucial hour —they are writing their names in fadeless letters in the history of mankind. (Applause.) . . .

Are we opposed to Prussian militarism? (Laughter.) (Shouts from the crowd of "Yes, Yes!") Why, we have been fighting it since the day the Socialist movement was born; (Applause) and we are going to continue to fight it, day and night, until it is wiped from the face of the earth. (Thunderous applause and cheers.) Between us there is no truce—no compromise. . . .

I hate, I loathe, I despise Junkers and junkerdom. I have no earthly use for the Junkers of Germany, and not one particle more use for the Junkers in the United States. (Thunderous applause and cheers.)

They tell us that we live in a great free republic; that our institutions are democratic; that we are a free and self-governing people. (Laughter.) This is too much, even for a joke. (Laughter.) But it is not a subject for levity; it is an exceedingly serious matter.

To whom do the Wall Street Junkers in our country marry their daughters? After they have wrung their countless millions from your sweat, your agony and your life's blood, in a time of war as in a time of peace, they invest these untold millions in the purchase of titles of broken-down aristocrats, such as princes, dukes, counts and other parasites and no-accounts. (Laughter.) Would they be satisfied to wed their daughters to honest workingmen? (Shouts from the crowd, "No!") To real democrats? Oh, no! They scour the markets of Europe for vampires who are titled and nothing else. (Laughter.) And they swap their millions for the titles, so that matrimony with them becomes literally a matter of money. (Laughter.) . . .

Who appoints our federal judges? The people? In all the history of the country, the working class have never named a federal judge. There are 121 of these judges and every solitary one holds his position, his tenure, through the influence and power of corporate capital. The corporations and trusts dictate their appointment. And when they go to the bench, they go, not to serve the people, but to serve the interests that place them and keep them where they are.

Why, the other day, by a vote of five to four—a kind of craps game— (Laughter) come seven, come 'leven—(Laughter) they declared the child labor law unconstitutional—a law secured after twenty years of education and agitation on the part of all kinds of people. And yet, by a majority of one, the Supreme Court, a body of corporation lawyers, with just one exception, wiped that law from the statute books, and this in our so-called Democracy, so that we may continue to grind the flesh and blood and bones of puny little children into profits for the Junkers of Wall Street. (Applause.) And this in a country that boasts of fighting to make the world safe for democracy! (Laughter.) The history of this country is being written in the blood of the childhood the industrial lords have murdered. . . .

How stupid and short-sighted the ruling class really is! Cupidity is stone blind. It has no vision. The greedy, profit-seeking exploiter cannot see beyond the end of his nose. He can see a chance for an "opening"; he is cunning enough to know what graft is and where it is, and how it can be secured, but vision he has none—not the slightest. He knows nothing of the great throbbing world that spreads out in all directions. He has no capacity for literature; no appreciation of art; no soul for beauty. That is the penalty the parasites pay for the violation of the laws of life. . . . Every move they make in their game of greed but hastens their own doom. Every blow they strike at the Socialist movement reacts upon themselves. Every time they strike at us, they hit themselves. It never fails. (Applause.) Every time they strangle a Socialist paper they add a thousand voices proclaiming the truth of the principles of Socialism and the ideals of the Socialist movement. They help us in spite of themselves.

Socialism is a growing idea; an expanding philosophy. It is spreading over the entire face of the earth. It is as vain to resist it as it would be to arrest the sunrise on the morrow. It is coming, coming, coming all along the line. Can you not see it? If not, I advise you to consult an oculist. There is certainly something the matter with your vision. It is the mightiest movement in the history of mankind. What a privilege to serve it! I have regretted a thousand times that I can do so little for the movement that has done so much for me. (Applause.) The little that I am, the little that I am hoping to be, I owe to the Socialist movement. (Applause.) It has given me my ideas and ideals; my principles and convictions, and I would not exchange one of them for all of Rockefeller's blood-stained dollars. (Cheers.) It has taught me how to serve—a lesson to me of priceless value. It has taught me the ecstasy in the handclasp of a comrade. It has enabled me to hold high communion with you, and made it possible for me to take my place side by side with you in the great struggle for the better day; to multiply myself over and over again; to thrill with a fresh-born manhood; to feel life truly worth while; to open new avenues of vision; to spread out glorious vistas; to know that I am kin to all that throbs; to be class-conscious, and to realize that, regardless of nationality, race, creed, color or sex, every man, every woman who toils, who renders useful service, every member of the working class without an exception, is my comrade, my brother and sister—and that to serve them and their cause is the highest duty of my life. (Great applause.) . . .

Yes, my comrades, my heart is attuned to yours. Aye, all our hearts now throb as one great heart responsive to the battle-cry of the social revolution. Here, in this alert and inspiring assemblage (Applause) our hearts are with the Bolsheviki of Russia. (Deafening and prolonged applause.) Those heroic men and women, those unconquerable comrades have by their incomparable valor and sacrifice added fresh lustre to the fame of the international movement. . . . The very first act of the triumphant Russian revolution was to proclaim a state of peace with all mankind, coupled with a fervent moral appeal, not to kings, not to emperors, rulers or diplomats but to *the people* of all nations. . . . When the Bolsheviki came into power and went through the archives they found and exposed the secret treaties—the treaties that were made between the Czar and the French Government, the British Government and the Italian Government, proposing, after the victory was achieved, to dismember the German Empire and destroy the Central Powers. These treaties have never been denied nor repudiated. Very little has been said about them in the American press. I have a copy of these treaties, showing that the purpose of the Allies is exactly the purpose of the Central Powers, and that is the conquest and spoliation of the weaker nations that has always been the purpose of war.

Wars throughout history have been waged for conquest and plunder. In the Middle Ages when the feudal lords, who inhabited the castles whose towers may still be seen along the Rhine, concluded to enlarge their domains, to increase their power, their prestige and their wealth, they declared war upon one another. But they themselves did not go to war any more than the modern feudal lords, the barons of Wall Street go to war. (Applause.) The feudal barons of the Middle Ages, the economic predecessors of the capitalists of our day, declared all wars. And their miserable serfs fought all the battles. The poor, ignorant serfs had been taught to revere their masters; to believe that when their masters declared war upon one another, it was their patriotic duty to fall upon one another and to cut one another's throats for the profit and glory of the lords and barons who held them in contempt. And that is war in a nutshell. The master class has always declared the wars; the subject class has always fought the battles. The master class has had all to gain and nothing to lose, while the subject class has had nothing to gain and all to lose—especially their lives. (Applause.) . . .

And here let me emphasize the fact—and it cannot be repeated too often—that the working class who fight all the battles, the working class who make the supreme sacrifices, the working class who freely shed their blood and furnish the corpses, has never yet had a voice in either declaring war or making peace. It is the ruling class that invariably does both. They alone declare war and they alone make peace.

> Yours not to reason why;
> Yours but to do and die.

That is their motto and we object on the part of the awakening workers of this nation. . . .

What a compliment it is to the Socialist movement to be persecuted for the sake of the truth! The truth alone will make the people free. (Applause.) And for this reason the truth must not be permitted to reach the people. The truth has always been dangerous to the rule of the rogue, the exploiter, the robber. So the truth must be ruthlessly suppressed. That is why they are trying to destroy the Socialist movement; and every time they strike a blow they add a thousand new voices to the hosts proclaiming that Socialism is the hope of humanity and has come to emancipate the people from their final form of servitude. (Applause.) . . .

We do not attack individuals. We do not seek to avenge ourselves upon those opposed to our faith. We have no fight with individuals as such. We are capable of pitying those who hate us. (Applause.) We do not hate them; we know better; we would freely give them a cup of water if they needed it. (Applause.) There is no room in our hearts for hate, except for the system, the social system in which it is possible for one man to amass a stupendous fortune doing nothing, while millions of others suffer and struggle and agonize and die for the bare necessities of existence. (Applause.) . . .

It is the minorities who have made the history of this world. It is the few who have had the courage to take their places at the front; who have been true enough to themselves to speak the truth that was in them; who have dared oppose the established order of things; who have espoused the cause of the suffering, struggling poor; who have upheld without regard to personal consequences the cause of freedom and righteousness. It is they, the heroic, self-sacrificing few who have made the history of the race and who have paved the way from barbarism to civilization. The many prefer to remain upon the popular side. They lack the courage and vision to join a despised minority that stands for a principle; they have not the moral fibre that withstands, endures and finally conquers. They are to be pitied and not treated with contempt for they cannot help their cowardice. But, thank God, in every age and in every nation there have been the brave and self-reliant few, and they have been sufficient to their historic task; and we, who are here today, are under infinite obligations to them because they suffered, they sacrificed, they went to jail, they had their bones broken upon the wheel, they were burned at the stake and their ashes scattered to the winds by the hands of hate and revenge in their struggle to leave the world better for us than they found it for themselves. We are under eternal obligations to them because of what they did and what they suffered for us and the only way we can discharge that obligation is by doing the best we can for those who are to come after us. (Applause.) . . .

The heart of the International Socialist never beats a retreat. (Applause.)

If you would be respected you have got to begin by respecting yourself. (Applause.) Stand up squarely and look yourself in the face and see a man! Do not allow yourself to fall into the predicament of the poor fellow who, after he had heard a Socialist speech, concluded that he too ought to be a Socialist. The argument he had heard was unanswerable. "Yes," he said to himself, "all the speaker said was true and I certainly ought to join the party." But after a while he allowed his ardor to cool and he soberly concluded that by joining the party he might anger his boss and lose his job. He then concluded: "I can't take the chance." That night he slept alone. There was something on his conscience and it resulted in a dreadful dream. Men always have such dreams when they betray themselves. A Socialist is free to go to bed with a clear conscience. He goes to sleep with his manhood and he awakens and walks forth in the morning with his self-respect. He is unafraid and he can look the whole world in the face (Applause and laughter) without a tremor and without a blush. But this poor weakling who lacked the courage to do the bidding of his reason and conscience was haunted by a startling dream and at midnight he awoke in terror, bounded from his bed and exclaimed: "My God, there is nobody in this room." (Laughter.) He was absolutely right. (Laughter and applause.) There was nobody in that room.

How would you like to sleep in a room that had nobody in it? (Laughter.) It is an awful thing to be nobody. That is certainly a state of mind to get out of, the sooner the better. . . .

To turn your back on the corrupt Republican Party and the corrupt Democratic Party—the gold-dust lackeys of the ruling class (laughter) counts for something. It counts for still more after you have stepped out of those popular and corrupt capitalist parties to join a minority party that has an ideal, that stands for a principle, and fights for a cause. (Applause.) This will be the most important change you have ever made and the time will come when you will thank me for having made the suggestion. It was the day of days for me. I remember it well. It was like passing from midnight darkness to the noontide light of day. It came almost like a flash and found me ready. It must have been in such a flash that great, seething, throbbing Russia, prepared by centuries of slavery and tears and martyrdom, was transformed from a dark continent to a land of living light.

There is something splendid, something sustaining and inspiring in the prompting of the heart to be true to yourself and to the best you know, especially in a crucial hour of your life. You are in the crucible today, my Socialist comrades! You are going to be tried by fire, to what extent no one knows. If you are weak-fibred and faint-hearted you will be lost to the Socialist movement. We will have to bid you good-bye. You are not the stuff of which revolutions are made. We are sorry for you (applause) unless you chance to be an "intellectual." The "intellectuals," many of them, are already gone. No loss on our side nor gain on the other.

I am always amused in the discussion of the "intellectual" phase of this question. It is the same old standard under which the rank and file are judged. What would become of the sheep if they had no shepherd to lead them out of the wilderness into the land of milk and honey?

Oh, yes, "I am your shepherd and ye are my mutton." (Laughter.)

They would have us believe that if we had no "intellectuals" we would have no movement. They would have our party, the rank and file, controlled by the "intellectual" bosses as the Republican and Democratic parties are controlled. These capitalist parties are managed by "intellectual" leaders and the rank and file are sheep that follow the bellwether to the shambles. . . .

The capitalist system affects to have great regard and reward for intellect, and the capitalists give themselves full credit for having superior brains. When we have ventured to say that the time would come when the working class would rule they have bluntly answered "Never! it requires brains to rule." The workers of course have none. And they certainly try hard to prove it by proudly supporting the political parties of their masters under whose administration they are kept in poverty and servitude. . . .

These are the gentry who are today wrapped up in the American flag, who shout their claim from the housetops that they are the only patriots, and who have their magnifying glasses in hand, scanning the country for evidence of disloyalty, eager to apply the brand of treason to the men who dare to even whisper their opposition to Junker rule in the United States. No wonder Sam Johnson declared that "patriotism is the last refuge of the scoundrel." He must have had this Wall Street gentry in mind, or at least their prototypes, for in every age it has been the tyrant, the oppressor and the exploiter who has wrapped himself in the cloak of patriotism, or religion, or both to deceive and overawe the people. (Applause.) . . .

They are continually talking about your patriotic duty. It is not *their* but *your* patriotic duty that they are concerned about. There is a decided difference. Their patriotic duty never takes them to the firing line or chucks them into the trenches.

And now among other things they are urging you to "cultivate" war gardens, while at the same time a government war report just issued shows that practically 52 percent of the arable, tillable soil is held out of use by the landlords, speculators and profiteers. They themselves do not cultivate the soil. They could not if they would. Nor do they allow others to cultivate it. They keep it idle to enrich themselves, to pocket the millions of dollars of unearned increment. Who is it that makes this land valuable while it is fenced in and kept out of use? It is the people. Who pockets this tremendous accumulation of value? The landlords. And these landlords who toil not and spin not are supreme among American "patriots." . . .

In the present system the miner, a wage-slave, gets down into a pit three or four hundred feet deep. He works hard and produces a ton of coal. But he does not own an ounce of it. That coal belongs to some mine-owning plutocrat who may be in New York or sailing the high seas in his private yacht; or he may be hobnobbing with royalty in the capitals of Europe, and that is where most of them were before the war was declared. The industrial captain, so-called, who lives in Paris, London, Vienna or some other center of gayety does not have to work to revel in luxury. He owns the mines and he might as well own the miners.

That is where you workers are and where you will remain as long as you give your support to the political parties of your masters and exploiters. You vote these miners out of a job and reduce them to corporation vassals and paupers.

We Socialists say: "Take possession of the mines in the name of the people." (Applause.) Set the miners at work and give every miner the equivalent of all the coal he produces. Reduce the work day in proportion to the development of productive machinery. That would at once settle the matter of a coal famine and of idle miners. But that is too simple a proposition and the people will have none of it. The time will come, however, when the people will be driven to take such action for there is no other efficient and permanent solution of the problem. . . .

Of course that would be Socialism as far as it goes. But you are not in favor of that program. It is too visionary because it is so simple and practical. So you will have to continue to wait until winter is upon you before you get your coal and then pay three prices for it because you insist upon voting a capitalist ticket and giving your support to the present wage-slave system. The trouble with you is that you are still in a capitalist state of mind. . . .

There are few men who have the courage to say a word in favor of the I.W.W. (Applause.) I have. (Applause.) Let me say here that I have great respect for the I.W.W. Far greater than I have for their infamous detractors. (Applause.)

It is only necessary to label a man "I.W.W." to have him lynched. War makes possible all such crimes and outrages. And war comes in spite of the people. When Wall Street says war the press says war and the pulpit promptly follows with its *Amen*. In every age the pulpit has been on the side of the rulers and not on the side of the people. That is one reason why the preachers so fiercely denounce the I.W.W. . . .

Political action and industrial action must supplement and sustain each other. You will never vote the Socialist republic into existence. You will have to lay its foundations in industrial organization. The industrial union is the forerunner of industrial democracy. In the shop where the workers are associated is where industrial democracy has its beginning. Organize according to your industries! Get together in every department of industrial service! United and acting together for the common good your power is invincible.

When you have organized industrially you will soon learn that you can manage as well as operate industry. You will soon realize that you do not need the idle masters and exploiters. They are simply parasites. They do not employ you as you imagine but you employ them to take from you what you produce, and that is how they function in industry. You can certainly dispense with them in that capacity. You do not need them to depend upon for your jobs. You can never be free while you work and live by their sufferance. You must own your own tools and then you will control your own jobs, enjoy the products of your own labor, and be free men instead of industrial slaves.

Organize industrially and make your organization complete. Then unite in the Socialist party. Vote as you strike and strike as you vote.

Your union and your party embrace the working class. The Socialist party expresses the interest, hopes and aspirations of the toilers of all the world.

Get your fellow-workers into the industrial union and the political party to which they rightfully belong, especially this year, this historic year in which the forces of labor will assert themselves as they never have before. This is the year that calls for men and women who have the courage, the manhood and womanhood to do their duty.

Get into the Socialist Party and take your place in its ranks; help to inspire the weak and strengthen the faltering, and do your share to speed the coming of the brighter and better day for us all. (Applause.)

When we unite and act together on the industrial field and when we vote together on election day we shall develop the supreme power of the one class that can and will bring permanent peace to the world. We shall then have the intelligence, the courage and the power for our great task. In due time industry will be organized on a co-operative basis. We shall conquer the public power. We shall then transfer the title deeds of the railroads, the telegraph lines, the mines, mills and great industries to the people in their collective capacity; we shall take possession of all these social utilities in the name of the people. We shall then have industrial democracy. We shall be a free nation whose government is of and by and for the people.

And now for all of us to do our duty! The clarion call is ringing in our ears and we cannot falter without being convicted of treason to ourselves and to our great cause.

Do not worry over the charge of treason to your masters, but be concerned about the treason that involves yourselves. (Applause.) Be true to yourself and you cannot be a traitor to any good cause on earth.

Yes, in good time we are going to sweep into power in this nation and throughout the world. We are going to destroy all enslaving and degrading capitalist institutions and re-create them as free and humanizing institutions. The world is daily changing before our eyes. The sun of capitalism is setting; the sun of Socialism is rising. It is our duty to build the new nation and the free republic. We need industrial and social builders. We Socialists are the builders of the beautiful world that is to be. We are all pledged to do our part. We are inviting—aye challenging you in the name of your own manhood and womanhood to join us and do your part.

In due time the hour will strike and this great cause triumphant—the greatest in history—will proclaim the emancipation of the working class and the brotherhood of all mankind. (Thunderous and prolonged applause.)

PART VI
The War to Make the World Safe for Capitalism

W ITH some important exceptions and defections, the American Left opposed World War I as a conflict of capitalistic, imperialistic powers who were fighting in the name of a superannuated nationalism. But America's entrance into the war polarized the Left between those who believed that, after all, England was preferable to "feudal" Germany and those who could see no difference to the working class between one oppressor and another. William English Walling, Upton Sinclair, and A. M. Simons, among others, departed from the official Socialist position to support Woodrow Wilson. The official and majority position continued to assert that the international working class had everything to lose and nothing to gain from this exercise in greed and violence. Millions of workers would die, millions more would be hurt, and the eventual outcome would merely retard the social and political liberation of oppressed classes all over the world.

The first document (12) reprinted here was a flyer circulated by anonymous anarchists who appealed to the individual's conscience to refuse induction into the military. (This foreshadowed the "Hell no—we won't go" position of the Vietman war resistors of the 1960's.) A number of anarchists were convicted under the Espionage Act (in a case upheld by the Supreme Court) for distributing material such as this.

Documents 13 and 14 were issued by the Socialist Party. The first, a

"War Proclamation" that was offered by Morris Hillquit, was adopted at a national convention of the Socialist party in St. Louis, April 1917, only hours after the United States officially entered the war. It clearly spelled out the majority of the Socialists' opposition to the war and to America's involvement, as well as laid out the tactics of resistance recommended to workers and accepted by party members. (However, a number of leftwing members of the party were suspicious of the sincerity of the statement and of the motives of some of its leading advocates, especially suspicious of men such as Victor Berger and Meyer London, the New York Socialist congressman, who did not in fact vote against war expenditures). But as a declaration of principle, this St. Louis proclamation was firmer and more consistent with Socialist principles than almost any statement of any European Socialist party.

In Document 14, a manifesto adopted at an emergency convention of the Socialist party in Chicago, September 1919, the party condemned the work of the patriarchal peacemakers at Versailles and Paris. And, once again, the party committed itself to the primacy of political action, with American workers allegedly "ready in cases of emergency to reinforce the political demands of the working class by industrial action." Perhaps because the party's perception of international politics was less clouded by domestic squabbling over tactics, its teasing out of the political realities behind the Versailles Peace and the League of Nations was realistic and unsentimental. The decades following the "peace" give special weight to part of this display of political explication.

Finally, the impact of the war hysteria on rudimentary civil rights is shown in the following speech (Document 15) of Victor Berger (1860–1929). Berger was a dominant force in the moderate wing of the Socialist party, which he had helped to found, a leader in Milwaukee politics, and was elected to Congress in 1910, the first Socialist represented there. His opposition to the war changed his usually ordered life, and forced him to defend his moderate politics as a buffer between capitalism and what he called Bolshevism. His Milwaukee newspaper was banned from the U.S. mails, and he and four other Socialists were indicted for obstructing the draft in 1917. In January 1919, Judge Kenesaw Mountain Landis declared all five guilty, and sentenced each of them to twenty years in Leavenworth. Two years later, the Supreme Court overturned this decision because of Landis's manifest prejudices against the defendants. Meanwhile, Berger was out on bail and was again elected to Congress from Wisconsin's fifth congressional district. Still affected by the mood that had produced Wilson's Espionage Act, the House of Representatives appointed a special committee to investigate Berger's "case," to determine whether he had a right to a seat in the House. In the speech reprinted here, Berger defended his right to the seat, declared that democracy itself was on trial, warned the representatives of the many dangers of excluding him, and argued that he was no more guilty than Wilson himself. The House refused to seat him by a vote of 309 to 1, and in a special election in December 1919, he was reelected from Wisconsin; the House again refused to admit him; after another election he was finally allowed to take the seat to which he had now been properly elected three different times. He was subsequently reelected for two additional and consecutive terms. His ultimately successful struggles in the courts and in Congress revealed the crudity and repressiveness of the war administration. Berger's victories should be attributed to the return of peace, rather than to the justice of his case.

---

[12]

REFUSE TO KILL OR BE KILLED

ANONYMOUS ANARCHISTS

YOU are against murder and bloodshed, you have no special grievance against the working class of Germany. All you ask for is to get along peacefully, express yourself, make a living, and take care of your family. You don't want war and you didn't ask the president or any one else to declare war.

But you will ask: What can I do if I am drafted and ordered to fight? Well; what would happen if you did obey the president and fought for your country? You would probably be killed and lose what little you have, and your family would suffer. Now, if you don't become a professional murderer (a soldier) and refuse to obey the president, nothing worse can happen to you, can it? Oh, but you will say, "I would have a chance to live." Well, those ten million men who were killed in Europe, and those twenty million who were injured, didn't have much of a chance, did they? And those who lived didn't get much joy out of life. It isn't a very happy

SOURCE: New York Senate, Joint Legislative Committee Investigating Seditious Activities, *Revolutionary Radicalism,* part 1, "Revolutionary and Subversive Movements Abroad and at Home" 1 (Albany, 1920): 854–855.

feeling to realize that you have deliberately killed hundreds of inoffensive fellows just like yourself, and who never did you any harm, and who didn't want to fight any more than you do. You may think that you could avoid killing anyone. Nearly everybody who puts on a uniform thinks that, but when once you put on a soldier's clothes and get into the crowd of trained murderers, you are lost and you will do just as you are ordered. No man is brave or strong or lucky enough to escape killing when once he has the uniform on. Now this is the truth, and the history of a hundred million men in arms proves it. Don't try to bluff yourself or anyone else. You must realize that if you join the army you will do just as you are told to do, and if you have any courage or humanity to assert, the time to do it is before you get into the uniform.

You may agree with all of this, but still you ask, "What can I do?" We don't believe in telling people what to do. You have a mind and a conscience and you believe in brotherhood and real democracy. If you think murder is wrong, REFUSE TO JOIN THE ARMY or any military body. Then if the government wants to kill you or put you in jail, you will have done your part, and have been faithful to your conscience and humanity, and the world will be the better for your courage and determination.

No matter what the government of the other fellow does, let's you and I be faithful to mankind and REFUSE TO GO TO WAR.

WAR PROCLAMATION AND PROGRAM ADOPTED AT NATIONAL CONVENTION, SOCIALIST PARTY, ST. LOUIS, MO., APRIL 1917

SOCIALIST PARTY

THE Socialist Party of the United States in the present grave crisis, solemnly reaffirm its allegiance to the principle of internationalism and working-class solidarity the world over, and proclaims its unalterable opposition to the war just declared by the Government of the United States.

Modern wars as a rule have been caused by the commercial and financial rivalry and intrigues of the capitalist interests in the different countries. Whether they have been frankly waged as wars of aggression or have been hypocritically represented as wars of "defense," they have always been made by the classes and fought by the masses. Wars bring wealth and power to the ruling classes, and suffering, death and demoralization to the workers.

They breed a sinister spirit of passion, unreason, race hatred and false patriotism. They obscure the struggles of the workers for life, liberty and social justice. They tend to sever the vital bonds of solidarity between them and their brothers in other countries, to destroy their organizations and to curtail their civic and political rights and liberties.

The Socialist Party of the United States is unalterably opposed to the system of exploitation and class rule which is upheld and strengthened by military power and sham national patriotism. We, therefore, call upon the workers of all countries to refuse support to their governments in their wars. The wars of the contending national groups of capitalists are not the

SOURCE: New York Senate, Joint Legislative Committee Investigating Seditious Activities, *Revolutionary Radicalism*, part 1, "Revolutionary and Subversive Movements Abroad and at Home" 1 (Albany, 1920): 613–618.

concern of the workers. The only struggle which would justify the workers in taking up arms is the great struggle of the working class of the world to free itself from economic exploitation and political oppression, and we particularly warn the workers against the snare and delusion of so-called defensive warfare. As against the false doctrine of national patriotism we uphold the ideal of international working-class solidarity. In support of capitalism, we will not willingly give a single life or a single dollar; in support of the struggle of the workers for freedom we pledge our all.

The mad orgy of death and destruction which is now convulsing unfortunate Europe was caused by the conflict of capitalist interests in the European countries.

In each of these countries, the workers were oppressed and exploited. They produced enormous wealth but the bulk of it was withheld from them by the owners of the industries. The workers were thus deprived of the means to repurchase the wealth which they themselves had created.

The capitalist class of each country was forced to look for foreign markets to dispose of the accumulated "surplus" wealth. The huge profits made by the capitalists could no longer be profitably reinvested in their own countries, hence, they were driven to look for foreign fields of investment. The geographical boundaries of each modern capitalist country thus became too narrow for the industrial and commercial operations of its capitalist class.

The efforts of the capitalists of all leading nations were, therefore, centered upon the domination of the world markets. Imperialism became the dominant note in the politics of Europe. The acquisition of colonial possessions and the extension of spheres of commercial and political influence became the object of diplomatic intrigues and the cause of constant clashes between nations.

The acute competition between the capitalist powers of the earth, their jealousies and distrusts of one another and the fear of the rising power of the working class forced each of them to arm to the teeth. This led to the mad rivalry of armament, which, years before the outbreak of the present war, had turned the leading countries of Europe into armed camps with standing armies of many millions, drilled and equipped for war in times of "peace."

Capitalism, imperialism and militarism had thus laid the foundation of an inevitable general conflict in Europe. The ghastly war in Europe was not caused by an accidental event, nor by the policy or institutions of any single nation. It was the logical outcome of the competitive capitalist system.

The 6,000,000 men of all countries and races who have been ruthlessly slain in the first thirty months of this war, the millions of others who have been crippled and maimed, the vast treasures of wealth that have been destroyed, the untold misery and sufferings of Europe, have not been sacrifices exacted in a struggle for principles or ideals, but wanton offerings upon the altar of private profit.

The forces of capitalism which have led to the war in Europe are even more hideously transparent in the war recently provoked by the ruling class of this country.

When Belgium was invaded, the government enjoined upon the people of this country the duty of remaining neutral, thus clearly demonstrating that the "dictates of humanity," and the fate of small nations and of democratic institutions were matters that did not concern it. But when our enormous war traffic was seriously threatened, our government calls upon us to rally to the "defense of democracy and civilization."

Our entrance into the European War was instigated by the predatory capitalists in the United States who boast of the enormous profit of $7,000,000,000 from the manufacture and sale of munitions and war supplies and from the exportation of American food stuffs and other necessaries. They are also deeply interested in the continuance of war and the success of the Allied arms through their huge loans to the governments of the Allied powers and through other commercial ties. It is the same interests which strive for imperialistic domination of the Western Hemisphere.

The war of the United States against Germany cannot be justified even on the plea that it is a war in defense of American rights or American "honor." Ruthless as the unrestricted submarine war policy of the German government was and is, it is not an invasion of the rights of the American people, as such, but only an interference with the opportunity of certain groups of American capitalists to coin cold profits out of the blood and sufferings of our fellow men in the warring countries of Europe.

It is not a war against the militarist regime of the Central Powers. Militarism can never be abolished by militarism.

It is not a war to advance the cause of democracy in Europe. Democracy can never be imposed upon any country by a foreign power by force of arms.

It is cant and hypocrisy to say that the war is not directed against the German people, but against the Imperial Government of Germany. If we send an armed force to the battlefields of Europe, its cannon will mow down the masses of the German people and not the Imperial German Government.

Our entrance into the European conflict at this time will serve only to multiply the horrors of the war, to increase the toll of death and destruction and to prolong the fiendish slaughter. It will bring death, suffering and destitution to the people of the United States and particularly to the working class. It will give the powers of reaction in this country the pretext for an attempt to throttle our rights and to crush our democratic institutions, and to fasten upon this country a permanent militarism.

The working class of the United States has no quarrel with the working class of Germany or of any other country. The people of the United States have no quarrel with the people of Germany or any other country. The American people did not want and do not want this war. They have not been consulted about the war and have had no part in declaring war. They have been plunged into this war by the trickery and treachery of the ruling class of the country through its representatives in the National Administration and National Congress, its demagogic agitators, its subsidized press, and other servile instruments of public expression.

We brand the declaration of war by our government as a crime against the people of the United States and against the nations of the world.

In all modern history there has been no war more unjustifiable than the war in which we are about to engage.

No greater dishonor has ever been forced upon a people than that which the capitalist class is forcing upon this nation against its will.

In harmony with these principles, the Socialist Party emphatically rejects the proposal that in time of war the workers should suspend their struggle for better conditions. On the contrary, the acute situation created by war calls for an even more vigorous prosecution of the class struggle, and we recommend to the workers and pledge ourselves to the following course of action:

1. Continuous, active, and public opposition to the war through demonstrations, mass petitions, and all other means within our power.
2. Unyielding opposition to all proposed legislation for military or industrial conscription. Should such conscription be forced upon the people we pledge ourselves to continuous efforts for the repeal of such laws and to the support of all mass movements in opposition to conscription. We pledge ourselves to oppose with all our strength any attempt to raise money for payment of war expense by taxing the necessaries of life or issuing bonds which will put the burden upon future generations. We demand that the capitalist class, which is responsible for the war, pay its cost. Let those who kindled the fire, furnish the fuel.

3. Vigorous resistance to all reactionary measures, such as censorship of press and mails, restriction of the rights of free speech, assemblage, and organization, or compulsory arbitration and limitation of the right to strike.
4. Consistent propaganda against military training and militaristic teaching in the public schools.
5. Extension of the campaign of education among the workers to organize them into strong, class-conscious, and closely unified political and industrial organizations, to enable them by concerted and harmonious mass action to shorten this war and to establish lasting peace.
6. Widespread educational propaganda to enlighten the masses as to the true relation between capitalism and war, and to rouse and organize them for action, not only against present war evils, but for the prevention of future wars and for the destruction of the causes of war.
7. To protect the masses of the American people from the pressing danger of starvation which the war in Europe has brought upon them, and which the entry of the United States has already accentuated, we demand—
    (a) The restriction of food exports so long as the present shortage continues, the fixing of maximum prices and whatever measures may be necessary to prevent the food speculators from holding back the supplies now in their hands;
    (b) The socialization and democratic management of the great industries concerned with the production, transportation, storage, and the marketing of food and other necessaries of life;
    (c) The socialization and democratic management of all land and other natural resources now held out of use for monopolistic or speculative profit.

These measures are presented as means of protecting the workers against the evil results of the present war. The danger of recurrence of war will exist as long as the capitalist system of industry remains in existence. The end of wars will come with the establishment of socialized industry and industrial democracy the world over. The Socialist Party calls upon all the workers to join it in its struggle to reach this goal, and thus bring into the world a new society in which peace, fraternity, and human brotherhood will be the dominant ideals.

[14]

MANIFESTO OF THE SOCIALIST PARTY ADOPTED AT THE NATIONAL EMERGENCY CONVENTION, CHICAGO, SEPTEMBER 1919

SOCIALIST PARTY

THE capitalist class is now making its last stand in its history. It was intrusted with the government of the world. It is responsible for the prevailing chaos. The events of recent years have conclusively demonstrated that capitalism is bankrupt, it has become a dangerous impediment to progress and human welfare. The working class alone has the power to redeem and to save the world.

In every modern country, whether monarchial or republican in form, the capitalist class was in control, monopolized the national wealth and directed the industrial processes.

Its rule has been one of oppression, disorder and civil and international strife.

The capitalist interests of every leading nation fully exploited the resources of their country and reduced their peoples to wretchedness and then set out to conquer the markets of the world for the sale of their surplus commodities, for the investment of their surplus capital and for the acquisition of additional sources of raw materials and national wealth.

Struggle for Market Grows Desperate

A new era dawned upon the world, the mad era of capitalist imperialism. The weak peoples of the globe were subjugated by the strong nations. Asia, Africa, Central and South America with their hundreds of millions

SOURCE: New York Senate, Joint Legislative Committee Investigating Seditious Activities, *Revolutionary Radicalism*, part 1, "Revolutionary and Subversive Movements Abroad and at Home" 1 (Albany, 1920): 618–624.

of peaceful inhabitants were forcibly parcelled out into colonies, so-called —protectorates and spheres of influence for the capitalist conquerors.

The struggle for foreign markets became ever more desperate and acute. A violent clash among competing imperialistic nations became even more imminent and threatening.

The great rival powers of the world were uneasily and distrustfully watching each other and arming against each other. Millions of workers were taken from productive labor and trained in the savage art of killing their fellowmen. Civilizing and life-sustaining activities were subordinated to the mad race for military and naval supremacy. The nations of Europe groaned under the oppressive burdens of great armaments and became frantic with fear of mutual attacks. Capitalism in its full development caused human society to revert to the primitive conditions of savage tribal warfare.

Statesmen at Versailles Blinded by Greed

Then came the inevitable collapse. The world was precipitated into the most savage and inhuman slaughter in history.

Millions of young men were killed. Millions more were maimed and crippled. Countries were devastated and depopulated. Industries were disorganized. Famine, disease and misery ravaged the people of many lands.

Finally, the ghastly combat ended. The Central Powers, vanquished and exhausted, laid down their arms. Imperialistic statesmen of victorious Allies dictated a so-called peace. It is a peace of hatred and violence, a peace of vengeance and strangulation. The reactionary statesmen at the Versailles Peace Conference were blinded by greed, passion and fear. They refused to heed the terrible lesson of the Great War. They have left open the old international sores and have inflicted innumerable and grievous new wounds upon a distracted world.

To strengthen their precarious rule of violence and reaction, the triumphant representatives of Allied capitalism have created an executive committee of their governments, which they have the insolence to parade under the counterfeit label of a League of Nations.

Weaker Nations Will Be Bullied

The true aim of this alliance of capitalist powers is to safeguard their plunder, to bully and dominate the weak nations, to crush proletarian governments and to thwart everywhere the movements of the working class.

It was the worldwide struggle between the working class and the capitalist class which dictated the decisions of the Versailles Conference. This is clearly shown on the one hand by the desperate attempts to crush Soviet Russia and by the destruction of Soviet Hungary, on the other hand, by its recognition of the unsocialistic coalition government of Germany.

The so-called League of Nations is the capitalist black international against the rise of the working class. It is the conscious alliance of the capitalists of all nations against the workers of all nations.

Workers Must Rebuild Social Order

It now becomes more than ever the immediate task of international Socialism to accelerate and organize the inevitable transfer of political and industrial power from the capitalist class to the workers. The workers must reorganize the economic structure of human society by eliminating the institution of the private ownership of natural wealth and of the machinery of industry, the essence of the war breeding system of international commercial rivalry. The workers of the world must reorganize the economic structure of human society by making the natural wealth and the machinery of industry the collective property of all.

The workers of the world are already ushering in the new order of true civilization.

The workers of Germany and Austria are now the dominant political powers. While the leaders of the workers of these two countries have as yet proved too timid to use their political power for the abolition of economic exploitation, the masses are showing an ever-increasing determination to end the impossible government copartnership between capital and labor and to establish in its place a genuine Socialist industrial democracy.

The workers of Great Britain, France and Italy, the workers of the newly created nations, and the workers of the countries which remained neutral during the war are all in a state of unprecedented unrest. In different ways, and by different methods, either blindly impelled by the inexorable conditions which confront them, or clearly recognizing their revolutionary aims, they are abandoning their temporizing programs of pre-war labor reform. They are determined to control the industries, which means control of the governments.

In the United States, capitalism has emerged from the war more reactionary and aggressive, more insolent and oppressive, than it has ever been.

Having entered the war "to make the world safe for democracy," our government has enthusiastically allied itself with the most reactionary imperialism of Europe and Asia. In the preparation of the infamous Peace Treaty acts of violence and of plunder were sanctioned by our peace delegates. Acts of infamy were masked by our eloquent President in idealistic and sanctimonious phrases.

And, while thus serving as an accomplice of black reaction abroad, our administration and the capitalist interests behind it were busily engaged in the ruthless work of suppressing civil rights and liberties at home.

Patriotism Screens Capitalists

Under the pretext of wartime necessity, Congress and State Legislatures enacted drastic laws, which effectively nullified the right of political criticism and opposition, freedom of speech, of the press and of assemblage. Although these laws were clearly unconstitutional, our courts skilfully avoided declaring them invalid. The Socialist Party, which during the war was the only party of peace and progress and the sole political defender of civil rights and labor's interests in the United States, was brutally outlawed. Its press was crippled, many of its meetings were dispersed, a great number of its defenders were persecuted and jailed.

Under the cloak of false patriotism and behind a barrage of terroristic jingo sentiment, deliberately incited by them, the capitalists of America launched an orgy of profiteering which all but ruined the nation. The administration permitted a relatively small number of men to make profits amounting to billions of dollars, while the price of the necessaries of life rose to overwhelming heights.

While the war created thousands of new millionaires, the shortsighted workers of the United States were appeased by increases of their nominal wages, which left them behind their prewar standards of life. While the vain, conservative labor leaders were bribed by meaningless posts of honor, the courageous spokesmen for the radical labor groups were put behind prison bars.

Spirit of Revolt Grows Steadily

It is not surprising, therefore, that the end of the war has found the organized workers of America far behind their brothers in Europe, who are everywhere strengthening their forces to throw off the chains of industrial and political subjugation.

But even in the United States the symptoms of a rebellious spirit in the ranks of the working masses are rapidly multiplying. The widespread and extensive strikes for better labor conditions, the demand of the 2,000,000 railway workers to control their industry, the sporadic formation of labor parties apparently, though not fundamentally, in opposition to the political parties of the possessing class, are promising indications of a definite tendency on the part of American labor to break away from its reactionary and futile leadership and to join in the great emancipating movement of the more advanced revolutionary workers of the world.

Pro-War Socialists Repudiated

Recognizing this crucial situation at home and abroad, the Socialist Party of the United States at its first National Convention after the war, squarely takes its position with the uncompromising section of the International Socialist movement. We unreservedly reject the policy of those Socialists who supported their belligerent capitalist governments on the plea of "National Defense," and who entered into demoralizing compacts for so-called civil peace with the exploiters of labor during the war and continued a political alliance with them after the war.

We, the organized Socialists of America, declare our solidarity with the revolutionary workers of Russia—

In the support of the government of their Soviets, with the radical Socialists of Germany, Austria and Hungary in their efforts to establish working-class rule in their countries, and with those Socialist organizations in England, France, Italy and other countries, who during the war as after the war, have remained true to the principles of uncompromising international socialism.

The people of Russia, like the American Colonists in 1776, were driven by their rulers to the use of violent methods to obtain and maintain their freedom. The Socialist Party calls upon the workers of the United States to do all in their power to restore and maintain our civil rights to the end that the transition from capitalism to Socialism may be effected without resort to the drastic measures made necessary by autocratic despotism.

Russian Blockade Must Be Lifted

We are utterly opposed to the so-called League of Nations. Against this international alliance of capitalistic governments, we hold out to the world the ideal of a federation of free and equal Socialist nations.

A genuine and lasting peace can be built only upon the basis of reconciliation among the peoples of the warring nations and their mutual co-operation in the task of reconstructing the shattered world.

We emphatically protest against all military, material or moral support which our government is extending to Czarist counter-revolutionists in Russia and reactionary powers in Hungary, and demand the immediate lifting of the indefensible and inhuman blockade of those countries.

We demand the unconditional and immediate liberation of all class war prisoners convicted under the infamous Espionage Law and other repressive legislation.

We demand the immediate and unconditional release of all conscientious objectors.

We demand the full restoration to the American people of their constitutional rights and liberties.

Workers Must Take Industries

The great purpose of the Socialist Party is to wrest the industries and the control of the Government of the United States from the capitalists and their retainers. It is our purpose to place industry and government in the control of the workers with hand and brain, to be administered for the benefit of the whole community.

To insure the triumph of Socialism in the United States the bulk of the American workers must be strongly organized politically as Socialists, in constant, clearcut and oppressive opposition to all parties of the possessing class. They must be strongly organized in the economic field on broad industrial lines, as one powerful and harmonious class organization, co-operating with the Socialist Party, and ready in cases of emergency to reinforce the political demands of the working class by industrial action.

To win the American workers from their ineffective and demoralizing leadership, to educate them to an enlightened understanding of their own class interests, and to train and assist them to organize politically and industrially on class lines, in order to effect their emancipation, that is the supreme task confronting the Socialist Party of America.

To this great task, without deviation or compromise, we pledge all our energies and resources. For its accomplishments we call for the support and co-operation of the workers of America and of all other persons desirous of ending the insane rule of capitalism before it has the opportunity to precipitate humanity into another cataclysm of blood and ruin.

Long live the International Socialist Revolution, the only hope of the suffering world!

RIGHT OF A DULY ELECTED REPRESENTATIVE TO A SEAT IN CONGRESS, SEPTEMBER 15, 1919

VICTOR L. BERGER

MR. Chairman and gentlemen of the committee—this is not the time for fine phrases. This committee is making history. It is not Victor Berger's seat in the National House of Representatives alone that is in the balance —representative government as such is in the balance.

I was told that the cards are stacked against me, that arguments are useless, that the Milwaukee Socialist is to be unseated in obedience to the dictates of certain capitalist influences because he is a Socialist and because he is of German extraction. . . .

While I am well aware that the capitalist octopus in America is frightened by what is going on in Europe—particularly in Russia—while I know that there is a great deal of prejudice against Socialists, and especially against Socialists of German descent, I refuse to believe that sane men—and members of Congress at that—who favor a democratic form of government would deliberately try to destroy that kind of government.

I was indicted upon orders "from above" on the charge of conspiracy to interfere with the armed forces, and found guilty of that charge by a hand-picked Federal jury, each member of which, according to a statement in the Chicago *Herald-Examiner,* had the OK of the American Protective League—which means a branch of the Secret Service—before he was put on the jury. The same jury undoubtedly would have found many members of the Sixty-fifth Congress guilty of the same charge if the jury had been selected for that purpose.

The overt acts which formed the "conspiracy" consisted in the reprinting of the Socialist Party proclamation against wars adopted at the Social-

SOURCE: Victor L. Berger, *Voice and Pen of Victor L. Berger: Congressional Speeches and Editorials, The Milwaukee Leader,* 1929, pp. 577–589, 592–603.

ist convention at St. Louis, and in printing of five editorials in which *The Milwaukee Leader* expressed its disagreement with the policies of the national administration regarding participation in European wars.

There were four men indicted with me. The prosecution did not charge that we had ever met to discuss the alleged "conspiracy," nor that we had ever planned or ever mentioned it to one another by means of correspondence or otherwise.

What the prosecution did charge was that five men holding similar opinions with regard to the war conspired by means of "a meeting of minds." This legal fiction outrages common sense, of course. Under this construction any man of any party or of no party anywhere in the United States could be indicted, convicted, and sentenced to 20 years in the penitentiary if his opinions upon public questions were offensive to the men temporarily in power.

You have heard these articles read here—these articles and many others written at that time—and also articles printed for many years before the indictment and some written after the indictment. Even the most rigorous construction of any of these articles by a man with a sane mind will not bear out the charge. And the suggestion that any of them is pro-German must sound just as ridiculous to you after you have listened to them. They are international and pro-humanity.

The American Socialists believed that the American people did not want war; that they were plunged into it by the plutocrats and profiteers of the country—their demagogic agitators, their press, their photoplays, their advertisements, and other instruments of public expression; this is what the American Socialists believed and still believe.

Many Republicans and Democrats believed and said the same. And some papers and some men in Congress have criticized the national administration and the war in stronger language than I did. Among these were some of the foremost representatives of the Republican and Democratic Parties—men like James R. Mann, Claude Kitchin, Frank Mondell, W. E. Mason, and Champ Clark. We have read extracts from their speeches at this hearing.

I shall add here only a few of President Woodrow Wilson's remarks as to this war and its causes. At a time when the Socialists and *The Milwaukee Leader* attacked the German Kaiser and Germany most bitterly for being a party to the World War, Mr. Wilson said:

May 13, 1915:

Recalling the humane and enlightened attitude heretofore assumed by the Imperial German Government in matters of international right. . . .

May 13, 1915:

. . . having learned to recognize the German views and German influence in the field of international obligations as always engaged on the side of justice and humanity. . . .

Of course, that happened before Mr. Wilson knew that he was going "to make the world safe for democracy" and fight the "Huns." President Wilson went on like this:

February 3, 1916:

We believe that we can show our friendship for the world and our devotion for the purposes of humanity better by keeping out of this trouble than by getting into it.

May 5, 1916:

There are two reasons why the chief wish of America is for peace. One is that they love peace and have nothing to do with the present quarrel. . . .

May 27, 1916:

With its [the war's] causes and objects we have no concern.

October 5, 1916:

The singularity of the present war is that its origin and objects have never been disclosed.

December 18, 1916:

I take the liberty of calling attention to the fact that the objects of the statesmen of the belligerents on both sides are virtally the same.

Under the convenient legalistic term of "conspiracy," as construed by some of our Federal judges "as a meeting of minds," whether the persons accused have ever met or not—and with an act like the "espionage" law, which forbade men even to think against the war—the gentlemen in Congress (mentioned above) could have been indicted and found guilty of "conspiracy," individually and collectively.

They could be indicted, tried, and found guilty for the alleged utterances of persons whom they have not known and for articles they have never seen—if the right kind of a panel could be gotten together by the United States authorities.

They could be indicted far away from their homes, compelled to give bail in another state, and convicted there by a Federal jury. The gentlemen whose names I have mentioned above were protected from that tyrannical procedure only because they were members of Congress at the time.

But does the Constitution only protect members of Congress during a war? And how long will it protect even members of Congress if you permit this sort of procedure?

What happened to me is that: A citizen of Milwaukee, Wis., I was indicted in Chicago, in the State of Illinois. I was compelled to furnish bail there, amounting to $100,000. I am under bail for $45,000 more on other indictments in some places in Wisconsin for the same articles.

Republicans and Democrats could be punished in exactly the same fashion for any opposition to a hostile national administration. President Wilson was recently quoted in the papers as having said that certain Senators "should be hanged" because they do not approve of his treaty. Suppose he insists that this idea be incorporated in a law? Well, these Senators happen to be very prominent Republicans, so there is little likelihood that they will be hanged even on Mr. Wilson's say so.

But we American Socialists surely were doomed beforehand as "German Socialists" and as "Bolsheviki" in the capitalist press.

The minions of the Department of Justice were in possession of all our books and files. These spies had opened my letters and the letters of other defendants for many months, before and after the indictment. And although there was not even the shadow of evidence to connect any of us— or the Socialist Party—with "German propaganda," the prosecution continually hinted at "German propaganda."

The Milwaukee Leader and I have been persecuted under the espionage act in an unprecedented manner. *The Milwaukee Leader* has not only lost its second-class mailing rights by order of Postmaster General Burleson, but he has also deprived us of the right to receive any and all kinds of mail, letters included.

It was a crime to say or to write that this war was caused by commercial rivalry. To doubt that this was an "idealistic war" meant that the doubting Thomas was immediately arrested—as a pro-German or at least a Socialist.

Spokesmen of the Republican Party in the United States Senate, however, now frankly admit that it was a war for commercial supremacy.

Senator Harding of Ohio declared a few months ago in open session that "from the very beginning it was a lie to say that this was a war to make the world safe for democracy."

And President Wilson, at the St. Louis Coliseum, September 5, 1919, enlightened the world as follows:

> The real reason that the war that we have just finished took place was that Germany was afraid that her commercial rivals were going to get the better of her, and the reason why some nations went into the war against Germany was that they thought that Germany would get the commercial advantage of them.

Nevertheless, in 1917 Postmaster General Burleson suppressed about 60 weekly Socialist publications and took away the second-class mailing right from *The Milwaukee Leader* and tried his level best to kill the paper—for saying the same thing in 1917 that Woodrow Wilson and everybody else is saying now. Or was it a crime to tell the truth—until Mr. Wilson himself accepted it as his own?

At the present time America is the only civilized country in the world which still has political prisoners. And our national administration keeps on adding to their number.

Of course, the Attorney General denies that there is such a thing as a "political crime" in America. He claims that we Socialists are to be punished for violating a certain provision of a law—the espionage act—not for our Socialist ideas.

But while my co-defendants and I were told at the beginning of our trial in Chicago by the United States district attorney that "the Socialist Party was not on trial"—a few minutes after we had been found guilty by the hand-picked jury, the same United States district attorney triumphantly declared in an interview to the papers that "Bolshevism has received its fatal blow by this verdict."

Now, Socialism is not Bolshevism.

Socialism is the collective ownership and democratic management of the social means of production and distribution—while Bolshevism, as far as I understand it, is communism combined with syndicalism.

And this is my chance to say a few words explanatory of Socialism.

Socialism stands for a new civilization.

Surely no educated man believes that the present conditions are the end of all things. That we have not reached the end of our national development is clear. Every new invention and every new political question prove that to us.

And it would be sad indeed if we had reached "the end." We then should soon be on a level with China. And I need not explain that the Socialist movement is not to be traced to the irresponsible work of individual agitators or eccentric persons. The very name of our movement, "Social-Democracy," proclaims the aims of the Socialists.

In regard to the political form, we demand the rule of the people, i.e., democracy. In regard to the economic sphere and the spirit which shall manifest itself in this form and give life to it, we demand Socialism; that is, the collective ownership of the means of social production and distribution.

Thus we shall have Social-Democracy—a democracy which is founded on economic independence, upon the political and industrial equality of opportunity for all.

Determined opponents of the present capitalistic system of industry as the Socialists are, still they never claim that the concentration of capital is the cause of all evil.

We look the facts square in the face.

The trusts are the legitimate outcome of competition. The trust is the "survival of the fittest" under capitalism. The trust appears after competition has virtually destroyed competition.

Socialists, therefore, do not try to smash the trusts as such. On the contrary, the Socialists appreciate so fully the advantage of industrial production on a large scale that we wish its most perfect development—and wish to give its benefits to everybody—which is impossible under the capitalist system. For that reason we want to nationalize the trusts.

The control of production by the people as a whole means the highest possible perfection of industry on a large scale and means the extension of its advantages to all the people. And we all deeply feel the disadvantages of the private ownership of the means of production and distribution on a large scale. We observe how the railroads and other public service corporations corrupt our legislatures.

We notice how our life insurance savings and bank deposits are simply furnishing funds for high financiers to underwrite industrial ventures. We witness how the successful largest factory owners combine into trusts, which are "financiered" by the banks, and how the meat trust, the oil trust, the steel trust, and all the other trusts are "regulating prices," and how, moreover, some of these trusts are ruining the health of the people.

We all see it. We all feel it. And we all know it.

But it is said that the Socialists are revolutionists.

Very well! We are revolutionary, not in the vulgar meaning of the word, however, which is entirely wrong, but in the sense illustrated by history, the only logical sense.

I believe it is foolish to expect any results from riots and dynamite, from murderous attacks and conspiracies, in a country where we have the ballot, as long as the ballot has not been given a full and fair trial. We want to convince the majority of the people. As long as we are in the minority, we, of course, have no right to force our opinions upon an unwilling majority.

Besides, as modern men and true democrats, we have a somewhat less romantic and boyish idea of the development of human things and social systems.

And we know that one can kill tyrants and scare individuals with dynamite and bullets, but one can not develop a system in that way. Lenin and Trotski are finding this out to their dismay.

Therefore, no true Socialist ever dreams of a sudden change of society. We may have revolutions, if neither the capitalists nor the workmen make good use of their brains, but greater than all revolutions is evolution.

We know perfectly well that force serves only those who have it, that a sudden overthrow invariably breeds dictators, that dictatorship can promote only subjection, never freedom.

I have even proposed a general and methodical arming of all people as the safest means of preventing sudden upheavals and of preserving genuine democracy. That would, as a matter of course, also end the dictatorship of the plutocracy.

In short, the Socialists do not expect success from a smaller or bigger riot, but from a real revolution, from the revolutionizing of minds, the only true revolution there is.

It is clear that this revolution of the minds cannot be brought about in a day or two, nor can it be arranged according to the pleasure of a few. It can only be attained by patient work and intelligent organization. Therefore, the Socialists concentrate their whole force on education, agitation and organization.

And education always means enlightenment and humanity, and organization means order.

We want to observe closely the course of things, the development of economic and political conditions. We want to find out, if possible, where this development leads. Then, supported by this knowledge, we want to put ourselves in line with the march of civilization, so that civilization will carry us, instead of crushing us, which it would do, if, knowingly or not, we should stand opposed to it.

Thinking men of all classes become Socialists not because we like to be "different" from other people. We are Socialists because we have recognized that the economical development of the present capitalist system leads towards Socialistic production. Not that we wish to urge upon humanity "our" Socialistic Republic, but that the Socialistic Republic has urged itself upon us as the next stage of civilization and will urge itself some day upon all civilized humanity.

In a hazy way, however, our opponents attempt to convey the idea that the Socialists incite class antagonism and class hatred. And there are some honest men who believe that the Socialists create class hatred by explaining the class struggle. There are some well-meaning men in this country who still believe that because this is a republic there are no classes in the United States. They claim that everybody here is the equal of everybody else. Nothing of the kind.

As a matter of fact, under the present capitalist system, we have three classes, roughly speaking, in America.

The first class is the capitalist class, composed of wealthy bankers, railway magnates, corporation directors, trust magnates, etc., who have made money and are active in business, and people who are doing nothing and inherited their wealth. That class forms about 2 percent of the Nation. In the income tax figures for 1917 we find 206 men with millionaire yearly incomes—10 of them with annual incomes of more than $5,000,000 and 196 with yearly incomes ranging from $1,000,000 to $5,000,000. I have no figures for 1918.

The next class is the middle class, composed chiefly of small manufacturers, merchants, farmers, and some professional men. This class forms about 24 percent of the Nation.

The third class is the proletariat, made up of wageworkers, small farmers, and some persons in professional occupations. That class forms about 74 percent of the Nation.

It is unnecessary for me to dwell on the difference in the lives, modes of living, and general standard of the different classes. But the existence of classes is nothing new and the class struggle is many thousands of years old. It began the moment civilization began. . . .

A statesman of old Rome said that the Romans could hold their slaves only because they had never counted themselves and their masters. However, since we have universal suffrage, there is a good chance to count ourselves and our masters at every election.

Nor would the claim that God had ordained class rule hold good today. Not even the most stupid worker would believe Ogden Armour that God has ordained that he and the other big packers should form a trust to uphold the price of meat. Nor would anyone believe our magnates of the steel trust that they are descended from the gods—and must rule.

Unless plutocracy can persuade the majority of the people to close up the public schools and make illiterates of the next generation, and unless it can also persuade them to give up the electoral franchise, plutocracy is doomed. So much is clear.

And that is the reason why we Socialists can look with such equanimity and complacence into the future. The future belongs to some form of Socialism.

And now you understand, gentlemen, while the Socialists are not Bolsheviks—if they had only the choice between Bolshevism and plutocracy, and no other choice, then they would stand for Bolshevism in preference to plutocracy.

In short, it will depend very much upon the action of the capitalist class and the behavior of capitalist Governments during the next few years as to what is going to happen to the capitalist class, not only in European countries, but also in America.

It will depend on our rulers whether we shall have an orderly evolution, which I have always preached and propagated, or a violent revolution which we Socialists have always tried to avoid.

Just now the plutocrats believe that they can quell the uprising of the working class by using force and by enacting special restrictive legislation. But remember, the Czar of Russia tried force to suppress ideas. Where is the Czar now? Where is his wife? Where are his children?

Prince Bismarck, one of the greatest statesmen Germany has ever produced, tried the enactment of special restrictive legislation against the Socialists. Bismarck lived long enough to regret it. Where is Germany now? If the Socialists can not save Germany—Germany can not be saved.

But even at that I believe that a verdict like the one rendered in Landis' court in Chicago—and a sentence like his—would have been impossible under the Czar in Russia or under the Kaiser in Germany.

I believe that for the articles that I have printed and for which I was found guilty and sentenced to serve 20 years in the penitentiary, I should not have been punished 20 minutes in prison in Germany under the Kaiser or under the Czar in Russia.

Under acts passed by Congress as "war measures," however, many men have been sentenced to terms of imprisonment far exceeding the heaviest sentences for much worse offenses under the regime of the Czar or the Kaiser.

For the ruling class in America, capitalism and Americanism have come to mean the same thing. The words "profit" and "patriotism" were used as synonyms by our profiteers during the war and ever since.

And all opposition to capitalistic, commercial, or imperialistic wars was regarded as "high treason." And all opposition to profiteering was denounced as disloyalty and "German propaganda."

Bolshevism and socialism also mean the same thing to the capitalist class and its press. And "Government" and the "national administration" were purposely confounded by the people who wanted war because it helped their business.

The capitalists fear Socialism. They point to poor Russia, which is undergoing the pangs of rejuvenation—where a new society is to be born out of chaos and pain—as an example of Socialism.

This is not the time nor the place to explain Bolshevism in Russia and to tell the difference between Bolshevism and Socialism—but there can be no doubt that the Bolshevist revolution is the natural result of Czarism and of the methods the Czars used against the Socialists and liberals in Russia.

And if our authorities refuse the representatives elected by legal voters admission to legislative bodies—then the working people may be forced to discard their belief in representative government and in the ballot.

The Bolshevists do not favor representative government. They preach "direct action" and the "dictatorship of the proletariat."

The Bolshevists want to break entirely with the past. The Socialists do not believe that a complete break is either possible or desirable. But, as I said before, the outcome will largely depend upon the attitude of the "powers that be"—whether the Socialists or the extremists will prevail.

Remember, less than two years ago the Kaiser was one of the most powerful men in the world. Less than three years ago the Czar was the autocrat of 170,000,000 people. Where are they today? And do you really believe that a revolution which did not stop before Kaiser and Czar will stop before the majesty of the money bag?

It is true, our capitalist rulers may form a so-called league of nations. It is an alliance of the plutocratic governments against the Socialist and the communist nations of Europe—the alliance to be directed and governed by the British plutocracy. Such a league will furnish no relief against armaments, high taxes, and wars. On the contrary, there will be more armaments than ever, and more wars than ever.

And since ideas can not be excluded by bayonets, the Communists may eventually win simply because of persecution. The present civilization may be lost entirely, the good in it will go down with the bad, which would be deplorable.

I repeat that I have nothing to retract from the articles that I have written or from the speeches I have made. All my predictions have come true. And a great deal more will come true than I have predicted.

This was the worst imperialistic war ever known in the history of the world. Every honest man who has any brains admits it now. . . .

As for America in particular—what have we gained in this war and by this war? What has America gained except billions of debts and a hundred thousand of cripples? And we have lost most of our political democracy. Can anybody think of a single thing, worth while, that we have gained through this war? And even a casual reader of the daily newspapers will admit that an imperialistic peace of the worst kind is the result of the much-heralded peace conference in Paris. All the predictions of the Socialists—and especially my predictions in *The Milwaukee Leader*—have come true, I am sorry to say.

And because I am a student of the world's history, because I can see clearly, because I warned my fellowmen, my countrymen, of the events that were bound to happen if we pursued a certain course, therefore I was indicted, found guilty, and sentenced to serve 20 years in the penitentiary.

This incident of being found guilty in Judge Landis' court for exercising my constitutional right of free speech and a free press should have nothing to do, however, with my being seated in the House of Representatives.

And it would be ridiculous, of course, to pay much attention to the plea of the attorney for my Democratic opponent, Mr. Carney, that I must be excluded and Mr. Carney seated (although he received almost 6,000 votes less than I did) in order to make at least the Sixty-sixth Congress "safe," since I am sure to be re-elected if Carney is not seated.

If my re-election is as certain as the attorney for Carney claims, then that is only one more reason to seat me, because I am the true choice of the electorate of the Fifth District of Wisconsin.

Of course, it is the natural and usual thing that the people should re-elect the man who expresses their ideas, especially if the man has proved to be true in face of persecution and prison. . . .

It seems that the statesmen of the Democratic Party, including Woodrow Wilson, do not know the history of the origin of their own party. If they did they never would have passed the so-called espionage act—which is patterned after the old alien and sedition acts, only made very much more drastic and cruel. Even the truth of a statement is not permissible as a defense under Wilson's law. And the maximum punishment was raised from 3 years in 1798 to 20 years in 1917.

Yes, from time immemorial, the Bird of Liberty was a jailbird, and it got to be more so since Woodrow Wilson "made the world safe for democracy."

Gentlemen, it may depend upon your decision in this case to a great extent whether the common people are to lose all faith in political elections and representative government—whether they are to turn to "direct action" and "soviets."

The tendency manifest among workmen of our country today is decidedly against "politics" and in favor of "direct action." The only "politics" the workingmen know in this country (with the exception of very few places in the Middle West and the Northwest) is capitalistic politics. And this "politics" is so discredited that even the Boston policemen will not trust the promises of politicians, but prefer "direct action" and the strike. . . .

In one instance after the other, labor unions are showing their willingness to accept the strike, and especially the general strike, as their sole weapon, and they are willing to use this weapon to enforce all of their demands, political and economic.

It is due to this tendency that at the special convention of the Socialist Party of America held during the first week of September, this year, a part of our organization split off. They started the Communist Labor Party and the Communist Party, neither of which has any faith in representative government and parliamentarism.

Now, I do not believe in the present capitalist system. I am convinced that it has outlived its usefulness and must make room for a new order of society. I believe in sane and orderly methods, however, to bring about that necessary change, provided we are permitted to use sane and orderly methods.

And if you gentlemen would only have your ears to the ground and not trust to the capitalist newspapers entirely for your information—if you gentlemen would read the signs of the times, even between the lines of these capitalistic papers—you would soon come to the conclusion that besides furnishing a bad precedent it would be foolish and criminal to deprive the Socialist Party—a party casting over a million votes—of its sole representative in Congress.

As a matter of fact, a large number of Socialists in Congress would be a blessing to the country—they and their measures might possibly stand between present society and chaos.

Special legislation to keep "undesirable" members out of Congress surely will work both ways. Some day it may be used by Socialists or other radicals against the representatives of the capitalist class, especially if the present decision will furnish a sufficient precedent.

Every thinking man should keep in mind that over half of the white race is in a chaotic stage of revolution at the present time, out of which revolution must develop an orderly Socialist reign within the next five years. Every thinking American should take into consideration that England, France and Italy will soon join the world-wide social revolution.

Can America alone escape a world-wide movement of the white race?

It will avail our statesmen nothing to hide their heads in the sand of reaction and to forbid immigration, or even to deport rebels. You can not build a Chinese wall against ideas.

There are 10,000,000 men and women in this country always on the brink of pauperism and starvation. You can not expel all of them. You can not kill all of them. You need them under the capitalist system as a reserve army of labor for your industries.

You cannot solve this question. And yet this question must be solved. Our reactionaries may soon rue the day when they persecuted the representatives of evolutionary Socialism and thus invited a cataclysm which is bound to bury the present system and its defenders.

To sum up: I have always been proud of the Socialist record of observance of law. I have always tried to change or repeal such laws as, in my opinion, were harmful. My work was always constructive. I have always striven to conserve what is best in capitalist civilization as an inheritance for coming generations.

The law under which suppression of free speech and of free press was enforced is a flat denial of rights guaranteed every citizen by the Constitution of the United States. The manner in which that unjust and inherently unconstitutional law was used to procure my conviction for a crime which I never in word, deed, or spirit contemplated, was a travesty upon justice.

My case is still pending in the courts on an appeal. I am confident that the verdict will be reversed by the higher tribunal. I believe that the higher court will hold that I was within my constitutional rights in printing these editorials. A man can not be considered guilty, especially in a political case of this kind, until the highest court in the land has spoken. And in the opinion of real democrats, he will not be considered guilty at any time.

The Fifth District of the State of Wisconsin is entitled to be represented by the man of its own choice. I say again, it is not the personal case of Victor Berger—representative government is on trial.

And the particular question now is: Does the National House of Representatives desire to unseat the regularly elected and regularly certified representative of the Fifth District of Wisconsin because he stood honestly and loyally by his principles?

PART VII
The Communist Party

THE history of the organization of the Communist Party in America is an involuted and frustrating record of schism and often arid intellectual, ideological, and personal conflict. The nature of the political context, however, made a degree of schismatic fervor and ill-will both necessary and desirable. The loose heterogeneity of the Socialist Party, from a more radical perspective, made a rigorous and organized revolutionary effort within that structure impossible. Hoping to build on the exciting model of the Bolsheviks, the American Communists sought a disciplined, clear-eyed, and dedicated political organization that would lead the way into the American phase of international revolution. The Russian Revolution seemed to prove that anything was possible, and the establishment of soviets in Europe, as well as domestic crises like the Boston police strike and the steel strike, seemed to show that *the* revolution was imminent. This somewhat manic sense of real possibilities is the essential context for comprehending the organization of Communism in the United States.

The basic outline of the schisms that led to a Communist Party is this: a group called the Left Wing Section broke away from the Socialist Party; this group itself broke into two rival factions, the Communist Party and the Communist Labor Party; these two finally combined (after other subschisms) into a United Communist Party. The real ideological, political, and psychological differences that underlay these fissions and fusions cannot be hidden by so simple an outline.

A manifesto of the Left Wing (Document 16) was published in February 1919. (In November, four Communists were indicted for publishing this manifesto; massive government raids on their offices opened the curtain on the national Red Scare, the Palmer Raids, and a national epidemic of political hysteria.) Starting from the conviction that the Old Guard of the Socialist Party failed to honor its own St. Louis war resolution (see 13 for this text), the left-wingers formally organized themselves as an independent caucus of the Socialist Party in a meeting in New York that was attended by about 100 members of the party. This caucus condemned the basic tactical commitments of the SP to reform, political evolution, and electoral action as hopelessly middle class, compromised, and futile. It established its own journal, *Revolutionary Age,* edited by Louis Fraina, and in April 1919, started its own newspaper, *New York Communist,* edited by John Reed.

The first major question for the Left Wing was whether to try to take over the Socialist Party or to secede from it in order to start a new Communist Party; because agreement was not possible between the contending factions, they finally took separate paths. The Socialist Party responded by expelling the entire membership affiliated with the Left Wing, altogether about 30,000 members. When the New York State Committee of the SP voted to revoke the charters of locals affiliated with the Left, Reed's newspaper playfully reported the impending purge: "We're Gonna Be Expelled! Help!!" [1] By now the Left could not care less because it was only a question of who was going to kick whom out first.

The SP lost most of its membership in its purges, but it retained control of its own major committees and party leadership. One left-wing faction, including Fraina and most of the National Council of the Left Wing Section, believed that the SP could not, and should not, be taken over, and they formed the Communist Party in a Chicago convention in September 1919 (their first program is Document 17). The remainder of the Left Wing, including John Reed and Benjamin Gitlow, went to the SP convention also being held in Chicago at the same time, but by fraud and political muscle the Socialists turned the challenge back, so the insurgents bolted the convention and formed the Communist Labor Party in their own convention held in the IWW hall that was filled by eighty-two delegates from twenty-one states. The Communist Party convention met at the headquarters of the Russian Federation, and the festivities began when the Anarchist Squad of the Chicago police tore down the red banners, made a few arrests, and Fraina spoke of the end of factionalism, the beginning of real unity on the real Left.

The distance between the CP and the CLP was occasionally more rhetorical than substantial, but there were important ideological and ethnic

[1] *New York Communist,* 19 April 1919, p. 8.

differences. Many East European radicals moved leftward in the United States *after* the Bolshevik successes, and most of the membership of the first CP was dominated by the Russians on their borrowed glamour. The leadership of the Russian Federation seemed to assume that their language and origin automatically made each a potential Lenin. Their demand for complete ideological purity (i.e., complete conformity with their often distorted reading of Lenin) turned them away from even an attempt to connect with the American working class. The CLP had more English-speaking leaders, was more concerned with finding a mass constituency without sacrificing principle, and resented the ideological megalomania of the Slavic Federation's leadership in the CP. Political orthodoxy versus a mass base was one of the major conflicts between the two Communist parties, and the fact that both must eventually point out that the posed alternatives were fake did not lessen the vitriol they heaped on each other. The CP, in fact, was bitterly critical of the CLP for being too American: "The Socialist Party and the Communist Labor Party agree on one thing—an 'American' movement, not a 'foreign' movement, is necessary. It is appropriate that the Communist Labor Party, which has not yet severed the umbilical cord binding it to the Socialist Party, should express this treacherous ideology of 'Americanism.' " [2] Perhaps the "Americanism" of the CLP was proved by its failure to mention black workers in its first program, and the equally crippling "internationalism" of the CP in its bald assertion that the black problem in America was simply an aspect of the worldwide working-class struggle. The conflict of "American exceptionalism" versus the solidarity of the international working class was to blight the American Left for decades to come.

Just after their respective founding conventions, the CP and the CLP had a combined enrolled membership of between 25,000 and 40,000. The foreign language federations that comprised the bulk of the CP were Russian, Ukrainian, South Slavic, Polish, Lithuanian, Jewish, Lettish, and Hungarian. The intense government persecution of both aliens and radicals in late 1919 and 1920 finally drove most of the leadership underground and to its senses. The Palmer Raids constituted a common danger to the CP and the CLP, and precipitated a move toward unity. In May 1920, these groups finally were reorganized into a United Communist Party.

The content and flavor of this toughening militance are seen better in an individual than in official party proclamations. On 14 August 1919, Dr. Maximilian Cohen, the secretary of the Left Wing Section of New York

[2] Quoted in Theodore Draper, *The Roots of American Communism* (New York: Viking Press, 1957), p. 187.

and a founder of the first CP, was interrogated by the New York Lusk Committee, the group that finally led to the expulsion from the legislature of five properly elected Socialist assemblymen, to mass arrests, and to the seizure of about twenty-five tons of material. Cohen's testimony (Document 18) was taken in the office of the attorney general of New York, and his elan and dedication are perfectly clear.

---

[16]

PROBLEMS OF AMERICAN SOCIALISM

MANIFESTO AND PROGRAM OF THE LEFT WING OF THE AMERICAN SOCIALIST MOVEMENT

AT the present moment the Socialist Party of America is agitated by several cross-currents, some local in their character, and some a reflex of cleavages within the European Socialist movements. Many see in this internal dissension merely an unimportant difference of opinion, or, at most, dissatisfaction with the command of the party, and the desire to replace those who have misused it with better men.

We, however, maintain that there is a fundamental distinction in views concerning party policies and tactics. And we believe that this difference is so vast that from our standpoint a radical change in party policies and tactics is necessary.

This essential task is being shirked by our party leaders and officials generally. In view of the impending change in the tactics of organized labor in this country, we must hurry to readjust the Socialist movement to the new conditions or find ourselves left behind by the march of events.

Already there is formidable industrial unrest, a seething ferment of discontent, evidenced by inarticulate rumblings which presage striking occurrences. The transformation of industry from a war to a peace basis has

SOURCE: "Manifesto and Program of the Left Wing of the American Socialist Movement," *The Revolutionary Age* 1, no. 17 (8 February 1919): 4–6.

thoroughly disorganized the economic structure. Thousands upon thousands of workers are being thrown out of work. Demobilized sailors and soldiers find themselves a drug on the labor market, unless they act as scabs and strike-breakers. Skilled mechanics, fighting desperately to maintain their war-wage and their industrial status, are forced to strike. Women, who during the war have been welcomed into industries hitherto closed to them, are struggling to keep their jobs. And to cap the climax, the capitalists, through their Chambers of Commerce and their Merchants' and Manufacturers' Associations, have resolved to take advantage of the situation to break down even the inadequate organizations labor has built up through generations of painful struggle.

The temper of the workers and the soldiers, after the sacrifices they have made in the war, is such that they will not endure the reactionary labor conditions so openly advocated by the master-class. A series of labor struggles is bound to follow—indeed, is beginning now. Shall the Socialist Party continue to feed the workers with social reform legislation at this critical period? Shall it approach the whole question from the standpoint of votes and the election of representatives to the legislature? Shall it emphasize the consumer's point of view, when Socialist principles teach that the worker is robbed at the point of production? Shall it talk about Cost of Living and taxation, when it should be explaining how the worker is robbed at his job?

There are many signs of the awakening of Labor. The organized Trade Unions, against the definite commands of their leaders, are resorting to independent political action, in an effort to conserve what they have won and wrest new concessions from the master-class. What shall be our attitude toward the awakening workers?

On the basis of the class struggle we shall go among them, impregnating them with revolutionary Socialism; we shall teach them solidarity; we shall teach them class-consciousness; we shall teach them the hopelessness of social reform; we shall teach them the meaning of Revolution. And the industrial unrest, the ferment of discontent, will compel them to listen!

Capitalist Imperialism

Among the many problems immediately confronting us are those new questions springing from Capitalist-Imperialism, the final and decisive stage of Capitalism. How shall the Socialist Party meet these problems?

Imperialism is that stage of Capitalism in which the accumulated capital or surplus of a nation is too great for the home market to reinvest or absorb. The increased productivity of the working class, due to improved machinery and efficiency methods, and the mere subsistence wage which permits the worker to buy back only a small portion of what he produces, causes an ever-increasing accumulation of commodities, which in turn become capital and must be invested in further production. When Capitalism has reached the stage in which it imports raw materials from undeveloped countries and exports them again in the shape of manufactured products, it has reached its highest development.

This process is universal. Foreign markets, spheres of influence and protectorates, under the intensive development of capitalist industry and finance in turn become highly developed. They, too, seek for markets. National capitalist control, to save itself from ruin, breaks its national bonds and emerges full-grown as a capitalist League of Nations, with international armies and navies to maintain its supremacy.

[This is] the new situation the Socialist Party must meet. From now on the United States will no longer hold itself aloof, isolated and provincial. It is reaching out for new markets, new zones of influence, new protectorates; not alone, and not in competition with other capitalist nations, but in cooperation with them. They will divide the world among them. And the League of Nations will be the instrument through which they will work.

The master-class of America will soon attempt to use organized labor for its imperialistic purposes. But a restless and discontented working class cannot pile up profits. Therefore in this country we may soon expect the master-class, in true Bismarckian fashion, to grant factory laws, medical laws, old-age pensions, unemployment insurance, sick benefits, and the whole category of bourgeois reforms, so that the workers may be kept physically and mentally fit to produce the greatest profits at the greatest speed.

Dangers to American Socialism

There is danger that the Socialist Party of America might make use of these purely bourgeois reforms to attract the workers' votes, by claiming that they are victories for Socialism, and that they have been won by Socialist political action; when, as a matter of fact, the object of these master-class measures is to prevent the growing class-consciousness of the workers, and to divert them from their revolutionary aim. By agitating for these reforms, therefore, the Socialist Party would be playing into the hands of our American imperialists.

On the basis of the class struggle, then, the Socialist Party of America must reorganize itself—must prepare to come to grips with the master-class during the difficult period of capitalist readjustment now going on. This it can do only by teaching the working class the truth about present-day conditions; it must preach revolutionary industrial unionism, and urge the workers to turn their craft unions into industrial unions, the only form of labor organization which can cope with the power of great modern aggregations of capital. It must carry on its political campaigns, not merely as means of electing officials to political office, as in the past, but as a year-around educational campaign to arouse the workers to class conscious economic and political action, and to keep alive the burning ideal of revolution in the hearts of the people.

For New Policies and Tactics

We believe that the time has come for the Socialist Party of America to adopt the following course of action: to throw off its parliamentary opportunism and to stand squarely behind the Soviet Republic of Russia, the Spartacus Group in Germany, and the revolutionary working-class movement in Europe. Thus it will be ready when the hour strikes in this country—and it will strike soon—to take the leadership of the revolutionary proletariat in its struggle with the capitalist class, instead of obstructing its path with the palliative of parliamentary reforms and lead the workers forward to the dictatorship of the proletariat, the final phase of the class struggle, necessary to the ushering in of the Cooperative Commonwealth.

Political Action

Realizing that the vital difference between revolutionary Socialism and "moderate Socialism" lies in their varying conceptions of political action, and realizing too that on this point revolutionary Socialists are most misunderstood and misrepresented, we append a detailed explanation of the scientific Socialist conception of political action.

Since we assert with Marx that *"the class struggle is essentially a political struggle,"* we can only accept his own oft repeated interpretation of that phrase. The class struggle, whether it manifest itself on the industrial field or in the direct struggle for governmental control, is essentially a struggle for the capture and destruction of the capitalist political state. This is a political act. In this broader view of the term "political," Marx includes revolutionary industrial action. In other words, the objective of Socialist industrial action is also "political," in the sense that it aims to undermine the state, which *"is nothing less than a machine for the oppression of one class by another and that no less so in a democratic republic than under a monarchy."*

Participation in Elections

Political action is also and more generally used to refer to participation in election campaigns for the immediate purpose of capturing legislative seats. In this sense also we urge the use of political action as a revolutionary weapon.

But both in the nature and the purpose of this form of political action, revolutionary Socialism and "moderate Socialism" are completely at odds.

We contend that such political action is a valuable means of propaganda; and further, that the capture of legislative seats is an effective means of capturing the political state, but—and here is the vital point for the "moderate Socialist" goes no further—we hold that this capture of the political state is merely for the purpose of destroying it. The nature of Socialist parliamentary activity should be purely destructive.

"Moderate Socialism" aims to "simply lay hold of the ready-made machinery and wield it for its own purposes"—the attainment of Socialism. And so the "moderate" falls into the error of believing that parliamentary activity is constructive—that he can eventually legislate Socialism into existence.

This error leads to two dangerous practices: (1), making parliamentary activity an end in itself; and (2), making essentially destructive political action the instrument for constructing the Socialist order. To avoid these dangers, and to strengthen Labor's political arm, the Socialist ballot must be supported by the might of *"the industrial organization of the working class."* Only the economic organization of the working class can build the new society within the frame of the old.

Revolutionary Industrial Unionism

"Moderate Socialism" constantly overlooks this fact. We must continually remind the working class that *Labor's economic organizations are naturally the school for Socialism. All political parties, and without exception, whatever their complexion may be, warm up the working class only for a season, transitorily.*

Only through his industrial organization can the worker receive training in the control of production. It is by means of this weapon that the working class will eventually take over and hold the mines, mills and factories, not for the purpose of destroying them but for their permanent control and development. Thus, the only thing worth taking from capitalist society and keeping the highly developed means of production and distribution—will be won for the working class by its *Revolutionary Economic Organization.*

Because of its constructive nature, our Economic Arm, unlike our Political Arm, may take "a little at a time." Our economic movement is not unlike a military movement. All means are used to win a war—infantry attacks, heavy and light artillery, bombardments, sieges, and guerrilla fighting. In the industrial struggle the working class employs strikes, boycotts, and the like. The political movement, however, has for its object only the storming of the political citadel of capitalist tyranny: therefore the Political Arm cannot compromise. Our political movement should be the essence and incarnation of our revolutionary aim. With Liebknecht we say, "To parliamentarize is to compromise, to logroll, to sell out."

Syndicalism and Parliamentarism

In characteristic utopian fashion the Syndicalists forget that the Social Revolution must in part grow "within the capitalist shell." They forget that the state, the engine of oppression employed by the capitalist class, must be destroyed through capture by the working class.

In equally characteristic utopian fashion, the "moderate Socialist," with his pure and simple parliamentarism, forgets that *"because of its destructive object and because of its structure, which is arbitrary and determined by geographical lines, the Political Arm of Labor cannot be used as a means of taking away from the capitalists and holding for the working men the means of production."*

Thus the utopian Syndicalist fails to utilize the political weapon; and the 20th Century Utopian Socialist misuses the political weapon and fails altogether to utilize the industrial weapon.

A combination of these two methods is necessary to the revolutionary Socialist movement, and this combination the Left Wing intends to effect.

Program

1. We stand for a uniform declaration of principles in all party platforms both local and national and the abolition of all social reform planks now contained in them.
2. The party must teach, propagate and agitate exclusively for the overthrow of Capitalism and the establishment of Socialism through a Proletarian Dictatorship.
3. The Socialist candidates elected to office shall adhere strictly to the above provisions.
4. Realizing that a political party cannot reorganize and reconstruct the industrial organizations of the working class and that that is the task of the economic organizations themselves, we demand that the party assist this process of reorganization by a propaganda for revolutionary and industrial unionism as part of its general activities. We believe it is the mission of the Socialist movement to encourage and assist the proletariat to adopt newer and more effective forms of organization and to stir it into newer and more revolutionary modes of action.
5. We demand that the official party press be party owned and controlled.
6. We demand that officially recognized educational institutions be party owned and controlled.
7. We demand that the party discard its obsolete literature and publish new literature in keeping with the policies and tactics above mentioned.

Immediate Demands

1. We demand that the National Executive Committee call an immediate emergency national convention for the purpose of reorganizing party policies and tactics to meet the present crisis.
2. We demand that the American Socialist Party shall not participate in the proposed Lauzanne Conference engineered by "moderate Socialists" and social patriots.
3. We demand that the Socialist Party of America issue a call for an international congress of those groups of the Socialist movement that participated both in the Zimmerwald Conference in September 1915 and the Kienthal Conference in 1916, and those groups that are in agreement with them today.

4. We demand the unequivocal endorsement of the Russian Socialist Federated Soviet Republic.
5. We demand the unequivocal indorsement of the Spartacus Group of Germany.
6. We demand the unequivocal endorsement of the Left Wing movements of Europe.

---

[17]

THE COMMUNIST PARTY MANIFESTO AND PROGRAM

THE world is on the verge of a new era. Europe is in revolt. The masses of Asia are stirring uneasily. Capitalism is in collapse. The workers of the world are seeing a new life and securing new courage. Out of the night of war is coming a new day.

The spectre of Communism haunts the world of capitalism. Communism, the hope of the workers to end misery and oppression.

The workers of Russia smashed the front of international Capitalism and Imperialism. They broke the chains of the terrible war; and in the midst of agony, starvation and the attacks of the capitalists of the world, they are creating a new social order.

The class war rages fiercely in all nations. Everywhere the workers are in a desperate struggle against their capitalist masters. The call to action has come. The workers must answer the call!

The Communist Party of America is the party of the working class. The Communist Party proposes to end capitalism and organize a workers' industrial republic. The workers must control industry and dispose of the products of industry. The Communist Party is a party realizing the limitations of all existing workers' organizations and proposes to develop the revolutionary movement necessary to free the workers from the oppression of Capitalism. The Communist Party insists that the problems of the American worker are identical with the problems of the workers of the world.

SOURCE: "The Communist Party Manifesto and Program," *The Communist* 1, no. 1 (27 September 1919): 6–9.

The War and Socialism

A giant struggle is convulsing the world. The war is at end, but peace is not here. The struggle is between the capitalist nations of the world and the international proletariat, inspired by Soviet Russia. The Imperialisms of the world are desperately arraying themselves against the onsweeping proletarian revolution.

The League of Nations is dividing the world financially and territorially. It is directing the fight against the workers. It is the last effort of Capitalism to save itself. . . .

The war made a shamble of civilization. It proved the utter incapacity of capitalism to direct and promote the progress of humanity. Capitalism has broken down.

But the Socialist movement itself broke down under the test of war. The old dominant moderate Socialism accepted and justified the war. It acted against the proletarian revolution and united with the capitalists against the workers. Out of this circumstance developed the forces of revolutionary Socialism now expressed in the Communist International. . . .

The Socialist parties accepted the war as a war for democracy—as if democracy under Imperialism is not directly counter-revolutionary. They justified the war as a war for the independence of nations. Not the proletarian class struggle, but nationalism, social-patriotism and social-imperialism determined the policy of the dominant Socialism. The coming of Socialism was made dependent upon the workers cutting each others' throats in the struggles of their own ruling class! . . .

American Socialism

Socialism in the United States, prior to the appearance of the Socialist Labor Party, was a movement of isolated and indefinite protest. It was the spur of middle-class movements, while itself split by Socialist and Anarchist factions.

The Socialist Labor Party, after casting off the non-Socialist elements, developed as a consistent party of revolutionary Socialism. Particularly, the S. L. P. realized the importance of imparting a Socialist character and consciousness to the unions. The Socialist Labor Party, together with the experience of the Western Federation of Miners and the American Labor Union, developed the theory and practice of Industrial Unionism.

The struggle of the Socialist Labor Party against the old unionism developed a secession from the party of elements who considered protecting the reactionary American Federation of Labor more important than revolutionary Socialism. These, together with bourgeois and agrarian radicals, organized the Socialist Party.

The Socialist Party was a party of moderate socialism. Its policy was that of government ownership of industry, not the proletarian conquest of power. It maintained that the middle class and the lesser capitalists are necessary in the Socialist struggle against capitalism. The Socialist Party asserted in substance: Socialism is a struggle of all the people against the trusts, making the realization of Socialism depend upon the "unity of the common people," the workers, the small capitalists and investors, the professions. In short the official policy of the Socialist Party was to attain Socialism by means of capitalist democracy.

The Socialist Party stultified proletarian political action by limiting it to elections and participation in legislative reform activity. The party favored reactionary trade unionism as against revolutionary industrial unionism.

The Socialist Labor Party developed a purely theoretical activity, of real value, but was isolated from the masses. The Socialist Party attained a considerable membership, but largely of a petty bourgeoisie character. The war brought in new industrial proletarian elements but the party still isolated itself from revolutionary theory and practice. The proletarian masses in the Socialist Party required simply the opportunity to develop a revolutionary proletarian policy.

The Socialist Party under the impulse of its proletarian membership adopted a militant declaration against the war. But the officials of the party sabotaged this declaration. The official policy of the party on the war was that of liberal pacifism. The party bureaucracy united with the People's Council which propagandized a Wilson peace. The 1918 party platform accepted the Wilson "fourteen points" as adopted by the pro-war Interallied Labor and Socialist Conference.

The war and the proletarian revolution in Russia sharpened the antagonism between the party policy and the revolutionary proletarian temper in the party. Revolt broke loose. The Socialist Party was crushed. The Communist Party is the response to this revolt and to the call of the Communist International. . . .

The Program of the Party

The Communist Party is the conscious expression of the class struggle of the workers against capitalism. Its aim is to direct this struggle to the conquest of political power, the overthrow of capitalism and the destruction of the bourgeois state.

The Communist Party prepares itself for the revolution in the measure that it develops a program of immediate action, expressing the mass struggles of the proletariat. These struggles must be inspired with revolutionary spirit and purposes.

The Communist Party is fundamentally a party of action. It brings to the workers a consciousness of their oppression, of the impossibility of improving their conditions under capitalism. The Communist Party directs the workers' struggle against capitalism, developing fuller forms and purposes in this struggle, culminating in the mass action of the revolution.

I

The Communist Party maintains that the class struggle is essentially a political struggle; that is, a struggle to conquer the power of the state.

(a) The Communist Party shall keep in the foreground its consistent appeal for proletarian revolution, the overthrow of capitalism and the establishment of a dictatorship of the proletariat. As the opposition of the bourgeoisie is broken, as it is expropriated and gradually absorbed in the working groups, the proletarian dictatorship disappears, until finally the state dies and there are no more class distinctions.

(b) Participation in parliamentary campaigns, which in the general struggle of the proletariat is of secondary importance, is for the purpose of revolutionary propaganda only.

(c) Parliamentary representatives of the Communist Party shall not introduce or support reform measures. Parliaments and political democracy shall be utilized to assist in organizing the working class against capitalism and the state. Parliamentary representatives shall consistently expose the oppressive class character of the capitalist state, using the legislative forum to interpret and emphasize the class struggle; they shall make clear how parliamentarism and parliamentary democracy deceive the workers; and they shall analyze capitalist legislative proposals and reforms palliatives as evasions of the issue and as of no fundamental significance to the working class.

(d) Nominations for public office and participation in elections are limited to legislative bodies only, such as municipal councils, state legislatures and the national congress.

(e) The uncompromising character of the class struggle must be maintained under all circumstances. The Communist Party accordingly, in campaigns and elections, and in all its other activities shall not co-operate with groups or parties not committed to the revolutionary class struggle, such as the Socialist Party, Labor Party, Non-Partisan League, People's Council, Municipal Ownership Leagues, etc.

II

The Communist Party shall make the great industrial struggles of the working class its major campaigns, in order to develop an understanding of the strike in relation to the overthrow of capitalism.

(a) The Communist Party shall participate in mass strikes, not only to achieve the immediate purposes of the strike, but to develop the revolutionary implications of the mass strike.

(b) Mass strikes are vital factors in the process out of which develops the workers' understanding and action for the conquest of power.

(c) In mass strikes under conditions of concentrated capitalism there is latent the tendency toward the general mass strike, which takes on a political character and manifests the impulse toward proletarian dictatorship.

In these general mass strikes the Communist Party shall emphasize the necessity of maintaining industry and the taking over of social functions usually discharged by the capitalists and the institutions of capitalism. The strike must cease being isolated and passive; it must become positive, general and aggressive, preparing the workers for the complete assumption of industrial and social control.

(a) Every local and district organization of the Party shall establish contact with the industrial units in its territory, the shops, mills and mines —and direct its agitation accordingly.

(b) Shop Committees shall be organized wherever possible for the purpose of Communist agitation in a particular shop or industry by the workers employed there. These committees shall be united with each other and with the Communist Party, so that the party shall have actual contact with the workers and mobilize them for action against capitalism.

III

The Communist Party must engage actively in the struggle to revolutionize the trade unions. As against the unionism of the American Federation of Labor, the Communist Party propagandizes industrial unionism and industrial union organization, emphasizing their revolutionary implications. Industrial Unionism is not simply a means for the everyday struggle against capitalism; its ultimate purpose is revolutionary, implying the necessity of ending the capitalist parliamentary state. Industrial Unionism is a factor in the final mass action for the conquest of power, as it will constitute the basis for the industrial administration of the Communist Commonwealth.

(a) The Communist Party recognizes that the A. F. of L. is reactionary and a bulwark of capitalism.

(b) Councils of workers shall be organized in the shops as circumstances allow, for the purpose of carrying on the industrial union struggle in the old unions, uniting and mobilizing the militant elements; these councils to be unified in a central council wherever possible.

(c) It shall be a major task of the Communist Party to agitate for the construction of a general industrial union organization, embracing the I. W. W., W. I. I. U., independent and secession unions, militant unions of the A. F. of L., and the unorganized workers, on the basis of the revolutionary class struggle.

IV

The Communist Party shall encourage movements of the workers in the shops seeking to realize workers' control of industry, while indicating their limitations under capitalism; concretely, any movement analogous to the Shop Stewards of England. These movements (equally directed against the union bureaucracy) should be related to the Communist Party.

V

The unorganized unskilled workers (including the agricultural proletariat) constitute the bulk of the working class. The Communist Party shall directly and systematically agitate among these workers, awakening them to industrial union organization and action.

VI

In close connection with the unskilled workers is the problem of the Negro worker. The Negro problem is a political and economic problem. The racial oppression of the Negro is simply the expression of his economic bondage and oppression, each intensifying the other. This complicates the Negro problem, but does not alter its proletarian character. The Communist Party will carry on agitation among the Negro workers to unite them with all class-conscious workers.

VII

The United States is developing an aggressive militarism. The Communist Party will wage the struggle against militarism as a phase of the class struggle to hasten the downfall of Capitalism.

VIII

The struggle against Imperialism, necessarily an international struggle, is the basis of proletarian revolutionary action in this epoch.

(a) There must be close unity with the Communist International for common action against the Imperialism.

(b) The Communist Party emphasizes the common character of the struggle of the workers of all nations, making necessary the solidarity of the workers of the world.

INTERROGATION OF
DR. MAXIMILIAN COHEN

JOINT LEGISLATIVE COMMITTEE OF THE
STATE OF NEW YORK

SOME of the statements made by Doctor Cohen in the course of his examination are here given and will, we believe, make clear the meaning of the general strike. Doctor Cohen said "the agricultural workers would organize and immediately take over the factory or the dairy just as they would take over an industry or a store or anything else."

Doctor Cohen, being further questioned, replied as follows:

Q: Instead of delivering it and selling it, they would deliver it to you people?

A: Yes, exactly, to the strike committee. . . .

Q: You mean to assume the government to the exclusion of the elected representatives?

A: We are not interested at all in what Congress would do. . . .

If capitalism is, as we believe it is, on the verge of a breakdown in all countries, which brings with it a greater and greater discontent and a growing class consciousness among the unskilled workers, who are in the vast majority, and they will organize and listen to our propaganda, the time must necessarily come when a state of chaos is at hand. The workers and Soviets on one hand, and the constituent assemblies on the other hand, both wrestling for power. That will be the situation. Whether or not it will be orderly depends on you people, because we want to assume these organizations.

Q: But if there is any resistance?

A: Well, you will show the resistance, we will not; you will fight to retain power and the workers will fight to wrest it away from you. On the one hand the Workers' Council, on the other hand the Constituent Assemblies.

SOURCE: New York State, Joint Legislative Committee Investigating Seditious Activities, *Revolutionary Radicalism*, part 1, "Revolutionary and Subversive Movements Abroad and at Home" 1 (Albany, 1920): 876–881.

What you are trying to get from me is an admission that force will be necessary.

Q: No, no; if you have any other way to do it, we would like to know your idea.

A: The question of force does not rest with us. We base our philosophy on life itself—mass action. Our Socialist brethren berate us for our loose way of talking, but we say mass action is dependent on life itself. We cannot make a narrow definition of it, because it involves all of life itself.

Q: Laying all the cards right on the table, let us get at this a little. My understanding is that the Communist Party is purely and simply a propaganda organization?

A: Right.

Q: For the express purpose of encouraging and stimulating in the workers' minds the idea that they must organize, industrially, economically, politically—

A: In the Communist Party.

Q: No necessarily.

A: Necessarily.

Q: Well, in co-operation with it. For instance, the W. I. I. U. is pretty close to the Socialist Labor Party, isn't it?

A: No, it is an industrial organization—

Q: Isn't that about the relation there would be between the industrial organization and the Communist Party?

A: No, because if a revolutionary crisis were to come, you would find the Communist Party would stand aloof as a party, but individually their representatives were in the Soviets even at the time the Mensheviki were in control. Now, then, the workers' councils will be the revolutionary organizations. They will be composed of all the workers' organizations, skilled or unskilled, that will have organized and sent representatives to the Soviets, and the Soviets will be the actual revolutionary organizations, not the Bolsheviks or the Communist Party. If that is what you mean, you are right.

Q: What do you mean by social revolution?

A: Social revolution means the overthrow of the existing system.

Q: In what way?

A: It is immaterial, but it is not by the methods of the present ruling class, that is plain.

Q: What other way?

A: By organizing the revolutionary workers, making them class conscious.

It is like the depositors in a bank: So long as there is a feeling that the bank is stable, they will deposit their money, but as soon as a doubt gets in their minds, there is a mass movement, a panic seems to enter them all at once, and they will rush pell mell to draw out the money.

Q: Their own money?

A: I just want to develop my idea: The workers will be in the same position as the depositors in the bank, to the present government. They will feel that they have lost all faith in it—through our propaganda, I admit, and through the gradual breakdown of the existing system—wages will not rise to meet it and they will feel they are always on the ragged edge. When that condition prevails and we can instil into their minds doubt and distrust and lack of faith in the present capitalistic methods . . . to meet the tremendous reforms necessary. The reforms granted in Germany under Bismarck, they did not do any good. We have to show them that all social reformers are worthless to them and that the one thing they must do is to organize in the Communist Party. When that stage has reached its development, and the breakdown of industry comes, the revolutionary organizations will probably spring into existence and will attempt to take over the control of the government from your capitalist class—

Q: How?

A: Well, let us see, in Russia they made a raid on the—of course, they abolished all the constituent assemblies—but they raided the offices of the powers that be, and installed themselves, and immediately organized Red Guards to protect themselves in their newly found power.

Q: And you would approve of that method?

A: Unquestionably.

Q: That would mean, of course, force.

A: Well, suppose the capitalist class did not desire to come to us, would use force against us—

Q: Of course you don't expect they would desire to go to you?

A: Then the onus is on your side, not ours. We merely protect ourselves. We all know enough to know that no ruling class will give up power without a fight. But we must have the initiative. All submerged classes must assume the initiative if they are to get what they want.

Q: Therefore the onus of the result rests with you?

A: Of course, if we establish a dictatorship of the proletariat we will accept whatever onus is involved.

Q: Whether the result is successful or not?

A: You see, of course, it is a peculiar situation: We are being tried in the capitalist court, and there can be no justice, because we tell you frankly what we aim for is the overthrow of your government.

Q: And you expect to take all the institutions and all of the property of the capitalists?

A: Communize it, nationalize it, immediately.

Q: Well, you mean take it away from the present owners and do what you please with it?

A: Yes.

Q: You don't expect a man is going to give up property and money without resistance, therefore you are going to supply the means of taking it from him, and you have the initiative in bringing about the means, therefore it cannot be done except by force.

A: It can be done without force, but if force is used, we blame you people because you are prepared to use force. Now we are going to win over the army and navy—

Q: How would you try to win it over?

A: Through propaganda. How do you think any revolutionary organization ever won anybody over, except through propaganda?

Q: Then you will try to win over the army and navy, the members of which have sworn to uphold the government, and to resist the efforts of anyone who seeks to overthrow the government, and you will try to get them in such a frame of mind as to be untrue to that oath, and not do that which they are sworn to do, to wit, to uphold law and order?

A: To tell you frankly, we don't care a fig for your oaths. We don't hold them as meaning anything to us, because necessarily if we did we would have to stop and go out of business.

Q: You are not under oath now, but if you were put under oath, would that mean anything to you? As a gentleman, you would tell the truth. You have been very frank and I would take your word as well without an oath as with an oath.

A: My oath would mean nothing at all to me.

Q: It would mean nothing to you?

A: Nothing at all.

Q: May I ask, is that anything personal with you, that is the general principle?

A: No, that is the principle of all revolutionary organizations.

Q: I certainly want to say that I want to express my personal respect for your frankness.

A: I must be frank or be untrue to my principles. They are universal so far as those who hold these beliefs are concerned. If I were to get on the stand and say that I don't believe in a class war and in overthrowing the capitalist government, I would be lying. I know if I come before your capitalistic court I must be convicted. I cannot help myself.

Q: Are these the same ideas that actuate and are followed by the men who publish this Revolutionary Age?

A: Well, you must make allowance for human equation, but barring that, that is the principle that actuates every member of the Left Wing and every convert that comes into the Left Wing. Ever since the inception of the Socialist movement—if it were not for its hesitancy—they have preached the overthrow of the capitalist system.

Q: That is rather an indefinite term.

A: We will say the capitalist class. I mean the system that bases its mode of production on profits, rent, interest and capital.

Q: Do you mean by that our present form of government as now constituted?

A: Exactly.

Q: That is a capitalistic government?

A: Yes.

Q: And you understand that the United States government is a capitalistic government?

A: Yes.

Q: And when you say that you want to abolish the capitalist government, you mean the United States government?

A: I mean the United States government in so far as the term applies to this country. If we are carrying on revolutionary propaganda in this country, we mean the overthrow of the United States government; and in France, it would mean the overthrow of the French government, that is it exactly.

Q: And when the words "capitalist system" appear in any of your Communist publications, you mean the United States government?

A: In so far as it functions for the capitalist class, and it does today function for the capitalist class.

Q: Doesn't it function for the laboring class?

A: No.

PART VIII
Strike

Fʀᴏᴍ the close of the war throughout the twenties, the Left's immediate context was made up of industrial conflict, union decline, a general rise in real prosperity, and the spreading effectiveness of industrial paternalism, including the growing use of company unions. The wartime labor shortage, Wilson's request that employers recognize collective bargaining, and the tough pressures of industrial mobilization resulted in substantial gains for organized labor, with the AFL adding over 2 million workers to its membership. But when the pressure was released, when war contracts were canceled, veterans returned to the labor market, employers got meaner and government weaker, a period of intense conflict, sometimes warfare, hit a growing number of firms and industries. The million workers who struck in 1918 grew to over 4 million by the next year.

The conflict between even the most moderate wing of the Left and the AFL is shown in the following exchange (Document 19) between Morris Hillquit (1869–1933) and Samuel Gompers. Presumably to get a clearer picture of American industrial relations, a Senate commission allowed Hillquit and Gompers to interrogate each other. The bitterness of the debate came from an irreconcilable ideological and personal conflict. Hillquit was an extraordinary debater, partly as a result of his legal training and his leadership of the Socialist Party, which he had helped to organize. When Hillquit ran for mayor of New York City in 1917 he got 150,000 votes, 22 percent of the total cast, and he was one of the leaders of the LaFollette movement in 1924. One of the most moderate spokesmen of the American Left at the time, Hillquit was nevertheless an intransigent enemy of all that Gompers represented.

The steel strike of 1919 was a crucial struggle. The enormous power of the steel trust had always prevented the unionization of steel and iron workers, and until this basic industry could be included in its victories, organized labor in America would remain malformed. A call went out of an AFL meeting in Chicago in 1918 to begin organizing the iron and steel workers, even though the leadership of the AFL was reluctant to test its muscle and prestige against the steel industry. William Z. Foster (1881–1961) led the effort in Chicago, and was eventually to lead the murderous strike that followed. Until Foster joined the Communist Party in 1921, and seized temporary control some years later, he was basically a labor organizer. Coming from a working-class background, his path to communism led through the Populists, the Bryan wing of the Democratic Party, the Socialist Party, and the Wobblies. Unyieldingly committed to industrial rather than craft unionism, and eventually equally opposed to dual unionism, Foster worked within the AFL for radical reform. Although his radical reputation and position were hateful to the AFL leadership, his extraordinary effectiveness as an organizer gave him some internal leverage.

Because of the steel trust's brutal repression of organizers and workers, anger and frustration became widespread, and a grassroots demand for a strike overcame the deepening distaste of the AFL leadership for action. At the very last minute Gompers withdrew his support and urged postponement. But Judge Elbert H. Gary, chairman of the board of the United Steel Corporation, refused to deal with the strike leaders. On 22 September 1919 about 365,000 men went on strike in fifty different cities. The violence of the employers, the hunger of the winter, and the ferocity of the government's antiradicalism broke the strike and destroyed the union. Full production resumed in January, just at the height, depth, of the Palmer Raids.

Foster failed in this strike, and he argued (in Document 20) that the usual radical stupidity about conservative labor unions contributed to the disaster. Furthermore, he said, with the simplicity of those days, unions were by their very nature anticapitalistic so that the steel strike, though lost, could teach important lessons, especially to those on the left who continued to be hypnotized by dual unionism. When the Communist Party finally abandoned this alleged misapprehension, Foster joined it and gave the party the image of native leadership that Debs and Haywood had given to the Socialists and Wobblies.

Michael Gold (1894–1967) described the human feel of the coal strike of 1922 (Document 21). He was an editor of *The Masses, The Liberator,* and the *New Masses,* an early advocate for the proletarianization of American writing, and with his *Jews without Money* (1935), a reasonably successful novelist. Although the proletarian fiction that was so often discussed, analyzed, lamented, and criticized throughout the 1930's was never a genuine force or even a movement, there was the sort of politically and emotionally sensitive reporting that is reflected here. Gold's considerable literary skill was best turned to social description and literary criticism rather than to the demands of a fully articulated imaginative work.

In the last text of this section (Document 22), Jay Lovestone (b. 1899), one of the most significant figures of the faction-ridden turmoil of the 1920's, pressed the Left's case against the government. He viewed the several agencies and divisions of the government as the political committee of American capitalism, always and absolutely at war against the best interests of American workers. Although there is neither need nor space to recount the dreary internal squabbling on the left in general, and among the Communists in particular, a few of the highlights, lowlights, will convey something of the suffocating context in which the Left struggled to survive through its own internal blood-letting as well as through the Coolidge and Hoover prosperity. And Lovestone is the key.

When the red hysteria of the early twenties drove the United Communist Party underground, the Soviet Comintern demanded an open and legal party, which surfaced as the Workers Party. Lovestone worked to make the WP more than a necessary evil, more than the tip of the submerged iceberg. He believed that the WP should in fact become the effective agency of communism in the United States, until in 1922 the two factions —over and under the table—were about equal in size. William Z. Foster secretly favored the underground organization. Both factions argued their case in Moscow, and the official word came down in favor of legality. Thereafter, and because of uncertainty about the direction of political movement within the Soviet Union, Lovestone reinvigorated an old debate, one that was infinitely more significant than the internal factionalizing of the hysterics. He ultimately became the advocate within the party of the concept of American exceptionalism. With Foster in full opposition, Lovestone and his followers argued that capitalism was at a different stage of development in the United States than anywhere else, including Europe; that therefore the American party should proceed along lines dictated by an analysis of the United States political economy rather than by a mindless conformity to any other strategy worked out for any other country. In 1929 the Comintern ordered Lovestone and his circle to the Soviet Union to defend themselves before a special commission created to investigate American factionalizing. Stalin himself condemned American exceptionalism.

Henceforth, the era of factions within the Communist Party was over, for the very good reason that all the factions except one had been destroyed. This so-called beginning was the actual end of the official Communist Party as a genuine political force in the United States. Stalin's disdain not only for the American Communist Party but for America as a whole led the Comintern to its offhanded refusal to think seriously about the American situation. The party discipline meant, of course, that the American members could not rethink, much less argue, their case. It is with the dismissal of Lovestone and his followers that the party became entirely subject to political direction which it could not influence. Henceforth party energies spilled into scholastic exegesis rather than thought, intense intramural hatred rather than common effort, and an otherworldly ignorance of the nation whose political economy the party sought to reconstruct with the support of American workers.

---

[19]

HILLQUIT VS. GOMPERS

COMMISSION ON INDUSTRIAL RELATIONS

MR. Hillquit: . . . In your experience with the labor movement and its ever forward march toward greater and greater improvement, and a greater and greater share of social justice, can you point out any line where the labor movement will stop and rest contented so long as it may receive short of the full product of its work?

Mr. Gompers: I say that the workers, as human beings, will never stop in any effort, nor stop at any point in the effort to secure greater improvements in their condition, a better life in all its phases. And wherever that may lead, whatever that may be, so far in my time and my age I decline to permit my mind or my activities to be labeled by any particular ism.

Mr. Hillquit: Do not try to attach any ism to me, please; but the question I ask is whether you maintain—whether the American Federation of Labor and its authorized spokesmen have a general social philosophy, or work blindly from day to day?

SOURCE: U.S. Congress, Senate, *Industrial Relations: Final Report and Testimony Submitted to the Congress by the Commission on Industrial Relations* . . . , 64th Cong., 1st sess., 1916, 2, pp. 1528–1530.

Mr. Gompers: I think your question————

Mr. Hillquit (interrupting): Inconvenient.

Mr. Gompers: No. I will tell you what it is, it is a question prompted to you, and is an insult.

Mr. Hillquit: It is not a question prompted to me.

Mr. Gompers: It is an insult.

Mr. Hillquit: Why? Why, Mr. Gompers?

Mr. Gompers: To insinuate that the men and women in the American Federation of Labor movement are acting blindly from day to day.

Mr. Hillquit: I have not insinuated————

Mr. Gompers (interrupting): Your question implies it.

Mr. Hillquit: I am giving you an opportunity to deny.

Mr. Gompers: If a man should ask me whether I still beat my wife, any answer I could make would incriminate me if I answered yes or no. If I answered that I did not, the intimation would be that I had stopped. If I answered that I did, that I was continuing to beat her.

Mr. Hillquit: But Mr. Gompers, this question bears no analogy to that story————

Mr. Gompers (interrupting): Your question is an insult and a studied one.

Mr. Hillquit: Now, will you state whether you will or whether you will not answer my question?

Mr. Gompers: Will you repeat the question?

Mr. Hillquit: My question was whether the American Federation of Labor as represented by its spokesmen has a general social philosophy, or whether the organization is working blindly from day to day? Now, that is a plain question.

Mr. Gompers: Yes; it is a plain question; it is a plain insult.

Chairman Walsh: Do you refuse to answer it on the ground that it is insulting?

Mr. Gompers: Yes, sir.

Chairman Walsh: That is all, then.

Mr. Hillquit: Then, inform me upon this matter: In your political work of the labor movement is the American Federation of Labor guided by a general social philosophy, or is it not?

Mr. Gompers: It is guided by the history of the past, drawing its lessons from history, to know of the conditions by which the working people are surrounded and confronted; to work along the lines of least resistance; to accomplish the best results in improving the condition of the working people, men and women and children, today and tomorrow and tomorrow—and tomorrow's tomorrow; and each day making it a better day than the one that had gone before. That is the guiding principle and philosophy and aim of the labor movement—in order to secure a better life for all.

Mr. Hillquit: But in these efforts to improve conditions from day to day you must have an underlying standard of what is better, don't you?

Mr. Gompers: No. You start out with a given program, and everything must conform to it; and if the facts do not conform to your theories, why, your declarations, or, rather, your actions, betray the state of mind "so much the worse for the facts."

Mr. Hillquit: Mr. Gompers, what I ask you is this: You say you try to make the conditions of the workers better every day. In order to determine whether the conditions are better or worse you must have some standards by which you distinguish the bad from the good in the labor movement, do you not?

Mr. Gompers: Certainly. Well, is that————

Mr. Hillquit (interrupting): Now, just————

Mr. Gompers (interrupting): Well, one moment. Does it require much discernment to know that a wage of $3 a day and a workday of 8 hours a day in sanitary workshops are all better than $2.50 a day and 12 hours a day and under perilous conditions of labor? It does not require much conception of a social philosophy to understand that.

Mr. Hillquit: Then, Mr. Gompers, by the same parity of reasoning, $4 a day and seven hours a day of work and very attractive working conditions are still better?

Mr. Gompers: Unquestionably.

Mr. Hillquit: Therefore————

Mr. Gompers (interrupting): Just a moment. I have not stipulated $4 a day or $8 a day or any number of dollars a day or eight hours a day or seven hours a day or any number of hours a day, but the best possible conditions obtainable for the workers is the aim.

Mr. Hillquit: Yes; and when these conditions are obtained————

Mr. Gompers (interrupting): Why, then, we want better.

Mr. Hillquit (continuing): You will still strive for better?

Mr. Gompers: Yes.

Mr. Hillquit: Now, my question is, Will this effort on the part of organized labor ever stop until it has the full reward for its labor?

Mr. Gompers: It won't stop at all.

Mr. Hillquit: That is a question————

Mr. Gompers (interrupting): Not when any particular point is reached, whether it be that toward which you have just declared or anything else. The working people will never stop————

Mr. Hillquit: Exactly.

Mr. Gompers (continuing): In their effort to obtain a better life for themselves and for their wives and for their children and for humanity.

Mr. Hillquit: Then, the object of the labor union is to obtain complete social justice for themselves and for their wives and for their children?

Mr. Gompers: It is the effort to obtain a better life every day.

Mr. Hillquit: Every day and always————

Mr. Gompers: Every day. That does not limit it.

Mr. Hillquit: Until such time————

Mr. Gompers: Not until any time.

Mr. Hillquit: In other words————

Mr. Gompers (interrupting): In other words, we go further than you. [Laughter and applause in the audience] You have an end; we have not.

Mr. Hillquit: Then, Mr. Gompers, you want to go on record as saying that the American Federation of Labor, in its endeavors and striving goes farther than the Socialist Party————

Mr. Gompers (interrupting): When you say you have a goal————

Mr. Hillquit (interrupting): I have not finished the question.

Chairman Walsh: Finish your question, Mr. Hillquit.

Mr. Hillquit: If the Socialist Party has for its present purpose the abolition of the present system of profits and wages, and seeks to secure to the workers the full measure of the product of their labor, if they—their purposes eventually seek to obtain that by gradual steps—then I understand you to say that the American Federation of Labor goes beyond it.

Mr. Gompers: I have said this, and I say that no categorical answer, yes or no, can be given to that question. I say this, that the fact that what I said to you yesterday, after the close of your statement is—as a clever sophist you take the cake; but it is cleverness and sophistry.

Mr. Hillquit: That is becoming almost personal, Mr. Gompers.

Chairman Walsh: Yes; I think so.

Mr. Gompers: As just indicated, the abolition of private profits and wages —there are quite a number of employers who quite agree with you, who would reduce wages and take wages away entirely. The question of the cooperative Commonwealth and the ownership of the means of production and distribution is implied by it. Now, let me say————

Mr. Hillquit (interrupting): It is not, Mr. Gompers.

Mr. Gompers: Well, all right.

Mr. Hillquit: I am not proposing any system. I want your aims and the limits of your aims.

Mr. Gompers: By your question, you want to place me in the position of saying that I am for the system of society which some of you dreamers have conceived of, and then say that I go beyond it.

Mr. Hillquit: I do not, Mr. Gompers, you interrupted me————

Mr. Gompers (interrupting): Well, you interrupted me, so we are even. And I say that the movement of the working people, whether under the American Federation, or not, will be simply following the human impulse for improvement in their condition, and wherever that may lead, they will go, without having a goal up to yours or surpassing yours, but it will lead them constantly to the material and physical and social and moral well-being of the people.

Mr. Hillquit: Then, Mr. Gompers, you would not say that the difference between the program of the American Federation of Labor and that of the Socialist Party is a quantitative one—that the Socialist Party wants more than the American Federation of Labor. You would not say that, would you?

Mr. Gompers: I don't know that it is necessary that the comparison—that I should answer as to the comparison. It is not interesting at all, nor is it a contribution to the subject which the commission desires to ascertain.

Mr. Hillquit: You decline to answer that point?

Mr. Gompers: The question is not germane to the subject under inquiry, and is not necessary.

Chairman Walsh: I would like to hear it answered if possible, Mr. Gompers. If it is not possible for any reason, very well.

Mr. Gompers: May I hear the question read?

(Question read.)

Mr. Gompers: The Socialist Party proposition—socialism is a proposition to place the working people of the country and of the world in a physical material strait-jacket.

Mr. Hillquit: Pardon me, Mr. Gompers, I have not asked your opinion about what you consider to be the tendencies of the cooperative commonwealth. I am speaking merely about the aim to abolish the wage system and the program to secure to the workers the full product of their labor; and I am asking you, in this respect, whether we demand more than the American Federation has ultimately in view.

Mr. Gompers: I think you demand something to which the American Labor movement declines to give its adherence.

Mr. Hillquit: Then do I understand you to say that the American labor movement would countenance the abolition of the wage system and the return of the full reward of labor to the workers?

Mr. Gompers: Your question is an assumption and is unwarranted, for as a matter of fact we decline to commit our labor movement to your species of speculative philosophy.

Mr. Hillquit: I have not introduced speculative philosophy, Mr. Gompers. If I can not make myself clear, please tell me so.

Chairman Walsh: May I be permitted here to ask the stenographer to read that last question?

Mr. Hillquit: Certainly, Mr. Chairman.

(The question read as follows:) "I am speaking merely about the aim to abolish the wage system, and about the program to secure to the workers the full product of their labor, and I am asking in this respect whether we demand more than the American Federation of Labor has ultimately in view?"

Chairman Walsh: That is with reference to getting the full product of labor alone?

Mr. Hillquit: Yes.

Chairman Walsh: Now, can you answer that directly, Mr. Gompers?

Mr. Gompers: No; that is impossible to answer yes or no. . . .

---

[20]

THE GREAT STEEL STRIKE AND ITS LESSONS

WILLIAM Z. FOSTER

FOR those progressives who will look upon the steel campaign from an evolutionary standpoint—that is by a comparison with past experiences—it will stand out in its true light as marking a great advance in trade-union methods and practices. It is true that the unions in the campaign made many mistakes, quarreled seriously among themselves, and put forth only a fraction of their real strength; but when one considers that they substituted a group of twenty-four unions for individual action in other campaigns; established a standard initiation fee instead of the multitude that existed be-

SOURCE: William Z. Foster, *The Great Steel Strike and Its Lessons* (New York: B. W. Huebsch, Inc., 1920), pp. 255–265. © 1920 by B. W. Huebsch, Inc. All Rights Reserved. Reprinted by permission of The Viking Press, Inc.

fore; adopted modern methods of organizing in place of the antiquated system previously prevailing; organized a joint commissariat, carried on a successful organizing campaign and waged a great strike together, one must admit that a tremendous stride forward has been made. The conclusion is bound to be optimistic and full of enthusiasm for the future.

But unfortunately there are large bodies of progressives who do not judge from the evolutionary viewpoint when it comes to trade unionism. These range all the way from the mildest liberals and friends of Labor to the most extreme I. W. W.'s. They form an influential group. Theirs is the idealistic method; more or less clearly, these elements hold in their mind's eye a smooth-running, intelligent, imaginary "one big union." This they use as an inelastic criterion by which to judge the trade unions. And the natural result is that, even in such cases as the steel campaign, the unions cut a sorry figure. Their weaknesses are unduly emphasized; their progressive innovations lose their import and seem but makeshift imitations of the real thing. The conclusions are necessarily pessimistic. The true significance of the epoch-making movement is lost. This viewpoint is so general and its consequences so far-reaching and detrimental, not only to the steel unions but to the whole labor movement, that perhaps a discussion of it may not be amiss at this point.

For many years radicals in this country have almost universally maintained that the trade unions are fundamentally non-revolutionary; that they have no real quarrel with capitalism, but are seeking merely to modify its harshness through a policy of mild reform. They have been pictured as lacking both the intelligence to want industrial freedom and the courage to demand it. And so often have these ideas been repeated, so slight has been the inquiry into their soundness, that they have come to be accepted in a large degree by virtually the entire left wing of the labor movement. To these ideas, more than anything else, is due the current idealistic labor pessimism, the unsympathetic attitude toward, and general lack of understanding of the trade unions.

Yet their falsity is readily apparent when one takes into consideration the real situation. It is an indisputable fact that the trade unions always act upon the policy of taking all they can get from their exploiters. They even overreach themselves sometimes, as a thousand lost strikes eloquently testify. Their program is directly anti-capitalistic. But let me quote from a booklet, written by myself several years ago, entitled, "Trade Unionism; The Road To Freedom," page 18:

It is idle to say that the trade unions will rest content with anything short of actual emancipation. For they are as insatiable as the veriest so-called revolu-

166

tionary unions. In the measure that their strength increases, so do their demands. They have sent wages up: 2, 3, 4, 5, 6, 7, 8 dollars per day, and hours down: 12, 11, 10, 9, 8, 7, 6, per day with all kinds of other concessions sandwiched in between. And now they are more radical in their demands than ever before in their history. Permanently satisfied trade unions under capitalism would be the eighth wonder of the world, outrivalling in interest the famous hanging gardens of Babylon. They would be impossible. With its growing power, Organized Labor will go on winning greater and greater concessions, regardless of how profound they may be. It is purest assumption to state that the trade unions would balk at ending the wages system.

So far as the tendency of their demands is concerned, there can be no question about that to anyone who will look at them squarely; the trade unions may be depended upon always to check exploitation through the wages system as far as their power enables them. The big question is whether or not they will be able to develop enough power to stop this exploitation altogether. As for me, I am confident that they will. In every country they are constantly adding to and solidifying their ranks; building ever more gigantic and militant combinations and throwing them athwart the exploiter's path. It is safe to say that if they cannot finally stop him it will be because it does not lie within the realms of possibility for the working class to produce a sufficiently powerful organization.

Why, then, have these strongly anti-capitalistic qualities been so long and generally ignored and the trade unions considered merely as palliative bodies? In my opinion it is because they, like various other aggressive social movements, have more or less instinctively surrounded themselves with a sort of camouflage or protective coloring, designed to disguise the movement and thus to pacify and disarm the opposition. This is the function of such expressions as "A fair day's pay for a fair day's work," "The interests of Capital and Labor are identical," etc. In actual practice little or no attention is paid to them. They are for foreign consumption. The fact that those who utter them may actually believe what they say does not change the situation a particle. Most movements are blind to their own goals anyway. The important thing is the real trend of the movement, which is indisputably as I have stated above, on the one hand constantly expanding organization, and on the other constantly increasing demands. The trade unions will not *become* anti-capitalistic through the conversion of their members to a certain point of view or by the adoption of certain preambles; they *are* that by their very makeup and methods. The most that can be done is to clarify their aims and intensify their efforts towards freedom.

If the trade unions instinctively throw dust in the eyes of their enemies, they do it for an altogether worthy purpose, the elevation of the standard of well-being for the mass of the people. In the case of the capitalist class we see the same principle applied to an utterly vicious end. The whole trend of the great employing interests is to set up an oligarchy of wealthy parasites, neither toiling nor spinning, yet for whom the whole body of workers would be compelled to labor in degradation and poverty. And if unopposed, they would not only bring about this condition, but in so doing would rob the people of every right they have—free speech, free press, free assemblage, legislative representation, trial by jury, and all the rest. But do they openly avow their purpose? Most assuredly not, for they know that powerful though they are they would be swept away by a wave of popular opposition. Therefore, through their newspapers and innumerable other propaganda agencies, they proceed to cover up their nefarious schemes of exploitation and oppression with hypocritical cloaks of patriotism, religion, benevolence, and the like. Their practice is one thing, their preaching something entirely different. Thus we have Garys and Rockefellers actually enslaving their workers by the most brutal methods and at the same time seeking to convince the public that what they are trying to do is to protect these workers from union domination, to preserve to them their sacred right to work for whomever they please, etc. Men such as these are knifing America and doing it in the name of 100 percent Americanism. They are social camouflagers par excellence.

The question may be pertinently asked, why, if camouflage is such a potent weapon in social as well as military warfare, should the true nature and tendency of the trade unions be pointed out, thus stripping the movement of its philosophic protection and leaving it bare before its enemies? The answer is that the camouflage works both ways; it deceives friends as well as enemies. It has thus to a great extent cost the unions the support of the whole left wing of the labor movement. Its advantages are outweighed by its disadvantages.

In what I have called the left wing of the movement there are large and ever-increasing numbers of workers and sympathizers who refuse to face the prospect of a society forever based upon the wage system. They demand an organization that is making for its abolition and the substitution therefore of a system of industrial justice. If they were to look sharply, they would see that the trade-union movement is traveling faster than any other body toward the end they wish to reach. But unfortunately, looking sharply is not their method. They habitually attach too much importance to surface indications and not enough to real results. They go almost entirely by preambles and manifestoes. Consequently, taking the trade-union slogans at their face value and finding them altogether unsatisfactory, they turn their backs upon the trade-union movement and give support to the organizations which have the sort they want, the I. W. W., the W. I. I. U., etc.

This belief, that the trade unions are inherently conservative bodies, is the basis of the strong conviction that they are hopeless and that they must be supplanted by a new organization, aiming to abolish the wage system. The conception is found in some degree or other among virtually all radicals. And it has done incalculable harm to the unions. It has cost them the support of thousands of militants, of the best and most intelligent that the working class produces. These might have done a wonderful work; but their time and energies have been worse than wasted in trying to build up organizations such as the I. W. W. When one considers that the life of nearly every labor union depends upon the activities of a very small fraction of its membership, it is clear that this constant drain upon its best blood must have seriously hindered the advance of the trade-union movement. Many have complained at the slow progress it has made; but the marvel is rather that it has been able to progress at all.

This devitalizing drain must be stopped, and the great body of progressives and radicals won over to a whole-hearted support of the trade unions. I consider this one of the most important tasks confronting the labor movement. But it can be accomplished only by driving home to these elements the patent facts that the trade unions are making straight for the abolition of capitalism and that they are going incomparably faster towards this goal than any of the much advertized, so-called revolutionary unions, in spite of the latter's glittering preambles. They must be taught that the weaknesses of the trade unions are but the weaknesses of the working class, and that as the latter gradually improves in education and experience, the unions will correspondingly take on higher forms and clearer aims. You cannot have perfect organizations with imperfect workers to build upon. In a word, the progressives must be won over from the idealistic and utopian to the evolutionary point of view.

Indeed, it must be granted that insistence upon the real goal and tendency of trade unionism will provoke the capitalist class into greater opposition against the movement. But this will be trebly offset by the added support which the unions will get from the large numbers of militants who now stand apart from them because of lack of understanding. The power of even a few such men, proceeding intelligently along practical lines, is one of the marvels of the labor movement. It may be confidently expected, therefore, that when the many thousands of these, now indifferent or hostile, begin to work together, setting up their own press and systematically furthering amalgamation and federation projects to bring the unions into closer cooperation, initiating and prosecuting organizing campaigns, retiring to private life such officials as now find themselves at the head of the Amalgamated Association, etc., vast changes for the better are bound to occur in the labor movement.

The trade unions have cost the workers untold efforts to build, and in the main they seem loath to give them up, despite the blandishments of utopian dual unions. Apparently, it is through the old unions that the workers will eventually achieve their industrial freedom, save, perhaps, in such cases as the United Garment Workers, where conditions in the organization were so utterly hopeless that there was nothing to do but form a new body, the Amalgamated Clothing Workers. But this was an exceptional case. Most of the unions are moving steadily onward and upward, and they have an unshakable grip upon the workers in their respective spheres. This being so, the logical thing to do is systematically to set about improving and strengthening them. If this is done, then, instead of the wild, desperate, dualistic outbreaks and strikes, which have characterized the American labor movement for years, and done it incalculable harm, the discontented rank and file will find relief through an orderly and rapid progress within the folds of the organizations they already have. The sooner these facts are recognized the better for American Labor.

During the past few years much has been said about the wonderful progress being made by the English trade-union movement. This, I venture to assert, is due largely, if not altogether, to the absence among the radicals of England of the idealistic, dualistic attitude toward the unions which exists so widely here, and which has produced the I. W. W. and its great body of sympathizers. The English radicals have a better conception than ours of the trade unions; for, flesh and blood of the labor movement, they pit their policies and energies against the conservatives, and win. They are the ones who are writing the highly-praised programs, and driving onward the great wage movements. They are practical and constructive. Unlike so many of our radicals they do not waste their time and strength in empty, pessimistic criticism of the trade unions, and in vain, foolhardy attempts to tear the whole labor structure to pieces and to reconstruct it according to the dream of Daniel De Leon.

In England the turning point came ten years ago when she felt the great wave of sentiment for revolutionary unionism then sweeping the world. The question was whether this movement should realize its aims through the old unions or by starting new ones. The existing unions were notoriously conservative. Several of our leading radicals had said they were even more hopeless than our own organizations and strongly urged the formation of an English I. W. W. But fortunately, Tom Mann and his colleagues, with a deeper knowledge of trade unionism, were able to forestall this movement and to direct the strong stream of progressive thought and energy into the old unions. The result was magical. Within two years the great and successful strikes of the transport workers, railroaders and miners had occurred, and the renaissance of the English labor movement was assured. British workingmen will never realize the invaluable service which Tom Mann rendered them in saving England from an I. W. W. dual movement, with its tremendous waste of power and its weakening effect upon the trade unions.

How long are American progressives going to continue deceiving themselves with the words of high-sounding preambles? When are they going to quit chasing rainbows and settle down to real work? These are important considerations indeed. The hour when our militants generally adopt English methods, and turn their whole-hearted attention to building up and developing the trade-union movement,—that hour will be the dawn of a new day for American Labor.

---

[21]

PALM SUNDAY IN THE COAL FIELDS

MICHAEL GOLD

EXCEPT for attending a meeting of the Central Labor Union in Pittsburgh, and drinking, in a barroom decorated with the Soviet arms, seidels of a wonderful drink that really tasted like beer, smelt like it, and had all the other ancient virtues of beer, I saw little of the labor soul of the city —that soul which is present in every city in every nation on the globe— (though outsiders never see it and come away depressed).

Two and a half hours outside of Pittsburgh, however, I at last found myself in the heart of the great coal strike.

SOURCE: Michael Gold, "Palm Sunday in the Coal Fields," *The Liberator* 5, no. 5 (May 1922): 5–9.

I had wandered into Brownsville, a town of 10,000 inhabitants, which is the center of the coke industry and of the coal mines that feed this industry.

They were talking steel here, I found. . . . All of the coke used in the steel mills about Pittsburgh comes from the Brownsville and Connellsville fields. They are probably the most important coal fields in America for that reason, and for the past thirty years Frick and his fellow-Christians had seen that no union got a foothold here, using the blacklist, the blackjack, the assassin's revolver and other New Testament methods of persuasion to accomplish this. There had been no union held here since Frick and his comrades in Christ had shot the Knights of Labor out of existence in 1894.

Everyone, bosses and union officials alike, had imagined that this region would forever be the peaceful home of starvation wages, the open shop, and deputy-sheriff Americanism. Secretary Hoover had depended on this, too, and he had cheered the coal barons by announcing at the opening of the miners' strike that there was a surplus of four months' coal supply on hand, and that the miners would be starved into submission at the end of that time. Hoover had reasoned, in his New Republican way, that the Brownsville region would go on scabbing, as in the past. But a great miracle had happened. There had been a wonderful spontaneous movement of the masses; 28,000 miners in this sector, and as many more in the Connellsville area, had joined the union; every day hundreds more were downing tools and joining the strike.

As a result, three big steel plants had already been forced to shut down for want of coke, the Pittsburgh papers said. Hoover's helpful little capitalistic estimate discouraged no one any longer; it was proven false as the complexion of a chorus girl, or the heart of a Wilson liberal; it was as dead, in the light of events, as a herring or Pharaoh's scented, mouldy mummy.

The strike in the non-union fields was like America's entry into the war; it spelt victory, sooner or later, for all the miners of the nation. By good fortune I had chanced into this region, the most important strategic point in the great fight that had begun on April 1st to save the miners' union from destruction.

Hundreds of miners in their Sunday clothes were lounging about Brownsville's main street as I came into the town. They were big, brawny, self-contained men, of all the races in the world, and they stood about on the sidewalks in the yellow sunlight of the warm spring afternoon, smoking, chewing, and talking in quiet tones of the strike.

The stores were all open, and women moved in and out of them, like bees to and from a comb. . . . Spring was in the air; there was in this town of lounging men the spring atmosphere of freedom, of holiday and of strange, unspoken unrest. Something silent and great was happening unseen beneath the mould of all the ploughed fields; and something was happening here. Grim-lipped big men walked up and down the sidewalks, with badges pinned on their coats, and police clubs swinging from their hands. They were keeping law and order. And the miners sat about the restaurants and the ice-cream parlors, and stood about the streets and thought and argued and talked to each other. Something great was happening.

The union hall was on the other side of the river, in an old murky frame building that had still the sign of a defunct co-operative store written across its face. In the long, dark hall on the first floor the organizers were seated at a table, conferring with the committee of men from different mines who poured in all the afternoon. They seemed to arrive from everywhere; one after another they announced the mines they came from, and as the names were repeated exultantly around the hall, one got the feeling as if the whole state of Pennsylvania was stopping work. It was a gay feeling.

"The crowd at the Lambert mine struck this morning," a huge, slow-moving American in blue overalls announced diffidently, almost as if he did not care. "The whole bunch is out; and I guess you'd better send us an organizer, and tell us how to get fixed for a local charter."

Then one of the organizers would take the name and location of the mine, and would arrange for a meeting the next afternoon. An international organizer for the United Mine Workers named William Feeney was in charge of the campaign in this section. He sat at the table near a dingy window, a frail, patient-looking man with a long Irish upper lip and friendly, blue Irish eyes, who moved calmly and deliberately about this business, and seemed like the executive of some big corporation in his quiet business suit, white collar and natty bow tie. I had heard about him before I had come here; Feeney, I was told, had been one of the most daring organizers in the steel strike; he was considered a little conservative in his views, but everyone agreed loudly that "Feeney had guts"; and everyone said that he was honest and loyal, and would fight all the chariots of hell for the miners' union, which was his religion and life.

The miners' union is the religion of every worker in this district. In New York one gets the illusion that the class struggle is an intellectual concept that one can argue about, take or let alone. In these mining districts it is a living reality, and one can no more dodge it than one can escape from the weather. The miners' union is part of the trees and the hills, the sky and the air of this landscape. It grew here, out of the needs and dangers of the miners' lives. They suffered and struggled, and then a union was formed; and through it they found some relief. They know that the union is their only defence; for forty years fathers have been handing down its precepts to their sons in this region, and no one questions that the union is necessary or unnecessary; it is there; it must be there, so long as the boss is there.

I talked to some of the other organizers who were helping Feeney in the work. One of them, Bill Henderson, a short, vigorous bantam of a man, compact as a mainspring, and with the alert light of a born fighter snapping in his eyes, told me about the meeting he had held yesterday at the Revere mine.

"I organized five hundred men up there," he said, his eyes burning. "It was the proudest moment of my life, too, and I'll tell you why. Thirty years ago my daddy was working in that mine, and he went out when the Knights of Labor called their big strike in '94. We lived in a tent up on the hillside, our family; I was only a wee boy, but I remember it all. I remember that we had mighty little to eat for a long time, and I remember my mother crying over us one night when she thought we were all asleep. And I remember that my daddy was blacklisted after the strike was lost, and how we wandered on from town to town till we found a place where they didn't know him. I tell you I was proud to go back there and organize those 500 men. I wish my daddy were alive; he'd have been proud, too."

The whole countryside was filled with stories of this Knights of Labor strike of thirty years ago. Everywhere I found miners who remembered it vividly, and who remembered all the other battles the region had been through. Other countrysides have their folklore and mythology, but in the nation of the miners there are only stories and histories of the wars for the union.

In the hall there was a lean, sombre-eyed miner in neat clothes, named Frank Gaynor, an American of Irish-Dutch descent and about forty-five years old. He looked as if he were a successful small-town merchant, but he was out on strike down at Roscoe, and had come here to volunteer in the work of organizing the non-union mines. He, too, told me some of the traditions of this region.

Gaynor's father had died when he was six years old, and at nine the boy went down into the mines to work with his grandfather, an ardent member of the Knights of Labor. His grandfather had been a miner since his own ninth year in this world, and could remember the days when there were no mule-carts or steam-cars in the mines, and the men had to transport the coal they had mined with wheelbarrows to the pit-mouth.

Gaynor was seventeen years old, and had graduated to pickwork when the big strike came in '94. This Monongahela Valley was aflame with it, and all around Brownsville meetings were held daily, the organizers walking from place to place because they had not the fare to ride. Most of the mines emptied their workers into the union, and in this section only Star Junction, or Stickle Hollow as it was then called, had not struck. Organizers were beaten up and chased out of the region there, and finally the miners decided to march on it en masse. These miners' parades are another tradition with them; the gesture of man instinctively militant and personally loyal to each other in an emergency. Five thousand men were in line that day, Gaynor said; some had walked ten and twelve miles to the assembling place; it was spring, and they were all hot and tired when they reached Stickle Hollow.

Suddenly, from behind a clump of bushes in the road near the mines, a band of deputy sheriffs fired on the peaceful, unsuspecting, unarmed regiment of miners. Seventeen of them were killed; many more wounded.

"It was awful to see our fellows lying there in their blood," said Gaynor; "good fellows, the best in the world. They were killed for daring to strike. I was young then, and the sight made a lifelong impression on me. It taught me a lesson I've never forgotten. No one has forgotten it around that region. The kids hear the story on their daddy's knee; they drink in its lesson with their mother's milk. The coal operators and their gunmen have been the best agitators for a union I know."

The coal operators were still continuing this form of agitation. The day previous there had been a miners' march through Masontown, a place about twelve miles from Brownsville. A squadron of members of the State Constabulary (Cossacks they are called by the workers of Pennsylvania) had suddenly appeared and ridden their horses full tilt into the parade. One miner had had his leg broken; about thirty others had been injured; there had been quite a lot of loyal union men made in the brief, uneven scuffle. . . .

I heard many other such stories. There are thousands of them; they are the reality of the labor movement; they are the reasons why thousands of Fourth of July speeches by corporation-owned Congressmen, tons of Americanization literature written by lecherous, booze-soaked press agents and paid for by murderous bosses, miles of editorials by prostitute newspapermen and oceans of oily lies flowing from the ministerial sewers can never divert Labor from the path on which its feet have been set by history.

Workingmen know the facts about the class struggle; the facts have been shot into them with gunmen's bullets, beaten into them with Cossacks' clubs; they remember these facts; and forget soon enough, thank God, the lessons American social service has tried to teach them.

In all the newspapers this great coal strike was now being discussed. Everyone knew the academic questions involved in the situation. The miners and the bosses had an agreement that expired on April 1st, when it was provided that they meet to make another wage agreement for the following two years. The operators had refused to renew the argument. They wanted to make local settlements in each of the separate districts. They wanted to abolish the check-off; they wanted to cut wages; they wanted other concessions.

That was the faint, far-off newspaper story millions of Americans read, half-understanding, half-irritated because the miners and the operators could not iron out these tiny quarrels that after all amounted to nothing.

But they amounted to everything in the world for these men in this Brownsville union headquarters. Here were the men who made the strike a reality. These miners "knew" the facts. Big, strong men in overalls, jumpers, flannel shirts, hob-nailed boots, men of ten or twelve races, Lithuanians, Poles, Italians, Austrians, Croatians, Slavs, Negroes, Welsh, Irish, British and Americans—bold men, men who faced death every day in the hot, dripping, airless mines; men with mutilated hands, powder-marked faces; these men had formed a union to get them a living wage for their wives and children, and to protect them against the gunman, the thug and the spy. They had fought for that union, and their fathers had fought before them. The union was their self-respect; it was their children's bread; and now the bosses were making a fierce new attempt to smash it.

I traveled about for several days with organizers in the non-union fields.

On Palm Sunday I went with Bill Henderson and a Pole and a Czecho–Slovak organizer to the mining camp of Bowood.

It was a warm, golden day, rich with spring odors and spring sunlight. In Masontown, where we left the car-line and got into a wild, young, untamed Ford for the five-mile ride inland, the churches were emptying, and miners and their women-folk dressed in their finest were moving leisurely up the main street. They were all carrying palms, the sacred palms with which the Jews hailed Jesus on that sunny, holy day when he passed through them on his ass on the way up to Jerusalem.

It was in Masontown, a few days before, that the state troopers had charged into the parade of miners, and had injured thirty of them. We saw one of the troopers resting his horse before a church and sitting quietly as if in meditation. He was a lusty young chap, with ruddy cheeks and broad shoulders and big muscles under his dark-green uniform; as fine an animal as the splendid horse he was straddling.

"The dirty Cossack!" the Polish organizer muttered, scowling darkly. "The damn trouble-maker; the damn murderer!"

Every labor man in the State of Pennsylvania hates the State troopers. These "Cossacks" are the most highly paid and best trained set of assassins of labor unionism in this wide country. They possess military efficiency—they crack heads skillfully, and trample women and children without a blunder in technique. Wherever they come they bring riot and death. They seem to love their jobs, these young men; it is more than the high pay that makes them work so hard; they enjoy being Cossacks, as some men enjoy war with its legalized rapine and slaughter.

A crowd of men and boys swarmed into the road as we galloped up in the Ford before the grocery and butcher store at Bowood, where the meeting was to be held. I sat around on the porch and waited while the organizers talked over matters with the local committee.

The miners gathering around were of the same type I had seen everywhere in this region—men of ten or twelve races, big, stalwart men with the blue tattoo marks of powder and rock on their faces, and with fingers missing and fingers gnarled and twisted on their hands.

A small group of American miners was looking at a cartoon in a Philadelphia newspaper. It was the usual "non-partisan" thing that newspapers are so fond of printing in big strikes. It was called "Passing the Buck," and showed the Coal Operators, the Banker, the Railroads, and the Coal Miner passing the buck of high coal prices to each other, while a figure dressed like Uncle Sam, and marked "The Public," was standing beside a tiny heap of coal, scratching his head in bewilderment.

The miners sneered at this cartoon in their quiet way. "I'd like to meet this guy Public sometime," drawled a tall young chap; "I'd jest like to kick his backside and see whether he's real enough to feel it."

A huge Hungarian miner with a flat nose, high cheekbones, and a chest like the bulge of a stove, was busy at another spot on the porch, explaining his views of life, liberty and happiness to a squat, brawny Austrian with a thin, long moustache like a Mongol's, who was sucking his pipe and listening, his derby back on his head.

The Hungarian was in roaring good spirits. He was dressed in a clean white shirt, collarless and coatless, and his beady little eyes beamed with delight.

"Me strike, sure!" he shouted, thumping himself on the chest with a fist hard and round as a sledge. "Me strike twelve times in last two years—me like strikes. Me strike in Mesaba range with I. W. W.—me strike with anyone. I say to the boys, Ah, g'wan and strike! Me live once under blanket in winter with my children—for strike! G'wan, boys, it's summer now—me say—put up tent in fields, go fishing, strike! The bosses are all no good! The bosses in our mine bought big searchlight—cost two million dollar—what for? Me load forty tons a day, and the boss's gal she wears diamonds. What for?"

The mines in these non-union fields, some of them, had not been working for many months. I met on this porch a tall, self-possessed, middle-aged American miner, who spoke with a drawl, and who told me the most remarkable story I heard in this section. This man had ten children. And he had been out of work for the past fourteen months. On April 1st, when the union miners walked out, his mine opened up again, to scab on the rest of the country. The mine was soon rushed with orders.

This man and his comrades put in about a week's work, and then they walked out on strike.

I will repeat this statement.

The man and his comrades put in a week's work, and then they walked out on strike. After fourteen months of idleness. For the sake of a union. Ten children. Middle-aged and worn-looking; sad, brown, loyal, friendly eyes; square jaw, long nose, lanky figure in blue overalls, a torn black jacket, broken shoes. For the sake of a just cause.

"The whole family of us jest lived out in a tent all last summer," he said. "My ole woman's game, though it's hard on her, more th'n me. Yes, I've been blacklisted in a few places, that's what made it hard to connect up elsewhere. No, none of my kids was big enough to get into the army. I'd 'a' larruped them with a rawhide if they did—we'll do all our fighting right here in Fayette County—there's enough to go round. I fought a detective once—he put me into the hospital for five weeks, but say, he was laid up for nine! And once I saw the State Cossacks ride their horses over a bunch of miners' kids that got in their way. Yes, I seen it; I seen them bleeding and crying. I'll do my fighting at home."

The meeting was held in the back yard. Henderson and the other two organizers stood on the steps leading up to the house, and the crowd of men and boys filled the yard. The soft wind was blowing. The smell of grass in the sun was everywhere. A little dog ran about the edges of the crowd and whined for attention. A rooster crowed; there was a cow chewing patiently on the grass of the next field. Bill Henderson's militant words rang out like shot in this sylvan place, and the crowd pressed up and drank in every syllable. It was a proletarian holiday.

When Henderson called all who wanted to join the union to raise their hands, every hand went up, and every voice joined in the solemn oath which miners take when initiated into their union, an oath never to scab, never to betray a brother, never to desert.

I heard the oath repeated by about four thousand other miners later in the afternoon at Uniontown, where Bill Feeney and others spoke. It was thrilling to hear this mob of strong men repeat in deep, manly voices after him the litany and vow, sacred as the vow of the Athenian citizens, that symbolizes the miners' attitude toward their union.

There had been not a single union meeting held in Uniontown for thirty years, I was told; this meeting was a red page in the miners' history. I asked why it was that the non-union men were flocking so unanimously into the union now. The reason was simple. In the non-union fields Frick and the other operators were paying one-third of the wages paid in the other fields, under the union contract. The non-union miners had been starving on the job; they had no redress against bad supers and pit bosses; for years the operators had been teaching them the value of a union, and they had at last learned the bitter lesson.

The half million miners of the nation are not striking for any big positive end at the present moment; they are fighting to keep the union intact. It is the most serious fight they have ever been in; yet they are only on the defensive, in a negative position. They have no choice in the matter; but some day, when conditions are not stacked so badly against them, they are going to strike for bigger and more constructive ends. They are going to strike for nationalization of the mines, and control of production, slack work, technical improvements, wages, bosses and other matters by the miners themselves. They are going to strike for the ownership of their mines—of the mines where they live the greater part of their lives, where they mine coal.

John Brophy, president of District No. 2 of the United Mine Workers, is the leading spokesman for this larger program of the miners' union. In the Brownsville district, I found many miners who knew about this program, and were solidly behind it.

One was a lively, slangy, happy, scrappy young miner named Delbarre, an artist in living dressed in a battered derby hat, a ragged dingy suit, and a flannel shirt. Delbarre is president of the council of all the Brownsville unions; he stumps about on a wooden leg, and is called "Peggy" by everyone. Peggy Delbarre is one of the "radicals" in this district, but he is not the talky radical we know around New York. He has been a leader in all the union movements in this district; and he is simple, honest, unambitious and popular. And he works.

He has a rich sense of humor. "Say, kid," he answered with his wide, homely grin when I asked how long he had been a miner, "say, guy, I was a miner when I was a spermatozoa playing around in my daddy's insides. It's in my blood."

I went with Peggy Delbarre, Frank Gaynor, and a breezy, slangy young American miner, Louis Seignor, who was the son of Polish immigrants and spoke both languages fluently, on a long auto ride one day to Fairchance, where the men of seven or eight mines had walked out and were waiting to be formed into locals.

Peggy was a volunteer organizer, and so were the other two men in the car. On the ride they told me of the preliminary work that had been done to get the men to strike in the non-union fields.

A committee of a hundred volunteers had been formed in Brownsville Labor Council, and these volunteers had taken the strike circulars into the non-union fields long before April 1st. They had tacked the circulars on walls and houses in the towns, they had distributed them to miners on the "man-trips" into the mines, they had talked and pleaded and argued. Some of them had been beaten up, and run off the company property, but they had won, anyway. Their work had probably saved the whole miners' union in this fight, for, as I have said, these non-union fields are probably the most important strategic points in the whole country. And they had brought the strike here; it is the work of such rank-and-filers, unrecorded and unrewarded, that maintains the labor organizations of this country.

Our first meeting was at Fairchance. Five or six hundred miners were waiting in the road near the general store as we drove up. It was another beautiful spring day.

We met in a small stuffy hall, the floor of which seemed to bend under the strain of this unusual mass. The miners stood with bare heads, and listened while Peggy Delbarre made his speech. He told them about the strike; he told them what the Mine Workers' Union stood for; he warned them against using violence; he gave a few practical lessons in organization.

"And don't forget we're all Americans. I'm an American, though both my parents were French. Forget what these hundred percenters try to tell you; they've got no monopoly on this country; they were only the first to steal it away from the Indians. Don't let racial differences stand in your way. Labor is a nation all its own, inside the other nation. Labor didn't get any nearer the last Republican and Democratic conventions than cleaning the spittoons, but that doesn't matter; we dig the coal for America, we're the real Americans; we keep the works going; we've got the real power."

180

He gave the men the union oath, and then they elected their president, secretary and treasurer. Louis Seinar spoke to them in Polish, and Gaynor made a fiery miners' speech full of deep, real passion.

We had tire trouble on the road, and were two hours late in reaching another meeting in Croatian Hall, on the outskirts of Uniontown. It was coming dusk, but the miners had waited patiently there; not one had lost his faith that the organizers would fail to appear. These miners, too, were organized, and given the oath to repeat.

"They're all jolly now; they feel as if they were going on a big picnic," said Peggy. "Later, when things get hard, there'll be a reaction, but most of 'em will stick anyway. That's what unions are good for; they teach the workers solidarity and discipline."

It was dark now. A few stars had lifted their silver faces to the world. The moon was appearing in the purple sky. We rushed up and down the steep roads, sharp as the inclines of a roller coaster at Coney Island. The wind beat against our faces, cool and laden with blossom perfume.

"Give her the gas," someone shouted, and the car leaped forward and hummed along with the roar of an aeroplane. Peggy sat at the wheel and laughed and sang. The dark masses of trees fled by like defeated ghosts. We caught the glimpse of immense bouquets of peach and cherry blossoms in the gloom. It was great to be moving, to be alive. We were going somewhere. Life was going somewhere. The American labor movement was going somewhere. This miners' strike would be won, and other strikes for greater ends would be won. Some day the miners would sit in the congress of workers that ruled America. Some day the men who were near to the sources of life, the men who were brave enough to make steel and mine coal, would be building a new civilization in America, a new art and culture, a new society. It would be a brave culture, a heroic culture for strong men and women, a culture near to the sources of life. It would move along in beauty under the stars, it would laugh and sing.

[22]

THE GRAND OFFENSIVE AGAINST THE WORKERS

JAY LOVESTONE

The Government's Labor Policy During the War

Our participation in the World War had a beneficial effect on the trade unions. In the course of the war the membership of the American Federation of Labor doubled. The railway unions especially made great gains. They won a foothold on many systems which had previously refused to deal with them. In this phenomenal rise the organizations of the unskilled workers grew at a particularly rapid pace. The membership of the United Brotherhood of Maintenance of Way Employees and Railway Shop Laborers rose to 325,000 in 1919. In 1920 the membership of the International Seamen's Union totalled 115,000. Many other industries that had previously successfully resisted unionization became strongly organized.

The Government recognized the utter impossibility of winning the war without an effective mobilization of the labor forces. This knowledge on the part of the Government was in a large measure responsible for many gains made by the unions. Formal invitation to assure the accomplishment of this task was extended by the Government to the Railway Brotherhoods, the American Federation of Labor and many other labor bodies. This policy of the National Government was clearly expressed by the War Labor Board:

> The right of workers to organize in trade unions and to bargain collectively thru chosen representatives is recognized and affirmed. This right shall not be denied, abridged, or interfered with by the employers in any manner whatsoever.

Speedy, unrestricted output in industry is today indispensable to a nation at war if it is to be saved from defeat. The Government found it easier to achieve this output by dealing with organized workers who were directed and controlled by a conservative or reactionary leadership than by

SOURCE: Jay Lovestone, *The Government—Strikebreaker: A Study of the Role of the Government in the Recent Industrial Crisis* (New York: Workers Party of America, 1923), pp. 9–16.

trusting to the undirected whims and wishes of a dissatisfied, unorganized mass of workers. The Government was compelled by the sheer necessity of avoiding disaster during the war, to adopt this policy towards the unions.

Besides, the successful prosecution of the war required *Burgfrieden*— class peace. When the United States entered the war the country was in the throes of great industrial unrest. In 1916 and 1917 there were reported by the Department of Labor 8,239 strikes and lockouts. The year 1917 was a record year of 4,324 strikes reported by the Department of Labor. Contentment at home is also a condition prerequisite for attaining the end to which the Government subdued everything else—victory in war. The Government was therefore compelled by political as well as economic conditions to adopt at least a seemingly non-hostile attitude towards the labor unions.

"Wait till the War Is Over"

The more conscious and far-sighted representatives of the capitalists, their political leaders and skilled diplomats saw in the working-class revolution in Russia and the flames of war a menace to the whole capitalist fabric of exploitation and oppression. These spokesmen of the employing class saw the need of subjecting everything else to the one end of a victory of Allied Imperialism—an end in which they could find their only hope for securing their system. In the interest of this greater aim, some ground was temporarily yielded to the workers.

But the American capitalists only grudgingly and resentfully attuned themselves to this condition. They were whetting their knives for more blood. In the powerful conclaves of Wealth and Privilege the slogan was: "Wait till the War Is Over." The capitalists were marshalling their forces for the "grand offensive" against the working class.

This campaign to crush the workers was somewhat delayed by the continuation of the war prosperity. But the capitalists lost no time. Their Government, their press, and their detective agencies were busily preparing the ground for a "fight to the finish."

The Reversion to Normalcy

The declaration of the Armistice was a signal for an intensified labor struggle in the United States. For two years following the cessation of hostilities, America grappled with the problems of readjusting its machinery of production and exchange to a peace basis. This readjustment has not yet been completed; if it ever will be.

By the fall of 1920 we were well on our way to a peace basis. And with the return to "normalcy" the economic crisis in which America found itself on the eve of the World War gripped the United States more deadly than ever. The great depression began in the latter months of 1920. The year 1921 was the worst the United States had known.

But the reversion to "normalcy" also brought with it the greatest industrial crisis in our history—the overwhelming strike wave in 1922. Never before had the country witnessed such bitter class conflicts. Textile workers, soft stonecutters, granite cutters, miners and railwaymen were the vanguard of the heroic army of resistance to the employers' wage-cutting and union-smashing offensive. Never before in our industrial history have there been such large numbers on strike and never before have the workers remained out for such long periods. Outwardly, these and the many other strikes appear only as disputes over wages or hours of labor. Fundamentally, the strikes of 1922 were far more significant. They were a revolt against the powerful campaign waged by the captains of finance and industry to uproot every vestige of working-class organization. The strikers fought these battles primarily to uphold these organizations which they had built up thru years of painful struggle.

The Government in Its True Role

Many workers maintain that the Government is the centralized, directing organ of capitalist oppression—the executive committee of the employing class. The history of the "grand offensive" against the workers, the great Open-Shop drive of 1920 completely bears out this truth. By means of its policy of repression in the Steel and Mine Strikes of 1919 and the vicious "Red Raids" of 1920 the Government prepared the ground for the country-wide attack on the working class.

In the Steel Strike troops were freely put at the disposal of the mill owners. Complete denial of the freedom of speech and assembly followed. Police brutality, Black Cossack terrorism, assaults and arrests were the order of the day. In the Pittsburgh district meetings were prohibited as soon as the organization campaign opened. The sheriff of Clairton ordered on September 21st that "there should not be any meetings of any kind anywhere." That the object of this campaign of terrorism was to break up the campaign of unionization was evident. Apropos of this situation the Department of Labor plainly said:

This denial of free speech and free assemblage had an undeniable influence on the strike. In Duquesne, for example, where meetings were prohibited, approximately 50 percent of the men were reported to be organized. In Cleveland and Lackawanna, where the men were allowed to meet, approximately 80 percent were reported to be organized and the mills practically closed down when the strike was called.

The victory achieved by the Steel Trust thru the aid of the Government lent great impetus to the Open-Shop drive. The policy of Gary's corporation "not to deal with union labor leaders at any time" became the battle-cry of the Open-Shop warriors.

In the Mine Strike the Government pursued the same strike-breaking policy. The Democratic President Wilson declared the strike illegal. On October 24, 1919, he said that:

From whatever angle the subject may be viewed, it is apparent that such a strike in such circumstances would be the most far-reaching plan ever presented in this country to limit the facilities of production and distribution of all the necessities of life. *A strike under these circumstances is not only unjustifiable; it is unlawful.* (Our italics.)

This declaration is a model anti-union statement. It has served as the source of inspiration to several of Harding's anti-labor messages.

The Democratic Attorney-General Palmer spoke almost the very words subsequently used by his Republican successor, Daugherty, during the Railroad strike. On October 29, 1919, Palmer declared:

The illegality of the strike can and will be established without in any way impairing the right to strike, and the general right to strike is not the issue in any sense whatsoever in the present situation. This is true because the circumstances differentiate this case from the case of any other strike that has ever taken place in this country. It does not follow that any strike is lawful merely because the right to strike is recognized to exist. (Our italics.)

In the same statement Palmer pretended to be solicitous of the laborer's inherent right to work and posed as a defender of the "right kind" of unionism. He announced:

Indeed, I am hearing from many sources that large numbers of the miners themselves do not wish to quit work and will not do so if assured the protection of the Government of which they properly feel themselves a part. It is probably unnecessary for me to say that such protection will everywhere be given, so that men may exercise their undoubted right of continuing to work under such times and conditions as they shall see fit. *The facts present a situation which challenges the supremacy of the law, and every resource of the Government will be brought to bear to prevent the national disaster which would inevitably result from the cessation of the mining operations.* (Our italics.)

Here we have an official endorsement of Government strikebreaking. We have the same hypocritical talk of the "right to work"—by strikebreakers—to the detriment of the working class. The unbridled hypocrisy of all this talk of the "right to work" yells for help when one thinks of the fact that this same Government did not utter a single word or take a single step towards guaranteeing this much-vaunted inherent right to the millions of honest workers who were unemployed in 1914 and who refused to betray their brother-workers who may have been striking then.

Our Democratic Congress was not to be outdone by the President and the Attorney-General. The Senate made haste to endorse their strikebreaking activities and adopted the following resolution (S. Con. Res. 15—House of Representatives concurring):

Whereas, the enforcement of the law and the maintenance of order for the security of life and property and the protection of the individual citizen in the exercise of the constitutional rights is the first and paramount duty of the Government and must be at all times vigorously and effectively safeguarded by the use of every means essential to that end: therefore be it

Resolved by the Senate (*the House of Representatives concurring*), That we hereby give the National Administration and all others in authority the assurance of our constant, continuous, and unqualified support in the use of such constitutional and lawful means as may be necessary to meet the present industrial emergency and in vindicating the majesty and power of the Government in enforcing obedience to and respect for the Constitution, and the laws, and in fully protecting every citizen in the maintenance and exercise of his lawful rights and the observance of his lawful obligations.

On November 8, 1919, the Government's lawyers, the Department of Justice, procured for the coal operators an injunction restraining the union officials from aiding the strike in any way by "messages of encouragement or exhortation," or from using any of the union funds for strike benefits. This injunction was based on the Lever Anti-Profiteering Act, a law enacted supposedly to stop profiteering while the war was on. This law was not used against the capitalists. It was turned against the workers. On November 14, 1919, came the declaration of the reactionary labor leaders calling off the strike under the plea of "we won't fight our Government." This confession of bankruptcy was a grim monument to the power of the United States Government as strikebreaker.

The Government Organizes Wholesale Raids on Workers

Thru the "Red Raids" of January 1920, the Government threw its last spadeful of earth in preparing the ground for the subsequent powerful Open-Shop drive. Thousands of militant workers were arrested. Hundreds were deported. The attack was launched against the foreign-born workers who form a very large proportion of our working class. In this attack the Communist Party of America was driven underground and the Government succeeded in intimidating hundreds of thousands of foreign-born workers. The industrial unrest gripping the country was given a Red tinge. "Un-Americanism," "disloyalty," "treason" and "bolshevism" were the stock-in-trade of the Government's fake advertising campaign of the Open-Shop drive. The object was twofold: to blind and divide the workers by injecting the nationality issue into the struggle, and to break the morale of the whole working class by meting out severe punishment to its most advanced advocates. By a campaign of unparalleled brutality the militant spirit of the workers was dealt a crushing blow. The ground was fully prepared for the heavy artillery of the employers to open up its infernal barrage on the workers.

PART IX
The Literary
Class Struggle

A year after Wall Street's crash, Michael Gold (see Document 21) tried to open the literary veins of Thornton Wilder (Document 23). As Edmund Wilson later reported, this attack made it "plain that the economic crisis is to be accompanied by a literary one." [1] Gold's attempt to devastate Wilder was more than pique or even literary disagreement; it was an ideological struggle between Communist and liberal theories and practice of literature. The *New Republic,* where Gold's attack occurred, was deluged by letters from readers, was itself moved to comment editorially (on Gold's side), and finally had to refuse further space to the controversy. The ensuing debate throughout literary America centered around crucial moral, intellectual, and political confusion: what is the relationship of the writer and intellectual to the working class? What is proletarian literature? Where and how does creative fiction fit into the political struggle? Can middle-class authors write working-class novels, poetry, plays, movies, journalism? These questions were not unique to the thirties, but this decade was especially agitated by them.

In the middle of the decade, on 26 April 1935, in the Mecca Temple of New York City, a congress of American writers convened in order to defend culture against fascism. Over 200 writers were delegates, a somewhat smaller number were guests, including writers from Mexico, Cuba, Germany, and Japan. Four thousand spectators filled the hall. The leading radical authors of the country delivered formal papers and participated in discussions (Document 24). The heart of this congress was contained in re-

[1] Edmund Wilson, "The Literary Class War," 4 May 1932, in *The Shores of Light* (New York: Noonday, 1952), p. 539.

marks by Josephine Herbst, a novelist of the Left: "It would be a very dark world today were it not for the hope reposing in the working class. This is a marvelous time in which to be alive. It is immeasurably better than 1890, when literature was devoted to *trivia*. Today we have everything *but* triviality to write about." [2] The discussions at this first congress covered the usual questions with great intensity. Richard Wright, then a young black writer who had not yet established himself, spoke briefly of the special isolation of the black writer, and of the special need for better black history. Waldo Frank (b. 1889) was elected to head the League of American Writers that was organized by this congress, and his extemporaneous address to the delegates closed this unique meeting.

Also in 1935 an anthology of proletarian literature was published with an introduction (Document 25) by Joseph Freeman (1897–1965). Freeman was one of the leading literary radicals in the nation, a founder of the *New Masses* in 1926, a correspondent for Tass for five years, and helped to found the *Partisan Review*. He wrote a brilliant and significant autobiography, *An American Testament* (1936), which offended the Soviets, and for which he was read out of the American Communist Party. In the following essay, Freeman argued that art was an instrument of the class struggle; that the class affiliation of authors necessarily constituted a perceptual grid which defined their realities; and that no felt experience, especially proletarian experience, was intrinsically alien to art. His analysis of liberal literary criticism was particularly successful.

James T. Farrell (b. 1904), who had already published the *Studs Lonigan* trilogy (1932, 1934, 1935), formally joined the debate in 1936 with a full-length book, *A Note on Literary Criticism* (part of the concluding chapter follows as Document 26). Farrell was solidly of the Left, both politically and literarily, and yet he was concerned that throwing literature into the service of politics in too mechanical and formalistic a fashion might damage both. His special enemy on the left was rigid leftism, and the following sensible plea for flexibility, for a sustaining life behind the "revolutionary cultural movement," was his personal attempt to find a way through the already knotted ideological maze that threatened to trap even the most dedicated revolutionary artists.

Finally, the *Partisan Review*'s editorial statement of 1937 (Document 27) shows that political factionalizing had to create literary counterparts. The editorial statement of the very first issue of this magazine, with its promise to avoid sectarianism, should now be kept in mind:

[2] Reported in Henry Hart, ed., *American Writers' Congress* (New York, 1935), p. 15.

We propose to concentrate on creative and critical literature, but we shall maintain a definite viewpoint—that of the revolutionary working class. Through our specific literary medium we shall participate in the struggle of the workers and sincere intellectuals against imperialist war, fascism, national and racial oppression, and for the abolition of the system which breeds these evils. The defense of the Soviet Union is one of our principal tasks.

We shall combat not only the decadent culture of the exploiting classes but also the debilitating liberalism which at times seeps into our writers through the pressure of class-alien forces. Nor shall we forget to keep our own house in order. We shall resist every attempt to cripple our literature by narrow-minded, sectarian theories and practices.[3]

The 1937 statement closes the literary class struggle, at least in the sense that now the war was fought mostly within the Left itself. Now the *Partisan Review* dissociated from the Communist Party, declared itself opposed to the Communist Left, and received payment in vitriolic kind. *Partisan Review*'s search for a literature independent of organized politics presaged an impassable crack in the bridge between art and organized struggle. The decade closed, in this regard, approximately where it had opened, and the long, sometimes rigorous, sometimes helpful, sometimes arid discussion about the political role of the intellectual, it seemed, might never have taken place.

---

[23]

WILDER: PROPHET OF THE GENTEEL CHRIST

MICHAEL GOLD

HERE'S a group of people losing sleep over a host of notions that the rest of the world has outgrown several centuries ago: one duchess's right to enter a door before another; the word order in a dogma of the Church; the divine right of Kings, especially of Bourbons."

[3] *Partisan Review* 1, no. 1 (February–March 1934), p. 2.
SOURCE: Michael Gold, "Wilder: Prophet of the Genteel Christ," *New Republic* 64 (22 October 1930): 266–267. Reprinted by permission of *The New Republic,* © 1930 (Renewed 1958) Harrison-Blaine of New Jersey, Inc.

In these words Thornton Wilder describes the people in his first book, *The Cabala*. They are some eccentric old aristocrats in Rome, seen through the eyes of a typical American art "pansy" who is there as a student.

Marcantonio is the sixteen-year-old son of one of the group; he is burned out with sex and idleness, and sexualizes with his sister, and then commits suicide. Another character is a beautiful, mad princess, who hates her dull Italian husband, falls in love with many Nordics and is regularly rejected by them. Others are a moldy old aristocrat woman who "believes," and a moldy old Cardinal who doesn't, and some other fine worm-eaten authentic specimens of the rare old Italian antique.

Wilder views these people with tender irony. He makes no claim as to their usefulness to the world that feeds them; yet he hints that their palace mustiness is a most important fact in the world of today. He writes with a brooding seriousness of them as if all the gods were watching their little lavender tragedies. The style is a diluted Henry James.

Wilder's second novel was *The Bridge of San Luis Rey*. This famous and vastly popular yarn made a bold leap backward in time. Mr. Wilder, by then, had evidently completed his appraisal of our own age. The scene is laid in Lima, Peru; the time is Friday noon, July 20, 1714. In this volume Wilder perfected the style which is now probably permanent with him; the diluted and veritable Anatole France.

Among the characters of San Luis Rey are: (1) A sweet old duchess who loves her grown daughter to madness, but is not loved in return; (2) A beautiful unfortunate genius of an actress who after much sexualizing turns nun; (3) Her tutor, a jolly old rogue, but a true worshipper of literature; (4) Two strange brothers who love each other with a passion and delicacy that again brings the homosexual bouquet into a Wilder book, and a few other minor sufferers.

Some of the characters in this novel die in the fall of a bridge. Our author points out the spiritual lessons imbedded in this Accident; viz.: that God is Love.

The third novel is the recent *The Woman of Andros*. This marks a still further masterly retreat into time and space. The scene is one of the lesser Greek islands, the hour somewhere in B.C.

The fable: a group of young Greeks spend their evenings in alternate sexual bouts and lofty Attic conversations with the last of the Aspasias. One young man falls in love with her sister, who is "pure." His father objects. Fortunately, the Aspasia dies. The father relents. But then the sister dies, too. Wistful futility and sweet soft sadness of Life. Hints of the coming of Christ: "and in the East the stars shone tranquilly down upon the land that was soon to be called Holy and that even then was preparing its precious burden." (Palestine.)

Then Mr. Wilder has published some pretty, tinkling, little three-minute playlets. These are on the most erudite and esoteric themes one could ever imagine; all about Angels, and Mozart, and King Louis, and Fairies, and a Girl of the Renaissance, and a whimsical old Actress (1780) and her old Lover; Childe Harold to the Dark Tower Came; Proserpine and the Devil; The Flight into Egypt; a Venetian Prince and a Mermaid; Shelley, Judgment Day, Centaurs, God, The Woman in the Chlamys, Christ; Brigomeide, Leviathan, Ibsen; every waxwork in Wells's Outline, in fact, except Buffalo Bill.

And this, to date, is the garden cultivated by Mr. Thornton Wilder. It is a museum, it is not a world. In this devitalized air move the wan ghosts he has called up, each in "romantic" costume. It is an historic junkshop over which our author presides.

Here one will not find the heroic archaeology of a Walter Scott or Eugene Sue. Those men had social passions, and used the past as a weapon to affect the present and future. Scott was the poet of feudalism. The past was a glorious myth he created to influence the bourgeois anti-feudal present. Eugene Sue was the poet of the proletariat. On every page of history he traced the bitter, neglected facts of the working-class martyrdom. He wove these into an epic melodrama to strengthen the heart and hand of the revolutionary workers, to inspire them with a proud consciousness of their historic mission.

That is how the past should be used; as a rich manure, as a springboard, as a battle cry, as a deepening, clarifying and sublimation of the struggles in the too-immediate present. But Mr. Wilder is the poet of the genteel bourgeoisie. They fear any such disturbing lessons out of the past. Their goal is comfort and status quo. Hence, the vapidity of these little readings in history.

Mr. Wilder, in a foreword to his book of little plays, tells himself and us the object of his esthetic striving:

"I hope," he says, "through many mistakes, to discover that spirit that is not unequal to the elevation of the great religious themes, yet which does not fall into a repellent didacticism. Didacticism is an attempt at the coercion of another's free mind, even though one knows that in these matters beyond logic, beauty is the only persuasion. Here the schoolmaster enters again. He sees all that is fairest in the Christian tradition made repugnant to the new generations by reason of the diction in which it is expressed.

. . . So that the revival of religion is almost a matter of rhetoric. The work is difficult, perhaps impossible (perhaps all religions die out with the exhaustion of the language), but it at least reminds us that Our Lord asked us in His work to be not only gentle as doves, but as wise as serpents."

Mr. Wilder wishes to restore, he says, through Beauty and Rhetoric, the Spirit of Religion in American Literature. One can respect any writer in America who sets himself a goal higher than the usual racketeering. But what is this religious spirit Mr. Wilder aims to restore? Is it the crude self-torture of the Holy Rollers, or the brimstone howls and fears of the Baptists, or even the mad, titanic sincerities and delusions of a Tolstoy or Dostoievsky?

No, it is that newly fashionable literary religion that centers around Jesus Christ, the First British Gentleman. It is a pastel, pastiche, dilettante religion, without the true neurotic blood and fire, a daydream of homosexual figures in graceful gowns moving archaically among the lilies. It is Anglo-Catholicism, that last refuge of the American Literary snob.

This genteel spirit of the new parlor-Christianity pervades every phrase of Mr. Wilder's rhetoric. What gentle theatrical sighs! what lovely, well-composed deaths and martyrdoms! what languishings and flutterings of God's sinning doves! what little jewels of Sunday-school wisdom, distributed modestly here and there through the softly flowing narrative like delicate pearls, diamonds and rubies on the costume of a meek, wronged princess gracefully drowning herself for love (if my image is clear).

Wilder has concocted a synthesis of all the chambermaid literature, Sunday-school tracts and boulevard piety there ever were. He has added a dash of the prep-school teacher's erudition, then embalmed all this in the speciously glamorous style of the late Anatole France. He talks much of art, of himself as Artist, of style. He is a very conscious craftsman. But his is the most irritating and pretentious style pattern I have read in years. It has the slick, smug finality of the lesser Latins; that shallow clarity and tight little good taste that remind one of nothing so much as the conversation and practice of a veteran cocotte.

Mr. Wilder strains to be spiritual; but who could reveal any real agonies and exaltations of spirit in this neat, tailor-made rhetoric? It is a great lie. It is Death. Its serenity is that of the corpse. Prick it, and it will bleed violet ink and *apéritif*. It is false to the great stormy music of Anglo-Saxon speech. Shakespeare is crude and disorderly beside Mr. Wilder. Neither Milton, Fielding, Burns, Blake, Byron, Chaucer nor Hardy could ever receive a passing mark in Mr. Wilder's classroom of style.

And this is the style with which to express America? Is this the speech of a pioneer continent? Will this discreet French drawing room hold all the blood, horror and hope of the world's new empire? Is this the language of the intoxicated Emerson? Or the clean, rugged Thoreau, or vast Whitman? Where are the modern streets of New York, Chicago and New Orleans in these little novels? Where are the cotton mills, and the murder of Ella May and her songs? Where are the child slaves of the beet fields? Where are the stockbroker suicides, the labor racketeers or passion and death of the coal miners? Where are Babbitt, Jimmy Higgins and Anita Loos's Blonde? Is Mr. Wilder a Swede or a Greek, or is he an American? No stranger would know from these books he has written.

But is it right to demand this "nativism" of him? Yes, for Mr. Wilder has offered himself as a spiritual teacher; therefore one may say: Father, what are your lessons? How will your teaching help the "spirit" trapped in American capitalism? But Wilder takes refuge in the rootless cosmopolitanism which marks every *émigré* trying to flee the problems of his community. Internationalism is a totally different spirit. It begins at home. Mr. Wilder speaks much of the "human heart" and its eternal problems. It is with these, he would have us believe, that he concerns himself; and they are the same in any time and geography, he says. Another banal evasion. For the human heart, as he probes it in Greece, Peru, Italy and other remote places, is only the "heart" of a small futile group with whom few Americans have the faintest kinship.

For to repeat, Mr. Wilder remains the poet of a small sophisticated class that has recently arisen in America—our genteel bourgeoisie. His style is their style; it is the new fashion. Their women have taken to wearing his Greek chlamys and faintly indulge themselves in his smart Victorian pieties. Their men are at ease in his Paris and Rome.

America won the War. The world's wealth flowed into it like a red Mississippi. The newest and greatest of all leisure classes was created. Luxury-hotels, golf, old furniture and Vanity Fair sophistication were some of their expressions.

Thorstein Veblen foretold all this in 1899, in an epoch-making book that every American critic ought to study like a Bible. In *The Theory of the Leisure Class* he painted the hopeless course of most American culture for the next three decades. The grim, ironic prophet has been justified. Thornton Wilder is the perfect flower of the new prosperity. He has all the virtues Veblen said this leisure class would demand: the air of good breeding, the decorum, priestliness, glossy high finish as against intrinsic qualities, conspicuous inutility, caste feeling, love of the archaic, etc. . . . .

All this is needed to help the parvenu class forget its lowly origins in

American industrialism. It yields them a short cut to the aristocratic emotions. It disguises the barbaric sources of their income, the billions wrung from American workers and foreign peasants and coolies. It lets them feel spiritually worthy of that income.

Babbitt made them ashamed of being crude American climbers. Mr. Wilder, "gentle as the dove and wise as the serpent," is a more constructive teacher. Taking them patiently by the hand, he leads them into castles, palaces and far-off Greek islands, where they may study the human heart when it is nourished by blue blood. This Emily Post of culture will never reproach them; or remind them of Pittsburgh or the breadlines. He is always in perfect taste; he is the personal friend of Gene Tunney.

"For there is a land of the living and a land of the dead, and the bridge is love, the only survival, the only meaning." And nobody works in a Ford plant, and nobody starves looking for work, and there is nothing but Love in God's ancient Peru, Italy, Greece, if not in God's capitalist America 1930!

Let Mr. Wilder write a book about modern America. We predict it will reveal all his fundamental silliness and superficiality, now hidden under a Greek chlamys.

---

[24]

DISCUSSION AND PROCEEDINGS OF THE AMERICAN WRITERS' CONGRESS

HENRY HART

THE second session of the American Writers' Congress opened on the morning of April 27 [1935] in the auditorium of the New School for Social Research. The chairman was John Howard Lawson. He announced that because of the number of papers, and the need to devote most of the last session to the organization of the League of American Writers, discus-

SOURCE: Henry Hart, ed., *American Writers' Congress* (New York: International Publishers, 1935), pp. 165–171, 176–183, 188–192. Reprinted by permission of International Publishers Co., Inc.

sion of the individual papers would have to be grouped at the end of each session instead of occurring at the end of each paper. In the main this worked out well—speakers did not duplicate each other. Before presenting the first speaker, who was Joseph Freeman, Mr. Lawson read aloud the names of those writers who had been suggested, by those who had worked for months to prepare for the Congress, as the actual presiding committee of the Congress. The nominees, all of whom were accepted by the delegates, were: Michael Blankfort, Harry Carlisle, Jack Conroy, Malcolm Cowley, Joseph Freeman, Michael Gold, Eugene Gordon, Henry Hart, Granville Hicks, Orrick Johns, John Howard Lawson, Meridel Le Sueur, Isidor Schneider, Edwin Seaver, Bernhard J. Stern and Alexander Trachtenberg. Paul Romaine was appointed recording secretary.

Two papers at the session provoked most of the discussion. These were Edwin Seaver's "The Proletarian Novel" and Kenneth Burke's "Revolutionary Symbolism in America."

Martin Russak dissented from Seaver's contention that the proletarian novel, by definition, could be one that treated any subject matter provided it did so from the standpoint and in the interest of the proletariat. "I think the proletarian novel has got to be," he said, "and is already becoming, a novel that deals with the working class. I don't think our novels should be concerned with the emotions and reactions and values of the upper or middle classes or the lumpen proletariat. I don't think the life experiences of hoboes and tramps, as depicted in some of our writing recently, are legitimate subject matter.

"I think that, if we completely understood the nature of class division, we would not say that all people are the same. In the working class we have a distinct kind of human being, a new type of human being, with an emotional life and psychology, that is different, and distinct, and with which we should deal."

Michael Gold, in discussing Jack Conroy's paper, took issue with Mr. Russak, but also warned against the danger of "our literary movement becoming a petty bourgeois movement." He said:

"I think some of the discussion this morning was interesting because it again contrasted two points of view which have been battling in our world of proletarian literature as long as I can remember.

"We know that our enemies have taken up the cry that proletarian literature is a literature of men with hairy chests, of slums and so forth, and that no bourgeois writer can approach these things. On the other hand, we have had all the proletarians insisting that the bourgeois writers and their themes have no place in the revolutionary movement. I think we got a little conception of that from Martin Russak. If anything has been cleared up in the last few years, it has been this point: that the revolution is a revolution led by the working class, and the lower middle classes are its allies. There is therefore room in the revolution for literature from all these groups. The viewpoint, as Edwin Seaver said, is what is important. The man with the revolutionary mind and approach can write a revolutionary book.

"So I think we must stand equally against the idea that proletarian literature has a place only for novels about the working class, the idea that was more or less implied this morning, as well as against the idea that novels about the workers are not important.

"Someone said that when we are dealing with a class myth we can juggle this class myth around. The very acceptance of this conception . . . that the working-class myth is on a par with other myths, with fascist myths, is a surrender at a very vital point. We cannot accept any such classification, as many of the liberals do, that communism and fascism are equal schemes for solving the problems of society, for socializing society. We cannot accept the idea that the class struggle is a myth, or that the working class is a myth.

"I think the tone of many of our papers this morning showed that our literary movement is in danger of becoming a petty bourgeois movement. I think we must guard against that. It cannot become that. It must not become that. It is our main task to see that a strong working class is developed in the United States to lead the revolutionary vanguard. We may not lead it. So I think one of the basic tasks of every writer is to stimulate and encourage and help the growth of proletarian literature which is written by workers.

"I think all of us must learn to become teachers of the working class. We must assemble around ourselves a group of talented workers who wish to write, just as Gorky did it twenty-five years ago in Russia. We must realize that only this literature can answer these intellectual abstractions into which petty bourgeois people fall.

"A great body of proletarian literature will show the concrete facts. It will show our face. It will be the greatest argument we can present to those people who juggle with the theories of communism and fascism. We must build up a picture of what the working class in this country looks like. We must use this as a final and clinching argument—this picture of real life, of real working-class struggle. We must use this as the final answer we can give to the intellectual abstractions of the bourgeoisie."

The discussion of Kenneth Burke's paper centered chiefly around the reasons for resisting his suggested substitution of the symbol "people" for "worker."

It began with Allen Porter's observations that one of the propaganda devices employed by the exploiting class during periods of struggle was making the demands of the workers appear as antipathetic to the "good of the *people*."

"Distinguishing between the workers and the people," he said, "is deliberately undertaken to confuse, as, for example, when Father Coughlin [the rightwing radio priest] and General Johnson [the head of the National Recovery Act] last summer attacked the general strike in San Francisco on the grounds that the workers were 'holding up the people.' By using the symbol 'all of the people' the inference was made that the common interest was opposed to the interests of the workers. The same symbol was used during the general strike of 1926 in Great Britain in precisely the same way. The *workers* were attacking the *people*. The attempt to substitute 'people' for 'worker' is very dangerous from our point of view. Historically, it has been the ruse of the exploiting class to confuse the issue. Moreover, the word 'people' is historically associated with demagoguery of the most vicious sort."

Friedrich Wolf supported this view, saying:

"A great danger reposes in this formulation of 'the people.' Hitler and Rosenberg used it. They said, let us not talk any more about the workers, let us talk about the people. In 1918 it was precisely this very same thing that the German reformist leaders utilized. Scheideman and Ebert said we must have a policy that will cover the worker and the small merchant and the middle bourgeoisie. Hitlerism is a continuation of this policy. Hitler knew enough to use this ideological device as a supplement to his blackjacks and machine guns. Utilization of the myth of *'das Volk,'* the people, is an essential part of the reformist approach. In my own country it has directly resulted in the fascists taking power. The symbol 'worker' must be reserved to indicate the preponderant mass of the population—the actual workers and farmers. Substitution of the symbol 'people' confuses the interests of this fundamental and all-important class and renders a picture of society that is not merely un-Marxian but one which history has proven to be necessary for the continuation of the power of the exploiting class."

Joseph Freeman, in agreeing with the attacks upon Burke's suggestion, declared that it was necessary to show why the proletariat "is the sole revolutionary class." "If we consider the matter from the viewpoint of reality first and then from the literary viewpoint, it is possible we may have no disagreement with Burke," he said and continued:

"The symbol of the *people* came with the bourgeois revolution. The bourgeoisie demanded the abolition of class privileges. Therefore it had the following of all the people. Then it turned out that the people were divided into classes. The word people then became a reactionary slogan—not because of any philosophy of myths, but because it concealed the reality, the actual living antagonism between the social classes. The type of myth represented by the word *people* can go so far that reality can be concealed even in the name of the proletarian revolution, even in the name of Lenin. Consider carefully the demagogy of the fascist government of Mexico. When I was in Mexico, I found state governors—one of whom became president of the republic—who used to hand out Lenin's portrait to peasant delegations. The official organ of the ruling reactionary party publishes special pro-Soviet supplements on November 7. It also published in full the call for our own Writers' Congress. So revolutionary are the Mexican workers and peasants, that nobody in Mexico can play politics without saying 'three cheers for the red flag' and 'three cheers for the *proletarian* revolution.' Even the Catholic church and its political exponents do this.

"If the *proletariat* can become a dangerous political myth in the hands of the reaction, how much more dangerous is the vague symbol of the *people*. We must not encourage such myths. We are not interested in the myth. We are interested in revealing the reality. We set up the 'symbol' of the worker because of the role which the worker plays in reality. When Hitler first came into power, most of the American bourgeois correspondents in Berlin were against him. Why were Burchell of the *Times* and the other American reporters so enthusiastic about Dimitroff and the other Communist workers on trial? Because the workers are in the most effective position to fight the reaction. Even the most proletarian of writers and intellectuals cannot call a general strike. They cannot switch off the electric lights, halt the street-cars, stop the factories, tie up the ships; they can't go out into the streets and take rifles and fight. We heard Friedrich Wolf tell us last night why the German writers and intellectuals came over to the working class. He told us how the poet Erich Muhsam died in a Nazi prison singing the *International*. Why this change? Under the bloody repression of fascism, the intellectuals recognized this tremendously significant fact, that the workers alone are socially, industrially, politically in a position to shut off industry under capitalism, to take it over under socialism. The intellectuals learned that the workers alone can give militant and effective leadership to the fight against reaction.

"This is due to the social position of the proletariat. That is why it is the only revolutionary class in modern society. If some of us call for the 'positive' symbol of the people to replace the 'negative' symbol of the worker, it is because we feel that the proletariat is a concept too narrow to include the intellectuals. But we do not need to be afraid. There is no real conflict involved here. We want to be included in the progressive class— and we are included. The proletariat alone can create a just society for the whole of the people. The proletarian is not merely someone who works. An English journalist told me the other day [that] the Prince of Wales is getting a nervous breakdown. He works too hard. As a matter of fact, the Prince of Wales does work hard—and we know what he is working for. But this does not make him a proletarian. The proletarian is the man who has nothing to sell but his labor power. He not only works but depends upon his labor solely for his existence. That is why he is the most exploited and oppressed man in capitalist society; that is why he is the only one in a position to break with that society completely. The intellectual cannot lead the fight for the new world. He has his own vested interests in the old. He finds it hard to break with the old culture. He goes to school for sixteen years, takes his Ph.D., absorbs the old ideas, functions with them—and now he feels that the proletariat wants to expropriate him of the old culture. That is terrible. He feels that the term *people* will include not only him but his old ideas. But he need not fear. The proletariat takes over all that is best in the old culture.

"What must be kept in mind above all is the leading role which the worker plays in the transformation of society. The worker has nothing to lose but his chains. He alone is forced by his position to be revolutionary, and he alone can liberate the people. If we do not get lost in 'myths,' if we stick to the reality, it is only in the working class that the other exploited classes of society—including the intellectuals—can find leadership."

Kenneth Burke was then asked to reply to these criticisms and in the course of doing so, said:

"I was not disappointed in the response I expected when bringing up this subject. But I wish that someone had discussed the issue from my point of attack, the problem of propaganda. I think we are all agreed that we are trying to defend a position in favor of the workers, that we are trying to enlist in the cause of the workers. There is no issue about that. The important thing is how to make ourselves effective in this particular social structure. I am trying to point out that there is a first stage where the writer's primary job is to disarm people. First you knock at the door —and not until later will you become wholly precise.

"As for my use of the word myth, I was speaking technically before a group of literary experts, hence I felt justified in using the word in a special sense. A poet's myths, I tried to make clear, are *real,* in the sense that they perform a necessary function. They so pattern the mind as to give it a grip upon reality. For the myth embodies a sense of relationships. But relationships cannot be pointed to, in the simple objective way in which you could point to a stone or a house. It is such a sense of *relationships* (I have sometimes called them 'secondary reality') that I had in mind when using the word myth.

"As for the charge that I made Communism appear like a religion: It may be a weakness on my part, but I have never taken this matter very seriously. As the Latin *religio* signifies a binding *together,* I take religion and Communism to be alike insofar as both are systems for binding people together—and the main difference at the present time resides for me in the fact that the Communistic vocabulary does the binding job much more accurately than the religious vocabulary. Let us compromise by saying that Communism is an ethic, a morality. But whenever you talk about an ethic, you must talk about much the same sort of things as you would if you were talking purely and simply about religion.

"As for the use of the term *people:* one speaker in rebutting me actually corroborated me when he said that Lenin used the term *people* up to 1917. I think that we are exactly in the same position as Russia prior to 1917.

"I probably should not have used the words *positive* and *negative* to distinguish the two types of symbol. I did not mean that there is anything negative about the worker symbol in itself, but only insofar as it *tends to* overly restrict a writer's range of interests and emphases. In practice it *tends to* focus a writer's attention upon traits that enlist our *sympathies—* whereas by a *positive* symbol I meant one that enlists not only our *sympathies* but also our *ambitions.*

"Some speakers have made the point that there is no contradiction between the *worker* and the *people.* I emphatically agree. But it was pointed out that in California the demagogues were able to give the appearance of a contradiction, to make it seem as though the workers were aligned against the people. And it is precisely this demagogic trick which the propagandist must combat. I think your symbolism has to be so molded that this apparent contradiction between workers and people cannot be set up. If you emphasize the worker symbol exclusively you give the reactionaries the best opportunity to make it seem that the *workers* and the *people* are opposed. But if you amalgamate the worker symbol with the people symbol, the very thing that was done in California cannot be done.

"I think that finishes up all the points that were made. The fundamental thing that I want to emphasize again is my belief that there is a different problem confronting the propagandist from that which confronts the organizer. The propagandist's main job is to disarm. In the course of disarming, he opens himself to certain dangers. He cannot draw a distinct line because if he did, he would not be able to advance into outlying areas. The organizer must cancel off these other dangers. After getting these people into your party, you can give them a more accurate sense of what you are aiming at. But in the first stage, the propagandist must use certain terms which have a certain ambiguity, and which for that very reason give him entrance into other areas."

At the fourth session, on Sunday morning, presided over by Eugene Gordon, some of the best discussion occurred. Some of this related to ideas discussed at the various commissions on Saturday night.

Charles Quinn, a miner from Gallup, New Mexico, in direct and homely words, praised Albert Maltz's play *Black Pit*. He said it was a pity it could not be taken from mining camp to mining town. He urged the delegates to write short sketches, skits, one-act plays that *could* be acted before miners. He invited the writers to go among the miners and learn about their life, their struggles and their ambitions. "We are looking for stories and books that reveal the truth about ourselves to us," he said, "not for novels or books or plays written by somebody on a pedestal looking down on us."

Granville Hicks, at the conclusion of his paper, made some extemporaneous remarks concerning the critics' commission which he had attended the night before. "Some of us were discussing the magazine which will be issued by the League of American Writers," he said. "Though there was some disagreement, it seemed to be the feeling that it ought to be as broad as the League itself.

"Therefore, so far as criticism was concerned, it could not limit itself entirely to the Marxist critics; since we are asking other critics to come into the League, they should be given a voice in the organ. It should be made perfectly clear that this magazine will not be primarily, exclusively, officially, a Marxist organ. It is an organ of the League, representing many different points of view.

"We also discussed at length the reason why there has been so much talk about the critics trying to catalog, trying to force writers and critics into particular categories. We discussed the fact, for example, that many different points of view have been represented in the *New Masses* within the last few months. Nevertheless, when anybody wants to take Marxism, or wants to take particular tendencies in Marxist criticism, he will pick out any one of those articles and treat it as if it was our official statement of the Marxist position. So if you want to attack Marxist criticism, all you have to do is to pick out one of twenty different opinions and say that all Marxism is included therein.

"How that particular impression has grown up is somewhat of a problem. Nevertheless, we recognize that it has. We would like to have it understood that there is no individual, no magazine, nobody that can or should attempt to say what is the official Marxist position in criticism.

"We believe, of course, that there is a correct Marxist position. Everyone of us believes that he has it, and all that we say is that other people should realize that each of us is expressing what he believes to be the correct Marxist principle, and no one can say, except as an individual, that his is the Marxist position, that this is wrong and that is right, or somebody else is or is not right or wrong. Whoever believes himself a Marxist and wishes to study Marxism has a perfect right to express himself as a Marxist, and everybody else has a perfect right to disagree with him. I think that should be clearly recognized. It is only his own basis. If that would be generally recognized, then instead of having a lot of talk about the narrowness and dogmatism of Marxist critics, we would have some useful talk about this precise dogmatism of John Jones. In other words, let's stop talking about Marxist criticism as a body, when we mean the particular faults or the particular merits of a particular person."

Revolutionary writers must not neglect the child, the Congress was warned by the young editor of *New Pioneer,* Martha Campion. "It is very important that some of our good writers begin to write for children," she said. "The kids who are fifteen now will in three years be eighteen—old enough to be drafted into the army, old enough to scab, and old enough to be drafted into the Storm Troops, too."

Robert Gessner, the poet, said he had been struck by the sure knowledge of their audience displayed by the dramatists and the confusion displayed at the poets' commission concerning the audience for poetry. He observed that the poets' confusion probably derived from the poet feeling himself to be a special person, above the class struggle.

"The proletarian poet has not been sufficiently revolutionary," he said. "Most of the revolutionary poetry has been of the ostrich variety. Last night the Yiddish writers remarked that by reading their poetry directly to mass audiences of Jewish workers they were able to get many helpful suggestions and an enthusiastic response. Maxim Gorky, at the writers' congress in Moscow, pointed out that any poet who removes himself from the characters about whom he writes is living an abortive life. It is a question of contact. Workers have appeared at this Congress and asked us to come and see them as they actually are, live their life and learn of their problems at first hand. One thing that keeps revolutionary writers from doing so is the fear that their technique would be lost. Leave your technique on the fence. It will come trotting after you with its tail between its legs."

Alfred Hayes objected to what he called "Robert Gessner's contemptuous criticism." He said that there are many more poets writing revolutionary poetry than there were five years ago and that it is of a superior quality. Concern with revolutionary themes, he said, has entailed difficulties which other poets do not need to face, and which have not yet been solved.

"It may be that the poets who are writing today will be forgotten," he said, "and a whole new group of poets will arise who will be the genuine expression of the working class. If the poetry now being written does not give voice to the real human conflicts of today, it will die and a different poetry will take its place. But before that poetry comes, I think we should deal with the poetry of today and accept it as a genuine feeling and attitude toward the working class."

J. S. Balch, of St. Louis, in discussing the short story, alluded to the popular fallacy that "a proletarian writer is one who hasn't been able to hit *Harper's Bazaar,* a writer who goes in for proletarian literature because it is easy." "We all know how false and absurd that is," he said. "But I have had occasion to read a great number of short stories in manuscript and I find they fall into definite categories. Many have what I call the proletarian happy ending. At the end you wave a red flag or have a strike and that is supposed to make a man a proletarian writer. Usually it comes at the end of a painfully unintegrated story and is absolutely valueless—as art, as propaganda, as a short story."

Richard Wright made some moving remarks on the isolation of the young Negro writer. "You may not understand it," he said. "I don't think you can unless you feel it. You can understand the causes, and oppose them, but the human results are tragic in peculiar ways. Some of the more obvious results are lack of contact with other writers, a lack of personal culture, a tendency toward escape mechanisms of ingenious, insidious kinds. Other results of his isolation are the monotony of subject matter and becoming the victim of a sort of traditional Negro character.

"I think that this isolation can be ended, but it will take terrific effort. In this respect the whole left movement can do something. As the Negro worker moves leftward, the Negro merchant will also become a little more sympathetic. After all, they are parasites. They are dependent upon what the Negro workers earn. And if the merchants become a little more sympathetic, the newspapers and the general run of people will feel it. A better attitude, coming from the bottom upward, will prevail.

"The young Negro writer, too, can help himself by a thorough understanding of his own history. This is a rather peculiar thing. Negro history has been distorted from two points of view, from the point of view of the ruling class and from the point of view of certain Negro historians who have colored the history in racial terms.

"This last point is perhaps the most important, one which indicates how completely isolated a great many young Negro writers are. Some of them are unaware of the vast field of experimental fiction that is being carried on in the little magazines."

Merle Colby warned against what he considered to be one of the gravest dangers confronting the revolutionary writer. "I think a writer should *write*," he said. "Several times at this Congress I have asked about so-and-so, who was a remarkable writer. I was told that he has changed his name, that he has grown a mustache, and that he is organizing a trade union.

"It seems to me that this is very serious, for, under the pretense of actually engaging in the class struggle we stop writing. There are about three hundred writers here, and perhaps we produce on an average ten or twelve books a year. That average is altogether too small. We fancy ourselves men of action. Well, writing is the worst sort of gruelling work. Almost everything else is easier. Let us stick to our lasts."

The last participant in the discussion was Edward Dahlberg, who declared that the revolutionary movement must "build up our writers." He declared that the neglect of them in the bourgeois literary media must not be duplicated in the revolutionary press. "What has really happened," he said, "is that the person who engages in controversies and in critical discussions is immediately charged with having a personal animus against this person and that person, simply because he passionately believes in literature and wants to build up a literature. You can't build up a literature without passion, and if you have no passion, you had better stop writing altogether."

The fifth and last session, presided over by Michael Gold, was the fullest and most dramatic of all. A proportionate share of the papers were read, several guests spoke at length, and all the work of organizing the League of American Writers was executed.

Also at that session Albert Maltz reported on the playwrights' commission, held the evening before. Mr. Maltz has summarized his report on the activities of that commission as follows:

"The Playwrights' Commission consisted of an examination into the state of health of the workers' theaters and a prospectus for their immediate future.

"Invited to the Commission were not only the playwrights attending the Congress, but other theatrical workers. There were present representatives of the New Theater of Philadelphia, the Theater of Action, the Theater Union, the New Theater League and *New Theater* magazine. No report can be made for the Group Theater since its representative was unable to attend.

"John Howard Lawson reported on workers' movies. He said that there is lying fallow now an artistic weapon of such magnitude that beside it the workers' theaters can only be puny by comparison. This is the medium of the motion picture. Last year Pudovkin's *Mother,* an eighteen-millimeter film, was shown in almost every industrial center, small town and farming community in the country. In one stroke we were given an example of how a workers' art can reach not thousands, but millions of people. There are in New York City now two organizations, the Film and Photo League and the New York Kino, which are producing workers' films. Their development depends upon two things: the interest of writers in preparing scenarios of high quality which come within the scope of the technique of these organizations, and the development, or rather, the organization of existing channels for showing these films. To those who have seen some of the short pictures already produced it will be apparent that they are limited by scenario and not by their technical ability in producing—a combination of ingenuity and energy compensating to a great degree for lack of funds and equipment. And there is wanting, as well as writers, those who will be sufficiently interested in the medium, to give time and energy to the necessary organizational work in the same manner that many have already given these things to the workers' theaters. The future of cheap workers' films of high artistic quality is within our hands if we take it. The result can only be something that will surpass all previous attempts to develop a working-class art which can reach wide masses of people.

"Dr. Friedrich Wolf declared that in two or three years the revolutionary theaters of the United States had accomplished what had taken sixteen years in Germany, and that, on the other hand, there was apparent a great need for cooperation between the existing theaters and theater workers. Dr. Wolf was empowered to arrange a medium of exchange for the newest Soviet plays and the newest American revolutionary plays. We here, he said, do not know at all the new Soviet plays, and in the Soviet Union the only American plays are the plays of the Broadway theater.

"Manuel Gomez, reporting on the Theater Union, said that in two seasons five hundred thousand people have seen the four Theater Union plays. Of this number 75 percent have been workers, a great many of whom never attended a theater before. A Theater Union play is now faced by the bright prospect of a ten weeks' benefit audience signed up in advance. This may be compared with the Theater Guild, which has a subscription audience of only five weeks. Regular Dramatist Guild royalties are paid and scripts are wanted for future productions. In the two years since the founding of the Theater Union, professional theaters modeled after it have sprung up in Philadelphia, Los Angeles, San Francisco and New Orleans, which are doing Theater Union scripts and all other revolutionary plays they can get their hands on for average runs of three weeks.

"Peter Martin, reporting on the Theater of Action, said that the Theater of Action, formerly the Workers' Laboratory Theater, began as and still is a mobile theater—the mobility for many years revolving literally about the subway, with actors carrying their scenery under their arms. Working with amateur actors, and in the most extreme personal and collective poverty, this group, in five years, writing its agit-prop plays 'on the collective run,' played in workers' halls, before picket lines, in front of factory gates and on the waterfront before two hundred and fifty thousand workers in five hundred performances. The Theater of Action is beginning to actively branch out from its 'cartoon' forms into the use of short and long realistic plays. In a few weeks it will open in an uptown theater a full-length realistic play, *The Young Go First*. Behind this production is a dual purpose: one, the establishment of a stationary repertory theater with a permanent company; two, the insuring of a source of funds whereby the mobility of the theater can be extended within and without New York City. Long and short plays will be toured through the country. However valuable and influential the permanent theaters may be, they are, by their nature, open to easy censorship. But the mobile theater performs, and is gone. We must not in any way divert valuable energies from this mobile theater into the stationary. Both must develop side by side. In 1932 in Berlin there were five stationary theaters. They were closed by Hitler. But the presence of mobile theaters kept things functioning. Instead of waiting for workers to come to the theater (which was no longer possible) groups toured throughout the country. A playwright for the Theater of Action becomes a member of the theater organization. He is offered royalties while his play runs and a home and food while the play is being re-written or is in rehearsal. Scripts are needed.

"Herbert Kline, reporting on the New Theater League, explained that it is organized on a minimum program of a struggle against war, fascism and censorship. Its purpose is threefold: to develop the ideology of the workers' theaters and to see that they advance as quickly as possible along artistic lines in order that their work may not, as has occurred in the past in many instances, be hamstrung by artistic and political backwardness, frequently a product of their isolation; secondly, to send out organizational information and to help in the creation of new workers' theaters; and, finally, to act as a source for repertory.

"Herbert Kline also reported on *New Theater,* declaring that it is not just a cultural organ, but a reporter, an ideological guide and an organizer as well. There is nothing that reflects so well the growth in the workers' theater movement as the growth of *New Theater* itself. From May 1934 to January 1935 its circulation grew from two thousand to twelve thousand.

"In conclusion, the Playwrights' Commission of this Congress found that there are today in the United States three hundred functioning workers' theaters. How many there will be a week from now we cannot tell. They are springing up everywhere with a vitality so tremendous that in a great many places they are taking over the old little theaters which have been functioning for many years.

"Not all of these theaters can do long plays—but some can and *all* can produce plays lasting from fifteen minutes to an hour.

"Their tremendous need is for scripts. The various central offices of the New Theater League are flooded with more and more insistent demands for scripts.

"The poets, I am told, discussed in their commission last night methods for getting an audience for their poetry. This is undoubtedly a slander. But in any instance, the workers' theater movement says to them: 'Write your best poetry and write it in the play form. There are three hundred workers' theaters begging for scripts.' To novelists whose books may sell from three hundred to two thousand copies, the workers' theater movement says: 'There is already established an audience of over a million waiting to hear what you have to say—if you will write in the play form.' It is particularly necessary for established, revolutionary playwrights to help in overcoming this script famine. A dozen good examples of the short form from professionals will result not only in helping the situation but in helping to guide and create two dozen young playwrights who look to their work for instruction.

"The New Theater League has worked out a form of royalty payment which, although small, becomes a sizable sum in view of the number of theaters, and writers may feel assured of a steady and increasing revenue if their plays are at all worth producing.

"In the time allotted it has been almost impossible to indicate with any fullness the true growth and vigor of the new revolutionary theater movement. But this new theater in America is booming as is no other revolutionary art today. Write for it and help it grow." . . .

Jack Conroy then announced the name of the man nominated to head the League of American Writers—Waldo Frank. The nomination was unanimously approved.

Mr. Conroy read the names of the following nominees for the Executive Committee, all of whom were approved: Kenneth Burke, Harold Clurman, Malcolm Cowley, Waldo Frank, Joseph Freeman, Michael Gold, Henry Hart, Josephine Herbst, Granville Hicks, Matthew Josephson, Alfred Kreymborg, John Howard Lawson, Albert Maltz, Isidor Schneider, Edwin Seaver, Genevieve Taggard, and Alexander Trachtenberg.

The personnel of the National Council, as finally approved, follows: Nelson Algren, Michael Blankfort, Maxwell Bodenheim, Van Wyck Brooks, Sterling Brown, Fielding Burke, Alan Calmer, Robert Cantwell, Harry Carlisle, Eugene Clay, Merle Colby, Jack Conroy, Edward Dahlberg, Leonard Ehrlich, James T. Farrell, Kenneth Fearing, Angel Flores, Horace Gregory, Robert Herrick, Sidney Howard, Orrick Johns, Joshua Kunitz, Tillie Lerner, Meridel Le Sueur, Robert Morss Lovett, Grace Lumpkin, Lewis Mumford, Moishe Nadir, Clifford Odets, M. J. Olgin, Joseph Opatoshu, Paul Peters, Rebecca Pitts, William Rollins, Jr., George Sklar, Agnes Smedley, Lincoln Steffens, James Waterman Wise, and Richard Wright.

The report of the resolutions committee was then read by Michael Blankfort. Resolutions were passed demanding the release of revolutionary intellectuals in all parts of the world, including Ludwig Renn, German novelist, and Carl von Ossietsky, foremost German publicist; Korea Sanda, who first gained recognition as Emperor Jones in a Japanese version of the O'Neill play, and Ryokichi Sugimoto, imprisoned in Japan; Jacques Rouhain, Haitian novelist and poet, charged with conspiring against the government of Stenio Vincent because he possessed pamphlets on the Scottsboro case; Juan Marinello and Rejino Pedroso and other editors of *Masas* imprisoned in Cuba for their editorials against American imperialist control of that country through a military dictatorship; and almost twenty Chinese writers imprisoned by Chiang Kai-shek.

Resolutions were passed protesting against the suppression of civil rights, the burning of schools and the closing of institutions of higher learning and the murder of intellectuals in Cuba; against the censorship and suppression of the press in Mexico, and against the burning of the headquarters of the Mexican Communist Party; against the various deportation and sedition bills proposed in the state legislatures of this country; against William Randolph Hearst and all his publications; against the terror in Gallup and the results of the trials in Sacramento; against the persecution of Mooney, Angelo Herndon and the Scottsboro boys.

The invitation from Romain Rolland, André Malraux, Louis Aragon and Henri Barbusse to send delegates to the Congress for the Defense of Culture in Paris at the end of June was accepted and the Executive Committee was authorized to send delegates. The proposal for a Pan-American Writers' Congress was endorsed.

Michael Gold called upon Waldo Frank, secretary of the League of American Writers. As Mr. Frank walked down the aisle and mounted the platform the delegates rose. Visibly moved, Waldo Frank said:

"There has probably never been a time in my career when it was more necessary that I should have been prepared beforehand to speak. But I have prepared nothing, and I suppose it is just as well, because we are all tired. The one thing to say now is the reverse of the old order: not 'hail and farewell,' but 'farewell and hail.'

"There has been a great deal of excited discussion here, although much of it was indirect, on the subject of dogmatism. Granville Hicks this morning pointed out that the two attitudes which have characterized revolutionary literature in the last fifteen years—the dualism of the old *Masses* and *Liberator* and the sectarianism of more recent times—have been buried. There is as yet no definite orthodox set of literary doctrines and dogmas to direct us as writers. We have to create our philosophy of revolutionary writing as we live our lives. We have to create it out of our experience, as men and women living in this revolutionary age, and also out of our experience as writers. We are going to create this philosophy through our work and through the responses to our work. We have only begun. All that has gone before might be called a sort of a false dawn, or, if you will, the very earliest part of the dawn before the sun rises.

"We can honestly say, I think, that now the sun is rising. Meridel Le Sueur made a very fine point in her talk this morning. She spoke of this great period of ferment, and the need of warmth. She used, I am glad to say, a word which I have used a great deal—the word 'organic'—organic experience. Malcolm Cowley pointed out in the session at Mecca Temple that the renaissance which we have so far is analogous in a way to the literary ferment of Germany which Hitler has, I am sure only temporarily, abolished, or dimmed.

"We have been in this period of ferment, fellow writers. We need the warmth, we need the freedom that has been spoken of by these delegates. But we also need the discipline, the ruthless intellectual and aesthetic training. Ferment is not enough. We need to build, to give and to take hard knocks. We need to be armed against any premature crystallizations; because the great danger in our American cultural life has been premature crystallization, which is another name for miscarriage.

"I want to say that I am surer now than I was when I wrote my paper for the Mecca Temple meeting, that there will be no miscarriage. I am certain of that now. I am certain that there is here in us not only the ferment, the warmth, the energy, but there is also the will to hard thinking, the will to the hard experiencing of our parts in the revolutionary struggle. The philosophy which will create us as writers must come out of our way of living and of thinking and feeling. That is what our revolutionary way of life must be—a way of living.

"But we have to understand ourselves more complexly still, not only as revolutionary fellow-workers, but as a craft within a craft; and that takes great clarity and ruthless heroism. We have to believe in our own work and in the necessity of the autonomy of our own work as craftsmen and writers. This is very hard in an agitated period like this. It is very hard, as I said the other night, when there are so many immediate tasks, which we must participate in—tasks in the daily struggle.

"And it is precisely out of this furnace of contradictions, as it were, that the writer, if he really can hold himself to his clear views, creates the sort of hard, durable stuff of which his work—our creative work—must be born in order that it may live and that it may gain its end.

"I want to make one other point which came to me last night in connection with some of the younger writers here. I was rather surprised to find that there were writers around who felt that such old gray-beards as Jim Farrell and Ed Dahlberg and myself—and others too—were perhaps not giving to their problems the specific consideration that the younger writers need. Let me say to these younger writers that if we failed to do this, we gray-beards, it was because we haven't realized that we are not all the same age; it is because (I am sure, in my own case at least) all of us here have felt so young, felt so in the beginning of things, that these differentiations in age didn't really come to us at all. But when I do think of the youngest writers—and there are probably writers here who are twenty years younger than I am and that is a lot these days, particularly when one thinks of twenty years ahead—let me say, very sincerely, that my own participation here is primarily concerned with them: and if I shall continue to give my time, it is because I am passionately devoted to there being a world in which these youngest writers may live.

"Insofar as that is so, insofar as we are all fighting that there may be a world in which youth—in the creative sense of the word—may live, age drops off. Age has a way of dropping off, at any rate, in the revolutionary movement. The youngest writers of Europe today are the men of whatever number of years who have grown up in the revolutionary movement. The old—many of them not yet thirty—are the reactionary writers; not men like Romain Rolland, who is young at seventy, like André Gide, who is young at sixty-five. Insofar as you keep alive, you don't get old. And I think I can say that insofar as we keep alive today—we will find ourselves in the revolutionary movement, because this is the place of life.

"I don't have to tell you how important this Congress is. I don't have to speak the sort of words which would really express what we feel about its significance; because these words are the sort of words we are schooled and trained to shrink from. They are the sort of words—serious, deep and solemn words fraught with universal significance—which we can feel perhaps best to-day in silence. Let me end then, as I said, as a beginning. We have reversed the old, old greeting: *ave atque vale,* 'hail and farewell,' into 'farewell and hail.'

"Let me end with a quotation from a great revolutionary fighter, a man I have just mentioned, Romain Rolland. I remember twenty years ago at the time of the War reading these words of his. He happened to be a friend of mine, and it was his example perhaps as much as any which during those first years of the War changed me in a direction which I think now is nearing a goal since it has brought me to so many comrades. With these words I should like not to end this Congress, but to begin the League of American Writers. Romain Rolland said: 'Everything remains to be said. Everything remains to be done. Let us get to work!' "

When the applause died down James Farrell arose and suggested that the Congress conclude its final session by singing the *International*. This was done.

[25]

PROLETARIAN LITERATURE IN THE UNITED STATES

JOSEPH FREEMAN

WHATEVER role art may have played in epochs preceding ours, whatever may be its function in the classless society of the future, social war today has made it the subject of partisan polemic. The form of polemic varies with the social class for which the critic speaks, as well as with his personal intelligence, integrity, and courage. The Communist says frankly: art, an instrument in the class struggle, must be developed by the proletariat as one of its weapons. The fascist, with equal frankness, says: art must serve the aims of the capitalist state. The liberal, speaking for the middle class which vacillates between monopoly capital and the proletariat, between fascism and communism, poses as the "impartial" arbiter in this, as in all other social disputes. He alone presumes to speak from above the battle, in the "scientific" spirit.

Wrapping himself in linen, donning rubber gloves, and lifting his surgical instruments—all stage props—the Man in White, the "impartial" liberal critic, proceeds to lecture the assembled boys and girls on the anatomy of art in the quiet, disinterested voice of the old trouper playing the role of "science." He has barely finished his first sentence, when it becomes clear that his lofty "scientific" spirit drips with the bitter gall of partisan hatred. Long before he approaches the vaguest semblance of an idea, the Man in White assaults personalities and parties. We are reading, it turns out, not a scientific treatise on art but a political pamphlet. To characterize an essay or a book as a political pamphlet is neither to praise nor to condemn it. Such pamphlets have their place in the world. In the case of the liberal critic, however, we have a political pamphlet which pretends to be something else. We have an attack on the theory of art as a political weapon which turns out to be itself a political weapon.

The liberal's quarrel with the Marxists does not spring from the desire

SOURCE: Joseph Freeman, "Introduction," in Granville Hicks et al., eds., *Proletarian Literature in the United States* (New York: International Publishers, 1935), pp. 9–28. Reprinted by permission of International Publishers Co., Inc.

to defend a new and original theory. After the ideas are sifted from the abuse, the theories from the polemics, we find nothing more than a series of commonplaces, unhappily wedded to a series of negations. The basic commonplace is that art is something different from action and something different from science. It is hard to understand why anyone should pour out bottles of ink to labor so obvious and elementary a point. No one has ever denied it, least of all the Marxists. We have always recognized that there is a difference between poetry and science, between poetry and action; that life extends beyond statistics, indices, resolutions. To labor that idea with showers of abuse on the heads of the "Marxists–Leninists" is not dispassionate science but polemics, and very dishonest polemics at that.

The problem is: what, in the class society of today, is the relation between art and society, art and science, art and action. It is true that the specific province of art, as distinguished from action or science, is the grasp and transmission of human experience. But is any human experience changeless and universal? Are the humans of the twelfth century the same in their specific experience as the humans of the twentieth? Is life, experience, thought, emotion, the same for the knight of 1300, the young merchant of 1400, the discoverer of 1500, the adventurer of 1600, the scientist of 1700, the factory owner of 1800, the banker of 1900, the worker of 1935? Is there no difference in the "experience" grasped and transmitted by Catholic and Protestant poets, by feudal and bourgeois playwrights, by Broadway and the Theatre Union? Is Heine's social experience the same as Archibald MacLeish's? Is the love experience of Pietro Aretino the same as T. S. Eliot's?

We may say that these are all personal differences: experience is an individual affair and individuals differ from age to age. Yet nothing is more obvious than the social, the *class* basis of fundamental differences. Greeks of the slave-owning class, for all their individual differences, had more in common with each other than any of them has with the bourgeois poets of the Romantic school; the Romantics, for all their individual differences and conflicts, had more in common with each other than with individuals of similar temperament in Soviet letters or American fiction.

Art, then, is not the same as action; it is not identical with science; it is distinct from party program. It has its own special function, the grasp and transmission of experience. The catch lies in the word "experience." The liberal critic, the Man in White, wants us to believe that when you write about the autumn wind blowing a girl's hair or about "thirsting breasts," you are writing about "experience"; but when you write about the October

Revolution, or the Five-Year Plan, or the lynching of Negroes in the South, or the San Francisco strike you are not writing about "experience." Hence to say: "bed your desire among the pressing grasses" is *art;* while *Roar China,* Mayakovsky's poems, or the novels of Josephine Herbst and Robert Cantwell are *propaganda.*

Studying the life of their own country, Soviet critics observed that the poet deals with living people, not with abstractions. He conveys the tremendous experience of the revolution through the personal experience of individual beings who participate in it, fight for or against it, help to forward or retard its purposes, are in turn refashioned by it. He describes people who make friends and enemies, love women and are loved by them, work mightily to transform the land. All this the artist—if he is an artist and not an agitator—does with the specific technique of his craft. He does not repeat party theses; he communicates that experience out of which the theses arose. In so far as the artist's deepest thoughts and feelings are bound to the old régime, in so far as he experiences life with the mind and heart of a bourgeois, the experience he conveys will be seen with the eyes of the bourgeois. Such a poet will best understand all those weaknesses of the revolution which have their roots in the old, that is near and dear to him; he will be blind to the greatness of the revolution which springs from the new, that is alien to him. He will create a false picture of Soviet reality; he will discourage people who read and believe him. But whether an artist grasps the true course of the revolution or is blind to it, his work is not divorced from science and action and class.

No party resolution, no government decree can produce art, or transform an agitator into a poet. A party card does not automatically endow a Communist with artistic genius. Whatever it is that makes an artist, as distinguished from a scientist or a man of action, it is something beyond the power of anyone to produce deliberately. But once the artist is here, once there is the man with the specific sensibility, the mind, the emotions, the images, the gift for language which make the creative writer, he is not a creature in a vacuum.

The poet describes a flower differently from a botanist, a war differently from a general. Ernest Hemingway's description of the retreat at Carpornetto is different from the Italian general staff's; Tretiakov's stories of China are not the same as the resolution on that country by a Comintern plenum. The poet deals with experience rather than theory or action. But the social class to which the poet is attached conditions the nature and flavor of his experience. A Chinese poet of the proletariat of necessity conveys to us experiences different from those of a poet attached to

Chiang Kai-shek or a bourgeois poet who thinks he is above the battle. Moreover, in an era of bitter class war such as ours, party programs, collective actions, class purposes, when they are enacted in life, themselves become experiences—experiences so great, so far-reaching, so all-inclusive that, *as experiences,* they transcend flirtations and autumn winds and stars and nightingales and getting drunk in Paris cafés. It is a petty mind indeed which cannot conceive how men in the Soviet Union, even poets, may be moved more by the vast transformation of an entire people from darkness to light, from poverty to security, from weakness to strength, from bondage to freedom, than by their own personal sensations as loafers or lovers. He is indeed lost in the morass of philistinism who is blind to the *experience,* the *emotion* aroused by the struggle of the workers in all capitalist countries to emancipate themselves and to create a new world.

Here lies the key to the dispute current in American literary circles. No one says the artist should cease being an artist; no one urges him to ignore experience. The question is: what constitutes experience? Only he who is remote from the revolution, if not directly hostile to it, can look upon the poet whose experiences are those of the proletariat as being nothing more than "an adjunct, a servitor, a pedagogue, and faithful illustrator," while the poet who lives the life of the bourgeois, whose experiences are the self-indulgences of the philistine, "asserts with self-dependent force" the sovereignty of art. Art, however it may differ in its specific nature from science and action, is never wholly divorced from them. It is no more self-dependent and sovereign than science and action are self-dependent and sovereign. To speak of art in those terms is to follow the priests who talk of the church, and the politicians who talk of the state, as being self-dependent and sovereign. In all these cases the illusion of self-dependence and sovereignty is propagated in order to conceal the class nature of society, to cover the propagandist of the ruling class with the mantle of impartiality.

In the name of art and by the vague term experience, accompanied by pages of abuse against the Communists, the ideologues of the ruling class have added another intellectual sanction for the *status quo.* What they are really saying is that only *their* experience is experience. They are ignorant of or hate proletarian experience; hence for them it is not experience at all and not a fit subject for art. But if art is to be divorced from the "development of knowledge" and the "technique of scientific action," if it is to ignore politics and the class struggle—matters of the utmost importance in the life of the workers—what sort of experience is left to art? Only the experience of personal sensation, emotion, and conduct, the experience of the parasitic classes. Such art is produced today by bourgeois writers. Their experience is class-conditioned, but, as has always been the case with the bourgeoisie, they pretend that their values are the values of humanity.

If you were to take a worker gifted with a creative imagination and ask him to set down his experience honestly, it would be an experience so remote from that of the bourgeois that the Man in White would, as usual, raise the cry of "propaganda." Yet the worker's life revolves precisely around those experiences which are alien to the bourgeois aesthete, who loathes them, who cannot believe they are experiences at all. To the Man in White it seems that only a decree from Moscow could force people to write about factories, strikes, political discussions. He knows that only force would compel *him* to write about such things; he would never do it of his own free will, since the themes of proletarian literature are outside his own life. But the worker writes about the very experiences which the bourgeois labels "propaganda," those experiences which reveal the exploitation upon which the prevailing society is based.

Often the writer who describes the contemporary world from the viewpoint of the proletariat is not himself a worker. War, unemployment, a widespread social-economic crisis drive middle-class writers into the ranks of the proletariat. Their experience becomes contiguous to or identical with that of the working class; they see their former life, and the life of everyone around them with new eyes; their grasp of experience is conditioned by the class to which they have now attached themselves; they write from the viewpoint of the revolutionary proletariat; they create what is called proletarian literature.

The class basis of art is most obvious when a poem, play, or novel deals with a political theme. Readers and critics then react to literature, as they do to life, in an unequivocal manner. There is a general assumption, however, that certain "biologic" experiences transcend class factors. Love, anger, hatred, fear, the desire to please, to pose, to mystify, even vanity and self-love, may be universal motives; but the form they take, and above all the factors which arouse them, are conditioned, even determined, by class culture. . . .

Art at its best does not deal with abstract anger. When it does it becomes abstract and didactic. The best art deals with specific experience which arouses specific emotion in specific people at a specific moment in a specific locale, in such a way that other people who have had similar experiences in other places and times recognize it as their own. Jack Conroy, to whom a Proustian salon with its snobbish pride, envy, and shame is a closed world, can describe the pride, envy, and shame of a factory. We may recognize analogies between the *feelings* of the salon and those of the factory, but the objects and events which arouse them are different. And since no feeling can exist without an object or event, art must of necessity deal with specific experience, even if only obliquely, by evasion and flight. The liberal critic who concludes that all literature *except proletarian literature* is equally sincere and artistic, that every poet *except the proletarian poet* is animated by "experience," "life," "human values," has abandoned the search before it has really begun. The creative writer's motives, however "human" they may be, however analogous to the motives of the savage, are modified by his social status, his class, or the class to which he is emotionally and intellectually attached, from whose viewpoint he sees the world around him.

Is there any writer, however remote his theme or language may seem at first glance from contemporary reality, however "sincere" and "artistic" his creations may be, whose work is not in some way conditioned by the political state in which he lives, by the knowledge of his time, by the attitudes of his class, by the revolution which he loves, hates, or seeks to ignore? What is the *real* antagonism involved in the fake and academic antagonism between "experience" on the one hand and the state, education, science, revolution on the other? This question is all the more significant since the best literary minds of all times have agreed on some kind of social sanction for art, from Plato and Aristotle to Wordsworth and Shelley, to Voronsky, and I. A. Richards. Recent attempts to destroy the "Marxo–Leninist aesthetics" fall into a morass of idealistic gibberish. The term "experience" becomes an abstract, metaphysical concept, like "life" or the "Idea" or the "Absolute." But even the most abstract metaphysical concept, like the most fantastic dream, conceals a reality.

Let us examine one typical example of this metaphysical concept. Recently a bourgeois critic cited the following words by Karl Marx: "At a certain stage of their development, the material forces of production in society come in conflict with the existing relations of production, or, what is but a legal expression for the same thing, with the property relations within which they had been at work before. From forms of development of the forces of production, these relations turn into their fetters. Then comes the period of social revolution. With the change of the economic foundation, the entire immense superstructure is more or less rapidly transformed." The critic commented that this was a *true scientific description of a social law;* in the future some "intellectually inventive" artist might write a poem in which this thought would be "greatly and spontaneously portrayed." But, he added, no man "can get into a position to experience a revolution concretely in those terms." Therefore, the attempt "to convey the conception in concrete images and pictures will be *normally a tour de force.*"

Our author himself underlined the word *normally.* That indeed is the significant word not only in the essay, but in the entire campaign which bourgeois ideologues have been conducting against proletarian literature. If Karl Marx's law is true, as the conservative critic admits, then the process it describes involves every individual in capitalist society, even when he is utterly ignorant of Marx's formulation. The worker may never have heard of Marx, but he knows that the factory is overstocked with goods, that he is unemployed, that he is unable to purchase the goods he has produced. He may not know the phrases about the conflict between the material forces of production and the existing relations of production; he may accept the explanation of demagogues like Roosevelt, General Johnson, Father Coughlin, Huey Long, or Phil La Follette; but he knows the *facts,* his "experience" consists of those facts.

Let us now suppose that a given worker is a gifted story-teller, yet ignorant of Marxian theory. He accurately describes his own specific experiences at the moment when the social revolution breaks out, as many Russian, German, Hungarian, Mexican, and Chinese workers have done. Such a worker would not be writing an *illustration* of the *Communist Manifesto* any more than the bee's conduct is an illustration of Fabre's famous book. The worker's experience, however, would sustain Marx's theory, otherwise the theory would not be true. The worker's poetic rendering of the specific experience would be art, as Marx's summation of that experience is science. Nor would such a story be for the *worker* or the intellectual *writing from the worker's standpoint a tour de force.* It would be a "natural," "free" expression of experience.

But is the worker or the intellectual who identifies himself with the worker *normal?* Remember, the conservative critic I cited only said that *normally* the attempt to convey Marx's concept in concrete images and pictures would be a *tour de force.* From the viewpoint of the bourgeois aesthete, the worker is apparently not normal, just as the experience of the worker or of the crushed middle classes is not experience. The "normal" poet is the bourgeois poet; "experience" is bourgeois experience. It is only if we make that false assumption that the *tour de force* becomes inevitable. Only when an aesthete lives the life of a bourgeois and attempts intellectually to be "Communist" does the dualism here involved arise. For the Man in White art develops out of experience and experience is bourgeois;

he can conceive of writing about proletarian life, which Marx has described scientifically, only as an intellectual *tour de force,* only by reading a Communist book and then "with a teacherly intention and a sufficiently deliberate ingenuity" attempt to "show" the Marxian concept, admittedly true, in images and pictures. Such a man, naturally, is compelled to a *tour de force,* to very bad "proletarian art"; he proceeds from the general to the specific instead of from the specific to the general.

We have had such writings in the revolutionary press, nearly always from intellectuals new to the movement. It is well known that American Marxist critics have fought against this tendency. We have maintained for years that to put a Comintern resolution in rhyme does not make proletarian poetry. It is better for the poet honestly to describe his real experiences, his doubts and inner conflicts, and the external circumstances which brought him to the revolutionary movement, than to fake his feelings by rehashing and corrupting political manifestoes which we prefer to read in their original form. But the intellectual who sympathizes with the proletariat in the abstract and continues his bourgeois life in the concrete is bound to resort to a *tour de force.* Such a poet can only write of his bourgeois experience; he must violate his real feelings when he attempts to translate Marxian science into art. It is when the intellectual describes his own conflicts sincerely that he can create revolutionary art; it is when he has transformed his life, when his experience is in the ranks of the advanced proletariat that he begins to create proletarian art.

Art varies with experience; its so-called sanctions vary with experience. The experience of the mass of humanity today is such that social and political themes are more interesting, more significant, more "normal" than the personal themes of other eras. Social themes today correspond to the general experience of men, acutely conscious of the violent and basic transformations through which they are living, which they are helping to bring about. It does not require much imagination to see why workers and intellectuals sympathetic to the working class—and themselves victims of the general social-economic crisis—should be more interested in unemployment, strikes, the fight against war and fascism, revolution and counter-revolution than in nightingales, the stream of the middle-class unconscious, or love in Greenwich Village.

At the moment when the creative writer sits at his desk and composes his verses or his novel or his play, he may have the illusion that he is writing his work for its own sake. But without his past life, without his class education, prejudices, and experiences, that particular book would be impossible. Memory, the Greeks said, is the mother of the muses; and memory feeds not on the general, abstract idea of absolute disembodied experience, but on our action, education, and knowledge in our specific social milieu. As the poet's experience changes, his poetry changes. . . .

American writers of the present generation have passed through three general stages in their attempts to relate art to the contemporary environment. Employing the term *poetry* in the German sense of *Dichtung,* creative writing in any form, we may roughly designate the three stages as follows: Poetry and Time, Poetry and Class, Poetry and Party.

From the poetic renaissance of 1912 until the economic crisis of 1929, literary discussions outside of revolutionary circles centered on the problem of Time and Eternity. The movement associated with Harriet Monroe, Carl Sandburg, Ezra Pound, Sinclair Lewis, Sherwood Anderson, Gertrude Stein, Ernest Hemingway was one which repudiated the "eternal values" of traditional poetry and emphasized immediate American experience. The movement had its prophet in Walt Whitman, who broke with the "eternal values" of feudal literature and proclaimed the here and now. Poetry abandoned the pose of moving freely in space and time; it focused its attention on New York, Chicago, San Francisco, Iowa, Alabama in the twentieth century.

The economic crisis shattered the common illusion that American society was classless. Literary frustration, unemployment, poverty, hunger threw many writers into the camp of the proletariat. Once they were compelled to face the basic facts of class society, such writers of necessity faced the problem of poetry and class. It was impossible to share the experiences of the unemployed worker and continue to create the poetry of the secure bourgeois. Poetry, however, tends to lag behind reality. Suffering opens the poet's eyes but tradition ties his tongue. As a member of society he was forced to face the meaning of the class struggle; as a member of the ancient and honorable caste of scribes, he continued to be burdened with antiquated shibboleths about art and society, art and propaganda, art and class.

In the past five years many writers have fought their way to a clearer conception of their role in the contemporary world. At first they split themselves into apparently irreconcilable halves. As *men,* they supported the working class in its struggle for a classless society; as *poets,* they retained the umbilical cord which bound them to bourgeois culture. The deepening of the economic crisis compelled many writers to abandon this dichotomy. The dualism paralyzed them both as men and as poets. Either the man had to follow the poet back to the camp of the bourgeoisie, or the poet had to follow the man forward into the camp of the proletariat. Those who chose the latter course accepted the fact that art has a class basis; they realized that in a revolutionary period like ours, poetry is inseparable from politics. The choice was influenced chiefly by the violence of the class struggle in America today; it was also influenced by echoes of that struggle in the realm of letters. On the one hand, there were writers trained in the revolutionary movement with definite ideas on the question of poetry and class, who reasoned with the hesitant and the confused; on the other, it became more and more evident that the writers who proclaimed the "independence" of poetry from all social factors were themselves passionate and sometimes unscrupulous political partisans. The poet poised uncertainly between the two great political camps of our epoch now saw that it was no longer an abstract question of art and class, but the specific challenge: which class?

The solution of this problem raised new ones. The working class is itself divided, and the poet feels the cleavage acutely. He now faces the question of poetry and party. There are those who say: "I am, both as man and poet, on the side of the proletariat, but I cannot get mixed up with the party of the proletariat, the Communist Party." The poet cannot be above class, but he must be above party. There are others who say with Edwin Seaver: "The literary honeymoon is over, and I believe the time is fast approaching when we will no longer classify authors as proletarian writers and fellow-travellers, but as Party writers and non-Party writers."

Current discussions of this problem are fruitful. They would be more fruitful if the history of revolutionary literature were generally known. It is because most of us know little of that history that partisans of the old order are able to falsify the role of the poet. They distort the past, the present, and the future; and since they fill the pages of the conservative and liberal press, their lies and libels are bound to have some effect even on writers who are on the side of the proletariat. . . .

To followers of Karl Marx the connection between poetry, politics, and party was so obvious, that wherever the Socialist movement developed there grew up around it groups of Socialist writers and artists. Where the class struggle was latent, the Socialist movement was weak; where the movement was weak, the art it inspired was weak. Where the class struggle was sharp, the movement was strong; where the movement was strong, the art it inspired was strong. . . .

In every epoch, proletarian art is identified with the political movement of the working class. During the first two decades of our century, American revolutionary writers were influenced by or directly affiliated with the Socialist Party or the I.W.W. In the third decade, they moved in the orbit of the Communist Party which emerged as the political vanguard of the workers. They were writers, and not politicians; and they developed on the periphery of the organized movement. But their outlook on life was molded by the October Revolution and by the struggles of the workers in all countries for a similar social transformation. Around their own, independent magazine—the *New Masses,* founded in the spring of 1926—they created the foundations of an American art and literature corresponding to the class conflicts of our epoch.

During the twenties, the *New Masses* group was small. It was isolated both from the mass organizations of the workers and from the mass of the intellectuals, who, despite liberal reservations, were at this time attached to the existing social system. One or two novels, occasional stories and poems, were all that American left-wing writers were able to produce in the creative field. Proletarian literature was in its propaganda stage. The handful of revolutionary writers active in the Coolidge–Hoover era devoted themselves chiefly to criticism. They analyzed contemporary American literature from a Marxist viewpoint and agitated for a conscious proletarian art. They exposed the decay of bourgeois culture before it became generally apparent, and indicated future literary trends.

In this period, the revolutionary writer suffered from a dualism which forced him to be sectarian. His social allegiance was to the proletariat; his literary peers were attached to the bourgeoisie. Hence he had no literary milieu; he worked in isolation. That was why he was prolific in critical writing, an intellectual process, and backward in creative writing, an emotional-imaginative process. He was able to tell what kind of literature the revolutionary movement needed; he was rarely able to produce it. The historic conditions necessary for such a literature did not appear until the economic crisis overwhelmed the country and altered the life of its people.

Most men of letters come from the middle classes, which have both the education and the incentive for literary production. These classes shared the pangs of the crisis together with the workers and farmers. The unemployment, poverty, and insecurity which spread over the country hit the educated classes like a hurricane; writers and artists, among others, were catapulted out of privileged positions; and many of those who remained economically secure experienced a revolution in ideas which reflected the profound changes around them. And at the very moment when our own country, to the surprise of all except the Marxists, was sliding into a social-economic abyss, the new social-economic system of the Russian workers and peasants showed striking gains.

The contrast between the two worlds loomed up above the wreckage of old illusions. Writers and artists, like other members of the educated classes, began to read revolutionary books, pamphlets, and newspapers;

they came to workers' meetings; they discovered a new America, the land of the masses whose existence they had ignored. They saw those masses as the motive power of modern history, as the hope for a superior social system, for a revival and extension of culture.

At first the middle-class writer who "went left" was a divided being. As a citizen he supported Foster and Ford in the 1932 elections; he went to the aid of the striking miners in Kentucky and was beaten up by the police; he called for the liberation of Tom Mooney and the Scottsboro boys. As a writer he remained where he was. He continued to hope that the old themes of middle-class personal existence would serve as well as in the old days. But the crisis became deeper; it forced him further toward the viewpoint of the workers. There came a time when many writers who had all their lives ignored politics and economics suddenly abandoned the poem, the novel, and the play and began to write solemn articles on unemployment, fiscal policy, and foreign trade. This politicalization of the man of letters was a step toward his transformation *as a poet*.

One more thing was needed to complete that transformation: direct contact with the proletarian audience. At the beginning of the crisis, the writers and artists who had grown up in the working-class movement and kept alive the tradition of proletarian literature, founded literary groups like the John Reed Clubs, dramatic groups like the Theatre Union, film and photo leagues, music and dance organizations. The growth of the workers' movement was accompanied by a growth of proletarian literature. The workers and their middle-class allies, in their struggles against capitalist exploitation, against fascism, against the menace of a new world war, furnish the themes of the new literature; they also furnish the audience of the revolutionary theatre and magazines.

In the past five years, American proletarian literature has made striking progress. The arguments against it are dying down in the face of actual creative achievement. Life itself has settled the dispute for the most progressive minds of America. The collapse of the prevailing culture, the pressure of the economic crisis, the ruthless oppression of monopoly capital, the heroic struggle of the workers everywhere for the abolition of man's exploitation of man—this whole vast transformation of the world through the inexorable conflict of social classes has produced a new art in this country which has won the respect even of its enemies.

[26]

A NOTE ON LITERARY CRITICISM

JAMES T. FARRELL

THE living stream of literature is a process, intertwined with other processes in society. The products of this process give us understanding; they enable us to feel aspects of life more deeply; and they afford us pleasure. At various times, and according to the character of the literary output and its audience and of the society of which both are parts, one of the elements —understanding, feeling, or pleasure—may gain an ascendancy over the others; when, for instance, literature heightens our understanding and intensifies our awareness, it contributes what it is capable of toward the changing of society.

We have discussed the twin processes of growth and decay in society. A whole body, even a whole tradition, of modern literature—such as the naturalistic novel—has been instrumental in making man aware of the decay and the loss of religious belief that are so prevalent today. The role, here, of "exposure" literature has been utterly misunderstood. We must distinguish literature from propaganda and agitation, as I have used the words, not because of any necessary hierarchy of importance in literature, propaganda, and agitation, but because of the possibilities inherent in the function of each. No function of any of these can be said to shut the door absolutely on the rest. Literature may be propaganda, according to my definition of propaganda; but when it is, it must contain that internal consistency and that essential external reference which I have described in applying the concept of necessity to literature.

It should be clear, now, that the effect of living literature on its reader is not the same as the effect of an advertising slogan upon a prospective customer. It cuts much deeper into the human consciousness. It cuts beneath stereotyped feelings and crystallized thoughts, furnishing the material from which extended feelings and added thought are developed. It is one of the agents serving to work out within the individual consciousness the twin processes of growth and decay in a way corresponding to the

SOURCE: James T. Farrell, *A Note on Literary Criticism* (New York: Vanguard Press, 1936), pp. 214–221. © 1936, 1963 by James T. Farrell. Reprinted by permission of the publisher, The Vanguard Press.

226

objective working-out of these processes in society. It destroys old faiths and ideals, and creates new ones, or at least lays the basis for their creation. What is important in such literature is its content, and that content is not to be taken as merely synonymous with formal ideology, generalized themes, and the explicitly stated ideas of its writers. Rather it is the shaping of life itself into literary form—a way of feeling and thinking and seeing life that the creative artist conveys to his audience—the structure of events, the quality of the characterizations, the complex impact of the work itself.

Criticism, in the literary process, should become the agent that makes for the understanding and evaluation of works of literature. It should create the atmosphere through which a maximum of value and effect, rather than a minimum, is produced by our living literature. It should strive to make the meanings of books clear, to draw out these essential meanings and refer and assimilate them in a wider social area. In performing these functions, criticism will evidently be making judgments, and on the basis of analysis; the criteria for these judgments being not alone internal to the literary process, and not alone external. Like the books to which they are applied they have both a subjective or aesthetic side and an objective or functional side. These criteria must be rationally established, tested by reference to experience, and used flexibly. In other words, they cannot be absolutized and fixed; they cannot be invented. They must have applicability to the literary work that is being judged. . . .

When literary criticism fails to play such a role as this, it is failing to function as it should. It is reneging on its duties and thereby sowing the seeds of confusion; for it is making no contribution toward that clarity, that lucidity, that understanding, which are rightfully asked of the critic. The critic must, as I have said, refer the book to life in an *essential* way: He must understand the book as a work of literature, reproducing elements from life, re-creating a sense of them. He must also understand the author's terms, the premises explicitly or implicitly established by the author. And this understanding cannot be merely in terms of formal ideology; it must also relate to the internal structure of events in the book. These tell the critic what the author is trying to say; they provide the clue to estimating how well, and how truthfully, the author has rendered life. The critic is thus enabled to judge the meaning of the work, both in terms of its inherent worth and in terms of its reference to other but related meanings.

It is to be assumed, of course, that the critic has some original equipment. If he lacks original equipment in sensory capacities, in imagination, in powers of reasoning, then not all the formulae in the world, not all the

227

external categories he may devise, not all his academic learning, will help him. Technique without the ability to apply it is futile. It results in formalism.

This equipment, however, can be assumed in most persons who undertake criticism. A fairly adequate power of thinking, understanding, and feeling is presumably common among them. What I challenge is the way they make use of what equipment they have—their view of the functions of literature and their procedure in measuring and legislating rather than judging it. And I am convinced that if a critic follows such a procedure—unless he seeks to judge, evaluate, relate, understand, feel, and enjoy works of living literature—his critical efforts are vain. He falls into functional extremism. He adds to the number of tasks left for others to perform in the future. He fails to advance lucidity of thinking and thus turns criticism into an instrument for confusion. Or else he sinks into impressionism, his criticism becoming totally subjective. And subjectivism leads him finally—whether he is gifted or not—into sensationalism.

We have had enough of aberrations in criticism. We have had enough extra-literary critical legislation. We have had enough blindness and sentimentalism. The health of both living literature and the revolutionary movement to which it is more and more attaching itself demands that these aberrations be exposed and liquidated. It is because of this present need that I agree with Maxim Gorky, who writes: "I do not want to give our enemies the opportunity to laugh at us by emphasizing the coarseness, the lack of culture and, very often, even the ignorance of our critics. Perhaps our critics are very well equipped ideologically, but something seems to deter them from stating with the utmost clarity and simplicity the science of dialectic materialism as applied to questions of art."

It is time, I think, that revolutionary criticism should concern itself with its proper tasks, and in a thorough and adequate way. The pious expression of generalized conclusions is insufficient. The harping cry that criticism must be raised above the level of personalities, the search for personal motives rather than for ideas and criteria of judgment behind critical evaluations—such serve only to advertise a paucity and degradation of ideas. Critics who have ideas to express need not indulge in pious assent to "Marxian" generalizations which should be assimilated before one calls oneself a "Marxist." And the factors that have militated against our revolutionary criticism thus far have been mechanical legislation leading to these pieties; and sentimentalism leading to equally empty pities. And in each case, these different tendencies either begin or end in mechanism crudity. They absolutize standards, and they absolutize Marx. For several years this process has gone on; its nature and contents have been suggested in my analysis. Its fruits in misunderstanding are incalculable. Again to quote Maxim Gorky: "For many years a certain professor, writer and critic exalted mediocre writers to the height of classic authors. Serious critics paid no attention to his activities, which were hardly beneficial to the young people who heard him lecture. Now he admits that 'in the last few months he recognized some of his mistakes'! . . . A Russian proverb says: 'Words once uttered cannot be revoked'; consequently the mistakes of the professor remain."

The mistakes of our critics remain, too, and they harm the revolutionary cultural movement, which has much to assimilate, much to understand, much to produce. If it is going to assimilate what is alive from the traditions it has inherited, fight what is dead within them, and carry forward to the future, enlarging and expanding these traditions and creating new ones, it must now stop cooking up recipes for culture. It must understand, must produce culture. And to do that, it must liquidate its sins; it must pay now, with understanding, for the forged checks it has issued during the last few years. For it has been perpetuating old errors, and the point has now been reached where it is inexcusable to keep on doing this. For these are errors that Engels recognized years ago. I conclude with a statement from one of his letters:

Marx and I are partly to blame for the fact that younger writers sometimes lay more stress on the economic side than is due to it. We had to emphasize this main principle in opposition to our adversaries, who denied it, and we had not always the time, the place or the opportunity to allow the other elements involved in the interaction to come into their rights. But when it was a case of presenting a section of history, that is, of a practical application, the thing was different and there no error was possible. Unfortunately, however, it happens only too often that people think they have fully understood a theory and can apply it without more ado from the moment they have mastered its main principles, and those even not always correctly. And I cannot exempt many of the more recent "Marxists" from this reproach, for the most wonderful rubbish has been produced from this quarter too.

EDITORIAL STATEMENT

Partisan Review

AS our readers know, the tradition of aestheticism has given way to a literature which, for its origin and final justification, looks beyond itself and deep into the historic process. But the forms of literary editorship, at once exacting and adventurous, which characterized the magazines of the aesthetic revolt, were of definite cultural value; and these forms *Partisan Review* will wish to adapt to the literature of the new period.

Any magazine, we believe, that aspires to a place in the vanguard of literature today, will be revolutionary in tendency; but we are also convinced that any such magazine will be unequivocally independent. *Partisan Review* is aware of its responsibility to the revolutionary movement in general, but we disclaim obligation to any of its organized political expressions. Indeed we think that the cause of revolutionary literature is best served by a policy of no commitments to any political party. Thus our underscoring of the factor of independence is based, not primarily on our differences with any one group, but on the conviction that literature in our period should be free of all factional dependence.

There is already a tendency in America for the more conscious social writers to identify themselves with a single organization, the Communist Party; with the result that they grow automatic in their political responses but increasingly less responsible in an artistic sense. And the Party literary critics, equipped with the zeal of vigilantes, begin to consolidate into aggressive political-literary amalgams as many tendencies as possible and to outlaw all dissenting opinion. This projection on the cultural field of factionalism in politics makes for literary cleavages which, in most instances, have little to do with literary issues, and which are more and more provocative of a ruinous bitterness among writers. Formerly associated with the Communist Party, *Partisan Review* strove from the first against its drive to equate the interests of literature with those of factional politics. Our reappearance on an independent basis signifies our conviction that the totalitarian trend is inherent in that movement and that it can no longer be combatted from within.

SOURCE: "Editorial Statement," *Partisan Review* 4, no. 1 (December 1937): 3–4.
© 1937 by *Partisan Review*.

But many other tendencies exist in American letters, and these, we think, are turning from the senseless disciplines of the official Left to shape a new movement. The old movement will continue and, to judge by present indications, it will be reenforced more and more by academicians from the universities, by yesterday's celebrities and today's philistines. Armed to the teeth with slogans of revolutionary prudence, its official critics will revive the petty-bourgeois tradition of gentility, and with each new tragedy on the historic level they will call the louder for a literature of good cheer. Weak in genuine literary authority but equipped with all the economic and publicity powers of an authentic cultural bureaucracy, the old regime will seek to isolate the new by performing upon it the easy surgery of political falsification. Because the writers of the new grouping aspire to independence in politics as well as in art, they will be identified with fascism, sometimes directly, sometimes through the convenient medium of "Trotskyism." Every effort, in short, will be made to *excommunicate* the new generation, so that their writing and their politics may be regarded as making up a kind of diabolic totality; which would render unnecessary any sort of rational discussion of the merits of either.

Do we exaggerate? On the contrary, our prediction as to the line the old regime will take is based on the first maneuvers of a campaign which has already begun. Already, *before it has appeared, Partisan Review* has been subjected to a series of attacks in the Communist Party press; already, with no regard for fact—without, indeed, any relevant facts to go by— they have attributed gratuitous political designs to *Partisan Review* in an effort to confuse the primarily literary issue between us.

But *Partisan Review* aspires to represent a new and dissident generation in American letters; it will not be dislodged from its independent position by any political campaign against it. And without ignoring the importance of the official movement as a sign of the times we shall know how to estimate its authority in literature. But we shall also distinguish, wherever possible, between the tendencies of this faction itself and the work of writers associated with it. For our editorial accent falls chiefly on culture and its broader social determinants. Conformity to a given social ideology or to a prescribed attitude or technique will not be asked of our writers. On the contrary, our pages will be open to any tendency which is relevant to literature in our time. Marxism in culture, we think, is first of all an instrument of analysis and evaluation; and if, in the last instance, it prevails over other disciplines, it does so through the medium of democratic controversy. Such is the medium that *Partisan Review* will want to provide in its pages.

PART X
Depression

THE American Left, as others did also, always sustained itself on the conviction that time was on its side. At every point in the twentieth century, Marxist analysts concluded that the American political economy would necessarily crash, that political consciousness would therefore rise, that total polarization would occur, and that the cooperative commonwealth would spring from the debris of capitalism's failure. The Great Depression of the 1930's seemed to vindicate the Left's beliefs about America's political economy. The Depression was an enormous challenge for the Left, whose progress now absolutely depended on clarity and unity, both of which however, along with almost everything else during these austere years, were in short supply.

Having to confront the political genius of Franklin Delano Roosevelt, the American Left very quickly abandoned ideas of actual political victory, and devoted itself, as usual, to the longer haul, to building consciousness, to education, and to organizing the cadres that one day would hopefully lead the way into socialism of one kind or another. Given the objective chaos of capitalism, and remembering the now familiar liberal nonsense about how the entire nation presumably moved leftward in the 1930's, it is important to point out that the American Left, even during the Great Depression, was on the defensive. Its economic predictions were turning out to be better than its political ones, and this was in itself a major problem for the theorists on the left. Radical spokesmen, although they would not say so in public, knew that this was so. They knew it because the millions of unemployed turned not to them but to the Democratic Party.

In February 1933, one month before Roosevelt's inauguration, V. F. Calverton (1900–1940) analyzed the meaning of liberalism in American civilization (Document 28). Calverton was an ideological maverick, required his own magazine to contain his independence, and broke with the

Communists in 1931. His view of the retrogressive character of home-grown liberalism, however, could have been accepted by most of the Left, even if his attachment to the idea of American exceptionalism seemed to be still a willful attachment to heresy. Calverton concluded that liberalism's final if unwitting achievement would be the rise of fascism in the United States.

In brief Document 29 which follows, there is at least a suggestion about the growing militance of college students. Unlike the goldfish-eaters of the 1920's, the students at New York City colleges went on strike against repressive university administrations. Athletes—"jocks"—formed antistrike vigilante groups, and faculties remained "above the battle," "neutral," and therefore politically dangerous. But these sporadic and essentially disorganized student actions did not constitute, as the author of this article assumed, the political coming of age of the American student. But insofar as this was premonitory of the campuses of the late sixties, we can usefully view these early student strikes as background.

An analysis of Roosevelt appeared in *The American Socialist Quarterly* in the summer of 1933 (Document 30). Written by one of the journal's editors, the article displayed the official SP view of "That Man." (This journal was soon declared to be "the official theoretical organ of the Socialist Party of America.") All the New Deal was described as either a public relations gimmick or an outright lie. But the myth of Roosevelt as a beneficent Big Daddy seemed to grow right in the face of damning evidence to the contrary. The idea of a self-limiting capitalism was inherently contradictory, but this is what FDR probably believed himself, and this is the idea he sold to the nation. This was what the Left had to withstand. The confident tilt of the president's cigarette holder seemed to be more persuasive to more people than reasoned analysis.

Earl Browder (b. 1891) reported for the Central Committee to the eighth Communist Party convention in Cleveland in early April 1934. He was for many difficult years at, or near, the head of the American CP, and his career began with the birth of the party in 1919 and officially ended when Moscow insisted that he be replaced in 1945. In the following section of Browder's long report (Document 31), he leveled his heaviest political artillery against the New Deal. He said that FDR's program had the same goal as fascism, that it was "the same as Hitler's program." He conceded that American workers were still hypnotized by FDR, but he thought that growing labor organization revealed a growing resistance to the New Deal. As he saw and described it, the New Deal was a program designed to save capitalism by giving more to the rich while taking more from the poor. Browder's vehemence on this score probably made his reversal of field difficult: he soon was defending the New Deal and Roosevelt under the rubric of the Popular Front against war and fascism.

Lewis Corey understood the American middle class better than anyone else. He had been instrumental in organizing the CP in 1919 under his original name, Louis C. Fraina. After rumored scandals, spectacular trials in Moscow that exonerated him, and a still mysterious disappearance in Mexico, he emerged with his new name as a calmer professor of political economy in a small Midwestern college. He published *The Crisis of the Middle Class* in 1935 (from which Document 32 is taken), an acute perception of the proletarianization of the petit bourgeoisie during the Depression.

The final word here belongs to Norman Thomas (1884–1968), the SP's presidential candidate in six elections, former clergyman, and a devoted pacifist and civil libertarian. The following transcript (Document 33) of a speech he gave over CBS Radio on 2 February 1936 was printed as a pamphlet and sold for 2 cents. It was important that he try to distinguish himself from Roosevelt because a growing number of articulate liberals were already saying that FDR was actually implementing Thomas's socialism. He insisted that the New Deal was state capitalism, not socialism, and would tend toward fascism if greater resistance did not form. Thomas's clergylike mildness was somewhat pale next to the old fire of Debs, but as he pointed out many times, there is nothing mild about socialism. He was a true believer in his own variant of socialism and pacifism, but militance did turn to mildness and fair play in his hands. Distrusted by the more angry Left, Thomas became the respected resident socialist for many American liberals. Nonetheless he understood Roosevelt and the New Deal, and this radio speech was delivered by an authentic voice of the American Left.

[28]

BACKWARD MARCH: THE LIBERAL COMMAND (AN EXAMINATION OF THE RETROGRESSIVE ROLE OF AMERICAN LIBERALISM)

V. F. CALVERTON

THE time has come when American history must be re-evaluated and re-written. It is only today, when certain forces in American life have reached a point of focus contributive of a clarity impossible in the past, that this re-evaluation can be attempted with success. In the nineteenth century, the American scene was in a state which was too muddled and confused to inspire such a re-evaluation. At that time the interests at stake, the conflicts of purpose between classes, sections, groups, and individuals, were too blurred to be recognized clearly in terms of what they were to become. Today we can see them as the interrelated and indisseverable parts of a cultural process which is as definite and clear-cut as the lines of a skyscraper.

The class lines which in the nineteenth century were so uncertain and nebulous, so bewilderingly criss-crossed and intersecting, have become clear and precise in the twentieth century. It is in the light of that new clarity that American history must be rewritten.

During the first two-thirds of the nineteenth century, America was a nation created by small men, men without social station or distinction, men without means but with pluck and courage and determination, men who were individualistic-minded, democratic-spirited, and patriotic to the core. That America was animate with aspiration, impregnated with a belief in its future. When Mrs. Trollope traveled through the America of that day she was constantly annoyed by the bombardment of patriotism which greeted her on every side, in villages, towns, and cities, as also was de Tocqueville who found the Americans the most obstreperous chauvinists he had ever encountered. That patriotism, born on the rising tide of expansion of that day, penetrated throughout the length and breadth of our

SOURCE: V. F. Calverton, "Backward March: The Liberal Command. An Examination of the Retrogressive Role of American Liberalism," *Modern Monthly* 1, no. 1 (February 1933): 27–33.

life. It was shared by the politicians, the literati, the well-to-do, and the populace on the street. It was in the writing of American history, symbolized in the work of Bancroft, that that spirit became most unrestrained and vociferous. In the eyes of Bancroft, for example, everything American was sacred; everything this country ever attempted was right; from the founders of the country to the leaders of that day no blemish was to be noted, so noble had been their intentions and so fruitfully had they been fulfilled. Like the cherry-tree Washington of Weems' biography, the country and its leaders were sheathed in a mist of fabled rectitude and virtue.

As long as the country remained in its expanding stage, that tendency of interpretation continued to dominate the spirit of American history. When the twentieth century arrived, however, and the days of expansion were over, and the small man found himself being beaten over the head by the big man in the field of business, as well as agriculture, that tendency ceased. Since that time the halo which once enshrouded American institutions and leaders has disappeared. Beginning with the era of the muckrakers, things American began to look exceedingly sick and shoddy. With the advance of liberal scholarship, an outgrowth of the muckraking decade and of the spirit of defeat which had come upon the land with the defeat of the small man on the economic field, the American scene was subjected to a new interpretation. Exposing as it did the monetary machinations behind many of our most lauded achievements, the liberal tradition encouraged the tendency to scoff and sneer at American traditions. It was out of that tendency that the "debunkers" of American history sprang. The achievements of the Revolutionary War were debunked; the importance of the Civil War was debunked; the pertinence and place of various individuals in the historical process were debunked—in fact, everything was debunked with an indiscriminate enthusiasm which betrayed the lack of historical insight involved in the whole approach. Instead of seeing the development of America as part of its progressive advance as a historic whole, and evaluating its phenomena and its leaders in relationship with that development, the debunkers adjudge everything and everybody in reference to the immediate criteria of today, stressing with a narrow-mindedness culpably characteristic of defeatist historians the corruption involved in the *means* but neglecting entirely the significance involved in the *ends*. It is easy to attack the motivations behind many of the leaders in the Revolutionary War or the Civil War or the Reconstruction period, but it is a much more difficult and valuable task to determine the significance of those events in relationship to the historic advance of the country as a unit.

The great problem confronting and challenging us today, therefore, is not that of debunking our past but of re-evaluating it in terms of our revolutionary tradition. In a word, we must learn not to scoff at our revolutionary past but to build upon it.

What we must see is that in every phase of our development there have been progressive as well as reactionary forces at work, and if the progressive forces of one day lose their progressiveness in the next that is no reason why we should disregard the important influence which they exerted at the time they were progressive. What we must do is to evaluate every period in terms of the forces active at the time, differentiating those that were progressive from those that were retrogressive, showing in just what ways those that were progressive tended to shape the developments in our society which are important to understanding its character today and its possibilities of change tomorrow.

By employing that approach, it can be seen at once that things American must be adjudged by different standards than things European, since American social and economic conditions have been so different from those present in Europe. American history is usually misjudged because of the neglect of that difference. In discussing the theme of this article, for example, it can be said at once that if we mean by a revolution what the French Revolution of 1789 signifies or the Bolshevik Revolution of 1917, then America has had no revolutionary history at all. What is necessary to stress at this point, in keeping with our previous observations, is that America has evolved differently from European countries, creating a different cultural pattern in the process, and developing a different series of social struggles with different revolutionary implications. It is those differences which must be understood first if there is to be any appreciation of the significance and challenge of our revolutionary history.

In Europe the great social struggles of the seventeenth, eighteenth, and early nineteenth centuries were those fought between the landed aristocracies and the commercial and industrial bourgeoisie. In America those struggles took on an entirely different character. The earliest approach to a landed aristocracy that America ever had was in the patroon system and the vast landed estates which had been dealt out by English kings as special grants to various individuals who stood high in royal favor. But that landed aristocracy, largely Tory in extraction, which, due to the rapid rise in power of the merchant class, had never been able to function effectively, disappeared with the close of the Revolutionary War. Its representatives or defendants, Tories in the main, were driven out by force by the bourgeoisie who were the patriots of the period. The Revolutionary War, then, was a progressive war in that it dealt the first death blow to American feudalism. After the Revolutionary War, the only remnant of feudalism which persisted was the presence of the plantation aristocracy in the South. The struggle between the North and the South which developed with violent intensity during the first half of the nineteenth century, reaching its climax in the Civil War, marked the last conflict between the landed aristocracy and the bourgeoisie in the nation. The Civil War meted out the final death blow to feudal institutions in this country. After the Civil War, the class struggle in America changed character and became a conflict between the upper bourgeoisie and the petty bourgeoisie, big business and small business, with the growing proletariat of the time allying itself politically with the cause of the latter. The landed class disappeared as a separate social force and became absorbed into the maw of the commercial and industrial structure. Big business in the form of the banks, the loan associations, and the railroads, sunk its tentacles into the land, mortgaging it beyond redemption. The small farmer and the small businessman found themselves face to face with the same foe, big business in the guise of the financier and the industrialist. The struggle between those two forces absorbed the *revolutionary* energy, of the American people throughout the nineteenth century and in decreasing degree continues to do so even today.

Now the very fact that the struggle against feudalism in America assumed in the Civil War the form of a sectional conflict instead of a national conflict of classes, thwarted the development of a revolutionary ideology on the part of the bourgeois forces which were bent upon the destruction of the feudal way of life. *In all European countries, for example, the battle which the bourgeoisie carried on against feudalism led to the creation of a revolutionary ideology which found dynamic expression in economics, politics, religion, and ethics.* Freedom of speech, press, religion, became the great rallying cries of the revolutionary bourgeoisie in Europe. The struggle for the right to economic freedom, that is freedom for the middle class from the restrictions of the aristocracy, lent the cause of the European bourgeoisie a fierce fighting character, which found its summation in the liberal idealism of the eighteenth and nineteenth centuries. The fact that that conflict followed sectional instead of national class lines in this country robbed us of that heritage of progressive liberal idealism, *and twisted and distorted our whole political outlook in such ways that class interests became blurred by sectional prejudices, with antagonistic classes resolving their conflicts with each other (which under different conditions would have led them to open strife) into a mutual alliance against their accepted sectional foe.* Even today the South provides a clear-cut example of the confusing consequences of that alliance. Active as various aspects of the class struggle are in the South today, the South as a whole, proletarians as well as sharecroppers, poor whites as well as successful bourgeoisie, stand politically as one in their uncompromising support of the Democratic Party. (Only the religious issue in the preceding election could in any way shake the strength and solidity of that union.) In short, their sectional hostility to the North, derivative from the struggle between the two sections in the Civil War, is still greater than their class hostility to each other. This sectional fact has definitely held back the development of a nation-wide revolutionary outlook along class lines in this country.

Paradoxically enough, because of the factors we have stressed, *liberalism has been forced to play an economically retrogressive instead of progressive role in American life.* The progressive liberal tradition developed by the bourgeoisie in England, for example, sprang out of its fight against the aristocracy and the necessity of destroying the feudal way of life. The so-called liberal tradition in America, on the other hand, developed as a definite defense against the advancing bourgeois way of life. Its energies were wasted in a futile attempt to hold back the progressive development of capitalist enterprise.

In European countries liberalism derived its fighting vigor from the intensity of its conflict with the landed class. Its revolutionary fight for its various freedoms, freedom of speech, freedom of press, freedom before the law, lent its cause a challenging progressive character, for it was those freedoms which were necessary to the advance of middle class society at that time. Moreover, its whole philosophy became identified with the advancing forms of bourgeois enterprise. In this country, on the other hand, as we noted before, the reverse occurred. Liberalism in America became identified with the retrogressive instead of progressive forms of bourgeois enterprise, and hence developed a backward instead of forward-looking philosophy of life. Without appreciating the significance of that difference, it is impossible to understand the singular development of American political and social thought.

Beginning with Jefferson, American liberalism favored agrarianism as opposed to industrialism and fought the introduction of manufactures into American life; it advocated decentralization instead of centralization of government and enterprise, with the result that it defended competition as the basis of progress and attacked all forms of corporate organization and control. Aiming to preserve competition instead of to destroy it, it devoted its energies to retarding the progressive role that big business, by the very nature of its objectives, was scheduled to perform, namely, to eliminate competition within the respective industries by the organization of corporations, trusts, and monopolies to take the place of the myriad-fold competing enterprises and proprietors.

In brief, American liberalism from the very start was reactionary in that it defended competition instead of opposing it, thereby helping to hold back the progressive advance of our economic life. Sentimentally, to be sure, it stood up for the cause of the individual, defending his rights against those of big business and the centralized state; realistically, however, it fought to preserve a way of life which early in the nineteenth century had begun to become retrogressive. It defended the interests of the small farmer and the small businessman against those of the large capitalist and financier, although it was the large capitalist and financier, the Rockefellers, the Carnegies, the Morgans, who were to make possible the reorganization of our economic life in such ways as to prepare the groundwork for a more cooperative world wherein competition would not exist and individualism would disappear. It was in that sense that American liberalism was retrogressive instead of progressive in its outlook. It was as capitalistic in its logic as big business, save that it wanted capitalism to proceed on a small scale instead of a vast, concentrated one. It wanted a world which was filled with predatory wolves and foxes but in which there were no all-powerful lions. What it did not see was that it was the lions, though at the cost of life of the smaller animals, who brought order out of chaos, lifting the world in which they lived from a lower to a higher state of existence.

Indeed, we can say at this point that the whole development of revolutionary thought in this country has been impeded and distorted by the retrogressive character of American liberalism. In the early conflict between Jefferson and Hamilton, for instance, it was the conservative Hamilton who was right in his emphasis upon the importance of encouraging industries and in his advocacy of a sound national finance, while it was the liberal Jefferson who was wrong in his hostility to industries and in his opposition to every form of national control. A century later, American liberalism was guilty of the same fallacy. Bryan had not advanced a step beyond Jefferson in his economic philosophy, except that he did not attack the development of industries,—industries having grown by that time to so large a stature that the only thing possible to attack were their tendencies toward expansion.

In fact the whole history of American liberalism stretching from Jefferson to Bryan, and then down to Wilson and LaFollette, did nothing more than comprise new and ever more pathetic testimonies of the futile, economically backward character of the liberal cause. Industrialism having planted itself ineradicably in our soil, Jefferson's stand on the question could no longer be defended. But the attempt of the later liberals to restrain the development of industry was essentially no less retrogressive an influence. Woodrow Wilson's platitudes about "the new freedom" were no more sound or progressive than Theodore Roosevelt's Billy Sunday-like denunciations of the trusts, or LaFollette's infantile proposals that we return to the days of 1776. Franklin D. Roosevelt's voluble promises to restore power to the "forgotten man" retain the same anachronistic echo. Without exception, then, American liberalism, changing though it did with new conditions, has continued throughout our history to play a retarding role in our economic life. However much it altered its program, under the pressure of changing social forces, it constantly remained, from the days of Jefferson to those of Wilson, backward-gazing in its economic outlook. Caught in the beginning by environment and a philosophy which were predominantly agrarian, it became handicapped almost at birth with an economic myopia which eventually proved to be an immedicable affliction. Because of the affliction it was the conservatives in America, paradoxical as it may seem, who were progressive in economic vision and the liberals who were retrogressive. Hamilton was economically more progressive than Jefferson at the end of the eighteenth century, and the Republican Party was economically more progressive than the Democratic at the end of the nineteenth. Today neither party has a progressive economic role to perform. Both are equally retrogressive. Progress now lies in a new, collectivistic direction which only a radical proletarian party can convert into a program of action.

It is only by understanding the backward role which American liberalism has played in our history that we can understand the pathetic lack of social clarity in the philosophies of such outstanding American "progressives" as John Dewey, William Graham Sumner, Charles A. Beard, James Harvey Robinson, Frederick C. Howe, Herbert Croly, Jane Addams, Walter Weyl, Lincoln Steffens, Harry Elmer Barnes, and others, and realize why America has created no sociological school of consequence. Enamored of the backward-looking philosophy of American liberalism, with its emphases upon agrarian democracy and equality and upon individualism and the inspiration of the competitive drive, these so-called progressives expended their ardor and energy in fighting futile battles with an enemy that grew stronger with every attack they hazarded against it. Lilliputian zealots advancing upon a Brobdignagian foe, their tragic struggle seems almost comic in present-day perspective. Lacking the strength which communicates itself to those allied to a progressive cause, they were never able to endow their liberalism with the insight and intelligence which characterized European liberalism at its heyday of development.

The only progressive influence that American liberalism ever exercised was in providing early in the nineteenth century the necessary incentive and inspiration to encourage the masses to go West and populate the country, but even that influence behaved like a boomerang once the migrations were in full swing, for its immediate political impact was to combat the rise of industry and defend the cause of agriculture. Indeed, the land issue assumed such a commanding aspect that even when a liberal thinker acquired a degree of social-mindedness he tended to go off on a tangent like Henry George with his lopsided emphasis upon the panacea-like qualities of the Single Tax. But it was that same land factor with its individualistic challenge which also misled the others, tending to make them believe, one in this way, one in another, that the individual and not society was the center of things, and that reform to possess significance must be dedicated to a defense of individual interests even at the cost of those of society. Identified with the small agrarianite on one side and the small urbanite on the other, it was inevitable that their logic should be retrogressive in emphasis. The democracy they were interested in was not the industrial or proletarian democracy of the modern radical but the democracy of the small farmer and the small businessman and entrepreneur in the cities. In a word, they were not interested in proletarians as proletarians, but in proletarians as potential bourgeois. They were determined to think of American society as a classless phenomenon, uncognizant that what they were doing was supporting the middle class, first as agrarianites and later on as urbanites as well, with its futile stress upon an individualistic economic outlook which had been rendered anachronistic by the technical processes of production and social organization.

It was in the twentieth century that liberal thought in America became most dangerously retrogressive. By virtue of its false promises and compelling rhetoric it was able to conceal from the minds of millions of Americans the existence of certain ineradicable fundamentals. In the form of the platitude-mongering Wilson, who was willing to have young men die for old men's dividends, while he spread peace over the no-man's land of posterity, liberalism cashed in on its thirty pieces of silver and crucified itself on the wrong cross. It thought that it was Jesus but found out when it was too late that it was Judas in disguise. By talking about love of humanity instead of trying to discover how to create it, it succeeded only in spreading more hate and horror in a world that was already stinking with it from every nostril, buttock, and mouth. But Wilson's folly was not singular. It was the product of his generation, of the whole liberal way of thought. Before the War it had been in the educational philosophy of John Dewey, in the mystic nationalism of Herbert Croly, and in the pacifism of Jane Addams.

Products of the ideology of the lower middle class, they couldn't see the fundamentals involved in all issues which they discussed. Wilson couldn't see that a League of Nations can't function in a capitalist world; and Dewey couldn't see that democracy in education cannot prevail in a plutocracy and that vocationalized education in our system of society is but another way of perpetuating the prevailing plutocracy—any more than Charles Beard today, still a votary of the liberal tradition, can see that economic planning cannot be successful in an economic system which continues to defend private property and the profit motivation.

Although the American liberalism of the nineteenth century is dead, as well as that derivative of the Wilsonian tradition, twentieth-century postwar liberalism has one more retrogressive function to perform, namely, to abet the rise of an American fascism which will ultimately repudiate everything which the liberal tradition once stood for—but which the liberals will believe is liberal still.

---

[29]

RUMBLINGS IN THE COLLEGES

RICHARD DICHTER

THE recent simultaneous strikes at New York University and the College of the City of New York have again focused the attention of the American student on the strike as a weapon in the struggle against reactionary and tyrannical university administrations. It is only within the last year that students in America have resorted to the strike with any frequency. During the era of high powered football teams and million dollar gates, student strikes were rarities. With one exception the few that occurred were in protest against stringent conduct regulations. In 1925 at Howard Univer-

SOURCE: Richard Dichter, "Rumblings in the Colleges," *Common Sense* 1, no. 8 (30 March 1933): 23.

sity, a Negro school, 600 students struck when five of their fellows were dismissed for refusing to observe the existing military training regulations. The strike was short and successful, for the same evening the students were reinstated. These early strikes, although spontaneous and infrequent, were indications of the revolutionary capabilities of the American students.

In Europe and Latin America the students have long used the strike not only to gain campus reforms, but to aid revolutionary political movements. In Havana, the strike of the University students two years ago was a direct blow at the Machado regime. Previous to the March Revolution in Spain the students walked out on general strike to protest the dismissal of a professor with republican tendencies. The authorities were forced to close the universities for a month for fear the strike might lead to the overthrow of the monarchy. The strikes of European and Latin American students are characterized by greater political maturity and better organization than in the United States.

The strike at Columbia University last year ushered in a new era. It heralded the beginning of a left-wing movement on the campus. Numerous strikes of a definite political character followed. Of particular importance are those which occurred at Commonwealth College and at Kincaid, Illinois, High School. At Commonwealth, a "labor" college in Arkansas, the students walked out on strike when the administration refused them representation on the governing board of the school. They wanted a voice in order to insure the admittance of Negro applicants. During the two-day tenure of the strike the school was completely controlled by the strikers. Expulsions and arrests finally broke the strike. But the fact that students in a southern college had demanded the admittance of Negroes and struck for it illustrates the definite swing leftward.

At Kincaid, Illinois, the mine workers had been out on strike against a wage cut. The school board purchased a load of coal mined by scabs. When students became aware of it they walked out in protest. This was the first time that American students had actively supported workers by striking.

The Columbia strike laid the basis for the tactics that were later to be used at New York University and City College. On the morning of the strike at the latter, students picketed at every entrance to the college. A mass meeting was in progress in the center of the campus. Volunteer committees "pulled" students from classes. At noon a committee presented a set of demands to the administration. The strike proved highly successful. The administration acceded to the strikers' demands. The faculty, with the exception of sixteen members who came out in favor of the strike, remained neutral. The more obvious opposition came from a small group of "vigilantes" headed by athletes.

This last year has witnessed a marked change in the American student. Social problems, which previously held the interest of a small group only, are becoming the table talk of increasing numbers. This new interest can be traced to the unstable economic position in which a great majority of students find themselves. They are in ever increasing numbers swinging leftward. Open opposition to reactionary administrative policy marks their political development. Attempts to throttle student expression or abrogate academic freedom are meeting more determined and better organized student opposition. The suspension of 19 students at City College for participating in a public trial of the administrative officers was answered with a strike by the students. The suspension of the New York University *Daily News* because it criticized the administration resulted in a three-hour protest strike. American students are fast losing their reluctance to use their strongest weapon, the strike, against administrative reaction.

---

[30]

ROOSEVELT

DAVID P. BERENBERG

THE Roosevelt myth grows. In the New York subway cars the slogan "As Right As Roosevelt" has appeared. The papers are daily filled with encomiums on his greatness. The rise in the stock market, the increase (pathetically small to date) in production, in employment, and in wages, whatever improvement occurs in international relations—are all laid at his door. It will not be long before all the blessings of nature will be attributed to him. This is the day of his rising star. He will go the way of all folk heroes.

A more objective examination of his accomplishments can hardly be said to justify the enthusiasm that he has awakened. Now that the banking holiday is over, 80% of the banks have reopened. Little by little the oth-

SOURCE: David P. Berenberg, "Roosevelt," *The American Socialist Quarterly* 2, no. 3 (Summer 1933): 45–52.

ers are being reorganized, but there is no assurance that all will open. Between $3,000,000,000 and $5,000,000,000 are still tied up in banks that may or may not eventually reopen their doors. Worse, there is no banking legislation in sight that will give the nation what it most needs, a centralized bank with governmental responsibility for its operations, and with a rigid elimination of private banking. A measure pending before the House does promise to guarantee deposits within certain limits, but without full governmental responsibility for all banking operations, this measure might in another banking crisis mean the guarantee of money lost in private speculation by the tax payer. And while this measure, the Glass–Steagall Bill, is before the House, J. P. Morgan tells the Senate Investigating Committee that the private banker is a public asset, a sentiment with which, so far at least, the government is in basic agreement. . . .

In the early days of the Roosevelt administration there was much talk, and grave talk, of a compulsory federal 30 hour week, and of a minimum wage law. Cool critics of the administration realized that this meant a protracted fight in the Supreme Court to establish the legality of such measures, with every indication that the Supreme Court would turn thumbs down upon them. Nevertheless socialists and even some clear sighted non-socialists welcomed the gesture. To have fought this issue through the courts would have been a tremendous achievement in the education of the *genus Americanus*. This is apparently not to be. The Roosevelt administration seems to have been frightened away from this brave adventure; the counsellors of "reason" and legalism seem to have won the day. Instead of national 30 hour law and a minimum wage law we are to have industrial self-regulation in the National Recovery Act through a federal dictator who will, however, have no power really to dictate. This policy of self-regulation and of permitting industry to work out such questions as the shortening of the work week and the maintenance of wages is a surrender to Hooverian principles.

Beer has come back. We were told that this would mean a vast increase in employment and greatly increased revenue for the government. Statistics as to increased employment directly or indirectly through the return of beer are not available. It is fair to assume that the increased employment and wage figures which amount to from 3 to 4% in the large industrial states in April and in May include the men and women directly and indirectly employed in the manufacture and distribution of beer. Perhaps in time this figure will increase. In the meantime it is well to note that while there have been small increases in the number employed and in payrolls in May as compared with April, the figures for both these months are markedly lower than for the corresponding months in 1932. . . . At best, the 110 million dollars which the government may hope to gain from beer does not by half meet the expected quarter of a billion which we were promised.

Hence, the present worry in Congress about taxes. The House has rejected the sales tax and has increased the normal income tax rates, while the surtaxes remain the same. In the meantime we hear that neither J. P. Morgan nor any of his partners has paid an income tax in 1931 or in 1932. True, this circumstance cannot be laid at the door of the Roosevelt administration. On the contrary, we owe it to the fumbling good intentions of the administration that such facts are at last beginning to come to life. The discovery may lead to a revision of the entire income tax law and may end at last the whole principle of permitting exemptions for the manipulation of capital losses, although it is difficult to see how evasions of this type can be guarded against. What we may expect to see is some clumsy experimentation with the capital levy. In the meantime the budget is not balanced. Deficits grow and expenses increase. Through the increase in the income tax in the lower brackets vast sections of the population will be called upon to pay additional levies to the government in the name of re-employment; this in addition to the increase in the price of food-stuffs already pointed out above.

The Roosevelt administration, like that of the older Roosevelt, knows the value of a good show. The best performance in recent years, exceeding in humor even the Teapot Dome investigation and the Seabury revue, is now in progress in Washington. J. P. Morgan, Jr., is telling us how he runs the country and how little the law means to a private banker who has his own code of ethics. So far he has managed to implicate Mr. Woodin, our Secretary of the Treasury, who has the power to open and close banks, Mr. Norman Davis, who is entrusted as Ambassador-at-large with the maintenance of peace, Mr. Raskob, whose property interests in the administration may prove to be enormous, and, of course, Mr. Owen D. Young, not to speak of hundreds of minor officials and politicians.

So soon as the Senate investigation began really to disclose important matters, Senator Glass launched an attack on the attorney for the committee, Mr. Pecora. Mr. Pecora is of Tammany Hall; it ought not to be hard for Senator Glass to find something unpleasant and inconvenient in his record. It is hard to see what this will profit the Senator. Even his attack on Mr. Pecora has permanently identified him in the popular mind as a Morgan henchman.

Congress has passed and the President has signed a Securities Bill which is intended to prevent the defrauding of the public through the issue of worthless stock. All enterprises floating stock issues for public sale are to be required to furnish correct information concerning the financial status of the business. In the face of misleading bank statements it is difficult to see what benefit will be derived from such a law. It is the easiest thing in the world to issue a correct and misleading statement. The administration, according to its publicity staff, expects great results from this law. This betrays the fundamental failure of the administration to grasp its problems. It typifies the usual pursuit of unconsequential matters and the intentional neglect of the real issues. . . .

Of the 250,000 men who were to be put to work [in the Civilian Conservation Corps] at $30 a month in labor camps for reforestation purposes, it is now reported that some 90,000 have been enrolled, and that enrollments are proceeding at the rate of 10,000 a week. In passing let it be noted that insofar as the total unemployment figures show, this rate of reemployment hardly takes up the slack. It was at first planned to give these men a military regime. When protest against militarization of the unemployed arose, we heard less about the employment of army officers to supervise the reforestation work. Now it is announced that the three or four thousand army officers who were slated for the camps will not be retired but will be transferred to the reforestation camps for supervising the work. Does this mean that this army of 250,000 is to receive military or even semi-military training and that what is intended as a measure to relieve unemployment is being transformed into a measure for the surreptitious creation of a reserve army 250,000 strong? In any case it is clear from the many desertions and changes of heart, that the unfortunate enlisters in the reforestation corps are not exactly lying on a bed of roses.

In international affairs the Roosevelt administration seems to be expending its energy very largely in the continuation of the policy of talk and hokum. While the British government and the French government pointedly expressed themselves on the question of Hitler's treatment of the Jews and on his suppression of all political opposition, the Roosevelt government was ominously silent. It contented itself with watchful waiting. Dr. Rosenberg, the Nazi errand boy with the suspiciously Semitic name, was able to say that while Sir John Simon treated him very brusquely, he was able to get along very well with Norman Davis. Too well?

Roosevelt's speech about war was hailed the world over as a great contribution to the cause of peace. In a sense it was, in that it dispelled for the moment the strained situation that had arisen between Germany on the one hand and England and France on the other. It also gave Hitler a much needed opportunity to reconsider his position and to deliver a speech . . . in which he all but retracts his own former truculence. But if the Roosevelt administration and the world, delude themselves with the belief that the Roosevelt charm, and the magic of the Roosevelt words have permanently checked the war danger, or the Hitler insanity, they will be sadly deceived. The Wilson administration fell under the spell of its own fine words and glittering ideals. We all know what they led to. The Roosevelt administration, which in so many things is following in the footsteps of the Wilson regime, may in this too lead us with the best intentions in the world into another war.

What is left of the administration is the myth. It may very well be that the depression through natural processes has reached the bottom of the trough and that the present mild upward trend is a true indication of solid economic recovery. If it is, the myth will live long that it was the Roosevelt administration that brought fair weather. We shall then never be able to convince the casual man that the same measures would have been damned as subversive of all that is good and sound, had the depression continued. It ought not to be difficult for a socialist to think his way through the convolutions of the Roosevelt mythology. Should on the other hand the depression continue in fact, the poverty of the Roosevelt concept, of a planned production within the limits of the capitalist property and profit economy, will become evident. The pseudo-communism of his brain trust, and more particularly the pseudo-Machiavellianism of one of its members should be recognized for what they are: the last and desperate effort on the part of people who realize that the capitalist system is doomed, but who cannot emotionally reconcile themselves to the destruction of the capitalist class to which they belong, to save that class by causing it to accept a voluntary reduction of powers. Some socialists are bound to fall victim to the charms of a self-limiting capitalism, but the well grounded socialist will know that capitalism never limits itself and that the neo-Rooseveltian era will not bring a solution of our problems.

In the meantime, despite the rise in stock and commodity prices, despite beer and psychology, despite minute improvements in wage and employment figures, there are still 12,000,000 or more without work, the danger of war still threatens, the dead hand of the mortgage holder continues still to squeeze the farmer. The Morgan disclosures tend only to reveal to us the vast power and scope of the dead hand. The masses will ultimately realize that they have once more been swindled. The Morgans, the Roosevelts and the less naive members of the "Brain Trust" expect the development of this mood of disillusionment, and confidently hope to channel it into a course that will prove harmless to them and their interests. If necessary they will establish a "Dictatorship" which will wipe out the last vestiges of mass rights and powers, but which will leave the basic property concepts intact.

The question for us to decide is: Shall they be permitted to carry out their intentions? Is it our task, for the socialists, to channel the disillusionment that is sure to come into a different course? If there is to be a Dictatorship, why should it not be a Dictatorship of the workers which will preserve and increase the rights and powers of the masses and wipe out the last vestiges of the existent property concepts.

---

[31]

THE UPSURGE OF THE MASS STRUGGLES AND THE WORK OF THE COMMUNIST PARTY

EARL BROWDER

THE United States, stronghold of world capitalism, exhibits at the same time its deepest contradictions. The blows of the economic crisis struck heaviest, relatively, here. The contrast between mass hopes and illusions in 1929, and bitter reality in 1934, is greater than almost anywhere else. The greatest accumulated wealth and productive forces, side by side with the largest mass unemployment and starvation of any industrial country, stare every observer in the face. Revolutionary forces in the United States, developing more slowly than elsewhere, are yet of enormously greater potentiality and depth.

All capitalist contradictions are embodied in Roosevelt's "New Deal" policies. Roosevelt promises to feed the hungry, by reducing the production of food. He promises to redistribute wealth, by billions of subsidies to the banks and corporations. He gives help to the "forgotten" man, by

SOURCE: Earl Browder, *Communism in the United States* (New York: International Publishers, 1935), pp. 30–35. Reprinted by permission of International Publishers Co., Inc.

speeding up the process of monopoly and trustification. He would increase the purchasing power of the masses, through inflation which gives them a dollar worth only 60 cents. He drives the Wall Street money changers out of the temple of government, by giving them complete power in the administration of the governmental machinery of the industrial codes. He gives the workers the right of organization, by legalizing the company unions. He inaugurates a regime of economy, by shifting the tax burden to the consuming masses, by cutting appropriations for wages, veterans, and social services, while increasing the war budget a billion dollars, and giving ten billions to those who already own everything. He restores the faith of the masses in democracy, by beginning the introduction of fascism. He works for international peace, by launching the sharpest trade and currency war in history.

Roosevelt's program is the same as that of finance capital the world over. It is a program of hunger, fascization and imperialist war. It differs chiefly in the forms of its unprecedented ballyhoo, of demagogic promises, for the creation of mass illusions of a saviour who has found the way out. The New Deal is not developed fascism. But in political essence and direction it is the same as Hitler's program.

Under cover of these mass illusions, Roosevelt launched the sharpest, most deep-going attack against the living standards of the masses. Even though the workers were still under the influence of illusions about Roosevelt (these illusions continue to stand up under repeated blows!) they could not but recognize what was happening to them. They answered with a wave of strikes. More than a million workers struck in 1933 in resistance to the New Deal policies. Over 750,000 joined the trade unions.

During this period the unemployed movement also deepened and consolidated itself, in spite of a serious lag. Especially important, it reacted to the new forms of government relief, the C. W. A. and forced labor camps, and began a movement on those jobs to protect living standards. The movement for the Workers' Unemployment Insurance Bill began to take on a broad mass character.

Struggles involving the masses of impoverished farmers, veterans, students, professionals, stimulated by the strike wave, gathered about the rising working class movement, and to a greater degree than ever before came in political contact with the workers.

This first wave of struggle against the Roosevelt "New Deal" was stimulated and clarified by the fact that the Communist Party, from the beginning, gave a bold and correct analysis of the "New Deal," and a clear directive for struggle against it. Events since last July confirmed entirely the analysis then given. Every serious effort to apply that program to struggle has brought gains for the workers. There is no need to revise our analysis. Now we can sum up the results of nine months' experience.

What has happened to the "New Deal"? Has it failed? Many workers, in the first stages of disillusionment, come to that conclusion. They are disillusioned with the result, but still believe in the intention. The S. P. and A. F. of L. leaders try to keep them in this stage. But this conclusion is entirely too simple. The "New Deal" has not improved conditions for the workers and exploited masses. But that was never its real aim; that was only ballyhoo; that was only bait with which to catch suckers. In its first and chief aim, the "New Deal" succeeded; that aim was to bridge over the most difficult situation for the capitalists, and to launch a new attack upon the workers with the help of their leaders, to keep the workers from general resistance, to begin to restore the profits of finance capital. . . .

Without the collaboration of the A. F. of L. leadership, it must be emphasized, this program could never have been carried out over the resistance of the workers. This truth, which we pointed out in advance, is now the boast of Green, Lewis & Co., in their conferences with Roosevelt, Johnson [head of the National Recovery Act] and the employers. Whenever a strike has been broken, the main "credit" belongs to Green and his associates. Every vicious code provision against the workers, for company unions, has borne the signature of Green & Co. Section 7a, the new "charter for labor," turned out in reality to be the legalization of company unionism and compulsory arbitration. Even the A. F. of L. leaders are allowed to organize only where and when this is required to block the formation of revolutionary or independent trade unions. The Wagner Bill to interpret Section 7a, now before Congress, which received such vigorous support and high praise from Socialist and A. F. of L. leaders, is already, even before passage, openly admitted to be legal confirmation of the company unions, the enforcement of compulsory arbitration. . . .

Now, for a brief glance at the results of the "New Deal" as registered in governmental statistics.

First, the Reconstruction Finance Corporation: Payments authorized by the R. F. C. up to the end of 1933, amounted to $5,233,800,000. More than 80 per cent of this enormous sum went directly to banks, insurance companies, railroads, mortgage loan companies, credit unions, etc., in loans or purchase of preferred stock; and for what is called "agricultural credit" which means advances to financial institutions holding uncollectable farm mortgages. About 12 per cent went for "relief," payment for forced labor on municipal and state work. These enormous subsidies, the size of which staggers the imagination, are the source of a large part of the renewed profits of the big corporations.

Second, inflation and price-fixing: These measures have resulted in such rise in living costs that even the A. F. of L. leaders, close partners of Roosevelt and Johnson, have to admit a decided drop in the purchasing power of employed workers. An indication is the drop of 9 per cent, from September to December, in the volume of consumers' goods actually purchased.

Third, the Government budget: Here we find the realization of Roosevelt's promise to remember the "forgotten man." The shift of the burden of taxes, the basis of the budget, comparing the current year with 1928–1929, is as follows:

Government income from taxation on corporations, rich individuals, and wealthy middle class, declined from $2,231,000,000 to $864,000,000 —a saving to the rich of $1,467,000,000. At the same time, taxation of workers and consuming masses increased from $1,571,000,000 to $2,395,000,000—an increase of the tax burden amounting to almost the total taxes now paid by the rich.

On the expenditure side of the budget, changes took the following direction: To banks, corporations, wealthy individuals and property owners, increased payments of 413 per cent. Expenditures for war purposes, increased by 82 per cent. Against these increases, economy was practiced by reducing wages of government employees, and veteran allowances, by 38 per cent and 27 per cent.

Fourth, distribution of National Income: Roosevelt promised that he would begin to remedy the maldistribution of the national income, whereby the rich get too much and the poor get too little. . . . Actually, what happened in 1933 was that the purchasing power of the workers went backward (a fact testified by the A. F. of L. and the Bureau of Labor Statistics) while property income took a sharp rise. A recent report of a group of large selected corporations which in 1932 showed a loss of about 45 millions, showed that in 1933 they had been restored to the profit side of the ledger by about a half-billion dollars.

Fifth, the workers' housing: In estimating the social effects of the shift of national income away from the workers and to property owners, it must be remembered that even in 1932 the majority of workers lived just at or even below the subsistence level. Every loss of income has been a direct deduction from daily necessities of life. This is sharply expressed in the catastrophic worsening of housing conditions. The epidemic of tenement house fires, burning to death hundreds of men, women and children, is but a dramatic revelation of one corner of the inhuman conditions under which growing millions are reduced.

Sixth, breaking up the home: A barometer of the degeneration of living standards is the growing army of wandering, homeless people, especially children. The "New Deal" proposed to turn the army of unattached boys into a military reserve through the Civilian Conservation Corps. Some 380,000 boys were so recruited in 1933; but in spite of this mass militarization, all reports agree that a larger number than before of homeless youth wandered the country.

Seventh, collapse of the school system: Conditions in the school system in rich America reflect the catastrophic situation of the masses. No improvement is to be seen under the "New Deal," but on the contrary, a sharp worsening takes place. Just a few details, presented not by Communist agitators but by the U.S. Commissioner of Education, George F. Zook, and the National Education Association, describing the current school year, after Mr. Roosevelt's "New Deal" was at work. Over 2,290,000 children of school age cannot find a place. Over 2,000 schools in rural communities failed to open this year in 24 states (the other 24 states, probably, being ashamed to report because their conditions are worse!). Some 1,500 commercial schools and 16 institutions of higher learning have been completely liquidated. School terms in nearly every large city are from 1 to 2 months shorter than they were 70 to 100 years ago. The average term in the United States, 170 school days per year, is less than that for France, Germany, England, Sweden, Denmark. School teachers' wages are generally from 4 to 24 months in arrears, although interest on bonds is paid promptly. In Chicago, where teachers are behind in their wages by $25,000,000, the committee enforcing the economy program contains, among its 29 members, all affiliated with big business, 5 directors of the largest banks, and 14 residents of exclusive Lake Shore Drive ("the Gold Coast"). Unemployed teachers are estimated at a quarter million. Teachers' wage rates have been cut by 27 per cent. In 14 states even this reduced salary is far behind in payment.

It is impossible to go into all the ramifications of the result of a "successful" New Deal program. We have shown enough to expose fully that the "success" was in giving more to the rich, and taking away from the poor even that which they had.

MIDDLE CLASS AND
THE WORKERS

LEWIS COREY

IN addition to being property conscious the middle class is animated by an antagonism to the workers. Defend property! Against labor! They are manifestations of a rallying call which is in complete disaccord with the existing conditions and needs of the masses of lower salaried employees and professionals, who are propertyless and dependent on jobs for a livelihood. For these groups property consciousness and antagonism to labor are an ideological inheritance completely at variance with the realities of their existing situation. This is the most significant aspect of the split personality of the middle class and its incapacity to formulate a class program expressing the concrete economic interests of all groups.

I

The old middle class of independent enterprisers was antagonistic to the workers. Even in the guild system, where workers and small producers were closely united, the masters exploited the journeymen and gradually converted them into proletarians. In the bourgeois revolutions, particularly the Jacobin, the lower middle class rallied the propertyless workers to the struggle; their support was necessary, and the workers responded because they had no independent program and identified their interests with petty-bourgeois democracy. But the workers were betrayed and abandoned by the middle class. The small producers who arose after the industrial revolution were necessarily and more completely antagonistic to the workers, for handicraftsmen constantly decreased and the capitalist, whether big or small, must get his profits by appropriating an increasing yield of surplus value from the workers. As the middle class waged its struggle against

SOURCE: Lewis Corey, *The Crisis of the Middle Class* (New York: Civici, Friede, 1935), pp. 244–249, 252–259. © 1935 by Lewis Corey. Reprinted by permission of Crown Publishers, Inc.

concentration and trustification, in defense of independent small enterprise, it sought the support of the wage-workers—but on a middle class program which generalized its interests as the people's interests, and always strictly within the limits of the capitalist order. That was the essential character of American populism and progressivism. The underlying tendency was to discourage and repress the independent action of labor.

As they grew in numbers and emerged as an industrial proletariat, organized by the collective mechanism of capitalist production itself, the wage-workers moved increasingly toward action independent of the middle class. The ugly reality of capitalism made a mockery of the ideals of the bourgeois revolution. Workers were denied democratic rights and secured them only after bitter struggles, particularly in Europe. Increasing misery marked the earlier stages of industrial capitalism; the betterment of conditions was agonizingly slow and incomplete, while the rate of exploitation mounted. Trade unions arose and socialism issued its challenge to capitalism. The challenge emphasized the temporary historical nature of capitalism, which was itself creating the conditions of a new social order: economic collectivism, the objective basis of socialism, and the proletariat, the class carrier of socialism.

Trade unionism and socialism, by and large, strengthened the middle class antagonism to labor. The class was rarely neutral in strikes. It created the myth of "the public" whose interests transcended the struggle between labor and capital; in practice the myth favored the capitalist exploiter. And propertied enterprisers were frightened by the socialist proposal for the socialization of productive property.

But the middle class was still in the radical stage. Its lower layers were in contact with the propertyless workers and it was still engaged in the struggle against monopoly. Many small producers, especially the surviving handicraftsmen, were being thrust downward into the proletariat. Hence a radicalism, mainly in the lower middle class, which often assumed the form of petty-bourgeois socialism. The mixed elements of this "socialism" included defense of handicraft labor and other forms of small industry, cooperative workshops as the basis of a new social order. nationalization of big enterprises and the broadening of democracy. This petty-bourgeois socialism, most clearly developed in Europe, was doomed to disaster, for it represented the disappearing pre-industrial small producers and accepted the relations of capitalist production. In many struggles, especially for democratic rights, the lower middle class and the workers united their forces. But the radical middle class was constantly vacillating between capitalism and socialism, between the bourgeoisie and the proletariat.

257

Antagonism to the workers was necessary to the small industrial capitalists in the middle class. It still is today. They are employers and exploiters of labor; although increasingly crushed by capitalism, they are inseparably entangled in capitalist relations. The antagonism to labor, in varying degrees, dominates other types of enterprisers, among them small shopkeepers and independent professionals. But the economic interests of these groups are not antagonistic to labor, for the masses of small storekeepers and professionals must depend for their livelihood on labor's patronage; they quickly feel the effects of lower standards of living, of unemployment and wage cuts, among the workers, and may combine with them in the struggle against capitalist exploitation. On the whole, however, the antagonism to labor conforms to the interests of the old middle class of independent small enterprisers.

But antagonism to labor is wholly opposed to the interests of the masses of lower salaried employees and professionals. Capitalism has proletarianized them, and it increasingly thrusts them downward to the economic level of wage-workers. That produces a substantial identity of interests that *must* break through inherited antagonisms and ideological differences.

II

Salaried employees and professionals were clearly members of the middle class in the earlier stages of capitalism. A gulf separated them from the wage-workers. Professionals were practically all self-employed; a profession was measurably a form of independent property. Salaried employees were scarce (wage-workers developed much more rapidly); they became a big group only after collective large-scale industry assigned to them the tasks of management, administration and supervision. Their scarcity value and highly skilled functions, in spite of the proletarian relation involved in the sale of their skill to an employer, assured salaried employees security, good incomes and social standing; they were "on the make," salaried dependence being largely a mere transition to the independence of one's own enterprise. But economic collectivism proletarianized their functions while multiplying their numbers. Most salaried employees were converted economically into wage-workers and most professionals into salaried employees by corporate enterprise and its specialization and simplification of tasks formerly performed by highly skilled persons.

One group, however, retained and strengthened its privileges. The small upper layer of higher salaried employees became more closely identified with capitalism as corporate enterprise increased its importance, income and power; the members of this group may be called institutional capitalists, for they perform the more decisive functions of the older independent enterprisers. But the great masses of lower salaried employees moved downward. Their scarcity value, privileges and income were increasingly impaired as collective activity transformed their work into mechanical routine and the multiplication of their numbers created a labor reserve among them. These occupational changes depressed the social standing of lower salaried employees, but they clung pathetically to middle class ideals and, especially in the United States, scorned strikes, unionism and identification with labor.

As the masses of lower salaried employees moved downward the wage-workers moved upward, after the increasing misery of the industrial revolution. Their standards of living rose, especially among the skilled industrial workers, and their personal and class independence was invigorated by unionism and socialism. The economic differences separating the masses of lower salaried employees and the wage-workers are small and becoming constantly smaller. . . .

Of the 9,200,000 salaried employees in 1930, not more than 1,250,000 had incomes of $3,000 up: the incomes of over 85% were below $3,000. *Millions of organized skilled workers earned more than the majority of lower salaried employees.* Nor did this mean, as capitalist apologists claim, that wage-workers were moving upward into the middle class, for their standards of living were even then nothing to brag about; *it meant that the masses of lower salaried employees were economically moving downward into the proletariat,* and the process has accelerated since 1930. However stubbornly they still maintain the middle class antagonism to labor, capitalism makes them one with the dispossessed workers.

There is still a differential between the earnings of wage-workers and lower salaried employees. But it is significant of the proletarianizing tendency of capitalism that the differential has steadily decreased. While the average earnings of clerical employees on the railways in 1890 were 13 % higher than the wage-worker's average, they were only 0.6% (or $10 yearly) higher in 1924; in New York the differential in favor of clerical earnings decreased from 74% in 1914 to 34% in 1923. The breakdown of differentials, which affected the majority of lower salaried employees, was accompanied by another development: small as was the increase in real wages the increase in real salaries was still smaller. Proletarianization included a breakdown in the differentials of security and privileges, of confidential relations with the employer, and of the opportunity to move upward into higher jobs.

Middle class demagogues use the breakdown of differentials to incite the lower salaried employees against the workers, particularly against union workers. It is an effort to becloud the issue. For the masses of lower salaried employees moved downward more than the workers moved upward. And, in the 1920's, differentials in the earnings of lower and higher salaried employees became greater; the most flagrant expression was the constantly mounting salaries of corporation officers. Profits, moreover, greatly increased, partly because of the depressed earnings of lower salaried employees. It was possible to pamper salaried employees when they were few; but as they became numerous and enlarged the salary bills, aggravating the problem of overhead costs, capitalist enterprise began to apply scientific management and rationalization. Salaries as fixed costs had to become variable costs and smaller in amount. Lower salaried labor and wage labor, approaching one another in economic condition, are equal objects of capitalist exploitation. It is significant of proletarianization, and of the split in the "new" middle class, that lower salaried employees increased much more rapidly than higher salaried and the differentials in their earnings became greater.

Another, and strikingly significant, aspect of proletarianization is the exposure now of lower salaried employees to all the rigors of depression. They were formerly protected by their security and privileges. Few salaried employees were discharged and salaried earnings were largely maintained, while the wage-workers bore the brunt of depression. . . .

That security was destroyed in the depression of the 1930's, and it is gone forever. The earnings, employment and privileges of lower salaried employees (*not* the higher) were mercilessly slashed, almost as mercilessly as among the workers. . . . While the proportion of lower salaried employees thrown out of work was slightly smaller than that of wage-workers, it was larger by 25% in manufactures. . . . Unemployment among technicians was catastrophic; it included 50% of the pharmacists, 65% of the engineers, especially civil engineers, because of the almost complete stoppage of construction, and 90% of the architects and draftsmen. . . . By 1934, over 200,000 teachers were unemployed; 5,680 college teachers were dismissed in 1933–34. . . . At least two-thirds of the 15,000 members of the American Federation of Musicians were unemployed. . . . Clerical salaries were cut as savagely as wages; by 1935, office workers in New York City were earning as little as $12 weekly. . . . The earnings of nurses, which before the depression were not much over $1,200 yearly, dropped to $478 in 1932. . . . Pharmacists and drug clerks had their salaries cut up to 50% or more, with NRA codes establishing minimums of $13 to $16 weekly. . . . School appropriations were severely reduced while the number of pupils rose, and there was one cut after another in salaries; by 1933–34, the average teacher's salary was only $1,050 yearly, a decline of 20%, with many salaries as low as $450 and still lower among Negro teachers. . . . The extent to which the salaries of technicians were cut appears clearly in the minimum of $14 weekly established for qualified chemists by one NRA code; in another code technical employees got 35¢ to 45¢ an hour. . . . Earnings declined seriously among independent professionals. The net income of a group of more successful physicians was 40% lower in 1932 than in 1929, and the decline was greater among the lower groups, many physicians being forced out of practice. This condition was general among other types of independent professionals. . . . Thousands of trained men desperately accepted the jobs of skilled and unskilled workers; millions of lower salaried employees and professionals were forced on relief.

Nor was the breakdown of security, privileges and earnings merely a result of the unusual severity of the depression of the 1930's, for the depression of 1894 was almost as severe. It was the result of occupational changes that broke down the differentials favoring the lower salaried employees, an expression of their practical proletarianization.

It is not a temporary breakdown. The condition is permanent and must become worse as prosperity fails to revive on any considerable scale. One significant proof is that, during the slight economic revival after 1933, *more wage-workers were re-employed than lower salaried employees.* Not that the workers are favored, but they are directly productive and salaried labor is part of the overhead costs which must be cut ruthlessly as industry goes on iron rations and profits become lower. Hence rationalization and scientific management are applied more completely, lessening security, privileges and earnings. Many salaried employees work in superstructural enterprises which flourish only when there is a high level of prosperity. There is, moreover, a definite ratio between the number of employed wage-workers and of lower salaried employees and professionals; as one moves downward the other must also move downward. The prospect is one of permanent unemployment, more insecurity and impoverishment. For the increasing misery of capitalist decline engulfs millions of lower salaried employees and professionals. They may think they are "different" and "better," that as members of the middle class, even if only of the "new" middle class, they are deserving of special treatment, but the capitalist employers treat them as they do the workers.

[33]

IS THE NEW DEAL SOCIALISM?

NORMAN THOMAS

THE air rings, the newspapers are filled with the politics of bedlam. There are still around 10,000,000 unemployed in the United States. Re-employment lags behind the increase of production, and the increase of money wages in industry lags behind both. The burden of debt piles higher and higher. The world, and America with it, drifts toward a new war of inconceivable horror—war from which we shall not be delivered by spending out of our poverty more than a billion dollars a year on naval and military preparations without so much as squarely facing the issue: what are we protecting and how shall we protect it?

In this situation the leaders of our two major political parties have begun speaking, or rather shouting. And what do they say? First, President Roosevelt makes a fighting speech to Congress and the nation defending the record he has made, but proposing no new program. Scarcely has he finished his speech when the AAA decision of the Supreme Court and the enactment of the bonus legislation by Congress compel him to seek new laws and new taxes.

Then Mr. Roosevelt's one-time dearest political friend and sponsor, Alfred E. Smith, rushes to the fray. This erstwhile man of the people chooses a dinner of the Liberty League at which to proclaim the religion of Constitution worship, favorable incidental mention of the Holy Bible, Washington as the nation's capital and the Stars and Stripes forever.

It was attended, the newspapers tell us, by twelve Du Ponts—twelve apostles, not of liberty but of big business and the profits of war and preparation for war. Indeed, the record of Mr. Smith's new friends shows that that organization is as much entitled to the name Liberty League as was the disease commonly known as German measles to be called liberty measles in the hysteria of war. . . .

Yet basically beneath all the alarms and confusion these worthy warriors, happy and unhappy, are acting upon a common assumption—an as-

SOURCE: Norman Thomas, *Is the New Deal Socialism?* (Chicago: National Office of the Socialist Party, 1936), pp. 2–11.

sumption which is dangerously false. All of them are assuming the durability of the profit system, the security of a capitalist nationalist system in which our highest loyalties are to the principle of private profit and to the political power of an absolute jingoistic nationalist State. They assume that prosperity is coming back again to stay for a while.

Impartial in Smith–Roosevelt Fray

Mr. Roosevelt and his followers assume that prosperity is coming back because of the New Deal. Al Smith and the rest of Roosevelt's assorted critics assume that it is in spite of the New Deal and perhaps because of the Supreme Court. Mr. Hoover plaintively protests that the catastrophic depression of January–February 1933, was due merely to the shudders of the body politic anticipating the economic horrors of the New Deal.

As a Socialist, I view the Smith–Roosevelt controversy with complete impartiality. I am little concerned to point out the inconsistencies in Al Smith's record, or to remind him that in 1924 and 1928, when I happened to be the Socialist candidate for high office against him, more than one of his close political friends came to me to urge me as a Socialist not to attack him too severely since he really stood for so many of the things that Socialists and other progressive workers wanted.

But I am concerned to point out how false is the charge that Roosevelt and the New Deal represent socialism. What is at stake is not prestige or sentimental devotion to a particular name. What is at stake is a clear understanding of the issues on which the peace and prosperity of generations —perhaps of centuries—depend. A nation which misunderstands socialism as completely as Al Smith misunderstands it is a nation which weakens its defense against the coming of war and fascism.

But, some of you will say, isn't it true, as Alfred E. Smith and a host of others before him have charged, that Roosevelt carried out most of the demands of the Socialist platform?

This charge is by no means peculiar to Mr. Smith. I am told that a Republican speaker alleged that Norman Thomas rather than Franklin D. Roosevelt has been President of the United States. I deny the allegation and defy the allegator and I suspect I have Mr. Roosevelt's support in this denial. Matthew Woll, leader of the forces of reaction in the American Federation of Labor, is among the latest to make the same sort of charge.

Roosevelt Not Socialist

Emphatically, Mr. Roosevelt did not carry out the Socialist platform, unless he carried it out on a stretcher. What is true is that when Mr. Roosevelt took office he had to act vigorously.

We had demanded Federal relief for unemployment. Hence any attempts Mr. Roosevelt made at Federal relief could perhaps be called by his enemies an imitation of the Socialist platform. It was an extraordinarily poor imitation. We demanded Federal unemployment insurance. Hence any attempt to get Federal security legislation could be regarded as an imitation of the Socialist platform. It was an amazingly bad imitation.

Indeed, at various times Mr. Roosevelt has taken particular and rather unnecessary pains to explain that he was not a Socialist, that he was trying to support the profit system, which, by the way, he defined incorrectly. In his last message to Congress his attack was not upon the profit system but on the sins of big business.

His slogan was not the Socialist cry: "Workers of the world, workers with hand and brain, in town and country, unite!" His cry was: "Workers and small stockholders unite, clean up Wall Street." That cry is at least as old as Andrew Jackson.

What Mr. Roosevelt and his brain trust and practical political advisers did to such of the Socialist immediate demands as he copied at all merely illustrates the principle that if you want a child brought up right you had better leave the child with his parents and not farm him out to strangers.

Reformism

Some of it was good reformism, but there is nothing Socialist about trying to regulate or reform Wall Street. Socialism wants to abolish the system of which Wall Street is an appropriate expression. There is nothing Socialist about trying to break up great holding companies. We Socialists would prefer to acquire holding companies in order to socialize the utilities now subject to them.

There was no socialism at all about taking over all the banks which fell in Uncle Sam's lap, putting them on their feet again, and turning them back to the bankers to see if they can bring them once more to ruin. There was no socialism at all about putting in a Coordinator to see if he could make the bankrupt railroad systems profitable so they would be more expensive for the government to acquire as sooner or later the government, even a Republican party government, under capitalism must.

Mr. Roosevelt torpedoed the London Economic Conference; he went blindly rushing in to a big army and navy program; he maintained, as he still maintains, an Ambassador in Cuba who, as the agent of American financial interests, supports the brutal reaction in Cuba. While professing friendship for China, he blithely supported a silver purchase policy of no meaning for America except the enrichment of silver mine owners which nearly ruined the Chinese Government in the face of Japanese imperialism. These things which Al Smith or Alf Landon might also have done are anything but Socialist.

Mr. Smith presumably feels that the President's Security Bill, so-called, was socialism. Let us see. We Socialists have long advocated unemployment insurance or unemployment indemnity by which honest men who cannot find work are indemnified by a society so brutal or so stupid that it denies them the opportunity to work. This insurance or indemnification should be on a prearranged basis which will take account of the size of the family. It should be Federal because only the national government can act uniformly, consistently and effectively.

What did Mr. Roosevelt give us? In the name of security, he gave us a bill where in order to get security the unemployed workers will first have to get a job, then lose a job. He will have to be sure that he gets the job and loses the job in a State which has an unemployment insurance law.

He will then have to be sure that the State which has the law will have the funds and the zeal to get the money to fulfill the terms of the law. This will largely depend upon whether it proves to be practical and constitutional for the Federal Government to collect a sufficient tax on payrolls so that 90 percent of it when rebated to employers to turn over to the State officers will be sufficient to give some kind of security to those who are unemployed!

The whole proceeding is so complicated, the danger of forty-eight competing State laws—competing, by the way, for minimum, not for maximum benefits—is so dangerous that the President's bill can justly be called an in-Security bill.

"Billions of Words"

If Mr. Smith means that the program of public works either under PWA or WPA is Socialist, again he is mistaken. We do not tolerate the standards of pay set on much WPA work—$19 a month, for instance, in some

States in the South. We do insist not upon talk but upon action to re-house the third of America which lives in houses unfit for human habitation, which is possible given the present state of the mechanic arts in a nation of builders.

The administration, having spent billions of words, not dollars, on housing with little result, is now turning the job over to private mortgage companies. Would not Al Smith or Alf Landon do the same?

But even if Mr. Roosevelt and the New Deal had far more closely approximated Socialist immediate demands in their legislation, they would not have been Socialists, not unless Mr. Smith is willing to argue that every reform, every attempt to curb rampant and arrogant capitalism, every attempt to do for the farmers something like what the tariff has done for business interests, is socialism.

Not only is it not socialism, but in large degree this State capitalism, this use of bread and circuses to keep the people quiet, is so much a necessary development of a dying social order that neither Mr. Smith nor Mr. Hoover in office in 1937 could substantially change the present picture or bring back the days of Andrew Jackson, Grover Cleveland or Calvin Coolidge.

What Roosevelt has given us, and what the Republicans cannot and will not substantially change, is not the socialism of the co-operative commonwealth. It is a State capitalism which the Fascist demagogues of Europe have used when they came to power. The thing, Mr. Smith, that you ought to fear is not that the party of Jefferson and Jackson is marching in step with Socialists toward a Socialist goal; it is that, unwittingly, it may be marching in step with Fascists toward a Fascist goal.

I do not mean that Mr. Roosevelt himself is a Fascist or likely to become a Fascist. I credit him with as liberal intentions as capitalism and his Democratic colleagues of the South permit. I call attention to the solemn fact that in spite of his circumspect liberalism, repression, the denial of civil liberty, a Fascist kind of military law, stark terrorism has been increasing under Democratic Governors for the most part—in Indiana, Florida, Georgia, Alabama, Arkansas and, of course, in California, where Mr. Roosevelt did not even come to the aid of an ex-Socialist, Upton Sinclair, against the candidate of the reactionaries.

I repeat that what Mr. Roosevelt has given us is State capitalism; that is to say, a system under which the State steps in to regulate and in many cases to own, not for the purpose of establishing production for use but rather for the purpose of maintaining in so far as may be possible the profit system with its immense rewards of private ownership and its grossly unfair division of the national income.

Today Mr. Roosevelt does not want fascism; Mr. Hoover does not want fascism; not even Mr. Smith and his friends of the Liberty League want fascism. The last-named gentlemen want an impossible thing: the return to the unchecked private monopoly power of the Coolidge epoch.

Must Abolish the Profit System

All the gentlemen whom I have named want somehow to keep the profit system. Socialism means to abolish that system. Those who want to keep it will soon find that out of war or out of the fresh economic collapse inevitable when business prosperity is so spotty, so temporary, so insecure as it is today, will come the confusion to which capitalism's final answer must be the Fascist dictator.

In America that dictator will probably not call himself Fascist. He, like Mr. Roosevelt in his address to Congress, will thank God that we are not like other nations. But privately he will rejoice in the weakness of our opposition to tyranny. Under the forms of democracy we have not preserved liberty. It has not taken black shirts to make us docile.

Given the crisis of war or economic collapse we, unless we awake, will accept dictatorship by violence to perpetuate a while longer the class division of income. We shall acknowledge the religion of the totalitarian state and become hypnotized by the emotional appeal of a blind jingoistic nationalism. Against this Fascist peril and its Siamese twin, the menace of war, there is no protection in the New Deal, no protection in the Republican Party, less than no protection in the Liberty League.

Who of them all is waging a real battle even for such civil liberties and such democratic rights as ostensibly are possible in a bourgeois democracy? When Al Smith appeals to the Constitution is he thinking of the liberties of the Bill of Rights or is he thinking of the protection the Constitution has given to property?

As a Socialist I was no lover of NRA or AAA. NRA, at least temporarily, did give the workers some encouragement to organize, but at bottom it was an elaborate scheme for the stabilization of capitalism under associations of industries which could regulate production in order to maintain profit. AAA was perhaps some relative help to many classes of farmers. It was no help at all to the most exploited agricultural workers and share-croppers, but rather the opposite. And it was, as indeed it had to be under capitalism, primarily a scheme for subsidizing scarcity.

This was not primarily the fault of AAA. It was the fault of the capitalist system which Roosevelt and Smith alike accept; that system which makes private profit its god, which uses planning, in so far as it uses planning at all, to stabilize and maintain the profits of private owners, not the well-being of the masses. In the last analysis the profit system inevitably depends upon relative scarcity. Without this relative scarcity there is no profit and there is no planning for abundance which accepts the kingship of private profit.

When the world went in for great machinery operated by power it went in for specialization and integration of work. It doomed the old order of the pioneers. The one chance of using machinery for life, not death, is that we should plan to use it for the common good. There is no planned production for use rather than for the private profit of an owning class which does not involve social ownership. This is the gospel of socialism.

Abundance Possible

We can have abundance. In 1929, according to the Brookings Institute—and that, remember, was our most prosperous year—a decent use of our capacity to produce would have enabled us to raise the income of the 16,400,000 families with less than $2,000 a year to that modest level without even cutting any at the top.

Instead, without any interference from workers, without any pressure from agitators, the capitalist system so dear to Al Smith and his Liberty League friends went into a nose-spin. The earned income dropped from $83,000,000,000 to something like $38,000,000,000 in 1932, and the temporary recovery, of which the New Deal administration boasts, has probably not yet raised that income to the $50,000,000,000 level. It has, moreover, burdened us with an intolerable load of debt.

What we must have is a society where we can use our natural resources and machinery so that the children of the share-croppers who raise cotton will no longer lack the cotton necessary for underclothes. What we must have is a society which can use our resources and our mechanical skill so that the children of builders will not live in shacks and slums.

It is not that Socialists want less private property. We want more private property in the good things of life. We do not mean to take the carpenter's kit away from the carpenter or Fritz Kreisler's violin away from Fritz Kreisler, or the home or farm in which any man lives and works away from him.

We do intend to end private landlordism, and to take the great natural resources—oil, copper, coal, iron; the great public utilities, power, transportation; the banking system, the distributive agencies like the dairy trust, the basic monopolies and essential manufacturing enterprises out of the hands of private owners, most of them absentee owners, for whose profits workers with hand and brain are alike exploited. And we intend to put these things into the hands of society.

Tax Private Wealth

We intend to make this change to social ownership in orderly fashion. In the meantime we can avert fresh economic collapse by the road of crazy inflation or cruel deflation only by an orderly process of taxing wealth in private hands, by a graduated tax, approaching expropriation of unearned millions, in order to wipe out debt and to help in the socialization of industry.

We do not mean to turn socialized industries over to political bureaucrats, to Socialist Jim Farleys, so to speak. The adjective doesn't redeem the noun. For instance, we intend that a socialized steel industry shall be managed under a directorate representing the workers, including, of course, the technicians in that industry, and the consumers.

We can do it without conscription and without rationing our people. We ought not to pay the price Russia has paid because we are far more industrially advanced than was Russia and should learn from Russia's mistakes as well as her successes.

Goal Is True Democracy

Our goal, Mr. Smith, is true democracy. It is we who lead in the fight for liberty and justice which you in recent years have sadly ignored. It is we who seek to make freedom and democracy constitutional by advocating a Workers Rights' Amendment in the interest of farmers, workers and consumers, giving to Congress power to adopt all needful social and economic legislation, but leaving to the courts their present power to help protect civil and religious liberty.

Our present judicial power of legislation is as undemocratic as it is in the long run dangerous to peace. Remember the Dred Scott decision! Congress rather than the States must act because these issues are national. The religion of the Constitution with the Supreme Court as the high priests and the Liberty League as its preacher will never satisfy human hunger for freedom, peace and plenty.

The Constitution was made for man and not man for the Constitution. We Socialists seek now its orderly amendment. We seek now genuine social security, real unemployment insurance. We seek now a policy which will make it a little harder for American business interests to involve us in war as a result of a mad chase after the profits of war.

These, gentlemen who quarrel over the way to save capitalism, are the things of our immediate desire. But deepest of all is our desire for a federation of co-operative Commonwealths. Some of you may like this far less than you like the New Deal, but will you not agree that it is not the New Deal?

You said, Mr. Smith, in a peroration worthy of your old enemy, William Randolph Hearst, that there can be only one victory, of the Constitution.

And this is our reply: There is only one victory worth the seeking by the heirs of the American Revolution. It is the victory of a fellowship of free men, using government as their servant, to harness our marvelous machinery for abundance, not poverty; peace, not war; freedom, not exploitation.

This is the victory in which alone is practicable deliverance from the house of our bondage. This is the victory to which we dedicate ourselves.

PART XI
The Black Beginning

THE following brief and tentative leftward glance (Document 34) by W. E. B. Du Bois (1868–1963) shows a little of the black perception of pre-war socialism. This short statement reveals something of how a sensitive and educated black American was driven to socialism almost, apparently, by default. Du Bois was already an especially clear-minded social critic, as illustrated by his repudiation of Booker T. Washington's program, and by his participation in the creation of the NAACP. He thought that Washington represented "the old attitude of adjustment and submission," [1] and Du Bois began to view radicalism as a way for black people at least to think about liberation. His own movement leftward was marked by quitting the NAACP in 1934, rejoining in 1944, and leaving finally in 1948. In 1911 he joined the Socialist Party, but quit to support Woodrow Wilson. He then became increasingly critical of the Socialists for their failure to include American blacks in their social planning or vision.[2] During the Depression he began moving toward the Communist Party, which he joined only in 1961, two years after he had received the Lenin Peace Prize, and one year after he gave up his American citizenship in order to become a citizen of Ghana.

Black radicalism was slow to gather, slower even than white. Racial oppression combined with economic repression effectively submerged black Americans to a prepolitical level. Their struggle was one of sheer survival, and there can be only occasional politics in the jungle. The consequence was atomization, a sensible attachment to the techniques of personal endurance, and a deep distrust of organized activity, black or white, except

[1] W. E. B. Du Bois, *The Souls of Black Folks* (New York, 1903), p. 48.
[2] See, especially, his "Socialism and the Negro Problem," *The New Review* 1, no. 5 (1 February 1913): 138–141; and "Opinion," *The Crisis* 22, no. 6 (October 1921): 245–247.

for the church. These generalizations, however, apply to urban blacks less often than to those who were still rural, as Marcus Garvey's black nationalist movement showed.

It was recognized almost from the start that objective oppression carried with it a tragic inner uncertainty. The unfolding of American racism obscured or obliterated the black past, community, and culture. It is easy to understand that some of this white view of black people should be accepted by some blacks, that the sense of black inferiority on which the white exploiters absolutely insisted should also infect some blacks, perhaps many. Document 35 is an early attempt to resist this black acceptance of white prejudice. Arguing that blacks could train themselves not only to accept, but to approve of, black skin color, this editorial concludes with an anticipation of the slogan of the late 1960's that "black is beautiful."

Shortly after Franklin Roosevelt was inaugurated, Du Bois explained (Document 36) the peculiar position of the black proletariat in America. Advocating a general Marxist interpretation of American capitalism, he insisted that black workers suffered most from the bigotry of the white proletariat. This required a revision of orthodox Marxism. Even the facts of the Depression did not convince American whites to make a common workers' alliance with blacks, so an internal black organization was necessary for defense. This white workers' racism prevented the Socialist Party from taking a clearer and cleaner line on black liberation, and although the Communist Party did call for an end to discrimination, the white —black labor split meant that a proletarian revolution was nowhere in sight.

In 1928 the Comintern applied Stalin's concept of nationalities to American blacks, and advocated self-determination within the southern black belt. Ten years later, Richard Wright (b. 1908) published *Bright and Morning Star,* first in the *New Masses* and later as a booklet, the royalties of which he assigned to the Earl Browder Defense Fund. In the concluding section of this story (Document 37), Wright has Johnny-Boy, a black revolutionary committed to the Comintern's idea of a black republic, being tortured by white crackers who want him to inform on his political partners. Johnny-Boy's old mother goes to the terrible scene to shoot Booker, a certain informer, and if she could get off a second shot, to kill her son to give him a more merciful death. Richard Wright's literary power and black rage are amply displayed here, as they were to be in a more extended fashion in his most important novel, *Native Son,* two years later.

The party policies of black national self-determination and of the Popular Front, as both applied to black America, were explicated (Document 38) by James W. Ford, the black vice-presidential candidate on the Communist Party ticket. Ford quoted from the Comintern on the question of national self-determination, an idea which was described in the late sixties as "the internal colony": ". . . the Party must come out openly and unreservedly for the right of Negroes to national self-determination in the Southern states, where the Negroes form the majority of the population." Concerned that black nationalism must lead some to black separatism, Ford again relied on the Comintern's now awkward language to explain that the CP opposed reactionary separatism, while it supported the "rational-revolutionary" variety. The rise of fascism and the creation of the Popular Front meant cooperation, not separatism. American blacks presumably had been instructed about fascism's threat to blacks in Italy's Ethiopian campaign. Now, in the name of unity against fascism, the CP supported all the social uplift and other black institutions, including the NAACP, Urban League, and church organizations, just as it was now backing the New Deal. Grasping at straws, Ford also insisted that the CP's attachment to black liberation had converted the party from an isolated grouplet to a part of the "democratic majority." No such movement occurred, and the mass of American blacks continued to fight for breath rather than for organization. Ford's sense of a significant black political movement to the left was a delusion, pure and simple.

---

[34]

SOCIALIST OF THE PATH

W. E. B. DU BOIS

I am a Socialist of the Path. I do not believe in the complete socialization of the means of production—the entire abolition of private property in capital—but the Path of Progress and common sense certainly lead to a far greater ownership of the public wealth for the public good than is now the case. I do not believe that government can carry on private business as well as private concerns, but I do believe that most of the human business called private is no more private than God's blue sky, and that we are approaching a time when railroads, coal mines and many factories can and

SOURCE: W. E. B. Du Bois, "Socialist of the Path," *Horizon* 1 (February 1907): 7–8.

ought to be run by the public for the public. This is the way, as I see it, that the path leads and I follow it gladly and hopefully.

Negro and Socialism

In the socialistic trend thus indicated lies the one great hope of the Negro American. We have been thrown by strange historic reasons into the hands of the capitalists hitherto. We have been objects of dole and charity, and despised accordingly. We have been made tools of oppression against the workingman's cause—the puppets and playthings of the idle rich. Fools! We must awake! Not in a renaissance among ourselves of the evils of Get and Grab—not in private hoarding, squeezing and cheating, lies our salvation, but rather in that larger ideal of human brotherhood, equality of opportunity and work not for wealth but for Weal—here lies our shining goal. This goal the Socialists with all their extravagance and occasional foolishness have more stoutly followed than any other class and thus far we must follow them. Our natural friends are not the rich but the poor, not the great but the masses, not the employers but the employees. Our good is not wealth, power, oppression and snobbishness, but helpfulness, efficiency, service and self-respect. Watch the Socialists. We may not follow them and agree with them in all things. I certainly do not. But in trend and ideal they are the salt of this present earth.

---

[35]

EDITORIAL

The Crisis

IT was in Chicago. John Haynes Holmes was talking.

He said: "I met two children—one as fair as the dawn—the other as beautiful as the night." Then he paused. He had to pause for the audience guffawed in wild merriment. Why?

It was a colored audience. Many of them were black. Some black faces there were as beautiful as the night.

Why did they laugh?

Because the world had taught them to be ashamed of their color.

SOURCE: "Editorial," *The Crisis* 20 (October 1920): 263, 266.

Because for 500 years men had hated and despised and abused black folk.

And now in strange, inexplicable transposition the rising blacks laugh at themselves in nervous, blatant, furtive merriment.

They laugh because they think they are expected to laugh—because all their poor hunted lives they have heard "black" things laughed at.

Of all the pitiful things of this pitiful race problem, this is the pitifullest. So curious a mental state tends to further subtleties. Colored folk, like all folk, love to see themselves in pictures; but they are afraid to see the types which the white world has caricatured. The whites obviously seldom picture brown and yellow folk, but for five centuries they have exhausted every ingenuity of trick, of ridicule and caricature on black folk: "grinning" Negroes, "happy" Negroes, "gold dust twins," "Aunt Jemimas," "solid" headed tacks—everything and anything to make Negroes ridiculous. As a result if *The Crisis* puts a black face on its cover our 500,000 colored readers do not see the actual picture—they see the caricature that white folk intend when *they* make a black face. In the last few years a thoughtful, clear-eyed artist, Frank Walts, has done a number of striking portraits for *The Crisis*. Mainly he has treated black faces; and regularly protests have come to us from various colored sources. His lovely portrait of the bright-eyed boy, Harry Elam, done in thoughtful sympathy, was approved by few Negroes. Our photograph of a woman of Santa Lucia, with its strength and humor and fine swing of head, was laughed at by many.

Why?

"O———er—it was not because they were black," stammer some of my office companions, "but they are *too* black. No people were ever so—"

Nonsense! Do white people complain because their pictures are too white? They ought to, but they do not. Neither do we complain if we are photographed a shade "light."

No. It is not that we are ashamed of our color and blood. We are instinctively and almost unconsciously ashamed of the caricatures done of our darker shades. Black *is* caricature in our half-conscious thought, and we shun in print and paint that which we love in life. How good a dark face looks to us in a strange city! How the black soldiers, despite their white French sweethearts, yearned for their far-off "brown-skins." A mighty and swelling human consciousness is leading us joyously to embrace the darker world, but we remain afraid of black pictures because they are the cruel reminders of the crimes of Sunday "comics" and "Nigger" minstrels.

Off with these thought-chains and inchoate soul-shrinkings, and let us train ourselves to see beauty in black.

MARXISM AND THE
NEGRO PROBLEM

W . E . B . DU BOIS

KARL MARX was a Jew born at Treves, Germany, in March 1818. He came of an educated family and studied at the Universities of Bonn and Berlin, planning first to become a lawyer, and then to teach philosophy. But his ideas were too radical for the government. He turned to journalism, and finally gave his life to economic reform, dying in London in 1883, after háving lived in Germany, Belgium, France, and, for the last thirty-five years of his life, in England. He published in 1867 the first volume of his monumental work, *Capital*.

There are certain books in the world which every searcher for truth must know: the Bible, the *Critique of Pure Reason,* the *Origin of Species,* and Karl Marx' *Capital*.

Yet until the Russian Revolution, Karl Marx was little known in America. He was treated condescendingly in the universities, and regarded even by the intelligent public as a radical agitator whose curious and inconvenient theories it was easy to refute. Today, at last, we all know better, and we see in Karl Marx a colossal genius of infinite sacrifice and monumental industry, and with a mind of extraordinary logical keenness and grasp. We may disagree with many of the great books of truth that I have named, and with *Capital,* but they can never be ignored. . . .

What now has all this to do with the Negro problem? First of all, it is manifest that the mass of Negroes in the United States belong distinctly to the working proletariat. Of every thousand working Negroes less than a hundred and fifty belong to any class that could possibly be considered bourgeois. And even this more educated and prosperous class has but small connection with the exploiters of wage and labor. Nevertheless, this black proletariat is not a part of the white proletariat. Black and white work together in many cases, and influence each other's rates of wages. They have similar complaints against capitalists, save that the grievances

SOURCE: W. E. B. Du Bois, "Marxism and the Negro Problem," *The Crisis* 40 (May 1933): 103–104, 118.

of the Negro worker are more fundamental and indefensible, ranging as they do, since the day of Karl Marx, from chattel slavery, to the worst paid, sweated, mobbed and cheated labor in any civilized land.

And while Negro labor in America suffers because of the fundamental inequities of the whole capitalistic system, the lowest and most fatal degree of its suffering comes not from the capitalists but from fellow white laborers. It is white labor that deprives the Negro of his right to vote, denies him education, denies him affiliation with trade unions, expels him from decent houses and neighborhoods, and heaps upon him the public insults of open color discrimination.

It is no sufficient answer to say that capital encourages this oppression and uses it for its own ends. This may have excused the ignorant and superstitious Russian peasants in the past and some of the poor whites of the South today. But the bulk of American white labor is neither ignorant nor fanatical. It knows exactly what it is doing and it means to do it. William Green and Mathew Woll of the A. F. of L. have no excuse of illiteracy or religion to veil their deliberate intention to keep Negroes and Mexicans and other elements of common labor in a lower proletariat as subservient to their interests as theirs are to the interests of capital.

This large development of a petty bourgeoisie within the American laboring class is a post-Marxian phenomenon and the result of the tremendous and worldwide development of capitalism in the 20th Century. The market of capitalistic production has gained an effective worldwide organization. Industrial technique and mass production have brought possibilities in the production of goods and services which out-run even this wide market. A new class of technical engineers and managers has arisen forming a working-class aristocracy between the older proletariat and the absentee owners of capital. The real owners of capital are small as well as large investors—workers who have deposits in savings banks and small holdings in stocks and bonds; families buying homes and purchasing commodities on installment; as well as the large and rich investors.

Of course, the individual laborer gets but an infinitesimal part of his income from such investments. On the other hand, such investments, in the aggregate, largely increase available capital for the exploiters, and they give investing labors the capitalistic ideology. Between workers and owners of capital stand today the bankers and financiers who distribute capital and direct the engineers.

Thus the engineers and the saving better-paid workers form a new petty bourgeois class, whose interests are bound up with those of the capitalists and antagonistic to those of common labor. On the other hand, common labor in America and white Europe far from being motivated by any vision of revolt against capitalism, has been blinded by the American vision of the possibility of layer after layer of the workers escaping into the wealthy class and becoming managers and employers of labor.

Thus in America we have seen a wild and ruthless scramble of labor groups over each other in order to climb to wealth on the backs of black labor and foreign immigrants. The Irish climbed on the Negroes. The Germans scrambled over the Negroes and emulated the Irish. The Scandinavians fought forward next to the Germans and the Italians and "Bohunks" are crowding up, leaving Negroes still at the bottom chained to helplessness, first by slavery, then by disfranchisement and always by the Color Bar.

The second influence on white labor both in America and Europe has been the fact that the extension of the world market by imperial expanding industry has established a worldwide new proletariat of colored workers, toiling under the worst conditions of 19th-century capitalism, herded as slaves and serfs and furnishing by the lowest paid wage in modern history a mass of raw material for industry. With this largess the capitalists have consolidated their economic power, nullified universal suffrage and bribed the white workers by high wages, visions of wealth and the opportunity to drive "niggers." Soldiers and sailors from the white workers are used to keep "darkies" in their "places" and white foremen and engineers have been established as irresponsible satraps in China and India, Africa and the West Indies, backed by the organized and centralized ownership of machines, raw materials, finished commodities and land monopoly over the whole world.

How now does the philosophy of Karl Marx apply today to colored labor? First of all colored labor has no common ground with white labor. No soviet of technocrats would do more than exploit colored labor in order to raise the status of whites. No revolt of a white proletariat could be started if its object was to make black workers their economic, political and social equals. It is for this reason that American socialism for fifty years has been dumb on the Negro problem, and the Communists cannot even get a respectful hearing in America unless they begin by expelling Negroes.

On the other hand, within the Negro groups, in the United States, in West Africa, in South America and in the West Indies, petty bourgeois groups are being evolved. In South America and the West Indies such groups drain off skill and intelligence into the white group, and leave the black labor poor, ignorant and leaderless save for an occasional demagog.

In West Africa, a Negro bourgeoisie is developing with invested capital and employment of natives and is only kept from the conventional capitalistic development by the opposition and enmity of white capital, and the white managers and engineers who represent it locally and who display bitter prejudice and tyranny; and by white European labor which furnishes armies and navies and Empire "preference." African black labor and black capital are therefore driven to seek alliance and common ground.

In the United States also a petty bourgeoisie is being developed, consisting of clergymen, teachers, farm owners, professional men and retail businessmen. The position of this class, however, is peculiar: they are not the chief or even large investors in Negro labor and therefore exploit it only here and there; and they bear the brunt of color prejudice because they express in word and work the aspirations of all black folk for emancipation. The revolt of any black proletariat could not, therefore, be logically directed against this class, nor could this class join either white capital, white engineers or white workers to strengthen the color bar.

Under these circumstances, what shall we say of the Marxian philosophy and of its relation to the American Negro? We can only say, as it seems to me, that the Marxian philosophy is a true diagnosis of the situation in Europe in the middle of the 19th Century despite some of its logical difficulties. But it must be modified in the United States of America and especially so far as the Negro group is concerned. The Negro is exploited to a degree that means poverty, crime, delinquency and indigence. And that exploitation comes not from a black capitalistic class but from the white capitalists and equally from the white proletariat. His only defense is such internal organization as will protect him from both parties, and such practical economic insight as will prevent inside the race group any large development of capitalistic exploitation.

Meantime, comes the Great Depression. It levels all in mighty catastrophe. The fantastic industrial structure of America is threatened with ruin. The trade unions of skilled labor are double-tongued and helpless. Unskilled and common white labor is too frightened at Negro competition to attempt united action. It only begs a dole. The reformist program of socialism meets no response from the white proletariat because it offers no escape to wealth and no effective bar to black labor, and a mud-sill of black labor is essential to white labor's standard of living. The shrill cry of a few Communists is not even listened to, because and solely because it seeks to break down barriers between black and white. There is not at present the slightest indication that a Marxian revolution based on a united class-conscious proletariat is anywhere on the American far horizon.

Rather race antagonism and labor group rivalry are still undisturbed by world catastrophe. In the hearts of black laborers alone, therefore, lie those ideals of democracy in politics and industry which may in time make the workers of the world effective dictators of civilization.

---

[37]

BRIGHT AND MORNING STAR

RICHARD WRIGHT

FOR the most part she walked with her eyes half shut, her lips tightly compressed, leaning her body against the wind and the driving rain, feeling the pistol in the sheet sagging cold and heavy in her fingers. Already she was getting wet; it seemed that her feet found every puddle of water that stood between the corn rows.

She came to the edge of the creek and paused, wondering at what point was it low. Taking the sheet from under her apron, she wrapped the gun in it so that her finger could be upon the trigger. Ahll cross here, she thought. At first she did not feel the water; her feet were already wet. But the water grew cold as it came up to her knees; she gasped when it reached her waist. Lawd, this creek's high! When she had passed the middle, she knew that she was out of danger. She came out of the water, climbed a grassy hill, walked on, turned a bend and saw the lights of autos gleaming ahead. Yeah; theys still there! She hurried with her head down. Wonda did Ah beat im here? Lawd, Ah *hope* so! A vivid image of Booker's white face hovered a moment before her eyes and a surging will rose up in her so hard and strong that it vanished. She was among the autos now. From nearby came the hoarse voices of the men.

"Hey, yuh!"

She stopped, nervously clutching the sheet. Two white men with shotguns came toward her.

"Whut in hell yuh doin out here?"

She did not answer.

"Didnt yuh hear somebody speak t yuh?"

SOURCE: Richard Wright, *Bright and Morning Star* (New York: International Publishers, 1938), pp. 39–48. Reprinted by permission of International Publishers Co., Inc.

"Ahm comin aftah mah son," she said humbly.

"Yo *son?*"

"Yessuh."

"Whut yo son doin out here?"

"The sheriffs got im."

"Holy Scott! Jim, its the niggers ma!"

"What yuh got there?" asked one.

"A sheet."

"A *sheet?*"

"Yessuh."

"Fer whut?"

"The sheriff tol me t bring a sheet t git his body."

"Waal, waal . . ."

"Now, ain tha somethin?"

The white men looked at each other.

"These niggers sho love one ernother," said one.

"N tha ain no lie," said the other.

"Take me t the sheriff," she begged.

"Yuh ain givin us *orders,* is yuh?"

"Nawsuh."

"We'll take yuh when wes good n ready."

"Yessuh."

"So yuh wan his body?"

"Yessuh."

"Waal, he ain dead yit."

"They gonna kill im," she said.

"Ef he talks they wont."

"He ain gonna talk," she said.

"How yuh know?"

"Cause he ain."

"We got ways of makin niggers talk."

"Yuh ain got no way fer im."

"You thinka lot of tha black Red, don yuh?"

"Hes mah son."

"Why don yuh teach im some sense?"

"Hes mah son," she said again.

"Lissen, ol nigger woman, yuh stand there wid yo hair white. Yu got bettah sense than t blieve tha niggers kin make a revolution . . ."

"A black republic," said the other one, laughing.

"Take me t the sheriff," she begged.

"Yuh his ma," said one. "Yuh kin make im talk n tell whos in this thing wid im."

"He ain gonna talk," she said.

"Don yuh wan im t liv?"

She did not answer.

"Cmon, les take her t Bradley."

They grabbed her arms and she clutched hard at the sheet and gun; they led her toward the crowd in the woods. Her feelings were simple; Booker would not tell; she was there with the gun to see to that. The louder became the voices of the men the deeper became her feeling of wanting to right the mistake she had made; of wanting to fight her way back to solid ground. She would stall for time until Booker showed up. Oh, ef theyll only lemme git close t Johnny-Boy! As they led her near the crowd she saw white faces turning and looking at her and heard a rising clamor of voices.

"Whos tha?"

"A nigger woman!"

"Whut she doin out here?"

"This is his ma!" called one of the men.

"Whut she wans?"

"She brought a sheet t cover his body!"

"He ain dead yit!"

"They tryin t make im talk!"

"But he will be dead soon ef he don open up!"

"Say, look! The niggers ma brought a sheet t cover up his body!" . . .

"Now, ain tha sweet?"

"Mabbe she wans t hol a prayer meetin!"

"Did she git a preacher?"

"Say, go git Bradley!"

"O.K.!"

The crowd grew quiet. They looked at her curiously; she felt their cold eyes trying to detect some weakness in her. Humbly, she stood with the sheet covering the gun. She had already accepted all that they could do to her.

The sheriff came.

"So yuh brought yo sheet, hunh?"

"Yessuh," she whispered.

"Looks like them slaps we gave yuh learned yuh some sense, didnt they?"

She did not answer.

"Yuh don need tha sheet. Yo son ain dead yit," he said, reaching toward her.

She backed away, her eyes wide.

"Naw!"

"Now, lissen, Anty!" he said. "There ain no use in yuh ackin a fool! Go in there n tell tha nigger son of yos t tell us whos in this wid im, see? Ah promise we wont kill im ef he talks. We'll let im git outta town."

"There ain nothin Ah kin tell im," she said.

"Yuh wan us t kill im?"

She did not answer. She saw someone lean toward the sheriff and whisper.

"Bring her erlong," the sheriff said.

They led her to a muddy clearing. The rain streamed down through the ghostly glare of the flashlights. As the men formed a semi-circle she saw Johnny-Boy lying in a trough of mud. He was tied with rope; he lay hunched and one side of his face rested in a pool of black water. His eyes were staring questioningly at her.

"Speak t im," said the sheriff.

If she could only tell him why she was here! But that was impossible; she was close to what she wanted and she stared straight before her with compressed lips.

"Say, nigger!" called the sheriff, kicking Johnny-Boy. "Heres yo ma!"

Johnny-Boy did not move or speak. The sheriff faced her again.

"Lissen, Anty," he said. "Yuh got mo say wid im than anybody. Tell im t talk n hava chance. Whut he wanna pertect the other niggers n white folks fer?"

She slid her finger about the trigger of the gun and looked stonily at the mud.

"Go t him," said the sheriff.

She did not move. Her heart was crying out to answer the amazed question in Johnny-Boy's eyes. But there was no way now.

"Waal, yuhre astin fer it. By Gawd, we gotta way to *make* yuh talk t im," he said, turning away. "Say, Tim, git one of them logs n turn that nigger upside-down n put his legs on it!"

A murmur of assent ran through the crowd. She bit her lips; she knew what that meant.

"Yuh wan yo nigger son crippled?" she heard the sheriff ask.

She did not answer. She saw them roll the log up; they lifted Johnny-Boy and laid him on his face and stomach, then they pulled his legs over the log. His knee-caps rested on the sheer top of the log's back and the toes of his shoes pointed groundward. So absorbed was she in watching that she felt that it was she who was being lifted and made ready for torture.

"Git a crowbar!" said the sheriff.

A tall, lank man got a crowbar from a nearby auto and stood over the log. His jaws worked slowly on a wad of tobacco.

"Now, its up t yuh, Anty," the sheriff said. "Tell the man what t do!"

She looked into the rain. The sheriff turned.

"Mabbe she think wes playin. Ef she don say nothin, then break em at the knee-caps!"

"O.K., Sheriff!"

She stood waiting for Booker. Her legs felt weak; she wondered if she would be able to wait much longer. Over and over she said to herself, Ef he came now Ahd kill em both!

"She ain sayin nothin, Sheriff!"

"Waal, Gawddammit, let im have it!"

The crowbar came down and Johnny-Boy's body lunged in the mud and water. There was a scream. She swayed, holding tight to the gun and sheet.

"Hol im! Git the other leg!"

The crowbar fell again. There was another scream.

"Yuh break em?" asked the sheriff.

The tall man lifted Johnny-Boy's legs and let them drop limply again, dropping rearward from the knee-caps. Johnny-Boy's body lay still. His head had rolled to one side and she could not see his face.

"Jus lika broke sparrow wing," said the man, laughing softly.

Then Johnny-Boy's face turned to her; he screamed.

"Go way, ma! Go way!"

It was the first time she had heard his voice since she had come out to the woods; she all but lost control of herself. She started violently forward, but the sheriff's arm checked her.

"Aw naw! Yuh had yo chance!" He turned to Johnny-Boy. "She kin go ef yuh talk."

"Mistah, he ain gonna talk," she said.

"Go way, ma!" said Johnny-Boy.

"Shoot im! Don make im suffah so," she begged.

"He'll either talk or he'll never hear yuh ergin," the sheriff said. "There other things we kin do t im."

She said nothing.

"What yuh come here fer, ma?" Johnny-Boy sobbed.

"Ahm gonna split his eardrums," the sheriff said. "Ef yuh got anythin t say t im yuh bettah say it *now!*"

She closed her eyes. She heard the sheriff's feet sucking in mud. Ah could save im! She opened her eyes; there were shouts of eagerness from the crowd as it pushed in closer.

"Bus em, Sheriff!"

"Fix im so he cant hear!"

"He knows how t do it, too!"

"He busted a Jew boy tha way once!"

She saw the sheriff stoop over Johnny-Boy, place his flat palm over one ear and strike his fist against it with all his might. He placed his palm over the other ear and struck again. Johnny-Boy moaned, his head rolling from side to side, his eyes showing white amazement in a world without sound.

"Yuh wouldnt talk t im when yuh had the chance," said the sheriff. "Try n talk now."

She felt warm tears on her cheeks. She longed to shoot Johnny-Boy and let him go. But if she did that they would take the gun from her, and Booker would tell who the others were. Lawd, hep me! The men were talking loudly now, as though the main business was over. It seemed ages that she stood there watching Johnny-Boy roll and whimper in his world of silence.

"Say, Sheriff, heres somebody lookin fer yuh!"

"Who is it?"

"Ah don know!"

"Bring em in!"

She stiffened and looked around wildly, holding the gun tight. Is tha Booker? Then she held still, feeling that her excitement might betray her. Mabbe Ah kin shoot em both! Mabbe Ah kin shoot *twice!* The sheriff stood in front of her, waiting. The crowd parted and she saw Booker hurrying forward.

"Ah know em all, Sheriff!" he called.

He came full into the muddy clearing where Johnny-Boy lay.

"Yuh mean yuh got the names?"

"Sho! The ol nigger . . ."

She saw his lips hang open and silent when he saw her. She stepped forward and raised the sheet.

"Whut . . ."

She fired, once; then, without pausing, she turned, hearing them yell. She aimed at Johnny-Boy, but they had their arms around her, bearing her to the ground, clawing at the sheet in her hand. She glimpsed Booker lying sprawled in the mud, on his face, his hands stretched out before him; then a cluster of yelling men blotted him out. She lay without struggling, looking upward through the rain at the white faces above her. And she was suddenly at peace; they were not a white mountain now; they were not pushing her any longer to the edge of life. Its awright . . .

"She shot Booker!"

"She hada gun in the sheet!"

"She shot im right thu the head!"

"Whut she shoot im fer?"

"Kill the bitch!"

"Ah *thought* somethin wuz wrong bout her!"

"Ah wuz fer givin it t her from the firs!"

"Thas whut yuh get fer treatin a nigger nice!"

"Say, Bookers dead!"

She stopped looking into the white faces, stopped listening. She waited, giving up her life before they took it from her; she had done what she wanted. Ef only Johnny-Boy . . . She looked at him; he lay looking at her with tired eyes. Ef she could only tell im! But he lay already buried in a grave of silence.

"Whut yuh kill im fer, hunh?"

It was the sheriff's voice; she did not answer.

"Mabbe she wuz shootin at yuh, Sheriff?"

"Whut yuh kill im fer?"

She felt the sheriff's foot come into her side; she closed her eyes.

"Yuh black bitch!"

"Let her have it!"

"Yuh reckon she foun out bout Booker?"

"She mighta."

"Jesus Chris, whut yuh dummies *waitin* on!"

"Yeah; kill her!"

"Kill em *both!*"

"Let her know her nigger sons dead firs!"

She turned her head toward Johnny-Boy; he lay looking puzzled in a world beyond the reach of voices. At leas he cant hear, she thought.

"Cmon, let im have it!"

She listened to hear what Johnny-Boy could not. They came, two of them, one right behind the other; so close together that they sounded like one shot. She did not look at Johnny-Boy now; she looked at the white faces of the men, hard and wet in the glare of the flashlights.

"Yuh hear tha, nigger woman?"

"Did tha surprise im? Hes in hell now wonderin whut hit im!"

"Cmon! Give it t her, Sheriff!"

"Lemme shoot her, Sheriff! It wuz mah pal she shot!"

"Awright, Pete! Thas fair ernuff!"

She gave up as much of her life as she could before they took it from her. But the sound of the shot and the streak of fire that tore its way through her chest forced her to live again, intensely. She had not moved, save for the slight jarring impact of the bullet. She felt the heat of her own blood warming her cold, wet back. She yearned suddenly to talk. "Yuh didnt git whut yuh wanted! N yuh ain gonna nevah git it! Yuh didn't kill me; Ah come here by mahsef . . ." She felt rain falling into her wide-open, dimming eyes and heard faint voices. Her lips moved soundlessly. *Yuh didnt git yuh didnt yuh didnt . . .* Focused and pointed she was, buried in the depths of her star, swallowed in its peace and strength; and not feeling her flesh growing cold, cold as the rain that fell from the invisible sky upon the doomed living and the dead that never dies.

---

[38]

THE MARXIST-LENINIST POSITION ON THE NEGRO QUESTION

JAMES W. FORD

IN 1928, the Communist Party, guided by the Communist International, came to a full scientific, Marxist-Leninist understanding of the Negro question in the United States, as a national question.

In October of that year, following the Sixth World Congress of the Communist International, the Party adopted a resolution which stated:

The various forms of oppression of the Negro masses who are concentrated mainly in the so-called "Black Belt" provide the necessary conditions for a national revolutionary movement among the Negroes.

To accomplish this task, the Communist Party must come out as the champion of the right of the oppressed Negro race (nation) for full emancipation. While continuing and intensifying the struggle under the slogan of full social and political equality for the Negroes, which remains the central slogan of our

SOURCE: James W. Ford, "The Struggle for the Building of the Modern Liberation Movement of the Negro People," *Communist* 18 (September 1939): 822–828.

Party for work among the masses, the Party must come out openly and unreservedly for the right of Negroes to national self-determination in the Southern states, where the Negroes form the majority of the population.

The opportunist Lovestone leadership rejected the full implications of industrialization in the country and the development of capitalism following the Civil War. Instead, they preached that the industrialization of the South would "sweep away the remnants of slavery," and thus the Negro question would be "solved," or could be put off until the time of the socialist revolution!

Due to conscious distortions which sought to identify this position with reactionary Negro separatism, there was brought in confusion among the Party ranks on the question of self-determination. In the main, however, there was clarity. For, on the question of separatist tendencies among Negroes, the resolution stated:

The general reaction of Communists to separatist tendencies among the Negroes . . . cannot mean that Communists associate themselves at present, or generally speaking, during capitalism, indiscriminately and without criticism with all separatist currents of the various bourgeois or petty-bourgeois Negro groups. For there is not only a *national-revolutionary,* but also a reactionary Negro separatism, for instance, that represented by Garveyism.

With clarity on the Negro question from the basic Marxist-Leninist viewpoint, there followed the expulsion of Lovestone from the Communist Party. With the expulsion of the Lovestoneites and the establishment of unity in the Party, the program on the Negro question was cleared of opportunist views. This armed the Party politically for a decisive step forward in organizing the national liberation movement of the Negro masses. With a Leninist-Stalinist line, with unity established in the Party, the attention of the Party was directed toward mass work among the Negro people.

Immediately, the Party heeded the warning of its resolution to conduct "an aggressive fight against all forms of white chauvinism . . . accompanied by a widespread and thorough educational campaign in the spirit of internationalism within the Party, utilizing for this purpose to the fullest possible extent the Party schools, the Party press, and the public platform, to stamp out all forms of antagonisms, or even indifference, among our white comrades toward the Negro work."

Attacking white chauvinism within its own ranks, notably and dramatically expressed in the public trial of one of its members in 1930, the Party placed the Negro question before the entire country as a major problem on the agenda of American social and political history. It was this trial which prepared the Party membership and a large section of the American masses for the practical attainment of the objectives set forth in its resolutions.

Grasping a deeper understanding of the Negro people's movement as it relates to the land question, the Communists penetrated the deep South and helped organize thousands of Negroes into the Sharecroppers' Union and other organizations for the protection and extension of their basic rights. Indeed, it was this deepened understanding that made possible the development of the Scottsboro issue into an epic political struggle that stirred America—and the world. This struggle threw the spotlight of world opinion on the lynching and national oppression of the Negroes in the United States and won the support of the entire labor movement and wide sections of the progressive forces, North and South. Likewise, the widely supported struggle for the freedom of Angelo Herndon reaffirmed the legal right of the Communist Party to conduct activities in the South. These struggles, occurring in the midst of the great crisis, marked the beginning of a change in class relations within the Negro people. For the first time in history the Negro workers were acting as an independent force, fighting for their own and their people's demands.

Stemming from these struggles were movements for the immediate needs of the Negro people—the right to vote, to jury service, to hold public office, the abolition of the ancient chain gang laws. These movements are today changing the South to the benefit, not only of the Negro people, but of democracy in the entire nation.

The worst sufferers from the world economic crisis of capitalism were the Negro people. Economic insecurity affected whole sections of the Southern population. The pioneering work of the Communist Party to alleviate these sufferings was evidenced by the great nationwide unemployed demonstration held on March 6, 1930. Drawing tens of thousands of Negroes into common economic action with whites, these mass outpourings established the basis for Negro and white labor solidarity, both among the unemployed and in the unions.

The People's Front Movement and the Negro People

The offensive of fascism, by its hideous racism and its depredations against weaker nations, soon impressed itself upon the Negro people as a menace to their security. Ethiopia, subjected to the savage rapine of Italian fascism, became the focal point of the Negro people's fight against Nazi-fascist barbarism. Bleeding Ethiopia filled them with undying hatred against fascism and its bestiality. Out of this struggle, conducted on an international scale, and which the Communists helped to initiate, grew organizations uniting the Negro people for continued struggle against fascist dangers at home as well as abroad.

The aggressor policy of fascism in Europe, Asia and Africa, as well as its penetration of Latin America, the Caribbean, and the West Indies, has placed the slogan "for the right of self-determination" in a new light. The progressives and, above all, the Communists, must assume the task of preventing the fascists from using this slogan demagogically for reactionary purposes.

Following the Seventh World Congress of the Communist International and the development of a program for the people's front, life itself was already developing, in skeleton form, the Negro sector of this front in America. The Communist Party immediately set its tasks in regard to the problems growing out of the new situation.

The issue now in the world is democracy against fascism. This requires the utmost development of labor unity as a cementing factor in the construction of a powerful democratic front movement—unity of labor, the toiling farmers, the Negro people, and the middle classes against capitalist reaction, fascism and war.

For the Negroes the central task is the promotion of unity around their principal organizations: The National Association for the Advancement of Colored People, the National Negro Congress, the Southern Negro Youth Congress, the Urban League and the many other organizations of the Negro people, including the powerful church groups. The success of the movement for unity demands a more intensive mass mobilization of the Negro people, together with their friends and allies, for daily struggle against Negro discrimination—in unions, on jobs, in regard to relief and educational facilities; in a word, for full equal rights. To some extent many far-seeing Negro leaders are beginning to tackle this task; and in most instances their efforts have been rewarded with a ready response of the masses. The first serious effort in this regard was the First National Negro Congress called in Chicago in 1936.

Having acquired experience in, and developed leaders through, the mass work among the Negroes, the Communist Party was able to render valuable aid toward the accomplishment of this task. This aid was expressed concretely in the contributions of the Negro Communists, especially, to the National Negro Congress. In the midst of this broad movement the Communists helped it avoid the pitfalls that had beset previous movements of upsurge. Identifying itself with the Negro proletariat, now risen to a leading position in the people's movement, it assisted the movement in steering clear of narrow racialism and toward a broad unity movement of all the oppressed. Without its contact with the maturing Negro working class this assistance would not have been possible.

The Negro volunteers who fought and died in Spain, and those who are now breaking with the Japanese-inspired "unity of darker races" ideology in giving aid to the embattled Chinese people, are eloquent witnesses to the growth of advanced working-class influence among Negroes.

The Communists recognize that the fight for the rights of the Negroes is the task, not only of the Negro people, but of the country's democratic forces as a whole. It is particularly the task of the white working-class, whose historic ally in the struggle for its own emancipation is the Negro people.

On the basis of this principle the Communists have consistently conducted the struggle against the anti-Negro prejudices and restrictions of the labor movement and the people's organizations. This struggle has borne significant fruit: notably, the C.I.O. program expressed in its convention resolutions calling for full Negro equality. To be noted also is the increased pressure within the A. F. of L. and the Railroad Brotherhoods for the removal of color bars on the job and in the unions. . . .

In this way the labor movement, on the Negro question, as on other economic, social, and political issues, asserts its leadership in the democratic camp of which the New Deal is the political symbol.

This increasing support given the New Deal by labor, and the vital need of that support, brings the consistent New Dealers to realize the necessity for, and actively to promote, the unity of labor and the unity of Negro and white. And since Negro and white unity can come about only in the course of removing anti-Negro restrictions, we see the leading New Dealers speaking and acting in behalf of the abolition of these restrictions.

The Communist Party supports the New Deal as the political expression of the democratic front and strives to unite the Negro people's movement with it. The Party points out that in the interest of maintaining the New Deal and democracy against the attacks of the Hoover–Garner forces the people and the government must effectively meet the burning problems which confront the Negro masses. For, with the Negroes constituting the balance of power in at least seven states, their votes will have very important bearings, and even be decisive in the 1940 elections. Therefore, passage of the Anti-Lynching Bill, abolition of the disgraceful poll tax; and amending the Social Security Act, liberalizing the benefit provisions in the interests of Negro domestics and agricultural workers, must become a part of the political program of the New Deal. Independently, the Communists will continue to fight for these demands of the Negro people in the interest of democracy and America's well-being.

Under the aegis of the New Deal, the Southern Human Welfare Conference, held in Birmingham, in November 1938, opened up a new phase of the struggle against the feudal restrictions placed upon the Negro people and the South as a whole. The Southern Negro Youth Conference, following the Human Welfare Conference, disclosed the forces among the Negroes willing and ready to take their places in this basic struggle for democracy in the country. The Communists, through their pioneering work in the South, may justly claim to have laid the foundation for these great social movements. This new phase of the struggle for Negro rights in America, as reflected generally in contemporary social and political life, marks also the transition of the Communist Party from a minority, fighting almost alone on this issue, into a definite part of the democratic majority. No other field of work demonstrates this fact more than the Party's work among Negroes.

New times and new conditions bring new methods of attack and struggle by monopoly capital and reaction against the forward movement among the Negro people. This movement is achieving stability and solidarity. But reaction is resorting to demagogy, deceit, stool pigeons and spies to disrupt and disorganize it. Among the most common types of spies and disrupters are the Trotskyites and Lovestoneites. Types similar to the traitors in the struggles of the Negroes prior to and during the slave period are evident today.

A changed attitude is to be noted in the principal organizations of the Negro people toward labor and the relationship of labor to the problems of the Negro people. Labor organization among the Negro workers has reached heights never before known. An estimated 500,000 Negro workers are now organized into the C.I.O. and the A. F. of L. This change offers great hope for the advancement of the modern liberation movement of the Negro people, for their immediate needs and their ultimate freedom.

PART XII
International
Politics and
World War II

Fᴿᴏᴍ the summer of 1935 through the summer of 1939 the American Left, along with almost everybody else, was caught up in the politics and psychology of a deteriorating world. Fascism meant war, and the deep desire to hide from this fact gave the Fascists time to prepare to fight better. From the Comintern's announcement of the Popular Front through the Spanish Civil War, the Moscow purges, the Hitler-Stalin pact, and the German invasion of Poland, all the world was buffeted by events which demanded an ultimate appeal to fire. All the nations pretended that Hitler's open persecution of the Jews either would go away or did not justify their own serious intervention. The Western nations pretended that Germany's demand for "living space" would be satisfied after they gave Czechoslovakia away. The desire to avoid war led to a blindness which contributed to the coming of war, but war was planned in Berlin and Tokyo, and the other powers had only to react.

Stalin's major decisions in this prewar period were largely based on the conviction that there would be war between Germany and the Soviet Union, and on the deeply held suspicion that the Western nations would find a way either to assist Hitler in his political madness or else to get out of his way. Most Americans apparently believed that the crisis had little to do with them, that a corrupt Europe was simply at it again, and that this time America really could stay out. Several pieces of neutrality legislation, as well as Roosevelt's failure to elicit a sympathetic response to his "Quarantine" speech of 1937, were symptoms of America's profound wish to stand away from history. Coolidge had said that America's business was business, and European politics was none of America's business. But, of course, there was some fear and some clarity inside the American cocoon, and American radicals, although they were more likely at least to recognize the world's existence, were also not immune to the comforts of the American political ostrich.

Some radical spokesmen participated in a symposium in September 1935 (Document 39). They were asked to answer the question, "What will you do when America goes to war?" Most of them predictably said that they opposed nationalistic and imperialistic war, that workers should fight only a revolutionary class war, and that they must not get swept up into a fervid and jingoistic psychology that would put them at the literal disposal of international capitalism. One man even recalled the Socialists' St. Louis war proclamation of 1917 (see Document 13) as a continuingly appropriate position. But the Communist Left, now closely tied to Soviet policy, was desperate for a way out of this consistent but, in the event of war involving the Soviet Union, potentially dangerous perspective. Because the way was not yet clear, one respondent simply announced that the best policy, whatever that might be, would be to "follow the general line laid down by the Communist International." The non-Communist Left, with Norman Thomas and America at large, could more easily maintain a nice pacifist consistency, but the Communists had to find a way to exempt the Soviet Union from their otherwise general condemnation of nationalistic conflict.

The first step in the Comintern's prewar maneuvering had, however, already been taken a few weeks earlier. At its seventh world congress, the Comintern announced the creation of the Popular Front: "in the face of Fascist danger, Communists may, while reserving for themselves freedom of political agitation and criticism, participate in election campaigns on a common platform and with a common ticket of the anti-fascist front. . . ." This had an enormous and immediate impact on the Communist parties of the world, with a Popular Front government established in France, with the ambiguous intervention of the Comintern in the Spanish Civil War, and even with important consequences for the little American party.

Earl Browder (see Document 31), who had been sent to Leavenworth penitentiary twice for his opposition to World War I, led the Popular Front in America. He was in charge of leading the party's dramatic reversal on almost every major domestic issue. As he argued in his report to the ninth CP convention in June 1936 (Document 40), the issue now was not capitalism or socialism, but fascism or democracy. This meant that the CP would now work with anti-Communist democrats who opposed fascism. In practical terms this meant an occasionally weird passion to Americanize the party, with an eventual celebration of FDR and the Democratic Party, baseball, Hollywood movies, and Paul Revere's birthday. In becoming respectable and reasonable, the official CP simply ceased providing a radical critique of America's political economy, a task that was now performed only by the non-Communist Left. The *Partisan Review,* for instance, already independent of the CP (see Document 27), was bitterly critical of the *New Masses,* a party organ, for its abandonment of a radical view of the New Deal. The non-Communist Left, in short, now attacked the CP for its almost miraculous rightward lunge. The Communists defended themselves on the ground that fascism was so important a threat that momentary cooperation was more realistic than ideological or intellectual consistency; they acted on an old political maxim: the enemy of my enemy is my friend.

Although the Popular Front psychology allowed the American CP to broaden its circle of sympathizers significantly, it obviously did so by diluting what it was, by accepting the idea of American exceptionalism for which Jay Lovestone (see Document 22) had been expelled from the party, and by turning its back on the meaning of New Deal liberal and reform politics. The Popular Front meant that the obviously genuine international crisis, about which the CP was clearer than others on the left, paralyzed the Communists in domestic politics, about which the non-Communist Left was clearer than the CP.

The outbreak of the Spanish Civil War in July 1936 was an occasion for these confused and increasingly hostile radical forces to try to work themselves out—somehow. The Left of the world combined at least rhetorically to condemn Franco's Spanish fascism, and to call for a defense of the republican Loyalists. Hitler and Mussolini seized the Spanish opportunity to rehearse some of their troops and weapons, especially the Luftwaffe, and an international republican brigade was assembled to help defend Spain against Franco's rebels. The Abraham Lincoln Brigade arrived from America, as others did from all over the Western world. Here was a chance for anti-Fascists to do something, actually to fight for what they believed. Many members of the international legions thought of themselves as fighting against Nazism and fascism as well as against Franco, and they saw the Spanish struggle as part of the international class conflict (see Document 41). Pursuing the Popular Front, the Comintern also intervened in Spain, partially against the non-Communist Left, including anarchists; pursuing a dream, the U.S. Congress prohibited arms shipments to either side in Spain, thereby hurting only the republicans because the fascists were supplied by Germany and Italy.

The last prewar act was the Hitler–Stalin pact of 23 August 1939. Coupled with the Moscow trials, this diplomatic dynamite was agony for American radicals, many of whom now left or drifted away from the party. Only the party's inner core accepted the official line: that the Soviet Union was buying time for military preparation, was protecting itself from an anticipated attack from, or sellout by, the capitalistic powers, and was seeking a momentary refuge from hostile encirclement.

After the beginning of the war in Europe, and especially after Pearl Harbor, the military alliance resulted in a political detente for the Left as well as for the center. Bipartisanship in foreign policy now really meant a moratorium on criticism, even from the organized Left. Although some grumbling about nationalistic wars was still occasionally heard from the non-Communist Left, American radicalism essentially and voluntarily closed shop for the duration.

The Trotskyists, never more than a tiny grouplet on the intellectual and trade union Left, did continue their critique of the contending capitalistic and totalitarian national behemoths. Formed by James P. Cannon in the late 1920's, this splinter grew increasingly critical of what it believed to be bureaucratic statism—Stalinism—in the Soviet Union, while it also maintained its hostility to capitalism. Cannon and others were expelled from the CP when they got caught in the Lovestone–Foster crossfire, with all sides eager to denounce the Trotskyists. Organized in the Fourth International, the Trotskyists wished a plague on the House of Stalin as well as on the House of Morgan. This was clearly a dangerous position to maintain in the face of the war, as Cannon expressed it himself:

> With the approach of the war Trotskyism as a doctrine and as a movement began to lose its "respectability." Many of the intellectuals, sniffing danger, arranged a somewhat hasty and undignified departure. In truth, there is not much left of that considerable army of drawing room heroes who used to admire Trotsky's literary style and confound the less intelligent periphery of Stalinism with nuggets of wisdom mined from Trotsky's writings. The collapse of the Trotskyist "cultural front" was taken by some people, especially the ex-fronters themselves, to signify a collapse of our movement.[1]

But, so far from collapsing, according to Cannon, "Trotskyism, embodied in the Fourth International, is the only revolutionary movement." [2]

[1] James P. Cannon, *The Struggle for a Proletarian Party* (New York: Pioneer Publishers, 1943), p. 6.
[2] *Ibid.*, p. 5.

The concluding document (42) of this section shows the Trotskyist perspective of the war, as well as its feel for the international political future. Written by Max Shachtman (b. 1903), who was expelled from the CP with Cannon, and who was in 1945 the National Secretary of the Trotskyist Workers Party and the editor of the leading Trotskyist journal (from which this article is taken), this extraordinary survey of the consequences of the war concludes that world polarization between America and Russia means that workers are everywhere worse off than they were before the war. "What has changed," Shachtman said, "are the names and addresses of the slaves, but not the slavery." The power of the postwar Soviets proved some of Trotsky's predictions wrong, he concluded, because now no one in his right mind could argue that Stalin's Russia was a workers' state, not even a degenerated workers' state. The Trotskyist conclusion was then clear: only an international workers' revolution could free the world from the horror of new nationalistic madness, and as they tried to free themselves from the power politics of the postwar world, the Trotskyists became even more isolated on the fringe of the Left.

[39]

WHAT WILL I DO WHEN AMERICA GOES TO WAR?

A SYMPOSIUM IN *Modern Monthly*

Questions

1. *What will you do when America goes to war?*
2. *Will your decision be altered if Soviet Russia is an ally of the United States in a war with Japan?*
3. *Would a prospective victory by Hitler over most of Europe move you to urge United States participation in opposition to Germany to prevent such a catastrophe?*

SOURCE: "What Will I Do When America Goes to War? A Symposium," *Modern Monthly* 9, no. 5 (September 1935): 264–271.

Answers

NORMAN THOMAS

1. I shall do all I can to keep the United States out of any new international war. If and when America enters a new war I shall keep out myself, do what I can to bring about prompt peace, and take whatever advantage I can of the situation in order to bring about that capture of power in government by the workers which is the true basis of freedom, peace and plenty.

2. My decision would not be altered on the basis of the present facts or any facts that are likely to exist. A war between Soviet Russia and the United States on one side and Japan and possibly some other powers on the other would not be fundamentally changed in character by the participation of Stalin's Soviet Russia. It would still be a war of rival imperialisms.

3. I suppose my answer to your third question is "No" but I think the question rather unfair. A prospective victory by Hitler over most of Europe is highly unlikely. The circumstances of such victory would not be conditioned primarily by the triumph of Fascism over democracy but by a host of other considerations. The nations of Europe will not fight against Hitler out of love for democracy and hatred for Fascism. They will fight because of competing national interests. Out of that sort of maneuvering no victory for a genuine workers' democracy can come. The victory we want over Fascism must be won by the workers themselves on other than a basis of nationalistic war. I view with profound regret the recent acts of the Communist International in going back to the position of the majority Socialists in 1914; that is to say, the position of supporting a possible "good war," in this case a war against Fascism, as that was allegedly a war against imperialism.

JAMES RORTY

1. What will I do when America goes to war? But I had supposed America was now in a state of war—the class war of workers against exploiters and against the capitalist state. I consider myself a worker. As such, if the United States, as a capitalist state, went to war, I should consider that my interest and duty continued to lie in the building of a revolutionary movement, the overthrow of the capitalist state, and the building of socialism.

2. In the hypothetical situation which you pose, I should consider that my best service to the Soviet Union would be to prosecute, in every way possible, the activities indicated in my answer to question one. And I should expect the Comintern to support and aid me. If the Comintern line at the moment didn't read that way, so much the worse for the Comintern line, for Russia, and for the hope of mankind. I think revolutionaries should be prepared to fight under revolutionary flags to defend the revolution in their own or in any other country. But the idea of revolutionaries fighting under capitalist flags makes me sick. Unless I am a complete illiterate, I am right in believing that it would have made Marx sick and Lenin sick.

3. Again, I am interested in only one war—the present war. I don't believe that pseudo-democratic states can be maneuvered into pulling revolutionary chestnuts out of fascist fires. I believe in trying to keep my eye on the ball, and the ball is the struggle of workers to organize, to take power, and to build socialism. Violence is a part of the present and future content of this struggle. Personally, I have a profound dislike and distrust of violence. I have no stomach for it—was a stretcher bearer in the last war— and shall never have any stomach for it. Its only justification is defensive self-preservation. But I am bound to admit that this justification exists and that I cannot properly exempt myself from the terms of struggle as prescribed by the present state of what we call civilization.

BERTRAM D. WOLFE

My person is not important enough for my individual solution to this problem to be of interest to your readers. Moreover, I am a member of the Communist Opposition; I believe it the most important sector of the revolutionary movement against war and capitalism, and voluntarily accept its decisions and discipline in matters of such importance. Its decisions would determine what part I, as an individual, would play in connection with the next war.

More important to your readers, I take it, would be a discussion of what criterion the Communist Opposition would employ in instructing its members and advising your readers and the masses generally as to their conduct when next America goes to War. I think I speak for the Communist Opposition when I say:

1. Organize now for the struggle against war and fight with all your might to prevent America's entrance into another war.

We must not wait until war is actually upon us. We are in a general war situation now. Every diplomatic, every military, every economic move that brings us a step nearer to the outbreak must be exposed, fought against, and used to awaken fresh numbers and organize additional forces. Even if this activity should not gather enough volume to prevent America's going to war, it will at least stave it off, and what is far more important, build the forces for further struggle against the war once it has begun and for its conclusion in a way favorable not to the imperialist war-makers but to the mass of the American people and the abolition of the present war-breeding system.

2. I think a war in which imperialist America should find itself an ally of Soviet Russia an extremely unlikely one. But conceding its abstract possibility, it would not alter our attitude towards American capitalism and its imperialist war aims. An alliance with the Soviet Union would not make "the leopard change its spots." American war aims would still be imperialist—the acquisition of power in Asia, the enslavement of the Asiatic masses, greater reaction at home, and inevitably attack on its own "ally." Did not the German and French armies unite against the Paris Commune? Did not its allies turn on Russia when it established a workers' government? The American ruling class would not cease to be capitalist, its war aims would not cease to be imperialist, merely because, for those very aims, it might enter into a temporary and unstable, not to say improbable, military cooperation with the Soviet Union against an enemy which would attack both at the same time. (The very description indicates the improbability and instability of the situation you have conjured up.)

We would approve of the Soviet government's utilization of the antagonism between Japan and the United States for the defense of the workers' land. We would continue to carry on our struggle against our own ruling class and its imperialist war aims. We would seek to turn the imperialist war of our ruling class into a civil war against that ruling class. Our victory would bring about a workers' America, which would be a real ally of workers' Russia, and would aid the Japanese workers in their struggle for a workers' Japan.

3. Your "prospective victory by Hitler over most of Europe" is another improbable speculation. But again, granting its reality for the sake of argument, our attitude would still be basically as above. A capitalist America would use Hitler as a slogan bogey-man, but its entrance and participation would still be imperialist in aim.

In wartime, capitalist republic, monarchy, or fascist dictatorship all look pretty much alike; no civil liberties, no freedom of organization, absolute militarization, iron terror against all opponents of the war-policy. And the victorious ruling class is likely to be the most arrogant and reactionary.

Revolution, like charity in the proverb, should begin at home. Only the German workers can settle with Hitler. Only the American working class can settle with American capitalism. And a good job at home would make it easier for the German workers to do a good job in Germany.

There is only one war in which the conscious workers can enlist. In all wars, there's only one side on which the conscious worker can be. And that is the side of the revolutionary workers in their struggle for a workers' world.

SCOTT NEARING

1. Follow the general line laid down by the Communist International. In such a crisis there will be real need for a centrally directed strategy and the Communist International is the logical direction of the strategy.

2. No, see above.

3. The stage of capitalist decline, of which Hitler is a symbol and spokesman, has already been reached all over Central Europe. This is a process, not a catastrophe. It cannot be "prevented." It must be outlived —superseded.

PAUL MATTICK

1. Personally, I take neither pleasure nor interest in going into any war whatever; still, to declare oneself against war seems to me silly and useless. One has to set material forces against it, not mere attitudes, and anyone who fails to take part in shaping those forces is also not against war, however much he may protest that he is. The question itself suggests the idea that one is supposed to come out for peace and against war, but I am opposed to capitalist peace just as much as to capitalist war. Nor do I have any choice between the two situations; I can only contribute to putting an end to a system which has to assure its existence on the tendency to alternate between war and peace. In order to be opposed to capitalist war, one must be opposed to capitalism, since the wars as well as the crisis belong among this system's conditions of existence. And so it goes without saying that I shall not in any case help to defend a system which I find thoroughly repulsive and by which my life is spoiled.

If America goes to war, that means under the present conditions that the chronic world crisis is to be further sharpened in a world war, in which the crisis seeks its solution. It is today senseless to look for the causes of war in the policy and the necessities of particular nations; the world war is the affair of world capitalism. In view of such a situation, the will and the design of the individual sink to ridiculous insignificance, and whether this person or that comes out for or against war becomes almost a matter of indifference. As things stand, today—and this holds just for today—there is little ground for assuming that the next war will be prevented through action of the working class. It is much more probable that we shall have to wait for the next world war to produce a new world-revolutionary situation, and so it is very difficult for a revolutionist not to hope for the war's acceleration. But he cannot come out in favor of war any more than in favor of peace; he has simply nothing to do with this world, but shapes for himself his *new* world.

The mass of workers is reactionary out of necessity, as it also grows revolutionary out of necessity. The individual, in his attitude toward war, has to consider not only himself but also the mass phenomena. What he *wants* to do does not exhaust the question; what he *can* do is of greater importance. The working class will probably today go to war for Capital just as it also works for Capital, and both for the same reasons. If this situation fails to change, then the revolutionary war-rejector will remain a voice in the wilderness and can only wait for the turn of events. His attitude toward the war situation is then practically only that of living through the non-revolutionary period. It is nonsense to hold as an axiom for all time that one must get into the war in order to be able some time to direct the weapons against his own bourgeoisie, just as it is also false to insist on refusal of military service under all conditions. The revolutionist cannot, in a time which presents no possibilities of action, have any interest in getting out of life. A dead man has ceased to be anything whatever, hence also to be a revolutionist. If staying away from the war involves greater danger to one's life than does taking part in the thing, the choice is not difficult, for it is just as stupid to die for an idea *and nothing else* as to die for capitalism. If refusal of military service is possible, only an idiot could, in my opinion, let himself be persuaded that one should take part in the war in order to convert it. It is not until the war machine ceases to function accurately and the masses rise up out of themselves that the revolutionizing possibility is present; but then it is certainly also a matter of indifference as to where the revolutionist happens to be. If by reason of the unfavorable situation, refusal to serve is of no real importance, then it is senseless to expose oneself. If it has a revolutionary significance, then one must exercise it, even though a war were favorable to the objective presuppositions for changing society, since one can never side in any capitalistic affray. There is no absolute and universally valid answer to the question here proposed. In the different concrete situations, the practical class struggle is likely to answer the question differently. And yet war sets no special task either for the individual or for the class: the historical task of the workers merely presses for its solution, which remains the same in war as in peace.

2. From the standpoint of the proletariat, it is today no longer permissible to reject certain wars and accept others. The enemy is world capitalism, so that even a Russo–American alliance against Japan would present the workers with no new tasks. State-capitalist Russia is interested in and bound up with the maintenance of world capitalism. As a support of imperialist capitalism, Russia herself must be regarded as an imperialist power. The Russian workers have the same tasks as the German or the American: the overthrow of world capitalism, hence also the overthrow of Russian state capitalism. Support of the Russian alliance policy amounts to promoting the next world war.

3. Anyone who were to answer the third question with Yes would be nothing more than an ordinary war monger. Germany cannot be differentiated from the other capitalist countries. Everywhere the same capitalism rules, differing only in degrees of development and unessential particulars. Anyone who chooses between Hitler, Stalin and Roosevelt has by that very circumstance declared that he takes up for a capitalism which he finds agreeable and thereby also announced his willingness to participate in the next war.

HERBERT ZAM

1. The Saint Louis Resolution and the Detroit Declaration of Principles of the Socialist Party both take a clear-cut position as to the attitude of Socialists in case of American participation in a war. Eugene Debs, C. E. Ruthenberg, Joseph Coldwell, J. O. Bentall and others have amply demonstrated that these resolutions mean not mere passive opposition, but active, uncompromising opposition to war. So long as we live in a capitalist society, there can be no other course. A revolutionist living in an imperialist country must hope for, and work for, the defeat of his own imperialist government, not in order to help the "enemy" but in order to utilize such a defeat to promote the revolutionary movement and eventually to overthrow the imperialist government.

Socialists will oppose all talk of "civil peace," of cessation of the class struggle in time of war. On the contrary, by every means at their disposal they will promote the class struggle, promote a mass movement in opposition to war and utilize the mass resentment to war for a more effective fight against capitalism.

Experience has shown that individual acts, such as refusal to register, are of little value. The most effective weapon, one which can paralyze the conduct of the war, is a general strike, initiated by the organized labor movement. The Socialists will work for such a strike in case of war.

2. *No!* The mere fact that the United States and Soviet Russia would be fighting a common enemy does not mean that they deserve equal support. The United States and Japan will be conducting an imperialist war and the position outlined above will apply. It is not only false, but extremely dangerous to believe that any imperialist government can, objectively or subjectively, be a "defender" of the Soviet Union. The slogan "defend the Soviet Union" *was and remains an appeal to the workers and not to the capitalist governments.* In different circumstances, the United States would just as readily fight with Japan, or some other imperialist country (say England) *against* the Soviet Union. Only a government which defends the interests of the toiling population in the United States, a workers' and farmers' government, will also be in a position to defend the Soviet Union. Only such a government will deserve support in case of war.

3. *No.* Revolutionary Socialists deny that capitalism in its present stage of development can conduct progressive wars. Those who try to quote Marx and Engels in favor of defensive wars are forgetting this. The social patriots of 1914 also tried to quote Marx and Engels against Lenin. The quotations sound no more convincing in the mouths of Stalin and Dimitroff than they sounded in the mouths of Scheidemann and Cachin.

The German catastrophe has demonstrated the futility of relying on bourgeois, "democratic" *parties* (Bruening, Hindenburg) to defeat fascism. It is even more futile to rely on bourgeois decadent capitalism. The fight against fascism must have an anti-capitalist direction, and cannot be conducted by elements whose sole objective is to maintain capitalism *with* its "democratic" institutions.

It is fallacious to believe (as the question implies) that all "democratic" countries will be against Germany in a war. It is highly likely, for example, that "democratic" England will be on Germany's side (remember the Anglo–German naval treaty) and that fascist Italy will be against Germany. Not their form of government, but their imperialist interests will determine alignments, in the future, as in 1914.

Should another world war break out, the hope of the working class, and all progressive elements, must lie not in the victory of this or that "democratic" country, but in a world revolution.

ALBERT WEISBORD

This depends on the kind of war.

It is the duty of the revolutionary movement to support the revolts of the proletariat against the bourgeoisie, the wars of the colonials against the imperialists and the struggle of the workers of the Soviet Union against their capitalist attackers.

In the case of a war between imperialist powers, of which America is one, whether these imperialist powers are Fascist (under Hitler or Mussolini) or "Democratic" (under Wall Street, Downing Street, or the Paris Bourse), it is the duty of the revolutionary organization in each imperialist country to throw all its forces into the movement of revolutionary defeatism. The workers of each imperialist country must cease firing on each other and must turn their guns against their real enemies, the capitalists of their own country, so safely in the rear. Thus we must brush aside the Socialists and others who oppose this policy.

Wherever the proletariat must support the war, is where America declares war on Japan presumptively at war against the Soviet Union, it nevertheless still remains the paramount duty of the American proletariat to overthrow the American capitalist system. To overthrow American capitalism is the only way really to mobilize the entire toiling population to turn the war into a war against all imperialisms and capitalisms, and is the only adequate method to defend the Workers' State against imperialist aggrandizement. Thus we must liquidate the Communist Parties of Stalin who prevent this with their Franco–Soviet pacts.

To sum up, under no circumstances, whether the workers are for or against the war itself, can they postpone for one moment the struggle against Wall Street and its capitalist government that enter the war for their own imperialist purposes and would use the working class as their cannon fodder.

Where the war is between imperialist countries only, say where "democratic" U. S. is fighting another imperialist nation such as Fascist Germany, the main revolutionary tasks of the American workers must be:

a) To organize strikes and physical demonstrations of every sort for the termination of the war, the strikes to culminate in general strikes and struggles of a nature that will paralyze entirely the capitalist system.

b) To organize mutinies and rebellions in the armed forces of the capitalist state, so that the soldiers will turn on their own officers and refuse to shoot the workers of the other imperialist country but will call on these other workers to start the revolution as we do ours.

c) To organize struggles against conscription and universal military service.

d) To organize armed labor defence corps against the Fascist or Vigilante groups that would terrify the working class into submission.

Where America is fighting a war historically progressive, as where it is supporting the Soviet Union (still a Workers' State today in spite of Stalinism) against Japan, here the tasks of the revolutionary forces are different. They must include:

a) The abolition of the standing or conscript army and the arming of the entire people into a huge Workers' Militia with its own control and elected officers.

b) The seizure of the factories under the control of the workers; the complete abolition of the profits of the capitalist class of the country; the entire industrial machinery of the country put at the disposal of the toilers and of the Workers' Militia formed.

c) The organization of Soviets as the best form for the mobilization of the whole people to carrying out of the war and to insure that the war will be an anti-imperialist war in which the workers will smash capitalism throughout the world.

d) While the working class is forcing through the above measures, it is absolutely imperative for it to continue its intransigeant struggle against the American bourgeoisie, to expose the reactionary character of the bourgeois methods of conducting the war. Through strikes and physical demonstrations of every sort the working class must compel the turning over of the war to the proletariat so as to make it a war for socialism and for the abolition of the capitalist system.

Other groups may approximate our program in phrases. In deeds, they will not have the slightest ability to carry through such a program. Their past betrayals, their present methods of work, their social composition, all are the best guarantees of a new collapse on their part.

Thus, in all this work, it is necessary to build up a new Communist International and a genuine Communist Party without delay. Such genuine Communist forces will know how to unite the masses in struggle and how to wipe out the resistance of the opportunists and Centrists of every variety.

Unceasing struggle against the historically defunct Socialist and Stalinist parties and Trotsky capitulators, stern preparation for illegal activity, iron discipline and firmest adherence to Marxist methods become more decisive than ever.

JOSEPH BRANDON

1. I find it very difficult to frame an answer to the first question. I am opposed to war, but I am not a pacifist. In the last war I took my stand

on the basis that as a wage worker I had nothing at stake in the war and therefore could not support it. Because I would not fight against the "fiendish" Kaiser, I became acquainted with the atrocities of the benign Uncle Sam.

In the last war I was an "absolutist"? This was the name given to those who refused all military service (even in non-combatant units), farm furloughs, and who would not work in jail. Naturally, such individuals suffered more than those who were not so extreme in their objections.

It would be easy for me to say that I would do the same thing again. Maybe I would. But the chances are that I will not be drafted and if I am not drawn into the clutches of the military, I feel that I owe it to my family to keep out of jail if I possibly can. I will not ram my head against a stone wall. I know that unless conditions develop to a point where it is possible to agitate against the war with some hope of success, the best thing a revolutionist can do is to "accept the fact" as Stuart Chase says.

What we must do, we have to do *now*. We must endeavor to make the American workers class conscious, not anti-war conscious. We must show that capitalism breeds wars, as garbage breeds maggots, and that as long as the profit system exists war is inevitable. That if mankind is to be saved from another catastrophe, the workers must organize for the abolition of capitalism. If we can convince the workers, and they organize their economic power for the purpose of attaining this end, then if war breaks out we may be in a position to do something. For if the workers are sufficiently organized, the declaration of war may become the tocsin for the social revolution. With an unorganized, undisciplined and misinformed working class, nothing anyone may do will prevent the mass slaughter.

2. The American working class has no interest in a war with Japan, even though Soviet Russia is an ally of the American government. No doubt many sentimentalists will be taken in by this question. One must ask oneself, however,—what will these nations be fighting for?

It will be conceded that both Japan and America will be motivated by imperialistic purposes. Where does Russia fit in this picture? If Russia acts in consonance with Marxian precepts it will not be drawn into such a conflict. If Russia is invaded, it must, of course, defend itself. But if Russia is holding territory which is a hangover of the Czar's imperialism, the best thing it can do is to relinquish such holdings rather than permit itself to be drawn into a war of destruction. It is imperative that Russia show the working class of the world that it is the one sane spot in an insane planet.

3. I cannot see why a victory for Hitler in Europe should alter the attitude toward war. Hitler can no more rule Europe than Napoleon could.

As a matter of fact a Hitler victory must necessarily be followed by revolutions in the defeated nations, with the result that in his victory, Hitler would meet his ultimate defeat.

Our war is not with Hitler or the Mikado. It is with the American capitalist class. Let us gird our loins for that struggle.

---

[40]

DEMOCRACY OR FASCISM

EARL BROWDER

1. Struggle against Fascism and for Peace

The world is torn between two main directions of development: on the one hand stand those forces striving to maintain the rights and living standards of the masses in the midst of capitalist crisis and decay, and to maintain world peace; on the other side are the forces of fascism, striving to wipe out popular rights and throw the full burden of the crisis onto the masses, and driving toward a new world war.

The camp of fascism, of the war-makers, is mighty and menacing. It is headed by Hitler fascism, the most bloody and bestial reaction the world has ever seen. It contains Mussolini, whose hands drip with the blood of Italians and Ethiopians alike. It includes the military-fascist government of Japan, which is carving a new empire out of the body of the Chinese people. In every capitalist country its forces are organizing, backed and inspired by the monopolists of finance capital, and, where not already in power, are preparing with all energy, ruthlessness, and demagogy, to seize control of government. In the United States, this camp is headed by the dominant leadership of the Republican Party, with its allies of the Liberty League, Hearst, Black Legion, Ku Klux Klan, Coughlin, and others.

The camp of progress and peace finds its stronghold in the Soviet Union, the country of socialist prosperity. To its banner are rallying all the growing armies of those who would resist fascism and war. Relying upon its mighty strength, the French people were able to gather in the great

SOURCE: Earl Browder, *The People's Front* (New York: International Publishers, 1938), pp. 19–23, 31–33. Reprinted by permission of International Publishers Co., Inc.

Front Populaire, which threw back the first assaults of French fascism and warded off the first threat of war by Hitler, and advanced the living standards of the masses and their organized strength. Seeing in it a powerful protector, the small nations of Europe whose existence is threatened, who find less and less assistance from the great capitalist powers, turn to the firm peace policy of the Soviet Union as their reliable refuge. Even those great countries ruled by the imperialist bourgeoisie, like the U.S.A., who for their own special reasons are not ready for war, who want to maintain the *status quo,* at least for a time, must turn, even though hesitatingly, toward collaboration with the Soviet Union. The oppressed nations look to it for inspiration and leadership. Within each capitalist country, all forces for peace, and especially the workers and farmers, are beginning to see in the policy of the Soviet Union the chief hope of peace and progress in the world.

There are voices which shout of the menace of fascism and war, even in radical and "revolutionary" phrases, but which cannot find anything to say about the mighty and growing forces for progress and peace. Such voices come from confusionists and panic-mongers, who consciously or unconsciously are the advance agents of fascism, spreading defeatism and demoralization among the masses, disarming them before the enemy.

It is possible to defeat the fascists and war-makers. It is possible to move toward progress, to maintain peace. But to do this requires that we recognize and make full use of all factors, even the smallest, that work toward this end, even temporarily. It requires a drive toward *one united international policy,* around which is rallied the growing armies of progress and peace. It requires the recognition of the role of the Soviet Union, and full utilization of this great power.

The confusionists and panic-mongers all have one common starting point for their defeatism, fatalism and hopelessness. They reject the Soviet Union as a great power for progress and peace; some of them, like the Trotskyists, are moved by definitely counter-revolutionary theories and hatreds; others, like Norman Thomas, because they are filled with doubts, reservations, hesitations, misconceptions. Wherever this influence, in whatever degree, prevails among the masses, there we have more division instead of more unity, more confusion instead of more clarity, more defeatism and demoralization instead of the growth of a militant united movement against fascism and war.

But the united People's Front is winning the masses more and more in every country. It is overcoming the demagogic slanders of the counter-revolutionists, it is dissolving the doubts and hesitations of the confused people. It must, it can, and it will win the majority of the toiling people of every country. . . .

2. Issues and Parties in the Elections

There are two chief and opposite directions of possible development in American political life in the 1936 elections. All parties and groups must be judged by their relation to these two fundamental political tendencies. One stems from the most reactionary circles of finance capital, Wall Street; its direction is toward fascism and war. The fundamental aims of this camp can be summarized in five points:

1. Restore capitalist profits by cutting wages, raising prices, checking the growth of trade unions, subverting them, and eventually wiping them out; squeeze out the poor farmers from agriculture, transforming them into propertyless workers.
2. Wipe out social and labor legislation, balance the budget by eliminating unemployment relief, cutting taxes of the rich and throwing the tax burden onto the poor by means of sales taxes.
3. Remove all remnants of popular influence upon the government, by vesting all final power in the hands of an irresponsible judiciary—the Supreme Court; drive toward the curtailment and eventual destruction of democratic liberties and civil rights; create the storm troops of reaction, Black Legions, Ku Klux Klans, etc.
4. Seize control of all governmental machinery, moving toward a full-fledged fascist regime, in "American" and "constitutional" ways.
5. Develop extreme jingoistic nationalist moods among the masses; drive toward war under cover of "American isolation" and "neutrality"; support to and alliance with Hitler and other fascists, preparing the new world war.

The other chief direction of possible development, insofar as it becomes effective, moves and must move toward an opposite set of fundamental aims, which can be stated as follows:

1. Restore and raise the living standards of the masses, by higher wages, shorter hours, lower prices, extending the trade unions to the basic industries and all workers, through militant industrial unionism; secure the farmers in possession of their farms, with governmental help and guarantee of a minimum standard of life.
2. Consolidate and extend social and labor legislation, with guarantee of a

minimum standard of life for all, financing this with sharply graduated taxes on incomes, property and accumulated surpluses, abolition of sales taxes, balancing the budget at the expense of the rich.

3. Curb the usurped power of the Supreme Court; maintain and extend democratic rights and civil liberties; dispersal of reactionary bands, abolition of the use of legal machinery to suppress the people's movements; extension of popular control over government.

4. Restore control of the government to representatives of the people's organizations, through a broad People's Front.

5. Unite with the peace forces of the whole world to restrain the war-makers, to keep America out of war by keeping war out of the world. . . .

The Issue: Democracy or Fascism   Fourth, we must clarify the question, is socialism the issue that will be decided in this election? The war-cry of the reactionaries is that Roosevelt's New Deal is socialism or even communism. Norman Thomas gave some aid to this idea in 1933, during the honeymoon of the New Deal. Carried away by his enthusiasm, he hailed it as "a step toward socialism," as "a revolution." Now he swings just as far in the opposite direction, and sees little difference between Roosevelt and Landon, even while praising Roosevelt's liberalism. We must declare Roosevelt's policies as not socialism, nor a step to socialism. He at most tries to smooth out some of the worst abuses of capitalism, in order to give it a longer life. The reactionary cry of "socialism" is directed to two ends: first, to alarm all people of property to stampede them toward fascism; second, to discredit socialism among the masses by identifying it with the failures of the New Deal.

Before the two major parties, "socialism" is not an issue, but merely a demagogic war-cry of reaction. For the broad masses also, socialism is not the issue today, but rather the issue is, whether to move on the reactionary road toward fascism, or to struggle to maintain democratic rights, living standards, and peace. For the Farmer-Labor Party movement the issue is not between socialism and capitalism, but whether to move on the reactionary or progressive roads. We Communists, throwing our lot in with the Farmer-Labor Party movement, agree to fight for the road of progress under capitalism, together with those who are not adherents of socialism as we are; while at the same time we point out that the only final guarantee of progress is to abolish capitalism and move to socialism.

Thus, we conclude that the direct issue of the 1936 elections is not socialism or capitalism, but rather democracy or fascism. At the same time we emphasize, and will always emphasize, that a consistent struggle for democracy and progress leads inevitably, and in the not distant future, to the socialist revolution.

This leads us to a concrete phase of utmost importance in the fight to defeat fascism in America, namely, by what means to combat and overcome the influence of the reactionaries among the broad masses. We identify the fascist trend with Wall Street, the Liberty League and the big capitalists; that is absolutely correct. At the same time, these fascist forces, playing upon the most backward instincts and moods among the masses, and even utilizing some of their more positive characteristics, exert tremendous and growing influence precisely among some of the most suffering and desperate strata of the population. Hearst, with his chain of demagogic newspapers, is the classic type. Father Coughlin, with his radio appeals to the common people and his Union for Social Justice, apes closely the technique of Mussolini and Hitler. Huey Long, before his death, was a veritable American Hitler in embryo, with his Share-the-Wealth Clubs and wild demagogy. All appeal to very real grievances among the masses, they touch the sore spots of a suffering population, they rouse popular passions—only to direct them away from the real criminals, the Hearsts, du Ponts, Morgans, and against "the Jewish bankers," against the foreign-born workers, against the Negroes, against "the Reds," the Protestants against the Catholics and vice versa, and now above all they cry out against the "communistic New Deal" and Roosevelt, until the election is over.

---

[41]

SPAIN'S "RED" FOREIGN LEGION

LOUIS FISCHER

Alicante, December 7
THROUGHOUT the centuries men have left their homes to fight on foreign soil for liberty. Byron, Lafayette, Kosciusko, and, in more recent times, John Reed—the list is long and illustrious.

Spanish democracy has been attacked. It has issued no call for foreign

SOURCE: Louis Fischer, "Spain's 'Red' Foreign Legion," *Nation* 144, (9 January 1937): 36–38.

friends, but Europe's anti-fascists have volunteered in thousands to serve in the army of the Spanish republic. Approximately 60 per cent are French and Belgians, factory workers for the most part. There are also Poles, Germans, Czechs, Swiss, Hungarians, Bulgarians, Italians, Serbs, several score white Russian émigrés who thus want to document a change of mind, a Mexican artillery officer, a New York Jew, an Egyptian, some Algerian Arabs, two Turkish officers; and recently Britishers have commenced to arrive. Enlistment of women is discouraged, yet they slip into groups and are content to lend a hand wherever it is needed, either in ministering to the wounded or in peeling potatoes.

Usually governments have set no difficulties in the path of these volunteers. Foreign offices may adopt any attitude toward the Spanish conflict, but free nations do not obstruct the expression of the individual citizen's idealism. Not a few of these soldiers of freedom, however, have had to steal across the frontiers of dictatorships and walk many miles, footsore and penniless, always evading the eyes of the police, before they reached hospitable soil.

Linguistically the International Column of the Spanish loyalist army is a Babel. Yet no greater unanimity of sentiment ever animated a modern fighting force. General Franco is a symbol of feudal backwardness, the tool of the interests which have kept the Spanish millions in cruel poverty. Nevertheless, the volunteers, when they march to the Madrid trenches, think less of Franco and Spain than of Hitler and Mussolini, and of the little Hitlers and Mussolinis of Europe. The members of the international brigades in Spain are not newcomers in the battle with fascism. As Socialists, Communists, pacifists, radicals, and liberals they have contended against fascism at home. "We are merely transferring our activities," a prominent intellectual in the brigade said to me, "to the most threatened sector of the world anti-fascist front, for if this sector crumbles the other sectors will be less secure."

The German, Yugoslav, Hungarian, Italian, and Polish émigrés, deprived of the possibility of attacking their national regimes directly, do so in Spain. The French feel that they strike a blow for their own Front populaire. August Wach, a dealer in electrical appliances, left Germany in 1933, opened a store in an Alsatian town, and prospered. In October he closed his shop and put up a sign: "Gone for an indefinite stay in Spain." Since then eight men in the same city have followed his example. A young German named Kroge, finding it trying to continue the underground struggle against Hitler in Bremen, went to Montevideo. He returned to Europe as soon as the Spanish civil war began and enlisted in the International

Brigade. "To me," a French Socialist declared when I interviewed him behind his machine-gun on the Madrid front, "this is chiefly target practice for Colonel de la Rocque's aristocrats."

To facilitate instruction and command, the foreigners are divided into units according to national origin. Thus there exists a Franco–Belgian battalion, an Italian battalion, a Balkan company, and so on. But in the barracks the men mix to share their experiences, military and civil. I went out to Madrigeras, a village near Albacete, where the Italians were billeted. A sham battle was scheduled for the storming of a castle. In a conversation between Captain Galliani, late of New York, who led one of the attacking parties, and Lukac, a Hungarian author, now commander of the second brigade at the front, it developed that they had fought against each other in the World War, Galliani in the Italian army, Lukac in that of the Dual Monarchy. Ludwig Renn, the German writer, recently released from a Nazi prison, was with us. He chatted with Major Vidal, commander of the base at Albacete. They had faced each other across no man's land at the Somme. Men once poised to kill one another are now bound together by a live community of interest.

Not all the men are World War veterans. Many received their military training as conscripts in various European armies. Experience in sports for some and the self-discipline of others make up for their lack of soldiering. All of them have fought bravely in Spain. In a month they won a reputation which thrills the Spanish republican army and causes the enemy to pause—this though their number is surprisingly small.

The figures have been exaggerated out of ignorance but also in malice. The first International Brigade reached the front in the early days of November with a full complement of 1,900 men. The second brigade got to the front on November 14. Its strength then was 1,550. To date these are the only foreign units which have borne arms in the cause of Spanish democracy—3,450 soldiers. Yet they have appreciably influenced the military situation.

The Spaniards are brave and temperamental but not martial. The last time Spain engaged in war was against Napoleon, over a hundred years ago. Ninety per cent of the regular Spanish army remained with Franco and Mola when they raised the standard of revolt. Great masses immediately entered the ranks of the government militia. But they were green, untutored, unofficered, unaccustomed to the whistle of bullets or the sight of an advancing foe.

The republic's "Foreign Legion," seeking unselfish political gains rather than loot, was originally conceived as a shock corps. On November 6, however, the rebels stood at the gates of Madrid; the militia had retreated headlong before the onslaughts of the Moors, who were rescuing Christian Spain from the will of its workers, peasants, and intellectuals. The idea of the great smashing offensive was therefore abandoned, and the International Column was thrown into the breach to save Madrid. It saved Madrid. Not alone, of course. With their backs to the walls of the capital, the government troops, aided now by newly arrived airplanes and inspired by the contagious example of the foreigners, likewise fought better. Franco encountered unexpected resistance. Since then the two international brigades have created a legend. They never retreat. They are not afraid to die —and that is a soldier's highest asset. Given an objective, they take it. The Moors were intrenched in a building of University City. They had machine-guns and hand grenades. The Hungarians were ordered to storm the building. They had only rifles and bayonets. They stormed it and captured it. They suffered 200 casualties out of a total strength of 300. A heavy loss, but the victory electrified thousands of men.

On other occasions the experienced internationalists stood firm when whole brigades melted away before the well-directed fire of the Moors. The Spaniards then realized that more might be killed in flight than in resistance. Formerly, when the Moors came on the scene, fright had seized the militia. Now the militia began to see Moorish heels high in the air. Moroccan daggers were shown in Madrid, trophies of successful skirmishes with the once-dreaded North Africans.

Spanish units lying next to the foreigners started to display finer fighting qualities. This spread down the line. Brigades competed for positions at the front. Could they not be on the left flank of the International Column? Might they not occupy the second-line trenches behind Kleber's brigade? Meanwhile the foreigners remained in the thick of battle. They refused to leave the trenches until absolutely certain that their sectors would be held. They were lousy; they had not bathed for fifteen days. At night, wrapped in one woolen blanket apiece contributed by French trade unions, they slept on ground covered with hoar frost. But of their own free will they stayed.

I was present in a cold staff dining-room when the arrangements were made for the relief of the first International Brigade by Colonel Gallo's excellent Spanish brigade. Commander Hans and Chief of Staff Ludwig Renn discussed all the details of the change. The enemy must not know that a new force was lying opposite. How achieve this? The Moors sometimes fired at night. Loyal Spanish troops always replied. The foreigners never did. Their nerves permitted them to refrain until and if their antagonists advanced. Gallo undertook to give strict orders against useless waste of ammunition to keep up courage. Everything was settled.

That evening I sat by General Kleber's fireside. Colonel Gallo entered. He was taking over from Hans, he reported, and all was proceeding well. But could not the internationalists be held at a convenient distance behind his trenches to be on hand in case of trouble?

When I visited the second International Brigade, it was in the second-line trenches on the northern Madrid front. The Spaniards felt secure in the first line with the foreigners just in the rear.

The Spanish army units take pride in cooperating with the International Corps. Immediately after they went into action on the Madrid front, the foreigners bore the brunt of many a hot battle, and their losses in the first fortnight were enormous. The first brigade went forward with 1,900 men early in November and counted 1,000 effectives a month later. The second brigade had 750 killed and wounded in three weeks of fighting. Today the rate of casualties is much lower. But the two brigades had to be reinforced. In the beginning new foreign soldiers were sent up from the base. But this interfered to some extent with the formation of a third international brigade. Moreover, it was held desirable from all points of view— military, political, and moral—to mix Spaniards with foreigners. The authorities accordingly ruled that the international units were to be reconstituted so as to consist of three foreign and two Spanish battalions. Rivalry immediately arose among the Spaniards. They all wanted to join the International Column. In the end two battalions of brave and hardened Asturias miners were chosen for the first International Brigade. The selection for the second brigade has yet to be made.

Behind the lines, far away in the eastern provinces, approximately 3,200 more foreigners are being trained, organized, and equipped for the struggle. Reports of 60,000 foreigners in the service of the Spanish government are therefore fantastic. Spanish republicans regret that the figures of Ambassador Ribbentrop and the Berlin *Börsen Zeitung* are untrue, and they will take measures, undoubtedly, to augment the size of the International Column. For the moment, however, these 3,200 in the hinterland plus the 1,800 survivors of the first two brigades represent the entire strength of the International Column in Spain. The government expects to add some 2,000 good Spanish soldiers to the 3,200 foreigners not yet engaged in the Madrid battle—a reserve for a future offensive. Meanwhile, contingents continue to arrive from various foreign lands.

The relations between the foreigners and the Spaniards, needless to say, are most cordial. The women of Albacete have volunteered to wash the laundry of the men of the column stationed in that town. The Spanish Ministry of Education has given the column a college building near the coast for use as a 400-bed hospital for its wounded. The same ministry donated a thousand bottles of cognac for the men in the cold trenches, and writing material, foreign books, radios, and gramophones for the men in barracks. Villages near Valencia supply the column with oranges, pomegranates, rice, lentils, onions, and other vegetables—free of charge. Martinez Barrio, president of the Cortes and civil governor of Albacete, is always ready to listen to the needs of the brigades and to assist in meeting them. Prime Minister Largo Caballero told me that when he received arms —they are still very scarce in republican Spain—his first thought would be of the International Column. The railway workers of Albacete built a huge armored car on their own initiative, fitted it with a machine-gun, and presented it to the third brigade at a public ceremony marked by wildly enthusiastic scenes.

I was sitting in the headquarters of one of the brigades at the front when a delegation from the shoemakers' union entered with a beautiful pair of boots and tremendous rolls of leather. They had instructions, they said, to make made-to-measure boots for the commander and anybody else designated. This, one of the delegates declared, was merely a token of their fraternal sentiments toward the foreigners.

I saw the second brigade go off to Madrid. Old Spanish men and women moved for an hour among the soldiers shaking hands individually with hundreds of them and saying "Saud" and "Victory." Meanwhile young boys would attract the notice of the foreigners by exclaiming "Eh, Franco," and then drawing a horizontal finger across their throats. As the train pulled out of the station, the soldiers stood at the windows with clenched fists raised, the Spaniards stood at attention with clenched fists raised, and all sang the International in a dozen languages. Women wept. Between the Spanish united front and the European united front as represented by the brigades there exists a powerful bond of friendship and common purpose. If the Spanish revolution wins, the left movements of the world will of course feel the stimulating influence. But even the process of helping Spanish democracy must have an encouraging and inspiring effect on parties depressed by the recent apparently irresistible encroachments of fascism. The International Column is therefore regarded by its sponsors as at least as necessary and beneficial to the outside proletariat as it is to the Spanish republic.

[42]

BALANCE SHEET OF THE WAR

MAX SHACHTMAN

THE war has come to an end on the same note on which it began—sudden, terroristic mass destruction. Hitler's blitzkrieg in Poland and later in the Low Countries and France stupefied and horrified the world. The ruins of Warsaw, Rotterdam, Stalingrad and Coventry became the symbols of fascism's New Order. A few years later, the Allies (imperialist democracy plus imperialist democracy plus totalitarian despotism) showed their vast technical and moral superiority over Hitlerism: they began with the repeated holocausts in Hamburg, which made the bombing of Rotterdam look like a Sunday duck-hunt, and ended with the extermination of a whole city by means of a single atomic bomb. Neither German fascism nor Japanese militarism could withstand these subtle proddings by Democratic Humanism. They succumbed, and victory fell to the Peace-Loving Nations and Prostituted Science.

The war, if we date its beginning with the attack on Poland, lasted six years. It was fought—both sides gave the solemn assurance—to make humanity a head taller. On the one side, there was the promise of the New Order. On the other, the promise to regain, preserve and extend democracy and freedom. The New Order was a reactionary imposture and is now a shambles—one head dangling at the other end of its heels, the other lost in oblivion, the third blithering for mercy. What has been gained by the victory of the Allies?

Item: Millions of dead, maimed, wounded, millions driven mad or half-mad, millions making up the most important productive force in society; millions—if a "sentimental" note may be introduced into a cool business calculation—of human beings. But do not sacrifices have to be made in the interests of progress? Very well, a few millions sacrificed to progress.

Item: Millions of fertile acres destroyed for years during the war and for years to follow, by the torch in Russia, by frenzied abuse in Germany, by brine in Holland, by bomb and flame-thrower in a dozen

SOURCE: Max Shachtman, "Balance Sheet of the War," *The New International* 11, no. 6 (September 1945): 163–167.

countries. Let that be written off in the name of progress and in consideration of the fact that anyway there are fewer mouths to feed —the dead feel no hunger.

Item: Tens of billions of dollars' worth of machinery, buildings, raw materials, plus military and naval products of all kinds destroyed on a global, scientific, systematic, planned, organized scale, exceeding in dimensions and social significance the destruction of all the previous wars of mankind put together.

Item: Tens of billions of dollars in war debts saddled upon the peoples all over the world for generations to come, at least until they rise to throw off the saddle and the rider.

Item: The fall of the fascists in Italy and the Nazis in Germany and the liberation of all the countries they dominated. But liberation only from *their* rule. Every one of these countries is poorer now than it was before the war; many of them poorer than they were during the war. Every one of these countries is less free and more enslaved than it was before the war; many of them not more free than they were under Mussolini or Hitler; some of them are even less free today than they were under the Axis.

Item: For every person liberated from Axis rule by the Allies, the Allies have enslaved not less than two or three persons. What has changed are the names and addresses of the slaves, but not the slavery.

Item: The old pre-war colonies are no nearer freedom and independence today, with the victory of democracy, than they were on the eve of the war which brought the temporary victory of the Axis. The former Italian colonies now have the right to speak English to their overseer instead of Italian. The former Japanese colonies now have the right to eschew Japanese and to speak instead in such democratic tongues as American, Dutch, English and—language forgotten by them since the last day of the Czars—Russian. The Indians still have the right to bow to the white sahibs from London and Glasgow until they are replaced by the white sahibs from Washington.

Item: The threat of world rule of the German–Japanese duumvirate, with Italy assisting, has been dispelled. The world is now ruled by the American–Russian duumvirate, with England assisting.

Item: In general, all over the world, the people are less free, have fewer rights, more restrictions on these fewer rights, than before the war; the people are poorer, hungrier, sicker, more exhausted than before the war.

Item: Our greatest progress—the atomic bomb! At one time even the artillery of capitalism opened the road to human progress by shattering the walls of feudal reaction. Now its weapons, from trench dagger and pistol to .88's and .90's and atomic bombs, merely destroy human life and social wealth. The atomic bomb is said to contain only about one pound of the deadly disintegrator in its war-head. There is no ground for disappointment in this. Capitalism is still capable of grandiose exploits. It started in this war with aerial bombs weighing only a few hundred pounds. After only a few years it had ten- and twelve-ton blockbusters, breath-taking, life-taking, property-taking rockets with bigger ones already on the drawing-boards, suicide planes and other testimonials to progress. At the war's end, the atomic bomb had the destructive power of a couple of thousand blockbusters. That was the *first* atomic bomb, and it could only destroy one city at a time. The Third World War, which *everybody* expects, will surely be ushered in by a far more highly developed, refined, cultured, civilized and democratic atomic bomb. On that score, capitalism has the greatest conceivable confidence.

There is the balance-sheet of only the more outstanding items of the war and the victory.

Why Hitler Lost the War

The war lasted six years, the war in Europe something less than that. Almost from the beginning we said that this would be a long war, that it *could* last ten or even twice ten years, that it could end not with a military victory but with a revolution. So far as the toll of destruction in life and wealth is concerned, the war was long enough, by any standard. However, the actual course and outcome of the war require a corrective that it is instructive to introduce even at the present time.

It can be said that in making an approximate judgment of the duration of the war, insufficient weight was attached to the strength of Russia under Stalinism, a strength which all underestimated—we less than others—and to the profligacy with which the bureaucracy poured its most abundant commodity, human life, into the tireless maw of the battlefield. More important even than this factor was the insufficient weight attached to the stunning economic potential of the United States which, productive enough to be the envy of the world in peaceful and "normal" times, proved to be even more productive, vastly more productive, in the preparation of modern engines of destruction and their dispatch to every war front of the world.

Yet even these correctives do not, in our view, make the picture or the prediction much more accurate. They do not even account decisively for the comparatively speedy defeat of the apparently impregnable Axis in Europe. Not even the atomic bomb would necessarily have accounted for it. In the frenetic race for superior means of destruction, the United States came in first, for a change, with the atomic bomb. But how far behind in the race was Germany? We do not know, and those who are in a position to have the facts are not divulging them. In any case, speculation on this point cannot very well replace a judgment of the events that occurred, that are known, that can be weighed.

Hitler broke his neck primarily on the basis of the failure of the fascist "New Order" in conquered Europe. *If* German imperialism had really been able to establish *order* in Europe; *if* it had really been able to *unite* Europe into a more or less harmonious and smoothly-functioning whole; *if* it had really been able freely to coordinate and utilize the massive resources, natural and human, economic and cultural, of the old continent; *if* it had really been able to subordinate Europe to a single, freely-united will —there is little doubt that it could have survived the joint efforts of the Allies. To put it more simply: it could have done this *if it had not been imperialist Germany.* The impregnability of a freely-united Europe, having at its command all the resources of the continent, the ability of such a Europe not only to resist the assault of any enemy but more than that, to revolutionize the rest of the world, is precisely what gives such power to the fundamental idea of a Socialist United States of Europe.

Fascism attempted to do what the proletariat (more accurately, the proletarian leadership) failed to do: unite Europe. But because it was fascism that made the attempt, it was doomed in advance to failure. Hitlerism could unite the continent only by converting it into a prison of the peoples and nations—rebelling peoples and nations. The rebellion, which continued to grow in scope and intensity, prevented the Hitlerite "unification" of Europe and, accordingly, prevented that thorough utilization of the continent's resources by which alone Germany could hope to win the war.

Almost from the beginning—that is, as soon as the conquered peoples began to stir again from the stupor into which their sudden defeat had hurled them—Hitler was compelled to carry on a war on two fronts, war in the literal sense. The two-front war that ruined Hitler was not the war with Russia and the Western Allies, but the war against the rival imperialisms, on the one side, and the war against the revolutionary peoples of the occupied countries, on the other. In paying tribute to the latter in his Paris speech, General Eisenhower may have conceived his words as a graceful diplomatic gesture and nothing more. But the fact is that in stating that Germany could not have been defeated without these warring peoples, Eisenhower was making a political declaration of first-rate political importance. . . .

Because of its importance for today and especially for tomorrow, it is worth while repeating: Hitlerism broke its neck on the "national question."

Once the war in Europe was won by the Allies, the war in Asia and the Pacific could not be in doubt for a minute. In Europe, the war donned the tattered garments of a crusade for democracy and freedom; millions of the people looked to the Allies as liberators if they were already conquered or as protected from hated fascism if they were threatened by it, as in England. But the war in Asia was as nakedly imperialistic and chauvinistic—racially chauvinistic in the authentic Nazi style—as any in history. There it was openly a question of holding tightly to the colonies-in-possession and of regaining those taken by the Japanese rival. "I am not the First King's Minister to preside over the liquidation of the British Empire," said Churchill, with approving nods from colleagues Sinclair, Attlee and Bevin. India and Ceylon—remain British. Burma—back to Britain. Singapore—back to Britain. The East Indies—back to Holland-*cum*-America. Hong Kong—back to Britain (with the consent of the Peerless Leader in the struggle for China's national freedom, Generalissimo—he is also a Generalissimo!—Chiang). Indo-China—back to France-*cum*-England-*cum*-America (and in reverse order of real power). The islands of the Pacific—to the United States, which, as the entire world knows, does not lust for an inch of foreign soil. Manchuria, its natural resources and its railroads—out of the hands of the base oppressor, Japan, and into the hands of the noble liberator, Russia. Dairen and Port Arthur—out of the hands of the foreign ruler, Japan, and into the hands not of Czar Nicholas this time but of Czar Joseph. Korea—part for Russia, part for the United States, with the Korean themselves allowed to publish a modest bulletin in Washington. The Philippines—independence postponed indefinitely, inasmuch as they are to be fortified and super-fortified as a military and naval base (i.e., a vassal) of the United States (against whom? Utterly prostrated and completely controlled Japan? Or perhaps against so notorious an aggressor nation as Costa Rica? There is a mystery worthy of the era of guaranteed peace inaugurated at the San Francisco Conference!).

The Far East is the scene of an orgy of the imperialist swine. For this,

Japanese peasant boys and American farm and factory lads fevered and hungered and died in jungles, on beaches and on mountain ledges from Port Moresby to Okinawa, from Myitkyina to Midway.

The Two War Victors

There were seven more or less "big powers" when the war began—with countries like Poland and Yugoslavia counting as "medium powers." The war has ended with only two decisive big powers, only two victors, the United States and Russia. Of the rest of what is jokingly referred to as the "Big Five," England limps piteously behind the Big Two; France is a wreck which the others simply forget, half the time, to inform of their conferences; and China is simply told to lie still while it is dismembered and consumed. The smaller members of the "United Nations" are here, in the words of Jan Masaryk at the San Francisco Conference, "to be seen and not heard." Other members, like Poland, Finland, Latvia, Lithuania, Estonia, Greece, Yugoslavia and Albania, to say nothing of former enemies like Rumania, Bulgaria, Hungary and Austria, can neither be heard *nor* seen. Italy, Germany and Japan are simply in prison.

The war therefore only accelerated the fundamental tendency of modern imperialist society. On a national scale it manifests itself in the growth of large-scale industry at the expense of small-scale industry, or monopoly at the expense of competition, of the big bourgeoisie at the expense of the middle classes; in the concentration of wealth at one pole and of poverty, misery and degradation at the other; in the reduction of the size of the ruling class combined with an enormous increase in the economic and political power of the monopolistic few—and in the increase in the numbers of the ruled and ruined classes. On an international scale, it manifests itself in the growth of world-monopolistic control by fewer and fewer great powers, on the one side, and the growth of the number of nations that have lost (or have been prevented from acquiring) economic and political power, that are subordinated to the diminishing number of increasingly powerful nations, that lose their national independence to one degree or another, that are maintained as or converted into spheres of influence, protectorates, vassals, semi-colonies or outright colonies of the great powers that subjugate, oppress, disfranchise and exploit them.

At the end of six years of the war for the Atlantic Charter, national sovereignty and independence—only two powers have emerged that enjoy full independence and are able to play a decisively independent role in world politics. *All* the other nations of the earth are dependent upon one or the other of them, to one degree or another. If England appears to be an exception, it is more a case of appearance than of reality. The former workshop and banker of the world can no longer play an independent role. Throughout the war it depended on the United States for its defense— without the transatlantic cousin it would have perished. One flip of the pen in Washington—the cutting off of lend-lease—and all England is plunged into a panic amid heartrending wailings and lamentations by Mr. Attlee and the late Mr. Churchill. Once it was England that moved pawns about on the European chessboard. Now it is the colossus across the sea that is determined to reduce and is reducing England to the role of its pawn on the European continent. Irony of ironies: England as the European *agent* (not equal, but agent) of the power that grew out of its old thirteen colonies! England standing hat in hand before the new banker of the world! England standing on the American breadline, its back bowed to the ground under the heaviest financial burden in its history! The spectacle, one would think, is enough to warm the heart of the editor of the *Chicago Tribune*.

There is no room in this picture for indignation or commiseration. It is not "cruelty" that drives America, but necessity. Twenty years ago, Leon Trotsky started fashioning the key to an understanding of this irresistible development and of the problems it creates in his brilliant and prophetic analysis *Europe and America*. The United States, this continent-land, this land of vast resources and wealth and ingenuity, this land bursting with economic miracles, has become the first power in the world. But too late! It appears on the scene in an epoch of international capitalist decay. Nowhere is there durable peace in the world; poverty lasts longer than prosperity; the world market does not expand, it contracts. To maintain itself, the United States, like any other capitalist power, must expand. To expand, it must cut down the share of the world market of one country after another. In Trotsky's winged phrase, the United States seeks to put declining Europe on rations, diminishing rations, in order that its own share, its own "ration," may more closely correspond to its productive capacity and appetite. The greater the share of the United States, the smaller the share of all the others. The smaller their share, the more dependent they become upon the American titan. What is economic dependence upon another country? The forerunner of political dependence. What is political dependence? The surest guarantee of economic dependence. What is imperialist war? The endeavor to determine by armed force the question of who will be dependent upon whom.

America has come too late, however. The great empires of modern capitalism were established and consolidated in another epoch, the epoch of the organic ascension of capitalism itself. The very rise of American imperialism, its very power, generates the most violent disturbances and convulsions throughout the world. Putting Europe on rations did not result in converting the Old World into a docile milch-cow of Wall Street. It only plunged the continent into an agonizing crisis, with Germany suffering most acutely. Germany—all Europe—had to break the tightening grip of American domination or be reduced to paralysis. It failed to find a way out of the crisis along the road of the socialist revolution. Such a revolution would not only have restored the economic health of Germany on an unprecedented scale, but would have ended with the unification of the continent on a socialist foundation with more than enough economic and political power to smash any further encroachments upon its life and liberty by American imperialism. Failing in one way, it found another: Hitlerism, which deserves to bear the trade-mark "Made in America" as much as "Made in Germany." Totalitarianized Germany thereupon proceeded to its own variety of unification of Europe, mobilizing as best it could the economic resources of the continent so that it could, eventually (that is, after the "coordination" subordination of England and, of course, the conquest of at least European Russia), come to direct grips with the super-rival, America. How and why this attempt failed has already been dealt with.

The victory of the United States in the war does not mean an end to the social convulsions which its very power generated in Europe (and not only Europe) before the war. On the contrary. After an interval, the United States, precisely because of its now greater power, will produce even more violent upheavals of all kinds in Europe, at least that part of Europe (the West) which is its particular field of dominion. Whether it does it directly, or indirectly through its European "agent" or the country, it must convert more and more into its agent, England, is of secondary importance. (Its very power will stimulate and accelerate upheavals in England, too, for that matter. The first one, for which the power of American imperialism is far from the last cause, is the rise of the Labor Government.) One way or another, Europe will resist the pressure exerted by hypertrophied American imperialism, because resistance is the condition for life. And the ensuing upheavals, convulsions, collisions and social disturbances of all kinds will inevitably have their repercussions in the United States in the form of tremors and then earthquakes shaking its own social structure and shaping its own political future. To quote Trotsky again, the further American imperialism extends its power in the world, the more this power rests on powder-kegs. American imperialism has not learned the big lesson of our time: This, the epoch in which the old empires are crumbling, is not the epoch in which new ones can be created and consolidated. It has learned *nothing* from the disaster of Hitlerite imperialism. How could it? Imperialism is not something that "learns," it is something that must be extirpated.

The Great Conqueror of the war—the Greatest Conqueror—is headed for what has so aptly been called the "gloom of victory."

Russia over Europe (Or the Death of a Theory)

With the necessary changes, the same prospect lies ahead for Stalinist Russia. The bureaucracy seems to have attained a power which nobody ever expected, not even the bureaucracy itself. It dominates an empire which only the more delirious of the old Czars ever dreamed of: in the West, along a line from Northern Finland south past the Baltic lands, through Stettin, Berlin, Prague, Vienna, Ljubljana, probably including Albania, with everything eastward—Northern Iran included, British Asia and China excluded—all the way through Manchuria, at least part of Korea, the southern half of Sakhalin and a few of the Kuriles. As with capitalist imperialism so with Stalinist imperialism—some of these lands are "spheres of influence," others "protectorates," still others vassals and puppets, and the rest colonies and semi-colonies.

In the Western European countries which Russia does not rule, it nevertheless possesses utterly subservient police agencies, the so-called Communist parties—but police agencies with a tremendous political and physical power among the masses and in affairs of state. It is in this respect—it is extremely important to note and consider—that Stalinist imperialism has an instrument at its disposal which no other imperialist power has or ever had, not even the Nazis with their international network of Nazi groups and grouplets.

Therewith, Russia has become the dominant power on the European continent. Mr. Bevin and, now that he has acquired the courage that comes with loss of office, Mr. Churchill have allowed themselves to bleat and whimper, in a most deferential and anonymous reference to Russia, about the substitution in Eastern Europe of one totalitarianism for another. Once the really big concessions, the big spoils, have fallen into Stalin's hands, he is ready to make concessions *pro forma* to his "Allies"—but only tiny ones and not too many of them. Thus, after protest from Washington about the Bulgarian (not the Brazilian) elections, and another protest from

London about the Bulgarian (but not the Greek) elections, in the best Stalino–Hitlerite manner, the Kremlin Khan has agreed, through his Sofia puppets, to postpone the vote. What will be changed? Nothing, except to give the G.P.U. more time in which to kill off all remnants of real and potential opposition to its rule in Bulgaria. Why should Stalin take seriously the protestations of British imperialism? What can it *do* to him? Refuse him loans and credits? It has none to refuse. Call him ugly names? Stalin's retort would be "crushing." Put him in a British prison? Ghandi, yes; Stalin, no. Send an expeditionary force against him? Against unarmed Indians, yes; against Stalin, no. The United States is in a far better position, of course, to exert pressure upon Stalin. But not as much as it would like to exert, not as much as it needs to exert to bring its now principal rival to his knees—far, far from it! Besides, Stalin is not without his own means of exerting pressure in the opposite direction, as he has amply demonstrated to all skeptics. He must pay respectful attention to the wishes of the United States; a timid, cowering attitude, necessary for France and even for England, is not necessary for Russia.

But the enslavement of Europe, even of Eastern Europe, does not mean the consolidation of the new Russian empire, the definitive triumph of Stalinist totalitarianism. The war is at an end, the masses are tired, exhausted, disoriented. As happened immediately after the spectacular victories of German imperialism, so now the masses are stunned by the Russian triumphs. But what Stalin looks upon as a garland of oak-leaves around his Caesarian brow will prove to be a noose around his criminal's throat. The incapacity of the reactionaries to learn anything fundamental from the disasters of their predecessors and compeers, is positively astonishing— and encouraging. As with Hitler so with Stalin: the noose will come alive in time and strangle him and his regime as surely as it did the Nazis.

How long will the masses of the conquered, occupied, humiliated and traduced countries suffer the heel of Stalinist imperialism? How long will they remain silent in the face of the spoliation and plunder of their lands and industries? How long will they endure the monstrous police-dictatorship with which the G.P.U. replaces the Gestapo? Just how long, is hard to say. That they *will* rebel against it in much the same way they rebelled against Hitlerism, may be foretold with absolute confidence. If not tomorrow, then the next day, Stalin, his G.P.U., his "Communist" and "Workers'" parties and his Quislings will have to confront what Hitler, Himmler, Quisling and Pétain confronted, and with the same outcome.

There is another aspect of the Stalinist triumph that has been referred to in these pages before. The net result of the "unconditional defense of the

Soviet Union" is so dismal, not to say disastrous, that nobody in the Fourth International is very anxious today to press the matter, at least not with the vigor of 1939! This is highly understandable and, up to a certain point, gratifying. The question is nevertheless not eliminated. Above all there remains the question of the class character of the Soviet Union.

Officially, the Fourth International still stands on the theory that Russia is a "degenerated workers' state" by virtue of the existence of nationalized property. For our part, we have dumped that monstrosity down the drain of history where it belongs. What has the rest of the International to say now? Is it content to repeat the old formulae as if nothing of importance has happened in the past six years to test this theory, or to require a reconsideration of it? It is encouraging to note, here too, that there have been no efforts made recently to defend the theory with the old intransigence, pugnacity and confidence. That is encouraging, but far from satisfactory for a Marxian movement which takes its theories seriously.

What we are witnessing, in the International, is the *death of a theory*. It is clear that *nobody* now defends the "workers' state" theory, certainly not in the old way and with the old arguments; nobody *can* defend it. The theory is dying of lack of nourishment, dying in the vacuum which events have created around it and which prevents it from breathing, dying of lack of visible means of support. Mercy would dictate that it be allowed to die in this quiet, obscure, inanitive way. But theoretical clarity demands that it be deliberately *killed* and properly interred—*en connaisance de cause,* as the French say—with a knowledge as to the reason why—and that it be replaced with a carefully-thoughtout alternative theory in consonance with the realities of the living process and the principles of Marxian science.

The basic analysis of the Fourth International, which means in this case of its leader, Trotsky, has proved to be false and untenable in the matter of the class nature of Russia. The predictions based on this analysis have been proved false and untenable. Whoever fails to take this as his point of departure in the now mandatory reexamination lacks either theoretical understanding or theoretical honesty—less than that even politeness prevents us from saying. Whoever fails to adopt the *political* conclusions that follow logically from such a reexamination for a Marxist is certainly lost.

The war is over. The proletarian revolution did not come and did not triumph in Europe—an unhappy statement, but one that must be made. Imperialism continues to dominate the world. Stalinist Russia remains in existence—certainly not weaker in world politics than before the war! No fundamental or even serious *social* change has occurred there, no change in the economic foundations or social structure—at least none that anyone has yet been able to point to and name and weigh. Property remains nationalized; the monopoly of foreign trade is more or less intact. In addition, in conquered Poland the means of production have been nationalized, including even medium-sized enterprises. The same process was completed years ago in the Baltic states. A similar process is now going on in Yugoslavia (in the form of bureaucratic police measures, it is true, but going on nonetheless). If capitalist private property has been or is being restored by the bureaucracy, it is not visible to the naked eye or under any kind of microscope. *Nobody,* we repeat, has been able to adduce concrete data to indicate even a trend in this direction.

Trotsky predicted, nine years ago (he stated it before then and repeated it afterward), that Stalinist Russia would not survive the coming war. He predicted, just as emphatically, that an imperialist outcome of the war— that is, an end of the war without a successful proletarian revolution— would see the end of the "workers' state" in any form, "degenerated" or otherwise, and this *regardless of a military defeat or a military victory by Russia. . . .*

PART XIII
The Cold War

THE McCarthy era was extremely hard for the American Left, as it was for everyone who was sane. The senator threw so wide a net that suspicion, even paranoia, characterized much of America's public life. Unable to do anything about communism's successes, however defined, in Eastern Europe and Asia, the Truman and Eisenhower administrations countenanced a wholesale assault on the ostensible internal danger from the Left. Radicals naturally protested that the McCarthyist bulldozer was smashing all civil rights along with their own (Document 43), but the almost national hysteria about "international monolithic Communism" was too intense for a successful liberal defense of liberalism. McCarthy had a relatively free hand while he was sniffing out reds and pinkos in the State Department, "defense" industries, and most universities and churches; but his crude attack on the Army backfired since many Americans continued to think of the military as the last line of defense against the very "enemy" McCarthy was supposed to be tracking down. When the chips were really down, the public seemed to choose the external threat as more real than the so-called internal one. After the Army–McCarthy hearings, the U.S. Senate bestirred itself and censured its junior member from Wisconsin. But the damage was done, McCarthyist legislation was on the books, and the mindless ideology of anticommunism sent reverberations out into the future.

One of McCarthyism's sorrier episodes was staged in the universities. Coupling their anti-intellectual reflexes to the witchhunt, the hatreds freed by McCarthy and what he represented attempted to redefine academic freedom as a barrier to socialist convictions. Hundreds, maybe thousands, of conservative academics turned their minds to the formidable intellectual task of proving that freedom demanded a purge of the academic Left. Doxey A. Wilkerson, the director of faculty and curriculum of the Marxist-oriented Jefferson School of Social Science, revealed (Document 44) the hopeless inadequacies in the virtually official assault on academic freedom. When this article appeared, the Jefferson School was itself under attack by the Subersive Activities Control Board, and the Attorney General was trying to force it to register, and shut down, under the terms of the McCarran Internal Security Act of 1950. Wilkerson's reconstruction of the argument being used against the academic Left was accurate: it was repeatedly said that academic freedom demanded the suppression of Communists because they necessarily had minds servile to Moscow, and they were therefore agents, not heretics. The sophistry of the witchhunters is matched only by the medieval scholastics who worried about angels dancing on pinheads. But they were powerful, with force borrowed from widespread national fear, from near official sanction, and from the obsequiety of American academia. To Harvard's very great credit, it resisted when so many others pushed and shoved to get into line.

The destruction of the Left, especially during the Eisenhower years, could not have occurred without the collapse of the middle, without the surrender of liberalism. Irving Howe, the editor of the independent socialist journal *Dissent,* in a brief and occasional article (Document 45), reflected almost casually on the political assumptions of literary people in order to get at the intellectual bankruptcy of liberalism in America. Following Eisenhower's cue, many liberals apparently discovered that something called the "American consensus" not only explained the past and present, but also described the only practicable future. But, as Howe shows, consensual thinking ignored both the source and the future of America's material condition, blinded itself to the existence of economic classes, and identified the nation with the professional sector of the middle class (a maneuver similar to that of the president of General Motors who said, with more justification, that what was good for GM was good for the country). The liberals' full-blown idealism, and their attempt to deny conflict, at least contributed to the strength of the McCarthyites who understood and reveled in power.

But the Left grew moribund as much from its own ineptitude as from the wild national attacks on it. The Khrushchev revelations at the twentieth Communist Party Congress, his attack on Stalin, was an inescapable repudiation of, among many more important things, the American Stalinists; all the squirming over the Moscow trials, the Hitler–Stalin pact, and the cold war itself, now in America as elsewhere, were suddenly questionable, and the questions had been raised in the highest possible quarter. The Foster leadership, always Stalinist and unreconstructable, of the CP was isolated further, and other internal factions developed (including a painful squabble over control of *The Daily Worker*). With entire lifetimes of political effort suddenly revealed as silly at best and counterrevolutionary at worst, perhaps a majority of the tiny residual membership drifted away. The outpouring of confessions of past errors, and criticisms of the party, showed how devastating de-Stalinization was. By the end of the decade, the CPUSA had virtually ceased to exist. Except for the dues and support of FBI infiltrators it would probably have been forced to close down altogether.

---

[43]

AN OPEN LETTER TO
THE U.S. SENATE

The Daily Worker

GENTLEMEN:

Confronted with some truths about his career, Sen. McCarthy has dropped on your desk an assortment of Daily Worker articles and editorials.

He hopes to "prove" that if you agree to censure him for the outrages he has committed (the doctored photos, the faked "FBI letter," his summons to his private agents in government, and his contemptuous refusal to answer the questions of the 1951–52 Hennings Committee), that you will then be "following the Daily Worker line."

If you dare to censure Sen. McCarthy you will be "taking orders from the Kremlin."

In short, McCarthy is trying to slip over on the U.S. Senate the same falsehood which he has tried to dump on this nation—that loyalty to McCarthy is loyalty to America, and disloyalty to McCarthy can only spell disloyalty or treason to America.

* * *

His argument is that an idea advocated by the Communists, or by the Daily Worker, becomes by this very fact a criminal argument, a disloyal and treasonable argument with which no American can dare to agree.

SOURCE: "An Open Letter to the U.S. Senate," *The Daily Worker* 31, no. 224 (10 November 1954): 1. Reprinted by permission of *The Daily World*.

And thus, if the Daily Worker and a Senate Committee—solely on the basis of the irrefutable facts—find that McCarthy spurned the Hennings Committee, that the Pepsi-Cola Washington agent guaranteed a $20,000 bank loan for him when Pepsi-Cola was interested in sugar quotas; and his "spy" cases were sordid forgeries manufactured for headlines—why then according to McCarthy, the Senate and the Daily Worker will have become political allies. With this argument, McCarthy hopes to put himself beyond the reach of questioning by his fellow Senators.

* * *

But what are the realities of the situation?

It is not true as McCarthy would have you believe that this is a battle between him and the Communists. He hopes to persuade you of this falsehood because you gentlemen are, after all, anti-Communists even when you are not too clear as to what you are opposing.

But in his anthology of Daily Worker editorials, McCarthy has carefully omitted most of the facts which go to show that the Communists are a small, though an exceedingly vigorous, minority in the wide national anti-McCarthy front of decent and patriotic Americans who are sick to their souls of this imitation-Hitler and his contempt for the American way of life.

For example, McCarthy has not placed on your desks the excoriating speech of Catholic Bishop Shiel of Chicago, which the Daily Worker published.

Nor does he give you the Daily Worker report of the opinion of Labor (March 10), railroad labor's weekly, which referred to "the dangerous fakery of McCarthyism . . . like Hitler he is determined to rule or ruin. His alleged fight on communism is just a mask. . . . He intends if he can to seize control of the GOP and hand it to himself as master. . . . He hopes to undermine democracy and put himself on top . . . as Hitler did in Germany."

Nor would he place before you the angry statement of the post of the Veterans of Foreign Wars (Stoughton, Wisconsin) which proved that McCarthy's "war record" is as fraudulent as the rest of his claims. (March 7, 1954.)

As for the anti-McCarthy feelings of most of the labor movement, many of the leading churches, you will find none of that on your desks in McCarthy's "little pink book."

* * *

We are quite proud to be a target of McCarthy's in this crusade of the nation to defend its decency from faked photos, forged documents, and sordid "spy" forgeries; though we are happy to be able to state that it is America which is despising and rejecting McCarthyism and no one section of it alone, surely not the Communists nor the Daily Worker alone.

If that were true, McCarthy would not be facing the Watkins Committee Report nor the censure of the Senate.

* * *

A final word, Sirs.

It is this. If McCarthy, caught with the goods by the Watkins Committee, or at least some of the goods, can try to save himself by shouting to you, "The Daily Worker agrees with you!," is it not time for thinking Americans to begin to question the entire McCarthy doctrine?

If McCarthy can be so obviously wrong in his agrgument that to agree with the Daily Worker on any subject is to be part of a conspiracy, can the nation follow him in his propaganda about the nature and aims of the Daily Worker itself?

In short, may not McCarthy be as deceitful about the purposes of the Daily Worker as he is about the relations of the Senate to the Daily Worker?

Certainly, the recent election defeats of McCarthyites like Representatives Kit Clardy, Fred Busbey, and Charles Kersten would indicate that such thinking is indeed beginning to appear in the country.

The majority of Americans—Communists, non-Communists and anti-Communists—on the basis of what they know, expect the Senate to vote a quick censure of Senator McCarthy.

But beyond this, the special session of the Senate has the further duty, it seems to us, of probing more deeply into the McCarthy conspiracy and unseating him. The 84th Congress in January also has the duty of re-examining those laws of thought-control and repression (the Smith Act, the Brownell–Butler law and the McCarran Act) which are the embodiments of the tyrannical spirit of McCarthyism.

Respectfully yours,
THE DAILY WORKER

MARXISTS AND
ACADEMIC FREEDOM

DOXEY A. WILKERSON

IT is not difficult to understand why, in this period, the dominant forces in our society move to stamp out the teaching and advocacy of Marxist doctrines which have been propagated in the United States for more than a century. In the first place, the challenge of socialist theory to capitalist society is more serious today than ever before, now that one-third of the world's people are on the road to socialism or communism under governments led by Marxist parties. Second, the drive to suppress the teaching of Marxism provides an effective cover for the suppression of all other teaching and advocacy which poses a serious challenge to the monopolies that dominate the foreign and domestic policies of our government.

But this understandable urge to suppress the teaching of Marxism, now intensified by the "Cold War," poses a troublesome dilemma for the leaders of a nation which has long fought to achieve and defend the Bill of Rights, and whose traditions call for what Mr. Justice Holmes characterized as "free trade in ideas"—*any ideas,* including those of Marxism–Leninism. The controlling forces in our country either must uphold the right to teach and advocate precisely those Marxist ideas which they consider false or dangerous—and thus subordinate their special interests to the democratic traditions of America; or they must try to suppress the teaching and advocacy of Marxist ideas—and thus expose themselves as enemies of our constitutional guarantees of free speech and association.

They have sought to resolve this dilemma by eating their cake and having it too—by proceeding to suppress the teaching of Marxism (and all other social and political ideas which McCarthyism chooses to label "communistic"), while trying to reassure our nation that only thus can academic freedom and democracy be preserved. And they have moved into action an imposing corps of intellectuals to "justify" this deft bit of political sleight-of-hand.

SOURCE: Doxey A. Wilkerson, "Marxists and Academic Freedom," *Masses and Mainstream* 6, no. 12 (December 1953): 38–46.

The essence of the ideological façade behind which McCarthyism now seeks to destroy the *right* to teach and advocate Marxism is the thesis (1) that American Marxists are servants of a "world Communist conspiracy" directed toward the overthrow of our government by force and violence; (2) that as "conspirators" bound to follow a Moscow-dictated "line" they are properly without the privileged domain of academic freedom; and (3) that the purging of Marxists from school and college faculties is necessary to safeguard academic freedom.

In one form or another, this thesis has been proclaimed from the White House, enacted by Congress and state legislatures into law, sanctified by the courts, and echoed time and again in the press and in academic halls. Even the Jenner Committee report piously asserts that the purpose of its invasion of the campus "is to protect and safeguard academic freedom" from the dire machinations of "hidden (Communist) conspirators (who) are waiting at every vantage point to attack and destroy the loyal people who are going quietly about the business of teaching our youth to the best of their ability."

The most zealous and persistent purveyor of this "line" in academic circles is Professor Sidney Hook of New York University; [1] and its typical formulation is illustrated in a letter which he, George S. Counts, Paul R. Hays and Arthur O. Lovejoy addressed to *The New York Times* of July 19, 1953 on behalf of the Commission on Academic Freedom of the American Committee for Cultural Freedom.

These educators write that they are very much disturbed over both the "Communists" and the Congressional committees which claim to be hunting Communists; and their problem is to formulate a rationale for curbing both. They begin by affirming the basic premise of McCarthyism, that "academic freedom everywhere in the world is under the implacable threat of Communist aggression"; but add: "The existence of the Communist conspiracy in our own midst has stirred deep and natural anxieties—anxieties which are being exploited by unscrupulous politicians." Then, asserting that "the existence of this conspiracy has raised hard and urgent questions not easily answered by the familiar formulas of civil freedom" they proceed to devise a "new" formula for denying academic freedom to Marxists:

Where does the Communist teacher fit into the scheme of academic freedom? The only reasonable answer is: He does not. A member of the Communist party has transgressed the canons of academic responsibility, has engaged his intellect to servility, and is therefore professionally disqualified from performing his functions as scholar and teacher.

[1] See, for example, his *Heresy, Yes—Conspiracy, No!* John Day Company.

Here, indeed, is a convenient ideological device. On the premise that American Marxists lack intellectual integrity and merely parrot ideas dictated to them by an alleged "world Communist conspiracy," it seeks to justify throwing Marxists to the McCarthyite wolves as a means toward preserving academic freedom for non-Marxists. This neat formula cannot, however, withstand critical examination.

In the first place, the growing revolutionary movements in many countries, which are usually cited as evidence of the so-called "world Communist conspiracy," cannot possibly be explained in terms of some secret plot or intrigue by a small group of "conspirators." Whether in the Tsar's Russia, Chiang Kai-shek's China, or Malan's South Africa—precisely as was true in King George's North American colonies during the late 1700's—powerful revolutionary movements can be understood only in the light of changes taking place in the material foundations of society. They are the political reflection of basic social changes which have made—or are in process of making—obsolete and no longer viable the existing social order. In response to these underlying social changes, the masses of oppressed people rally behind their revolutionary leaders in struggles against the decadent and obdurate ruling classes which oppress them. . . .

Many non-Marxist sociologists likewise understand that revolutionary movements arise, not from the machinations of "conspirators," but from underlying economic changes which make untenable the existing social organization and impel masses of people into struggles to change it. Thus Ogburn and Nimkoff say that a major revolution "is to be explained in terms of unequal rates of change in correlated parts of culture," that it is "an attempt to adjust a long-standing lag in the political sector" to prior "changes in the economic organization." [2] Sutherland and Woodward express similar views, with special emphasis on the bankruptcy of the ruling class as a precondition for basic revolutionary change:

> The big revolutions, involving an overthrow of a whole class and a complete reorganization of governmental machinery, are not brought about because of militant mass opposition alone. They come only when the governing class or faction has lost faith in its own right and ability to rule, when it has been deserted by the intellectuals who have gone over to the reform party, and when the seizure of power can be relatively easy and bloodless because administrative authority and organization are in a state of decay.[3]

. . . Those "Cold War" advocates mainly responsible for spreading the myth of a "world Communist conspiracy" know full well that the wide-

[2] William F. Ogburn and Meyer F. Nimkoff, *Sociology,* Houghton Mifflin Company, p. 924.
[3] Robert Sutherland and Julian L. Woodward, *Introductory Sociology,* J. Lippincott Company, p. 79.

spread proletarian revolutionary movements and colonial liberation movements of today could not possibly be created by an international clique of backroom "conspirators." They propagate this nonsense because, in the words of the recent declaration of the General Council of the Presbyterian Church; "In this form of warfare, falsehood is frequently preferred to fact if it can be shown to have greater propaganda value."

Consider the enormity of this "world Communist conspiracy" deceit. Today, under the leadership of Communists, some 800,000,000 people—in the Soviet Union, Eastern Europe and China—are cooperatively engaged in the socialist reconstruction and development of their societies. Scores of millions more, in every country in the world, are convinced that socialism is the necessary and inevitable next stage of social development, and are struggling to promote its achievement. Here is a social movement which has dominated world politics for nearly half a century. It involves more than one-third of mankind. Yet, the masters of "Cold War" strategy would have us interpret this vast historic development as the fruits of a "conspiracy"!

The "world Communist conspiracy" hoax is THE Big Lie of our times. It serves well as an ideological cover for the war-makers, for those to whom corporate profits take precedence over our traditional democratic liberties, for the advocates of thought-control. But it is a monstrous fraud on the American people.

Second, the premise that Marxists lack intellectual integrity is a shop-worn cliché which flies in the face of elementary logic. No American is under compulsion to accept Communist theory, let alone to join the Communist Party; nor does such acceptance offer the material and prestige awards now readily available to the intellectual willing to make a career out of anti-Communism. Indeed, adherence to Marxism today invites economic and professional ruin, and perhaps imprisonment. Why, then, do many Americans do it? A reasonable hypothesis would seem to be that they are convinced that Marxist theory is valid, and are more than ordinarily endowed with the courage of their convictions.

What arrogance to adjudge as "intellectually servile" those professionals and others who now embrace the highly unpopular views of Marxism–Leninism! What sophistry to predicate one's unwillingness now to defend genuine academic freedom on an alleged "world Communist conspiracy" which—even if it existed—would have no power to coerce the beliefs of American intellectuals!

Dr. Alexander Meiklejohn gave the effective answer to this nonsense in his reply to Sidney Hook in the *New York Times* several years ago. Analyzing the motives which lead "men and women of scholarly training and taste" to accept Communism, he concluded that ". . . in general, the only explanation which fits the facts is that these scholars are moved by a passionate determination to follow the truth where it seems to lead, no matter what may be the cost to themselves and their families." Further, examining the argument that Communists are intellectual slaves to a "line" dictated from Moscow, he observed that people join the Communist Party solely because they want to, and that "they do not accept Communist beliefs because they are members of the party. They are members of the party because they accept Communist beliefs." [4]

Third, it is a gross deception to pretend that academic freedom can be preserved for non-Marxists while it is denied to Marxists. The fallacy of this "line" is demonstrated empirically by the sad experiences of non-Marxists with the "book-burners" and academic purgers during the past year. It can also be demonstrated theoretically.

The classic concept of "academic freedom" is well formulated in the famous Association of American Universities statement of last March:

A university must . . . be hospitable to an infinite variety of skills and viewpoints, relying upon open competition among them as the surest safeguard to truth. Its whole spirit requires investigation, criticism and presentation of ideas in an atmosphere of freedom and mutual confidence. This is the real meaning of "academic" freedom. It is essential to the achievement of its ends that the faculty of a university be guaranteed this freedom by its governing board, and that the reasons for the guarantee be understood by the public. To enjoin uniformity of outlook upon a university faculty would put a stop to learning at its source. To censor individual faculty members would put a stop to learning at its outlet.

This is all very fine. But suppose the university scholar and teacher comes, through his studies, to the conviction that capitalism is a stage in the continuing history of social development, that in its present period of monopoly domination it is no longer compatible with the basic needs of mankind, and that capitalism will and should be replaced with socialism —through another historic social revolution, led this time by the working class. What then?

On the premise that "free enterprise (i. e., capitalism) is as essential to intellectual as to economic progress," the A. A. U. statement answers that such a scholar and teacher must be lacking in "professional competence . . . integrity and independence," and by "adopting a 'party line' . . . he forfeits not only all university support but his right to membership in the

[4] "Should Communists Be Allowed to Teach?" *New York Times Magazine,* March 27, 1949.

340

university." In short, on this question of fundamental social theory, the A. A. U. would "enjoin uniformity of outlook upon a university faculty" and "censor individual faculty members" who do not conform.

This internal contradiction in the A. A. U. statement is inherent in all such efforts to rationalize the suppression of Marxist belief and teaching while at the same time proclaiming the necessity for academic freedom. . . .

The Hook–A. A. U. formula for withholding academic freedom from Communists does not arise from any genuine anxiety over the intellectual integrity of Marxist teachers, but from opposition to the conclusions they have reached concerning the superiority of socialism as a base for democracy and peace. The "conspiracy" thesis is a deceit which enables one to pose as a champion of free inquiry while actually serving the contrary interests of those economic forces which dominate the Congress, subsidize the universities and grant petty favors to anti-Communist intellectuals. The whole business is a shameful fraud which has done untold damage to the cause of academic freedom.

Once we grant the inquisitors' right to purge the Marxists, we open wide the door for McCarthyism to darken the halls of learning. We thus encourage those forces in our national life that would turn our schools into agencies for producing such warped personalities and stultified intellects as were characteristic in Hitler Germany.

Truly effective defense of academic freedom must proceed from the proposition that it is the democratic right of the American people to learn, teach and advocate the truth as they see it; and it is the obligation of education administrations as well as government to protect this right.

It is not within the purpose of this analysis either to explain or to evaluate the teachings of Marxism–Leninism; but it is relevant to note the social consequences which necessarily flow from the vulgar distortions of Marxism now palmed off on American youth by much of our current "education."

The philosophical, economic and political theories of Marxism–Leninism have had in our century an influence on the minds of men and on world events surpassing even that of the great liberating ideas which—with the development of capitalism in the seventeenth, eighteenth and nineteenth centuries—swept out feudalism in Western Europe and in large measure shaped the institutions established in our country. Marxism today plays a decisive role in the lives of the vast populations in the Union of Soviet Socialist Republics, the Chinese People's Republic and the People's Democracies of Eastern Europe. It is a guiding force in the independence movements developing among colonial and semi-colonial peoples in Asia, Africa and Latin America. The largest political parties of France and Italy, with millions of members and supporters, are their respective Communist parties.

There is great interest in Marxist theory and socialist practice among educators and other intellectuals in Western Europe. Delegations of French teachers and doctors, for example, have visited the Soviet Union and reported their observations in professional journals and conferences. The leading officers of the British National Union of Teachers visited the Soviet Union in the summer of 1951, and later reported on their study of the Soviet educational system both in their official journal and at teachers' meetings in many parts of the country. A conference on Soviet educational policy and practice held in Sienna, Italy, December 1951, was attended by some five hundred of the country's leading educators, psychologists and philosophers.

In all of Western Europe—except, of course, in fascist Spain—Marxist scholars and artists play leading roles in the professional and cultural life of their nations. In Britain, for example, there are Professor Benjamin Farrington, of Swansea College in Wales, who writes and lectures for the London District Committee of the Communist Party; and Professor George Thompson of the University of Birmingham, a national officer of the Communist Party of Great Britain. Among British Marxists in the professional field, one thinks also of Christopher Hill of Oxford, Ronald L. Meek of Glasgow, J. D. Bernal, Maurice Dobb and others. There are comparable Marxists of recognized stature in education and the other professions in France, Italy and Latin America, not to mention the countries of Asia. Much the same is true in the field of art. During the past summer, for example, J. Alvarez del Vayo reported from Europe:

It is not easy to imagine President Eisenhower lending the authority of his presence to the opening of an exhibition of a Communist painter. But it was President Einaudi of Catholic Italy who ceremoniously opened the Picasso exhibition in Rome.

He also reports an international piano and violin competition held in Paris, at which both first and second prizes were won by Soviet violinists.

Thus, whatever may be one's attitude toward the teachings of Marxism–Leninism, it is a fact that these ideas constitute and are recognized as an important part of the intellectual life of our age; and their concrete expressions in social development are among the political phenomena toward which our country must formulate foreign and domestic policy. It would seem, therefore, that the requirement both of scholarship and of national interest should lead us to study and understand these ideas, and to guarantee that they are available to our youth in the general market-place of ideas. No other course is open to a democratic society which would base its policies on social reality.

It is in the light of these considerations that thoughtful Americans will evaluate current tendencies to turn our schools and colleges into "Cold War" propaganda mills grinding out the National Association of Manufacturers "line" on the Soviet Union and China as "bloody dictatorships," and the police-agent version of the world Marxist movement as a bandit gang devoted to violence, sabotage and murder.

Illustrative of such distortions is a two-page spread on "Tools for Detecting Communist Propaganda" in the October 1951 issue of *Strengthening Democracy,* a bulletin distributed regularly to New York City teachers by the Superintendent of Schools. Here are some of the views teachers are asked to be on the lookout for as evidence of "Communism":

Reactionary: Anyone who opposes Soviet Russia or Communist politics is . called a reactionary . . .

They say Negroes in the United States are oppressed . . .

"Under capitalism," they say, "workers suffer from depression and unemployment. . . ."

A much-heralded speech by the Chancellor of New York University was reported in the press under the headline: "N.Y.U. STUDYING COMMUNISM 'LIKE CANCER.'" One sincerely hopes that cancer is not being "studied" there or elsewhere in such obscurantist terms as are now common in our "Cold War" teaching about Communism.

Sound social policy cannot be built on fantasy; and efforts to do so threaten the very life and future progress of our country. It is an important social responsibility of our schools and colleges to teach our people the truth about Marxist–Leninist theory and practice. . . .

[45]

AMERICA, THE COUNTRY AND THE MYTH

IRVING HOWE

ONE frequently hears these days that socialists cling to a stereotyped picture of American life. Failing to see the subtle and even gross changes that have taken place during the past few decades, they focus on an abstraction called "capitalism" and thereby neglect the variety, the complexity, the rich substance of American life.

Perhaps. Like everyone else, radicals are mortal, and like everyone else they suffer from the shell-shocks of modern history. But let me abandon the impersonal "they" and speak in the uncomfortable "we." Often enough we do treat such abstract—yet useful because abstract—categories as "capitalism" and "class struggle" as if they were real objects or persons rather than tools for analysis. And in doing so we may fail to notice the many changes that have taken place in the structure, as in the quality, of American life, changes that do not, I think, add up to the removal of capitalism as a functioning system or of "capitalism" as a fluid category for social analysis, but which nonetheless merit some attention and study.

The criticism would, however, be much easier for us to accept if the liberals who advance it were not themselves so susceptible to it. One of the curiosities of our intellectual life at the present moment is the thoroughness with which the dominant school of liberalism—the school for which Sidney Hook is philosopher-politician, David Riesman sociologist and Lionel Trilling literary moralist—exempts itself from its own analysis and recommendations. Few things are more dogmatic today than the anti-dogmatism of the liberal intellectual, few things more closed than his famous open mind. The image of "America" that emerges from the writings of this school is as thoroughly abstract, reified, and unhistorical as any that may be charged against the most dogmatic radicals.

In a recent tribute to David Riesman, Mr. Lionel Trilling has written that no American novel of the past period suggests to him so "brilliantly"

SOURCE: Irving Howe, "America, the Country and the Myth," *Dissent* 2 (Summer 1955): 241–244.

as do Riesman's essays "the excitement of contemplating our life in culture as an opportunity and a danger." * This phrase about "opportunity and danger" may be taken as a summary of the numerous essays written on "America" (the idea, that is, not the country).

It is not very hard to put one's finger on the main stress of these writings. America is unique, different. Rising phoenix-like from the ashes of an exhausted world, America has achieved not merely material plenty but also an exciting, adventuresome and free-wheeling style of life. The patterns of our experience are not yet settled; things here are still open and fluid; it is as if we were living at a time when the frontier was still a reality rather than an exploited memory; as if the H-bomb, the war economy, McCarthyism, the crack-up of Europe, the victories of Stalinism in Asia, while distressing enough, could not mar the immaculate essence of the American triumph. In the literature of liberal mythology America ceases to be a nation among nations, the major segment of international capitalist economy, and becomes instead an embodiment of the heart's desire which the brutish European intellectuals, in their malice or stupidity, insist upon maligning. All the penalties of history, all the penalties paid and yet to be paid by Europe and Asia, cannot touch us; like Joseph in his many-colored coat, America is the invulnerable and prodigal son. For America is the land that has escaped; escaped from Europe; escaped from the heartbreak house of capitalism; escaped from atomic radiation (though its heart goes out to Japanese fishermen); escaped from *anomie* and *je m'en fiche;* escaped, in short, from history.

In an essay written by Mary McCarthy a few years ago, these notions received eloquent expression. "America the Beautiful" was her title, and for once she could hardly be suspected of irony. Americans, she wrote, were the last idealists or non-materialists on earth; the nation that was soon to choose Dwight Eisenhower and John Foster Dulles as its leaders she described as a "communion of ascetics." Somewhat similarly, one sometimes feels in reading Leslie Fiedler's essays on "America" that Huck Finn, oblivious to time and man's works, is still floating down the river, Natty Bumpo is still loose on the prairie, and Ishmael is still cozying with Queequeg rather than, as I happen to know, doing his basic training at Fort Riley.

Some people may interject that it is not very profitable to take seriously

* The "excitement" of reading Mr. Riesman's current essays may be found in passages such as this one: "Our intellectuals do not . . . allow themselves to praise Hollywood movies as much as, in my opinion, they deserve; they are like psychiatrists who do not dare give a patient a clean bill of health lest some other doctor find a hidden flaw."

the political writings of literary people; but I disagree. It is profitable. For in such writings one finds expressed, with whatever indulgence of the fancy, the assumptions that cut through almost all liberal thinking. Perhaps it is worth noting two or three of these assumptions:

1) A Refusal to Analyze Either the Origins or Prospects of Our Material Prosperity

Merely to insist that everything about the past decade can be understood by a sweeping reference to "war economy" is surely to oversimplify a good deal; but to write about American life without recognizing that war production, with all of its economic and moral instabilities, *has* played a crucial role in American prosperity is to do something worse: it is to undersimplify the American scene. In Mr. Riesman's *The Lonely Crowd,* a book notable for its shrewd observations of middle-class manners, no serious effort is made to relate the patterns of social life to the nature of our economy. And Mr. Riesman is far from alone in this failure. The many writers who, like him, proclaim the blessings of our material prosperity, even if they are not so rash as to invoke with him the Age of Pericles, seldom trouble to notice such limited and unexciting problems as trouble and disrupt the lives of millions of actual Americans. It is easier by far to write distinguished essays about "America."

2) The Assumption That America Is a Socially Homogeneous Nation

John Jay Chapman once remarked that in going to an Italian opera you might at least find out what could never be learned from reading Emerson's essays: that there are two sexes. One might say in defense of certain American sociologists that in their books, no matter how dreary, it is at least possible to learn what can seldom be discovered in the essays of the literary liberals: that there are two or more classes in America.

But surely the assumption that one can talk usefully about "America" as if it were a graspable object, or as if it were a person waiting to be psychoanalyzed, is as much a reification as the habit of discussing America simply as if it were a "model" of capitalism. And it may even be a much less useful assumption, for the Marxist categories have, at the very least, the virtue of being comparatively public and open to verification, while in the recent literary celebrations of America every man makes up his terms as he goes along, so that one must try to correlate Mr. Riesman's "other-directed community" with Miss McCarthy's "communion of ascetics."

3) The Assumption That America Consists Exclusively of the Middle Class or the Academic and Professional Segments of the Middle Class

Seldom made explicit, this assumption pervades the work of numerous American writers, with the result that a sociologist familiar with the manners of academic life is taken to be a student of American society as a whole. The "we" that appears in the impressionistic studies of "America" comes, upon inspection, to suggest little more than a very small segment of the population. And meanwhile the millions of flesh-and-blood persons who work in factories and belong to labor unions seldom if ever appear in the works of those who talk about our changing "national character."

To be sure, it is commonly said that the American workers are thoroughly middle class in outlook, but this statement is seldom anything but the result of intellectual carelessness. In many areas of value judgment and style of life the workers of America do *approach* the middle class; but this closeness of approach can be understood only if seen as a relationship between two distinct groups. And there are also many significant areas of experience—e.g., the factory with its inner patterns of fraternity, discipline and chaos—in which the life of the workers is radically different from that of the middle class.

But few segments of the population interest the literary liberals and the impressionistic sociologists less than the workers. To feel any interest in, let alone community with, the American workers is for most intellectuals to run the worst of all risks—the risk of being thought sentimental.

And so whole strata of the American population have been dismissed from the consideration of those who analyze and rhapsodize America. None of the students of "American character" thinks to look into the gradual decay of the New England textile towns or the social disruption of New York City under the pressure of Puerto Rican migration; none thinks it worth the trouble to inquire what the production crisis in Detroit means to the life of thousands of people; none so much as dreams of writing a sequel to James Agee's *Let Us Now Praise Famous Men,* in which we might learn what has happened to the life of the Southern sharecroppers during recent years. Under the pressures of the historical moment, the sense of social curiosity, to say nothing of the sense of social sympathy, has virtually disappeared.

For precisely this reason we must look for direct and simple reportage written by young writers who, without ideological preconceptions, will go into the cities and towns, looking, watching, responding. All that is needed —it is a very great deal—is what Edith Wharton once called "that sharpening of the moral vision which makes all human suffering so near and insistent that the other aspects of life fade into remoteness." Surely there must be a few young writers not so busy with exercises in national self-congratulation that they will tell us, as once Edmund Wilson and Sherwood Anderson and James Agee told us, what the quality of American life really is. . . .

PART XIV
The Black
Liberation Front

T HE black struggle shaped the contours of all protest and resistance movements during the 1960's. Of course there was no unified black effort; the splintering and personal empire building was as self-defeating on the black front as it had always been on the white. But the energy of black liberation leapt from peaceful and nonviolent boycott to legal battles for civil rights to anarchic urban rebellion to a cooler, more political, even angrier attempt to organize the ghettos first for self-defense and then for actual liberation. If the actual details of this liberation could never be found, the black activists devoted themselves, as white radicals had done for at least a century, to an abolition of the hated and hurtful present in the name of whatever would follow from it. The implication was clear: nothing could be as bad as the present, and therefore change was welcomed before the outcome could be known.

The voice of the Black Muslims, especially that of Malcolm X (1925–1965), provided the early emotional and cultural support for an increasing militancy that was based on black, not white, perceptions of black people living in America. Indeed, as Eldridge Cleaver was later to say, "Black history began with Malcolm X." Malcolm X did what few American black people had done before; he found a black rhetoric, a black tone, and a black audience whose response was tougher than the responses elicited by the more ordinary black leaders, "so-called" black leaders as he called them. Commissioned by Elijah Muhammad to organize Muslim temples during the late fifties, Malcolm X had become the Muslims' chief and most articulate spokesman. The media, of course, swung into their sort of action in order to display the Muslims between commercials.

349

Shortly before the 1960's began, a TV program, characteristically called "The Hate That Hate Produced," dumped the Muslims and Malcolm into the consciousness of the nation, and brought Malcolm into a continuing struggle with all the media, as well as with most of the traditional black leaders and spokesmen of more liberal persuasion. The following excerpt (Document 46) from Malcolm's *Autobiography,* which should be read in whole, shows his response to the hysterical reaction to this TV program, shows something of his style, and conclusively shows the agility and muscularity of his mind. He was expelled from the Muslims in 1963, formed the Organization of Afro–American Unity, went on a pilgrimage to Mecca the next year where he abandoned Elijah Muhammad's racism, and, as he predicted, was murdered while speaking in 1965.

During the prominence which Malcolm X had given them, the Muslims were often criticized by blacks for merely talking a good game, for not doing enough. While Malcolm's contribution to emerging black consciousness was crucial and indispensable, the black activism of the 1960's began with M. L. King's boycott of the Montgomery buses in 1956. The decade really opened on 1 February 1960 when four neatly dressed black freshmen sat-in at a Woolworth lunch counter in Greensboro, N.C. The sit-ins spread all over the South, and by April of the next year King's group helped to found the Student Non-Violent Coordinating Committee (SNCC) to organize the increasing use of this tactic. The Freedom Rides began in the spring of 1961, under the leadership of SNCC, already moving away from campus to local community organization, where it began also to conduct voter registration drives. After the big civil rights demonstrations of 1963—one organized by M. L. King in Birmingham, and another by Bayard Rustin in Washington—SNCC called for 1,000 northern students to come to Mississippi during the summer of 1964. This "Mississippi Summer," with Bob Moses in overall charge, was dedicated to community organizing and voter registration, and to teaching in Freedom Schools led by Staughton Lynd. One immediate and liberally practical result of this effort was the emergence of the Mississippi Freedom Democratic Party which challenged and lost to the regular state machine during the national election of that year. The principled dedication of SNCC to democratic participation and democratic leadership necessarily resulted in a loose-jointed organization which had continually to ask itself what its goals were, what it was doing, and what its tactics should be. The internal criticism was one of the healthiest aspects of SNCC, as the following staff memorandum (Document 47) will demonstrate. Despite the looseness, however, there was a firm commitment to discovering local initiative, to avoiding actions which would merely strengthen SNCC's institutional glamour.

In the summer of 1966, sandwiched between the summers of Watts and Detroit, SNCC, under the leadership of Stokely Carmichael and H. Rap Brown, moved into black power, necessarily moved away from white support, especially that of liberal white financial support, and brutally slapped down the white radicals who had worked with it in the recent past. Document 48 is SNCC's own explanation of why it took this step and what it intended. Malcolm's voice can be detected in this important statement, and it predictably raised anew all the confused questions and accusations about black racism. It was a fundamental challenge to the fetish of integration, and thus to a basic ingredient in something then called the "American technique for solving minority problems." This statement said that SNCC did not merely want a foothold in mainstream America, that it did not believe in the so-called melting pot, and that blacks would have to find their own way. SNCC's commitment to black power was a basic challenge to all the undusted assumptions of white America, and the instructions to the white Left to go home and organize white communities was good but painful advice. It also paralleled thinking that was already under way within the white Left, but this SNCC announcement galvanized the white Left to rethink its relationship to black militancy, to think harder about its own job, and to begin to think of the conditions necessary for some new coalition with an increasingly independent black movement.

SNCC's decision to cut itself off from, free itself of, white participation meant that SNCC would necessarily become more inward-looking, would become more and more interested in black, rather than white, attitudes. It would, henceforth, become involved with the black constituency rather than the white reaction. This is the meaning of H. Rap Brown's (b. 1943) defiance in his autobiographical statement (Document 49). He joined SNCC in 1963, and succeeded Stokely Carmichael as chairman from 1967 to 1968. From 1967 to 1970 he was continually under legal pressure on charges of arson, inciting to riot, gun carrying, and intimidation of an FBI investigator. Although SNCC was eventually to recede as a leading militant organization, Brown continued as a spokesman of the black Left. His analysis, reprinted here, of the relationship between capitalism and racism is a typical militant black response. It may be that Brown's great usefulness consists precisely in his ability to speak common attitudes in a voice reminiscent of Malcolm X. It is probably Brown's rhetoric rather than the cogency of his analysis that recommends him to his impressive audiences.

With the emergence of the Black Panther Party organized by Huey P. Newton and Bobby Seale in Oakland, 1967, the black struggle entered a new phase. The Panthers obviously intended to answer the old charge made against the Muslims for being too inactive. Coupling a usually fuzzy

Marxist analysis of American racism with the well-broadcast intention to defend themselves and their communities against intimidation and harassment "by all necessary means," the Panthers caught the attention of the media, the police, the FBI, and for a while growing numbers of young men in northern ghettos. Their demands and early manifesto (Document 50) were different from earlier black announcements to either white or black America; there was now no doubt that the black struggle was to be defined as that of an internal colony, aligned with all the efforts of the Third World, and committed to a radical diagnosis of, and prescription for, American corruption. Although there was always the danger that the Panthers would will to see a revolution right around the next corner, and then proclaim the existence of what they had willed, they clearly constituted a new force in black America. Metropolitan police departments also recognized that here was a movement with a difference. The inclusion of sections of the Declaration of Independence at the close of the Panther manifesto indicates their revolutionary intention—obviously, but equally indicates their often muted self-perception as being part of at least some American tradition. "Guns, baby, guns" was not a slogan designed to soothe frazzled white nerves, but there was nothing in Panther thought or talk that was antiwhite as such. As Marxists their analysis was likely to be more class- than race-oriented, but as blacks the issue of race in America was always at the front of their minds.

Eldridge Cleaver (b. 1935), as Minister of Information of the Panthers, often argued for the necessity of a white-black coalition; this in fact was his major contribution to the Panther literature, most of whose details had been worked out by others before he joined the party. Strongly influenced by Malcolm X while he was serving nine years in prison on a rape charge, Cleaver became disillusioned with the Muslims. When Malcolm was purged, when Allah did not come, and when the Muslims failed to provide even legal aid for blacks, Cleaver split with the Muslims and intended to carry on Malcolm's efforts to build an alliance between Afro-Americans and African blacks. But Huey Newton's clarity and presence apparently swept Cleaver into the Panthers, for whom he then became a vital spokesman. He, and the Panthers, demanded the decentralization of social and political institutions, radical structural change in American life, and coalition with white groups dedicated to human liberation within, and for, the internal black American colony. Cleaver often spoke of the presumed benefits to be derived from a UN-supervised black plebiscite in America, but the Panthers were also willing to participate in the traditional American electoral process, as Newton, Seale, and Kathleen Cleaver ran for congressional seats in California, and Cleaver ran for president on the Peace and Freedom ticket. An alliance with SNCC for a moment seemed to forecast SNCC's abandonment of a black-only policy, but by the time this happened SNCC was already moribund. Naturally, white radicals moved toward the Panther banner as one under which they would be allowed to work.

In Document 51 Cleaver wrote his account of the Oakland shooting that resulted in his being wounded and arrested, and resulted in the death of Bobby Hutton, a young Panther. He wrote this as an affidavit from the Vacaville Prison where he had been sent. Newton was already in prison; Cleaver himself was soon to go underground to avoid being returned to prison on what seems clearly to be a fake charge of parole violation; Seale was also in and out and back in jail; and the entire leadership of the party was in physical danger or already dead. The questions this record raised even for liberal white America could not be answered until fairer trials, with more representative juries, were held; as matters stood by the middle of 1970 the entire system of American justice was being tried along with the Panthers, and obviously neither could be vindicated unless both were. Eventually chased into exile, Cleaver's eloquent and authentic black voice seemed destined to become muted.

And yet, after all this has been said, one thing more is imperative. For all the honest social and even self-criticism, for all the years of trying to relate analysis to action, the black movement for liberation in this decade of the 1960's did not finally come up with a persuasive diagnosis of the full American situation. Cleaver's own rejection of cultural nationalism (because he thought it would be used as an excuse to avoid political revolution), his own confession that he did not have "the answers," and his great confusion about the proper relationship of the Panthers to traditional American political processes, all seem to indicate that it is not enough to invoke the name of Marx. And because the white movement leaned so heavily on that of the blacks, it is perhaps not surprising that these ultimate confusions should also have proved to be contagious. It is clear that Cleaver and the Panthers could proclaim a revolution; it is equally clear that they could not make one, anyway not in that decade. If one is to take them at their rhetorical surface, they seemed to believe that the revolution could be made by wishing very hard. But now it is a question whether they will survive legal harassment.

Finally it seems to be bone-deep ambivalence about America that keeps not only the Panthers, but most of the Left, black and white, somewhat off balance. When Cleaver says, for instance, that unless the government does its duty then revolution will be necessary, he seems to be saying that it is really up to the government, that he has not yet given up, and that if Big White Daddy will only earn his daily wage then all the radicals can close up shop—when he says this the confusion on the entire left becomes more visible. Can such a man be serious about his avowed anticapitalism? Is the entire Left serious, if it is still willing to run candidates for political office, accept government grants for urban renewal or whatever, and, perhaps most important, if it is not yet willing to think through the problems of living in a place that is not nineteenth-century Europe or twentieth-century Cuba? [1] That part of the American working class is now notoriously racist is enough of a theoretical challenge to any mechanistic Marxist. The enemy—racist, corporate, technocentric America—grows stronger as the revolutionary troops also grow stronger. In terms of sheer power this must be declared as no contest, a mismatch that it would be better to stay clear of. But this is not the final word, and the black movement of the sixties took the entire nation further and faster than could earlier have been imagined. What is coming will largely be influenced by the continuing struggle of the relatively few people on the white and black Left who, whatever their confusion, fight for a better chance to run their own lives.

---

[46]

AUTOBIOGRAPHY

MALCOLM X

IN late 1959, the television program was aired. 'The Hate That Hate Produced'—the title—was edited tightly into a kaleidoscope of 'shocker' images . . .* Mr Muhammad, me, and others speaking . . . strong-looking, set-faced black men, our Fruit of Islam . . . white-scarved, white-gowned Muslim sisters of all ages . . . Muslims in our restaurants, and

[1] This paragraph draws upon the analysis in Harold Cruse, "The Fire This Time?" *The New York Review of Books*, 8 May 1969, pp. 13–18.
* [Ed. note: All ellipses in this section appear in the original.]
SOURCE: Reprinted from "Excerpt from *Black Muslims* from THE AUTOBIOGRAPHY OF MALCOLM X" (New York: Grove Press, 1966), pp. 238–244. Reprinted by permission of Grove Press, Inc. and Hutchinson & Co., Ltd. Copyright 1965 by Alex Haley and Betty Shabazz.

other businesses . . . Muslims and other black people entering and leaving our mosques. . . .

Every phrase was edited to increase the shock mood. As the producers intended, I think people sat just about limp when the program went off.

In a way, the public reaction was like what happened back in the 1930s when Orson Welles frightened America with a radio program describing, as though it was actually happening, an invasion by 'men from Mars'.

No one now jumped from any windows, but in New York City there was an instant avalanche of public reaction. It's my personal opinion that the 'Hate . . . Hate . . .' title was primarily responsible for the reaction. Hundreds of thousands of New Yorkers, black and white, were exclaiming 'Did you hear it? Did you see it? Preaching *hate* of white people!'

Here was one of the white man's most characteristic behavior patterns —where black men are concerned. He loves himself so much that he is startled if he discovers that his victims don't share his vainglorious self-opinion. In America for centuries it had been just fine as long as the victimized, brutalized and exploited black people had been grinning and begging and 'Yessa, Massa' and Uncle Tomming. But now, things were different. First came the white newspapers—feature writers and columnists: 'Alarming' . . . 'hate-messengers' . . . 'threat to the good relations between the races' . . . 'black segregationists' . . . 'black supremacists,' and the like.

And the newspapers' ink wasn't dry before the big national weekly news magazines started: 'Hate-teachers' . . . 'violence-seekers' . . . 'black racists' . . . 'black fascists' . . . 'anti-Christian' . . . 'possibly Communist-inspired. . . .'

It rolled out of the presses of the biggest devil in the history of mankind. And then the aroused white man made his next move.

Since slavery, the American white man has always kept some handpicked Negroes who fared much better than the black masses suffering and slaving out in the hot fields. The white man had these 'house' and 'yard' Negroes for his special servants. He threw them more crumbs from his rich table, he even let them eat in his kitchen. He knew that he could always count on them to keep 'good massa' happy in his self-image of being so 'good' and 'righteous.' 'Good massa' always heard just what he wanted to hear from these 'house' and 'yard' blacks. 'You're such a good, *fine* massa!' Or, 'Oh, massa, those old black nigger fieldhands out there, they're happy just like they are; why, massa, they're not intelligent enough for you to try and do any better for them, massa—'

Well, slavery time's 'house' and 'yard' Negroes had become more sophisticated, that was all. When now the white man picked up his telephone and dialed his 'house' and 'yard' Negroes—why, he didn't even need to instruct the trained black puppets. They had seen the television program; had read the newspapers. They were already composing their lines. They knew what to do.

I'm not going to call any names. But if you make a list of the biggest Negro 'leaders,' so-called, in 1960, then you've named the ones who began to attack us 'field' Negroes who were sounding *insane,* talking that way about 'good massa.'

'By no means do these Muslims represent the Negro masses—' That was the first worry, to reassure 'good massa' that he had no reason to be concerned about his fieldhands in the ghettoes. 'An irresponsible hate cult' . . . 'an unfortunate Negro image, just when the racial picture is improving—'

They were stumbling over each other to get quoted. 'A deplorable reverse-racism' . . . 'Ridiculous pretenders to the ancient Islamic doctrine' . . . 'Heretic anti-Christianity—'

The telephone in our then small Temple Seven restaurant nearly jumped off the wall. I had a receiver against my ear five hours a day. I was listening, and jotting in my notebook, as press, radio and television people called, all of them wanting the Muslim reaction to the quoted attacks of these black 'leaders.' Or I was on long-distance to Mr Muhammad in Chicago, reading from my notebook and asking for Mr Muhammad's instructions.

I couldn't understand how Mr Muhammad could maintain his calm and patience, hearing the things I told him. I could scarcely contain myself.

My unlisted home telephone number somehow got out. My wife Betty put down the phone after taking one message, and it was ringing again. It seemed that wherever I went, telephones were ringing.

The calls naturally were directed to me, New York City being the major news-media headquarters, and I was the New York minister of Mr Muhammad. Calls came, long-distance from San Francisco to Maine . . . from even London, Stockholm, Paris. I would see a Muslim brother at our restaurant, or Betty at home, trying to keep cool; they'd hand me the receiver, and I couldn't believe it, either. One funny thing—in all that hectic period, something quickly struck my notice: the Europeans never pressed the 'hate' question. Only the American white man was so plagued and obsessed with being 'hated.' He was so guilty, it was clear to me, of hating Negroes.

'Mr Malcom X, why do you teach black supremacy, and hate?' A red flag waved for me, something chemical happened inside me, every time I heard that. When we Muslims had talked about 'the devil white man' he had been relatively abstract, someone we Muslims rarely actually came into contact with, but now here was that devil-in-the-flesh on the phone—with all of his calculating, cold-eyed, self-righteous tricks and nerve and gall. The voices questioning me became to me as breathing, living devils.

And I tried to pour on pure fire in return. 'The white man so guilty of white supremacy can't hide *his* guilt by trying to accuse The Honorable Elijah Muhammad of teaching black supremacy and hate! All Mr Muhammad is doing is trying to uplift the black man's mentality and the black man's social and economic condition in this country.

'The guilty, two-faced white man can't decide *what* he wants. Our slave foreparents would have been put to death for advocating so-called "integration" with the white man. Now when Mr Muhammad speaks of "separation," the white man calls us "hate-teachers" and "fascists"!

'The white man doesn't *want* the blacks! He doesn't *want* the blacks that are a parasite upon him! He doesn't *want* this black man whose presence and condition in this country expose the white man to the world for what he is! So why do you attack Mr Muhammad?'

I'd have *scathing* in my voice; I *felt* it.

'For the white man to ask the black man if he hates him is just like the rapist asking the *raped,* or the wolf asking the *sheep,* "Do you hate me?" The white man is in no moral *position* to accuse anyone else of hate!

'Why, when all of my ancestors are snake-bitten, and I'm snake-bitten, and I warn my children to avoid snakes, what does that *snake* sound like accusing *me* of hate-teaching?'

'Mr Malcolm X,' those devils would ask, 'why is your Fruit of Islam being trained in judo and karate?' An image of black men learning anything suggesting self-defense seemed to terrify the white man. I'd turn their question around: 'Why does judo or karate suddenly get so ominous because black men study it? Across America, the Boy Scouts, the YMCA, even the YWCA, the CYP, PAL—they *all* teach judo! It's all right, it's fine—until *black men* teach it! Even little grammar school classes, little girls, are taught to defend themselves—'

'How many of you are in your organization, Mr Malcolm X? Right Reverend Bishop T. Chickenwing says you have only a handful of members—'

'Whoever tells you how many Muslims there are doesn't know, and whoever does know will never tell you—'

The Bishop Chickenwings were also often quoted about our 'anti-Christianity.' I'd fire right back on that:

'Christianity is the white man's religion. The Holy Bible in the white man's hands and his interpretations of it have been the greatest single ideological weapon for enslaving millions of non-white human beings. Every country the white man has conquered with his guns, he has always paved the way, and salved his conscience, by carrying the Bible and interpreting it to call the people 'heathens' and 'pagans'; then he sends his guns, then his missionaries behind the guns to mop up—'

White reporters, anger in their voices, would call us 'demagogues,' and I would try to be ready after I had been asked the same question two or three times.

'Well, let's go back to the Greek, and maybe you will learn the first thing you need to know about the word "demagogue." "Demagogue" means, actually, "teacher of the people." And let's examine some demagogues. The greatest of all Greeks, Socrates, was killed as a "demagogue." Jesus Christ died on the cross because the Pharisees of His day were upholding their law, not the spirit. The modern Pharisees are trying to heap destruction upon Mr Muhammad, calling him a demagogue, a crackpot and fanatic. What about Gandhi? The man that Churchill called "a naked little fakir," refusing food in a British jail? But then a quarter of a billion people, a whole subcontinent, rallied behind Gandhi—and they twisted the British lion's tail! What about Galileo, standing before his inquisitors, saying "The earth *does* move!" What about Martin Luther, nailing on a door his thesis against the all-powerful Catholic church which called him "heretic"? We, the followers of The Honorable Elijah Muhammad, are today in the ghettoes as once the sect of Christianity's followers were like termites in the catacombs and the grottoes—and they were preparing the grave of the mighty Roman Empire!'

I can remember those hot telephone sessions with those reporters as if it were yesterday. The reporters were angry. I was angry. When I'd reach into history, they'd try to pull me back to the present. They would quit interviewing, quit their work, trying to defend their personal white devil selves. They would unearth Lincoln and his freeing of the slaves. I'd tell them things Lincoln said in speeches, *against* the blacks. They would drag up the 1954 Supreme Court decision on school integration.

'That was one of the greatest magical feats ever performed in America,' I'd tell them. 'Do you mean to tell me that nine Supreme Court judges, who are past masters of legal phraseology, couldn't have worked their decision to make it stick as *law?* No! It was trickery and magic that told Negroes they were desegregated—Hooray! Hooray!—and at the same time it told whites "Here are your loopholes." '

The reporters would try their utmost to raise some 'good' white man whom I couldn't refute as such. I'll never forget how one practically lost his voice. He asked me did I feel *any* white man had ever done anything for the black man in America. I told him, 'Yes, I can think of two. Hitler and Stalin. The black man in America couldn't get a decent factory job until Hitler put so much pressure on the white man. And then Stalin kept up the pressure—'

But I don't care what points I made in the interviews, it practically never got printed the way I said it. I was learning under fire how the press, when it wants to, can twist, and slant. If I had said 'Mary had a little lamb,' what probably would have appeared was 'Malcolm X Lampoons Mary.'

Even so, my bitterness was less against the white press than it was against those Negro 'leaders' who kept attacking us. Mr Muhammad said he wanted us to try our best not to publicly counterattack the black 'leaders' because one of the white man's tricks was keeping the black race divided and fighting against each other. Mr Muhammad said that this had traditionally kept the black people from achieving the unity which was the worst need of the black race in America.

But instead of abating, the black puppets continued ripping and tearing at Mr Muhammad and the Nation of Islam—until it began to appear as though we were afraid to speak out against these 'important' Negroes. That's when Mr Muhammad's patience wore thin. And with his nod, I began returning their fire.

'Today's Uncle Tom doesn't wear a handkerchief on his head. This modern, twentieth-century Uncle Thomas now often wears a top hat. He's usually well-dressed and well-educated. He's often the personification of culture and refinement. The twentieth-century Uncle Thomas sometimes speaks with a Yale or Harvard accent. Sometimes he is known as Professor, Doctor, Judge, and Reverend, even Right Reverend Doctor. This twentieth-century Uncle Thomas is a *professional* Negro . . . by that I mean his profession is being a Negro for the white man.'

Never before in America had these hand-picked so-called 'leaders' been publicly blasted in this way. They reacted to the truth about themselves even more hotly than the devilish white man. Now their 'institutional' indictments of us began. Instead of 'leaders' speaking as themselves, for themselves, now their weighty-name organizations attacked Mr. Muhammad.

'Black bodies with white heads!' I called them what they were. Every one of those 'Negro progress' organizations had the same composition.

Black 'leaders' were out in the public eye—to be seen by the Negroes for whom they were supposed to be fighting the white man. But obscurely, behind the scenes, was a white boss—a president, or board chairman, or a some other title, pulling the real strings.

It was hot, hot copy, both in the white and the black press. *Life, Look, Newsweek* and *Time* reported us. Some newspaper chains began to run not one story, but a series of three, four, or five 'exposures' of the Nation of Islam. The *Reader's Digest* with its worldwide circulation of twenty-four million copies in thirteen languages carried an article titled 'Mr. Muhammad Speaks,' by the writer to whom I am telling this book; and that led off other major monthly magazines' coverage of us.

Before very long, radio and television people began asking me to defend our Nation of Islam in panel discussions and debates. I was to be confronted by handpicked scholars, both whites and some of those Ph.D. 'house' and 'yard' Negroes who had been attacking us. Every day, I was more incensed with the general misrepresentation and distortion of Mr. Muhammad's teachings; I truly think that not once did it cross my mind that previously I never had been *inside* a radio or television station—let alone faced a microphone to audiences of millions of people. Prison debating had been my only experience speaking to anyone but Muslims.

From the old hustling days I knew that there were tricks to everything. In the prison debating, I had learned tricks to upset my opponents, to catch them where they didn't expect to be caught. I knew there were bound to be tricks I didn't know anything about in arguing on the air.

I knew that if I closely studied what the others did, I could learn things in a hurry to help me to defend Mr. Muhammad and his teachings.

I'd walk into those studios. The devils and black Ph.D. puppets would be acting so friendly and 'integrated' with each other—laughing and calling each other by first names, and all that; it was such a big lie it made me sick in my stomach. They would even be trying to act friendly toward me —we all knowing they had asked me there to try and beat out my brains. They would offer me coffee. I would tell them 'No, thanks,' to please just tell me where was I supposed to sit. Sometimes the microphone sat on the table before you, at other times a smaller, cylindrical microphone was hung on a cord around your neck. From the start, I liked those microphones better; I didn't have to keep constantly aware of my distance from a microphone on the table.

The program hosts would start with some kind of dice-loading, non-religious introduction for me. It would be something like'—and we have with us today the fiery, angry chief Malcolm X of the New York Muslims . . .'

I made up my own introduction. At home, or driving my car, I practiced until I could interrupt a radio or television host and introduce myself.

'I represent Mr. Elijah Muhammad, the spiritual head of the fastest-growing group of Muslims in the Western Hemisphere. We who follow him know that he has been divinely taught and sent to us by God Himself. We believe that the miserable plight of America's twenty million black people is the fulfillment of divine prophecy. We also believe the presence today in America of The Honorable Elijah Muhammad, his teachings among the so-called Negroes, and his naked warning to America concerning her treatment of these so-called Negroes, is all the fulfillment of divine prophecy. I am privileged to be the minister of our Temple Number Seven here in New York City which is a part of the Nation of Islam, under the divine leadership of The Honorable Elijah Muhammad—'

I would look around at those devils and their trained black parrots staring at me, while I was catching my breath—and I had set my tone.

They would outdo each other, leaping in on me, hammering at Mr. Muhammad, at me, and at the Nation of Islam. Those 'integration'-mad Negroes—you know what they jumped on. *Why* couldn't Muslims *see* that 'integration' was the answer to American Negroes' problems? . . .

---

[47]

WHAT IS SNCC?

SNCC STAFF MEMORANDUM

What Is SNCC?

SNCC is a group of organizers. In other words, SNCC is a staff and the staff's job is to organize. SNCC exists because a group of people decided to try to change something about the United States and to do it in a certain way.

SOURCE: SNCC Staff Memorandum, "What Is SNCC?" Mimeographed (n.p., 1964), pp. 1–2.

What Do We Organize?

We organize groups of people who feel the same needs. We organize them so they can gain enough power to get their needs met by people in this country who can meet their needs. These groups should be as independent as possible, should be led by people from within the group (rather than by the organizers or by "civil rights leaders"), and should develop programs themselves with our help.

The groups we organize should join together for strength. Thus an independent student union on a campus should be able to hook up with other student unions into a southwide student union or a statewide student union. A local political unit should be able to hook up to an FDP [Freedom Democratic Party] or other voters leagues in their congressional district. In other words, these groups should not affiliate with SNCC but with other groups like themselves. SNCC is the organizing group that helps them do this.

Where Do We Organize?

So far, we've organized mainly in rural areas and small towns in the Black Belt. There are, of course, other possibilities:

Urban South   We haven't had much luck here because 1) there is already an established, usually conservative leadership we have to fight and 2) the problems to be fought are complex. We should be thinking about the urban areas of the South because people are moving to cities. But we can't be all things to all men. Maybe we should have a pilot project that we really support and stay with in a city so we can learn more about how to work in urban areas.

Campuses   Certainly we should work to organize campuses. They should be organized around student problems, not problems we think are important and try to impose on them. Their problems are likely to be things like dress regulations, hours, academic freedom, even food. We can organize groups to deal with these problems within the context of democratic rights, as we do communities. They can hook up with each other on a statewide or southwide basis. We will relate to them through our campus organizers in the same way we relate to a community through our community organizers. Many of these students will be potential SNCC staff.

Northern Cities Friends of SNCC groups, we are told, want to engage in action. If we organize in the North, we should follow the same pattern as in the South . . . independent local groups. Friends' groups, who are organized to do fund raising and support work for SNCC, shouldn't be action groups. There is also the question of whether we should organize for action in the North at all. If we can't handle Southern urban areas, what are we doing in the North?

How Do We Organize?

We should organize in a way that allows local people to take the lead. We should make sure that local people understand each program we suggest and its implications. We should make sure we respect the way they think and work and not impose an organizing pattern that is foreign to them.

But all this is very abstract: everyone would agree. What we need to do is talk about what all this means *concretely*.

We should also organize with as little confusion and with as much staff democracy as possible.

Why Do We Organize?

Some of us organize because we grew up in left-wing homes and learned this was the thing to do. Some of us organize because we are angry about what has been done to us and others and organizing is a way to vent this anger. Some of us organize because we are tired of school. Some of us.
. . . .

The point is, very few of us organize out of any kind of pure motive. But most of us would agree that we want to see a world where people have control over the decisions that most effect them. We want a world where people grow up learning to care for others and learning many different things they can do with their lives rather than growing up learning to hate and being very limited in the choices they can make about their future.

We hope for this world, all of us (although we don't all believe it will ever really come about). And even though we and our programs are sometimes dull, or ugly, or too impatient, the hope is beautiful. Maybe we would be more patient with each other—and our organization would therefore become more democratic—if we remember that while we are all very different, we are joined together by a hope that is very beautiful.

THE BASIS OF BLACK POWER

SNCC STAFF WORKING PAPER

THE myth that the Negro is somehow incapable of liberating himself, is lazy, etc., came out of the American experience. In the books that children read, whites are always 'good' (good symbols are white), blacks are 'evil' or seen as savages in movies, their language is referred to as a 'dialect,' and black people in this country are supposedly descended from savages.

Any white person who comes into the movement has these concepts in his mind about black people, if only subconsciously. He can not escape them because the whole society has geared his subconscious in that direction.

Miss America coming from Mississippi has a chance to represent all of America, but a black person from either Mississippi or New York will never represent America. Thus the white people coming into the movement cannot relate to the black experience, cannot relate to the word 'black,' cannot relate to the 'nitty gritty,' cannot relate to the experience that brought such a word into existence, cannot relate to chitterlings, hog's head cheese, pig feet, ham hocks, and cannot relate to slavery, because these things are not a part of their experience. They also cannot relate to the black religious experience, nor to the black church, unless, of course, this church has taken on white manifestations.

White Power

Negroes in this country have never been allowed to organize themselves because of white interference. As a result of this, the stereotype has been reinforced that blacks cannot organize themselves. The white psychology that blacks have to be watched also reinforces this stereotype. Blacks, in fact, feel intimidated by the presence of whites, because of their knowledge of the power that whites have over their lives. One white person can come

SOURCE: SNCC Staff Working Paper, *The Basis of Black Power* (Ann Arbor: Radical Education Project, n.d.), pp. 1–4; first published in *The New York Times*, 5 August 1966.

into a meeting of black people and change the complexion of that meeting, whereas one black person would not change the complexion of that meeting unless he was an obvious Uncle Tom. People would immediately start talking about 'brotherhood,' 'love,' etc.; race would not be discussed.

If people must express themselves freely, there has to be a climate in which they can do this. If blacks feel intimidated by whites, then they are not liable to vent the rage that they feel about whites in the presence of whites—especially not the black people whom we are trying to organize, i.e., the broad masses of black people. A climate has to be created whereby blacks can express themselves. The reason that whites must be excluded is not that one is anti-white, but because the effects that one is trying to achieve cannot succeed because whites have an intimidating effect. Oft'times the intimidating effect is in direct proportion to the amount of degradation that black people have suffered at the hands of white people.

Roles of Whites and Blacks

It must be offered that white people who desire change in this country should go where that problem (racism) is most manifest. The problem is not in the black community. The white people should go into white communities where the whites have created power for the express purpose of denying blacks human dignity and self-determination. Whites who come into the black community with ideas of change seem to want to absolve the power structure of its responsibility for what it is doing, and saying that change can only come through black unity, which is the worst kind of paternalism. This is not to say that whites have not had an important role in the movement. In the case of Mississippi, their role was very key in that they helped give blacks the right to organize, but that role is now over, and it should be.

People now have the right to picket, the right to give out leaflets, the right to vote, the right to demonstrate, the right to print.

These things which revolve around the right to organize have been accomplished mainly because of the entrance of white people into Mississippi, in the summer of 1964. Since these goals have now been accomplished, whites' role in the movement has now ended. What does it mean if black people, once having the right to organize, are not allowed to organize themselves? It means that blacks' ideas about inferiority are being reinforced. Shouldn't people be able to organize themselves? Blacks should be given this right. Further, white participation means in the eyes of the black community that whites are the 'brains' behind the movement, and that blacks cannot function without whites. This only serves to perpetuate existing attitudes within the existing society, i.e., blacks are 'dumb,' 'unable to take care of business,' etc. Whites are 'smart,' the 'brains' behind the whole thing.

How do blacks relate to other blacks as such? How do we react to Willie Mays as against Mickey Mantle? What is our response to Mays hitting a home run against Mantle performing the same deed? One has to come to the conclusion that it is because of black participation in baseball. Negroes still identify with the Dodgers because of Jackie Robinson's efforts with the Dodgers. Negroes would instinctively champion all-black teams if they opposed all-white or predominantly white teams. The same principle operates for the movement as it does for baseball: a mystique must be created whereby Negroes can identify with the movement.

Thus an all-black project is needed in order for the people to free themselves. This has to exist from the beginning. This relates to what can be called 'coalition politics.' There is no doubt in our minds that some whites are just as disgusted with this system as we are. But it is meaningless to talk about coalition if there is no one to align ourselves with, because of the lack of organization in the white communities. There can be no talk of 'hooking up' unless black people organize blacks and white people organize whites. If these conditions are met, then perhaps at some later date —and if we are going in the same direction—talks about exchange of personnel, coalition, and other meaningful alliances can be discussed.

In the beginning of the movement, we had fallen into a trap whereby we thought that our problems revolved around the right to eat at certain lunch counters or the right to vote, or to organize our communities. We have seen, however, that the problem is much deeper. The problem of this country, as we had seen it, concerned all blacks and all whites and therefore if decisions were left to the young people, then solutions would be arrived at. But this negates the history of black people and whites. We have dealt stringently with the problem of 'Uncle Tom,' but we have not yet gotten around to Simon Legree. We must ask ourselves, Who is the real villain—Uncle Tom or Simon Legree? Everybody knows Uncle Tom, but who knows Simon Legree? So what we have now in SNCC is a closed society, a clique. Black people cannot relate to SNCC because of its unrealistic, nonracial atmosphere; denying their experiences of America as a racist society. In contrast, the Southern Christian Leadership Conference of Martin Luther King, Jr., has a staff that at least maintains a black façade.

The front office is virtually all black, but nobody accuses SCLC of being racist.

If we are to proceed toward true liberation, we must cut ourselves off from white people. We must form our own institutions, credit unions, co-ops, political parties, write our own histories.

To proceed further, let us make some comparisons between the Black Movement of the early 1900's and the movement of the 1960's—i.e., compare the National Association for the Advancement of Colored People with SNCC. Whites subverted the Niagara movement (the forerunner of the NAACP) which, at the outset, was an all-black movement. The name of the new organization was also very revealing, in that it pre-supposed blacks have to be advanced to the level of whites. We are now aware that the NAACP has grown reactionary, is controlled by the black power structure itself, and stands as one of the main roadblocks to black freedom. SNCC, by allowing the whites to remain in the organization, can have its efforts subverted in the same manner, i.e., through having them play important roles such as community organizers, etc. Indigenous leadership cannot be built with whites in the positions they now hold.

These facts do not mean that whites cannot help. They can participate on a voluntary basis. We can contract work out to them, but in no way can they participate on a policy-making level.

Black Self-Determination

The charge may be made that we are 'racists,' but whites who are sensitive to our problems will realize that we must determine our own destiny.

In an attempt to find a solution to our dilemma, we propose that our organization (SNCC) should be black-staffed, black-controlled, and black-financed. We do not want to fall into a similar dilemma that other civil rights organizations have fallen into. If we continue to rely upon white financial support we will find ourselves entwined in the tentacles of the white power complex that controls this country. It is also important that a black organization (devoid of cultism) be projected to our people so that it can be demonstrated that such organizations are viable.

More and more we see black people in this country being used as a tool of the white liberal establishment. Liberal whites have not begun to address themselves to the real problem of black people in this country— witness their bewilderment, fear, and anxiety when nationalism is mentioned concerning black people. An analysis of the white liberal's reaction to the word 'nationalism' alone reveals a very meaningful attitude of whites of any ideological persuasion toward blacks in this country. It means previous solutions to black problems in this country have been made in the interests of those whites dealing with these problems and not in the best interests of black people in this country. Whites can only subvert our true search and struggle for self-determination, self-identification, and liberation in this country. Reevaluation of the white and black roles must NOW take place so that whites no longer designate roles that black people play but rather black people define white people's roles.

Too long have we allowed white people to interpret the importance and meaning of the cultural aspects of our society. We have allowed them to tell us what was good about our Afro-American music, art, and literature. How many black critics do we have on the 'jazz' scene? How can a white person who is not part of the black psyche (except in the oppressor's role) interpret the meaning of the blues to us who are manifestations of the songs themselves?

It must be pointed out that on whatever level of contact blacks and whites come together, that meeting or confrontation is not on the level of the blacks but always on the level of the whites. This only means that our everyday contact with whites is a reinforcement of the myth of white supremacy. Whites are the ones who must try to raise themselves to our humanistic level. We are not, after all, the ones who are responsible for a genocidal war in Vietnam; we are not the ones who are responsible for neocolonialism in Africa and Latin America; we are not the ones who held a people in animalistic bondage over 400 years. We reject the American dream as defined by white people and must work to construct an American reality defined by Afro-Americans.

White Radicals

One of the criticisms of white militants and radicals is that when we view the masses of white people we view the overall reality of America, we view the racism, the bigotry, and the distortion of personality, we view man's inhumanity to man; we view in reality 180 million racists. The sensitive white intellectual and radical who is fighting to bring about change is conscious of this fact, but does not have the courage to admit this. When he admits this reality, then he must also admit his involvement because he is a part of the collective white America. It is only to the extent that he recognizes this that he will be able to change this reality.

Another common concern is, how does the white radical view the black community, and how does he view the poor white community, in terms of organizing? So far, we have found that most white radicals have sought to escape the horrible reality of America by going into the black community and attempting to organize black people while neglecting the organization of their own people's racist communities. How can one clean up someone else's yard when one's own yard is untidy? Again we feel that SNCC and the civil rights movement in general are in many aspects similar to the anti-colonial situations in the African and Asian countries. We have the whites in the movement corresponding to the white civil servants and missionaries in the colonial countries who have worked with the colonial people for a long period of time and have developed a paternalistic attitude toward them. The reality of the colonial people taking over their own lives and controlling their own destiny must be faced. Having to move aside and letting the natural process of growth and development take place must be faced.

These views should not be equated with outside influence or outside agitation but should be viewed as the natural process of growth and development within a movement; so that the move by the black militants and SNCC in this direction should be viewed as a turn toward self-determination.

It is very ironic and curious that aware whites in this country can champion anticolonialism in other countries in Africa, Asia, and Latin America, but when black people move toward similar goals of self-determination in this country they are viewed as racists and anti-white by these same progressive whites. In proceeding further, it can be said that this attitude derives from the overall point of view of the white psyche as it concerns the black people. This attitude stems from the era of the slave revolts when every white man was a potential deputy or sheriff or guardian of the state. Because when black people got together among themselves to work out their problems, it became a threat to white people, because such meetings were potential slave revolts.

It can be maintained that this attitude or way of thinking has perpetuated itself to this current period and that it is part of the psyche of white people in this country whatever their political persuasion might be. It is part of the white fear—guilt complex resulting from the slave revolts. There have been examples of whites who stated that they can deal with black fellows on an individual basis but become threatened or menaced by the presence of groups of blacks. It can be maintained that this attitude is held by the majority of progressive whites in this country.

Black Identity

A thorough re-examination must be made by black people concerning the contributions that we have made in shaping this country. If this re-examination and re-evaluation is not made, and black people are not given their proper due and respect, then the antagonisms and contradictions are going to become more and more glaring, more and more intense, until a national explosion may result.

When people attempt to move from these conclusions it would be faulty reasoning to say they are ordered by racism, because, in this country and in the West, racism has functioned as a type of white nationalism when dealing with black people. We all know the habit that this has created throughout the world and particularly among nonwhite people in this country.

Therefore any re-evaluation that we must make will, for the most part, deal with identification. Who are black people, what are black people, what is their relationship to America and the world?

It must be repeated that the whole myth of 'Negro citizenship,' perpetuated by the white elite, has confused the thinking of radical and progressive blacks and whites in this country. The broad masses of black people react to American society in the same manner as colonial peoples react to the West in Africa, and Latin America, and had the same relationship— that of the colonized toward the colonizer.

---

[49]

DIE NIGGER DIE!

H. RAP BROWN

RACISM stems from an attitude and it can't be destroyed under the capitalist system. You can't fight attitudes. If white people want to address themselves to that, fine. They're the ones with the attitude, but the Black Movement cannot address itself to attitudes. Fuck attitudes. Fuck a

SOURCE: H. Rap Brown, *Die Nigger Die!* (New York: Dial Press, 1970), pp. 98–101.

muthafucka who hates me, because if I ever get him on the wrong end of my gun he's in trouble. But Black people have always dealt with attitudes and attitudes always boil down to an individual thing. Change the laws and enforce 'em and let the attitudes take care of themselves. Because most of the laws in this country are built on attitudes, not justice, not equality, revolution is necessary. Racism, capitalism, colonialism and imperialism dominate the lives of people of color around the world—the people of Africa, Asia, Latin America, the colonized minorities who live inside the united states. Fanon says of racism, "It stares one in the face for it so happens that it belongs in a characteristic whole: that of the shameless exploitation of one group of men by another which has reached a higher stage of technical development. That is why military and economic oppression generally precedes, makes possible and legitimatizes racism. The habit of considering racism as a mental quirk, as a psychological flaw, must be abandoned." Racism does not operate as an individual force, it is an integral part of colonial oppression. We must understand that all colonized people are victims of racism and exploitation, but that all exploited people are not colonized. For instance, inside the united states we see some whites who are oppressed and who are exploited, but they do not suffer from the racism which is forced upon Blacks by whites, they in fact form a part of the colonizing race. Some of the most racist whites are the oppressed whites.

Our job is not to convert whites. If whites are dedicated to revolution then they can be used in the struggle. However, if they impede the struggle and are proven to be a problem then it is up to us to deal with them as with all problems. Our job now is to project what should be our common goal—the destruction of a system that makes slavery profitable.

Now there're a lot of people who say that the way you change laws is to destroy the power structure. I say you got to go beyond that. If you destroy the power structure, it can always be replaced by another power structure, whether it's white or Black. The power structure serves the system and the system is the thing which demands exploitation of people. You have to destroy the system. You can destroy the power structure and leave the system intact. But if you get the system, you got the power structure. That's the job which confronts us.

However we may twist our words and regardless of our personal, subjective feelings—the truth of the matter is that we cannot end racism, capitalism, colonialism and imperialism until the reins of state power are in the hands of those people who understand that the wealth, the total wealth of any country and the world, belongs equally to all people. Societies and countries based on the profit motive will never insure a new humanism or eliminate poverty and racism. However we may twist our words and regardless of our personal feelings—the stark reality remains that the power necessary to end racism, colonialism, capitalism and imperialism will only come through long, protracted, bloody, brutal and violent wars with our oppressors.

Liberation movements must be based upon political principles that give meaning and substance to the struggle of the masses of people, and it is this struggle that advances the creation of a people's ideology. Liberation movements from the very beginning must be dedicated to principles that speak to the needs of the poor and oppressed, or must evolve into this type of movement with these principles while the fighting is going on, for it is not evident that those who fight will assume power and implement decisions that appropriate the wealth of countries for all people. Rather to the contrary: the absence of these revolutionary political principles relates to the fact that some new rulers have settled for a new flag, a new style of dress, a seat in the UN, and/or accommodation with former colonial powers. A negotiated independence.

We must draw from all ideologies those principles which benefit the majority of mankind. We cannot limit ourselves to just one concept or ideology that was relevant in some other revolution. As Debray points out, and correctly so, in his book *Revolution within the Revolution:* "Revolutions cannot be imported nor exported." Certain changes have made even some of the most advanced ideologies obsolete. For example, socialism as it exists today *ideologically* may be impractical for certain oppressed peoples. But the political principles of socialism certainly have validity. This is why in Cuba and other liberated countries the principles of socialism are being incorporated into the ideologies of these countries. This again goes back to Fanon's observation that we must extend the Marxian analysis when we view colonialism. It is the political principles that make the ideology; as these principles are refined through struggle an ideology is created.

Many people have had these principles (principles that speak to the needs of the mass of humanity) in mind as they were waging a struggle for independence, but having failed to win independence by defeating the enemy through armed struggle, it was necessary for them to negotiate with the colonial powers. In this process of negotiation, the colonial powers granted political autonomy but maintained economic influence, control and investments. The mere act of negotiating freedom means that the control necessary to appropriate the entire wealth of the country did not fall to the new leaders. We should have learned by now from history that the process of negotiating freedom and not winning it by armed struggle has built-in limitations. We must be prepared to fight to the death to destroy this system known as capitalism, for it is this system that oppresses the majority of mankind.

Vanguard groups must begin to re-evaluate politics. What is known as politics in this country is meaningless. People have been told that politics means the Democratic and Republican parties; federal, state and local government; the vote. History shows that politics as it is defined by america is undesirable and dangerous to Black people, for the politics of capitalism has always been human oppression and exploitation. We must begin to relate to the politics of revolution. Chairman Mao says, "Politics is war without bloodshed and war is an extension of politics." Every action that we are involved in is political, whether it is religious, artistic, cultural, athletic, governmental, educational, economic or personal. There is no separation between church and state, art and politics, or politics and individual beliefs. Everything is inherently political. The only division occurs around the question of whose political interest one will serve.

---

[50]

WHAT WE WANT NOW! WHAT WE BELIEVE

THE BLACK PANTHER PARTY

What We Want

1. We want freedom. We want power to determine the destiny of our black community.
2. We want full employment for our people.
3. We want an end to the robbery by the white man of our black community.
4. We want decent housing, fit for shelter of human beings.
5. We want education for our people that exposes the true nature of this

SOURCE: "What We Want Now! What We Believe," *The Black Panther*, 16 March 1968, p. 4. Reprinted by permission of the Black Panther Party.

decadent American society. We want education that teaches us our true history and our role in the present-day society.

6. We want all black men to be exempt from military service.
7. We want an immediate end to *police brutality* and *murder* of black people.
8. We want freedom for all black men held in federal, state, county, and city prisons and jails.
9. We want all black people when brought to trial to be tried in court by a jury of their peer group or people from their black communities, as defined by the Constitution of the United States.
10. We want land, bread, housing, education, clothing, justice and peace.

What We Believe

1. We believe that black people will not be free until we are able to determine our destiny.
2. We believe that the federal government is responsible and obligated to give every man employment or a guaranteed income. We believe that if the white American businessmen will not give full employment, then the means of production should be taken from the businessmen and placed in the community so that the people of the community can organize and employ all of its people and give a high standard of living.
3. We believe that this racist government has robbed us and now we are demanding the overdue debt of forty acres and two mules. Forty acres and two mules was promised 100 years ago as retribution for slave labor and mass murder of black people. We will accept the payment in currency which will be distributed to our many communities. The Germans are now aiding the Jews in Israel for the genocide of the Jewish people. The Germans murdered 6,000,000 Jews. The American racist has taken part in the slaughter of over 50,000,000 black people; therefore, we feel that this is a modest demand that we make.
4. We believe that if the white landlords will not give decent housing to our black community, then the housing and the land should be made into cooperatives so that our community, with government aid, can build and make decent housing for its people.
5. We believe in an educational system that will give to our people a knowledge of self. If a man does not have knowledge of himself and his position in society and the world, then he has little chance to relate to anything else.

374

6. We believe that black people should not be forced to fight in the military service to defend a racist government that does not protect us. We will not fight and kill other people of color in the world who, like black people, are being victimized by the white racist government of America. We will protect ourselves from the force and violence of the racist police and the racist military, by whatever means necessary.

7. We believe we can end police brutality in our black community by organizing black *self-defense* groups that are dedicated to defending our black community from racist police oppression and brutality. The Second Amendment of the Constitution of the United States gives us a right to bear arms. We therefore believe that all black people should arm themselves for *self-defense*.

8. We believe that all black people should be released from the many jails and prisons because they have not received a fair and impartial trial.

9. We believe that the courts should follow the United States Constitution so that black people will receive fair trials. The 14th Amendment of the U.S. Constitution gives a man a right to be tried by his peer group. A peer is a person from a similar economic, social, religious, geographical, environmental, historical and racial background. To do this the court will be forced to select a jury from the black community from which the black defendant came. We have been and are being tried by all white juries that have no understanding of the "average reasoning man" of the black community.

10. When in the course of human events, it becomes necessary for one people to dissolve the political bonds which have connected them with another, and to assume among the powers of the earth, the separate and equal station to which the laws of nature and nature's God entitle them, a decent respect to the opinions of mankind requires that they should declare the causes which impel them to separation. We hold these truths to be self-evident, that all men are created equal, that they are endowed by their Creator with certain inalienable rights, that among these are life, liberty and the pursuit of happiness. That to secure these rights, governments are instituted among men, deriving their just powers from the consent of the governed,—that *whenever any form of government becomes destructive of these ends, it is the right of people to alter or to abolish it, and to institute new government, laying its foundation on such principles and organizing its powers in such form as to them shall seem most likely to effect their safety and happiness.*

Prudence, indeed, will dictate that governments long established should not be changed for light and transient causes; and accordingly all experience hath shewn, that mankind are more disposed to suffer, while evils are sufferable, than to right themselves by abolishing the forms to which they are accustomed. *But when a long train of abuses and usurpations, pursuing invariably the same object, evinces a design to reduce them under absolute despotism, it is their right, it is their duty, to throw off such government, and to provide new guards for their future security.*

---

[51]

SHOOT-OUT IN OAKLAND

ELDRIDGE CLEAVER

I think that the so-called shoot-out on 28th Street was the direct result of frantic attempts by the Oakland Police Department to sabotage the Black Community Barbecue Picnic, which the Black Panther Party had set up for April 7th in DeFremery Park. The shoot-out occurred the night before the scheduled picnic. We had been advertising the barbecue picnic over the radio (KDIA & KSOL) and we had leafleted the community very heavily and put up many posters, inviting the community to come out and share in the picnic. Also, members of the Black Panther Party had been driving all over East and West Oakland in a sound truck, for a week, telling the people about the picnic and inviting them to come out.

The barbecue picnic was a fund raiser for the Black Panther Party Campaign Fund and for the Huey P. Newton Defense Fund. We were uptight for funds for both of these operations. We were running three candidates for public office: Huey P. Newton for Congress in the 7th Congressional District of Alameda County; Bobby Seale for the 17th Assembly District seat in Alameda County; and Kathleen Cleaver for the 18th Assembly District seat in San Francisco. These campaigns were being run on less than a shoestring, and we came up with the idea of the barbecue picnic hoping to raise a little money. And, of course, there was a constant need of funds for Huey's defense.

SOURCE: Eldridge Cleaver, *Post-Prison Writings and Speeches,* ed. Robert Scheer (London: Jonathan Cape, Ltd., 1969), pp. 80–94. Copyright 1967, 1968, 1969 by Eldridge Cleaver. Reprinted by permission of Random House, Inc.

We knew that the Oakland Police Department was against the picnic because at first they tried to block clearance when we sought it from the park authorities to hold the picnic at DeFremery Park. They failed in that, but they did succeed in getting the park authorities to impose a lot of ridiculous and crippling rules upon us, such as no speeches at the park, no sound equipment, no passing out of campaign literature, etc. Also, there was constant harassment of the brothers and sisters who were operating the sound truck, and members of the Oakland Police Department had been very active in tearing down the posters we put up to advertise the picnic, just as they had been tearing down the posters we put up to advertise Huey and Bobby's political campaigns. Oakland police were also stopping and harassing party members whom they observed putting up these posters or passing out leaflets. We had invested about $300 in the picnic, so we were anxious for it to come off successfully and without incident.

We had noticed that whenever we staged a large fund-raising event, the Oakland police would move, first, to try to prevent it from happening; then, failing that, they would arrest a lot of party members and drain off whatever money was raised because we would then have to bail these party members out of jail and there were legal fees. We became very aware of this. This became very clear to us when we staged the Huey P. Newton Birthday Benefit Rally at the Oakland Auditorium on February 17. At first the Oakland police tried to refuse us the use of the auditorium on the grounds that such a rally would be a public nuisance and create a dangerous situation. We had to get Attorney John George to go down with us and threaten Mr. Luddekke, who operates the auditorium for the City of Oakland, with a civil suit, before they backed up and agreed to allow us the use of the facility. Even so, within a week after the rally, the Oakland Police Department and the Berkeley Police Department arrested a total of sixteen members of our party, including the notorious incident in which our Chairman, Bobby Seale, and his wife Artie were dragged from their bed in the wee hours of the morning and charged with conspiracy to commit murder. There was a lot of public outcry against the police for this blatant harassment and frameup and that charge was quickly dropped. But what a lot of people don't understand is that it was also very expensive to us. Even though the ridiculous charge was dropped, the real purpose of the cops was achieved successfully: to drain away our funds through exorbitant bails and legal fees.

So, in staging the barbecue picnic, we had this experience in mind, and we had cautioned all party members to be on their best behavior in order to avoid any incidents with the police that would provide a pretext for arrest.

Here I have to bring up the name of Captain McCarthy of the Oakland Police Department, because he is one of the chief instigators within the OPD against the Black Panther Party and he has a special grudge against me. When we were making the preliminary arrangements for the rally at the Oakland Auditorium, Mr. Luddekke kept urging us to get in touch with a Sergeant White of the OPD to discuss matters of security with him. Such a discussion seemed disgusting to us at first so we avoided it, but as the date of the rally drew nearer it was clear that it would be best if the matter were dealt with, so on either February 16th or 17th, I can't remember which, I called the number given me by Mr. Luddekke, talked to Sergeant White, and made an appointment to meet with him to discuss the subject of security at the auditorium during the rally.

Another member of the Black Panther Party, Mr. Emory Douglass, who is our Revolutionary Artist, accompanied me to this meeting, which was held at the headquarters of the Oakland Police Department. When we arrived there, we were met in the lobby by Sergeant White, who took us in to talk to a Captain McCarthy. Entering the room where Captain McCarthy was waiting, Sergeant White introduced us. Captain McCarthy stuck out his big ham of a hand to shake mine. I declined, to which the captain responded: "What's the matter, you too good to shake my hand or something?"

I replied: "In view of the present relationship between your organization and mine, I think that our shaking hands would be out of order."

The captain stared into my eyes. His were cold and murder blue, and his fat neck, stuffed inside his shirt and choked with his tie, turned red, the color creeping all the way up from his adam's apple to his face and I could see that it took an effort, or a sense of a more urgent interest, to keep him from throwing us out of his office. I made a mental note then to stay out of this pig's way because he was not likely either to forgive or forget me.

Two months later, this captain, backed up by a phalanx of Oakland cops with shotguns levelled at the ready, tried to kick down the door to St. Augustine's Church on 27th and West Street in Oakland and terrorized one of our meetings. On this raid, the captain brought with him and his pigs a white priest and a black preacher, and he used them to try to cool down Reverend Neil, whose church it was and who would not be cooled down by the pious entreaties of the captain's anointed accomplices. This occurred on April 3, three days before this same captain, this time with an army of pigs, directed the murderous attack upon members of the Black Panther Party in which one party member, Bobby Hutton, was viciously and wantonly shot to death by racist pigs who had long lain in wait for a chance to shed the blood of the Black Panthers.

On the night the pigs murdered Little Bobby, we had all been very busy making last minute arrangements for the barbecue picnic scheduled for the next day. The Brother who owns the Soul Food restaurant next to our office at 41st and Grove Street in Oakland was cooking the meat for us and we were running sisters back and forth between the restaurant, the stores, and David Hilliard's house at 34th and Magnolia Street where we were assembling the supplies for the next day.

The cops had been following our cars around all day long. During the day, several different cop cars, at different times, had parked directly across the street from our office and made no secret of the fact that they were watching us, with ugly pig scowls on their faces, that look that says to a black man, "I don't like you, nigger, and I'm watching you, just waiting for one false move." Increasingly, the cops had been following me around so much that I had learned to ignore them and to go on about my business as though they did not even exist.

A white man in Berkeley, who sympathized with the work that our party was doing and who wanted to help us out, called us up one day and said that he had read in our paper that we needed transportation badly and offered to give us two cars. I know that we got one of the promised cars, a white Ford several years old but in good shape, but I do not know if we ever got the other. This was a big help to us but also a headache, because the car had a Florida license plate and none of the brothers liked to drive it because you would invariably be stopped by the cops, particularly when driving through Oakland, and they would use the Florida license plate as a pretext for stopping the car. It took only a few days for the word to get around amongst the Oakland cops that the Panthers had a white Ford with a Florida license plate, and from then on the car was marked. For this reason, I took the responsibility of using the car most of the time because I had what is considered good I.D.—driver's license, draft card, Social Security card, and a variety of press cards from my job at *Ramparts* magazine. I even had one press card issued to me by the United Nations, guaranteed to slow down the already sluggish mental process of a pig cop, especially a dumb Oakland pig. Several brothers had been stopped driving this car and the cops put them through all kinds of changes: "Are you from Florida? How long have you been in California?" Once an Oakland cop stopped me in this car, and when he asked me whose car it was I told him that a white man from Florida had given it to the Black Panther Party. This seemed to make him very mad, and he said: "You expect me to believe that story? No white man in his right mind would give the Black Panthers a car."

"Maybe this white man is crazy," I said to him.

Anyway, that's why I started using this car more frequently than any of the others we had available to the party.

It is a rule of our party that no well known member of the party is to be out on the Oakland streets at night unless accompanied by two or more other people, because we felt that if the Oakland cops ever caught one of us alone like that there was a chance that such a one might be killed and there would be only racist pig cops for witnesses: Verdict of the Coroner's Inquest, "Justifiable Homicide." Period. After the way they tried to murder our leader, Minister of Defense Huey P. Newton, we were not taking any chances. So on the night of April 6, the car I was driving was being followed by two carloads of Panthers and I was on my way to David Hilliard's house at 34th and Magnolia. In the car with me were David Hilliard, Wendell Wade, and John Scott, all members of the Black Panther Party.

We were only a few blocks away from David's house when, all of a sudden, I was overcome by an irresistible urge, a necessity, to urinate, and so I turned off the brightly lighted street we were on (I think it was 30th Street, but I'm not sure, not being overly familiar with the area), pulled to the curb, stopped the car, got out and started relieving myself. The two Panther cars following us pulled up behind to wait. While I was in the middle of this call of nature, a car came around the corner from the direction that we ourselves had come, and I found myself in danger of being embarrassed, I thought by a passing car. So I cut off the flow, then, and awkwardly hurried around to the other side of the car, to the sidewalk, to finish what had already been started and what was most difficult to stop— I recall that I did soil my trousers somewhat. But this car, instead of passing, stopped, and a spotlight from it was turned on and beamed my way. I could see it was the cops, two of them. They got out of the car and stood there, not leaving the car, each standing just outside. One of them shouted, "Hey, you, walk out into the middle of the street with your hands up, quick!"

For the second time, I had to deal with a ticklish situation and I was so close to the end that I could not resist finishing. I shouted back to the cops, "O.K., O.K.!" I turned, trying to zip up my fly and get out into the middle of the street. Common sense told me that I'd best have my hands up by the time I cleared the front of my car. But before I cleared, the cop on the passenger side of his car started shouting and firing his gun, and then the other cop started shooting. I am not sure they were shooting at me because the lights from their car were shining brightly at me, blocking my vision. But the explosions from their guns sounded right in my face and so, startled, I dove for cover in front of my car. The Panthers in the other two cars started yelling at the cops and honking their horns and getting out of their cars, and the brothers who were in my car scrambled out of the passenger side.

Above my head, the windshield of my car shattered and I looked behind me. There was another cop car at the other end of the street, from which shots were also being fired at us. In fact, shots seemed to be coming from everywhere; it sounded like the entire block had erupted with gunfire. It took only a split second to see that they had us in a cross fire, so I shouted to the brothers, "Scatter! Let's get out of here!" Our best bet, it was clear, was to make it across the street and that's where we headed. As we started across, one of the Panthers, Warren Wells, got hit and let out an agonized yelp of pain as he fell to the ground. I dove for the pavement, in about the middle of the street, with bullets ricocheting off the pavement all around me and whizzing past my head. I was being fired at from several different directions and for the second time within the space of a few minutes I could taste death on my tongue. But I kept crawling across the street as fast as I could and I truthfully didn't know whether I had been hit or not, whether I was dead or dying. I was hurting all over from scraping against the pavement and I was still being shot at. I saw a couple of Panthers run between two houses and got to my feet and followed them. A cop with a shotgun was running after me, shooting. I didn't have a gun but I wished that I had! (O, how I wish that I had!!!)

As I ran between those two houses, I saw a Panther climbing over what looked like a fence. I hit it just as soon as he was over, only to find out, as I climbed up, that it was some sort of a shed and I was on top of it and the cop behind me was still shooting at me with the shotgun. I dove off and onto the ground on the other side, landing on top of Bobby Hutton. Before I had recovered from the jolt of my leap, I was wishing that I had never come over the top of that shed, that I had stayed there to face that cop with that blazing shotgun, because Little Bobby and I were boxed in. The shed at our backs spanned the space between the houses on either side of us, and although the area in front of us was clear all the way out to the street, we could not budge from that little nook because the street was filled with cops and they were pumping shots at us as though shooting was about to go out of style. In the dark, I could not see that Little Bobby had a rifle until it started to bark, producing a miraculous effect: the cops, cowardly pigs from their flat feet to their thick heads, all ran for cover. The few seconds that this gave us allowed us to find a door into the basement of the house to our right, and we dove inside. We were just in time to escape a murderous fusillade of shots that scoured the tiny area we had just abandoned.

But if jumping over the shed had been like going from the frying pan into the fire, entering that house defies description. The walls were like tissue paper and the pigs were shooting through them from all four sides at once. It was like being the Indians in all the cowboy movies I had ever seen. What saved us for the moment was an eighteen-inch-high cement foundation running around the cellar at the base of the wall. We lay down flat against the floor while the bullets ripped through the walls. This unrelenting fire went on for about half an hour, and then it stopped and the pigs started lobbing in tear gas. While the gas was being pumped in through the windows, Little Bobby and I took the opportunity to fortify the walls with whatever we could lay our hands on: furniture, tin cans, cardboard boxes—it was hopeless but we tried it anyway. While I was standing up trying to move a thick board over against the wall, I was struck in the chest by a tear gas canister fired through a window. It knocked me down and almost out. Little Bobby, weak from the gas, was coughing and choking, but he took all my clothes off in an effort to locate a wound in the dark, patting me down for the moist feel of blood.

The pigs started shooting again and we had to hit the deck. The material we had stacked along the wall was blown away by what sounded like machine gun fire. We decided to stay in there and choke to death if necessary rather than walk out into a hail of bullets. Above the din of gunfire, we could hear the voices of people yelling at the cops to stop shooting, calling them murderers and all kinds of names, and this gave us the strength and the hope to hang on. The tear gas was not as hard to endure as I had imagined it to be. My lungs were on fire, nose and eyes burning, but after a while I couldn't feel anything. Once Little Bobby told me he was about to pass out. He did, but he came to before long, and the two of us lay there counting the minutes and ducking the bullets that were too numerous to count. One of the shots found my leg and my foot with an impact so painful and heavy that I was sure I no longer had two legs. But it didn't seem to matter because I was also sure that it was only a matter of seconds before one of the bullets found a more vital spot. In my mind, I was actually saying goodbye to the world and I was sure that Little Bobby was doing the same thing. Lying there pinned down like that, there was nothing else to do. If there was I couldn't think of it. I said goodbye to my wife, and an image of her dancing for me, as I had watched her do so many times before, floated past my mind's eye, and I reached out to touch her, to kiss her goodbye with my fingers. Then my mind seemed to dwell on crowds of people, masses of people, millions of people, as though the whole human race, all the men and women who had ever lived, seemed to present themselves to my view. I saw images of parades, crowd scenes in auditoriums. I remembered the people at the rally in the Oakland Auditorium, the surging, twisting sea of people at the Peace and Freedom Party Convention at the Richmond Auditorium; these two events somehow coupled in my mind. I saw throngs of students at Merritt College, at San Francisco State College, and at UC Berkeley, and then I heard Little Bobby ask me, "What are we going to do?"

I felt an impotent rage at myself because all I could tell him was to keep his head down, that head with its beautiful black face which I would watch a little later, again powerless, as the mad dogs outside blasted him into eternity. Was it in cold blood? It was in the coldest of blood. It was murder. MURDER! and that must never be forgotten: the Oakland Police Department MURDERED Little Bobby, and they cannot have that as a victory. Every pig on that murderous police force is guilty of murdering Little Bobby; and lying, hypocritical Chief Gains is Murderer No. 1. And we must all swear by Little Bobby's blood that we will not rest until Chief Gains is brought to justice, either in the courts or in the streets; and until the bloodthirsty troops of the Oakland Police Department no longer exist in the role of an occupying army with its boots on the neck of the black community, with its guns aimed at the black community's head, an evil force with its sword of terror thrust into the heart of the black community. That's what Little Bobby would ask you to do, Brothers and Sisters, put an end to the terror—by any means necessary. All he asks, all Huey asks, all I ask, is what Che Guevera asked:

> *Wherever Death may surprise us*
> *It will be welcome, provided that*
> *This, our battle cry, reach some*
> *Receptive ear; that another hand*
> *Reach out to pick up the gun, that*
> *Other fighting men come forward*
> *To intone our funeral dirge*
> *To the staccato of machine gun fire*
> *And new cries of battle and victory.*

The rest of the story is madness, pain, and humiliation at the hands of the pigs. They shot firebombs into the cellar, turning it into a raging inferno, and we could not stand the heat, could not breathe the hot air with lungs already raw from the tear gas. We had to get out of there, to flee from certain death to face whatever awaited us outside. I called out to the pigs and told them that we were coming out. They said to throw out the guns. I was lying beneath a window, so Little Bobby passed me the rifle and I threw it outside, still lying on my back. Then Little Bobby helped me to my feet and we tumbled through the door. There were pigs in the windows above us in the house next door, with guns pointed at us. They told us not to move, to raise our hands. This we did, and an army of pigs ran up from the street. They started kicking and cursing us, but we were already beyond any pain, beyond feeling. The pigs told us to stand up. Little Bobby helped me to my feet. The pigs pointed to a squad car parked in the middle of the street and told us to run to it. I told them that I couldn't run. Then they snatched Little Bobby away from me and shoved him forward, telling him to run to the car. It was a sickening sight. Little Bobby, coughing and choking on the night air that was burning his lungs as my own were burning from the tear gas, stumbled forward as best he could, and after he had traveled about ten yards the pigs cut loose on him with their guns, and then they turned to me. But before they could get into anything, the black people in the neighborhood who had been drawn to the site by the gunfire and commotion began yelling at them, calling the pigs murderers, telling them to leave me alone. And a face I will never forget, the face of the captain with the murder blue eyes, loomed up.

"Where are you wounded?" he asked me.

I pointed out my wound to him. The Pig of Pigs looked down at my wound, raised his foot and stomped on the wound.

"Get him out of here," he told the other pigs, and they took me away.

Why am I alive? While at Highland Hospital, a pig said to me: "You ain't going to be at no barbecue picnic tomorrow. You the barbecue now!" Why did Little Bobby die? It was not a miracle, it just happened that way. I know my duty. Having been spared my life, I don't want it. I give it back to our struggle. Eldridge Cleaver died in that house on 28th Street, with Little Bobby, and what's left is force: fuel for the fire that will rage across the face of this racist country and either purge it of its evil or turn it into ashes. I say this for Little Bobby, for Eldridge Cleaver who died that night, for every black man, woman, and child who ever died here in Babylon, and I say it to racist America, that if every voice of dissent is silenced by your guns, by your courts, by your gas chambers, by your money, you will know, that as long as the ghost of Eldridge Cleaver is afoot, you have an ENEMY in your midst

April 19, 1968

PART XV
The New Left

THE emergence of a living and thinking Left in the 1960's could not have been predicted in the previous paralyzed decade. With the McCarthy and Eisenhower years as a background, the appearance of an authentic American Left seems miraculous. But viewed against the more immediate context of southern civil rights activities and the later war in Indochina, the re-creation of American radicalism was, for once, deeply relevant to domestic realities. The struggle in the South gave birth to a tentative white radicalism; American Third World foreign policy, from Cuba through Indochina, force-fed this infant Left so that it grew to have a greater certainty and a firmer grasp.

What finally emerged in the sixties was a more vital and independent Left than anything since the Wobblies (with whom the new Left had many similarities, especially of style, and, in 1970, a small number of young radicals actually joined what was left of the I.W.W.). What was new about the Left of the sixties resulted from its own conscious attempt to junk that radical past which had led to puppeteering and to suicide. The new Left's attempt to avoid a crippling political scientism as well as a merely mechanical application of Bolshevik texts to American life, its desire (futile, as it proved) to avoid the maniac factionalism of the old Left, and, above all, its independence from authority, especially Soviet authority, which it could neither influence nor control, gave the new Left the best chance for qualified success of any twentieth-century American movement. And that it was an American movement, although in step with an international student radicalism as well as with Third World insurgency, decisively marks off what is new about the new Left.

The mood that fed into the creation of the new Left came out of the writings of C. Wright Mills in the 1950's; out of the literature of the Beats, especially Jack Kerouac and Allan Ginsberg; out of the sit-ins, freedom rides, the formation of SNCC and of Fair Play for Cuba Committees on some campuses in the 1960–1961 academic year; and out of the ban-the-bomb protests. The new Left began with the formation of Students for a Democratic Society (SDS), an offshoot of the older Student League for Industrial Democracy, in the middle of June 1962 at Port Huron, Michigan. The *Port Huron Statement* (Document 52) was the founding vision of SDS, the first draft of which was written by Tom Hayden, a 21-year-old University of Michigan student. Hayden, along with Alan Haber, also a Michigan student and SDS's first president, issued the call for a convention to broaden and sharpen the analysis of American society, to breathe new life into the student Left. With eloquence and intelligence, the *Port Huron Statement* said that the American Dream is a nightmare, that the distance between American rhetoric and practice had become a chasm, and that an alternative future had to be constructed to save humanity. "Our work," the statement warned, "is guided by the sense that we may be the last generation in the experiment with living." This urgency breathes throughout the statement, as does the self-consciousness of a new start: "not even the liberal and socialist preachments of the past seem adequate to the forms of the present." Participatory democracy was defined as a technique and a goal in this statement which tried to avoid Marxist theory, which seems to have been an attempt to begin the world of radicalism anew, from scratch, in line with the self-consciousness of occupying a unique moment in time, a present presumably discontinuous with the past. Although the *Port Huron Statement* is the sound of the new Left's birth, its consciously political radicalism was not yet focused.

In 1963 SDS began the Economic Research and Action Project (ERAP), an attempt to organize the poor on a community level in several northern cities. This was intended to be the main thrust of SDS work, and it followed from the *Port Huron Statement*'s emphasis on participatory democracy. Determined to avoid privileged leadership whether of the charismatic, bureaucratic, or educational variety, the ERAP organizers sought to make a conscious political community out of the disorganized and disaffiliated poor, black and white. They were so committed to indigenous control that national coordination of the several projects was voted down in 1965. The next year Tom Hayden, who was now an organizer in a black section of Newark, explained how this kind of community work was an essential ingredient of a poor people's movement,[1] and Richard Flacks, an SDS leader and later faculty member of the University of Chicago and

[1] Tom Hayden, "The Politics of 'The Movement,'" *Dissent* 13 (January 1966): 75–87.

in California, wrote an important article (Document 53) showing the relationship of this community organizing to the concept of participatory democracy. But Flacks went an important step further when he argued, towards the end and almost as an afterthought, that the new Left had better look to the socialist tradition in America if it was ever going to be able to provide a model for democratizing national planning.

Not surprisingly, the appropriate techniques for grassroots organizing bothered many people. How could middle class students, in a favorite new Left phrase, "relate to" poor Americans? Even after SDS was almost entirely distracted by the Indochina war, the community organizers continued to debate how they were to achieve their local goals. One group insisted that draft resistance was the best issue for interesting and involving local people. Immediately after, a group of organizers working in Chicago and Cincinnati (JOIN) argued (Document 54) that a variety of bread-and-butter issues worked better than the draft, that students would have to learn how to shed their own cultural pasts, and that an enormous dedication was essential to elicit the local trust necessary to build "consciousness, confidence, and leadership." This serious article shows better than anything else what sort of tasks the organizers set themselves, and what personal costs they had paid and were willing to pay.

The Mississippi Summer of 1964, the first Berkeley actions, the beginning of regular bombing raids over North Vietnam and the protests which followed, the SDS-sponsored antiwar demonstration in Washington in April 1965, the teach-ins that followed their inauguration at the University of Michigan, and the explosion of Watts in the summer of 1965—these were in the background of a general public recognition in 1965 that a new Left actually existed. But characteristically, the Left continued to worry about what it was, even if others had by then perceived a somewhat new, and relatively unified, phenomenon. This was a sign of public relations hysteria especially in the liberally oriented media, and healthy caution at least on the part of the most responsible Left. A brief statement (Document 55) by two young editors of *Studies on the Left,* a scholarly radical journal first published at the University of Wisconsin in the late fifties, now can be seen as a pivotal argument in the development of a new Left. These editors said that whatever else the new Left was it had no theoretical clarity, without which mere activity would necessarily result in failure, as they described the activities of the southern and ghetto organizers as well as those of the antiwar protesters. They demanded a long view, patient and unglamourous work toward the creation of a revolutionary movement and party, and a stop to mindless fascination with the moment. They were clear about where the new Left would have to go: "The first step is for new Leftists to examine the content of their radicalism and determine if they are committed to a transformation of American capitalism into that higher form of society envisaged by Marx." They called, in short, for the sort of political focus that was missing from the *Port Huron Statement*.

The Left was failing to build a constituency outside of its own student precincts. According to Gregory Calvert, then a 29-year-old national secretary of SDS, in a justly celebrated speech (Document 56) at Princeton, this too was a result of borrowed categories, of inadequate analysis. The failure to build any kind of popular base, especially in the black South, was the root of the Left's crisis. Calvert argued that white middle class radicals had to face who and what they are, had to learn to work in white communities, particularly after SNCC told the whites to get out of the black struggle. But Calvert's real contribution to the Left was his suggestion that there is a "new" working class in America, made up of what is traditionally thought of as the middle class, the masses of people caught up in the technological economy of a postindustrial world. Students are the trainees of this class, and should seek to organize themselves on this basis. Here was a reason for continuing student organizing, one that offered hope that such activity was central to the larger radical intention of social reconstruction. This had the further advantage of attacking problems on the most local and personal level, so that it could not be said that students out of their own guilt were merely trying to free others, but would be working to free themselves; this, Calvert said, is the difference between liberal and radical motivation.

In the final document (Document 57) of this section, Carl Oglesby, a past president of SDS, sensitively fingers the perceptual and psychological development necessary to the creation of a revolutionary. What makes a rebel? And why can't he tell us what he will put in the place of the society that he is trying to destroy? Oglesby: "The fundamental revolutionary motive is not to construct a Paradise but to destroy an Inferno." The revolutionary's answer to the question about what he wants in the future is—not what we have now. Self-defense, as Calvert had also insisted, makes a rebel, not ideological blueprints of a shining tomorrow; but without those blueprints, or at least shadows of blueprints, the very act of self-defense is easily muddled; the sense of systemic injustice is indispensable to distinguishing friends from enemies. It is useful to give Oglesby the last word here, because his understanding of nuance is a useful antidote to the strident reductionism of too many of the new Left's hysterical pamphleteers.

[52]

PORT HURON STATEMENT, INTRODUCTION

TOM HAYDEN ET AL.

Agenda for a Generation

We are people of this generation, bred in at least modest comfort, housed now in universities, looking uncomfortably to the world we inherit.

When we were kids the United States was the wealthiest and strongest country in the world; the only one with the atom bomb, the least scarred by modern war, an initiator of the United Nations that we thought would distribute Western influence throughout the world. Freedom and equality for each individual, government of, by, and for the people—these American values we found good, principles by which we could live as men. Many of us began maturing in complacency.

As we grew, however, our comfort was penetrated by events too troubling to dismiss. First, the permeating and victimizing fact of human degradation, symbolized by the Southern struggle against racial bigotry, compelled most of us from silence to activism. Second, the enclosing fact of the Cold War, symbolized by the presence of the Bomb, brought awareness that we ourselves, and our friends, and millions of abstract "others" we knew more directly because of our common peril, might die at any time. We might deliberately ignore, or avoid, or fail to feel all other human problems, but not these two, for these were too immediate and crushing in their impact, too challenging in the demand that we as individuals take the responsibility for encounter and resolution.

While these and other problems either directly oppressed us or rankled our consciences and became our own subjective concerns, we began to see complicated and disturbing paradoxes in our surrounding America. The declaration "all men are created equal . . ." rang hollow before the facts of Negro life in the South and the big cities of the North. The proclaimed peaceful intentions of the United States contradicted its economic and military investments in the Cold War status quo.

SOURCE: Tom Hayden et al., *Port Huron Statement,* mimeographed (n.p., Students for a Democratic Society, 1962), pp. 3–8, 61–63.

We witnessed, and continue to witness, other paradoxes. With nuclear energy whole cities can easily be powered, yet the dominant nation-states seem more likely to unleash destruction greater than that incurred in all wars of human history. Although our own technology is destroying old and creating new forms of social organization, men still tolerate meaningless work and idleness. While two-thirds of mankind suffers undernourishment, our own upper classes revel amidst superfluous abundance. Although world population is expected to double in forty years, the nations still tolerate anarchy as a major principle of international conduct and uncontrolled exploitation governs the sapping of the earth's physical resources. Although mankind desperately needs revolutionary leadership, America rests in national stalemate, its goals ambiguous and tradition-bound instead of informed and clear, its democratic system apathetic and manipulated rather than "of, by, and for the people."

Not only did tarnish appear on our image of American virtue, not only did disillusion occur when the hypocrisy of American ideals was discovered, but we began to sense that what we had originally seen as the American Golden Age was actually the decline of an era. The worldwide outbreak of revolution against colonialism and imperialism, the entrenchment of totalitarian states, the menace of war, overpopulation, international disorder, supertechnology—these trends were testing the tenacity of our own commitment to democracy and freedom and our abilities to visualize their application to a world in upheaval.

Our work is guided by the sense that we may be the last generation in the experiment with living. But we are a minority—the vast majority of our people regard the temporary equilibriums of our society and world as eternally-functional parts. In this is perhaps the outstanding paradox: we ourselves are imbued with urgency, yet the message of our society is that there is no viable alternative to the present. Beneath the reassuring tones of the politicians, beneath the common opinion that America will "muddle through," beneath the stagnation of those who have closed their minds to the future, is the pervading feeling that there simply are no alternatives, that our times have witnessed the exhaustion not only of Utopias, but of any new departures as well. Feeling the press of complexity upon the emptiness of life, people are fearful of the thought that at any moment things might be thrust out of control. They fear change itself, since change might smash whatever invisible framework seems to hold back chaos for them now. For most Americans, all crusades are suspect, threatening. The fact that each individual sees apathy in his fellows perpetuates the common reluctance to organize for change. The dominant institutions are complex enough to blunt the minds of their potential critics, and entrenched enough to swiftly dissipate or entirely repel the energies of protest and reform, thus limiting human expectancies. Then, too, we are a materially improved society, and by our own improvements we seem to have weakened the case for further change.

Some would have us believe that Americans feel contentment amidst prosperity—but might it not be better be called a glaze above deeply-felt anxieties about their role in the new world? And if these anxieties produce a developed indifference to human affairs, do they not as well produce a yearning to believe there *is* an alternative to the present, that something *can* be done to change circumstances in the school, the workplaces, the bureaucracies, the government? It is to this latter yearning, at once the spark and engine of change, that we direct our present appeal. The search for truly democratic alternatives to the present, and a commitment to social experimentation with them, is a worthy and fulfilling human enterprise, one which moves us and, we hope, others today. On such a basis do we offer this document of our convictions and analysis: as an effort in understanding and changing the conditions of humanity in the late twentieth century, an effort rooted in the ancient, still unfulfilled conception of man attaining determining influence over his circumstances of life.

Values

Making values explicit—an initial task in establishing alternatives—is an activity that has been devalued and corrupted. The conventional moral terms of the age, the politician moralities—"free world," "people's democracies"—reflect realities poorly, if at all, and seem to function more as ruling myths than as descriptive principles. But neither has our experience in the universities brought us moral enlightenment. Our professors and administrators sacrifice controversy to public relations; their curriculums change more slowly than the living events of the world; their skills and silence are purchased by investors in the arms race; passion is called unscholastic. The questions we might want raised—what is really important? can we live in a different and better way? if we wanted to change society, how would we do it?—are not thought to be questions of a "fruitful, empirical nature," and thus are brushed aside.

Unlike youth in other countries we are used to moral leadership being exercised and moral dimensions being clarified by our elders. But today, for us, not even the liberal and socialist preachments of the past seem adequate to the forms of the present. Consider the old slogans: Capitalism Cannot Reform Itself, United Front Against Fascism, General Strike, All Out on May Day. Or, more recently, No Cooperation with Commies and Fellow Travellers, Ideologies are Exhausted, Bipartisanship, No Utopias. These are incomplete, and there are few new prophets. It has been said that our liberal and socialist predecessors were plagued by vision without program, while our own generation is plagued by program without vision. All around us there is astute grasp of method, technique—the committee, the ad hoc group, the lobbyist, the hard and soft sell, the make, the projected image—but, if pressed critically, such expertise is incompetent to explain its implicit ideals. It is highly fashionable to identify oneself by old categories, or by naming a respected political figure, or by explaining "how we would vote" on various issues.

Theoretic chaos has replaced the idealistic thinking of old—and, unable to reconstitute theoretic order, men have condemned idealism itself. Doubt has replaced hopefulness—and men act out a defeatism that is labelled realistic. The decline of utopia and hope is in fact one of the defining features of social life today. The reasons are various: the dreams of the older left were perverted by Stalinism and never re-created; the congressional stalemate makes men narrow their view of the possible; the specialization of human acitivity leaves little room for sweeping thought; the horrors of the twentieth century, symbolized in the gas-ovens and concentration camps and atom bombs, have blasted hopefulness. To be idealistic is to be considered apocalyptic, deluded. To have no serious aspirations, on the contrary, is to be "toughminded."

In suggesting social goals and values, therefore, we are aware of entering a sphere of some disrepute. Perhaps matured by the past, we have no sure formulas, no closed theories—but that does not mean values are beyond discussion and tentative determination. A first task of any social movement is to convince people that the search for orienting theories and the creation of human values are complex but worthwhile. We are aware that to avoid platitudes we must analyze the concrete conditions of social order. But to direct such an analysis we must use the guideposts of basic principles. Our own social values involve conceptions of human beings, human relationships, and social systems.

We regard *men* as infinitely precious and possessed of unfulfilled capacities for reason, freedom, and love. In affirming these principles we are aware of countering perhaps the dominant conceptions of man in the twentieth century: that he is a thing to be manipulated, and that he is inherently incapable of directing his own affairs. We oppose the depersonalization that reduces human beings to the status of things—if anything, the brutalities of the twentieth century teach that means and ends are intimately related, that vague appeals to "posterity" cannot justify the mutilations of the present. We oppose, too, the doctrine of human incompetence because it rests essentially on the modern fact that men have been "competently" manipulated into incompetence—we see little reason why men cannot meet with increasing skill the complexities and responsibilities of their situation, if society is organized not for minority, but for majority, participation in decision-making.

Men have unrealized potential for self-cultivation, self-direction, self-understanding, and creativity. It is this potential that we regard as crucial and to which we appeal, not to the human potentiality for violence, unreason, and submission to authority. The goal of man and society should be human independence: a concern not with image of popularity but with finding a meaning in life that is personally authentic; a quality of mind not compulsively driven by a sense of powerlessness, nor one which unthinkingly adopts status values, nor one which represses all threats to its habits, but one which has full, spontaneous access to present and past experiences, one which easily unites the fragmented parts of personal history, one which openly faces problems which are troubling and unresolved; one with an intuitive awareness of possibilities, an active sense of curiosity, an ability and willingness to learn.

This kind of independence does not mean egotistic individualism—the object is not to have one's way so much as it is to have a way that is one's own. Nor do we deify man—we merely have faith in his potential.

Human relationships should involve fraternity and honesty. Human interdependence is contemporary fact; human brotherhood must be willed, however, as a condition of future survival and as the most appropriate form of social relations. Personal links between man and man are needed, especially to go beyond the partial and fragmentary bonds of function that bind men only as worker to worker, employer to employee, teacher to student, American to Russian.

Loneliness, estrangement, isolation describe the vast distance between man and man today. These dominant tendencies cannot be overcome by better personnel management, nor by improved gadgets, but only when a love of man overcomes the idolatrous worship of things by man. As the individualism we affirm is not egoism, the selflessness we affirm is not self-elimination. On the contrary we believe in generosity of a kind that imprints one's unique individual qualities in the relation to other men, and to all human activity. Further, to dislike isolation is not to favor the abolition of privacy; the latter differs from isolation in that [it] occurs or is abolished according to individual will.

We would replace power rooted in possession, privileged, or circumstance by power and uniqueness rooted in love, reflectiveness, reason, and creativity. As a *social system* we seek the establishment of a democracy of individual participation, governed by two central aims: that the individual share in those social decisions determining the quality and direction of his life; that society be organized to encourage independence in men and provide the media for their common participation.

In a participatory democracy, the political life would be based in several root principles:

that decision-making of basic social consequence be carried on by public groupings;

that politics be seen positively, as the art of collectively creating an acceptable pattern of social relations;

that politics has the function of bringing people out of isolation and into community, thus being a necessary, though not sufficient, means of finding meaning in personal life;

that the political order should serve to clarify problems in a way instrumental to their solution; it should provide outlets for the expression of personal grievance and aspiration; opposing views should be organized so as to illuminate choices and facilitate the attainment of goals; channels should be commonly available to relate men to knowledge and to power so that private problems—from bad recreation facilities to personal alienation—are formulated as general issues.

The economic sphere would have as its basis the principles:

that work should involve incentives worthier than money or survival. It should be educative, not stultifying; creative, not mechanical; self-directed, not manipulated, encouraging independence, a respect for others, a sense of dignity and a willingness to accept social responsibility, since it is this experience that has crucial influence on habits, perceptions and individual ethics;

that the economic experience is so personally decisive that the individual must share in its full determination;

that the economy itself is of such social importance that its major resources and means of production should be open to democratic participation and subject to democratic social regulation.

Like the political and economic ones, major social institutions—cultural, educational, rehabilitative, and others—should be generally organized with the well-being and dignity of man as the essential measure of success.

In social change or interchange, we find violence to be abhorrent because it requires generally the transformation of the target, be it a human being or a community of people, into a depersonalized object of hate. It is imperative that the means of violence be abolished and the institutions— local, national, international—that encourage nonviolence as a condition of conflict be developed.

These are our central values, in skeletal form. It remains vital to understand their denial or attainment in the context of the modern world. . . .

The University and Social Change

There is perhaps little reason to be optimistic about the above analysis. True, the Dixiecrat–GOP coalition is the weakest point in the dominating complex of corporate, military and political power. But the civil rights, peace, and student movements are too poor and socially slighted, and the labor movement too quiescent, to be counted with enthusiasm. From where else can power and vision be summoned? We believe that the universities are an overlooked seat of influence.

First, the university is located in a permanent position of social influence. Its educational function makes it indispensable and automatically makes it a crucial institution in the formation of social attitudes. Second, in an unbelievably complicated world, it is the central institution for organizing, evaluating, and transmitting knowledge. Third, the extent to which academic resources presently are used to buttress immoral social practice is revealed first, by the extent to which defense contracts make the universities engineers of the arms race. Too, the use of modern social science as a manipulative tool reveals itself in the "human relations" consultants to the modern corporations, who introduce trivial sops to give laborers feelings of "participation" or "belonging," while actually deluding them in order to further exploit their labor. And, of course, the use of motivational research is already infamous as a manipulative aspect of American politics. But these social uses of the universities' resources also demonstrate the unchangeable reliance by men of power on the men and storehouses of knowledge: this makes the university functionally tied to society in new ways, revealing new potentialities, new levers for change. Fourth, the university is the only mainstream institution that is open to participation by individuals of nearly any viewpoint.

These, at least, are facts, no matter how dull the teaching, how paternalistic the rules, how irrelevant the research that goes on. Social relevance, the accessibility to knowledge, and internal openness—these together make the university a potential base and agency in a movement of social change.

1. Any new Left in America must be, in large measure, a Left with real intellectual skills, committed to deliberativeness, honesty, reflection as working tools. The university permits the political life to be an adjunct to the academic one, and action to be informed by reason.

2. A new Left must be distributed in significant social roles throughout the country. The universities are distributed in such a manner.

3. A new Left must consist of younger people who matured in the post-war world, and partially be directed to the recruitment of younger people. The university is an obvious beginning point.

4. A new Left must include liberals and socialists, the former for their relevance, the latter for their sense of thoroughgoing reforms in the system. The university is a more sensible place than a political party for these two traditions to begin to discuss their differences and look for political synthesis.

5. A new Left must start controversy across the land, if national policies and national apathy are to be reversed. The ideal university is a community of controversy, within itself and in its effects on communities beyond.

6. A new Left must transform modern complexity into issues that can be understood and felt close-up by every human being. It must give form to the feelings of helplessness and indifference, so that people may see the political, social, and economic sources of their private troubles and organize to change society. In a time of supposed prosperity, moral complacency, and political manipulation, a new Left cannot rely on only aching stomachs to be the engine force of social reform. The case for change, for alternatives that will involve uncomfortable personal efforts, must be argued as never before. The university is a relevant place for all of these activities.

But we need not indulge in illusions: the university system cannot complete a movement of ordinary people making demands for a better life. From its schools and colleges across the nation, a militant Left might awaken its allies, and by beginning the process towards peace, civil rights, and labor struggles, reinsert theory and idealism where too often reign confusion and political barter. The power of students and faculty united is not only potential; it has shown its actuality in the South, and in the reform movements of the North.

The bridge to political power, though, will be built through genuine co-operation, locally, nationally, and internationally, between a new Left of young people and an awakening community of allies. In each community we must look within the university and act with confidence that we can be powerful, but we must look outwards to the less exotic but more lasting struggles for justice.

To turn these possibilities into realities will involve national efforts at university reform by an alliance of students and faculty. They must wrest control of the educational process from the administrative bureaucracy. They must make fraternal and functional contact with allies in labor, civil rights, and other liberal forces outside the campus. They must import major public issues into the curriculum—research and teaching on problems of war and peace is an outstanding example. They must make debate and controversy, not dull pedantic cant, the common style for educational life. They must consciously build a base for their assault upon the loci of power.

As students for a democratic society, we are committed to stimulating this kind of social movement, this kind of vision and program in campus and community across the country. If we appear to seek the unattainable, as it has been said, then let it be known that we do so to avoid the unimaginable.

---

[53]

ON THE USES OF
PARTICIPATORY DEMOCRACY

RICHARD FLACKS

I

The most frequently heard phrase used for defining participatory democracy is that "men must share in the decisions which affect their lives." In other words, participatory democrats take very seriously a vision of man as citizen; and by taking seriously such a vision, they seek to extend the conception of citizenship beyond the conventional political sphere

SOURCE: Richard Flacks, "On the Uses of Participatory Democracy," *Dissent* 13 (November 1966): 701–708.

to all institutions. Other ways of stating the core values are to assert the following: each man has responsibility for the action of the institutions in which he is imbedded; all authority ought to be responsible to those "under" it; each man can and should be a center of power and initiative in society.

II

The first priority for the achievement of a democracy of participation is to win full political rights and representation for all sectors of the population. Democracy, in fact, is an issue for this generation of radicals largely because their political experience has been shaped by the Negroes' elemental struggle for a political voice in the U.S. This struggle has not been simply for the right to vote—though even this right has not yet been guaranteed —but, more broadly, it has been an effort to win a share of political power by poor Negroes. It has been the experience of Negroes in the North, where voting rights have been formally guaranteed, that Negroes as a group have remained systematically under-represented in the political process and that, where Negro representation exists, it operates in behalf of Negro middle-class interests and is highly dependent on the beneficence of white-dominated political machines. The results of this situation are plain to see in every Northern city. Thus the main thrust of radicals in the civil rights movement has to do less with breaking the barriers of legal segregation and formal exclusion than with attempting to build viable grass-roots organizations of poor Negroes, which would actually represent the needs of the poor and remain independent of white and middle-class domination. The ideology of "participatory democracy" has been useful in this effort, since it provides a rationale for avoiding premature "coalition" of grass-roots groups with more powerful white or middle-class organizations, for effectively criticizing "charismatic" styles of leadership which prevent rank-and-file people from learning political skills, for criticizing tendencies toward bureaucratism, demagoguery, and elitism which are predictable in mass movements. Moreover, "participatory democracy," unlike black nationalist ideology, which also helps to mobilize grass-roots Negroes, offers a possible bridge between Negroes and other groups of poor or voiceless people. Thus we find much of the same rhetoric and organizing technique being used by SNCC workers in Southern Negro communities, SDS organizers among poor whites in Chicago and Cleveland, and farm labor organizers among the multi-national grape workers in California.

398

Just how is participatory democracy being applied to the organization of economically disadvantaged groups? It has influenced the analysis of the problem of poverty in an affluent society, by stressing political voicelessness and lack of organization as a root cause of deprivation. This analysis leads to an emphasis on grass-roots organization and mobilization of the poor as the main way of ending poverty. Since the people involved lack political skill, organization requires a full-time staff, initially composed of students and ex-students, but soon involving "indigenous" leadership. This staff has the problem of allaying the fear, suspicion, and sense of inadequacy of the community—hence there has been a strong emphasis on building a sense of community between staff and rank-and-file, and of finding techniques which will facilitate self-expression, enable new leadership to emerge, enable people to gain dignity by participation, and the organization to become self-sustaining. Such techniques include: rotation of leadership, eschewing by staff of opportunities to "speak for" the organization, the use of "consensus" to foster expression by the less-articulate.

More important than such procedural techniques has been the attempt to generate institutions which help to bind people to the organization, to see immediate benefits from participation. Thus, in Mississippi, alongside the political organization (the Freedom Democratic party), a variety of related "projects" have grown up—community centers, freedom schools, a Poor People's Corporation to help finance small business enterprise, cooperatives, and the like. In Newark, the Newark Community Union has established its own radio station. In California, the Farm Worker Association established a credit union. In Cleveland, the SDS Community Project established a traveling street theater. Although these new institutions are sometimes viewed as alternatives to participation in "organized society" . . . in practice, they are a very important way of sustaining a developing organization. They enable people to participate in an organization in a continuing fashion, help develop organizational resources, train people for leadership, and give people a sense of the possibilities for social change. But they are in no sense a *substitute* for political activity, direct action, and the development of a program. These, and not the development of "parallel institutions," constitute the main functions of the local political parties, community unions, etc., which are developing in many urban slum and rural areas.

The emphasis on participatory democracy has helped these developing grass-roots organizations to formulate and articulate *issues and programs*. Although the constituencies of these organizations include the most impoverished sectors of society, it is remarkable that—particularly in the Northern cities—the main activity of these organizations has not been focused on economic issues. They have, rather, been struggling over issues of *control, self-determination* and *independence:* Shall the poor have a voice in the allocation of War on Poverty funds? Shall urban renewal be shaped by the people whose neighborhood is being renewed? Shall the police be held accountable by the community? Who is to decide the dispensation of welfare payments? Who makes the rules in the welfare bureaucracies? Who controls the ghetto?

The outcome of these grass-roots organizing efforts, of course, cannot be predicted. The civil rights movement, in its direct-action phase, began the process of bringing Negroes and the poor into the political arena—and the results, in terms of political alignments and issues, have already been substantial. The more recent efforts of political organization initiated by the participatory democrats will certainly increase the degree of Negro representation in the political process. These efforts are now being emulated by more established and less insurgent agencies—Martin Luther King's Southern Christian Leadership Conference, for example, in the massive organizing campaign in Chicago, used many of the techniques and rhetorical devices developed by SNCC and SDS.

It seems clear, then, that the poor are being organized and mobilized. But such mobilization can lead in two directions. On the one hand, there is the strong probability that the newly developed constituencies will take their place alongside other ethnic and interest groups, bargaining for benefits within the framework of the Democratic party. An alternative to this path is embodied in the vision of participatory democracy—the development of community-based, self-determining organizations, having the following functions:

Achieving community control over previously centralized functions, through local election of school and police administrators; by forming community-run cooperatives in housing, social services, retail distribution and the like; by establishing community-run foundations and corporations.

Maintaining close control over elected representatives; running and electing poor people to public office; ensuring direct participation of the community in framing political platforms and in shaping the behavior of representatives.

Acting like a trade union in protecting the poor against exploitative and callous practices of public and private bureaucracies, landlords, businessmen, etc.

III

The values underlying participatory democracy have, so far, achieved their fullest expression in efforts to organize and mobilize communities of disenfranchised people, but such democratizing trends and potentialities also exist in other sectors of society. The most obvious example is the nationwide effort by university students to change the authority structure in American higher education. For the most part, this activity has been directed at protest against arbitrary restrictions of student political expression, and against paternalistic regulations limiting students' rights to privacy and self-expression. The most dramatic and widely-known instance of this activity was that of the civil disobedience and student strikes at Berkeley in the fall of 1964. But the Berkeley situation has been repeated in less intense form on scores of campuses across the country. Student reform efforts have increasingly shifted from protest and direct action to demands for a continuing voice in the shaping of university policy. Some students now have demanded representation on administrative committees. Others have looked to the formation of organizations along the trade union model—organizations which would be independent of and could bargain with university administrators, rather than becoming participants in administration. Thus far, the impact of the student protest has been to generate a considerable degree of ferment, of re-examination and experimentation among college faculties and administrators, as well as efforts coercively to repress the protest.

Student protest has spread from the elite, liberal campuses to Catholic schools, and from there to other clerical bodies. The talk at Catholic seminaries now prominently includes "participatory democracy," and "New Left" clergymen have gone so far as to propose the establishment of a trade union for priests. But the University and the Church are not the only institutions witnessing challenges to existing authority structures. In recent years, there has been an enormous growth of unionization among schoolteachers and other white-collar workers, particularly among employees in the welfare bureaucracies. Now one can also observe ferment within the professions: young doctors and young lawyers are developing organizations dedicated to challenging the authority of the highly conservative professional societies, and to bringing an active sense of social responsibility to their professions.

It is not farfetched to predict that the idea of "Workers' control" will soon become a highly relevant issue in American life. American industrial unions have largely had to sacrifice the struggle for control in the work place for higher wages and fringe benefits; but at union conventions, control over working conditions is repeatedly urged as a high-priority bargaining demand. The impetus for making such a demand paramount, however, may first come from the ranks of white-collar and professional employees. The authority structure of the modern bureaucratic organization is plainly unsuited for a work force which is highly educated and fully aware of its competence to participate in decision-making. The first impulse of modern managers faced with threats to authority has been to make small concessions ("improve channels of communications"). But the exciting time will come when such insurgency turns from protest over small grievances to a full-fledged realization of the possibilities for first-class citizenship within public bureaucracies and private corporations. The forms of such democratization could include further unionization of the unorganized, worker representation in management, young-turk overthrows of entrenched leaderships in the professions, and, ultimately, demands for elections and recall of managers and administrators, and for employee participation in the shaping of policies and regulations.

IV

The most authoritarian sector of public decision-making in the U.S. is in the area of foreign policy. The American Constitution gives enormous power to the President to make foreign policy without substantial built-in checks from Congress. The scope of Presidential power has, of course, been greatly expanded by the technology of modern war; the unchecked power of the government to mobilize support for its policies has been greatly enhanced by the invention of conscription, by the mass media and their centralization, by covert intelligence operations, etc. It is not surprising that foreign policy has been the special province of elites in America and, since World War II, has been carried on within a framework of almost total popular acquiescence.

The simultaneous occurrence of the Vietnam War and the emergence of a New Left in America may generate change in this situation. Due largely to student initiative, we are witnessing more protest during time of war than in any other comparable period in U.S. history. Not only does this protest begin to shatter the foreign policy consensus, but it also shows signs of bringing about more permanent change in the structure of foreign policy decision-making.

First, the teach-ins and similar initiatives mark the emergence of an *independent public* in the foreign policy area—a body of people, satisfied neither with official policy nor with official justifications of policy, determined to formulate alternatives, stimulate debate and criticism, and obtain independent sources of information. This public is to be found largely in universities but now spills over to include much of the intellectual community in the country. Moreover, the teach-in as a technique for disseminating information suggests, at least symbolically, a significant breakthrough in the effort to find alternatives to the propaganda media controlled or manipulated by the state.

Second, the emerging foreign policy public has plainly had an at least transitory impact on Congress. The revival of Congressional independence with respect to foreign policy would be a signal advance of democracy in America.

Third, the attempts to find a non-religious moral ground for conscientious objection in time of war has led to a rediscovery of the Allied case at the Nuremberg Trials—a case which argued in essence that individuals were responsible for the actions of institutions taken in their name. This principle, taken seriously, is revolutionary in its implications for individual-state relations; and it converges, interestingly enough, with "participatory democracy." The Nuremberg principle is now being used as a basis for legal defense of draft-refusal and civil disobedience at draft boards; it inspires professors to refuse to grade their students and become thereby accomplices to Selective Service; it inspires intellectuals and artists to acts of public defiance and witness. In fact, it is possible that one positive outcome of the war in Vietnam will have been its impact on the moral sensibility of many members of the intellectual and religious communities —forcing them to rethink their relationship to the state and to the institutions of war.

It is possible, then, that an unforeseen by-product of the highly-developed society is the emergence of potential publics that are (a) competent to evaluate the propaganda of elites and (b) impatient with chauvinistic definitions of loyalty. The organization of such publics in the U.S. may be a significant outcome of the war in Vietnam. These publics do not have the power to change the course of this war, but the spread of their influence may be a factor in transforming the issues and alignments of American politics in the coming period. Moreover, the strength of these publics on the campus is now being reflected in the growing conflict over the role of the universities in national mobilization. The current campaign to prevent university participation in the Selective Service induction process may portend a more profound effort to make universities centers of resistance to encroaching militarization. The outcome of this particular struggle could be important in democratizing the structure of foreign policy decision-making.

V

The development of democratic consciousness in communities, organizations, and foreign policy decision-making will mean little if the national distribution of power remains undisturbed. This means that the social theory of the New Left must be centrally concerned with the development of relevant models for democratic control over public decisions at the national level.

It is clear that implicit in the New Left's vision is the notion that participatory democracy is not possible without some version of public control over the allocation of resources, economic planning, and the operation of large corporations. Such control is, of course, not missing in the United States. The federal government has taken responsibility for national planning to avoid slump, to control wages and prices, and to avoid inflation. Moreover, the postwar period has seen a tremendous increase in public subsidy of the corporate economy—through the defense budget, urban redevelopment, investment in research and education, transportation and communication, etc. In many ways the "two governments"—political and corporate—are merged, and this merger approximates an elitist corporatist model (hence breaking down even the modest pluralism which once characterized the system). The further development of this trend will foreclose any possibility for the achievement of democratic participation.

The demand for more national planning, once the major plank of American socialism, is now decidedly on the agenda of American political and corporate elites. The question for the Left has become how to *democratize* that planning. There are as yet no answers to this, or to the question of how to bring the large corporations under democratic control.

VI

Thus the main intellectual problem for the new radicals is to suggest how patterns of decentralized decision-making in city administrations, and democratized authority structures in bureaucracies can be meshed with a situation of greatly broadened national planning and coordination in the economy.

That no such programs and models now exist is, of course, a consequence of the disintegration of the socialist tradition in America and of the continuing fragmentation of American intellectual life. Unless the New Left consciously accepts the task of restoring that tradition and of establishing a new political community, the democratizing revolts which it now catalyzes are likely to be abortive.

VII

These tasks were, less than a generation ago, declared by many American intellectuals to be no longer relevant. Ideology, it was argued, had no place in highly developed societies where problems of resource allocation had become technical matters. But the reverse may be true: that ideological questions—that is, questions about the structure and distribution of power —are *especially* pertinent when societies have the capacity to solve the merely technical problems.

It seems clear that the issue in a highly developed society is not simply economic exploitation; it is the question of the relationship of the individual to institutional and state authority which assumes paramount importance. In America, today, the familiar mechanisms of social control—money, status, patriotic and religious symbols—are losing their force for a population (particularly the new generation) which has learned to be intensely self-conscious and simultaneously worldly; to expect love and self-fulfillment; to quest for freedom and autonomy. All this learning is a consequence of increasingly sophisticated educational opportunities, of increasingly liberated standards in family and interpersonal relations, of affluence itself. Against this learning, the classic patterns of elite rule, bureaucratic authority, managerial manipulation, and class domination will have a difficult time sustaining themselves.

The virtue of "participatory democracy," as a basis for a new politics, is that it enables these new sources of social tension to achieve political expression. Participatory democracy symbolizes the restoration of personal freedom and interpersonal community as central political and social issues. It is not the end of ideology; it is a new beginning.

TAKE A STEP INTO AMERICA

JOIN ORGANIZERS

THE Movement of Nov. 1967 carried a plan of action for white resistance written by a group of young white organizers. They intend to move into poor and working class white neighborhoods in a number of cities across the country, using the draft as an initial issue to build draft resistance groups and as a door opener to build a radical base in the community that is multi-issue in nature.

As a group of organizers presently working with Southern whites in Chicago and Cincinnati, we found "We've Got to Reach Our Own People: a plan for White Resistance" encouraging. We welcome others who believe that the movement must reach white workers. We welcome those whose radical work will not remain confined to the student community where too many "radicals" often unconsciously believe what liberal America has told us—"poor and working white people are the enemy." However, on the basis of our experiences, and out of a firm belief that people must learn from movement history (does everybody have to make the same mistakes?), we take this opportunity to put forward some serious criticisms we have of "We've Got to Reach Our Own People." Furthermore, we hope that by talking about our experiences living and working in poor and working class Southern neighborhoods, others will get some glimpse of what a neighborhood is about, and give serious thought to where, other than the campus, they might work effectively as radicals. . . .

The authors talk of establishing roots in working class communities now, so that the people there will "be approached by people who settle into their own communities, are familiar and militant about their community problems, and who gain respect and credentials in their community." This is an important and proper motivation, yet the would-be-organizer must understand that sinking roots is extremely difficult and slow, filled

SOURCE: JOIN Organizers (Mike James, Diane Fager, Bob Lawson, Junebug Boykin, Tom Livingston, Tom Malear, Bobby McGinnis, Virgil Reed, Mike Sharon, and Youngblood) "Take a Step into America," *Don't Mourn—Organize!* (San Francisco: The Movement Press, 1968), pp. 10–16; first published in *The Movement,* December 1967.

with the problems of people of DIFFERENT CULTURES AND AT THIS TIME DIFFERENT INTERESTS AND MOTIVATIONS checking each other out, growing together and learning to understand and live with differences. People who come out of the radical-student-hip culture will not shed easily (even though they may desire to do so) some of what must be shed or purged if they hope to become close and deeply involved BOTH POLITICALLY AND PERSONALLY with people in poor and working class neighborhoods.

It is not just a decision of sinking roots, but one of learning, changing, teaching and being taught, and growing together with people in a community. There is good and bad in both the culture most students come from and that of the people they hope to work with. Things in both must be purged, things of both cultures learned by those from the other, and new life styles developed as people take root in each other, in an idea, developing together as radicals and as organizers. Regis Debray talks of bourgeoise intellectuals, workers and peasants growing together, with extreme difficulty, in the guerilla band. It's a good point, one to be striven for, yet difficult and clearly not easily achieved, EVEN IN CUBA. Debray projects his own hopes and concerns; they are good.

People who are serious about helping a radical movement to grow among non-white collar white Americans will learn that organizing is very different from social work school courses, OEO training manuals, Alinsky speeches, articles about the movement in radical newspapers, and the important but naive prospectuses of both the early Economic Research and Action Projects and the recent "We've Got to Reach Our People."

Organizing is in part a slow, filled with personal hurts, learning and hardening process of making contacts, developing relationships, and building overlapping networks or spiderwebs of many contacts and relationships. It is coming aware of, understanding and knowing of people known in every bar on the Avenue; guys who know most people on most corners, key hustlers in many scenes; the matriarch in a group of buildings on a block; steady workers as well as work-for-awhile-hustle-for-awhile people; first shift workers and second and third shift workers (they're very different); on-my-own people and those who are deeply involved and dependent on relationships with people of three or four extended families; young guys into cars; those into music; and those into pool halls and small-time hustles; teenagers that run with the guys and those that are into steady chick scenes; what all-night restaurants of blue vinyl that catch a hodgepodge of comers on main thoroughfares are all about, as well as those restaurants with steamed windows, single brand music jukeboxes, and home-cooked-specialties where customer, waitress and owner all know one another, and if you don't, it at least reminds you of the place you hung out in your home town.

Students As Organizers

People leaving the radical student movement to make this important step will not, by and large, be able to conceal their backgrounds. NOR SHOULD THEY. Yet to be effective they can and must minimize certain traits that make it easy for new acquaintances in the neighborhood to write the organizer off as a kook or hippy (a label bestowed for many ways of being different other than just hair style or clothes). There will be many things in common, many pleasures, hardships and achievements shared between the "radical organizer" and the radicalized or organized, but it will not happen overnight. Eager radicals moving into a neighborhood, anxious to share ideas and see them grow, will experience, perhaps many times, something like drinking with someone in a bar, or talking on a corner or in a kitchen, picking up and "preach-teaching" on something said about cops or the war, only suddenly to find himself or herself being bid good-bye because they were too far out, came on too strong too quickly, hadn't been around long enough, or didn't have legitimacy. Legitimacy won't come from 4–6 or 8 years of college, superior knowledge, conceptualization or awareness; it won't come from "Hey, I'm for you, don't you understand how you're being messed over?" but from how you handle yourself, and, for a long time, who the hell you know. Very simply, it takes time, care, thinking, re-thinking, and a lot of feeling silly, ignorant, lonely, isolated, and self-conscious to grow into a community and have a whole lot of people know you and trust you.

Those who intend to leave the radical student community at this time or in the near future must deal with the fact that their concerns and style have developed in a social, political, economic and cultural scene very different from the one they will face in the neighborhoods they select to live and work in. The authors of "We've Got to Reach Our People" define resistance as "an effort to impede and disrupt the functioning of the military/political machinery wherever it is local and vulnerable." Resistance, defined this way, is a political concept, with an associated style that is carried over from the student political scene WHICH THEY ARE LEAVING. A poor or working class neighborhood IS A VERY DIFFERENT PLACE FROM A UNIVERSITY. The would-be organizer will be forced to learn that good! Resistance may not be the best organizing approach at North Texas State while it might be at San Francisco State; a good organizer gets a feel for the place he is working and thinks seriously about how to move there, learning as he makes mistakes. The same is true for the neighborhoods the authors intend to work in. They have not done their living-in research, are (by the sound of their article) not sensitive to the dynamics of the places they intend to live and work. It should be noted that NOWHERE IN THEIR PIECE DO THEY SPEAK OF LEARNING FROM THE PEOPLE THEY HOPE TO WORK WITH.

Build Consciousness, Confidence and Leadership

The writers of "We've Got to Reach Our Own People" state: "We join a resistance movement out of no great optimism about its capacity to end the war; indeed we call this a resistance, not a revolution, because entrenched power is too strong to be broken." We think radicals can be far more positive, planting seeds for a time when we don't have to talk of just impeding, but of moving toward power.

We believe that right now, in 1967 America (and let's not forget where the hell we are), the key issue is not resistance ("because entrenched power is too strong to be broken"), but the development of consciousness, confidence and leadership, and that, once again, is slow and difficult when you are working with people who are not radical intellectuals with 4–6–8 years of college like most of those who wrote the draft resistance proposal. . . . To us that means developing friendships, trust, educating, exposing, asking questions; in short, going through slow changes with people.

Real Issues

America, how it works and messes people up in this country and all over the world, outrages us sometimes to a point where rats and roaches seem silly. But housing problems, welfare, food prices, and cops are the kind of things most people in poor and working class neighborhoods know and must deal with every day of their lives, even though some don't like to admit it or talk about it. (Some of these who are hardest to reach—"I ain't got no problems"—are the most solid members or organizers ONCE THEY'VE BEEN ORGANIZED.) These issues we mention are hardly revolutionary, but what does it mean to be a revolutionary in this country? We don't have revolutionaries in this country, but we have some radicals building for a time when we can become revolutionaries.

Cops, the draft, welfare, credit, schools, housing, urban renewal, food prices, etc. and the kinds of issues that poor and working class people feel. That doesn't mean people are ready to rise up around ANY OF THEM. We have found that people willing to come together in a common struggle under any particular issue are a prize taken only after long hours, days, and weeks of battling years of conditioning by church, state and home. We work around these issues because people are aware of them and can, though not easily, become involved in working to solve them. To do so in their self-interest. We work with people around such issues because they are educational; they help people to learn, to grow, and make connections between issues—rats and roaches to urban renewal, or cops, the draft and the war to U.S. Imperialism. People who become involved around these issues begin to understand them in relation to other issues that affect them or people they know. People move from saying "you complain about everything" to an understanding that "the whole damn thing is rotten." Those who develop a sophisticated understanding and assume leadership will be much more able to understand and deal with the situation of their own people as objective conditions change, and by working around these issues they help to influence conditions by articulating for others just what it is that's behind the rat race.

Being Organized

Let's get it straight: all of us understand U.S. Imperialism and we hate it. Those of us who didn't learn about it while sitting on the terrace at Berkeley drinking coffee and discussing the morning coups reported in the 25¢ daily New York Times learned about it because we were organized. WE WERE ORGANIZED AROUND MANY THINGS TALKED ABOUT BY RADICAL ORGANIZERS, both former students and those who never went to college. THESE WERE THE THINGS WE HAD EXPERIENCED ALL OF OUR LIVES. We have always paid high rent for crummy or small furnished apartments—and now we know it. We have always paid more for food than people in the suburbs—and now we know why. We have sisters, brothers, friends who are married and work in factories, putting in overtime to make gyp payments on plastic covered couches and gold tinted table lamps. We have all worked in low-paying non-union factories. We have dealt with brutal cops all our lives (not just in recent demonstrations), and we are developing the confidence, understanding, and strategy among ourselves and others in our neighborhoods to deal with them. We have spent time in reformatories, jails and penitentiaries—two, three, four years, not summer vacations.

About two years ago guys in the neighborhood started to learn about JOIN, because it helped some people we knew: people on welfare, guys screwed by the day labor hiring halls, people evicted illegally, people needing a lawyer, guys who needed bond money. It was an OK thing; it helped poor people (although we didn't think of ourselves as poor—like poor people are winos on Wilson Avenue); but it was different and something to do. Once in awhile we'd read JOIN's newsletter that was under the door, or in a restaurant, or that was handed out on the street (and we would take [it] reluctantly, ESPECIALLY IF WE WERE IN A GROUP). Now there is an 8 page newspaper, 10,000 copies distributed door to door. The Firing Line was two years in developing, not because of cost, but because that was HOW LONG IT TOOK FOR THE ORGANIZATION TO DEVELOP AND FOR PEOPLE TO BE ORGANIZED TO RUN IT.

Young Guys

In the spring of 1966 young guys started to become a part of JOIN. There were a couple of guys who we'd seen around the neighborhood for awhile who started coming around the Friendship House (a now defunct, church-run recreation hall) with guys we knew. We talked, drank, played guitars. We talked about a thing called the movement, about bad buildings, cops, the war, black people, the draft; we talked about stuff that was happening round the country. These guys were organizers, like some of us are now.

In the summer 250 southern guys marched on the police station, telling the cops, the neighborhood and the press that southern white guys got treated as bad by the cops as Negroes and Puerto Ricans. We learned later that the march resulted in 75 cops being either fired permanently or transferred out of the district. Things slowed down for awhile around the cops —WE HADN'T ORGANIZED WELL ENOUGH. In the spring of 1967 we opened a recreation hall. It lasted awhile, we made some mistakes and eventually closed it because we ran out of money. We're trying to open another hall now. . . .

In the winter of 1967 two of us went to the JOIN school all day Fridays along with 12 other people who were active in JOIN. We learned about urban renewal, taxes, the city machine, the educational system, the press, the war in Vietnam, AND PEOPLE'S MOVEMENT AROUND THE WORLD. We saw movies on labor (The Inheritance, etc.), some SNCC films on voter registration, Viva Zapata, Salt of the Earth, Grapes of Wrath, etc. There's a new session of the school with 10 people. Junebug is the teacher.

Indigenous Organizers

Two years ago we hung on corners, talking about chicks and faggots and cars and music; drinking, and taking pills; sometimes hustling (pool, winos, queers), sometimes working in factories for awhile. Now when we meet guys in the neighborhood or MAKE CONTACT AGAIN with someone we know, we talk about a lot of the stuff we used to talk about, but we also talk about urban renewal, cops, the war, Cuba. It's important to realize that even though it isn't easy to hip neighborhood guys to all this stuff, it's easier for guys from the neighborhood or from the South to do it than for organizers who aren't from the neighborhood. That's because we know the guys better, know what they're about, and they know us and we're more trusted.

We talk about the draft. Sometimes someone we've talked to about stuff will come around if he thinks he's getting drafted, but a lot of guys don't seem too up tight about it until they get the word. Guys have a lot of ways to stay out. Some join the Navy to avoid the Army. Others aren't registered, or didn't tell their board when they moved North. Some guys have deferments because they got a wife and kid, or support their mother, or because they've got a police record. A few of the guys we talked to about cops, the war and the draft, who ended up going in when they got drafted, are now AWOL. In general we get to know guys and they know what we're about. They come when they need you, whether it be cops, draft, or bond money. That's one reason we want to open the hall again, to get neighborhood guys together and doing stuff.

The Draft vs. Multi-Issue Organizing

The authors of "We Have to Reach Our Own People" believe that at the best the draft issue can scatter seeds across the country which will provide a foundation for a movement against foreign and domestic imperialism. But the draft, while offering a good opportunity to reach high school students before they are draft age, is strategically a weak issue, especially when used as the key element for moving into a community.

We have learned from organizing efforts against urban renewal around the country these past few years that, when the opposition was in a position to establish a time table which you had to work against or organize around, or when the opposition was in a much stronger position to take initiative action, our backs were necessarily against the wall. Urban renewal is a defensive issue; we had to organize a resistance against domestic imperialism.

The draft is a similar type of issue. When we organized against urban renewal we always were faced with grant deadlines and meeting deadlines which we had to rush to meet. In the case of the draft the national government can take initiative action to alter the rules of the game we must play. Thus Congress held on to 2-S deferments in the face of certain massive protest from students disaffected over looking their class privilege. The effect of that action was to reduce the total effect (possible threat) of the student anti-draft movement. We could have seriously hurt the war effort if the lottery bill had passed; now we are nuisances to the government.

It is reasonable to expect that when the resistance gains greater momentum that the national government will try another move like setting up a national service: "everybody's doing for his country; if you don't like the war then join the Peace Corps." These moves by the government don't destroy our movement, but they disrupt its momentum more effectively than we can now disrupt the government's ability to carry on the war.

Furthermore, there are other issues around the war which could be tried in poor and working class communities. The organizing required to move people on such issues would be difficult, but people are talking about digging deep roots in communities. The authors mention some of these issues —union suppression in a war effort, loss of wage gains with inflation, the war tax, loss of (token) government sponsored community development funds—but don't deal with them as issues to build around.

So, multi-issue organizing not only argues that you can reach more people in a community, for it is more in line with the reality of community, but also that single issue movements, in addition to the danger of becoming only a service, are more vulnerable to manipulation by the government.

Where Should Radicals Work?

The writers of "We've Got to Reach Our Own People" are understandably vague in their discussions of ethnicity and class. All of us in the movement—activists, organizers, and researchers (e.g., economists, anthropologists) must give a lot of thought to where working class America is located, and what it is—culturally, socially, politically and economically. For example, the authors use the terms "poor whites," "working class whites," "lower working class whites," "low paid whites," "poor and working class whites," and "lower class white working class communities." OK, what are the differences in terms of culture, job, habits, interests, sense of self as a group, aspirations, attitudes, etc.? What do these differences mean in terms of where radicals select to live and work? We must learn about them through some research, and mostly through work, discussion and self-criticism.

At a time when we have only a limited number of activists making the break with the student movement, we think it is important to give a lot of thought of what whites, what ethnic groups we work with. Poles, Italians, Portuguese, Germans, Greeks? Does it make a difference? We would like to suggest that radicals start to learn about, and begin to live and work with, people making up a group characterized by what we are temporarily referring to as "BASICALLY RURAL, COUNTRY AND WESTERN WHITE AMERICAN CULTURE."

What we are talking about are NON-WHITE COLLAR WORKERS (poor, transitional and working class whites) who are NOT OF EUROPEAN ETHNIC GROUP BACKGROUNDS. We are talking about a large portion of the South's 40 million white people, people who work in places like Durham, Birmingham, Memphis, Chattanooga, Nashville and Lawrenceburg; people in the Appalachian and Border cities: Ashville, Knoxville, Wheeling, Beckley, Huntington, Charleston, Evansville, Indianapolis, Youngstown, Cincinnati, St. Louis, people in Northern cities that have concentrations of people with the culture we're talking about: cities like Detroit, Benton Harbor, Flint, Cleveland, Columbus, Hammond and Chicago; mid- and southwestern cities like Kansas City, Topeka, Oklahoma City, Tulsa, Omaha, Wichita, Houston and Dallas; and it includes working people on the coast with kin who came West with grapes of wrath, people who now live in Los Angeles, Bakersfield, Stockton, San Jose, Fremont, Oakland, Richmond and Sacramento.

We are not talking about an ethnic group in the sense that Negroes, Mexicans and Puerto Ricans are ethnic groups. People of this group are not economically homogeneous. However, we think the kind of people we're talking about make up a distinguishable sub-culture in America, that is articulated (and in turn shaped) by Nashville (country and western music center of the world). People in this cultural group tend to work in unskilled and semi-skilled jobs, or in service industries. Large concentrations of them are located in cities. We think that when the overwhelming majority of the population lives in urban areas there is little political mileage in organizing creeks and hollers. So, when we say rural, we don't mean that's where people live now.

Discover America

Too many student radicals have a poor idea of what America is about. It's not their fault; mental pictures of the country are products of the distorting mass media. Cities like San Francisco and New York, the communication and culture centers of the country, appear hip, sophisticated and very middle class to residents and visitors alike, yet are, in fact, overwhelmingly working class cities. Student radicals must realize that cross country jaunts, digging truck stops, a past summer spent on a ranch, digging Bonnie and Clyde, and the reading of Kerouac's ON THE ROAD, Ginsburg's "Wichita, Vortex, Sutra," or Tom Wolf's CANDY COLORED TANGERINE FLAKE STREAM LINE BABY are not enough to give someone an understanding of people in this country. Probably 90% of those in the student movement have been reared, schooled and still spend 99% of their time in the middle class setting, even if it is now garnished with "groovy things."

The time has come for serious radicals to give serious attention to the people we speak of, basically with anglo–saxon protestants, the working class that is not in the European immigrant ethnic group bag. We sense it is probably the largest group of white people in the country, and the one from which the largest number of draftees are drawn. See, too many good radical kids, reared in liberal America, were falsely influenced by Amos 'n Andy—what about the Beverly Hillbillies? "Hillbillies," "white trash," "oakies," "shit kicker," "crackers," "red necks," and "ridge runners" aren't the gaunt (or even fat) characters out of a Hatfield and McCoy cartoon, singing purer versions of something the New Lost City Ramblers "preserved." They're a different trip, very large, with an essence and thrust in the society. Radicals should deal with it. . . .

Race is a problem, but let's blame it on capitalism and the failure of white radicals to organize among poor and working whites. We believe among whites of a rural background there is a populist consciousness that may be a factor in overcoming racism—IF ORGANIZERS ARE PRESENT. An organizer is also a teacher, and good teachers help people discover the truth.

New Projects: The Cincinnati View

We know that an organizer must operate from a position of trust with the people he or she is trying to organize. We cannot define trust or explain exactly how one gains it, but we think a certain mode of operation can help the organizer gain the trust of a community. Based on this premise, we are trying out the following model.

Rather than moving a project (office, large group of people, etc.) into a neighborhood, we think a small number of people should move into a city. These organizers should make contacts with the radical/peace/liberal people in the city, but should try to isolate themselves from these already organized folks. (From them we learned a lot about the city, regarding concentrations of hillbillies, industrial area, the power structure). Then, in order to understand the community they are going to organize, the organizers should submerge themselves in that community—the life style and culture should be understood. Besides gaining understanding, submergence helps the organizer move freely and relate realistically to the people. The reason for a small number of organizers and the isolation from a familiar circle of friends is two-fold: 1. so a student culture is not brought into the community, for it is alienating for neighborhood people, and keeps organizers from immersing themselves in the community; and 2. the isolation and loneliness will drive the organizers into the community for friendship and fun.

One of the friendship networks important for organizers to tie into is locating a place of work where people from the neighborhood work or frequent. For instance, men and women could work in factories where neighborhood people work; women could become waitresses in local cafes or retail clerks in local stores; men could work at the local gas station. Other places to tap into friendship networks are your building, block, bars, pool halls, cafes, laundromats, service stations, small stores, etc. An organizer should be straight about his political views (though be careful about over organizing—giving someone a copy of the Movement, GUERILLA WARFARE, and Ramparts all at once); it will be easier if the organizer understands the community and they trust him—someone who lives in the same place, works a similar job and has mutual friends can't be all that bad or kooky.

416

The Courses of Action

By building these types of relationships with people two courses of action will probably open up. Since "issues"—bad housing, police brutality, credit cheating, the draft—are daily occurrences in poor and working class communities, THE ORGANIZERS GROUP OF FRIENDS COULD BECOME THE NUCLEUS of a solid organization that begins to have actions in the neighborhood. Or if this doesn't occur, after the organizers are well established and have some base in the community (6–12 mos.?), they COULD BEGIN FORMALLY ORGANIZING—setting up an office, going door to door, passing out leaflets, having actions.

In either case the organization would grow out of a deep understanding of the community and the organizers would have some legitimacy within the community. (Contrast this with 10 students descending on a community, passing out leaflets about urban renewal or the draft.) This way a solid radical vanguard could be built in and of that community. This group would deal with issues vital to that community thus creating the radicalizing experiences necessary for people to become radicals. It is important that organizers don't usurp roles that should belong to the organized, that the organization doesn't become the organizer's organization rather than the community's. Example. The JOIN theater group might be tight for a month or more; then a steady member becomes absent; skits could be performed if other organizers were used, but that deters them from their work and doesn't help in the effort to reach new people. Because the organization that would develop from either of these courses of action would be of and by people in the community IT WOULD BE MORE SOLID—BASED ON PERSONAL TRUST AND COMMITMENT—AND MORE RADICAL—BECAUSE OF THE INDEPTH ORGANIZING THAT PRECEEDED THE ORGANIZATION—than one set up by a larger group of organizers who had little understanding of the community.

In choosing a neighborhood, people should use the library for census tracts, chamber of commerce reports, etc. We visited neighborhoods at night (because that's when people are on the streets). We looked for the following things: Southerners, housing conditions, amount of street life at night, the sense of community, amount of employment in the area (preferably a large amount), amount of transiency (largely hearsay). As we narrowed down our choices we began going into bars and cafes checking the jukeboxes for country and western music and the types of music (we were

interested in workers rather than winos). We made a choice—more an educated guess—on what would be the best community to organize in. Although we think we made the "right" choice, we are consciously remaining
mobile in case we don't think this is that good an area.

It Isn't So Bad

Our experiences in southern neighborhoods in urban centers suggests that
we can organize people into a radical community union. Our analysis of
the country tells us that we must begin, somehow, reaching more poor and
working whites if we are to build a powerful radical movement. So, we
urge other radicals to TAKE A STEP INTO AMERICA—IT ISN'T SO BAD. Confront white America: give poor and working people an alternative to Wallace, Reagan and Kennedy; build for the revolution—it's out there!

---

[55]

SOCIALISM AND THE NEW LEFT

MARTIN J. SKLAR AND JAMES WEINSTEIN

UNDERLYING much of the activity of new Left groups—whether it be
repeated demonstrations against the war or organizing projects among the
poor—is a shared sense that their activity will change American society
fundamentally. In the ghettos the specific content of the political programs
seldom goes beyond the standard demands of liberal pressure groups, and
is consistent with the "pluralist" idea that if an "excluded group" orga-
nizes and makes enough noise it will receive some rewards within the system as it is now constituted. In the peace movement repeated demonstrations increasingly serve to bolster the system by proving that it permits
ritualistic dissent, and by allowing the demonstrators to believe that they
have discharged their responsibilities by publicly taking a stand (or by demoralizing them as they witness their own impotence). In New York, for
example, the peace organizations planned, *in advance of the resumption of*

SOURCE: Martin J. Sklar and James Weinstein, "Socialism and the New Left," *Studies on the Left* 6, no. 2 (March–April 1966): 62–64, 66–70.

bombing North Vietnam, to demonstrate the following day—a procedure that could not prevent the bombing, but that would show the world that some Americans are more moral than others.

Of course, many activists in the movements recognize these circumstances. The failure to change them is perhaps most commonly attributed to the power and flexibility of America's great corporations and their political representatives. We do not raise these questions to be carping. But we suggest that the reasons lie closer to home. In view of the state of radical politics inherited by the new Left in the late 1950's, its accomplishments are impressive. Yet it is becoming clear that the new movements are at, or are fast approaching, states of crisis, that the initial usefulness and success of their anti-ideological stances have worn thin, and that the need now is to search for theoretical clarity about revolutionary politics in the United States.

Before we can do that some questions have to be answered about the old Left and its failures. This is necessary because many old Left concepts operate under new Left trappings, and because many of the arguments against ideology (in the sense of theory) are the result of unthinking equations of Marxism or Socialism with the organizational and political concepts of the Communist and Socialist Left in the United States between 1920 and 1965.

In 1962 we wrote that although *Studies on the Left* had been called a theoretical organ for the new Left in the United States, we could not identify a movement that could call itself *the* new Left. Almost four years later there is still a great deal of confusion over what and who the new Left is; but it is clear that there is a new ideological framework of Left politics and within that, as Hal Draper has recently pointed out, a new Left type. Unfortunately, the most usable definitions of the new Left, both of its encompassing framework and of its organizations and leaders, are negative. We know what the new Left is against, what it rejects, at least at any given moment; no one knows what it is for.

The new Left is essentially a student movement. Most of its members and activists are from middle class families, many from upper middle class families. They come to radicalism out of a feeling that American society has failed to live up to its potentials and to its articulated values. That is, the rhetoric of democracy and liberalism is seen as fraudulent, as a mask behind which the large corporations carry on neo-colonial wars and manipulate public tastes, opinions and perceived needs so as to create vast new markets for products that degrade as much as they satisfy. These new radicals are not motivated, as many who grew up in the 1920's and 1930's were, by a notion that American capitalism's failure consists in its inability to satisfy the material needs of most Americans despite a great unused productive capacity. They see poverty, and they react to it as something immoral. Their radicalism is not created by a consciousness of material poverty, however; they are more concerned about the poverty of human relationships and values. In other words, the new radicals become radicals first, then fighters in the ghetto or in the South. . . .

For our present purposes, two points must be made about the American Communists. First, they never applied Marxist theories to a serious analysis of American society. During their "left" periods they mimicked the pre-revolutionary Russians. During their united front period (essentially from 1935 to the present) they mimicked American liberalism, except in foreign policy where they mechanically followed the Russians. Second, their concepts of organization were copied from the Russian experience, despite the basically different conditions and problems facing American Socialists. The effect of this in isolating them from traditional American radicalism and from the new Left can be seen in its effects on the Progressive Labor Party. Although it is part of the new insurgency, PLP's style of work and concepts of party organization (what it calls the Leninist party) have created a gulf between it and the new radicals almost as wide as that separating the new Left from the Communist party.

Anti-Communist Socialists fare no better with the new Left, despite (maybe because of) their tireless reiteration that they are the "democratic Left." This is in part because they lack any convincing intention of transforming American society, a condition which flows from their gradual acceptance of American democratic capitalism as preferable to Communism as it has developed in Russia. This attitude toward Communism in Russia and the United States was facilitated by the unceasing attacks of Communists on Socialists even before the Socialists had adopted the attitudes they now have; however, it also reflects an inability to understand social development in its specific historical context. That is, it is the result of an identification of post-industrial Socialism with the process of industrialization under Socialist auspices that has gone on in Russia, China, Eastern Europe and Cuba. But it is not this that creates the near contempt of so many new leftists for men like Irving Howe and others of the League for Industrial Democracy. That view comes from the role that "Socialists" have played since 1946 as ideologues for the Cold War, which is to say, as the ideological defenders of American neo-colonialism. It was, after all, the right wing Socialists who laid the ideological basis of McCarthyism.

The ideological framework in which the new Left has developed is Socialist, but it is not part of the old debates described above. This is not to say that the archetype new leftist is a Socialist; he is not necessarily that, although he is anti-capitalist in the sense that he is opposed to the values which sustain the capitalist system. But there is a set of attitudes, an intellectual milieu, within which the new Left germinated. The earliest enunciation of these views was made by *Monthly Review,* the first Socialist journal that was non-Communist, but not anti-Communist. That is, it was committed to Socialism, critical of the Soviet Union but against the Cold War, and on the side of the social revolutions throughout the world that were and are the main victims of Cold War policies. Before 1956 that position was novel and difficult to take and maintain. After the Twentieth Congress in the Soviet Union, which exposed Stalinist terror even for Communists to see, and after the Cuban revolution, which proved that revolution could occur and be successful under non-Communist auspices, the need for a new look at revolutionary politics became much more readily apparent. In that atmosphere, *Studies on the Left, New University Thought, Root and Branch* and many other small magazines came into being.

It would be difficult to trace the connections between these ideological predecessors and what we now know as the new Left. Yet in the origins of SLATE, Free Speech Movement and the Vietnam Day Committee at Berkeley, of TOCSIN at Harvard, of SNCC and of the Students for a Democratic Society, there are many direct connections, in addition to the more important general framework of ideas reflected in *Studies* and the other journals.

Unfortunately, the archetype new radical defined by Hal Draper has chosen to remain unconscious of all this. He would prefer not to think of theory. He chooses, not as a temporary necessity but as a positive good, to be uncommitted to any system of ideas about the transformation of society. One of the reasons he does so is outlined above: there are no immediately usable alternative theories. Another reason is that present prospects appear so bleak: the system seems to be infinitely flexible and impenetrable. A third reason is that few of the new radicals are willing to make the kind of commitment required to build a revolutionary movement and party. To spend a year or two working full time in the movement between graduation and settling down to life's work is one thing. To commit oneself to the lifetime job of slowly building a new theory and revolutionary party is another. The first has a glamour and sense of immediacy and fulfillment that the second does not. It is easier to feel radical by rejecting everything about middle class life, to wear the old clothes of the ghetto and live in mock poverty, than it is to accept who and what you are and still try to revolutionize society.

But there is among the new radicals a growing awareness that *activity,* although essential within a worked-out political perspective, leads nowhere by itself. This is a result of the increasing frustrations experienced by organizers in the South, in ghetto projects and in the peace movement. Demonstrations never change power relationships, at best they cause those in power to grant concessions. On the war in Vietnam they do not even do that. The repeated and increasingly large demonstrations against the war have produced few lasting gains because there is no political movement of opposition which can recruit from the demonstrators and continue their education as radicals. In recognition of this and in the hope of moving toward a new socialist politics, some are beginning to search for new theory and are beginning to study the American past. Others, swinging from an extreme anti-electoral bias, are becoming fully involved in political campaigns, but in so doing they are reliving the patterns of old Left popular front electoral action. Instead of viewing electoral activity as an educational and organizing device, so that after the election independent, self-conscious radical constituencies have been created, this activity is designed to win. That means that programs are but partially developed, that large territories are tackled without attention being given to continuing relationships with groups of voters, that compromises are made to get votes. In other words, that the mindless living for the moment of the united front is being repeated.

The essential work now involves developing in outline, and to a degree programatically, a view of the new post-industrial society posited by present-day capitalism, and to begin building a new movement around this view. William Appleman Williams has taken a first step in this direction in suggesting that Socialists should reject programs of further consolidation and centralization. These, Williams argues, are more in line with the needs and values of the liberal guardians of the large corporations. Socialist ideals of community, equality, democracy and free individual development require not only social ownership and control of the nation's industrial plant, not only planning, but also units of government and of economic organization small enough to encourage and permit anyone to participate in the decisions that establish the framework of his life. These suggestions, of course, only indicate a direction in which Socialists should look as they work out new programs and visions. To assess and go beyond these suggestions is the intellectuals' part in the process of building a new revolutionary movement.

The easiest and least useful thing one can do is to decry the deficiencies of others; the difficult and most urgent task is to determine where we go from there. The first step is for new leftists to examine the content of their radicalism and determine if they are committed to a transformation of American capitalism into that higher form of society envisaged by Marx. If they are, then all of their activities should be consciously determined by an intention to build a revolutionary movement and then a party that has the perspective of gaining power in the United States. Such an outlook requires taking the long view as well as the short, thinking ten, fifteen, maybe twenty-five or fifty years as well as ten days, weeks or months ahead.

Assuming that liberalism will remain the dominant political ideology of the large corporations—that is, that the basic commitment to formal democracy will be maintained and the socially disruptive programs of the ultra-right will continue to be rejected—then electoral politics will continue to be central to the political consciousness of Americans. This will mean that the electoral arena must be entered and electoral politics developed in such a way as to build growing, solidly-based constituencies. . . . That is, the purpose of all such activity should be what Eugene V. Debs always insisted it should be: to make Socialists, not merely votes. Success cannot be measured by adding up the numbers who demonstrate or get arrested or vote in a particular election. Whatever the form of radical activity, its value to us and to those who share our long range perspective can be estimated finally in terms of how many new, consciously Socialist individuals merge and organize within a developing movement.

---

[56]

IN WHITE AMERICA

GREGORY CALVERT

. . . THE movement for radical social change in America is going through an important period of self-re-examination which is reflected in a myriad of ways: the often compulsive concern with ideology, the desperate attachment to militant tactics, the frustration, pessimism and despair in the life of full-time activists. This crisis has its roots in a very important failure —the failure of the Southern-based movement in the black community to

SOURCE: Gregory Calvert, *In White America* (Ann Arbor: Radical Education Project, n.d.), pp. 1–4; first published in *The National Guardian,* 25 March 1967.

423

mobilize a sufficiently powerful mass of people to alter the American system in any significant way. As a friend of mine, long-time SNCC staff member, put it: "We thought we could move enough people to move America, but America turned out to be incredibly more rigid than we had ever expected. We were on the move, but America just wouldn't budge. I look back now and wonder what sort of simple ideas we must have had in our heads to have ever believed in that possibility."

If we face up to this crisis honestly, if we look American reality hard in the face, two things emerge. First, we have to admit that—like it or not —we live in urban industrial capitalist America, in white America and not in the rural South. We owe SNCC a deep debt of gratitude for having slapped us brutally in the face with the slogan of black power, a slogan which said to white radicals: "Go home and organize in white America which is your reality and which only you are equipped to change." Secondly, we are thus forced to ask ourselves whether in white America there exists the possibility for organizing a truly radical, an authentically revolutionary movement for change. Finally, we must face the fact that unless such a potential exists, then the basic arguments of the Progressive Labor Party or other Third-World oriented groupings bear serious reading. If a mass movement cannot be built in white America, then individuals with revolutionary hopes and perspectives must orient themselves toward Third-World revolutions and develop those methods of activity which will maximize the impact of peasant-based revolutions on the structure of the American imperialist monster. The problem is a search for a constituency, for an agent of social transformation, for "the revolutionary class." If no such constituency can be developed, then our only hope lies with external agencies, with revolutionary developments in the Third World.

Let me say that I am not overflowing with optimism regarding the possibility of building such a movement. There are two things which go through my mind: 1) American corporate capitalism is an incredibly brutal and dehumanizing system, whether at home or abroad, but, 2) it is also fantastically adept at masking its reality at home. Some have called it "benevolent fascism," and there lies a key to its operation: it operates domestically by intimidation, regimentation, and conditioning, and prefers not to use overt repressive force. Why? because to do so is to reveal itself for what it is, and to open the possibility of rebellion.

The importance of American aggressive imperialism for the development of a domestic movement, the importance of Vietnam and the Vietnams to come, is that it reveals America to America, that the liberal façade is shattered and the American expansionist system reveals its brutality and aggressiveness and its dehumanizing horror in all its nakedness.

I am going to speak today about the problem of consciousness in American society and about the possibility of developing radical or revolutionary consciousness. I approach the problem of organizing from this viewpoint because 1) the objective conditions of oppression in America seem to be manifest and 2) because those objective conditions are not perceived, and 3) because the major problem to which organizers must address themselves in this period is the problem of false consciousness.

Revolutionary Consciousness

Let me posit a first principle: All authentically revolutionary movements are struggles for human freedom. . . . Revolutionary mass movements are not built out of a drive for the acquisition of more material goods. That is a perversion and vulgarization of revolutionary thought and a misreading of history. Revolutionary movements are freedom struggles born out of the perception of the contradictions between human potentiality and oppressive actuality. Revolutionary consciousness interprets those social economic and political structures which maintain the existing gap between potentiality and actuality as the objective conditions of oppression which must be transformed. Revolutionary consciousness sees the transformation of those oppressive conditions as the act of liberation and sees the realization of the previously frustrated human potentiality as the achievement of freedom. The bonds of oppression are broken and the new reality is constructed.

What is fundamental to this process is the mass perception of the contradiction between potentiality and actuality. In a given historical situation that contradiction may take the concrete form of economic deprivation in the face of the possibility of material abundance, and the struggle for liberation may take the form of a drive to eliminate the conditions which prevent the achievement of that abundance. In a situation of economic abundance, the drive for freedom will rest on different perceptions and will set different goals. But the struggle in either case is a struggle for freedom, the form of which depends on the given stage of historical development—that is, on the level of development of human potentiality.

There is only one impulse, one dynamic which can create and sustain an authentic revolutionary movement. The revolutionary struggle is always and always must be a struggle for freedom. No individual, no group, no class is genuinely engaged in a revolutionary movement unless their struggle is a struggle for their own liberation.

Radical versus Liberal Consciousness

The point which is important to understand is clearly illustrated by the difference between radical or revolutionary consciousness and "liberal" consciousness. The profound gap which separates a liberal reform movement from a revolutionary freedom movement is revealed in the dynamics of the participants.

Liberal reformists (including revisionist social democrats inside and outside the CP) react out of guilt motivation, that is, the contradiction to which they address themselves is the contradiction between what they have (comfort, goods, security) and who they are (which they posit as the universally human), on the one hand, and what others (the poor) do not have (the poverty and lack of opportunity of the poor) and what others are (the immediacy of satisfactions in underclass life perceived as uncivilized behavior). Their conscience reveals to them the injustice of their unearned position and their own self-image, as universally valid for humanity, is challenged by the life-style of the underclass. Their response is to close the gap, to resolve the contradictions and the accompanying psychological tensions by means of activity to "raise" the underprivileged to their own social-economic level and to draw them into the same nexus of relationships in order to impose on them their own image of humanity.

The liberal reformist is always engaged in "fighting someone else's battles." His struggle is involved in relieving the tension produced by the contradictions between his own existence and life-style, his self-image, and the conditions of existence and life-style of those who do not share his privileged, unearned status.

The liberal reformist accepts and defends his own self-image, his own vision and experience of humanity, and generalizes it to all men. He wants everyone to be "white, happy, and middle class." Should those toward whom his good works are directed (e.g., SNCC with its statement of Black Power) ever challenge his view of the human-universal, he reacts by rejecting them, however subtly or brutally.

The liberal does not speak comfortably of "freedom" or "liberation," but rather of justice and social amelioration. He does not sense himself to be unfree. He does not face the contradictions between his own human potential, his humanity, and the oppressive society in which he participates. To deal with the reality of his own unfreedom would require a shattering re-evaluation of his subjective life-experience.

Liberal consciousness is conscience translated into action for others. It may or may not include alienation or a sense of the meaninglessness of one's experience. When these latter elements are present, they are interpreted in a personalistic fashion (as personal guilt) and the solutions envisioned are privitized (e.g., a trip or a trip to the psychiatrist). Liberal consciousness is rarely consciousness of personal oppression, and, therefore, interprets oppression in the society as based on "misunderstanding" or "irrationality." Individual therapy or cultural liberalization and education are seen as the means of correction.

Radical or revolutionary consciousness perceives contradiction in a totally different fashion. The gap is not between oneself, what one is, and the underprivileged but is the gap between "what one could be and the existing conditions for self-realization. It is the perception of oneself as unfree, as oppressed—and finally it is the discovery of oneself as one of the oppressed who must unite to transform the objective conditions of their existence in order to resolve the contradiction between potentiality and actuality. Revolutionary consciousness leads to the struggle for one's own freedom in unity with others who share the burden of oppression. It is, to speak in the classical vocabulary, class consciousness because it no longer sees the problem as someone else's, because it breaks through individualization and privitization, because the recognition of one's own unfreedom unites one in the struggle of the oppressed, because it posits a more universally human potentiality for all men in a liberated society.

The problem in white America is the failure to admit or recognize unfreedom. It is a problem of false consciousness, that is, the failure to perceive one's situation in terms of oppressive (class) relationships. Only when white America comes to terms with its own unfreedom can it participate in the creation of a revolutionary movement.

When we have talked about the "new radicalism" about the "freedom movement," with a passionate conviction, we have been talking about a movement which involves us, you and me, in a gut-level encounter with disengagement from, and struggle against, the America which keeps us in bondage. It may have begun in a very personalistic fashion, out of a private sense of our individual alienation from the U.S. corporate-liberal capitalist monster and from "the bomb" which was the logical but unthinkable conclusion. But, it has and must move beyond the level of our own bewilderment, confusion, and despair about America. It moves to the final realization of our common oppression.

We should realize that Marx was quite correct when he said the true revolutionary consciousness was class consciousness. What he meant by

427

that was that in order to change society people must realize that they are united in common struggle for their own liberation from objective conditions of oppression. . . . He was saying to people that their struggle was the struggle of unfree men—not for individual salvation—but a struggle for collective liberation of all unfree, oppressed men.

What has held the new radicalism together, what has given it its life and vitality, has been the conviction that the gut-level alienation from America-the-Obscene-and-the-Dehumanized was a sincere and realistic basis for challenging America. What has often left the new radicals impotent and romantic is their failure to understand the dynamics of the society which produced their gut-level alienation, that is their failure to understand that what seemed humanly and emotionally real could be understood in terms of a fundamental and critical analysis of American corporate-liberal capitalism. There was a crying out of their own being against America, but a failure to understand why that revolt was authentically related to the necessity and the possibility of revolutionizing America.

That situation has begun to change. The new radicals are beginning to produce an analysis of America which enables them to understand themselves and the greater reality of American society in a way which authenticates their own revolt as a realistic basis for understanding the way in which we can be freed. It begins to relate the anarchist demand, "I want freedom," to the revolutionary socialist analysis which points the way to collective liberation.

False Consciousness and Radicalization

If the analysis is correct and if false consciousness is the major obstacle to organizing a revolutionary movement, then it would seem to follow that our primary task at this stage of development is the encouragement or building of revolutionary consciousness, of consciousness of the conditions of unfreedom. A question immediately arises, however—"To what extent is consciousness of unfreedom subject to the influence of variables which are independent of the question of economic remuneration or consumption level?" That is to say, since the society can buy people off with goods, are there other sufficiently potent radicalizing experiences apart from economic deprivation which radicals can work with?

This is an important and complex question. It is perhaps the failure of the old Left to arrive at a satisfactory answer to that question which was responsible for its fervent attachment to the concept of the inevitability of the collapse of capitalism—the catastrophic event which would reveal both the objective contradictions of the system and create the proper subjective response on the part of the exploited.

Without necessarily ruling out the possibility of such an economic cataclysm in the capitalist world, the new left is hardly notable for its faith in the inevitability of the event. Thus deprived of the *deus ex machina* which the old Left was certain existed in the wings, we new leftists have been driven by a special urgency which gives rise to a variety of inventive activities designed to reveal to people their unfreedom and to offer them alternatives and hope. Certainly the organizing of the new radicals has been one of their most characteristic features.

In the end, however, our ability to organize and to radicalize in an effective manner depends on more than our sensitivity to individual human beings. It requires the kind of careful analysis and conceptualizing which has produced the so-called Port Authority Statement (I hope you realize that the intent of the title was humorous!). The whole notion of the "new working class" provides a powerful tool for understanding the present structure of advanced industrial capitalism.

First, it breaks through the "myth of the great American middle class." Not only are millions of Americans held captive by that notion, but it has also been a major psychological obstacle for most radicals. If white America is mostly middle class, and if being middle class means not being oppressed, then there is no possibility for finding the resources upon which a radical movement can be built in white America. What we have come to understand is that the great American middle class is not middle class at all. None of the 19th Century definitions of the bourgeoisie apply: not the upper bourgeoisie—the owners of capital; not the petty bourgeoisie—the owners of small property; not, finally, even the professional bourgeoisie, which in the 19th Century meant those favored few whose education gave them independence within the economic system. The vast majority of those whom we called the middle class must properly be understood as members of the "new working class": that is, as those workers who fill the jobs created by a new level of technological development within the same exploitive system.

Secondly, it enables us to understand the special role of students in relation to the present structure of industrial capitalism. Students are the "trainees" for the new working class and the factory-like multiversities are the institutions which prepare them for their slots in the bureaucratic machinery of corporate capitalism. We must stop apologizing for being students or for organizing students. Students are in fact a key group in the creation of the productive forces of this super-technological capitalism. We have organized them out of their own alienation from the multiversity and have raised the demand for "student control." That is important: because that is precisely the demand that the new working class must raise when it is functioning as the new working class in the economic system. It is that demand which the system cannot fulfill and survive as it is. That is why it is potentially a real revolutionary demand in a way that demands for higher wages can never be.

Thirdly, we can see that it was a mistake to assume that the only radical role which students could play would be as organizers of other classes. It is still important, vitally important that student organizers continue to involve themselves in ghetto organizing, in the organizing of the underclass. That work is a vital part of the movement and it is first from ghetto community organizing that the demand for control was clearly articulated. But it is now important to realize that we must organize the great majority of students as the trainees of the new working class. We must speak to them of the way in which the new working class is created—of the meaningless training which is passed off as education and of the special coercive devices like the Selective Service System with its student deferments designed to channel them into the multiversity.

Finally, we must be sensitive to those places in the social strata where false consciousness is being broken down, where the middle class myth is crumbling, where groups are beginning to struggle for their own freedom. In terms of the concept of the new working class, certain groups have begun to respond: social workers, teachers, the medical profession. All of these are service groups, it is true, and, interestingly, there is in all these areas a characteristic contradiction between a high level of articulated aspiration and increasingly oppressive conditions. We need radicals in all those areas in order to articulate more clearly the political ramifications of the demands for control and meaningful work.

Though there has as yet been no mass organizing on the part of engineers, it is encouraging to note that an engineering student at Iowa State University (the cow college of the corn belt) was just elected student body president on a platform calling for student control which brought nearly 10,000 students to the ballot boxes.

We must be sensitive to the fact that a mass movement in America will take time to develop and that it requires the involvement of a broad range of social strata, old and new working class, students and underclass. What counts is that America is beginning to break up, that the myth of the great American middle class is crumbling, that white Americans as well as black Americans are beginning to recognize their common oppression and are raising their demands for freedom which can be the basis of a movement which could revolutionize America.

[57]

THE REVOLTED

CARL OGLESBY

EVERYONE in the rich world has heard that there is another world out there, almost out of sight, where two thirds of all of us are living, where misery and violence are routine, where Mozart has not been widely heard nor Plato and Shakespeare much studied.

There is a world, that is, which, according to the mainstream intuitions of mainstream middle-class America, must be somebody's exaggeration, a world which is fundamentally implausible. For the most part, we really believe in it, this poor world, only to the extent that we have it to blame for certain of our troubles. It is the "breeding ground," we say (a favorite term, packed with connotations of the plague), of those discontents which harass us. Most ordinary rich-world people would much prefer never even to have heard of Vietnam or Mozambique, not to mention the nearly thirty other states of the world where long-term insurgencies are under way.

The main fact about the revolutionary is that he demands total change. The corresponding fact about most Americans is that they are insulted by that demand. But what of that demand's moral force? When the statistics of world poverty reach us, as they now and then do, we can respond in several characteristic ways. Sometimes we cluck our tongues, shake our heads, and send a check off to CARE. Sometimes we tell tales about brave missionaries of either the Baptist or the AID persuasion. Someone might name the Alliance for Progress. And someone else might cough. When the statistics are voiced by the poor man's machine-gun fire, we are more decisive. While waiting for our bombers to warm up, we develop our poor-devils theory, according to which the wretched have been duped by Com-

SOURCE: Carl Oglesby, "The Revolted," in Carl Oglesby and Richard Shaull, *Containment and Change* (New York: Macmillan, 1967), pp. 140–156. © Carl Oglesby and Richard Shaull, 1967.

munist con men. It is a bad thing to be hungry; we can see that. But it is better to be hungry and patient than hungry and Red, for to be Red proves to us that all this hunger was really just a trick. It is probably the case that a Communist *has* no hunger.

In the land of remote-controlled adventure, the office-dwelling frontiersman, the automated pioneer—how can matters be seen otherwise?

Middle-class America is the nation to which the forthcoming obsolescence of the moral choice has been revealed.

Middle-class America is the condition of mind which supposes that a new, plastic Eden has been descried upon a calm sea, off our bow. A point here and there, a firm rudder, a smart following breeze, a bit of pluck, and we shall make port any time now in this "American Century."

Middle-class America regards itself as the Final Solution. Its most intense desire is not to be bothered by fools who disagree about that.

What must be difficult for any nation seems out of the question for us: To imagine that we may from time to time be the enemies of men who are just, smart, honest, courageous, and *correct*—who could think such a thing? Since we love rose arbors and pretty girls, our enemies must be unjust, stupid, dishonest, craven, and *wrong*.

Such conceptions are sometimes shaken. After the 1965 battle of Plei Me, Special Forces Major Charles Beckwith described NLF guerrilla fighters as "the finest soldiers I have ever seen in the world except Americans. I wish we could recruit them." After the same battle another American said of a captured Viet Cong, "We ought to put this guy on the north wall and throw out these Government troops. He could probably hold it alone. If we could get two more, we would have all the walls [of the triangular camp] taken care of." Major Beckwith was intrigued with the "high motivation" and "high dedication" of this enemy force and suggested an explanation: "I wish I knew what they were drugging them with to make them fight like that."

That curiosity, at least, is good. Why do men rebel? Let us try to find out what could possibly be so wrong with so many of the world's men and women that they should fight so hard to stay outside the Eden we think we are offering them.

I make three assumptions. First, everyone who is now a rebel *became* a rebel; he was once upon a time a child who spoke no politics. The rebel is someone who has changed.

Second, men do not imperil their own and others' lives for unimpressive reasons. They are sharp accountants on the subject of staying alive. When they do something dangerous, they have been convinced that not to do it was more dangerous. There are always a few who can evidently be persuaded by some combination of statistics and principles to put their lives on the line. Lenin, for example, did not materially *need* the Russian Revolution. His commitment was principled and it originated from a basic detachment. But I am not trying to describe the Lenins. I am after those nameless ones but for whom the Lenins would have remained only philosophers, those who (as Brecht put it) grasp revolution first in the hand and only later in the mind.

Third, I assume that the rebel is much like myself, someone whom I can understand. He is politically extraordinary. That does not mean that he is psychologically so. My assumption is that what would not move me to the act of rebellion would not move another man.

It is safe to say first that revolutionary potential exists only in societies where material human misery is the denominating term in most social relationships. No one thinks that bankers are going to make disturbances in the streets. Less obviously, this also implies that privation can be political only if it is not universal. The peasant who compares his poverty to someone else's richness is able to conceive that his poverty is special, a social identity. To say that hunger does not become a rebellious sensation until it coexists with food is to say that rebellion has less to do with scarcity than with maldistribution. This states a central theme: revolutionary anger is not produced by privation, but by understood injustice.

But the self-recognized victim is not at once his own avenger. He is first of all a man who simply wants to reject his humiliation. He will therefore re-create his world via social pantomimes which transfigure or otherwise discharge that humiliation. "They whipped Him up the hill," sang the black slave, "and He never said a mumbling word." That divine reticence is clearly supposed to set an example. But it also does much more. In such a song, the slave plays the role of himself and thus avoids himself, puts his realities at the distance of a pretense which differs from the realities only to the extent that it *is* a pretense. The slave creates for the master's inspection an exact replica of himself, of that slave which he is; and even as the master looks, the slave escapes behind the image. It is not that he pretends to be other than a slave. Such an act would be quickly punished. He instead pretends to be what he knows himself to be, acts out the role of the suffering and humiliated, in order to place a psychic foil between himself and the eyes of others. The American Negro's older Steppinfetchit disguise, or the acutely ritualized violence of ghetto gangs: these are intentional lies which intentionally tell the truth. The victim-liar's inner reality, his demand for freedom, precludes telling the truth. His outer reality, his victimhood, precludes telling a lie. Therefore he *pretends* the truth, pretends to hold the truth in his hand and to pass judgment on it. And by choosing to enact what he *is* he disguises from himself the fact that he had no choice.

A crucial moment comes when something ruptures this thin membrane of pretense. What can do that? A glimpse of weakness in his master sometimes; sometimes the accidental discovery of some unsuspected strength in himself. More often it will be the master's heightened violence that confronts the slave with the incorrigible authenticity of his slave act. A black man sings blues about his powerlessness, his loneliness; he has taken refuge behind that perfect image of himself. The white master, for no reason, in mid-song, takes the guitar away, breaks it, awaits the slave's reaction. The slave is at that moment forced into his self-image space, is psychologically fused with this truth-telling pretense of his: He *is* powerless; he *is* lonely. He cannot now enact himself; he must *be* that man of whom he had tried to sing. This encounter strips life of its formality and returns it to pure, primitive substance. For the victim, there is no longer even the fragile, rare escape of the simultaneous re-enactment of reality. He lives wholly now in his victim space, without manners, not even allowed to mimic the horror of victimhood in the same gesture that expresses it. He is nothing now but the locus of injustice.

Grown less random, injustice becomes more coherent. Confronted at every instant by that coherence, the victim may find that it is no longer so easy to avoid the truth that his suffering is *caused,* that it is not just an accident that there are so many differences between his life and the life of the round, white-suited man in the big hillside house. He begins to feel singled out. He rediscovers the idea of the system of power.

And at that same moment he discovers that he also may accuse. When the victim sees that what had seemed universal is local, that what had seemed God-given is man-made, that what had seemed quality is mere condition—his permanent immobility permanently disappears. Being for the first time in possession of the stark idea that his life could be different were it not for others, he is for the first time someone who might move. His vision of change will at this point be narrow and mundane, his politics naive: Maybe he only wants a different landlord, a different mayor, a different sheriff. The important element is not the scope or complexity of his vision but the sheer existence of the idea that change can happen.

Then who is to be the agent of this change? Surely not the victim himself. He has already seen enough proof of his impotence, and knows better than anyone else that he is an unimportant person. What compels him to hope nevertheless is the vague notion that his tormentor is answerable to a higher and fairer authority. This sheriff's outrageous conduct, that is, belongs strictly to this particular sheriff, not to sheriffness. Further, this sheriff represents only a local derangement within a system which the victim barely perceives and certainly does not yet accuse, a hardship which High Authority did not intend to inflict, does not need, and will not allow. (Once Robin Hood meets King Richard, the Sheriff of Nottingham is done for.)

We meet in this the politics of the appeal to higher power, which has led to some poignant moments in history. It is the same thing as prayer. Its prayerfulness remains basic even as it is elaborated into the seemingly more politically aggressive mass petition to the king, a main assumption of which is that the king is not bad, only uninformed. This way of thinking brought the peasants and priests to their massacre at Kremlin Square in 1905. It prompted the so-called Manifesto of the Eighteen which leading Vietnamese intellectuals published in 1960. It rationalized the 1963 March on Washington for Jobs and Freedom. The Freedom Rides, the nonviolent sit-ins, and the various Deep South marches were rooted in the same belief: that there was indeed a higher power which was responsive and decent.*

Sometimes mass-based secular prayer has resulted in change. But more often it has only shown the victim-petitioners that the problem is graver and change harder to get than they had imagined. The bad sheriffs turn out to be everywhere; indeed, there seems to be no other kind. It turns out that the king is on their side, that the state's administrative and coercive-punitive machinery exists precisely to serve the landlords. It turns out that the powerful know perfectly well who their victims are and why there should be victims, and that they have no intention of changing anything. This recognition is momentous, no doubt the spiritual low point of the emergent revolutionary's education. He finds that the enemy is not a few men but a whole system whose agents saturate the society, occupying and fiercely protecting its control centers. He is diverted by a most realistic despair.

But this despair contains within itself the omen of that final shattering

---

* What was new was the way these forms enlarged the concept of petition. Instead of merely writing down the tale of grievance, they reproduced the grievance itself in settings that forced everyone to behold it, tzar included, and to respond. The Vietnam war protest demonstrations are no different. The speeches they occasion may sometimes seem especially pugnacious. But inasmuch as the antiwar movement has never been able to dream up a threat which it might really make good, this fiercer face-making has remained basically a kind of entertainment. The main idea has always been to persuade higher authority—Congress, the UN, Bobby Kennedy—to do something. Far from calling higher authority into question, these wildly militant demonstrations actually dramatize and even exaggerate its power.

reconstitution of the spirit which will prepare the malcontent, the fighter, the wino, the criminal for the shift to insurgency, rebellion, revolution. He had entertained certain hopes about the powerful: They can tell justice from injustice, they support the first, they are open to change. He is now instructed that these hopes are whimsical. At the heart of his despair lies the new certainty that there will be no change which he does not produce by himself.

The man who believes that change can only come from his own initiative will be disinclined to believe that change can be less than total. Before he could see matters otherwise, he would have to accept on some terms, however revised, the power which he now opposes. The compromises which will actually be made will be arranged by his quietly "realistic" leaders and will be presented to him as a total victory. He himself is immoderate and unconciliatory. But the more important, more elusive feature of this immoderation is that he may be powerless to change it. He could only compromise with rebelled-against authority if he were in possession of specific "solutions" to those "problems" that finally drove him to revolt. Otherwise there is nothing to discuss. But the leap into revolution has left these "solutions" behind because it has collapsed and wholly redefined the "problems" to which they referred. The rebel is an incorrigible absolutist who has replaced all "problems" with the one grand claim that the entire system is an error, all "solutions" with the single irreducible demand that change shall be total, all diagnoses of disease with one final certificate of death. To him, total change means only that those who now have all power shall no longer have any, and that those who now have none—the people, the victimized—shall have all. Then what can it mean to speak of compromise? Compromise is whatever absolves and reprieves an enemy who has already been sentenced. It explicitly restores the legitimacy of the very authority which the rebel defines himself by repudiating. This repudiation being total, it leaves exactly no motive—again, not even the *motive*—for creating that fund of specific proposals, that *conversation,* without which a compromise is not even *technically* possible.

"What do you want?" asks the worried, perhaps intimidated master. "What can I give you?" he inquires, hoping to have found in this rebel a responsible, realistic person, a man of the world like himself. But the rebel does not fail to see the real meaning of this word *give.* Therefore he answers, "I cannot be purchased." The answer is meant mainly to break off the conference. But at one level, it is a completely substantive comment, not at all just a bolt of pride. It informs the master that he no longer exists, not even in part.

At another level, however, this answer is nothing but an evasion. The master seems to have solicited the rebel's views on the revolutionized, good society. The rebel would be embarrassed to confess the truth: that he has no such views. Industry? Agriculture? Foreign trade? It is not such matters that drive and preoccupy him. The victorious future is at the moment any society in which certain individuals no longer have power, no longer exist. The rebel fights for something that will not be like *this*. He cannot answer the question about the future because that is not his question. It is not the future that is victimizing him. It is the present. It is not an anticipated Utopia which moves him to risk his life. It is pain. "Turn it over!" he cries, because he can no longer bear it as it is. The revolutionary is not *by type* a Lenin, a Mao, a Castro, least of all a Brezhnev. He is neither an economist nor a politician nor a social philosopher. He may become these; ultimately he must. But his motivating vision of change is at root a vision of something absent—not of something that *will* be there, but of something that will be there *no longer*. His good future world is elementally described by its empty spaces: a missing landlord, a missing mine owner, a missing sheriff. Who or what will replace landlord, owner, sheriff? Never mind, says the revolutionary, glancing over his shoulder. Something better. If he is thereupon warned that this undefined "something" may turn out to make things worse than ever, his response is a plain one: "Then we should have to continue the revolution."

The fundamental revolutionary motive is not to construct a Paradise but to destroy an Inferno. In time, Utopian ideas will appear. Because the world now has a revolutionary past, it may seem that they appear at the same moment as destructive anger, or even that they precede and activate or even cause it. This is always an illusion produced by the predictive social analytic which revolutionist intellectuals claim to have borrowed from history. We may be sure that the people have not said: Here is a plan for a better life—socialism, Montes called it. He has proved to us that it is good. In its behalf, we shall throw everything to the wind and risk our necks. Rather, they have said: What we have here in the way of life cannot be put up with anymore. Therefore, we must defend ourselves.

It happens that at least the spirit of socialism will be implied by the inner dynamics of mass revolt: What was collectively won should be collectively owned. But it cannot be too much emphasized that the interest in developing other social forms, however acute it will become, follows, *does not precede,* the soul-basic explosion against injustice which is the one redemption of the damned. When Turcios takes his rebel band to a Guatemalan village for "armed propaganda," there is no need to talk of classless societies. Someone kneels in the center of the circle and begins to speak of his life, the few cents pay for a hard day's labor, the high prices, the arrogance of the *patrón,* the coffins of the children. It is this talk—very old talk, unfortunately always new—which finally sets the circle ringing with the defiant cry, *"Si, es cierto!"* Yes, it is true. Something will have to be done.

Revolutionary consciousness exists for the first time when the victim elaborates his experience of injustice into an inclusive definition of the society in which he lives. *The rebel is someone for whom injustice and society are only different words for the same thing.* Nothing in the social world of the master is spared the contempt of this definition, which, as soon as it exists, absorbs everything in sight. No public door is marked overnight with a device that permits its survival. The loanshark's corner office and the Chase Manhattan Bank, Coney Island and Lincoln Center, look very much the same from 137th Street. They are all owned by someone else.

Everywhere he looks, the man-who-is-being-revolted sees something which is not his. The good land which the *campesino* works belongs to the *hacienda.* That belongs to the *patrón.* As often as not, the *patrón* belongs to the United Fruit Company. And that prime mover unmoved belongs to nothing. It can only be for a brief moment that the *campesino* gazes with unashamed wonder at these skyscrapers. For all the justice they promise him, they might as well be so many rocks. He is soon unimpressed and grows apathetic toward Western grandeur. *The rebel is someone who has no stakes.* He is an unnecessary number, a drifter into a life that will be memorable chiefly for its humiliations. No use talking to him about the need to sustain traditions and preserve institutions or to help society evolve in an orderly way toward something better bit by bit. He very well knows that it is not in his name that the virtue of this orderliness is being proved. *The rebel is an irresponsible man whose irresponsibility has been decreed by others.* It is no doing of his own that his fantasy is now filled with explosions and burning Spanish lace.

But this new consciousness, this radical alienation from past and present authority, does not lead straightway to political action. A commitment to violence has only just become possible at this point. We have a man who certainly will not intervene in a streetcorner incident in behalf of the "law and order" of which he considers himself the main victim. He will even betray a government troop movement or shelter an "outlaw." But he may also find a tactical rationale for joining a "moderate" march or applauding a "reasonable" speech or doing nothing at all. At odd moments, he will abide talk of reform. Maybe things left to themselves will get better. He will keep the conversation open and the switchblade closed.

What is wrong with this man who thinks things can change without being changed? Who knows everything and does nothing?

Nothing is wrong with him but the fact that he is a human being. All these excuses, these cautions and carefully rationalized delays, add up to one thing: *He wants to be free.* He therefore temporizes with freedom. His desire for an independent private life has been intensified everywhere by the conditions that prohibit it. He has understood his situation and the demands it makes. He knows he is being asked to become a historical object. But he seems to recognize in this demand an old familiar presence. He has been drafted before by this history, has he not? Is the new allurement of rebellion really so different at bottom from the old coercion of slavery? Are his privacy and freedom not pre-empted equally by both? Is the rebel anything more than the same unfree object in a different costume, playing a new role? When the slave kills the master, argues Sartre, two men die. He meant that the slave dies too and the free man materializes in his place. Very well, the image is nearly overwhelming. But where is the freedom of this ex-slave who, instead of cutting cane, is now sharpening knives? That he has removed himself from one discipline to another does not hide the fact that he remains under discipline. It will be said that he at least chose the new one. But that does not diminish the servitude. When the slave conceives rebellion and remains a slave, one may say that he has chosen his slavery. That makes him no less a slave, no more a free man. In fact, the free man was glimpsed only in the moment at which he said: *I can! I may!* At that moment, the whole world shook with his exhilaration. Everywhere, he saw commotion and uncertainty where there had been only stillness and routine before. He stops at the window of a firearms dealer. He does not go in. He proceeds to the window of an agency of escape. This is not irresolution; it is freedom, the liquidity of choice. When he changes *I may* into *I will,* when he has taken the rifle and changed *I will* into *I am,* this man who was for one moment a profuse blur of possibilities, a fleeting freedom, has disappeared into another pose, has transformed himself into another image: that of the rebel.

Of all people, Sartre should have been distant enough from his partisanship to see that in this case freedom was only the possibility of transition from one binding contract to another—*and therefore not freedom.* As the slave found himself isolated from freedom by the master's power, so the rebel finds himself isolated from it by the decision which his life has forced upon him not merely to be a slave no longer, but *to be this rebel.*

Once again, he is not his own man. Once again his future, which was for one moment molten, has hardened into a specific object.

Do not be deceived by the high-mindedness of these concepts. Freedom is not an ecstasy reserved for enlightened Europeans. It is not as if its subtleties confine their influence to the bourgeois radicals who anatomize and name them. The psychiatric appendices to Fanon's *The Wretched of the Earth* often read like case-study illustrations for Sartre's *Being and Nothingness.* Drop-outs on Lexington Avenue are jangling and illumined with this torment. Freedom is not something which only certain men will discover only under certain conditions, and its goodness is not limited by the well-known fact that there are better and worse, nobler and baser ways in which it can be lost. We must not get it into our heads that the rebel *wants* to be a rebel. We must not think that he hurls his Molotov cocktails with a howl of glee, much less with a smirk on his face. We have to catch the wince, the flinch, those moments when he unaccountably turns aside. For the slave, there is simply no way to put an end to his current servitude except to exchange it for another. He is not at liberty to be just a nonslave. He is only free to choose between two hard masters. He will struggle to escape this fork, to liberate himself from these titles, to balance on the peak between them. But always he is about to be blown off on one side or the other. For him, it is a clear case of either/or.

I think Camus misses this. I cannot otherwise understand how he could believe himself to be making a useful, relevant moral point when he affirms that men should be "neither victims nor executioners." This is excellent advice for the executioner. It is less illuminating for the victim, perhaps even beyond his depth. The victim does not belong to that category of men for whom action can be regulated by such advice. This does *not* mean that he will recognize himself as the object of Camus's brilliant epithet, "privileged executioner," much less that he somehow prefers to be such a thing. What is so poignant about the victim, in fact, is the desperation with which he seeks to *enter* that category, to become *available* to Camus, for that is the category of free men. It is ruthless to assume that not ourselves but others are so appallingly strange as to choose shattered lives—as if pursuit, revenge, estrangement made up a career.

On the contrary. The rebel will have resisted his rebellion fiercely. The same inner agility that guarded his spirit from his body's subjugation, the same good guile that kept him from becoming for himself that slave which he could not help being for others—this talent for inner survival now stands up to ward off the new version of the old threat. At the moment at which he is most accelerated by his revulsion, he may also be most alarmed to see that he is about to be *reduced* to that revulsion, that he is in danger of becoming it—of becoming a revolted one, a revolutionary. He will for a long time affect a kind of reserve; he will not permit the loss of what Harlem has named his "cool," a word which could only be translated into the languages of oppressed people—"native tongues." To be cool is to float upon one's decisions, to remain positioned just barely beyond the reach of one's commitments. To be cool is to act freedom out without quite denying that there is a hoax involved. It is to tantalize oneself with the possibility that one may do *nothing,* at the same time never letting anyone forget the *fatefulness* of one's situation. Since he wants to be free, the slave cannot renounce rebellion. Since he cannot renounce rebellion, he craves freedom all the more hungrily. That tension can only be controlled by irony: The slave-rebel evades both captivities by refusing to destroy either.

But the evasion is only a more precarious form of the older ritualized self-enacting, and it dooms itself. As soon as the slave defines himself as *other* than the slave, he has already defined himself as the rebel, since the slave is precisely that person who cannot otherwise define himself without committing the act of rebellion.

How can he be said to make a choice when to choose anything at all is already to stand in rebellion?

This man's predicament can almost be touched with the hands. He wants nothing but freedom. That simple demand pits him against the injustice of being defined by the master. It also pits him against the internal and external forces that pressure him to define himself. The choice seems to lie between submitting to murder and committing suicide. Freedom is always escaping him in the direction of his anger or his fatigue. Desiring only that his objective life can have some of the variousness and elasticity of his subjective life, he is always rediscovering that this will be possible only if he forgoes variousness for concentration, elasticity for discipline. *The revolutionary is someone who is nothing else in order to be everything else.*

"We have come to the point," writes someone from the Brazilian underground, "of making a rigorous distinction between being leftist—even radically leftist—and being revolutionary. In the critical situation through which we are now living, there is all the difference in the world between the two. We are in dead earnest. At stake is the humanity of man."

Anyone who wants to know where revolution's strange capacity for terror and innocence comes from will find the answer vibrating between these last two sentences. How can ordinary men be at once warm enough to want what revolutionaries say they want (humanity), cold enough to do without remorse what they are capable of doing (cutting throats), and poised enough in the turbulence of their lives to keep the aspiration and the act both integrated and distinct? How is it that one of these passions does not invade and devour the other? How is it that the knife that is still wet from a second person's blood and a third person's tears can be raised in an intimate salute to "humanity"?

Thus the rebel's picture of himself: a dead-earnest soldier for the humanity of man. If we join him in accepting that picture, if we take the rebel's *machismo* as offered, then we shall probably convince ourselves that he is trapped in a deadly moral contradiction which can be resolved in only one of two ways. Most sympathetically, stressing his aspirations, we should then decide that he is *tragic,* someone driven to disfigure what he most highly prizes. Least sympathetically, stressing his actions, we should find in him the hypocrite *criminal* who cynically pretends that death is only relatively evil.

Both views are wrong. When the "criminal" affirms that he is "in dead earnest," his tone of voice attributes to himself a decision that has originated elsewhere. "In dead earnest" is a euphemism for "desperate." When the "tragic" figure affirms that his cause is "the humanity of man," he has either forgotten the way he came or he has failed to see that negating one thing is not the same as affirming its opposite. "The humanity of man" is a euphemism for "survival."

This abstract man has come through a good many changes. From one whose reaction to his own victimhood was resignation and ritual flight, he has become a self-conscious victim who understands that no one will change things for him, that he may himself take action, and that there is such a thing as revolution. Wretched man has come to the edge of violence. But he is not yet revolutionary man. He may very well piece together an entire habit of life out of hesitation, ambiguity, reserve. He is oblique, ironic, elegant, and cool, someone whose detachment tries not to become treachery, whose sympathy tries not to become irreversible involvement.

What drives him over the divide? What is the difference between the Guatemalan, Mozambiquan, Brazilian farmers who have joined Turcios, Mondlane, Alepio in the mountains, and those likeminded ones who have remained onlookers in the villages? What is the difference between the "revolutionary" and the "radical leftist" which the Brazilian informs us is so critical?

If I am correct in assuming that men resist danger and want freedom from *all* servitudes, then it follows that rebellion does not take place until it has become compulsory. The rebel is someone who is no longer free to choose even his own docile servitude. He has been driven to the wall. Somebody is even trying to pound him through it. He has been reduced from the slave to the prisoner, from the prisoner to the condemned. It is no longer a matter of standing before two objects and choosing which he shall be. Totally possessed by his predicament, and therefore in its command, he is no longer able to make even a subjective distinction between that predicament and himself. His anger, like his previous humiliation, was for awhile still something which he could set beside himself and contemplate or enact: his *situation* not his *person*. But this changes. In spite of himself, he is pushed into the same space which he formerly quarantined off for his anger. He is fused with it—with the poverty, estrangement, futurelessness which gave it its murderous content. He is turned into the venom from which he has tried to stand apart. Except for rebellion, there is nothing. The strange apparent freedom of the rebel, and hence that pride of his which is so enormous when it arrives as to dwarf everything else, a psychic flood which sweeps everything before it, lie in his having finally affirmed the only life that is available to him: *The rebel is someone who has accepted death.*

It is this deprivation of choice that makes the difference between the "revolutionary," who may not be at all "radical," and the "radical," who may never become "revolutionary."

Who determined that this most severe and absolute of reductions should have taken place? We contented Westerners prefer to think that it was the rebel himself. This gives us the right to treat him as though he were a criminal. This is what allows us to single out for pity those "innocent women and children" whom our bombs also destroy, as if there is nothing wrong in killing adult male rebels. But this distinction, because it presupposes that the rebel has had a choice, obliges us to concoct a whole new second definition of man, a definition to place beside the one which we reserve for ourselves. The rebel will in that case be for us the very astounding slave who found it in his power to walk away from his slavery.

There is a more mundane explanation.

Here is someone who was lucky. He was *educated*. It was systematically driven into his head that justice is such and such, truth this, honor that. One day he surfaced from his education. Powerless not to do so, he observed his world. Having no measures other than those that had been nailed into his brain, and unable to detach them, he found himself possessed by certain conclusions: There is no justice here. Innocently, meaning no harm, he spoke the names of the guilty. No doubt he vaguely expected to be thanked for this, congratulated for having entered the camp of Socrates and Bruno. Matters were otherwise and now he is in prison making plans. This happened.

Here is another, a humbler person. Belly rumbling but hat in hand, he goes before the mighty; does not accuse them of being mighty, far from it; points out politely that there is unused grain in the silos, and untilled land; makes a modest suggestion. His son is dragged from bed the following dawn to see someone whipped for having dangerous ideas. This happened.

A third spoke of a union. He survived the bomb that destroyed his family, but it appears that no one will accept his apologies.

Another who joined a freedom march believing that men were good; he saw an old black man fall in the heat, where he was at once surrounded by white men who said, "Watch him wiggle. Let him die." This is memorable.

A quiet one who spoke for peace between the city and the countryside. It is whispered to him that he must hide; the police have his name; he has committed the crime of neutralism. Where shall this quiet one go now that he is a criminal?

A scholar speculates in a public article that aspects of his nation's foreign-trade system are disadvantageous to development. A week later he hears that his name has been linked with the names of certain enemies of society. Another week, and he finds that he may no longer teach.

One day someone's telephone develops a peculiar click.

Two bombs go off in San Francisco. No clues are found. Two pacifists are shot in Richmond. The police are baffled. Gang beatings of a political nature occur in New York. There are no arrests. The murder toll in Dixie mounts year by year. There are no convictions. One group proposes to rethink the idea of nonviolence. Its supporters are alarmed. Another group arms itself. Its supporters disaffiliate.

Stability, after all, must be ensured. The *peace* must be kept.

But the master seems to grow less and less confident with each of his victories. Now he requires the slave to affirm his happiness. Suspicion of unhappiness in the slave becomes ground for his detention; proved unhappiness constitutes a criminal assault upon the peace. The master is unsure of something. He wants to see the slave embracing his chains.

Trying only to reduce his pain for a moment, the slave forces his body to fade away. The backward faction acquires hard proof from this that its assessment of the situation has been correct. "See this docility? After all, the whip is the best pacifier."

Exasperated, the slave spits out a curse. Shocked to discover that a slave can have learned to curse, the advanced faction hastens forward with a principled rebuke: "Bad tactics! No way to change the hearts of men!"

It is almost comic. As though he were really trying to produce the angry backlash, the master grinds the slave's face deeper and deeper into the realities of his situation. Yet the master must be blameless, for he is only trying to satisfy his now insatiable appetite for security, an appetite which has actually become an addiction. He only wants to know that he is still respected, if not loved, that matters stand as matters should, and that no threat to the peace is being incubated here. "I love you, master," whispers the slave, squinting up between the two huge boots, thinking to steal a moment's relief. To no one's real surprise, he is promptly shot. The master's explanation rings true: "He was a liar. He *must* have been. Liars are untrustworthy and dangerous."

The rebel is the man for whom it has been decreed that there is only one way out.

The rebel is also the man whom America has called "the Communist" and taken as her enemy. The man whom America now claims the right to kill.

PART XVI
In the University

T HE student movement of the 1960's developed from protest against the forms of university administration at Berkeley in 1964 to an almost nationwide protest, affecting some 450 colleges and universities, of the killing of four white students at Kent State University as well as of Nixon's decision to send American troops into Cambodia. The apparent swirl and formlessness of student militancy can be shaped by stressing the organizing causes: civil rights, black liberation, educational reform, opposition to the Indochina war and the draft, and, in places and at moments, radical social reconstruction.

Late in 1964, at a massive sit-in at Sproul Hall at the University of California's Berkeley campus, Mario Savio gave a speech (Document 58) that was recorded. He had been involved in the Mississippi Summer of 1964, was then a major in philosophy, and soon dropped out of school to lead the Free Speech Movement that was developing. Because of the civil rights' background, it was consistent that this first explosion of an American campus should center around a typical civil rights issue of free, if obscene, speech. But, also, for the first time, something of the loosening of style that was later to characterize the Yippies added to the worries of officials, and added to the fun of the participants even though 800 were arrested. Savio began by asserting that the struggles for civil rights in Mississippi and at Berkeley were the same fight: democratic participation was the goal of the oppressed on both battlefields. But at Berkeley the peculiarly academic enemy was flushed out so that he—or rather, it—could not be mistaken. The FSM came up against what Savio described "as the greatest problem of our nation—depersonalized, unresponsive bureaucracy." In effect, Savio demanded that the university simply live up to standard rules, including due process of law. But fundamentally this early ferment was aimed at somehow avoiding the bureaucratization of personal-

447

ity that the university seemed to be demanding; the slogan, "Don't Fold, Spindle, or Mutilate" that students chanted, indicated that the facelessness of an American career as controlled by the urgencies of a technologically sophisticated economy provided the mass pressure behind the Berkeley action. The student movement thus began from the civil rights efforts in the South, and from the students' rejection of human standardization inside as well as outside the university.

The most complex and significant student strike occurred at San Francisco State College during the 1968–1969 academic year, flared out of deepening frustration; this strike was related to the crises at Columbia, Harvard, and elsewhere. The San Francisco State strike involved not only people at the college, but unions, Third World communities all over the state, and, of course, the whole political apparatus of California. This strike continues to reverberate as politicians and university administrators continue to exploit it for immediate political advantage, and as the wounds it left refuse to heal. In the rather long narrative which follows (Document 59), the strike committee provided a record which is close to the general student mood, especially as that mood was by now importantly directed by increasingly militant and politically sophisticated black students. The San Francisco State strike centered around the Black Student Union demands, with which this document opens, with the active participation of Third World groups, the support of SDS, other usually unaffiliated students, and finally a union of teachers, teaching assistants, and some community groups. This narrative runs from 27 September 1968 to 16 February 1969, during which these issues engulfed California and demanded the attention of the entire nation.

The issues of black studies, student control, and easier access of minority peoples to higher education were dramatized but not solved by this single strike. It in fact raised an enormous number of questions and problems with which the Left has had to deal ever since, not the least of which was a reconsideration of the wisdom in closing down, rather than pressing for changes in, universities. It also demanded a broadening of the whole critique of the political economy of which the university is a symptom and a product. As this is being written (July 1970) it is reasonably clear that the relationship between the universities and the political economy needs more thought and analysis, and that this radical pressure internal to the colleges and universities is far from over. The trajectory from the civil rights orientation of the first Berkeley movement to a wide-ranging critique of American institutional life will surely continue into the future, with more and more searching crises to come as a result.

[58]

AN END TO HISTORY

MARIO SAVIO

LAST summer I went to Mississippi to join the struggle there for civil rights. This fall I am engaged in another phase of the same struggle, this time in Berkeley. The two battlefields may seem quite different to some observers, but this is not the case. The same rights are at stake in both places—the right to participate as citizens in democratic society and to struggle against the same enemy. In Mississippi an autocratic and powerful minority rules, through organized violence, to suppress the vast, virtually powerless, majority. In California, the privileged minority manipulates the University bureaucracy to suppress the students' political expression. That "respectable" bureaucracy masks the financial plutocrats: that impersonal bureaucracy is the efficient enemy in a "Brave New World."

In our free speech fight at the University of California, we have come up against what may emerge as the greatest problem of our nation— depersonalized, unresponsive bureaucracy. We have encountered the organized status quo in Mississippi, but it is the same in Berkeley. Here in Berkeley we find it impossible usually to meet with anyone but secretaries. Beyond that, we find functionaries who cannot make policy but can only hide behind the rules. We have discovered total lack of response on the part of the true policy makers. To grasp a situation which is truly Kafkaesque, it is necessary to understand the bureaucratic mentality. And we have learned quite a bit about it this fall, more outside the classroom than in.

As bureaucrat, an administrator believes that nothing new happens. He occupies an a-historical point of view. In September, to get the attention of this bureaucracy which had issued arbitrary edicts suppressing student political expression and refused to discuss its action, we held a sit-in on the campus. We sat around a police car and kept it immobilized for over thirty-two hours. At last the administrative bureaucracy agreed to negotiate. But instead, on the following Monday, we discovered that a committee had

SOURCE: Mario Savio, "An End to History," *Humanity*, December 1964. © Humanity. Reprinted by permission of Humanity.

been appointed, in accordance with usual regulations, to resolve the dispute. Our attempt to convince any of the administrators that an event had occurred, that something new had happened, failed. They saw this simply as something to be handled by normal University procedures.

The same is true of all bureaucracies. They begin as tools—means to certain legitimate goals—and they end up feeding their own existence. The conception that bureaucrats have is that history has in fact come to an end. No events can occur, now that the Second World War is over, which can change American society substantially. We proceed by standard procedures as we are.

The most crucial problems facing the United States today are the problem of automation and the problem of racial injustice. Most people who will be put out of jobs by machines will not accept an end to events, this historical plateau, as the point beyond which no change occurs. Negroes will not accept an end to history here. All of us must refuse to accept history's final judgment that in America there is no place in society for people whose skins are dark. On campus students are not about to accept it as fact that the University has ceased evolving and is in its final state of perfection, that students and faculty are respectively raw material and employees, or that the University is to be autocratically run by unresponsive bureaucrats.

Here is the real contradiction: The bureaucrats hold history as ended. As a result significant parts of the population both on campus and off are dispossessed, and these dispossessed are not about to accept this a-historical point of view. It is out of this that the conflict has occurred with the University bureaucracy and will continue to occur until that bureaucracy becomes responsive or until it is clear that the University can not function.

The things we are asking for in our civil rights protests have a deceptively quaint ring. We are asking for the due process of law. We are asking for our actions to be judged by committees of our peers. We are asking that regulations ought to be considered as arrived at legitimately only from the consensus of the governed. These phrases are all pretty old, but they are not being taken seriously in America today, nor are they being taken seriously on the Berkeley campus.

I have just come from a meeting with the Dean of Students. She notified us that she was aware of certain violations of University regulations by certain organizations. University Friends of SNCC, which I represent, was one of these. We tried to draw from her some statement on these great principles—consent of the governed, jury of one's peers, due process. The best she could do was to evade or to present the administration party line.

It is very hard to make any contact with the human being who is behind these organizations.

The university is the place where people begin seriously to question the conditions of their existence and raise the issue of whether they can be committed to the society they have been born into. After a long period of apathy during the fifties, students have begun not only to question, but, having arrived at answers, to act on those answers. This is part of a growing understanding among many people in America that history has not ended, that a better society is possible, and that it is worth dying for.

This free speech fight points up a fascinating aspect of contemporary campus life. Students are permitted to talk all they want so long as their speech has no consequences.

One conception of the university, suggested by a classical Christian formulation, is that it be in the world but not of the world. The conception of Clark Kerr by contrast is that the university is part and parcel of this particular stage in the history of American society; it stands to serve the needs of American industry; it is a factory that turns out a certain product needed by industry or government. Because speech does often have consequences which might alter this perversion of higher education, the university must put itself in a position of censorship. I can permit two kinds of speech: speech which encourages continuation of the status quo, and speech which advocates changes in it so radical as to be irrelevant in the foreseeable future. Someone may advocate radical change in all aspects of American society, and this I am sure he can do with impunity. But if someone advocates sit-ins to bring about changes in discriminatory hiring practices, this can not be permitted because it goes against the status quo of which the university is a part. And that is how the fight began here.

The administration of the Berkeley campus has admitted that external, extra-legal groups have pressured the University not to permit students on campus to organize picket lines, not to permit on campus any speech with consequences. And the bureaucracy went along. Speech with consequences, speech in the area of civil rights, speech which some might regard as illegal, must stop.

Many students here at the University, many people in society, are wandering aimlessly about. Strangers in their own lives, there is no place for them. They are people who have not learned to compromise, who for example have come to the University to learn to question, to grow, to learn —all the standard things that sound like clichés because no one takes them seriously. And they find at one point or another that for them to become part of society, to become lawyers, ministers, business men, or people in government, very often they must compromise those principles which were most dear to them. They must suppress the most creative impulses that they have; this is a prior condition for being part of the system. The university is well structured, well tooled, to turn out people with all the sharp edges worn off—the well-rounded person. The university is well equipped to produce that sort of person, and this means that the best among the people who enter must for four years wander aimlessly much of the time questioning why they are on campus at all, doubting whether there is any point in what they are doing, and looking toward a very bleak existence afterward in a game in which all of the rules have been made up—rules which one can not really amend.

It is a bleak scene, but it is all a lot of us have to look forward to. Society provides no challenge. American society in the standard conception it has of itself is simply no longer exciting. The most exciting things going on in America today are movements to change America. America is becoming ever more the utopia of sterilized, automated contentment. The "futures" and "careers" for which American students now prepare are for the most part intellectual and moral wastelands. This chrome-plated consumers' paradise would have us grow up to be well-behaved children. But an important minority of men and women coming to the front today have shown that they will die rather than be standardized, replaceable, and irrelevant.

BLACK STUDENTS UNION DEMANDS AND EXPLANATIONS (FROM A BSU POSITION STATEMENT)

SAN FRANCISCO STATE STRIKE COMMITTEE

The Demands

1. That all Black Studies courses being taught through various other departments be immediately part of the Black Studies Department and that all the instructors in this department receive full-time pay.

   Explanation—At the present time the so-called Black Studies courses are being taught from the established departments which also control the function of courses. In order for a brother or sister to teach a Black Studies course he or she has to go before the assigned department head to receive permission to teach, which clearly shows that the power lies with the departments and the racist administrators, not the Black Studies department chairman, faculty and staff.

   At the end of the summer, before the Fall of 1968, the racist administration announced that 47 full-time teaching positions were unfilled. The Black Studies Department only received 1.2 teaching positions out of the total number of 47. The Black Studies Department instructors should receive full-time pay like the various other departments on the San Francisco State College campus.

2. That Dr. Hare, Chairman of the Black Studies Department, receive a full-professorship and a comparable salary according to his qualifications.

   Explanation—Dr. Hare is one of the best sociologists in the country and one of the most sought after, yet he makes less money than any Department chairman and all newly appointed deans and administrators.

SOURCE: San Francisco State Strike Committee, *On Strike—Shut It Down* (San Francisco: San Francisco State Strike Committee, 1969), pp. 1–3, 47–51, 54–60.

3. That there be a Department of Black Studies which will grant a Bachelor's degree in Black Studies—that the Black Studies Department, chairman, faculty, and staff have the sole power to hire faculty and control and determine the destiny of its department.

   Explanation—That the Black Studies Department have the power to grant Bachelor degrees—and that the Black Studies Department Chairman, faculty and staff have the sole power to hire and fire without the interference of the racist administration and the Chancellor.

4. That all un-used slots for Black students from Fall, 1968 under the Special Admissions program be filled in Spring, 1969.

   Explanation—That the 128 slots that were not filled by so-called "special admittees" be filled by any Third World student who wishes to attend SFSC in the Spring of 1969.

5. That all Black students wishing so, be admitted in Fall 1969.

   Explanation—In San Francisco 70% of all Primary, Jr. High School and High School students are Third World, but at SFSC only 4% of the entire student body are Third World students. In other words, the racist pig power structure does not want an abundance of "niggers" in their so-called "institutions of higher learning."

6. That twenty full-time teaching positions be allocated to the Department of Black Studies.

   Explanation—At the beginning of the Fall semester 1.2% of a teaching position was allocated to the so-called Black Studies Department. No department can function off of such a small number of teaching positions.

7. That Dr. Helen Bedesom be replaced from the position of Financial Aid officer and that a Black person be hired to direct it, that Third World people have the power to determine how it will be administered.

8. That no disciplinary action will be administered in any way to any student workers, teachers, or administrators during and after the strike as consequence of their participation in the strike.

   Explanation—That the racist administrators do not threaten the security and well-being of people who support and participate in the strike.

9. That the California State College Trustees will not be allowed to dissolve any Black programs on or off San Francisco State College campus.

   Explanation—On November 22–24, later postponed, the California State Trustees were to meet on the request of Pig Dumke to dissolve

454

the Associated Students on all State College campuses throughout the State. This means that we cannot create and maintain programs on campus and off campus. Everything we do will be controlled by the Pig Dumke. All programs such as the Associated Students, CSI, EC, etc., will have to have Pig Dumke's OK. If the Trustees dissolve creativity on campus and off campus, we will use our creativity in a prolonged and protracted war against them.

10. That George Murray maintain his teaching position on campus for 1968–69 academic year.

Explanation—That George Murray is one of the best English instructors on the campus. He was fired not because of a lack of teaching ability, but because of his political philosophy. He must be reinstated. He was teaching his students about the true nature of this society and the need for Third World people to obtain liberation by any means necessary.

The Third World Liberation Front Demands

1. That a School of Ethnic Studies for the ethnic groups involved in the Third World be set up with the students in each particular ethnic organization having the authority and control of the hiring and retention of any faculty member, director, and administrator, as well as the curriculum in a specific area of study.
2. That 50 faculty positions be appropriated to the School of Ethnic Studies, 20 of which would be for the Black Studies Program.
3. That in the Spring semester, the College fulfill its commitment to the non-white students in admitting those that apply.
4. That in the Fall of 1969, all applications of non-white students be accepted.
5. That George Murray and any other faculty person chosen by non-white people as their teacher be retained in their position.

On Strike—100 Days

Thursday, Sept. 27 [1968]

In the wake of the Eldridge Cleaver controversy at the University of California, the California State College Trustees move to have Black Panther Minister of Education George Murray removed from the S. F. State faculty. The

Trustees "request" that S. F. State President Robert Smith place Murray in a non-teaching position.

Tuesday, Oct. 1

Smith, feeling that the time is not right and the situation too explosive, "refuses" to act on the Trustees "request" regarding Murray.

Thursday, Oct. 24

Murray delivers speech at Fresno State College calling for oppressed people to take up a struggle against their slavemasters. The Trustees meeting on the Fresno State campus fires veiled threats at Murray.

Monday, Oct. 28

Black Students Union (BSU), seeing that all proper channels for the implementation of the Black Studies Program have been exhausted, call a student strike as a means of achieving their demands to begin on November 6th. Murray delivers speech suggesting that oppressed students may have cause for armed struggle on campus to protect themselves from racist administrators.

Wednesday, Oct. 30

San Francisco's Mayor Joseph Alioto blasts Murray's Monday speech and has the police Red Squad investigate the matter.

Thursday, Oct. 31

State College Chancellor Glenn Dumke orders Smith to suspend Murray. Smith balks at the order.

Leaflet Issued Nov. 1 by SDS: Support George Murray

Why are the Trustees frantically trying to save us from George Murray? The Trustees, contrary to liberal myths, are not rabid right-wing fanatics, but competent, successful businessmen—like Dudley Swim, member of the Board of Directors of Del Monte Corp. They are successful because they are able to extract super-profits from the labor of Black, Brown and white workers. When George Murray says that Black and non-white people have a right to rebel against being exploited by Dudley Swim and his ilk, he is directly threatening the corporate interests which control the State College system.

Corporation wizards who sit on the Board of Trustees are not there for their health, but to insure that the State Colleges meet their quotas of technicians and apologists to be the cogs in a system designed to serve the narrow interests of the corporate wealth. When George Murray says that students should not serve the oppressors, but *fight* them, he is a real threat to the role of higher education, that is, the role defined by the corporate interests of the Board of Trustees.

President Summerskill lost his usefulness to the Board of Trustees, for when push came to shove he was not a neutral force, but stood squarely with the Board of Trustees, and students clearly saw this.

President Smith has launched a "sharp attack" against Dumke. He called Dumke's order to suspend Murray, both as a teacher and student, "unprecedented." But what is Smith's plan? To stand up for and defend George Murray's right to fight for self-determination of Black people and the implementation of the Black Panther Party's program?

HELL NO! Smith's got a better plan (with the help of his friend, Benito Alioto) to get rid of Murray—slander Murray in the local ruling-class press, threaten him with felony indictments, and then fire him. What Smith is doing is pleading with the Trustees for more time so he can do a more efficient hatchet job. He is counting on student apathy and fear of the Black Liberation Movement to mitigate any reaction against Murray's dismissal (note Smith's memo of earlier this week on unmentioned perpetrators of campus violence).

Despite Smith's rhetoric, his position is quite clear. He is trying to make us believe that he is a "liberal," that he is a "neutral," that he is fighting the conservative Trustees and "leftist extremists" who are out to "destroy the university." He will tell us that he fought hard to retain Murray, but that it is "out of his hands." He will tell us that his decision is an administrative one.

SDS sees any attempt to investigate, suspend, or fire Murray as an act of racism, not an administrative decision. The suspending of Murray means that the Trustees consider those who speak and act for Black Liberation, criminals. This comes as no surprise since Black Liberation directly threatens the exploitative corporate interests of the Trustees and the whole system in general.

In an issue involving racism, there are no "neutrals" and no "liberals." SDS urges white students to take note of Smith's position and not to be fooled. Smith is the local representative of corporate wealth in this state, indeed the country. Thus, he is no "neutral" but objectively carries out the policies of a certain class that aims to smash the Black Liberation Movement.

The vast majority of white students have objectively no interest in common with the Board of Trustees and its racist policies which Smith represents. We must recognize the nature of the university and what Smith is doing and oppose the pending firing of Murray. SDS urges white students to act according to their own interests and the interests of the vast majority of the people in this country, and *fight this racist act*.

Friday, Nov.1
  Smith, waiting until the campus is virtually cleared for the weekend, orders
  Murray suspended.
Monday, Nov. 4

BSU calls a press conference re-iterating their demands and a call for the strike to begin on Nov. 6. SDS calls a mass meeting of all interested white students to muster support for the BSU strike and demands.

Tuesday, Nov. 5

Stokeley Carmichael addresses Third World students suggesting confrontation politics to heighten the contradictions within American racist institutions. White students begin to organize around the strike.

Wednesday, Nov. 6

THE STRIKE BEGINS. Students picket buildings, enter classrooms to argue with and try to convince the strike-breakers, and hold a rally culminating with a march on the Administration Building to get a statement from Smith. Smith states that he is too busy and doesn't have the time to face the students at this time. Concurrently the Third World students dismiss all classes one by one, disrupting those classes resisting. The S.F. Police Tactical Squad is called to maintain "law and order." But the students have established *just* law and order by closing the school.

Thursday, Nov. 7

Students continue picketing and classroom education. Noon rally ends with a march through the halls of classroom buildings by hundreds of strikers chanting "On strike, shut it down!" Classes are effectively disrupted. Third World Liberation Front (TWLF) adds five demands to strike goals.

Friday, Nov. 8

The strike grows. Most departments report attendance below 50%.

Monday, Nov. 11

Holiday. Strikers continue to organize.

Tuesday, Nov. 12

Students continue to picket and classroom educate despite Smith's hard line about classes being interrupted. An arbitration board is suggested by a strike-breaking Department Chairman. The TWLF reply, "No arbitrations, the demands are non-negotiable." Two students, discovering the Tactical Squad is occupying the boiler rooms on campus, are arrested.

Wednesday, Nov. 13

The strike continues to grow. Discussion groups are formed all over the campus. At noon the Tactical Squad appears in front of the BSU office and stands in formation intimidating students. Students hail Tac Squad with rocks, dirt clods, food, and wood. Tac Squad break formation and indiscriminately start clubbing students. Students fight back, liberating prisoners. Cops then draw guns and withdraw from campus. Tac Squad reappears ten minutes later and are forced off campus by 2000 strikers. Students and faculty demand that Smith close down the college. Smith closes campus indefinitely.

Monday, Nov. 18

Smith is ordered by Trustees to open the campus immediately. Smith asks all students to come to campus to engage in Departmental meetings to discuss the issues.

Tuesday, Nov. 19

Smith addresses students and faculty. His decision to reopen is rejected by students and faculty. Faculty calls for a Crisis Convocation to resolve the issues. Smith declares school will open Wednesday.

Wednesday, Nov. 20

Some classes reopen as Convocation goes on in hostile atmosphere. BSU–TWLF agrees to participate in Convocation as an educational tactic. Campus occupied by 200 plainclothes police and Tactical Squad in boiler rooms.

Thursday, Nov. 21

Classes and Convocation continue. BSU–TWLF demand that Smith suspend classes to establish atmosphere of good faith for Convocation. Smith refuses and striking students walk out of Convocation. Thousands of strikers march through buildings, closing down classes. Plainclothesmen attempting to stop the action and arrest leaders are hassled by strikers. Tac Squad appears to protect empty buildings on a closed campus.

Friday, Nov. 22

Alioto proposes negotiations. Academic Senate suggests Department meetings to discuss possibility of another Convocation. Smith cancels afternoon classes for Department meetings. Departments call for Convocation with no classes to be held and immediate withdrawal of all cops from the campus.

Leaflet Issued Nov. 25 by the Strike Committee: Rely on the People—Build the Strike!

A "crisis" convocation is being held based on the proposal put forward by President Robert Smith. The faculty passed a proposal to have a three day convocation beginning today, ending Wednesday, with classes called to resume on December 2. The focus of the discussion will revolve around the question of the fifteen demands put forward by the BSU–TWLF.

The convocation has positive and negative aspects. The positive aspect is that the issues became so clear during the last convocation that when Smith was confronted with the first demand he hemmed and hawed for 20 minutes and never replied directly. Thousands of students saw that Smith avoided the issues and avoided the 15 demands. He exposed himself through these actions as a puppet of the Board of Trustees and the corporate interests they represent.

Although the convocation has a positive aspect, the negative aspects should not be overlooked. The convocation, while it may be a good discussion, will never by itself win the 15 demands. The Third World students on campus have continually pointed out that it is only through protracted struggle against the administration and the Board of Trustees that the demands will be won. The administration sees this convocation as a week-long cooling-off period. They make this obvious by calling for classes to begin next week whether the demands are met or not.

The faculty has played a dual role in this strike. On one hand, many faculty members took a positive step by going out on strike and trying to win other faculty members to join them. But, on the other hand, the faculty has seen itself as a buffer zone between the administration, its cops, and striking students. We see this as an untenable position. In this strike one must clearly take either the administration side or the side of black and Third World liberation. When professors stopped students from fighting the cops, although their intentions may have been good, they are objectively taking the side against the strike and for the administration. And, by supporting Smith's plan to resume classes on December 2 whether or not the demands are met the faculty are taking a strike-breaking position. There is also the question of leadership in the struggle.

Certain segments of the faculty have tried to impress on students that they (the faculty) will resolve the issues of the strike. This says that 1) the faculty has the power to resolve the conflict and 2) they see themselves in the leadership position. Both of these hypotheses are wrong.

Students should realize that their power flows from the strength of the people involved in the struggle. It is this attitude, relying on ourselves, that will win. Winning will not come from relying on the faculty or administration. The faculty must be won to the idea that they must unite with white students supporting the Third World demands.

Also, the idea that some faculty members believe they are in a position to lead students in this fight must be defeated. The BSU–TWLF are in the leadership of this struggle. The position for the faculty and other white students is to support the demands. They, along with white students, must take the offensive in fighting racism among other white faculty, white students and in the white community.

Monday, Nov. 25
   BSU–TWLF approved convocation (televised to the community) begins while Trustees meet in Los Angeles to discuss the S. F. State crisis.
Tuesday, Nov. 26
   BSU–TWLF call an end to convocation when letters of suspension are received by some striking students. In Los Angeles Smith submits his resignation to the Trustees. Smith's reason for resigning—"an inability to resolve issues amidst the various political pressures." A half hour later the Trustees name S. I. Hayakawa to be their new lackey. Hayakawa orders the campus closed.
Wednesday, Nov. 27
   Students and faculty in defiance of Hayakawa's "closed campus" order occupy the campus to organize the strike and denounce Hayakawa.

Thanksgiving Holidays—Strike organizing continues.
Monday, Dec. 2

Hayakawa reopens the campus with a hardline "state of emergency" and 650 cops to maintain fascist law and racist order. Hayakawa attacks strikers' sound truck parked off campus, assaulting students, ripping out speaker wires and inciting to riot by littering the streets with "blue armbands" which were being passed out to students supporting Hayakawa's position. Rally is followed by marches on police-occupied classroom buildings resulting in a massive confrontation between thousands of striking students and 650 cops.

Leaflet Issued by Strike Committee on Dec. 2: Warning—Beware of Fanatics Masquerading As College Presidents

This morning a fanatic bearing a striking resemblance to our dignified president of the month, Hayakawa, viciously attacked the strike sound truck on 19th Ave. This unbalanced individual tore loose the speaker wires and began passing out mimeographed sheets with blue ribbons attached. At first we thought they were prizes for creative broadcasting. The paper turned out to be on the semantics of strike-breaking and the blue ribbon a booby prize for right-wing flunkies.

When it was pointed out that the man had no business being on a student's truck, the poor fellow started shoving students and screaming, "Don't touch me, I'm the president of the college." In the interest of safety on campus we demand that such fruitcakes be removed at once. That goes as well for the club-swinging, blue-suited Napoleons which the press so rightly denounced yesterday for their brutality in Chicago.

Tuesday, Dec. 3

Picket line formed by 30 students at classroom building is routed by 40 club-swinging Tac Squaders. Picketers are chased into student Commons where students are indiscriminately hassled and clubbed. At noon rally Third World community leaders speak in support of strike. March on classroom building is met with 650 cops. A bloody two-hour battle ensues between students and cops. Chicago repeats itself on the S. F. State campus. Hayakawa, summing up the day, stated that the day was his "most exciting day since he rode a roller coaster on his tenth birthday."

Wednesday, Dec. 4

Black community leaders meet with Hayakawa and denounce him. Hayakawa walks out. Third World community leaders march on campus in support of strike and join rally. Thousands of strikers march off campus to build community support for the strike. Community people picket Hall of Justice in protest of police on campus. Strikers picket City Hall in protest of police on campus. Strikers picket City Hall in protest of the same.

Thursday, Dec. 5

Noon rally with many working people from the Third World communities . . . ends with a march led by Third World community people and students on the Administration building to confront Hayakawa. This march is met by cops with drawn guns and mace protecting Hayakawa's office. A confrontation ensued resulting in the arrest of more students. The confrontation is carried to the streets tying up traffic in front of campus for 45 minutes.

Friday, Dec. 6

The strike is one month old. Hayakawa, in an effort to squelch growing community support, meets about 1½ demands. The strikers and community meet Hayakawa's deal with cries of "Bullshit, bullshit, bullshit." Strikers and community people march off campus in solidarity chanting, "We'll be back, we'll be back," and once again march at City Hall.

Saturday, Dec. 7

The Strike Committee hold a community rally at City Hall attended by several thousand strikers and supporters. The rally is followed with a march through downtown to S. F. Chronicle & Examiner building to protest racist, distorted coverage of the strike.

Sunday, Dec. 8

Third World community holds a rally at City Hall in support of the strike.

Monday, Dec. 9

Campus still occupied by 650 cops. Following noon rally and march on classroom building, a confrontation ensues in the rain. The police try a new tactic—mounted police in cavalry formation.

Tuesday, Dec. 10

Heavy rain forces rally indoors followed by a march off campus to build more community support. In a press conference the BSU–TWLF declares war on those forces controlling the college.

Wednesday, Dec. 11

Students walking picket lines attacked several times by Tac Squad. At noon rally 200 police surround strikers and wade in to arrest *one* strike leader in center of crowd. Students wearing blue armbands and wielding blackjacks attack striking students; when soundly trounced by the strikers, they ran behind the police lines.

Thursday, Dec. 12

Once again Tac Squad attacks picket line. As solidarity march leaves campus, cops attack and club students. Students stone the buildings and the cops.

Friday, Dec. 13

Tac Squad runs into picket line to arrest strike leaders. Hayakawa closes campus one week early for Christmas vacation to avert show of community support called for Monday, Dec. 16.

Dec. 14–Jan. 5   Christmas Holidays

TWLF and Strike Committee take advantage of the "Vacation" (including Hayakawa's "gift" of one week) to continue organizing and building the strike. Significant activities include:

* In answer to Hayakawa's avoidance of Third World Community Day the TWLF calls for Third World Community *Week* to be held on campus week of Jan. 6.

462

B.S.U. Demands and Explanations

* Rallies, Demonstrations, and Forums held to build Community support for the strike.
* Statewide support organized at other state colleges, universities, junior colleges and high schools.
* Strikers carry news of struggle across the nation and gain nationwide support for the strike.
* S. F. State SDS relates the struggle to the SDS National Council and presents and has passed a proposal calling for a Direction of the Student Movement to be aimed at attacking Racism and the Class Nature of the University.
* In preparation for Third World Community Week Hayakawa suspends more civil liberties: "Specifically, rallies, parades, be-ins, hootenannies, hoedowns, shivarees and all other events . . . are hereby forbidden on the central campus." Reagan calls for the college to be kept open "at the point of a bayonet if necessary."

Monday, Jan. 6

The third month of the strike begins with fascist law and racist order maintained by Hayakawa's occupying army of cops as the campus reopens. 3,000 pickets ring campus including hundreds of Third World and white community strike supporters. 300 professors (members of AFT Local 1352) go on strike for their own demands including "Resolution and Implementation of TWLF Demands" and "Amnesty for all involved in fight against Racism." TA's Union (AFT Local 1928) strikes in support of TWLF Demands. Classroom count shows strike 80–85% effective. Late in afternoon San Francisco Labor Council grants AFT Local 1352 Strike Sanction. "Scab Education" teams begin confronting Scab Students and Professors.

Tuesday, Jan. 7

Thousands of Students, Faculty, and Community People continue to picket, keeping attendance down to 14%. Clerical, Commons, and Library Workers honor picket line and join the strike. Teamsters honor picket lines and deliveries to college and dormitories stop. A thousand pickets defy Hayakawa's central camps ban and are surrounded by several hundred cops but the "power of the people" breaks through their lines.

The Following Leaflet Issued by the TWLF:
No Deals—Fight against Racism for Self-Determination—
Grant the 15 Demands for TWLF Now!

The strike at S. F. State began on November 6, 1968. It was called by TWLF. It has been directed by TWLF. It will continue to be directed by TWLF.

After two months of intensive struggle by TWLF and white students to win this TWLF demands, the AFT finally decided to go on strike. This in itself shows the difference in political consciousness between the faculty and students. After the teachers went out, the Labor Council voted to sanction the strike *only until the AFT economic demands are met.*

We view it as positive that the AFT has finally gone on strike. It must be clear, however, the AFT is, by their own admission, striking primarily for their own demands and only secondarily, under pressure, for the 15 demands of TWLF. Further, it is we the students who have initiated this strike to fight against racism. Because of the strength of our strike the AFT has taken the opportunity to gain some long outstanding demands.

The position of the TWLF has been from November 6, 1968 that the 15 demands are absolutely non-negotiable and the struggle for the demands has been characterized as a struggle against racism and for self-determination. We will fight until these demands are met.

We will not allow our principle to be confused or compromised by campus autonomy, due process or any other issues which do not relate directly to the 15 demands as we have defined them.

Further, we will not compromise the commitment of the thousands of courageous students by allowing the militancy of our struggle to be held back by anyone. In fact, we must be prepared to wage even sharper struggle against the enemy. We must take our inspiration from our working brothers and sisters in the communities—such as the Kaiser Hospital workers who went on strike and attacked the pigs!

We urge strikers to reaffirm their commitment to the struggle! Tighten up the picket lines! Fight even harder against racism and for the self-determination of all oppressed people around the world! The people will win.

THIRD WORLD LIBERATION FRONT

Wednesday, Jan. 8

Thousands continue to picket effectively, keeping attendance down to 15%. Strikebreaking cops rout picket line to open a path for scabs. A confrontation ensues with students fighting back. Cops call in cavalry and students are chased four blocks by galloping pigs on horses while students shell them with rocks, bottles, etc. Students and Faculty at San Jose State go on strike in support of S. F. State Strike. Informational picket lines set up at other state colleges. Injunction against AFT Local 1352 Strike is issued.

Attention Scabs

What are you doing By crossing the picket line you have consciously or not put yourself in a position against the strike of the BSU–TWLF. This is a strike against racism, both within the individual and the institution. It is a strike that recognizes the right of the oppressed Third World people to self-determination by any means necessary. Also it is a strike that speaks to the minimal needs of Third World people to function in a university. By crossing the line you have made your choice—there is no middle ground.

You are being used You are being used by Hayakawa and the Trustees to break the strike. Their position concerning the demands and the principles of the strike is clear—they will use any means necessary to crush it. You are part of those means. In labor struggles the bosses try to break strikes by recruiting scabs to carry on the functioning of the factory. He appeals to the narrow self-interest of the scab—a livable wage, a good job, etc. In this situation the boss (the Administration) has done the same. It has conditioned you to think that the factory must continue to function —further perpetuating its racist and oppressive role toward Third World people. Also it has appealed to your narrow self-interest by constantly pushing the attitude on you that *"I* have a right to go to school, *I* want to get *my* education."

Too many scabs have given lip service to the support of the 15 demands but still go to class. You are either lying or don't know the effect of what you are saying. You say you support the demands but not the tactics used to achieve them. What you really are saying is that you support the right of Third World people to better their conditions, but you don't support their efforts to achieve that better condition. What you really are saying is that you, a scab, know the best way for Third World students to win their demands. Friend, that is a pretty racist attitude.

But you scabs must realize that this struggle involves more than "your individual 'rights.' " It involves the human rights of all oppressed people to function in a university thereby serving the working people in their communities. It also involves the majority of white students who have physically put themselves on the line fighting racism which hurts them and keeps them from uniting with Third World people to fight the common enemy which is the source of all oppression—the corporate class. This selfish individualistic attitude of you scabs, which hurts the majority, yes, majority, of students can no longer be tolerated.

What Are the Consequences of Scabbing Despite the crap Hayakawa has been laying on the public, the school has been only 25–39% attended. The Commons workers, the maintenance workers, grounds, etc. have walked off their jobs. But you still have persisted to attend class.

Historically, workers on strike have not dealt so kindly with scabs as we have with you. In the current steel strike in Denison, Texas, the workers are armed and there have been several shoot-outs with scabs. Scabs have been beaten in numerous strikes. Not even police have been able to protect scabs when working people have been fighting for their lives against the bosses.

We students realize that you scabs aren't the real enemy. The real enemy is the administration just like the real enemy of the workers is the bosses. We know that you are being used by the administration, willingly or not, to perpetuate the functioning of a thoroughly decadent, racist institution. Though we know you aren't the enemy, and urge you not to cross the picket line, you are objectively acting as agents of Hayakawa and the Trustees and as such must be dealt with accordingly.—Issued by Strike Committee 1/8/69

Thursday, Jan. 9
   Picketing continues effectively paralyzing campus. AFT defies injunction. Cops rout picket line and mace dogs being walked on picket line. Enraged picketers fight back and chant, "Kill the pigs." Scab "education" continues. Stink bombs clear Library of scabs. Home of Edwin Duerr, Hayakawa's hatchet-man, is fire-bombed.
Friday, Jan. 10
   Picketing continues with strike more than 80% effective. College and dorms begin to feel effects of supplies being cut off due to Teamsters honoring strike. Scab "education" continues. Library "book-in" begins by strikers. Some scabs discover slashed tires on their cars.
Monday, Jan. 13
   Picketing continues with Third World Community Week entering its *second* week despite heavy rain. Several Third World leaders ripped off picket line by cops. Scab "education" escalates. "Book-in" continues. Garbage begins to pile up all over campus. Two S. F. State strikers arrested in Richmond while actively supporting the Oil, Chemical and Atomic Workers strike.
Tuesday, Jan. 14
   Picketing continues. Tac squad moves in on picket line to arrest TWLF strike leader and is repelled by fighting strikers. Cops call in reinforcements and one and a half hours later move in to make the arrest, engaging a defensive ring of aggressive fighting strikers. Strikers are clubbed, hassled and arrested in the ensuing confrontation, but cops also suffer several casualties. Stink bombs clear two classroom buildings. Incidence of flat tires rises on campus.
Wednesday, Jan. 15
   Picketing continues to keep attendance below 20%. Many toilets stopped up all over campus. The racist Department Chairmen of Political Science and History have their tires slashed and cars painted with the words, "Fascist Scab."
Thursday, Jan. 16
   Strike continues to be 80–85% effective. Smoke bomb clears Education Building. Bomb placed in Administration Building fails to explode, but effec-

tively stops business for several hours. Toilets all over campus effectively clogged. Scab "education" and "book-in" escalate. College is unable to feed dorms, and is forced to pay rebate to residents.

Friday, Jan. 17

Picketing continues to paralyze campus. Loyalist "Hayakawa Youth" have downtown rally, disrupted by strikers and community supporters of strike. Striking San Jose State students, in solidarity with S. F. Strikers, conduct mill-in in their Administration Building.

Monday, Jan. 20 through Wednesday, Jan. 22

Picketing continues and strikers organize for a rally on campus on Thursday.

Thursday, Jan. 23

Picketers move on campus to hold a rally of about 1000 people. Police charge and surround it, arresting 450 students and community supporters.

The mass arrest, rather than breaking the strike as the Administration and cops hoped, has greatly increased the determination of the strikers to fight and defeat those who will go to all lengths to maintain racism. In its fourth month the TWLF-called strike continues to build and grow. Strikes are continuing and threatening at most campuses of the State College system. Berkeley has called a TWLF strike. Administrators at S. F. State have been forced to institute a Pass/No Report grading system to keep 80% of its students (strikers) from flunking out. The campus has been paralyzed by TWLF strike and it is clear that the struggle will continue until the fifteen demands of the TWLF are met.

Thursday, Jan. 24 through Feb. 16

The strike continues with two thousand people joining the picket line on Thursday Jan. 30.—Striking teachers refuse to turn in grades—Final exam period is wrecked with scabbing teachers giving take home exams or none at all. The 450 arrestees appear in court Jan. 31 and disrupt proceedings by singing, chanting, etc. Tac squad outside courtroom readied for action—two people busted. State students migrate to Richmond to support striking oil workers. Over a hundred joined their picket line on Monday, February 3. Hayakawa begins sending out pre-suspension letters to all those busted on January 23. Plan to the strikers is to register for class use first few days to re-establish contact with those who support the strike but haven't been active and then pick up where things left off and *shut it down.*

PART XVII
Radical Women

In the magnitude and depth of social reconstruction which they demand, the several groupings of women liberationists are potentially the most revolutionary organizations in America today, not excluding the blacks. As soon as women perceived the important difference between being women radicals and radical women the precondition for politically conditioned sexual consciousness was met. Justifiably enraged by the subordinate roles assigned to women within the Left itself, women typists, mimeographers, and coffee-brewers began, in the late sixties, to stake out their own claim. The boundary they drew enclosed all society, east and west, public and private, included human as well as economic and political relationships, and left no aspect of behavior or association outside of their mounting anger. The very inclusiveness of their vision naturally impeded a unified, or even a clear, sense of purpose and direction. The most militant of the women's groups, because of their total human and social assault were, more even than the male-dominated and therefore more traditional new Left, desperately in need of theory when the confusion and swirl of competing groups, the pressure of emergency or at least urgent actions, and the almost omnipresent sniggering of men, including those firmly on the left, all worked against greater coherence.

Obviously taking important cues from the black power movement, some women radicals groped and reasoned their way to a position resembling black separatism. But as the Black Panthers have proved, there is an important difference between autonomy and separatism. The women would need, they said, their own maleless organizations in order to avoid falling into the almost reflexive passive roles society had assigned to them. They would constitute themselves as a social and political vanguard, in that already ancient concept, in order to lead a more sluggish constituency, including men, toward liberation for all. And they would by force of political will and imagination reconstruct their own individual perceptions so as to avoid the sort of self-hatred that inevitably flowed from an acceptance of the masters' view of the victims. As "black power" was an expression of pride, so the women liberationists sought a formula that would assist them in escaping the psychological as well as economic and political thralldom to the male chauvinists on the left as well as everywhere else.

Every time a woman rehearsed the list of attributes traditionally defined as feminine—including an inability to reason, excessive intuitiveness and emotionality, passivity, reliance on wile, supposed warmth and easy embarrassment, perhaps even natural rhythm—and pointed out that the list was identical to the catalogue of traits the slavemasters attributed to their slaves, every time this happened, the women were asserting their common cause with black liberation, at least implying the direction women would have to go, and explicitly displaying the human urgency of the problem. And in American as well as worldwide terms, this need not be a minority movement, even though only a tiny fraction of women had been organized. So the women, again like at least some of the blacks, had a universalist attitude toward themselves and their politics. Although the American context is the immediate occasion of their first efforts, they almost always seem to have at least one eye peeled on the rest of the world.

One of the early steps in the articulation of women's radicalism was taken by Naomi Jaffe, a leader of the New York SDS antidraft movement, and Bernadine Dohrn, a graduate of the University of Chicago law school, importantly involved in SDS, and both later attached to the militant Weatherwomen. In Document 60 they argue the essentially accurate but weak line that women as the high priestesses of consumption had a "vanguard economic role as consumers." This role determined their passivity but could be turned around and used against capitalism the moment women refused to play their socially defined role, as soon, that is, as women redefined themselves from consumers to human beings. The apparent freedom bestowed by increasing technology, especially as experienced in the Pill, was equally repressive because this freedom contributed to an expanded definition of women as available objects, a definition which is a cornerstone of intensifying exploitation by advertising. In any case, the particular oppressions of women were presumably to become their peculiar weapons against a political economy sufficiently strong to have debased the very psychology of the women to whom these authors now called.

Kathy McAfee, on the staff of a radical newspaper and active in SDS, and Myrna Wood, working with antiwar and women's liberation movements in Canada, attempted (in Document 61) to provide the necessary political dimension to the rapid growth of, and perhaps even more swift muddling in, the women's liberation movements. Acknowledging that meetings too often did not grow from amateur group therapy and professional bitching, they also tried to confront what was then an often-expressed male SDS attitude about women's liberation, that it constituted personal catharsis rather than political action. But McAfee and Wood insist that only through a heightened consciousness of the exploitation of women could an authentic class consciousness be created, so that, in their view, it is the men on the left who impede revolutionary intelligence and zeal. Until such time, for instance, as working class men can be led to see the centrality of their wives' degraded positions, those wives will continue to press for the very sort of social stability which will hurt their own husbands' economic aspirations and political efforts. The success of women's liberation, then, is presented as indispensable to working class consciousness and unity. The changing position of the working class is not discussed.

The most powerful statements by radical women concern the most concrete life situations of women in America and elsewhere. They accurately assert that the cultural conditioning of girls demands that every act in a woman's life is necessarily political. In a frontal attack on women's experiences in the kitchen and the bedroom, the radical women have revealed the human oppression of culturally settled routine. Pat Mainardi, a member of radical women in New York City, brilliantly displays (Document 62) the political implications of housework, and shows how far from trivial this is; equally important, she shows the power struggle as seen by men, in this case a self-defined leisure class. In Document 63 Anne Koedt, a founder of the New York Radical Feminists, argues that the very conception of female anatomy is also culturally defined quite literally to fit men's wishes: she says that the widely held assumption about the vaginal orgasm is nothing more, and nothing less, than male chauvinism at a basic level. If the current debate about the physiology of women's sexual response sustains this view, the radical women will win their most important victory against those chauvinists who perceive women as mere sexual vessels. The politics of liberation in this issue will depend on continuing work on the physiology of sex, while the politics implicit in the definition of women is now clearer than ever.

These two statements prove what the clearest radical women have tried to argue all along: the oppression of women is so total that every action is intrinsically political. And the way out is perceived to be through an autonomous movement that could encourage the creation of "women-defined-women, subjects not objects who are strong, independent, and together, who can transcend their own training to become able to think and act for themselves, each other, and for the movement." [1]

The increasing bitterness of some radical women was encapsulated in an article (Document 64) written by Robin Morgan on the occasion of a women's collective taking over control of *RAT,* an important underground newspaper formerly run by men. This is a manifesto of militancy, a declaration of independence from a male-dominated Left, as well as from all male domination in society as presently organized. She condemns the Weather Sisters for their surrogate *machismo,* but her own pitch is written with a clenched fist: "Goodbye to the illusion of strength when you run hand in hand with your oppressors; goodbye to the dream that being in the leadership collective will get you anything but gonorrhea." And the final confession and declaration: "We are the women that men have warned us about." Socialism was neither her answer nor her hope, as she demanded nothing less than a social reconstruction beyond any standards now known or articulated. The end of domination was the goal, and for that the entire masculine Left finally turned out to be not brothers-in-struggle, but pernicious oppressors.

There is no predicting the outcome of this intense Left factionalism, this battle for sexual hegemony. The guilt is there, as is the frustration, and the delight in newly found chances for expressing long squelched resentments and hatreds. This particular struggle will last at least on the left, if for no other reason than that the passions it has unloosed are so intense. Of course not all of the radical women go all the way with Robin Morgan when she declares that "Women are the real Left," but there it is. The kind of man-hating Morgan expresses is analogous to the Black Muslim's white-hating; her emphasis on sexual separatism is analogous to their demand for racial separatism. This analogy should show that this most bitter wing of women's liberation will not be able to make a contribution to the Left until a more politically conscious movement, as Malcolm X tried to lead, and the Panthers did lead, out of the Muslims, begins to move away from merely sexual or racial spleen. Whether this is more than the newest chapter in intramural bickering on the left will be proved only in the future. But it is likely that the ultimate winners will be the radical women who argue that the struggle, as always, is one of class, here freighted with sexism in the same way as it may also be racist.

[1] Elizabeth Ewen, unpublished statement, 1970, p. 1.

For now it is enough to point out the obvious: for the first time in the history of the Left, women are attempting to free themselves not only from their oppression as social victims, but from the Left itself, in order better to explore who they must become. It is a question whether this repudiates radicalism or whether it seeks to rephrase, rephase, and remake it. Let it all stop here for now, even though the end is not yet. Fortunately.

---

[60]

THE LOOK IS YOU: TOWARD A STRATEGY FOR RADICAL WOMEN

NAOMI JAFFE AND BERNADINE DOHRN

TWO tits and no head—as the representation, in glossy color, of the women's liberation movement—is an apt example of *Ramparts'* success in making a commodity out of politics.

Over the past few months, small groups have been coming together in various cities to meet around the realization that as women radicals we are not radical women—that we are unfree within the movement and in personal relationships, as in the society at large. We realize that women are organized into the movement by men and continue to relate to it through men. We find that the difficulty that women have in taking initiative and in acting and speaking in a political context is the consequence of internalizing the view that men define reality and women are defined in terms of men. We are coming together *not* in a defensive posture to rage at our exploited status vis-a-vis men; rather, in the process of developing our own autonomy, to expose the nature of American society in which all people are reified (manipulated as objects). We insist on a recognition of the organic connection of the unfreedom of all groups in society.

The consciousness that our underdeveloped abilities are not just personal failings but are deeply rooted in this society is an exhilarating and expressive breakthrough. There is the terror of giving up the roles through which we know how to obtain a certain measure of power and security.

SOURCE: Naomi Jaffe and Bernadine Dohrn, "The Look Is You: Toward a Strategy for Radical Women," mimeographed, February 1968, pp. 1–4.

473

But again and again there is the rejoicing in the unexplored possibilities of becoming vital potent human beings.

By refusing to be kept separate from other women by feelings of dislike, jealousy and competitiveness, we have begun to discuss and research ourselves in our context—to de-mystify the myth of women by analyzing the forces which have shaped us.

Women suffer only a particular form of the general social oppression, so our struggles to understand and break through society's repressive definition of us are struggles which have to attack the foundations of that society—its power to define people according to needs of an economy based on domination.

The dynamic of that economy is a changing technology, which creates an ever-greater scale of production. Lack of social control over this increasing production (the planned use of the productive forces for and by the people of the society) means that the goal of productivity is profit, and profit can only be sustained if markets can be found (or created) to absorb an increasing volume of goods.

This is the dynamic of imperialism—the relentless search for new markets which drains the resources of the Third World and cripples its independent economic development. It is also the dynamic of the domestic imperialism of consumption: the creation of internal markets through a process which defines persons as consumers and cripples their development as free human beings.

Women are the consummate products of that process. We are at the same time the beneficiaries and the victims of the productivity made possible by advanced technology. The innovations that offer us immediate freedom and also force us into the service of an overall system of domination and repression. The more we realize ourselves through consumption, the greater the power of commodities to define . . . us. "Women must be liberated to desire new products." (Market research executive.)

The same new things that allow us to express our new sense of freedom and naturalness and movement—swingy, body-revealing clothing, fun gimmicky accessories—are also used to force us to be the consumers of the endless flow of products necessary for the perpetuation of a repressive society. Mini-skirts and costume-clothes and high boots and transparent makeup *are* fun and expressive and pretty; at the same time they are self-expression through *things,* through acquiring rather than becoming—and it is the expression of all human needs through commodities which sustains an economy that has to produce and sell more and more goods in order to survive.

474

"But the real point about that swinging sixteen-to-twenty-four group is not their spending power, but the fact that they have become market leaders. They have created a climate that has enabled fashion to catch on as a new force in the market, driving apparel expenditures higher and higher." (Fortune Oct. '67.)

The same rise in productivity that requires more consumption of more goods also creates more leisure time—so leisure time becomes consumption time and consumption becomes increasingly a major sphere of life activity. A culture of consumption is created through the mass media, supported by the 16 billion dollars per year advertising industry, to channel all the potential human development into commodity form.

"Deeply set in human nature is the need to have a meaningful place in a group that strives for meaningful social goals. Whenever this is lacking, the individual becomes restless. Which explains why, as we talk to people across the nation, over and over again, we hear questions like these: 'What does it all mean?' 'Where am I going?' 'Why don't things seem more worthwhile when we all work so hard and have so darn many things to play with?' The question is: Can your product fill this gap?" (From an advertising agency report.)

The increased economic importance of consumption is reflected most deeply in the role of women, who are said to make 75% of all family consumption decisions and at whom 75% of all advertising is directed. This consumption culture shapes us as women and as people into an essentially passive mode of being, which in turn enables us to be exploited in the productive sphere in meaningless, low-paying clerical jobs. Women are culturally manipulated to see our work roles as being of secondary importance (since we are defined primarily by our sexual roles); we therefore serve as a reserve army of labor for the lowest status white collar jobs, drawn into the labor force when needed, and told to find fulfillment at home when employment is slack.

Or, as professional and semi-professional women, our very status as "independent women" is the source of our exploitation, forcing us into work and leisure roles which reinforce an illusory image of freedom and creativity. The work role demands of status and travel open new areas for the creation of commodity "needs," and professional women as consumers are used to create styles and tastes for the larger population.

So our passive roles as producers and consumers reinforce each other, and in turn are reinforced by and perpetuate our passive social-sexual roles. These roles are based on receptivity—being through acquiring objects, rather than becoming through projecting oneself onto the world to

475

change it (active mastery of the world). Real control over one's life is not the same as the illusion deliberately created by commodity culture through a choice of commodities. "Choosing oneself" on commodity form is a choice predefined by a repressive system.

The passive-receptive woman role, a product of the structure and development of American society, increasingly defines the culture of that society. Men too do not control their environment or project themselves onto it to change it (potency). Although active mastery is still considered a male mode, it is increasingly irrelevant to a society based on the compulsive consumption of commodities. "What is self but a permanent mode of selection?" (Advertising executive.)

The relationships of a market economy are reflected and reinforced in the dynamic and the forms of human relationships. The real needs of people are translated into a currency of possession, exclusivity and investment: a language of commodities where people are the goods. Both men and women are manipulated into functioning within these categories; it is the uniquely visible condition of women as primarily sexual creatures—as decorative, tempting (passive aggressive), pleasure giving objects—which exposes the broader framework of social coercion.

Psychology, as a social institution, works in the service of this pacification of human needs and desires. Its categories begin with a historically bound notion of the restrictive implications of female biology ("Anatomy as destiny." Freud). Concepts of women as mutilated men, penis envy, and the electra complex (a mechanical inversion of the oedipal situation) exemplify a society which produces people who are taught to experience themselves as objects. These definitions allow only the possibilities of a passive mode—at best, the liberation of a "creative" resignation to fulfillment through realizing our femininity.*

In our social-sexual roles, again, the innovations that offer us immediate freedom also force us into the service of an overall system of domination and repression. Technological emancipation from enslavement to our bodies (for example, The Pill as the Great Liberator) is offered to women as the realization of freedom now. ". . . almost every aspect of the New Girl's personality reflects her *final* freedom from the sexual status that was the fate of women in the past." (Playboy, Jan. '68.)

But this greatly expanded area of permissive erotic gratification and personal control occurs inside the context of greater social control and dehumanization. The desublimation is repressive. The liberating potential of

* Feminine-intuitive-unobtrusive-serving-non-castrating-warm-sensitive-cuddly-supportive-has-rhythm-smells good-sensuous-satisfying-creative, etc.

expressed sexuality is channeled into mutually exploitative relationships where people are objects, and into the market economy where sexuality is a cornerstone. Liberalized sex begins to define the shape and texture of leisure time—in a commodity framework. Again, we are beneficiaries and victims. Thus, a more sexually active role for women actually reinforces a broader passive mode of consumption.

If women are made into objects, the object-relationships between men and women make human communication and community impossible for both; if women are defined by their sexual roles, they are only a paradigm of the reified role structures that stifle the conscious creativity of men and women alike.

A strategy for the liberation of women, then, does not demand equal jobs (exploitation), by meaningful creative activity for all; not a larger share of power but the abolition of commodity tyranny; not equal reified sexual roles but an end to sexual objectification and exploitation; not equal aggressive leadership in the movement but the initiation of a new style of a non-dominating leadership.

Our strategy will focus on the unique quality of our exploitation as women, primarily in our vanguard economic role as consumers. Women power is the power to destroy a destructive system by refusing to play the part(s) assigned to us by it—by refusing to accept its definition of us as passive consumers, and by actively subverting the institutions which create and enforce that definition.

---

[61]

BREAD AND ROSES

KATHY MCAFEE AND MYRNA WOOD

A GREAT deal of confusion exists today about the role of women's liberation in a revolutionary movement. Hundreds of women's groups have sprung up within the past year or two, but among them, a number of very different and often conflicting ideologies have developed. The growth of these movements has demonstrated the desperate need that many women feel to

SOURCE: Kathy McAfee and Myrna Wood, *Bread and Roses* (Detroit: Radical Education Project, n.d.), pp. 1–5, 12–16; reprinted from *Leviathan* 1, no. 3 (June 1969).

escape their own oppression, but it has also shown that organization around women's issues need not lead to revolutionary consciousness, or even to an identification with the left. (Some groups mobilize middle class women to fight for equal privileges as businesswomen and academics; others maintain that the overthrow of capitalism is irrelevant for women.)

Many movement women have experienced the initial exhilaration of discovering women's liberation as an issue, of realizing that the frustration, anger, and fear we feel are not a result of individual failure but are shared by all our sisters, and of sensing—if not fully understanding—that these feelings stem from the same oppressive conditions that give rise to racism, chauvinism and the barbarity of American culture. But many movement women, too, have become disillusioned after a time by their experiences with women's liberation groups. More often than not these groups never get beyond the level of therapy sessions; rather than aiding the political development of women and building a revolutionary women's movement, they often encourage escape from political struggle.

The existence of this tendency among women's liberation groups is one reason why many movement activists (including some women) have come out against a women's liberation movement that distinguishes itself from the general movement, even if it considers itself part of the left. A movement organized by women around the oppression of women, they say, is bound to emphasize the bourgeois and personal aspects of oppression and to obscure the material oppression of working class women *and men.* At best, such a movement "lacks revolutionary potential." . . . In SDS, where this attitude is very strong, questions about the oppression and liberation of women are raised only within the context of current SDS ideology and strategy; the question of women's liberation is raised only as an incidental, subordinate aspect of programs around *"the* primary struggle," anti-racism. (Although most people in SDS now understand the extent of black people's oppression, they are not aware of the fact that the median wage of working women (black and white) is lower than that of black males). The male domination of the organization has not been affected by occasional rhetorical attacks on male chauvinism and, most important, very little organizing of women is being done.

Although the reason behind it can be understood, this attitude toward women's liberation is mistaken and dangerous. By discouraging the development of a revolutionary women's liberation movement, it avoids a serious challenge to what, along with racism, is the deepest source of division and false consciousness among workers. By setting up (in the name of Marxist class analysis) a dichotomy between the "bourgeois," personal and psychological forms of oppression on the one hand, and the "real" material forms on the other, it substitutes a mechanistic model of class relations for a more profound understanding of how these two aspects of oppression depend upon and reinforce each other. Finally, this anti-women's liberationist attitude makes it easier for us to bypass a confrontation of male chauvinism and the closely related values of elitism and authoritarianism which are weakening our movement.

I

Before we can discuss the potential of a women's liberation movement, we need a more precise description of the way the oppression of women functions in a capitalist society. This will also help us understand the relation of psychological to material oppression.

(1) *Male Chauvinism—The Attitude That Women Are the Passive and Inferior Servants of Society and of Men—Sets Women Apart from the Rest of the Working Class* Even when they do the same work as men, women are not considered workers in the same sense, with the need and right to work to provide for their families or to support themselves independently. They are expected to accept work at lower wages and without job security. Thus they can be used as a marginal or reserve labor force when profits depend on extra low costs or when men are needed for war.

Women are not supposed to be independent, so they are not supposed to have any "right to work." This means, in effect, that although they do work, they are denied the right to organize and fight for better wages and conditions. Thus the role of women in the labor force undermines the struggles of male workers as well. The boss can break a union drive by threatening to hire lower paid women or blacks. In many cases, where women are organized, the union contract reinforces their inferior position, making women the least loyal and militant union members. (Standard Oil workers in San Francisco recently paid the price of male supremacy. Women at Standard Oil have the least chance for advancement and decent pay, and the union has done little to fight this. Not surprisingly, women formed the core of the back to work move that eventually broke the strike.)

In general, because women are defined as docile, helpless, and inferior, they are forced into the most demeaning and mindrotting jobs—from scrubbing floors to filing cards—under the most oppressive conditions where they are treated like children or slaves. Their very position rein-

479

forces the idea, even among the women themselves, that they are fit for and should be satisfied with this kind of work.

(2) *Apart from the Direct, Material Exploitation of Women, Male Supremacy Acts in More Subtle Ways to Undermine Class Consciousness* The tendency of male workers to think of themselves primarily as men (i.e., powerful) rather than as workers (i.e., members of an oppressed group) promotes a false sense of privilege and power, and an identification with the world of men, including the boss. The petty dictatorship which most men exercise over their wives and families enables them to vent their anger and frustration in a way which poses no challenge to the system. The role of the man in the family reinforces aggressive individualism, authoritarianism, and a hierarchical view of social relations—values which are fundamental to the perpetuation of capitalism. In this system we are taught to relieve our fears and frustrations by brutalizing those weaker than we are: a man in uniform turns into a pig; the foreman intimidates the man on the line; the husband beats his wife, child, and dog.

(3) *Women Are Further Exploited in Their Roles As Housewives and Mothers, through Which They Reduce the Costs (Social and Economic) of Maintaining the Labor Force* All of us will admit that inadequate as it may be American workers have a relatively decent standard of living, in a strictly material sense, when compared to workers of other countries or periods of history. But American workers are exploited and harassed in other ways than through the size of the weekly paycheck. They are made into robots on the job; they are denied security; they are forced to pay for expensive insurance and can rarely save enough to protect them from sudden loss of job or emergency. They are denied decent medical care and a livable environment. They are cheated by inflation. They are "given" a regimented education that prepares them for a narrow slot or for nothing. And they are taxed heavily to pay for these "benefits."

In all these areas, it is a woman's responsibility to make up for the failures of the system. In countless working class families, it is mother's job that bridges the gap between week-to-week subsistence and relative security. It is her wages that enable the family to eat better food, to escape their oppressive surroundings through a trip, an occasional movie, or new clothes. It is her responsibility to keep her family healthy despite the cost of decent medical care; to make a comfortable home in an unsafe and unlivable neighborhood; to provide a refuge from the alienation of work and to keep the male ego in good repair. It is she who must struggle daily to make ends meet despite inflation. She must make up for the fact that her children do not receive a decent education and she must salvage their damaged personalities.

A woman is judged as a wife and mother—the only role she is allowed —according to her ability to maintain stability in her family and to help her family "adjust" to harsh realities. She therefore transmits the values of hard work and conformity to each generation of workers. It is she who forces her children to stay in school and "behave" or who urges her husband not to risk his job by standing up to the boss or going on strike.

Thus the role of wife and mother is one of social mediator and pacifier. She shields her family from the direct impact of class oppression. She is the true opiate of the masses.

(4) *Working Class Women and Other Women as Well Are Exploited as Consumers* They are forced to buy products which are necessities, but which have waste built into them, like the soap powder the price of which includes fancy packaging and advertising. They also buy products which are wasteful in themselves because they are told that a new car or TV will add to their families' status and satisfaction, or that cosmetics will increase their desirability as sex objects. Among "middle class" women, of course, the second type of wasteful consumption is more important than it is among working class women, but all women are victims of both types to a greater or lesser extent, and the values which support wasteful consumption are part of our general culture.

(5) *All Women, Too, Are Oppressed and Exploited Sexually* For working class women this oppression is more direct and brutal. They are denied control of their own bodies, when as girls they are refused information about sex and birth control, and when as women they are denied any right to decide whether and when to have children. Their confinement to the role of sex partner and mother, and their passive submission to a single man are often maintained by physical force. The relative sexual freedom of "middle class" or college educated women, however, does not bring *them* real independence. Their sexual role is still primarily a passive one; their value as individuals still determined by their ability to attract, please, and hold onto a man. The definition of women as docile and dependent, inferior in intellect and weak in character cuts across class lines.

A woman of any class is expected to sell herself—not just her body but her entire life, her talents, interests, and dreams—to a man. She is expected to give up friendships, ambitions, pleasures, and moments of time to herself in order to serve his career or his family. In return, she receives not only her livelihood but her identity, her very right to existence, for unless she is the wife of someone or the mother of someone, a woman is nothing.

In this summary of the forms of oppression of women in this society, the rigid dichotomy between material oppression and psychological oppression fails to hold, for it can be seen that these two aspects of oppression reinforce each other at every level. A woman may seek a job out of absolute necessity, or in order to escape repression and dependence at home. In either case, on the job she will be persuaded or forced to accept low pay, indignity and a prison-like atmosphere because a woman isn't supposed to need money or respect. Then, after working all week turning tiny wires, or typing endless forms, she finds that cooking and cleaning, dressing up and making up, becoming submissive and childlike in order to please a man are her only relief, so she gladly falls back into her "proper" role.

All women, even including those of the ruling class, are oppressed as women in the sense that their real fulfillment is linked to their role as girl-friend, wife or mother. This definition of women is part of bourgeois culture—the whole superstructure of ideas that serves to explain and reinforce the social relations of capitalism. It is applied to all women, but it has very different consequences for women of different classes. For a ruling class woman, it means she is denied real independence, dignity, and sexual freedom. For a working class woman it means this too, but it also justifies her material super-exploitation and physical coercion. Her oppression is a total one. . . .

What Is the Revolutionary Potential of Women's Liberation?

The potential for revolutionary thought and action lies in the masses of super-oppressed and super-exploited working class women. We have seen the stagnation in New Left women's groups caused by the lack of the *need to fight* that class oppression produces. Unlike most radical women, working class women have no freedom of alternatives, no chance of achieving some slight degree of individual liberation. It is these women, through their struggle, who will develop a revolutionary women's liberation movement.

A women's liberation movement will be necessary if unity of the working class is ever to be achieved. Until working men see their female co-workers and their own wives as equal in their movement, and until those women see that it is in their own interests and that of their families to "dare to win," the position of women will continue to undermine every working class struggle.

The attitude of unions, and of the workers themselves, that women should not work, and that they do not do difficult or necessary work, helps to maintain a situation in which (1) many women who need income or independence cannot work, (2) women who do work are usually not organized, (3) union contracts reinforce the inferior position of women who are organized, and (4) women are further penalized with the costs of child care. As a result, most women workers do not see much value in organizing. They have little to gain from militant fights for better wages and conditions, and they have the most to risk in organizing in the first place.

The position of workers' wives outside their husbands' union often places them in antagonism to it. They know how little it does about safety and working conditions, grievances, and layoffs. The unions demand complete loyalty to strikes—which means weeks without income—and then sign contracts which bring little improvement in wages or conditions.

Thus on the simple trade union level, the oppression of women weakens the position of the workers as a whole. But any working class movement that does not deal with the vulnerable position of totally powerless women will have to deal with the false consciousness of those women.

The importance of a working class women's liberation movement goes beyond the need for unity. A liberation movement of the "slaves of the slave" tends to raise broader issues of people's oppression in all its forms, so that it is inherently wider than the economism of most trade union movements. For example, last year 187 women struck British Ford demanding equal wages (and shutting down 40,000 other jobs in the process). They won their specific demand, but Ford insisted that the women work all three rotating shifts, as the men do. The women objected that this would create great difficulty for them in their work as housekeepers and mothers, and that their husbands would not like it.

A militant women's liberation movement must go on from this point to demand (1) that mothers must also be free in the home, (2) that management must pay for child care facilities so that women can do equal work with men, and that (3) equal work *with* men must mean equal work *by* men. In this way, the winning of a simple demand for equality on the job raises much broader issues of the extent of inequality, the degree of exploitation, and the totality of the oppression of all the workers. It can show how women workers are forced to hold an extra full time job without pay or recognition that this is necessary work, how male chauvinism allows the capitalist class to exploit workers in this way, how people are treated like machines owned by the boss, and how the most basic conditions of workers' lives are controlled in the interests of capitalism.

The workplace is not the only area in which the fight against women's oppression can raise the consciousness of everybody about the real func-

483

tions of bourgeois institutions. Propaganda against sexual objectification and the demeaning of women in the media can help make people understand how advertising manipulates our desires and frustrations, and how the media sets up models of human relationships and values which we all unconsciously accept. A fight against the tracking of girls in school into low-level, deadened service jobs helps show how the education system channels and divides us all, playing upon the false self-images we have been given in school and by the media (women are best as secretaries and nurses; blacks aren't cut out for responsible positions; workers' sons aren't smart enough for college).

Struggles to free women from domestic slavery which may begin around demands for a neighborhood or factory child care center can lead to consciousness of the crippling effects of relations of domination and exploitation in the home, and to an understanding of how the institutions of marriage and the family embody those relations and destroy human potential.

In short, because the material oppression of women is integrally related to their psychological and sexual oppression, the women's liberation movement must necessarily raise these issues. In doing so it can make us all aware of how capitalism oppresses us, not only by drafting us, taxing us, and exploiting us on the job, but by determining the way we think, feel, and relate to each other.

II

In order to form a women's liberation movement based on the oppression of working class women we must begin to agitate on issues of "equal rights" and specific rights. Equal rights means all those "rights" that men are supposed to have: the right to work, to organize for equal pay, promotions, better conditions, equal (and *not* separate) education. Specific rights means those rights women must have if they are to be equal in the other areas: free, adequate child care, abortions, birth control for young women from puberty, self-defense, desegregation of all institutions (schools, unions, jobs). It is not so much an academic question of what is correct theory as an inescapable empirical fact; women must fight their conditions just to participate in the movement.

The first reason why we need to fight on these issues is that we must serve the people. That slogan is not just rhetoric with the Black Panthers but reflects their determination to end the exploitation of their people. Similarly, the women's liberation movement will grow and be effective only to the extent that it abominates and fights the conditions of misery that so many women suffer every day. It will gain support only if it speaks to the immediate needs of women. For instance:

1. We must begin to disseminate birth control information in high schools and fight the tracking of girls into inferior education. We must do this not only to raise the consciousness of these girls to their condition but because control of their bodies is the key to their participation in the future. Otherwise, their natural sexuality will be indirectly used to repress them from struggles for better jobs and organizing, because they will be encumbered with children and economically tied to the family structure for basic security.

2. We must raise demands for maternity leave and child-care facilities provided (paid for, but not controlled) by management as a rightful side benefit of women workers. This is important not only for what those issues say about women's right to work but so that women who choose to have children have more freedom to participate in the movement.

3. We must agitate for rank and file revolt against the male supremacist hierarchy of the unions and for demands for equal wages. Only through winning such struggles for equality can the rank and file *be* united and see their common enemies—management and union hierarchy. Wives of workers must fight the chauvinist attitudes of their husbands simply to be able to attend meetings.

4. We must organize among store clerks, waitresses, office workers, and hospitals where vast numbers of women have no bargaining rights or security. In doing so we will have to confront the question of a radical strategy towards established unions and the viability of independent unions.

5. We must add to the liberal demands for abortion reform by fighting against the hospital and doctors' boards that such reforms consist of. They will in no way make abortions more available for the majority of non-middle class women or young girls who will still be forced to home remedies and butchers. We must insist at all times on the right of every woman to control her own body.

6. We must demand the right of women to protect themselves. Because the pigs protect property and not people, because the violence created by the brutalization of many men in our society is often directed at women and because not all women are willing or able to sell themselves (or to limit their lives) for the protection of a male, women have a right to self-protection.

This is where the struggle must begin, although it cannot end here. In the course of the fight we will have to raise the issues of the human relationships in which the special oppression of women is rooted: sexual objectification, the division of labor in the home, and the institutions of marriage and the nuclear family. But organizing "against the family" cannot be the basis of a program. An uneducated working class wife with five kids is perfectly capable of understanding that marriage has destroyed most of her potential as a human being—probably she already understands this—but she is hardly in a position to repudiate her source of livelihood and free herself of those children. If we expect that of her, we will never build a movement.

As the women's liberation movement gains strength, the development of cooperative child care centers and living arrangements, and the provision of birth control may allow more working class women to free themselves from slavery as sex objects and housewives. But at the present time, the insistence by some women's liberation groups that we must "organize against sexual objectification," and that only women who repudiate the family can really be part of the movement, reflects the class chauvinism and lack of seriousness of women who were privileged enough to avoid economic dependence and sexual slavery in the first place.

In no socialist country have women yet achieved equality or full liberation, but in the most recent revolutions (Vietnam, Cuba, and China's cultural revolution) the women's struggle has intensified. It may be that in an advanced society such as our own, where women have had relatively more freedom, a revolutionary movement may not be able to avoid a militant women's movement developing within it. But the examples of previous attempts at socialist revolutions prove that the struggle must be instigated *by* militant women; liberation is not handed down from above.

62

THE POLITICS OF HOUSEWORK

P A T   M A I N A R D I

Though women do not complain of the power of husbands, each complains of her own husband, or of the husbands of her friends. It is the same in all other cases of servitude; at least in the commencement of the emancipatory movement. The serfs did not at first complain of the power of the lords, but only of their tyranny.

JOHN STUART MILL
On the Subjection of Women

LIBERATED women—very different from Women's Liberation! The first signals all kinds of goodies, to warm the hearts (not to mention other parts) of the most radical men. The other signals—HOUSEWORK. The first brings sex without marriage, sex before marriage, cozy housekeeping arrangements ("I'm living with this chick") and the self-content of knowing that you're not the kind of man who wants a doormat instead of a woman. That will come later. After all, who wants that old commodity any more, the Standard American Housewife, all husband, home and kids. The New Commodity, the Liberated Woman, has sex a lot and has a Career, preferably something that can be fitted in with the household chores —like dancing, pottery, or painting.

On the other hand is Women's Liberation—and housework. What? You say that is all trivial? Wonderful! That's what I thought. It seemed perfectly reasonable. We both had careers, both had to work a couple of days a week to earn enough to live on, so why shouldn't we share the housework? So I suggested it to my mate and he agreed—most men are too hip to turn you down flat. You're right, he said. It's only fair.

Then an interesting thing happened. I can only explain it by stating that we women have been brainwashed more than even we can imagine. Probably too many years of seeing television women in ecstasy over their shiny waxed floors or breaking down over their dirty shirt collars. Men have no such conditioning. They recognize the essential fact of housework right from the very beginning. Which is that it stinks.

Here's my list of dirty chores: buying groceries, carting them home and putting them away; cooking meals and washing dishes and pots; doing the laundry, digging out the place when things get out of control; washing floors. The list could go on but the sheer necessities are bad enough. All of us have to do these things, or get someone else to do them for us. The longer my husband contemplated these chores, the more repulsed he became, and so proceeded the change from the normally sweet considerate Dr. Jekyll into the crafty Mr. Hyde who would stop at nothing to avoid the horrors of—housework. As he felt himself backed into a corner laden with dirty dishes, brooms, mops and reeking garbage, his front teeth grew longer and pointier, his fingernails haggled and his eyes grew wild. Housework trivial? Not on your life! Just try to share the burden.

So ensued a dialogue that's been going on for several years. Here are some of the high points:

"I don't mind sharing the housework, but I don't do it very well. We should each do the things we're best at." MEANING: Unfortunately I'm no good at things like washing dishes or cooking. What I do best is a little light carpentry, changing light bulbs, moving furniture (how often do *you* move furniture?). ALSO MEANING: Historically the lower classes (black men and us) have had hundreds of years experience doing menial jobs. It would be a waste of manpower to train someone else to do them now. ALSO MEANING: I don't like the dull stupid boring jobs, so you should do them.

"I don't mind sharing the work, but you'll have to show me how to do it." MEANING: I ask a lot of questions and you'll have to show me everything every time I do it because I don't remember so good. Also don't try to sit down and read while I'M doing my jobs because I'm going to annoy hell out of you until it's easier to do them yourself.

"We used to be so happy!" (Said whenever it was his turn to do something.) MEANING: I used to be so happy. MEANING: Life without housework is bliss. No quarrel here. Perfect Agreement.

"We have different standards, and why should I have to work to your standards? That's unfair." MEANING: If I begin to get bugged by the dirt and crap I will say, "This place sure is a sty" or "How can anyone live like this?" and wait for your reaction. I know that all women have a sore called "Guilt over a messy house" or "Household work is ultimately my responsibility." I know that men have caused that sore—if anyone visits and the place *is* a sty, they're not going to leave and say, "He sure is a lousy housekeeper." You'll take the rap in any case. I can outwait you. ALSO MEANING: I can provoke innumerable scenes over the housework issue. Eventually doing all the housework yourself will be less painful to you than trying to get me to do half. Or I'll suggest we get a maid. She will do my share of the work. You will do yours. It's women's work.

"I've got nothing against sharing the housework, but you can't make me do it on your schedule." MEANING: Passive resistance. I'll do it when I damned well please, if at all. If my job is doing dishes, it's easier to do them once a week. If taking out laundry, once a month. If washing the floors, once a year. If you don't like it, do it yourself oftener, and then I won't do it at all.

"I hate it more than you. You don't mind it so much." MEANING: Housework is garbage work. It's the worst crap I've ever done. It's degrading and humiliating for someone of *my* intelligence to do it. But for someone of *your* intelligence. . . .

"Housework is too trivial to even talk about." MEANING: It's even more trivial to do. Housework is beneath my status. My purpose in life is to deal with matters of significance. Yours is to deal with matters of insignificance. You should do the housework.

"This problem of housework is not a man–woman problem. In any relationship between two people one is going to have a stronger personality and dominate." MEANING: That stronger personality had better be *me*.

"In animal societies, wolves, for example, the top animal is usually a male even where he is not chosen for brute strength but on the basis of cunning and intelligence. Isn't that interesting?" MEANING: I have historical, psychological, anthropological and biological justification for keeping you down. How can you ask the top wolf to be equal?

"Women's Liberation isn't really a political movement." MEANING: The Revolution is coming too close to home. ALSO MEANING: I am only interested in how I am oppressed, not how I oppress others. Therefore the war, the draft and the university are political. Women's Liberation is not. "Man's accomplishments have always depended on getting help from other people, mostly women. What great man would have accomplished what he did if he had to do his own housework?" MEANING: Oppression is built into the system and I, as the white American male, receive the benefits of this system. I don't want to give them up.

*　*　*

Participatory democracy begins at home. If you are planning to implement your politics, there are certain things to remember:

1. He *is* feeling it more than you. He's losing some leisure and you're gaining it. The measure of your oppression is his resistance.

2. A great many American men are not accustomed to doing monotonous repetitive work which never issues in any lasting, let alone important, achievement. This is why they would rather repair a cabinet than wash dishes. If human endeavors are like a pyramid with man's highest achievements at the top, then keeping oneself alive is at the bottom. Men have always had servants (us) to take care of this bottom stratum of life while they have confined their efforts to the rarefied upper regions. It is thus ironic when they ask of women—where are your great painters, statesmen, etc. Mme Matisse ran a millinery shop so he could paint. Mrs. Martin Luther King kept his house and raised his babies.

3. It is a traumatizing experience for someone who has always thought of himself as being against any oppression or exploitation of one human being by another to realize that in his daily life he has been accepting and implementing (and benefiting from) his exploitation; that his rationalization is little different from that of the racist who says "Black people don't feel pain" (women don't mind doing the shitwork); and that the oldest form of oppression in history has been the oppression of 50 percent of the population by the other 50 percent.

4. Arm yourself with some knowledge of the psychology of oppressed peoples everywhere, and a few facts about the animal kingdom. I admit playing top wolf or who runs the gorillas is silly but as a last resort men bring it up all the time. Talk about bees. If you feel really hostile bring up the sex life of spiders. They have sex. She bites off his head.

   The psychology of oppressed peoples is not silly. Jews, immigrants, black men and all women have employed the same psychological mechanisms to survive: Admiring the oppressor, glorifying the oppressor, wanting to be like the oppressor, wanting the oppressor to like them, mostly because the oppressor held all the power.

5. In a sense, all men everywhere are slightly schizoid—divorced from the reality of maintaining life. This makes it easier for them to play games with it. It is almost a cliche that women feel greater grief at sending a son off to a war or losing him to that war because they bore him, suckled him, and raised him. The men who foment those wars did none of those things and have a more superficial estimate of the worth of human life. One hour a day is a low estimate of the amount of time one has to spend "keeping" oneself. By foisting this off on others, man has seven hours a week—one working day more to play with his mind and

not his human needs. Over the course of generations it is easy to see whence evolved the horrifying abstractions of modern life.

6. With the death of each form of oppression, life changes and new forms evolve. English aristocrats at the turn of the century were horrified at the idea of enfranchising working men—were sure that it signalled the death of civilization and a return to barbarism. Some workingmen were even deceived by this line. Similarly with the minimum wage, abolition of slavery, and female suffrage. Life changes but it goes on. Don't fall for any line about the death of everything if men take a turn at the dishes. They will imply that you are holding back the Revolution (their Revolution). But you are advancing it (your Revolution).

7. Keep checking up. Periodically consider who's actually *doing* the jobs. These things have a way of backsliding so that a year later once again the woman is doing everything. After a year make a list of jobs the man has rarely if ever done. You will find cleaning pots, toilets, refrigerators and ovens high on the list. Use time sheets if necessary. He will accuse you of being petty. He is above that sort of thing (housework). Bear in mind what the worst jobs are, namely the ones that have to be done every day or several times a day. Also the ones that are dirty— it's more pleasant to pick up books, newspapers, etc., than to wash dishes. Alternate the bad jobs. It's the daily grind that gets you down. Also make sure that you don't have the responsibility for the housework with occasional help from him. "I'll cook dinner for you tonight" implies it's really your job and isn't he a nice guy to do some of it for you.

8. Most men had a rich and rewarding bachelor life during which they did not starve or become encrusted with crud or buried under the litter. There is a taboo that says women mustn't strain themselves in the presence of men—we haul around 50 lbs. of groceries if we have to but aren't allowed to open a jar if there is someone around to do it for us. The reverse side of the coin is that men aren't supposed to be able to take care of themselves without a woman. Both are excuses for making women do the housework.

9. Beware of the double whammy. He won't do the little things he always did because you're now a "Liberated Woman," right? Of course he won't do anything else either. . . .

I was just finishing this when my husband came in and asked what I was doing. Writing a paper on housework. Housework? he said, *Housework?* Oh my god how trivial can you get. A paper on housework.

Little Politics of Housework Quiz

1. The lowest job in the army, used as punishment is *a) working 9–5 b) kitchen duty (K.P.)*.
2. When a man lives with his family, his *a) father b) mother* does his housework.
3. When he lives with a woman, *a) he b) she* does the housework.
4. *a) His son b) his daughter* learns preschool how much fun it is to iron daddy's handkerchief.
5. From the *New York Times*, 9/21/69: "Former Greek Official George Mylonas pays the penalty for differing with the ruling junta in Athens by performing household chores on the island of Amorgos where he lives in forced exile" (with hilarious photo of a miserable Mylonas carrying his own water). What the *Times* means is that he ought to have *a) indoor plumbing b) a maid*.
6. Dr. Spock said (*Redbook,* 3/69) "Biologically and temperamentally I believe, women were made to be concerned first and foremost with child care, husband care, and home care." Think about *a) who made us? b) why? c) what is the effect on their lives? d) what is the effect on our lives?*
7. From *Time,* 1/5/70, "Like their American counterparts, many housing project housewives are said to suffer from neurosis. And for the first time in Japanese history, many young husbands today complain of being henpecked. Their wives are beginning to demand detailed explanations when they don't come home straight from work and some Japanese males nowadays are even compelled to do housework." According to *Time,* women become neurotic *a) when they are forced to do the maintenance work for the male caste all day every day of their lives* or *b) when they no longer want to do the maintenance work for the male caste all day every day of their lives.*

63

THE MYTH OF THE
VAGINAL ORGASM

ANNE P. KOEDT

WHENEVER female orgasm and frigidity are discussed, a false distinction is made between the vaginal and clitoral orgasm. Frigidity has generally been defined by men as the failure of women to have vaginal orgasms. Actually the vagina is not a highly sensitive area and is not constructed to achieve orgasm. It is the clitoris which is the center of sexual sensitivity and which is the female equivalent of the penis.

I think this explains a great many things: First of all, the fact that the so-called frigidity rate among women is phenomenally high. Rather than tracing female frigidity to the false assumptions about female anatomy, our "experts" have declared frigidity a psychological problem of women. Those women who complained about it were recommended psychiatrists, so that they might discover their "problem"—diagnosed generally as a failure to adjust to their role as women.

The facts of female anatomy and sexual response tell a different story. There is only one area for sexual climax, although there are many areas for sexual arousal; that area is the clitoris. All orgasms are extensions of sensation from this area. Since the clitoris is not necessarily stimulated sufficiently in the conventional sexual positions, we are left "frigid."

Aside from physical stimulation, which is the common cause of orgasm for most people, there is also stimulation through primarily mental processes. Some women, for example, may achieve orgasm through sexual fantasies, or through fetishes. However, while the stimulation may be psychological, the orgasm manifests itself physically. Thus, while the cause is psychological, the *effect* is still physical, and the orgasm necessarily takes place in the sexual organ equipped for sexual climax—the clitoris. The orgasm experience may also differ in degree of intensity—some more localized, and some more diffuse and sensitive. But they are all clitoral orgasms.

SOURCE: Anne P. Koedt, "The Myth of the Vaginal Orgasm," in *Notes from the Second Year: Women's Liberation,* eds. Shulamith Firestone and Anne P. Koedt (New York: Radical Feminism, 1970), pp. 37–41. Copyright 1970, Anne Koedt.

All this leads to some interesting questions about conventional sex and our role in it. Men have orgasms essentially by friction with the vagina, not the clitoral area, which is external and not able to cause friction the way penetration does. Women have thus been defined sexually in terms of what pleases men; our own biology has not been properly analyzed. Instead, we are fed the myth of the liberated woman and her vaginal orgasm —an orgasm which in fact does not exist.

What we must do is redefine our sexuality. We must discard the "normal" concepts of sex and create new guidelines which take into account mutual sexual enjoyment. While the idea of mutual enjoyment is liberally applauded in marriage manuals, it is not followed to its logical conclusion. We must begin to demand that if certain sexual positions now defined as "standard" are not mutually conducive to orgasm, they no longer be defined as standard. New techniques must be used or devised which transform this particular aspect of our current sexual exploitation.

Freud—A Father of the Vaginal Orgasm

Freud contended that the clitoral orgasm was adolescent, and that upon puberty, when women began having intercourse with men, women should transfer the center of orgasm to the vagina. The vagina, it was assumed, was able to produce a parallel, but more mature, orgasm than the clitoris. Much work was done to elaborate on this theory, but little was done to challenge the basic assumptions.

To fully appreciate this incredible invention, perhaps Freud's general attitude about women should first be recalled. Mary Ellman, in *Thinking about Women,* summed it up this way:

> Everything in Freud's patronizing and fearful attitude toward women follows from their lack of a penis, but it is only in his essay *The Psychology of Women* that Freud makes explicit . . . the deprecations of women which are implicit in his work. He then prescribes for them the abandonment of the life of the mind, which will interfere with their sexual function. When the psychoanalyzed patient is male, the analyst sets himself the task of developing the man's capacities; but with women patients, the job is to resign them to the limits of their sexuality. As Mr. Rieff puts it: For Freud, "Analysis cannot encourage in women new energies for success and achievement, but only teach them the lesson of rational resignation."

It was Freud's feelings about women's secondary and inferior relationship to men that formed the basis for his theories on female sexuality.

Once having laid down the law about the nature of our sexuality, Freud not so strangely discovered a tremendous problem of frigidity in women. His recommended cure for a woman who was frigid was psychiatric care. She was suffering from failure to mentally adjust to her "natural" role as a woman. Frank S. Caprio, a contemporary follower of these ideas, states:

. . . whenever a woman is incapable of achieving an orgasm via coitus, provided her husband is an adequate partner, and prefers clitoral stimulation to any other form of sexual activity, she can be regarded as suffering from frigidity and requires psychiatric assistance. (*The Sexually Adequate Female,* p. 64.)

The explanation given was that women were envious of men— "renunciation of womanhood." Thus it was diagnosed as an anti-male phenomenon.

It is important to emphasize that Freud did not base his theory upon a study of woman's anatomy, but rather upon his assumptions of woman as an inferior appendage to man, and her consequent social and psychological role. In their attempts to deal with the ensuing problem of mass frigidity, Freudians created elaborate mental gymnastics. Marie Bonaparte, in *Female Sexuality,* goes so far as to suggest surgery to help women back on their rightful path. Having discovered a strange connection between the non-frigid woman and the location of the clitoris near the vagina,

it then occurred to me that where, in certain women, this gap was excessive, and clitoridal fixation obdurate, a clitoridal–vaginal reconciliation might be effected by surgical means, which would then benefit the normal erotic function. Professor Halban, of Vienna, as much a biologist as surgeon, became interested in the problem and worked out a simple operative technique. In this, the suspensory ligament of the clitoris was severed and the clitoris secured to the underlying structures, thus fixing it in a lower position, with eventual reduction of the labia minora. (P. 148.)

But the severest damage was not in the area of surgery, where Freudians ran around absurdly trying to change female anatomy to fit their basic assumptions. The worst damage was done to the mental health of women, who either suffered silently with self-blame, or flocked to the psychiatrists looking desperately for the hidden and terrible repression that kept from them their vaginal destiny.

Lack of Evidence?

One may perhaps at first claim that these are unknown and unexplored areas, but upon closer examination this is certainly not true today, nor was it true even in the past. For example, men have known that women suffered from frigidity often during intercourse. So the problem was there.

Also, there is much specific evidence. Men knew that the clitoris was and is the essential organ for masturbation, whether in children or adult women. So obviously women made it clear where *they* thought their sexuality was located. Men also seem suspiciously aware of the clitoral powers during "foreplay," when they want to arouse women and produce the necessary lubrication for penetration. Foreplay is a concept created for male purposes, but works to the disadvantage of many women, since as soon as the woman is aroused the man changes to vaginal stimulation, leaving her both aroused and unsatisfied.

It has also been known that women need no anesthesia inside the vagina during surgery, thus pointing to the fact that the vagina is in fact not a highly sensitive area.

Today, with extensive knowledge of anatomy, with Kinsey, and Masters and Johnson, to mention just a few sources, there is no ignorance on the subject. There are, however, social reasons why this knowledge has not been popularized. We are living in a male society which has not sought change in women's role.

Anatomical Evidence

Rather than starting with what women *ought* to feel, it would seem logical to start out with the anatomical facts regarding the clitoris and vagina.

The Clitoris   [It] is a small equivalent of the penis, except for the fact that the urethra does not go through it as in the man's penis. Its erection is similar to the male erection, and the head of the clitoris has the same type of structure and function as the head of the penis. G. Lombard Kelly, in *Sexual Feeling in Married Men and Women,* says:

> The head of the clitoris is also composed of erectile tissue and it possesses a very sensitive epithelium or surface covering, supplied with special nerve endings called genital corpuscles, which are peculiarly adapted for sensory stimulation that under proper mental conditions terminates in the sexual orgasm. No other part of the female generative tract has such corpuscles. (Pocketbooks; p. 35.)

The clitoris has no other function than that of sexual pleasure.

The Vagina   Its functions are related to the reproductive function. Principally, 1) menstruation, 2) receive penis, 3) hold semen, and 4) birth passage. The interior of the vagina, which according to the defenders of the vaginally caused orgasm is the center and producer of the orgasm, is:

like nearly all other internal body structures, poorly supplied with end organs of touch. The internal entodermal origin of the lining of the vagina makes it similar in this respect to the rectum and other parts of the digestive tract. (Kinsey, *Sexual Behavior in the Human Female,* p. 580.)

The degree of insensitivity inside the vagina is so high that "among the women who were tested in our gynecologic sample, less than 14% were at all conscious that they had been touched." (Kinsey, p. 580.)

Even the importance of the vagina as an *erotic* center (as opposed to an orgasmic center) has been found to be minor.

Other Areas   Labia minora and the vestibule of the vagina. These two sensitive areas may trigger off a clitoral orgasm. Because they can be effectively stimulated during "normal" coitus, though infrequent, this kind of stimulation is incorrectly thought to be vaginal orgasm. However, it is important to distinguish between areas which can stimulate the clitoris, incapable of producing the orgasm themselves, and the clitoris:

Regardless of what means of excitation is used to bring the individual to the state of sexual climax, the sensation is perceived by the genital corpuscles and is localized where they are situated: in the head of the clitoris or penis. (Kelly, p. 49.)

Psychologically Stimulated Orgasm   Aside from the above mentioned direct and indirect stimulations of the clitoris, there is a third way an orgasm may be triggered. This is through mental (cortical) stimulation, where the imagination stimulates the brain, which in turn stimulates the genital corpuscles of the glans to set off an orgasm.

Women Who Say They Have Vaginal Orgasms

Confusion   Because of the lack of knowledge of their own anatomy, some women accept the idea that an orgasm felt during "normal" intercourse was vaginally caused. This confusion is caused by a combination of two factors. One, failing to locate the center of the orgasm, and two, by a desire to fit her experience to the male-defined idea of sexual normalcy. Considering that women know little about their anatomy, it is easy to be confused.

Deception   The vast majority of women who pretend vaginal orgasm to their men are faking it to, as Ti-Grace Atkinson says, "get the job." In a new best-selling Danish book, *I Accuse* (my own translation), Mette Ejlersen specifically deals with this common problem, which she calls the "sex comedy." This comedy has many causes. First of all, the man brings a great deal of pressure to bear on the woman, because he considers his ability as a lover at stake. So as not to offend his ego, the woman will comply with the prescribed role and go through simulated ecstasy. In some of the other Danish women mentioned, women who were left frigid were turned off to sex, and pretended vaginal orgasm to hurry up the sex act. Others admitted that they had faked vaginal orgasm to catch a man. In one case, the woman pretended vaginal orgasm to get him to leave his first wife, who admitted being vaginally frigid. Later she was forced to continue the deception, since obviously she couldn't tell him to stimulate her clitorally.

Many more women were simply afraid to establish their right to equal enjoyment, seeing the sexual act as being primarily for the man's benefit, and any pleasure that the woman got as an added extra.

Other women, with just enough ego to reject the man's idea that they needed psychiatric care, refused to admit their frigidity. They wouldn't accept self-blame, but they didn't know how to solve the problem, not knowing the physiological facts about themselves. So they were left in a peculiar limbo.

Again, perhaps one of the most infuriating and damaging results of this whole charade has been that women who were perfectly healthy sexually were taught that they were not. So in addition to being sexually deprived, these women were told to blame themselves when they deserved no blame. Looking for a cure to a problem that has none can lead a woman on an endless path of self-hatred and insecurity. For she is told by her analyst that not even in her one role allowed in a male society—the role of a woman—is she successful. She is put on the defensive, with phony data as evidence that she better try to be even more feminine, think more feminine, and reject her envy of men. That is, shuffle even harder, baby.

Why Men Maintain the Myth

1. *Sexual Penetration Is Preferred*   The best stimulant for the penis is the woman's vagina. It supplies the necessary friction and lubrication. From a strictly technical point of view this position offers the best physical conditions, even though the man may try other positions for variation.

2. *The Invisible Woman*   One of the elements of male chauvinism is the refusal or inability to see women as total, separate human beings. Rather, men have chosen to define women only in terms of how they benefited men's lives. Sexually, a woman was not seen as an individual wanting to share equally in the sexual act, any more than she was seen as a person with independent desires when she did anything else in society. Thus, it

was easy to make up what was convenient about women; for on top of that, society has been a function of male interests, and women were not organized to form even a vocal opposition to the male experts.

3. *The Penis As Epitome of Masculinity* Men define their lives greatly in terms of masculinity. It is a *universal,* as opposed to racial, ego boosting, which is localized by the geography of racial mixtures.

The essence of male chauvinism is not the practical, economic services women supply. It is the psychological superiority. This kind of negative definition of self, rather than positive definition based upon one's own achievements and development, has of course chained the victim and the oppressor both. But by far the most brutalized of the two is the victim.

An analogy is racism, where the white racist compensates his feelings of unworthiness by creating an image of the black man (it is primarily a male struggle) as biologically inferior to him. Because of his power in a white male power structure, the white man can socially enforce this mythical division.

To the extent that men try to rationalize and justify male superiority through physical differentiation, masculinity may be symbolized by being the *most* muscular, the most hairy, the deepest voice, and the biggest penis. Women, on the other hand, are approved of (i.e., called feminine) if they are weak, petite, shave their legs, have high soft voices, and no penis.

Since the clitoris is almost identical to the penis, one finds a great deal of evidence of men in various societies trying to either ignore the clitoris and emphasize the vagina (as did Freud), or, as in some places in the Mideast, actually performing clitoridectomy. Freud saw this ancient and still practiced custom as a way of further "feminizing" the female by removing this cardinal vestige of her masculinity. It should be noted also that a big clitoris is considered ugly and masculine. Some cultures engage in the practice of pouring a chemical on the clitoris to make it shrivel up into proper size.

It seems clear to me that men in fact fear the clitoris as a threat to their masculinity.

4. *Sexually Expendable Male* Men fear that they will become sexually expendable if the clitoris is substituted for the vagina as the center of pleasure for women. Actually this has a great deal of validity if one considers *only* the anatomy. The position of the penis inside the vagina, while perfect for reproduction, does not necessarily stimulate an orgasm in women because the clitoris is located externally and higher up. Women must rely upon indirect stimulation in the "normal" position.

Lesbian sexuality could make an excellent case, based upon anatomical data, for the extinction of the male organ. Albert Ellis says something to the effect that a man without a penis can make a woman an excellent lover.

Considering that the vagina is very desirable from a man's point of view, purely on physical grounds, one begins to see the dilemma for men. And it forces us as well to discard many "physical" arguments explaining why women go to bed with men. What is left, it seems to me, are primarily psychological reasons why women select men at the exclusion of women as sexual partners.

5. *Control of Women*   One reason given to explain the Mideastern practice of clitoridectomy is that it will keep the women from straying. By removing the sexual organ capable of orgasm, it must be assumed that her sexual drive will diminish. Considering how men look upon their women as property, particularly in very backward nations, we should begin to consider a great deal more why it is not in the men's interest to have women totally free sexually. The double standard, as practiced for example in Latin America, is set up to keep the woman as total property of the husband, while he is free to have affairs as he wishes.

6. *Lesbianism and Bisexuality*   Aside from the strictly anatomical reasons why women might equally seek other women as lovers, there is a fear on men's part that women will seek the company of other women on a full, human basis. The establishment of clitoral orgasm as fact would threaten the heterosexual *institution*. For it would indicate that sexual pleasure was obtainable from either men *or* women, thus making heterosexuality not an absolute, but an option. It would thus open up the whole question of *human* sexual relationships beyond the confines of the present male–female role system.

[64]

GOODBYE TO ALL THAT*

ROBIN MORGAN

WHAT I want to write about are the friends, brothers, and lovers in the counterfeit male-dominated Left. The good guys who think they know what "Women's Lib," as they so chummily call it, is all about—and who then proceed to degrade and destroy women by almost everything they say and do: The token "pussy power" or "clit militancy" articles. The little jokes, the personal ads, the smile, the snarl. No more, brothers. No more well-meaning ignorance, no more co-optation, no more assuming that this thing we're all fighting for is the same: one revolution under *man,* with liberty and justice for all. No more.

Let's run it on down. White males are most responsible for the destruction of human life and environment on the planet today. Yet who is controlling the supposed revolution to change all that? White males (yes, yes, even with their pasty fingers back in black and brown pies again). It just could make one a bit uneasy. It seems obvious that a legitimate revolution must be led by, *made* by those who have been most oppressed: black, brown, and white women—with men relating to that the best they can. A genuine Left doesn't consider anyone's suffering irrelevant or titillating; nor does it function as a microcosm of capitalist economy, with men competing for power and status at the top, and women doing all the work at the bottom (and functioning as objectified prizes or "coin" as well). Goodbye to all that.

Run it all the way down.

Goodbye to the male-dominated peace movement, where sweet old Uncle Dave can say with impunity to a woman on the staff of *Liberation,* "The trouble with you is you're an aggressive woman."

Goodbye to the "straight" male-dominated Left: to PL who will allow that some workers are women, but won't see all women (say, housewives)

SOURCE: Robin Morgan, "Goodbye to All That," *The Every Other Weekly* 1, no. 12 (12 May 1970), pp. 6–7; reprinted from *Rat* (6 February 1970).

* (Editor's note: This article was initially written for the February 6, 1970 issue of *Rat*—an underground N.Y.C. paper—to explain the reasons for a women's collective taking over that publication.)

501

as workers (just like the System itself); to all the old Leftover parties who offer their "Women's Liberation caucuses" to us as if that were not a contradiction in terms; to the individual anti-leadership leaders who hand-pick certain women to be leaders and then relate only to them, either in the male Left or in Women's Liberation—bringing their hang-ups about power-dominance and manipulation to everything they touch.

Goodbye to the WeatherVain, with the Stanley Kowalski image and theory of free sexuality but practice of sex on demand for males. "Left Out!"—not Right On—to the Weather Sisters who reject their own radical feminism for the last desperate grab at male approval that we all know so well, for claiming that the *machismo* style and the gratuitous violence are their own style by "free choice" and for believing that this is the way for a woman to make her revolution . . . all the while, oh my sister, not meeting my eyes because WeatherMen chose Manson as their—and your— Hero. (Honest, at least . . . since Manson is only the logical extreme of the normal American male's fantasy [whether he is Dick Nixon or Mark Rudd]: master of a harem, women to do all the shitwork, from raising babies and cooking and hustling to killing people on order.) Goodbye to all that shit that sets women apart from women; shit that covers the face of any Weatherwoman which is the face of any Manson Slave which is the face of Sharon Tate which is the face of Mary Jo Kopechne which is the face of Beulah Saunders which is the face of me which is the face of Pat Nixon which is the face of Pat Swinton.

In the dark we are all the same—and you better believe it: we're in the dark, baby. (Remember the old joke: Know what they call a black man with a Ph.D.? A nigger. Variation: Know what they call a Weatherman? A heavy cunt. Know what they call a Hip Revolutionary Woman? A groovy cunt. Know what they call a radical militant feminist? A crazy cunt. Amerika is a land of free choice—take your pick of titles. Left Out, my Sister—don't you see? Goodbye to the illusion of strength when you run hand in hand with your oppressors; goodbye to the dream that being in the leadership collective will get you anything but gonorrhea.

Male chauvinism is an *attitude*—male supremacy is the *objective reality, the fact*. Goodbye to the Conspiracy who, when lunching with fellow sexist bastards Norman Mailer and Terry Southern in a bunny-type club in Chicago, found Judge Hoffman at the neighboring table—no surprise: *in the light they are all the same*.

Goodbye to Hip Culture and the so-called Sexual Revolution, which has functioned toward women's freedom as did the Reconstruction toward former slaves—reinstituted oppression by another name. Goodbye to the assumption that Hugh Romney is safe in his "cultural revolution," safe enough to refer to "our women, who make all our clothes" without somebody not forgiving that. Goodbye to the idea that Hugh Hefner is groovy 'cause he lets Conspirators come to parties at the Mansion—Goodbye to Hefner's dream of a ripe old age. Goodbye to the notion that good ol' Abbie is any different from any other up and coming movie star (like, say Cliff Robertson, who ditches the first wife and kids, good enough for the old days but awkward once you're Making It). Goodbye to his hypocritical double standard that reeks through all the tattered charm. Goodbye to lovely pro-Women's-Liberation Paul Krassner, with all his astonished anger that women have lost their sense of humor "on this issue" and don't laugh any more at little funnies that degrade and hurt them; farewell to the memory of his "Instant Pussy" aerosol-can poster, to his column for *Cavalier,* to his dream of a Rape-In against legislators' wives, to his Scapegoats and Realist Nuns and cute anecdotes about the little daughter he sees as often as any proper divorced Scarsdale middle-aged (38) father; goodbye forever to the notion that he is my brother who, like Paul, buys a prostitute for the night as a birthday gift for a male friend, or who, like Paul, reels off the names in alphabetical order of people in the Women's Movement he has fucked, reels off names in the best lockerroom tradition—as proof that *he's* no sexist oppressor.

Let it all hang out. Let it seem bitchy, catty, dykey, frustrated, crazy, Solanisesque, nutty, frigid, ridiculous, bitter, embarrassing, man-hating, libelous, pure, unfair, envious, intuitive, low-down, stupid, petty, liberating. We are the women that men have warned us about.

And let's put one lie to rest for all time: the lie that men are oppressed, too, by sexism—the lie that there can be such a thing as "men's liberation groups." Oppression is something that one group of people commits against another group specifically because of a "threatening" characteristic shared by the latter group—skin color or sex or age, etc. The oppressors are indeed *fucked up* by being masters (racism hurts whites, sexual stereotypes are harmful to men) but those masters are not *oppressed*. Any master has the alternative of divesting himself of sexism or racism—the oppressed have no alternative—for they have no power—but to fight. In the long run, Women's Liberation will of course free men—but in the short run it's going to *cost* men a lot of privilege, which no one gives up willingly or easily. Sexism is *not* the fault of women—kill your fathers, not your mothers.

Run it on down. Goodbye to a beautiful new ecology movement that could fight to save us all if it would stop tripping off women as earth-mother types or frontier chicks, if it would *right now* cede leadership to those who have *not* polluted the planet because that action implies power and women haven't had any power in about 5,000 years, cede leadership to those whose brains are as tough and clear as any man's but whose bodies are also unavoidably aware of the locked-in relationship between humans and their biosphere—the earth, the tides, the atmosphere, the moon. Ecology is no big *shtick* if you're a woman—it's always been there.

Goodbye to the complicity inherent in the Berkeley Tribesmen being part publishers of Trashman Comics; goodbye, for that matter, to the reasoning that finds whoremaster Trashman a fitting model, however comic-strip far out, for a revolutionary man—somehow related to the same Super-male reasoning that permits the first statement on Women's Liberation and male chauvinism that came out of the Black Panther Party to be made *by a man,* talkin' a whole lot 'bout how the Sisters should speak up for themselves. Such ignorance and arrogance ill befit a revolutionary.

We know how racism is worked deep into the unconscious by our System—the same way sexism is, as it appears in the very name of The Young Lords. What are you if you're a "macho woman"—female Lord? Or, god forbid, a Young Lady? Change it, change it to The Young Gentry if you must, or never assume that the name itself is innocent of pain, of oppression.

Theory and practice and the light-years between them. "Do it!" says Jerry Rubin in *Rat's* last issue—but he doesn't, or every *Rat* reader would have known the pictured face next to his article as well as they know his own much-photographed face: it was Nancy Kurshan, the power behind the clown.

Was it my brother who listed human beings among the *objects* which would be easily available after the Revolution: "Free grass, free food, free women, free acid, free clothes, etc.?" Was it my brother who wrote "Fuck your women till they can't stand up" and said that groupies were liberated chicks 'cause they dug a tit-shake instead of a hand-shake? The epitome of female exclusionism—"men will make the Revolution—and their chicks." Not my brother, no. Not my revolution. Not one breath of my support for the new counterleft Christ—John Sinclair. Just one less to worry about for ten years. I do not choose my enemy for my brother.

Goodbye, goodbye. The hell with the simplistic notion that automatic freedom for women—or non-white peoples—will come about ZAP! with the advent of a socialist revolution. Bullshit. Two evils pre-date capitalism and have been clearly able to survive and post-date socialism: sexism and racism. Women were the first property when the Primary Contradiction occurred: when one half of the human species decided to subjugate the other half, because it was "different," alien, the Other. From there it was an easy enough step to extend the Other to someone of different skin shade, different height or weight or language—or strength to resist. Goodbye to those simple-minded optimistic dreams of socialist equality all our good socialist brothers want us to believe. How liberal a politics that is! How much further we will have to go to create those profound changes that would give birth to a genderless society. *Profound,* Sister. Beyond what is male or female. Beyond standards we all adhere to now without daring to examine them as male-created, male-dominated, male-fucked-up, and in male self-interest. *Beyond all known standards,* especially those easily articulated revolutionary ones we all rhetorically invoke. Beyond, to a species with a new name, that would not dare define itself as Man.

I once said, "I'm a revolutionary, not just a woman," and knew my own lie even as I said the words. The pity of that statement's eagerness to be acceptable to those whose revolutionary zeal no one would question, i.e., any male supremacist in the counterleft. But to become a true revolutionary one must first become one of the oppressed (not organize or educate or manipulate them, but become one of them)—or realize that you are one of them already. No woman wants that. Because that realization is humiliating, it hurts. It hurts to understand that at Woodstock or Altamont a woman could be declared uptight or a poor sport if she didn't want to be raped. It hurts to learn that the Sisters still in male-Left captivity are putting down the crazy feminists to make themselves look okay and unthreatening to our mutual oppressors. It hurts to be pawns in those games. It hurts to try and change *each day of your life right now*—not in talk, not "in your head," and not only conveniently "out there" in the Third World (half of which is women) or the black and brown communities (half of which are women) but in your own home, kitchen, bed. No getting away, no matter how else you are oppressed, from the primary oppression of being female in a patriarchal world. It hurts to hear that the Sisters in the Gay Liberation Front, too, have to struggle continually against the male chauvinism of their gay brothers. It hurts that Jane Alpert was cheered when rapping about imperialism, racism, the Third World, and All Those Safe Topics but hissed and booed by a Movement crowd of men who wanted none of it when she began to talk about Women's Liberation. The backlash is upon us.

They tell us the alternative is to hang in there and "struggle," to confront male domination in the counterleft, to fight beside or behind or beneath our brothers—to show 'em we're just as tough, just as revolushunerry, just as whatever-image-they-now-want-of-us-as-once-they-wanted-us-to-be-feminine-and-keep-the-home-fire-burning. They will bestow titular leadership on our grateful shoulders, whether it's being a token woman on the Movement Speakers Bureau Advisory Board, or being a Conspiracy Groupie or one of the "respectable" chain-swinging Motor City Nine. Sisters all, with only one real alternative: to seize our own power into our own hands, all women, separate and together, and make the Revolution the way it must be made—no priorities this time, no suffering group told to wait until after.

It is the job of revolutionary feminists to build an ever stronger independent Women's Liberation Movement, so that the Sisters in counterleft captivity will have somewhere to turn, to use their power and rage and beauty and coolness in their own behalf for once, on their own terms, on their own issues, in their own style—whatever that may be. Not for us in Women's Liberation to hassle them and confront them the way their men do, nor to blame them—or ourselves—for what any of us are: an oppressed people, but a people raising our consciousness toward something that is the other side of anger, something bright and smooth and cool, like action unlike anything yet contemplated or carried out. It is for us to survive (something the white male radical has the luxury of never really worrying about, what with all his options), to talk, to plan, to be patient, to welcome new fugitives from the counterfeit Left with no arrogance but only humility and delight, to plan, to push—to strike.

There is something every woman wears around her neck on a thin chain of fear—an amulet of madness. For each of us, there exists somewhere a moment of insult so intense that she will reach up and rip the amulet off, even if the chain tears at the flesh of her neck. And the last protection from seeing the truth will be gone. Do you think, tugging furtively every day at the chain and going nicely insane as I am, that I can be concerned with the puerile squabbles of a counterfeit Left that laughs at my pain? Do you think, such a concern is noticeable when set alongside the suffering of more than half the human species for the past 5,000 years—due to a whim of the other half? No, no, no, goodbye to all that.

Women are Something Else. This time, we're going to kick out all the jams, and the boys will just have to hustle to keep up, or else drop out and openly join the power structure of which they are already the illegitimate sons. Any man who claims he is serious about wanting to divest himself of cock privilege should trip on this: all male leadership out of the Left is the only way; and it's going to happen, whether through men stepping down or through women seizing the helm. It's up to the "brothers"—after all, sexism is their concern, not ours; we're too busy getting ourselves together to have to deal with their bigotry. So they'll have to make up their own minds as to whether they will be divested of just cock privilege or—what the hell, why not say it, say it?—divested of cocks. How deep the fear of that loss must be, that it can be suppressed only by the building of empires and the waging of genocidal wars!

Goodbye, goodbye forever, counterfeit Left, counterleft, male-dominated cracked-glass mirror reflection of the Amerikan Nightmare. Women are the real Left. We are rising, powerful in our unclean bodies; bright glowing mad in our inferior brains; wild voices keening; undaunted by blood we who hemorrhage every twenty-eight days; laughing at our own beauty we who have lost our sense of humor; mourning for all each precious one of us might have been in this one living time-place had she not been born a woman; stuffing fingers into our mouths to stop the screams of fear and hate and pity for men we have loved and love still; tears in our eyes and bitterness in our mouths for children we couldn't have, or couldn't *not* have, or didn't want, or didn't want *yet,* or wanted and had in this place and this time of horror. We are rising with a fury older and potentially greater than any force in history, and this time we will be free or no one will survive.

Power to all the people or to none.

INDEX